Hippie Faggot Freak

The Making of a Gay Liberationist

A Memoir

Dale Mitchell

RATTLING GOOD YARNS
PRESS

Rattling Good Yarns Press
33490 Date Palm Drive 3065
Cathedral City CA 92235
USA
www.rattlinggoodyarns.com

Library of Congress Control Number: 2023943863
ISBN: 9781955826495

First Edition

For David

On my destroyed shelter
On my collapsed beacon
On the walls of my weariness...
I was born to know you
To sing songs of freedom to you.

—Paul Eluard

Duration. Success. No Blame.
Perseverance Furthers.

—I Ching

Contents

Preface

Thirty-five years after the close of this memoir, my mother told me a secret she'd promised my father she'd never reveal. It was in the fall of 2005, and we were dining at Jerry's, an upscale seafood restaurant on the road between Wrightsville Beach and Wilmington, North Carolina, where my parents had retired to a house they'd had built off the Pine Valley golf course. It was, they'd claimed, their dream house, although I suspect that was due more to the emptiness of their nest than the prestige of their address, a four-digit number on a gently curving drive named after the traitorous slaveholder Robert E. Lee.

Although my parents would never admit it, children brought little of the 'Ozzie and Harriet' happiness their era had promised. My would-be twin sisters, Nan and Jane, were stillborn, while neither my brother nor I turned out the way we were supposed to, a failure my father attributed to a lack of gumption and my mother, selfishness. If only we'd thought more about her, she complained, we would've turned out better. Instead, we thought only of ourselves and, worse, in ways that made her look bad. Like when my brother announced his engagement to a plumber's daughter. Or I dropped out of college to become a hippie faggot freak.

Both claimed my brother's 1977 divorce, an ugly break-up involving allegations of drug abuse and domestic violence, was the family's nadir. But that was only because it couldn't be covered up; at some point, absent wives and missing grandchildren had to be explained away. Not so with my homosexuality, the news of which I'd dropped in their lap ten years earlier and which they'd promptly swept under the rug. While my brother eventually made his way back into my parent's good graces, mostly through remarriage, I remained an outsider or, as my mother liked to tell her friends—despite the fact that I'd been with the same man since 1979—a "confirmed bachelor."

I'd like to think my mother opened up that night at Jerry's because she wanted to put "all that ugliness," as she liked to call my coming out, behind her. However, forty years into it, she still refused to utter the word 'gay' or refer to David, my partner of twenty-six years, as anything more than a friend. Indeed, her homophobia was so intense that, when David and I wed a few months after

i

gay marriage became legal in Massachusetts, I'd refused to tell her for fear she'd ruin the day for me. And, despite the headlines marriage equality garnered around the world, she never once inquired about our status or commented on the thin gold band that suddenly appeared on the third finger of my left hand.

No, I suspect my mother's openness that night was due mostly to her fondness for vodka and water. Before we'd even raised a fork, she'd already polished off one and was working on her second while fielding my many questions about my paternal grandfather, whose death from alcohol at sixty-two was so at odds with my family's staid storyline that I had long sensed an affinity. And so, every chance I got I returned to the man everyone called Bo, probing for the convergence that I hoped lurked behind my family's fine, upstanding middle-class facade.

Like the others before it, my interrogation was not going well. "Dale, I just don't know," or "Gosh, I never thought about it," my mother would reply with such maddening frequency I'd just about decided to give my inquiry up. At ninety-six, she had limited time left for setting the family record straight; and worse, she had started to become alarmingly addled. Earlier in the day, she'd conflated the 1937 Ohio River flood, from which my father had to be rescued in a rowboat, with the 1958 flooding of our suburban Wilmington, Delaware basement, which required nothing more than a sump pump. Soon, I feared she wouldn't even remember who I was, let alone a father-in-law who'd died some fifty years earlier.

Then, out of the blue, she dropped her bomb. She'd just finished slathering a dinner roll with butter and squinted at it as if she wasn't quite sure what she was handling. "You know, of course, that Bo was arrested for sodomy," she said, returning the roll to her bread plate.

Certain my two pricey glasses of red wine had gone to my head, I stared at her for a few astonished seconds. "Arrested for *what*??" I finally blurted out.

"You heard me," she replied, swigging the last of her vodka.

"No, honestly, I didn't."

My mother reached again for her dinner roll and, annoyed, bellowed, "For *sodomy*, I said!"

At that, the room fell into such a startled hush I could hear dishes being stacked in Jerry's kitchen. The woman at the table next to us, a deacon at my mother's church who'd risen to greet her on our way in, pulled nervously at her pearls. Her husband, the orthopedic surgeon who'd replaced my mother's hip when she broke it fifteen years earlier, cleared his throat. "Jane," he asked, turning to glare at me, "is everything all right?"

"Yes, quite, except that I'd like another drink," my mother smiled, jangling her ice cubes at a passing waitress.

"Certainly," the waitress, a grizzled Brit who'd waited on us during our previous three visits, replied. She removed my mother's empty tumbler and smiled. "Another vodka and water?"

My mother turned to me and scowled.

"Uhm, yes, please," I stammered, realizing that I'd once again failed her. As the "man of the table," a title I'd inherited after my father's death, I was expected to order her drinks. "And another one of these?" I asked, sheepishly pointing to my empty wine glass.

"Of course, another Gundlauch Bundschu," the waitress replied, winking knowingly. Earlier in the evening, when my mother had complained my taste for wine was unmanly, the waitress had rushed to my defense. "On no, dearie, all those old rules are dead. Nowadays, it's anything goes." She'd jabbed me with her elbow and laughed heartily. "Isn't that right, love?" Blushing, I'd mouthed a heartfelt thank you. It was the closest I'd ever heard anyone get to telling my mother it was okay to be gay.

When the buzz finally returned to the room, I slid my chair closer to her and returned to the subject of my grandfather's bust. "You can't be serious. For *sodomy*?"

My mother looked up from her plate and glared at me. "What, you think I'd make something like that up?"

"But how could you possibly know?"

"Because your father was the one the police called," she replied. She grimaced as if it had only been yesterday. "He was the one who had to go down and bail your grandfather out of jail."

"You're kidding."

"What, is that all you can say?"

"Sorry, but I just can't imagine bailing your own..." Trailing off, I recalled the time my father had bailed me out of a jail in Danville, Illinois, the Midwestern hellhole to which my parents had moved after another DuPont transfer. While the cops made sure he knew what I'd been busted for—I'd shoplifted a bottle of bubble bath—my gayness had only been implied. With sodomy, there was little room for doubt. The word practically screamed 'faggot.'

Picking at my salad, I wondered just how calamitous Bo's bust had been. As with so much in gay life, timing and location would have been critical. And while Jeffersonville, the southern Indiana river town where Bo had married into one of its most prominent families, was strictly Bible Belt, he might have gotten lucky on timing. Dabbing a piece of bread in olive oil, I asked my mother if she knew in what year Bo's bust had been.

"Let's see," she replied, noting that she and my father were still living in the Jeffersonville apartment they'd moved into after marrying. "You know the one on Riverside Drive?" she asked, her macular-clouded eyes blindly scouring the wall behind me. "The one around the corner from Mo and Bo?"

I nodded and smiled. Before we'd left Jeffersonville for Wilmington, Delaware, where my father had landed a plumb job in the home offices of DuPont, the chemical giant my parents referred to as simply 'the Company'— as if there were no others—my mother would point out the apartment building every time we drove by. There, she would say, on the second floor, with a striped canvas awning over a porch that looked across the Ohio at the big city bustle of Louisville, Kentucky, was where our family began.

She fondly recalled how spacious the flat was. "We couldn't really afford it. But you know how your father was." She smiled wistfully. "Always wanting the best..."

"Yes, yes," I interrupted, glancing at her half-empty vodka. Soon, she'd be too drunk to focus. "But when? What *year*?"

She woozily wiped a smudge of tartar sauce from the side of her mouth and recalled that she'd just finished giving Dean, my older brother, a bath in the kitchen sink. "He'd just turned two months so that would've meant..." Pausing, she turned suddenly ashen, and confessed she couldn't remember the year my brother was born. "Isn't that terrible?" she gasped. "What kind of a mother doesn't remember when her own son was born?"

Fearing another meltdown—the night before, she'd gotten teary-eyed and blamed herself for my brother's growing indifference—I assured her it was okay. At ninety-six, she was entitled to be a little fuzzy over dates. Then I reminded her that Dean was born ten years before me. "In 1939," I added, just in case she'd forgotten when I was born too.

I took a long swig of wine and shuddered over Bo's timing. 1939 was smack-dab in the middle of the anti-gay crackdown that ushered in a new era of repression, culminating in the Lavender Scare of the late McCarthy, early Eisenhower blacklist era. Censorship became universal; blackmail, routine; entrapment, official police policy; and termination, an employers' instantaneous, no-questions-asked response. Religion, science, philosophy, medicine, and law coalesced: homosexuality was suddenly immoral, unnatural, decadent, sick, and illegal, all in one neatly wrapped package.

Gripping the side of my chair, I recalled the camp, old-world word for what we later called coming out: "wrecked." Busted in 1939 on a sodomy charge in a southern Indiana Bible Belt town, Bo would've defined the word. He hadn't been just wrecked. He'd been ruined.

"Of course, 1939, now why couldn't I remember that?" my mother chirped. She stabbed a cherry tomato with her fork and smiled triumphantly; the previous two had catapulted off her plate and under our neighbor's table. "I don't know how you put up with an old lady like me."

"But Bo was editor of the town newspaper," I ventured, hoping against hope that his status as a member of Jeffersonville's elite would've somehow protected him.

"Not for long he wasn't," my mother replied dryly. While my father had managed to hush the arrest up, the price was my grandfather's erasure. "Retired" by the newspaper and banished by my grandmother to a spare room overseen by a mocking statue of Winged Victory—a wedding gift from her gruff, domineering father—he quickly took to drink. By the time I was born, he was a mere shadow—disgraced, humiliated, and impoverished. He'd even lost his pension.

"I see," I said, more familiar than I cared to admit with such downward spirals. I turned and stared into the mercury vapor glow of Jerry's strip mall parking lot and recalled an old photo I'd found in a large wooden box in the storage space over my mother's garage. Taken a few months before he'd married, Bo looks defiantly at the camera, his head feyly cocked to the side with the arm of his much butcher companion draped affectionately over his shoulder. On the back, he'd written in a script so florid it made my mother's near-perfect Palmer cursive look almost child-like: *Observe that look of mine: it's the limit.* Of his friend's look, he'd concluded: *Cliff's says "don't forget."*

Attacking my scallops, I anticipated the late-night call to my husband, David, announcing the news: *It's in my blood! My grandfather was gay! Gay!!* Much more measured, with a skeptical bent I often found maddening, I knew David would be unmoved. After all, he would ask, couldn't straights be busted for sodomy too?

I watched our waitress clear a table across the room and recalled what a Greenwich Village drag queen I'd once lived across the hall from had said of straight sexual privilege. What we had to bang out in toilets and parks—"In full view of everyone and, honey, I do mean *everyone*," she'd cried, rolling her eyes—straights got to do behind closed doors. Even their whores, she'd bitterly noted, did it in beds. As for her, she couldn't remember the last time she'd done it lying down, let alone on a sheet.

Before the start of the so-called "sexual revolution," only the privileged few could. Most gays either played it safe by abstaining or, succumbing to an overpowering need, did it outdoors, furtively, often in places patrolled by undercover cops. There they thought they'd be safe and, for the most part, they were, at least until, as with Bo, the handcuffs came out and off to jail they were hauled, humiliated and ruined.

I wiped my sweaty palms on my pants leg and, leaning across the table, hesitantly asked if my mother knew where Bo had been arrested. "I mean, was it outdoors?"

She grimaced as if she knew exactly what I was asking and nodded. "Down by the river," she muttered between teeth so tightly clenched I nearly had to ask her to repeat it.

"You mean the Ohio?" I asked, incredulous. Until we moved to Delaware, the river's edge was where my cousin Kay and I had played 'The Dying Swan.' She'd be the prince and I, the beautiful peasant girl he'd fallen in love with but who the prince's mother, the evil queen, had cast a spell on and turned into a swan.

I recalled the large granite slab on the river's banks, partially submerged, that we'd used as our stage. There, surrounded on one side by thick undergrowth and, on the other, by the Ohio's murky depths, we'd be so hidden from view that I could safely let out the girl trapped inside me. There, I'd let her shriek and twirl to her heart's content. None of the bullies who tormented me had any idea that she—or I, her host—were even there.

My head spun. Was that childhood play site also the spot where grown men met for sex? I scoured my memory for the telltale signs—used condoms, wads of rumpled tissue, torn pieces of yellowing porn—but I'd been too young to interpret them, even if they'd been there. Still, the possibilities intrigued me. Could I have sampled my first taste of freedom as a budding gay man at the very spot where my grandfather enjoyed his last?

"Why of course, it was the Ohio," my mother snipped. "Is there some other river in Jeff I don't know about?"

"No, of course not," I muttered as waves of vindication washed over me. For years, my mother and I had fought over what she insisted was a choice—made by me mostly to hurt her—and I, a fact of life we both needed to simply accept. And now here it was, four decades later: evidence that gayness was as much a part of my DNA as male-patterned baldness, a cleft chin, and blue eyes. I leaned back in my chair, shaken. On some level, she'd known all along.

"It was sad," my mother continued. "Bo was so kind and gentle—a sweetheart, really." She paused and smiled; back then, men were no more supposed to be gentle than they were to drink wine. "And, oh, what a lovely voice he had. When he sang, the whole room would light up." She swilled the last of her vodka and asked if I remembered that about him.

I reminded her that my only remembrance of Bo was the sterling silver cup engraved *To Dale from Bo-Bo* he'd given my parents to commemorate my birth. "I was two when he died, Mother. Two."

"Why, of course you were," she replied, a bit defensively. She patted her mouth with her napkin and smiled woozily. "I remember that. Of course, I do."

I glanced nervously at my mother's empty tumbler. After three vodka and waters, she could hardly be deemed a reliable reporter. However, she'd been much too guileless not to be believed. Besides, 'sodomy' was hardly a word a woman of her social standing would casually drop within earshot of a church deacon in a fancy restaurant like Jerry's.

I looked across the table at her and smiled. I'd been right to suspect an affinity; Bo and I were both gay, a fact our family not only refused to accept but had swept—not just once, but twice—under the rug. "Amazing," I muttered.

Then, as if on cue, my mother moved on and we finished our meal discussing the usual topics: the weather; her frustrations with her grandkids, whom she felt failed to give her due deference; her terror of going blind; her fears of having to move into a nursing home or, worse, in with my brother, a prospect she again made me promise I'd never let happen; and whether I was getting enough to eat. "Here, have some of mine," she said repeatedly, pointing to her flounder. "You know I can't finish it."

She never once asked about David or what the last forty years had been like for me as an out gay man. Had I ever been busted like Bo? Had I ever been beaten up, harassed, or fired from a job? Had I tried to kill myself? And what about those needle tracks from when I lived in Greenwich Village? Surely, she'd seen them, although she never once mentioned them.

And what about AIDS? Indeed, during the height of the epidemic, with friends dying all around us, she never once asked if David or I were sick. Questions like that would have implied acceptance—something proper, God-fearing, Southern ladies like her would never grant. And my mother, a working-class Hoosier who'd married far better than even her striving, evangelical mother dreamed possible, was nothing if not proper. "Tastefulness personified," was how one of her country club friends once described her.

But in the terse family code I'd become expert at cracking, my mother had finally given me what I wanted. There, in the margins of her story, was an apology for her betrayal when in late 1967, home from my first semester as an architectural student at Syracuse University, I came out to her, a revelation she greeted by throwing up. Two days later, she handed me the card of a shrink who'd promised her a cure and informed me it was either that or the draft; they would not pay to put a degenerate through college. Certain Vietnam would be the end of me—back then, gays had more to fear from our side than the other—I promised her the impossible: I would go straight.

After that, I embarked on my own downward spiral, a demented, late-Sixties update of my grandfather's in every way but one. I did not let it kill me—although by the time of that dinner at Jerry's the jury was still out on the hepatitis C I'd contracted while shooting speed with a bunch of Greenwich Village junkies known as the Horrible Fags. Stunned, I stared over the restaurant's bistro curtains at the rental car I'd parked outside. None of that had been necessary. Homosexuality was in my blood. My being gay was as natural as her being straight.

On the drive back to the gated community my mother had moved to a few years after my father's death, the local public radio station played Big Band music, her favorite. "Your father and I used to dance to this," she said, bouncing up and down in the passenger seat. She turned to me and beamed. "He was such a good dancer. Everyone said so."

Aglow from our unspoken reconciliation, I gave her that—an acknowledgment that my father, with whom I never got along, was at least a good dancer. I recalled the times I'd watched them as a kid foxtrot across our suburban Wilmington, Delaware living room, my father leading and my mother, her head on his shoulder, blissfully happy. "And, yes, a very good one at that," I added.

Back at her condo, I put the radio on full blast while she danced around the den in her stocking feet, all by herself. I sat in a swivel chair whose soiling betrayed her growing incontinence and, clapping along with the beat, shouted encouragement. "Yeah, that's it. Come on, Mom. Do it!"

Exhausted, she collapsed into the chair next to the TV and murmured, "Oh gosh, that was fun!" Then, we did what we had not done since my coming out destroyed nearly everything between us. We broke into giggles that, for a few gasping moments, reminded us of what we once were, before shame and recrimination intervened—a mother and her hopelessly sissy son, delighted by nothing so much as to be in each other's company.

Once we regained our composure, my mother came as close as she ever had to acknowledging our losses. "My, we haven't done that in a long time," she sighed before getting up to say goodnight. Passing, she bent down, took my face in her wrinkled, parchment-like hands and smiled. "It felt good, didn't it?"

Reeling, I could only nod and wait until, padding down the hall, she closed her bedroom door behind her and, finally alone, I could call David with the news: *It's in my blood! My grandfather was gay! Gay!! My mother told me so!!*

Incredulous, David asked if she'd finally uttered the word. I swallowed hard and admitted she had not. "Maybe next time," I added, certain there would be one.

I was wrong. My mother never returned to the story and, fearful she'd deny she ever told it, I never again pursued it. Like my coming out, Bo's sodomy bust returned to being one of the many elephants in the room my mother routinely worked around, blithely pretending they weren't there. As my dear friend and fellow gay liberationist Eric once said of her, denial was not just a river in Egypt.

And so, when four years later—three weeks after her one-hundredth birthday—my mother died as she had wished, in her own bed, with David holding her hand and me reciting the 23rd Psalm, 'sodomy' was as close to the word 'gay' as she ever got. And while I could not help feeling bitter about this, I also could not help interpreting the tear that formed in the corner of her left eye moments before her death as a gift—her death-bed confession that she regretted squandering our once-solid bond. Had she only relented and accepted me for who I am, she would have kept me, a mama's boy to the end. Instead, she rebuffed my every entreaty. I had no choice but to move on.

It was not easy. I came out to my parents a year-and-a-half before the Stonewall Rebellion issued the call to leave the closet behind. Before that, there were no signposts or paths on how to exist out in the open—only barriers. Shame and self-doubt were gay life's defaults; suicide—or at least a premature death, generally from alcohol or drugs, although sometimes, as in the case of the old-world gay icon, Judy Garland, both—were too often its end.

My father often claimed I lacked the quality he most admired in a man: gumption. While I proudly eschew many masculine trappings, the story that follows shows just how wrong he was. I had the gumption to make it through a time when being out was mostly considered a sign of madness, an act of willful self-destruction, or the perverse embrace of Marx's lumpenproletariat: low-life losers like drag queens, drug addicts, petty thieves, and prostitutes.

Many of the people featured in this memoir were exactly that. Back then, drag queens, junkies, drug dealers, pickpockets and whores were virtually the only ones around who had a hand to lend. And, no, I could have never made it on my own. I was too young; the times were too tough; and the repression too pervasive. Back then, the more experienced men who helped newcomers like me navigate our coming out were called 'gay mothers.' Nearly everyone had one. I was fortunate to have had many.

Most of my gay mothers were older, although the oldest was not yet thirty, the age at which the then-insurgent "youth culture" declared one to no longer be trustworthy. Two were actually my age, although both were what we called back then "precocious," meaning they'd come out much younger, one as early as thirteen. Another two were transgender, although back then we called them drag queens. One was even a straight woman—thoroughly cisgender, although what today might also pass as "queer." She introduced me to LSD, which was, along with Free Love, Free Speech, Freedom Summers, Sit-Ins, Be-Ins, Black Pride, Black Power, Flower Power, Maximum Feasible Participation, Self-Determination and guerilla warfare, also a gay mother. Another was a lover, although his influence was, as a mother's often can be, almost entirely negative. Through him—and the methamphetamine he got me hooked on—I saw up-close and personal the damage that self-loathing imparted to gay life. Yes, "internalized homophobia," as we later came to know it, was a gay mother too. Without experiencing its uniquely corrosive spin on guilt and shame, I might never have become the gay liberationist that the trajectory of this memoir points to.

A number of cultural touchstones were gay mothers as well. The first and perhaps most significant were *Time* and *Life*, the two Henry Luce periodicals whose weekly reports of a rapidly changing world a lonely and bullied gay kid like me regularly scoured for hints of an escape. The latter's 1964 exposé, "Homosexuality in America," proved seminal, offering not only assurances that there were others out there like me but also instructions on where to find them—in big city enclaves like Greenwich Village, of course, but also in small city "cruising" spots like, I later discovered, my hometown's main drag—and what I was to wear when I did—sneakers, fluffy sweaters, and tight pants: the so-called "gay uniform."

Time's coverage, though more episodic, was equally reassuring, offering me proof that—although always in the most disparaging of terms—gays could, with enough fame, money or chutzpah, survive out in the open. Through it, I came across my first hints of a gay mother—through trailblazers like Truman Capote, Tennessee Williams, Gore Vidal, Jean Genet, Jean Cocteau, Francis Bacon, Pier Paolo Pasolini, Luchino Visconti, Edward Albee, Kenneth Anger, James Purdy, Paul Goodman, Allen Ginsberg, William Burroughs, James Baldwin, Christopher Isherwood, W. H. Auden, Benjamin Britten, Ned Rorem, and, my personal favorite, Andy Warhol, in whose Silver Factory I imagined myself transformed from a sad, pathetic object of scorn into a venomous, fire-breathing superstar-faggot: the Pope Ondine. Even Walter Jenkins, the Presidential aide whose 1964 bust in a DC men's room was an object lesson in the dangers of entrapment, was a gay mother. As my first pick-up—"tricks," we called them back then—said of downtown Wilmington's cruising scene, it was wise of me to be so cautious. "Vice," he said, were everywhere.

There were, of course, women too, all also gleaned from magazines, who became the genre-shattering alter-egos through whom I also imagined myself free: the ultrachic Veruschka, the androgynous Twiggy, the transgender Christine Jorgensen, the icy Nico, the ballsy Nancy Sinatra, the demure Jennifer Jones, the regal Aretha Franklin, the fearsome Odetta, rebels like Fanny Lou Hamer of the Mississippi Freedom Democrats and Kathleen Cleaver of the Black Panther Party, rock stars like Janis Joplin of Big Brother and the Holding Company and Grace Slick of Jefferson Airplane, and vipers like Jiang Jing, Chairman Mao's white-boned demon, and Brigid Polk, the fat, demented, drug-shooting bull dyke of Warhol's *The Chelsea Girls*. But none ever came close to the beautiful lady whose photo, at age six, I'd clipped from the pages of *Look* magazine and who, clutching a dozen long-stemmed red roses and swooning in the arms of her handsome prince, was my first prima donna ballerina: Tchaikovsky's glorious Dying Swan.

There were books, plays and films too: Hubert Selby's *Last Exit to Brooklyn*, Franz Fanon's *Black Skins, White Masks*, John Rechy's *City of Night*, Genet's *Our Lady of the Flowers*, Amira Baraka's (then Leroi Jones) *Dutchman*, Edward Albee's *Who's Afraid of Virginia Woolf?*, Antonioni's *Blow-Up*, Resnais's *Last Year at Marienbad*, Buñuel's *Belle de Jour*, Godard's *Weekend*, Arthur Penn's *Bonnie and Clyde*, Paul Newman/Joanne Woodward's *Rachel, Rachel*, and Paul Morrissey/Andy Warhol's *Flesh*. Even Hollywood schlock like Russ Meyer's *Beyond the Valley of the Dolls* and the Jennifer Jones religious melodrama, *Song of Bernadette*, were gay mothers.

There was, of course, music too: Martha and the Vandellas' "Nowhere to Run," the Four Tops' "Reach Out, I'll Be There," the Beach Boys' "Wouldn't It Be Nice," the Beatles' "Strawberry Fields Forever," Aretha's "Ain't No Way," Dylan's "Visions of Johanna," James Brown's "Say It Loud: I'm Black and I'm Proud," the Stones' "Paint It Black," just about everything by the Velvet Underground—"Heroin," "Venus In Furs," "All Tomorrow's Parties, "Femme Fatale," "Sister Ray"—Nico's "I'll Keep It With Mine," Jefferson Airplane's "Plastic Fantastic Lover," and, of course, my grandfather's favorite piano piece, Debussy's "Clair de Lune." But nothing packed quite the wallop of Norman O. Brown's meditation on apocalypse, *Love's Body*, and Ingmar Bergman's back-to-back descents into the crisis of identity, *Persona* and *Hour of the Wolf*. These are the works that haunt this memoir, my gay mothers' emeritus.

I may have gotten the gay gene from my grandfather, but my gay mothers were the ones who taught me the ropes of life as an outsider: a gay man coming out in a time of rebellion. Through them, I learned to stand up and, against terrifying odds, be myself. Their love was tough and sometimes cruel, but it imparted resilience, a finger in the eye of hatred and adversity that got so many of us through. This book is a salute to them, the gay mothers who taught me the twisted, messy, sometimes ugly ways of survival in a time when we had no rights, only wrongs.

Yes, a few were ogres; one, monstrously so. Ironically, the more hideous these mentors were, the more powerful their allure. Back then, bad was an end unto itself, the rejection of good as sexy as the sculpted gym bodies of a later, more accepting time.

The one good my gay mothers never got me to reject was my love for my actual mother, although one tried very hard and, once, almost succeeded. Nor could my mother ever fully reject me. Despite the pressures of her time and place, she refused to give me up. Put bluntly, she loved me despite the fact that I was gay or, in the words of one of her icons, the Rev. Billy Graham, an "abomination."

More than a half century later, it is hard to imagine just how difficult that was for her. Back then, families were expected to submit their gay children to cures. No means—electroshock, castration, lobotomy—were deemed too barbaric. For children who refused, banishment was the family's only recourse; anything less would have been appeasement, a mollycoddling of evil, a treasonous embrace of the dreaded "other."

A deeply conservative, God-fearing Republican, my mother took great umbrage at the changes ushered in by the Sixties, the decade in which much of this memoir takes place. Once, during a Dick Cavett interview with Gloria Steinem, she lashed out at the feminist critique of traditional gender roles. "I don't know what's so wrong with female subservience," she snipped. "I rather like being taken care of!" Nevertheless, for years she resisted calls to "disown" me, a bourgeois euphemism for rejection that, like the draft's 4-F classification, underscored a gay man's utter unfitness.

One of the lessons my gay mothers taught me was to know the insults from which I'd never recover. Those, they'd advised, were to be avoided at all costs. For me, that fatal injury was to be disowned. I'd seen what it did to others and lived in terror of it happening to me. My mother made sure it did not.

While I owe much to my gay mothers, I could not have made it through without the real one. Although she'd be mortified to be found in their company, this book is a salute to her, as well.

I am not a writer by trade or training and there are a number of people I must acknowledge and thank for their inspiration, support, and encouragement throughout the process of bringing this remembrance to completion. First, there is my dear friend, comrade, and fellow gay liberationist, Bill Hoppe, whose premature death from AIDS in 1995 sent me careening down the rabbit hole of grief and commemoration that has ended up as this memoir. Hoppe came later in my life and thus does not appear in this story, although his spirit, as the linchpin of a "chosen family" that arose out of the ashes of gay liberation, permeates this work.

There is also Andrew Szanton, whose 1996 Harvard Extension memoir-writing class helped give shape and form to this project; Dr. Peter Kassel, whose guidance helped me sort through the waves of depression, shame, guilt, and rage this unearthing provoked; the fellow members of my former writers group, Brave New Writers, Deborah Blicher and Anne Stuart, whose criticism and comments on my endlessly evolving drafts helped move the process forward; my dear friend, Philip Gambone, author of his own recently published memoir, *As Far As I Can Tell*, whose enthusiasm for my work led him to recommend me to his publisher; and Ian Henzel and St Sukie de la Croix of Rattling Good Yarns Press, whose commitment to publishing our lived experiences is a significant contribution to LGBT history as well as our ongoing appreciation of the diversity that makes us a community.

And finally, I must acknowledge and thank from the depths of my heart my husband, David Imming, whose generosity of spirit gave me the space to work on a project others would have dismissed as mere vanity or, worse, madness. A woodworker of a decidedly minimalist bent, David's disdain for excess, cant, and sentimentality has been an inspiration. I can only hope the final product is worthy of his respect. While this memoir salutes the many who aided my emergence as a gay militant, *Hippie Faggot Freak* is dedicated only to David, the one who finally made me happy.

I have attempted to portray the events in this remembrance as accurately as my memory has allowed. Admittedly they occurred many years ago, although I have been working on this history for a very long time. The memories from which this work springs were, when first put to paper, if not exactly fresh, still indelibly raw. Inevitable gaps, particularly regarding dialogue, much of which is, by the way, cranially implanted, have been imaginatively filled in. Similarly, some names have been changed and chronology has in some cases been tweaked. No scene, however, has been invented, although each one has admittedly been filtered through a lens of moral outrage that no one at the time had the benefit of possessing. Back then, gay life was supposed to be rough. We were expected to just endure.

I am well aware of the skepticism that arises over memories revisited after such long intervals. However, I do not wish to engage here in a discussion of the historical value of the memoir or, more specifically, creative nonfiction. The lives of ordinary people, especially those from oppressed and/or marginalized groups, are rarely told and works like this I hope help fill that still-yawning gap. People like me not only make history; we feel its injustices in ways more privileged and distanced others never will. And feelings are very much what this memoir is about: the slow, painful expurgation of guilt and shame and the sudden—often blinding—dawning of power and pride, without which no liberation is ever possible.

I also hope there are many other works like this—ones of struggle, pain and yearning—in the pipeline. I have always thought lesbians, gay men, bisexuals, and transgender people, especially of the older variety, those from the bad old days before Stonewall, have compelling stories to tell. George Santayana famously said that those who ignore the past are condemned to repeat it. This memoir is offered up as my contribution to keeping the memory fresh of where we as a people—the first out, self-affirming homosexuals in human history—came from, in hopes that past will never be repeated.

To paraphrase Karl Marx, the point is not to interpret the world but to change it. Gay, lesbian, bisexual and transgender people have, to an astonishing degree—at least in the US—done that. We must remember why.

Dale Mitchell
Jamaica Plain, MA
January 2023

DALE MITCHELL

1

Everything Else is Dress-Up

"*Piercing*! She calls his screams *piercing*!" my father bellowed, jabbing his forefinger at a report card from my last year at the Jack and Jill Kindergarten. Located in a squat, cinder block bunker halfway between Jeffersonville and New Albany, the two rivalrous southern Indiana river towns that four generations of both sides of my family had called home, it was the place where I'd first come to think of myself as a mistake: a boy who, in every other respect but "down there," was a girl.

My father shook his head and glared at my mother. "Whoever heard of a word like that being used on a *boy*?!"

Frightened, I clutched my mother's neck and whimpered, "No, Mommy, please, don't let him take me." I listened to the rumble of coal emptying into our basement bin and tightened my grip. Next to it was the spot where my father gave me the punishments that he claimed hurt him much more than me, although he never once screamed during their administration. He didn't even well up. I, on the other hand, bawled my eyes out. "The belt," he called these terrors, although sometimes he resorted to a hairbrush.

Gently patting my back, my mother told my father to lower his voice. His shouting was upsetting me.

"I don't care. He should be upset." Scowling, my father read for her the plea Jack and Jill's director, Mrs. Vivian Oates Haum, had scrawled along the report card's left-hand margin. *Can you help us in reducing his piercing screams? Perhaps he could substitute laughter to express his enjoyment, please!* My father shook his head. "She's underlined that one twice."

"Underlined what?" my mother asked, nuzzling my blond buzz cut.

"'Please,'" he grumbled. "She's underlined 'please' twice." My father paused for the knock on the side of the house that signaled the end of our coal delivery—"Okay, Mr. Sims, see you next month. Yes, yes, I'll drop a check in the mail right away."—and tossed the report card onto the kitchen table. "I won't sign it. I can't. It isn't right." He pulled a fountain pen from the plastic pocket guard of the dress shirt I'd watched my mother iron the previous afternoon and placed it on the Formica table top in front of her. "This time, you'll have to."

My mother put on the reading glasses she kept on a chain around her neck and ran a red manicured nail down the report card's mimeographed column of boxes. "I don't know why you're so upset," she murmured, breezily ignoring the handwritten "more" Mrs. Haum had added after "Self-Control" or the exclamation point she'd placed next to "Excitable." "Everything else seems to be fine."

Shifting me onto a knee, she took my father's pen and signed her name in the gently sloping cursive that was, like her nails and perfectly coiffed hair, a mark of her undying faith in the power of appearances. As she'd often said, when something looked good, it generally was. And as nearly everyone said, I was a beautiful child: blond, blue-eyed, dimpled, and, around her anyway, deliriously happy.

Handing the pen back to my father, she smiled bravely and assured him I was merely going through a phase. "He's only five. Lots of boys his age are like this. He'll grow out of it. You'll see." She took my father by the hand and, drawing him in closer, whispered in pig Latin, the language my parents used whenever I wasn't supposed to know what they were saying, "I promise." *Eye-yay romise-pay*.

When, over my father's strenuous objections, my mother bought me a tutu, she made me promise I'd wear it only indoors. "Within these four walls," she demanded, standing beside the Magnavox hi-fi that she said proved, along with the basement Maytag and the garage's Hudson, how blessed we as a family were. I slipped on her gift and, fluffing out its ruffles, beamed. I was blessed too. My mother loved me no matter what—even in a frilly pink tutu.

"Cross your heart and hope to die?" she asked, the hi-fi's needle poised over a 78 recording of Tchaikovsky's *Swan Lake*. Eager to begin my dance, I made the sign across my chest and took the vow that, even at six, I knew I'd be unable to keep.

Satisfied, my mother placed the needle at the start of the record's final cut and watched me take my first leap. "Oh, isn't that pretty!" she cried. "Just beautiful," she purred when I broke into my first pirouette. And so, she continued until, by the end, I was a quivering heap of pink tulle in the middle of her living room floor and she, a proud mother applauding her sissy son's first dress rehearsal as a tutu'd and toe-shoed prima donna ballerina.

Crinkling his nose, our next-door neighbor, Billy, handed the photo back to me and said he didn't know; it didn't seem right.

Trembling, I took the picture from him. "Shhh," I whispered, nervously looking around to make sure my mother wasn't nearby, "it's a secret." My most prized possession, I'd cut the photo out of *Look* magazine and hidden it inside a coloring book. I'd brought it out just for him. Boyishly handsome, Billy was eight and I, two years younger, was about to enter first grade.

Smoothing out its crumpled edges, I stared at the cut-out longingly. A beautiful ballerina clutching a large bouquet of roses swooned in the arms of her handsome mate. I sighed. She was so lovely in her feathery cap and white frilly tutu, so serene in his strong arms. I looked at Billy and flushed. Only he could make me feel like her—a real prima donna ballerina.

"Ooh, she's so pretty," Billy's older sister, Janis, murmured. Disabled from polio, she had limped into the shady cave of a shrub border we used as our clubhouse. "I don't see anything wrong with it. Oh, come on, Billy. Go ahead!"

"Yeah, so what's a girl and what's a boy, anyway? The only difference is down there," I said, pointing at Billy's crotch. "Everything else is dress-up." I reached for the tutu I'd hidden inside a yew and told them it was a gift from my mother. "She says it's fine. I dance for her all the time. She says in make-believe you can be anyone you want."

"Yeah," Janis giggled, "let's play make-believe! We'll be the swans," she said, pointing at the two of us, "and you'll be the handsome prince, Billy. Just like here," she cried, grabbing my photo.

"Oh, all right," Billy replied. "But don't tell anybody."

I promised to keep our game a secret and, donning my tutu, recalled the dressing-down my father had given me after I'd danced 'The Dying Swan' for my grandmother Nanny's sixty-fifth birthday, an event attended by both sides of our family: the Potts's as well as the Mitchells. I was, he'd warned, "skating on thin ice."

I took the photo of the ballerina from Janis and sighed. I didn't care how thin the ice or deep the water; I'd danced alone long enough. It was time I swooned in the arms of a real-live boy.

I explained to Billy and Janis my ballet's plot. A handsome prince falls in love with a beautiful peasant girl. The prince's mother, the evil queen, is horrified and pays a witch to cast a spell on the girl. The witch entices her to drink a cup of magic brew she concocts from poison yew berries, worms, and frogs' eyes. The girl instantly turns into a swan and, in distress, flies to a faraway lake.

Abandoned and forlorn, the prince goes on a hunting trip. He comes upon her lake, mistakes her for prey, and shoots her. Mortally wounded, the swan flutters frantically across the surface of her pond. Realizing his mistake, the prince rushes to her side and watches helplessly as she swoons in his arms. As their lips touch, the swan flutters one last time and expires. The grief-stricken prince collapses across her and dies too. The music swells; the curse is broken; the lovers arise, embrace and, to thunderous applause, slowly ascend into heaven.

"Now, I'm the swan," I instructed my fellow dancers. "Janis, you're the evil queen. And, Billy, you're my handsome prince. Okay?"

"This is stupid," Billy sneered. "Who ever heard of anyone kissing a bird? Ugh!"

"Yeah," Janis cried, suddenly hesitant. "Remember?"

The three of us looked anxiously at each other. Earlier that week, Billy and Janis's father had invited us to watch him kill a goose a farmer friend a few miles outside of town had given him. Grabbing the bird by its neck, he'd spun it around until the body ripped from its head and landed on their garage's sawdust floor. Headless, it had chased us into the alley behind our houses before finally collapsing into a pool of its own blood.

"Bodies can live off their own energy," their father had said of the goose's terrifying stamina. "But only for a while. To survive, the head and the heart must be connected."

As he'd drained the blood from the bird's neck into a battered coffee can, he'd explained we'd just witnessed something called "centrifugal force." "When you spin something around real fast, it separates into its individual parts."

As the coffee can filled to overflowing, I'd wondered if centrifugal force might work on me too. If I spun around on my ballet shoes fast enough, might I be able to separate the girl on the inside from the boy on the outside? After all, only girls were supposed to feel the way I did about boys, Billy especially.

"Oh, come on," I exclaimed, determined to shake the goose's bloody hold. "This is about love, not some stupid old bird!"

When Janis agreed to join in, Billy shrugged and signed on too. "Great!" I said as my cheeks burned. Soon, I'd be in the arms of a real-live boy.

Billy and I flapped around our front yard to music I hummed while Janis hobbled after us in her rickety brace. Swooping back into our hiding place, Billy crouched down, pulled out a cap gun, aimed it in my direction and went *pow*! Falling into a swoon, I called for my lover. Darting out, Billy dropped to my side and, as I quivered in my tutu, nestled me in the soft down of his little-boy arms.

"Now kiss me," I whispered.

Startled, he scowled.

"Go ahead, Billy. The curse won't be broken unless you kiss the swan!" Janis cried, flapping about me like a fat, worried hen.

Bending over, his lips softly swept mine. "Ooh, yuck," he snarled. Wiping his mouth, he jumped to his feet and raced for his front door.

"Billy, Billy, wait a minute," Janis cried. "The story's not over. You're supposed to die in each other's arms."

Billy stopped and turned, his face contorted with rage. "I don't care. Boys aren't supposed to kiss boys. This game is for sissies. I'm going to tell."

Certain I'd get my father's belt if he learned what I'd been up to, I ripped the photo to shreds and buried it in a shallow grave I dug with my fingernails. Tearing off my tutu, I threw it across our front lawn and burst into tears. "Why me?" I cried at the cloudless blue sky. "Why do I have to be so different?"

"It's okay," Janis murmured, running to my side. "Don't worry. I'll make sure Billy doesn't tell." Stooping down, she told me she didn't care what I was—girl, boy, or something in between—she liked me no matter what. Then, she bent over and gave me the kiss that was supposed to release me from my curse.

Lying in the grass, I watched her hobble off to join her brother and burned with envy. Why couldn't I have a sister too? I listened to the creak of her brace and longed for one just like her, as crippled in her own way as I was in mine. With a sister like Janis, I'd have someone who'd love and understand me, no matter what. We'd be allies, united against a world that demanded we be someone we weren't.

I closed my eyes against a flood of tears and recalled my father's rage over the Betsy Wetsy doll my mother had gotten for me. "This is the last straw, Jane, I'm telling you," he'd fumed. "All this mollycoddling has got to stop!" A sister, I told myself, would help shore my mother up too, make her stronger, keep her from buckling under the pressure for me to conform—to be someone she knew I wasn't—someone even she'd never really wanted me to be either.

I had only a brother. Ten years older than me, he was my father's junior, the bearer of his name, although everyone called him Dean, after my father's father, the editor of the town newspaper who drank himself to death when I was only two. In high school when I was in kindergarten, Dean was a dark shadow haunting my childhood, a manly rebuke to my own obdurate effeminacy. Strangers, we eyed each other warily.

He was a tall, lean, good-looking blond with fair skin, a square jaw, and dreamy blue eyes. Model airplanes hung from his bedroom ceiling like trophies. He played the trumpet and marched in Jeffersonville's high school band with gold epaulets and a white plume in his hat. He bought junk cars and souped them up into hot rods that roared down the street on their way to our back-alley garage. He wore t-shirts with rolled-up sleeves, listened to Elvis Presley records, and slicked his hair back into a ducktail, real cool.

He always had a girlfriend. I'd befriend each one, hoping she'd end up my big sister. None of them ever did, mostly because he'd break up with them just as we'd start getting close. As my mother liked to say, Dean preferred getting girlfriends to having them. "Playing the field," she called it.

Halfway between my brother and me, my mother had twin girls. They were my would-be big sisters, Nan and Jane, the latter named after my mother, the former after a maiden great aunt. Shortly before they'd been due, my mother felt a stillness sweep over her womb and, rushing to her doctor, learned her babies had died. No one knew why or how, but then no one talked much about Nan and Jane either. After a while, it just seemed like a curse befell them—or at least that was what "stillborn" sounded like to my impressionable, young ears.

My mother had wanted nothing so much as those girls. Growing up, she'd been repeatedly tormented by her two younger brothers. When she was ten, they'd tied her to a pole in the basement and lit a fire around her. Smelling smoke, her mother had rushed down and stamped out the flames right before they'd engulfed her. Her brothers had claimed it was only a prank, but my mother knew better. Girls had to watch out for boys. They were ticking time bombs, set to go off without a moment's notice.

She'd hoped her firstborn would be a girl but Dean had turned out all boy—as moody and demanding as her husband, Hardin, the spoiled son of one of Jeffersonville's most prominent families. Sometimes, cleaning up after the two of them, she'd recall growing up, laughing and giggling with her girlfriends, the secrets they'd shared, the dressing up and the play-acting. Married, she'd made sure she always had a special girlfriend, but she was almost always the wife of one of my father's colleagues, and my mother had to be careful what she said and did around her. With a daughter, things would be different. With a girl, my mother could be herself—as silly and giggly as she wanted, as she had been when she too was a girl.

Right on schedule, Nan and Jane had dropped from her womb—two inert lumps of broken dreams. While my mother recuperated in the hospital, my father and her mother, a stern, no-nonsense evangelical, had struck down the girls' bedroom, boxed up their dolls and piled them into a pink ruffled heap next to the two rusty trash barrels out by the alley. By the time she returned home, there was nothing left to remind her of her lost little girls. It was almost as if she'd never been pregnant. She'd said my father and grandmother hadn't meant to be cruel. They'd simply wanted her back, like she had been, before the death of her dreams.

No one had bothered to ask if she was okay or what it was like delivering two dead babies. No one had comforted her or held her hand when grief overwhelmed her. Such things were not done back there, in southern Indiana, or then, during World War II, when people were expected to just buck up and get on with things. As my mother liked to say, she'd gotten through it like a real trooper, without any fuss or bother—"all by my lonesome."

Returning to her role as a loving wife and doting mother, my mother had quietly dropped her grief over her lost twins like two stones in a pond. Disappearing into the deep, they silently haunted our family life, dark and mysterious—two tiny faces lurking behind the façade of our middle-class contentment, screaming for tears.

Five years later and on the cusp of forty, my mother decided to try again, one last time. Hoping to regain what she had lost, she again prayed for a girl. In her place, she got a boy who loved pink, played with dolls, and announced his delight with ear-splitting screams. Watching him grow, she often recalled the irony of the old adage: beware of what you ask for, you just might get it.

My mother loved me nevertheless. After all, I was her last child and heartbreakingly sensitive, a crybaby from the start. Perhaps, her devotion simply derived from the fact that I was hers. Or, perhaps, in my piercing screams, she'd heard the far-off cry of her lost Nan and Jane. Protecting and nurturing me, she pretended not to see or, when she did, care how unalterably different I was. After all, she'd paid her dues with Nan and Jane. God couldn't possibly expect her to endure more, at least certainly not something like *that*— the dirty, ugly thing people snickered about when talk turned to the new hairdresser in town or another item in the *Evening News* about the men busted late at night down by the river. "Sodomy," the newspaper called their crimes.

My mother mentioned her twins only at the cemetery. There, on a hill overlooking the Ohio and, to its south, the rolling green of Kentucky, she pointed to their stones, flush with the grass and big enough only for a doll. "There are Nan and Jane. Someday, we'll all be together," she'd whisper, her grip tightening on my tiny hand.

Transfixed, I'd look down at their stones and feel our spirits comingle. Neither one or the other but both—a girl as well as a boy—I was the mistake through which my mother's longing for female companionship was sated, the gift she'd prayed God would bring her and which somehow He'd botched.

I waltzed out of my mother's closet and twirled in front of her full-length mirror. Her petticoat floated around me in a cloud of billowing crinoline. Thrilled, I turned to face my audience. "Look!" I cried, strutting before them like a proud, preening peacock.

Across the room, propped up against the pillows of her four-poster bed, lay my mother, a pale, five-foot-two protectress who kept the world at bay while I explored the frilly contours of my secret self. In her presence, I was the giggly, playful child she'd once proudly declared the happiest ever born. Away from her, the effects of name-calling had started to show. Shy and nervous, I'd become what my first-grade teacher, Mrs. Callahan, a kind, portly older woman who kept the bullies at bay with a whack of a ruler, called 'painfully sensitive,' a schoolmarm euphemism for what the boys at recess and my father in the basement with his belt put far more succinctly. I was, they all agreed, a crybaby, one of the worst.

To my right, sitting in a large wicker chair in a sunny bay overlooking Maple Street, one of Jeffersonville's busiest thoroughfares, was my great aunt Kitno. Married but childless, she was a jolly bear of a woman who, despite crippling arthritis, regularly got down on all fours to play Tiger with me. "Back! I'm not afraid of you," I'd shout as she'd lunge at me, claws bared and growling menacingly. Slowly bending to my will, she'd eventually relent and return to her cage, where she'd resume being my pet. "Meow," she'd purr, nibbling on goodies I'd feed her by hand.

Of all the grown-ups in my life, Kitno was the only one I played with. While my mother protected me, Kitno empowered me. She made me feel strong and brave, like I could take on my enemies and win. She also claimed, with a conviction that stunned even my mother, that I was a child who could do no wrong, a message I loved to hear, mostly because my father made me feel like I could do no right. "Bullheaded," he called my refusal to act more like a boy.

"Ooh, aren't you pretty," my mother cooed, looking up from her dog-eared, underlined copy of Norman Vincent Peale's *The Power of Positive Thinking*. A quilt of blue and pink calico my grandmother had made for her after Nan and Jane had died covered her feet and, on the nightstand to her right, was a photograph of my father in a fedora and tweed suit taken when he was a student at Indiana University, the first on either side of the family to go to college. She turned to Kitno and, smiling, nodded at me, "Have you ever seen anything so beautiful?"

Kitno pulled a bobby pin from between her teeth and beamed. "Just about the cutest thing you'd ever want to see," she cried in her harsh Hoosier twang. She jabbed the pin into the giant gray bun at the back of her head and beckoned me with fat, pendulous arms. "Come here, you little angel," she bellowed, "and let me give you a big hug."

I squealed with delight and instead darted back into my mother's closet. On tiptoes, I pulled a polka-dot sun dress from its hanger, slipped it over the petticoat and, after making sure the straps were properly crossed in the back, fastened them to the giant red buttons on the front of its bodice. Tearing through a mountain of shoe boxes, I found the open-toed sling-back pumps with Lucite heels and rhinestone straps that were my favorites and flushed. A few weeks earlier, when I'd modeled them for my mother's mother, Olive, a stern teetotaler who canned her own vegetables and made her own clothes, even she'd agreed I was a beauty.

The shoes flopped against my heels as I pranced back into the bedroom. Lighting a cigarette, my mother cried, "Oh my, Kitno, look at this!" Kitno glanced up from the stockings she'd rolled down to the tops of her black orthopedic shoes and, rubbing her swollen knees, nodded. "Have you ever seen anything so adorable?"

Giggling, I ran to my mother's vanity and rifled through her jewelry box. Pulling out the aquamarine bracelet that I wore to bed every night, I slipped it onto my left wrist and smiled as it sparkled in the late afternoon light. Aquamarines, my mother had said, were my birthstones. I pointed to my birthmark, a jagged pink moon the size of a quarter on the same wrist, and beamed. "Look!" I squealed, dazzled by the interplay of pink and blue—the latter for the boy I was on the outside, the former, the girl I was on the inside.

"Oh, how lovely," my mother and Kitno cooed in unison.

Rummaging through my mother's purse, I gathered up the tools to complete my transformation—a tube of lipstick, an eyelash curler, and a brown plastic compact with her initials, JPM, filigreed in gold on the top. I gently patted my face with powder, curled my eyelashes and colored my lips, just as I'd watched my mother do hundreds of times before. Trembling, I examined my creation in the vanity's triptych of mirrors and let out an ear-piercing scream. Finally, I was the same on the outside as I was on the inside, a girl through and through.

"Uh oh," my mother muttered, glancing at the clock radio next to the bed. Putting aside her book and tossing off her quilt, she walked over to me and, throwing her arms around me, claimed she'd been having so much fun she'd forgotten all about the time. "Soon, your brother'll be home from band practice and then, before you know it, there'll be your father, barreling through the door expecting dinner. And I haven't even peeled an onion." She turned to my great aunt and smiled. "Whaddya say, Kitno, time to bring this party to a close?"

Grumbling about her knees, Kitno rose slowly from her chair. "I don't know how you manage it all, Jane, I really don't," she muttered admiringly. Striding over to me, she gave me a bear hug and again claimed I was the most beautiful little boy she'd ever seen. Engulfed by her breasts, I inhaled the scent of stale perfume and closed my eyes, certain no one was loved more.

My mother rubbed the blond crew cut that my uncles called 'peach fuzz' and waited while Kitno slowly hobbled out of the room. Then she leaned over and whispered in my ear, "Now, honey, don't tell your father about any of this, okay?"

I noted the sudden seriousness of her tone and nodded. "Yes, Mommy, not a word."

"That's a good boy," she said and kissed me on the cheek. When I returned her kiss, I left a lipstick stain that she said would never do. "What would your father think?" she chuckled as she wiped away the smear with a Kleenex.

I listened as she descended the stairs and then dutifully removed my make-up, rehung her sundress and petticoat on their hangers, and returned her Lucite sling-back pumps with rhinestone straps to their shoe box. By the time my father returned home from work, I was back to being the boy he demanded I be more of, while the girl my mother and great aunt had so greatly admired rejoined Nan and Jane in their hiding place deep inside me, a cave not unlike the one in which Billy, Janis and I had once called our clubhouse.

"So, is that it, just the dance?" Randy, the fifth grader a half-block up Maple Street, asked after my audition for the neighborhood talent show he and his younger brother were organizing. He strode onto the makeshift stage his father had constructed from wood he'd found in the back alley and jotted down a note with a pencil he'd pulled from behind his ear. He looked back at me and smiled. "Got anything else you want to show us?"

Overhead, a chorus of cicadas heralded the start of another muggy Ohio River valley summer. Tucking my tutu back into my overalls, I felt my face flush. I knew my mother would be furious that I'd danced 'The Dying Swan' for others, but I could no longer help myself. I'd danced for her long enough; I needed to hear the applause of others—my peers and playmates. Friends.

"Yeah, come on, show us what you got," Stevie, Randy's younger brother, cried from a stool on the edge of the stage. A year ahead of me at school—he was going into third grade; I, second—he adjusted his cap and winked slyly at his scrappier, older brother.

"I don't know," I replied hesitantly. Other than my mother and my two favorite cousins, Kay and Betsy, no one had ever encouraged me to let more than my inner ballerina out.

"Yeah," Randy chimed in, returning Stevie's wink. "We know you got it. Maybe you're the headliner we've been looking for!"

"Headliner?"

"Yeah, you know," Randy replied, "the main attraction."

"Really?" I muttered, my heart racing. Randy and Stevie were the two toughest kids around. With their backing, no one would ever dare make fun of me again. I recalled the new taunt the bullies had started using on me—*sissy*, they'd sneer and then, snickering, run off—and felt my cheeks burn. Of all the names they hurled at me, it was the one I hated the most—the one that nearly always made me cry.

"Well, I can twirl a baton," I warily ventured. "I mean, I hardly ever drop it." Lying, I even said I could catch it behind my back.

"Just like a real drum majorette!" Stevie crowed.

Emboldened, I offered up more talent. I suggested a medley of songs from *South Pacific*; a reprive of the tap dance I'd done for our first-grade Christmas recital, *The Wedding of the Painted Dolls*; and, as a grand finale, a rendition of Kate Smith's *Bless This House*. I belted out the best lines, the ones near the end where her voice gets so big you're certain God can hear her, and beamed. After that, even my dad would be on his feet, cheering.

"So, you think that's it?" Randy asked, stepping closer.

I considered adding a xylophone solo but didn't want to seem too greedy. "Yeah," I murmured.

A brief, awkward silence followed. Then Randy grabbed me by the neck and threw me against the trunk of a giant maple. "You don't really think we'd let you do all that on our stage, do you?" Pointing at the pink tulle sticking out of my overalls, he claimed I'd make them both laughing stocks. Their father, he charged, would beat them to a pulp. "But that's what you want, isn't it?" Randy snarled, his eyes narrowing. "You want us to get in trouble!"

"No, no, honest I don't!"

"Yeah, you do. You're trouble. Big trouble." Releasing me, Randy demanded I put up my fists and fight. "Like a man," he snarled.

"No, *please*, I told you before, I don't like to fight," I stammered, welling up.

Unmoved, Randy persisted. "I'm gonna whup you. The only question is where." He smiled at his brother. "So, Stevie, whaddya say? Let's let him decide."

"Yeah," Stevie shouted, "let him decide!"

"Okay, you tell us," Randy demanded, his face so close I could've kissed him. "You want a black eye or a bloody nose?" Chuckling, he assured me he wouldn't give me both.

I burst into tears and begged him not to hurt me.

Randy laughed. "Oh look, Stevie, now he's *crying*!"

Stevie leapt off his stool and ran onto the stage. "*Crybaby! Crybaby!*" he whooped over and over.

"So, which will it be, a bloody this?" Randy persisted, tweaking my nose. "Or a black that?" he asked, poking me in the eye.

"Please stop, you're scaring me."

"Oh, look, Randy, we're scaring him," Stevie cried, mocking me.

"Tell you what," Randy said, loosening his grip. "I'll let you go if you promise one thing."

"Yeah, one thing," his brother squealed, jumping up and down.

"Anything," I whimpered. "Just, please let me go."

"You never set foot in our backyard again," Randy replied, his face hardening.

"Yeah," Stevie added, dancing around me like an Indian on the warpath. "We don't like you!"

"But why? What have I done?" I cried. The day before, the three of us had spent the afternoon in my backyard playing house, with Randy the husband, me his wife, and Stevie our adorable son. Home from a hard day at work, Randy had even greeted me with a kiss. When I'd told him I loved him, he'd smiled and told me he loved me too. He'd even told me I could touch him "down there" if I liked, although I'd been too scared to do anything like that.

"Because you're a sissy," Randy growled.

"Yeah, and we don't like sissies," Stevie shouted, jabbing me with a stick. "They make us want to *puke.*"

"Go on, get out!" Randy shouted, his eyes dark swirls of malice. Then, repeating their taunt over and over—*Sissy! Sissy! Sissy!*—they chased me down the alley to my own backyard where, next to a stand of pink hollyhocks I'd grown from seed, they stopped and yelled, "Just what do you think you are, anyway—*a girl*?!"

I wanted to say, yes, that was exactly what I thought I was, but blinded by tears, I instead tossed my tutu into the patch of hollyhocks and ran inside to my mother. There, she lifted me onto her lap and repeated the refrain about sticks and stones that, even at six, I knew was a lie. Bones at least healed but words, uh-huh, they never stopped hurting.

"What are we going to do with you?" my mother asked, her impotence as palpable as my tears.

Having no adequate answer, I wailed all the louder—a reaction that prompted her to suggest I spend the rest of the afternoon in the backyard playing by myself. "You could practice your baton," she said, wiping away my tears with a crumpled tissue she kept in the pocket of her apron. "What do you say about that?"

I slipped off her lap just as my father arrived home from the ordnance works which DuPont had opened at the start of the Korean War. "What's going on?" he grumbled as I darted past him, my baton's pink and silver Mylar streamers flapping wildly behind me.

I heard my mother whisper something and then my father cry, "Again?!" right as the porch door slammed behind me. Tossing my baton high, I ran into the backyard, where my imaginary big sisters, Nan and Jane, greeted me with piercing squeals—three prima-donna-ballerina-diva-drum majorettes together at last. *Eeeeeeee!*

Hearing shouts, I huddled in my pajamas at the top of the stairs, hugging my Betsy Wetsy doll. Suddenly, my brother jumped onto a landing connecting the entry hall of our Maple Street home to the kitchen/breakfast nook in the back and shouted, "Get away from me! Get away!!"

"I'll show you never to talk to me like that!" my father thundered, suddenly joining him. Slamming my brother against the wall, he whacked him across the face. Blood spurted from my brother's nose.

My brother wrestled away and disappeared into the kitchen, where my mother was washing the dinner dishes. Oh, good, I thought, she'll put a stop to this. Chasing after him, my father continued his rant. Over the din of overturned chairs and the slamming of the back door, he shouted it wasn't going to do my brother any good running away. He'd eventually catch up with him. Then he'd teach him a lesson he'd never forget. No son of his was going to talk back to him like that.

My mother said not a word.

Terrified my father was coming for me next, I ran to my bedroom, tossed Betsy Wetsy into the back of my closet, and pulled the covers over my head. While I had no idea what my brother had done, I knew quite well what my father thought of my dolls. Sometimes, he got so angry watching me play with them, I thought he was going explode.

Fortunately, my mother always managed to calm him down, sometimes as easily as with a cuddle and a kiss but mostly by assuring him I was still in that phase she claimed many boys my age went through. Soon, she promised, I'd grow out of it and become the real boy he insisted was his due. *Eye-yay romise-pay.*

That night, I had my first nightmare. A flying saucer appeared over our house and zapped it with lasers. Shouting we had to get out, my father raced into my room and pulled me out of bed. Fleeing to the front sidewalk, I watched in horror as my mother stayed behind to dance in her bedroom window. She was even laughing, as if relieved to finally be rid of us. In the spaceship hovering over the house, her long-lost twins, Nan and Jane, beckoned. Soon, they seemed to be saying, they'd all be together again.

No, Mommy, please, I cried, struggling against my father's grip. *Don't leave me, I promise to be good, please!* I bit my father's arm and screamed at him, *No, I don't want to be with you! I want to be with Mommy. Get away from me.*

He slapped me across the face and told me to never talk to him like that again. Then, smiling eerily, he announced that, from that point on, my brother and I were to do exactly as he said. No more back talk, he said, as my brother stood trembling off to the side, his face caked with blood. Then turning to me, he said only, "No more dolls."

I awoke screaming.

Curled up against my mother, I idly toyed with the cardboard hand fan I'd found on the seat of my folding chair, one of hundreds neatly arranged in rows under a yellow and white-striped circus tent. On one side was a photo of Rev. Billy Graham, the host of the "revival meeting" to which my grandmother had insisted we attend. On the other side was an advertisement for a local funeral home, one of the sponsors of Rev. Graham's Louisville "crusade."

Enrapt, my grandmother gripped my right thigh, vainly trying to control my fidgeting. On the other side of my mother my father leaned forward every few minutes to eye me menacingly. "I want you to sit quiet, you hear?" he'd said as we entered the tent. "This means a lot to ol' Nanny." I'd numbly nodded, not at all sure who Billy Graham was or what his so-called crusade was all about. Besides, it wasn't even Sunday and though my mother had told me there'd be a sermon, she'd said I hadn't needed to wear a sport coat and tie. And while I'd never heard a sermon in a t-shirt before, I'd made sure I put on my favorite, the one with a goldfish on the front warily eyeing a fishhook.

Graham's voice rose as he railed against a litany of social ills he called "abominations." Although I'd never heard the word before, there was something about his delivery that reminded me of my father the night he'd railed against my brother's back talk. And the way Graham kept repeating that word 'abomination' reminded me of all the times bullies had chased me home calling me a 'sissy' over and over and over. Terrified he was about to single me out, I leapt out of my chair, ran to the back of the tent, and took refuge under a folding table.

My parents weren't able to find me until the end of the revival. At first, my mother tried to gently coax me out of my hiding place but when I refused to budge, my father crouched down, grabbed my hand and dragged me, screaming, out of my hiding place. No one had the slightest idea what had provoked me, although one of Rev. Graham's admirers speculated on the way out that perhaps I was possessed.

On the drive home, I finally calmed down enough to ask what an abomination was, although I so mangled the word no one knew what I was talking about. Eventually, on the bridge over the Ohio, Nanny figured it out and, wrapping me in her arms, explained abomination meant "siding with the Devil." She kissed me on the forehead, then the cheek and smiled serenely. "Nothing you ever have to worry about."

She then looked sternly at my mother and asked, "Quite the sensitive one, isn't he, Jane? Is he often like this?" My mother blanched, as she often did when reproached by her mother, although my father grew so beet-red I again thought he was going to explode.

A hundred or so feet below us, the mighty Ohio rushed implacably onward, a torrent of water immune to every attempt to tame or redirect it.

The bronze cast of his sinewy body, naked except for a loin cloth, smoldered in the summer heat. His head, crowned in sharp, talon-like thorns, drooped and hid the compassion that even his tormenters had been unable to kill. His feet, bundled together and nailed to a cross, glowed from the adoration of supplicants who'd come before us.

When I'd once asked my mother why we were never among them, she'd explained we were Presbyterians, while the people who visited that cemetery were Catholics. Presbyterians and Catholics, she'd explained, didn't mix. When I'd asked why, she'd said Presbyterians believed in predestination, while Catholics believed in the Pope. When I'd asked what a Pope was, she'd said he was an old man who spoke Latin, which I figured was a variant of the pig-Latin my parents spoke whenever they wanted to keep things from me. When I'd asked what predestination was, she'd smiled. "It means God decides what you'll be."

"But what happens if you are bad?" I'd asked. "Does that mean God made you that way?" Ever since we'd gone to hear Billy Graham, I feared I was an abomination too.

"That's why God gave us Jesus Christ," my mother had replied. "Through Him, even bad people are saved."

I turned to the three girlfriends I'd come to the cemetery with. Although none of us were Catholic, each of us desperately wanted to be saved. Carol's mother said she was ugly; Susan's father told her she was too smart for her own good; and Donna, no matter how well behaved, could not make her parents stop fighting. I, of course, feared I was a mistake. A girl trapped in a boy's body. An abomination.

I stepped onto the small, geranium-lined plaza encircling the cross and faced Jesus. "Come on," I said, turning to my companions, "let's do it." The others followed suit, and together we huddled around the base of the crucifix.

"Isn't he beautiful?" Carol whispered. I looked up and nodded woozily. Not even the ballet dancer in the photograph I'd cut from *Look* magazine was more handsome. "Yeah," the others murmured in unison.

We knelt and clasped our hands to our chests, praying for a miracle like the ones we'd learned about in Sunday school. After all, if Jesus could cure lepers and raise people from the dead, shouldn't he be able to help us too?

Closing my eyes, I silently offered up my prayer. I explained that no matter how hard I tried, I was not who I was supposed to be. I confessed I was afraid of my father and begged Jesus to protect me. A shudder swept over me as I mouthed the plea I hoped would free me of my torment: Please, Lord, make me a boy, a real one, one my father can be proud of—one he'd never want to beat up.

I waited for a sign that Jesus had heard me—a lightning bolt, a voice from the clouds, a heaving of the ground—but other than the rumble of a far-off motorcycle and the cooing of some nearby mourning doves, there was nothing but silence. After a few minutes, Carol tapped me on the shoulder and informed me it was time to go; she and the others were getting bored.

As we ran back to our bicycles, Donna admitted she'd asked Jesus to marry her. At first, I said nothing, but when the others said they too wanted to be his bride, I stammered out my confession: I also wanted to marry Jesus. I braced myself for their taunts, but they simply nodded and said, of course, I did. "I mean, after all, Dale's a girl's name too," Susan, the smart one, said. Carol, the ugly one, nodded. As she noted, if my parents gave me a girl's name, then it certainly should be okay to act like one. "Besides, who cares anyway?" she asked, while I waited for the ground to open up and swallow us whole. At that, Donna took my hand and reminded me of the refrain I'd repeated over and over since our first tea party: the only difference between us was "down there." After that, everything else was just dress-up.

I looked across the street as a swirl of dust danced around the playground behind the decrepit, six-room Ingramville Elementary School each of us went to. Seeking a refuge from the boys' increasingly unnerving taunts, it was there that I'd first sought out the company of girls. In the cool of the school's deep overhang, we'd jump rope, make mud pies and build a make-believe family with the dolls that, over my father's increasingly loud protests, my mother still bought for me. They never once called me names or made me feel unwelcome. After all, as Susan, the smart one, had said, on some level, my mother—fathers, we'd already agreed, had little to do except, of course, yell at us—must've secretly wanted a girl.

I turned to my friends and smiled. "Come on," I said, hopping on my bike. "Let's go play hide and seek." Then, heading for Susan's backyard, we screamed at the tops of our lungs the chant that announced the coast was clear—everyone could stop hiding: *All-eee, all-eee in free. All-eee in free!*

2
Scary Noises

I sat on our back stoop and glumly watched our new puppy, a Dalmatian, gnaw on a bone. We'd named him Jeff, after Jeffersonville, the southern Indiana river town that we'd be leaving at dawn the next day. DuPont had transferred my father to its headquarters in Wilmington, Delaware, seven hundred miles from the doting canopy of the women in my life: my two grandmothers, Mo and Nanny; my great aunt Kitno; my aunts Gladdy, Bette, and Babe; my favorite cousins, Betsy and Kay; and Katie, the boisterous, hard-drinking woman who was my mother's best friend. In Wilmington, there'd be only my mother. I worried she couldn't hold up. As my father had started noting, by third grade, boys were supposed to have outgrown the dolls, tutus and piercing screams of delight I stubbornly clung to. When, he asked, was the phase my mother insisted I was still going through coming to an end? He was, he confessed, losing his patience.

"Soon, it'll be just you and me, boy," I grumbled and reached down to pet Jeff. Growling, he shot up from his bone and bit my hand. Yanking my bloody fist from his mouth, I ran to my mother in tears.

Dabbing my wound with Mercurochrome, my mother assured me Jeff hadn't meant to hurt me. "He just loves his bones. Imagine how you'd act if someone tried to take away the thing you love most."

Our new Wilmington home, a two-story, three-bedroom Colonial built of glinting Brandywine stone, was what my parents called a "step-up." Located in an early post-World War II suburban tract called Liftwood, it had features our Jeffersonville Queen Anne lacked: a gas-fired furnace; a master bedroom and bath; an attached garage; a screened-in porch; a den with a built-in cabinet for the TV; and a first-floor powder room for parties. Although we never used either, there was also a working fireplace in the living room and, adjoining my bedroom, a sundeck with a tar floor that melted in the summer sun and blistered the soles of my feet. In the back yard, there was even a flag pole that, hidden behind tall shrubs, my father couldn't be bothered with. Eventually, the pole rotted and fell over, although the wagon wheel herb garden at its base remained until my mother, claiming the herbs looked like weeds, pulled everything up and planted marigolds.

Wary of the reception I'd get from our new neighbors, I initially stayed close to home, exploring our half-acre yard so thickly planted with trees my father complained there was no room for a lawn and my mother no sunlight for tulips, the one flower she had luck growing. It had three apple trees; two peaches; three dogwoods, one pink; a mimosa; five crepe myrtles; six azaleas; two rhododendrons; a climbing wisteria; and smack dab in front of the house, a glorious weeping cherry. In spring, the yard's riot of blossoms became ball gowns for the fairy princess with whom I shared the garden, while in the fall, their leaves were the fuel for the backyard incinerations by which I got even with everyone who'd ever called me names. *Burn*! I'd hiss, dancing around the inferno like I was at a witches' Sabbath. Once, the flames shot so high my father came running with a hose, afraid I was about to set Liftwood ablaze.

But the best time was late summer when apples ripened by the bushel and my mother and I cooked them down, just her and me in the kitchen, for days on end. Our first summer, we ended up with so much apple sauce my father had to go out and buy a freezer, which he put in the basement next to the provisions we kept in case of an atomic bomb attack. Unlike Jeffersonville, Wilmington held regular air raid drills—a minute-long screeching of sirens during which cars were supposed to pull over and pedestrians run to the nearest bomb shelter. In Liftwood, everyone's shelter was their basement, although in Shelburne, one suburban tract over, a family built theirs in their backyard out of cinder block.

I'd throw a fit every time my parents threatened to clear-cut the yard for a lawn and tulip beds, although I did secretly wish one of the apple trees gone. Overhanging the sundeck next to my bedroom, it shattered my summer nights with a hailstorm of falling fruit. As they careened across its surface like a sack of upturned marbles, I'd lie in bed, certain that something was out there, coming for me. Terrified, I'd call for help but to no avail. *It's only apples. Go back to sleep*, my father would shout from the downstairs den or, if in the middle of the night, my parents' bedroom on the other side of the house.

One night, the scary noises came not from the sundeck but from my parents' bedroom. I thought I heard my mother say my name and I almost cried out: *Yes, Mommy, I'm here. Is everything okay?* Then, suddenly, I heard her hiss, "Go ahead if it'll make you feel better. Hit me." After that, the house fell into an eerie silence that lasted until dawn.

The next morning, my parents acted like nothing was wrong. My father sat in the breakfast nook, sipping his coffee and reading the Sunday paper, while my mother, in the kitchen, scolded me to get a move on; we were going to be late for church. As I ran upstairs to get dressed, I told myself I must've had another bad dream. As my mother had noted, I seemed to be having a lot of them since we'd left Indiana.

Still, I couldn't shake my mother's taunt: *Go ahead if it'll make you feel better. Hit me.* While I'd seen my father strike my brother and while he'd taken his belt to me numerous times, I'd never known him to raise a hand against her. Indeed, my mother had proclaimed with such conviction that their marriage was happier than just about anyone's they knew that I figured my imagination was once again running wild. Since we'd moved to Wilmington, my mother said that was happening more and more too. "I just don't understand where you get some of your ideas," she'd grumble.

Still, I worried there was more going on beneath the surface of our family life than what my mother was letting on. After all, my parents' shouting that night had been loud enough to awaken me. And they had come home late after a night of partying with friends. I'd noticed they fought more when they drank. My father got especially belligerent, but my mother also became what he called "hard-headed." After a few cocktails, she'd put her foot down over things she'd otherwise let slide. Besides, I was sure I'd heard my mother say my name. Not like she was calling out for me but more like she was protecting me. From my father.

But what had he proposed that had nearly brought them to blows? It couldn't have been my dolls or ballet lessons; they'd argued over both too many times for them to have gotten *that* angry. No, it had to be something more dire, something my mother knew I'd never accept—or forgive. Something so terrible, I'd no longer be me.

Then suddenly it dawned on me: what my mother had put a stop to was the plan my father had been pushing for the moment we'd settled into Liftwood. He wanted to ship me off to military school—the "good, swift kick in the pants" he claimed would cure me of my girly ways and give him the son to which he felt entitled.

After that, the apple tree's nightly barrages announced the arrival of an even more menacing presence. No longer was some imaginary monster about to break in and devour me but a real-live recruiter from the military school in which my father had secretly enrolled me was about to kidnap me. To get around my mother's opposition, my father had arranged for him to arrive late at night when she'd be asleep, and whisk me off to some undisclosed location where my deprogramming would begin.

Only my blood-curdling screams, which invariably sent my mother rushing to my side, foiled his plot, although my mother insisted my imagination was again running wild. "Your father would never do such a thing," she huffed when I finally worked up the courage to confess my terror. "He *loves* you!"

One afternoon, while my mother was off playing bridge, I decided to search for proof of my father's plot. Starting with the top drawer of his dresser, I at first encountered only mementos of the mild-mannered family man he was known to be: a stack of old check registers; a collection of plastic change purses; a cracked golf ball in a box with a handful of pucks; a wristwatch with a shattered glass face; and an old black and white photo of our family waving happily from the shoreline of a large, silvery lake. Then, stuffed between a candy tin full of silver dollars and a stack of old love letters from my mother, I found evidence of another kind of man: a revolver with a short, pitch-black nose and a handle sheathed in thick, nubby rubber. Carefully lifting it out, I'd peered into its stubby barrel and pointed it at the dresser's tiny mahogany mirror, big enough only for a face. Terrified, I carefully slipped the gun back under his socks and, ashen, slammed the drawer shut.

Trembling, I turned and, numbly staring at my parents' bed—the same one in which my mother had put her foot down over my father's plans to ship me off to military school—recalled the scene from the previous Sunday's dinner table. When my mother had tried to calm my father during another one of his tirades against my girly ways, he'd thrown down his napkin, shouted he wasn't going to put up with my whining and crying around much longer and stormed out of the dining room. What if he'd headed upstairs for the gun instead of running off to the garage for his pruning shears? After all, he'd seemed much more upset with me than he'd ever been with the hedges, whose propensity to grow at will kept him permanently on edge.

I never felt the same about my father after discovering that gun. Or, for that matter, my mother. After all, she had to know it was there. She did the laundry twice a week and the gun was right there, next to the dress socks she so neatly folded into tight little balls. Why hadn't she put her foot down about that?

After the gun, I never again trusted the postcard-perfect picture my mother painted of our family life. Nor did I ever again bother trying to see my father as the sensitive, caring, loving man she insisted he really was—if only I'd give him the chance. After the gun, I started listening to my own gut instead—the one that told me my father was a tyrannical bully and my mother a status-conscious coward who'd never leave him, no matter how rough he was on her children.

All my Liftwood friends were girls. While my mother liked to think this was mere happenstance—except for the Chandler boys, whom she agreed were strange, all the kids in the neighborhood my age were girls—I considered it a godsend. For the first time, I could run free without worrying about bullies or being called ugly names that sent me running home in tears.

The girls I befriended accepted me completely for who I was. Never once did they make fun of my fondness for dolls, jump rope, or playing horsey, a game which I usually led, and which involved prancing around like ballerinas and loudly whinnying. Nor did they care that I refused to play any sport but kickball, which, like horsey, allowed me to scream at the top of my lungs every time I successfully connected with the ball. As with my Jeffersonville girlfriends, we were, in every way but outwardly—or what we called "down there"—exactly the same.

There was Patty, who lived next door and loved to play canasta; Barbara, who was tall and lanky and did poorly at school; Molly, her younger sister, who was smarter but short and chubby; Janice, whose father drove a pick-up truck and who lived in a brick ranch house on Shipley Road, which technically put her outside of Liftwood; Anne, who had a Southern drawl, ate glue paste and pulled her hair out at night; and Linda, who was a math and science whizz and lived in one of the few houses in Liftwood sheathed in clapboard rather than Brandywine stone.

Sometimes, there was also Debbie, whose last name ended in a vowel. Our last names all ended in consonants and our fathers worked for either DuPont, Atlas, or Hercules, the three chemical giants headquartered in Wilmington. Debbie's father, who owned a construction company, worked for himself. Everyone's mother was stay-at-home, although Debbie's helped her husband out as his company's part-time bookkeeper. Because of this, my mother didn't approve of Debbie's mom, whose six children she said ran wild. My father, who also disapproved of Debbie's parents, said that was because they were Catholic. Catholics, he said, were told to have as many children as possible. He claimed that was because the Pope wanted to take over the world. Of all my girlfriends, Debbie was the only one my parents actively disliked.

Everyone in Liftwood had cleaning ladies who were called "girls" and who came in once a week to help the "Missus," as they called our mothers. Except for the garbage men and the liveried waiters and bartenders my parents brought in for their annual Kentucky Derby bashes, they were the only Blacks who ever set foot in Liftwood. There were no Jews, nearly all of whom lived in a small modernist enclave just outside Wilmington's city limits, and other than two poor white families who lived in a decrepit brick tenement on Shipley Road—people our neighbors called "trash"—everyone was solidly, proudly—indeed, smugly—middle class.

My girlfriends and I formed a tightly knit group and spent parts of nearly every day together. In summer, we'd ride bikes, roller skate, roam the woods, or swim at a private pool to which nearly every family in the area belonged. In winter, we'd ice-skate on a nearby creek called the Shellpot, go sledding on a hill that ended at the B&O railroad tracks, or play cards like canasta and board games like Clue or Monopoly, which we once modified so we could keep the same game going all season, an effort that provoked so much squabbling our mothers finally told us we had to find something else to do.

Periodically, my parents arranged for me to spend time with boys who lived outside of Liftwood. Generally, these were sons of my father's colleagues, a breed my parents called 'fellow DuPonters.' Almost all their friends were of this breed, and while I got along with their sons, I was always relieved to be back home with my Liftwood girlfriends.

The sole exception was Robert. He was cute and a bit of a roughneck and liked to horse around. Once he took me into the jalousie-enclosed storeroom on the back of their red brick ranch house to show me his penis. While my girlfriends and I had played doctor several times, Robert's showmanship felt very different. He even asked me to touch it. When my girlfriends and I exposed ourselves, we restricted ourselves to just looking. Robert's penis, though, thrilled me. I loved touching it. Once, on a dare, I even put it in my mouth, although when he told me he'd just peed I wanted to throw up.

The next time I saw Robert, I insisted he wash his penis before I touched it. Happy to oblige, he asked me to do something he called "jerking" him; he'd heard it made penises grow big and hard and shoot a sticky fluid he called "sperm." He said when that happened, he'd be a "real man." I tried my best but his penis stayed limp and nothing, thank God, came out of it.

That was when Robert said we'd probably have to wait until hair grew around our penises before anything would come out. "You know, like our Pops." I said that I too had seen that kind of hair around my father's penis but confessed he scared me too much to ever want to look like him. If and when I ever got pubic hair, I vowed I'd shave mine off.

It was then I confessed I was really a girl trapped inside a boy's body. To my great relief, Robert assured me my secret was safe with him. He even went so far as to say he was glad I'd told him. With me as a girl, at least on the inside anyway, he claimed our messing around wasn't the least bit dirty or shameful. Indeed, we weren't doing anything worse than what our parents did late at night, in the privacy of their own bedrooms.

Robert was the first boy I felt normal around, the only one who let me be me. I had no idea until we started playing around that had anything at all to do with "down there."

I hid behind my mother, afraid to even look at, let alone embrace, my grandmother.

Lying in a Louisville hospital bed with tubes coming out of her nose, Mo chuckled and acknowledged she probably did look scary. "But won't you give me one of your hugs?" she pled, trying to coax me into her arms. "You know how I live for them."

My mother gently pushed me forward and I walked over and gave her a tentative kiss on the cheek.

"There, angel, see how happy you've made your ol' Mo?" she cried, her voice weak and raspy but her smile sunny and bright.

The day before, my parents and I had returned to Indiana to see how Mo was doing after surgery for throat cancer. Only ten, I had no idea what cancer was, although I knew from the hushed tones with which my parents discussed her condition that it had to be bad. When they switched to pig Latin, which they used when I wasn't supposed to know what they were saying, I was sure Mo's days were numbered. *O's-may ot-nay oing-day ell-way*, they'd intone. *It's-yay erminal-tay.* Mo's not doing well. It's terminal.

After my mother, Mo was the woman in my family I loved most. Shy and thin as a rail, she never raised her voice or ever came close to disapproving of me. Even my father was more tolerant of me around Mo. My mother, who chafed under her own mother's stern and disapproving demeanor, loved being around Mo. Once, she even called Mo a "saint."

I agreed. Mo was the calm at the center of my brewing family storm. I'd spend a week with her in Jeffersonville every summer and feel even better going home than I did after playing with my Liftwood girlfriends. Sometimes, I imagined being around Mo was like having Nan and Jane as my big sisters.

There wasn't anything I did that Mo didn't praise. And so, when my father announced she'd started something called radiation, my fear of losing her turned into real panic. While I wasn't sure what radiation was, I knew it came from atomic bombs. That's why we had a bomb shelter in our basement. To protect ourselves from it.

My great aunt Kitno and her husband, Jim, a short, ruddy-cheeked Scotsman, were on the other side of Mo's hospital bed. Jim, standing, was dressed in his usual uniform, a tweed sports coat and a flannel shirt buttoned up to the neck, while Kitno, slumped in a chair sipping a Coke and complaining about her swollen ankles, wore a stained, rumpled housedress. Both appeared anxious. Kitno's hair was a mess. Jim's nose was red.

On the wall opposite Mo's bed, a TV my father had paid to have installed, filled in the gaps between Kitno's anxious fretting. The night before, I'd overheard my parents worrying about how Kitno was taking Mo's illness. As they'd noted, the two sisters were inseparable, having lived together since Bo, my deceased grandfather, had been forced out as editor of the *Jeffersonville Evening News* for reasons no one would talk about. Indeed, the two sisters were so close my parents worried Kitno wouldn't last long without Mo.

That was something that worried me too. I loved Kitno almost as much as Mo. Indeed, together, they were my biggest boosters, the only ones who'd never once made me feel strange or different.

A newscaster suddenly appeared on TV with what he called an important announcement. The reigning world heavyweight boxing champion, Ingemar Johannson, a dashing Swede whom Kitno called a "living doll," had agreed to defend his title against an up-and-coming Black boxer named Floyd Patterson. As the screen showed a clip of Patterson briskly bobbing around a ring, his bare chest gleaming with sweat, Kitno registered her disgust. "That Black ape," she snarled, "just who does he think he is?" She glared at the TV screen and shook her head. "Uppity nigger."

Horrified, I waited for one of my parents to chastise Kitno for her language, but both of them just chuckled and quietly shook their heads. As they'd noted many times before, Kitno was a "character," someone who spoke her mind, regardless of who she was around. While they agreed there was something refreshing about that, they acknowledged she wasn't to everyone's taste. One had to be careful about who you put in the same room with Kitno.

Only Mo disapproved of Kitno's outburst. As she noted, Cora, the Black maid who'd helped Mo raise her two kids and who'd stuck with her throughout her cancer treatments even though Mo was too poor by then to pay her, was part of the family. She'd countenance no disrespect. Grabbing a tissue, she loudly coughed up a thick glob of blood and sputum and then, exhausted, dropped her head back onto the pillow. "Besides," she rasped, pointing a long, gnarly finger at me, "there's the child."

"I was only speaking my mind, Bessie," Kitno replied, unrepentant. "Anyway, he's got to learn sometime. The races aren't meant to mix."

That night, while my mother tucked me into the bed my grandfather Bo had been exiled to for reasons no one would say, I confessed Kitno's outburst had upset me. How could someone so loving with me be so hateful toward others? Could Kitno one day say things about me like she had about Floyd Patterson?

My mother laughed; what could I possibly do to ever provoke something like that? Kitno worshipped the very ground I walked on.

I persisted. "But what she said was wrong, Mommy, wasn't it?" My eyes welled up. I was different too and, although no one had ever called me the names Kitno had used on Patterson, the ones people hurled at me were just as hurtful.

My mother patted me on the back and smiled. Kitno just didn't like "coloreds." It was a grown-up thing, she said; when I got older, I'd understand. When I told her I didn't want to understand things like that, she pulled my covers up, kissed me on the forehead and told me it was time to go to sleep. We had a long drive ahead of us. In the morning, we'd be heading home.

On the drive back to Wilmington, I pestered my parents with questions about my grandfather Bo, who'd died when I was only two. Other than basic biographical details—he'd been a piano player on an Ohio River steamboat who'd struck it rich by marrying the daughter of one of Jeffersonville's most prominent citizens—and the faint whiff of shame that surrounded his final years—he'd apparently drunk himself to death—no one said much about Bo. And, unlike Nan and Jane, whose gravesides we visited every time we returned to Indiana, I'd never even seen Bo's grave. I wanted to know why.

I never got very far. My mother would only say Bo had a lovely singing voice, while my father would grunt that he was a distant, rather cold father; they'd never been close. Kitno, never one to mince words, dismissed him as a dandy and a gold digger, while Jim, her husband, confessed that, back before he went on the wagon, Bo had been a great drinking buddy.

No one would say why Bo had his own bedroom, a tiny alcove at the top of the stairs overruled by a looming bronze statue of Winged Victory that Gog, Mo's father, had given them as a wedding present. I pushed and pushed against this silence but never got further than a begrudging acknowledgment that, around the time of Bo's hastily arranged retirement, he'd done something bad that Mo found unforgivable. What that was no one would say, although I was always happy when Mo told me during visits that I was to sleep in his bedroom.

I claimed the statue of Winged Victory was what made the room special but, in truth, it was Bo's spirit that drew me. I'd lie awake at night and feel his presence envelope me. Like the spirits of my would-be big sisters, Nan and Jane, Bo's would reassure me I was fine just the way I was. And, in truth, Bo's bedroom became one of the few places on Earth where I felt at peace with myself. I never once had a nightmare in his bed.

I took the news of Mo's death badly—so badly in fact, my mother considered calling the family doctor and having me sedated. Much of my grief was of course due to the loss of her love. But there was something else about Mo's death that I took badly: the loss of my connection to Bo. Mo had nurtured that connection by playing Debussy's "Clair de Lune," Bo's favorite piano piece, every day we spent together. I'd listen to it and feel him slowly encircle me. If he had lived, I was sure Bo would have loved me just like Mo had. Totally. Unconditionally.

We inherited Mo's piano after she died, but no one ever again played "Clair de Lune." In fact, no one ever mentioned Bo's name unless I brought it up, which I did repeatedly, all to no avail. The silence that enveloped him I grew to dread almost as much as the apples that fell onto our sundeck. After a while, I sensed that silence enveloping me too.

After Mo died, her companion Cora refused to work for Kitno and Jim and, although I repeatedly asked, no one seemed to know what became of her. Indeed, despite the fact that she'd helped raise them, neither my father nor his sister, my aunt Babe, was sure what Cora's last name was. They had no idea how to contact her or even if she was still alive. It was as if she'd been erased, just like Bo—and my would-be big sisters, Nan and Jane.

3
Dogs and Their Bones

My mother stopped me at the top of the stairs and demanded to know if I'd been in her jewelry box. Her face was red, and her eyes were narrow slits. I'd never seen her so angry.

Feigning ignorance, I asked what on earth was she talking about. "You mean that box on top of your sewing cabinet?"

"Yes," she hissed. "You know exactly what box I'm talking about. Someone's been rifling through it." Afraid the house had been broken into, she'd gone to my father, who'd suggested she speak to me.

"I need to know if it was you. If not, I'm going to have to call the police." She stuffed her fists into her house-coat pockets and fretted over the prospect of our house becoming a crime scene. What would the neighbors think? The police had never been called to Liftwood before.

Stung by her fury, I denied any involvement. That this was a bald-face lie—that the day before I'd gone into my mother's jewelry box to play with her aquamarine bracelet only to have it break while trying to stretch it over my eleven-year-old wrist—was irrelevant. What mattered was convincing her I'd outgrown the phase my father complained I was still hopelessly stuck in. I even feigned outrage. "I mean, what could I possibly want in your jewelry box? It's filled with girl things."

"Don't lie to me, young man," she replied. Her back stiffened as she grabbed me by the arm. "Look me in the eyes and tell me it wasn't you."

"I was not in your jewelry box, Mother," I replied stiffly, staring instead at a blue curlicue on the wallpaper over her right shoulder.

She released me and stormed down the stairs, warning me I'd better be telling the truth. She stopped at the bottom and glowered up at me. "You know what the police do to boys who lie, don't you?"

I shook my head. "No, what?"

"They put them in jail and throw away the key," she hissed before disappearing into the kitchen.

Certain the cops were on their way, I ran next door to Patty's house. As we played hand after hand of canasta, I worried my mother would also find evidence of my visits to her closet. That evening, while my parents sipped cocktails in the kitchen, I tiptoed into their bedroom and made sure my mother's handbags and shoes were in their proper place and all her dresses were hung correctly. While six-year-old boys might be forgiven an occasional foray into their mother's closet, eleven-year-olds were supposed to have moved on to more masculine pursuits, like collecting baseball cards, building model airplanes, and playing touch football. I had not.

My mother never did call the police, nor did she ever mention her missing aquamarine bracelet, which, in a panic, I'd tossed into the weeds of the next-door empty lot. However, two weeks later, she canceled my ballet lessons and allowed me to take piano only on the condition that I also learn clarinet. My tutu, baton, and all my dolls suddenly disappeared, and I was moved from the soprano to the tenor section of the church choir. Then, over my loud protests, I was enrolled in Boy Scouts. "Because your father and I say so," my mother sternly explained. They'd even signed me up for summer camp: two full weeks of no one but boys, pitched tents, merit badges, and campfire sing-alongs.

Gloating over his victory, my father boasted he'd make a son of me yet. Cocktail in hand, he goosed my mother into little squeals that made me jump with fright. Then, turning on me, he called me tiger and jabbed me in the ribs until, begging him to stop, I burst into tears.

After that, my ear became attuned to the drone of his Corvair turning into the driveway, the signal that he was home from work. Fleeing to my bedroom, I rode my toy horses to faraway places where no one made fun of anyone for how often they cried, who or what they played with, or what color their skin was. There was only one requirement—everyone had to wear an aquamarine bracelet—and one prohibition—no one was to ever call anyone "tiger." It was a land I came to call *Green Mansions* from the novel of the same name by William Hudson which, along with H.G. Wells' *War of the Worlds*, was the first grown-up book I read.

Three weeks later, my father dragged me out onto the driveway and said it was time I learned the proper use of a baseball mitt. "I don't want to hear it," he snarled in response to my protests. "I shoulda done this years ago."

Armed with the ball, my father glowered at me from his end of the driveway. Disabled by the tawny glove hanging limply at my side, I faced him, filled with dread. I fumbled each of his lobs and all of my returns missed him by yards, rolling under shrubbery or thudding loudly against the side of the house. One even cracked a garage door window, a humiliation my father refused to repair even when, five years later, he put the house on the market. "It's there to remind you," he snarled, although of what exactly—my preference for the company of girls, his disdain for me as a son, or the slow, terrifying withdrawal of my mother's protection—he didn't say.

My father punished my incompetence with a withering barrage. "No, not like that, look at me, not at the ground," he snarled after my first toss.

"Jeez, I'm here in front of the garage," he sneered, pointing to the backyard where my second ball landed. "You have to aim."

My next toss was even more off the mark. "Come on, I know you're not blind." He paused for emphasis and then said what others had been telling me for years: "My God, you throw just like a girl."

The blood rushed to my head and I grew queasy. Bursts of light coursed through the space between us. *He's going to call me a sissy*, I thought. *I know it. I can tell...*

Frantic, I tried to think of a ploy to head him off. As he demanded once more that I stand up straight like a man, I blurted out a request so monstrous I was sure it would shut him up. "Why don't you just get it over with and tell me you hate me?"

My father looked at me coolly from the shade of the garage's overhang. Behind him, all his tools were neatly stored in their proper places. The spade he used to chop stray roots from the mulched clearings he kept around our yard's trees leaned against a wall, next to a rake with its sharp, metal talons. The pruning shears he used to keep the hedges in line hung on a peg, next to a rubber mallet and a shiny scythe. The gas-powered lawnmower with a warning above its shoot to beware of flying objects was tucked between his new, steel-gray Corvair coupe and my mother's old, powder-blue, four-door Buick.

My father's eyes narrowed and he took two long, deep breaths. He nodded and smiled slightly. "I hate you," he said, so matter-of-factly it seemed hardly worth mentioning.

Stunned, I stared at my father through waves of heat radiating off the driveway's blacktop. All around him, our house's sheen of thick, quartz-flecked Brandywine stone glistened in the blinding July light. To my left, our weeping cherry arced gracefully over a patch of neatly clipped turf that my father, claiming there was nothing so beautiful as a lawn, obsessively watered.

A week earlier, saying we had to rid the cherry of its infestation, my father had handed me a stick with one end wrapped in a gas-soaked rag. Reaching into his pocket, he'd pulled out a cigarette lighter imprinted with his employer's logo, a bright red oval encircling the name DuPont, and below it, in bold black caps, the company's founding purpose: EXPLOSIVES SPECIALISTS. Lighting the rag, he told me to stuff the stick into the center of one of the ghostly white tents from which a swarm of caterpillars would soon ravage the tree's lush, green canopy. As it had sputtered and smoked, a hail of crackling larvae showered the ground around me. Exhilarated, I'd climbed onto a step stool and, with my father spotting me, burned out the tree's encampment of invaders, more than a dozen nests. As a pile of charred larvae sizzled on the ground around us, my father had patted me on the back. "Good job, son." Finally, I'd done something right.

My father released the ball from his fist. Silently we watched it drift slowly across our asphalt divide. Rolling inside the mitt I'd flung at my feet, it was the only lob I'd caught that day. He shook his head at the irony, turned, and then, without uttering another word, disappeared into the house.

Bursting into tears, I ran to my mother, who was bent over a nearby flower bed, deadheading pansies. That spring, she and I had planted two flats of seedlings, a ritual we'd shared since moving to Wilmington. Pansies, we'd agreed, were the happiest of flowers.

My mother held me at arm's length and reproached me. "Your father has feelings too. You must try to understand him better," she intoned, her eyes impenetrable pools of pale blue.

"But what about me? Who's going to understand me?"

Ignoring my query, my mother repeated her mantra: I must understand my father better. Then, without so much as wiping away my tears or giving me a hug, she turned and strode stiffly into the house to rejoin my father.

Abandoned, I stumbled into the shade of a sweet gum at the edge of our driveway. Next to it, a lamppost held a varnished shingle that proclaimed us a family: The Mitchells. Every Christmas, my father had strung the post with red and white lights, part of an over-the-top display that included lighting our foundation shrubbery and a twenty-foot cedar on the corner of our lot. The year before, he'd put on such a show it blew out all the neighbors' lights. People still laughed about it.

A crow cawed alarm from the TV antenna next to the sundeck. Locusts droned shrilly from a pair of white birches on the side of the house. By the driveway, wasps buzzed about the mimosa my father kept threatening to take out. "More trouble than it's worth," he'd repeatedly grumbled. "Messy, messy tree."

Crumpling into a heap, I howled at a cloudless blue sky, "Why, why me?" Beneath me, the sweet gum's litter of hard, nubby fruit scraped and poked at the spot on the small of my back my mother would rub while coaxing me out of my nightly terrors. No, no one was out there to get me, she'd murmur. Yes, she and my father would always be there to protect me. No, they wouldn't let go. Yes, she was sure of that, as sure as she was of anything. Why? Because no child has ever been loved more. *Anywhere, ever,* she'd coo, nuzzling me close.

When Robert broke things off during the summer between sixth and seventh grades, the summer we'd both started to sprout pubic hair, I sensed the walls closing in on me. I'd called him up to see if he wanted to play around and it was then that he'd told me boys weren't supposed to do what we did together. It no longer mattered what I said I was on the inside; on the outside, I was still a boy. And, as he noted, boys who played with other boys' penises had to be queer. His older brother had said so. Robert told me he never wanted to see me again.

Robert was the first person who ever used that word 'queer' on me. Many other slurs, of course, would follow, some in rapid succession—homo, pervert, faggot, cocksucker—but none ever stung quite like queer. Maybe it was because I liked what Robert and I did together, although I never did anything he didn't ask me to do. Or maybe it was because the word 'queer' seemed to invite real violence, much more so than even sissy, for which I'd already been beaten up. At any rate, starting with Robert, the names bullies called me shifted from a critique of my mannerisms—sissy, crybaby, fruit, pansy—to the denunciation of a sexuality everyone said was perverted, sick, disgusting, beyond the pale—a true, dyed-in-the-wool abomination.

I anxiously peered from behind the shower curtain. The bathroom was too hot and steamy to make anything out, although I was certain I would've heard him had he snuck in. He was everywhere I went, lurking in the distance. I couldn't see him, but I could feel him. Watching me. Touching himself down there and leering lewdly. What did he want?

I was twelve and in seventh grade, my first year of junior high. Terrified of what the pubic hair I'd started to sprout foretold, I shaved it off until I realized there was no point. Like everything else—my sexual fantasies, the increasingly crass taunts the bullies hurled at me, their growing threats of violence—my pubic hair just kept coming back.

I'd first encountered the man on my way out of a movie theater on Market Street in downtown Wilmington. The Queen Theater, it was called, and I'd just screamed my way through Alfred Hitchcock's *Psycho*, the first film my parents had let me see without an adult in tow. Mostly because my mother had started pressuring me into hanging around more boys, I'd gone with David, one of the few boys in junior high who wasn't too embarrassed to be seen with me.

I'd liked *Psycho*, mostly because I was able to scream at the scary scenes just like the girls in the theater. At one point, the screaming had gotten so loud David complained he couldn't hear what was going on, but I hadn't cared. I'd cared only about the screaming. Several times, it just erupted, all on its own, like at the beginning, when Janet Leigh and John Gavin appeared semi-nude in a hotel room. There had been nothing scary about that scene; the girls in the audience had just wanted to test their lung power. Or maybe it had been John Gavin without his shirt on. He'd certainly taken my breath away. And indeed, the din had been overpowering.

The man outside the theater had been a middle-aged white guy in a tattersall sport coat, tan pants, and a brimmed hat, the kind DuPonters wore to work. Standing in the doorway of a vacant storefront, he'd been too far away for me to see his eyes, but he'd managed to catch mine. Indeed, they'd burned a hole right through me. And then, once he'd gotten my attention, he'd reached down and groped himself. He'd even winked at me.

Appalled, I'd turned to David, who, oblivious, noticed my father's Corvair waiting for us on the corner. As we'd hopped into the car, I'd glanced back at the man. Smiling, he'd nodded and then tipped his hat as if to say, "Be seeing you."

I turned the shower off and reached for a towel. Downstairs, Jeff growled and then started barking. It was dark. My parents were out. What had the dog sensed? Could it be him, the man outside the movie theater?

I jumped into bed, pulled the covers over my head, and tried to figure out why the man had picked me out of the crowd. After all, there'd been hundreds of kids pouring out of the movie theater that afternoon. Was there something about the way I walked? Or held myself? Only yesterday, the boys at school had made fun of me for the way I carried my books. Keep them at your side, they'd instructed. Up against your chest was the way girls carried them.

Or maybe it was the way I dressed. My girlfriends said I dressed better than other boys, most of whom said they could care less about how they looked. I cared a lot. Indeed, one of my favorite past-times was clothes shopping. My mother complained my fashion sense was driving us into the poor house, although she never once refused me a purchase. She said that was because I was spoiled but I had another theory: my mother was pleased she finally had someone taking after her. After all, my mother was a clotheshorse too.

And why had that man grabbed himself *down there*? The boys in the locker room at school said only homos did stuff like that. Did he think I was a homo too?

But I couldn't possibly be. The boys in the locker room said homos liked to kiss each other and I liked to kiss girls. And as if to prove it, I even took up with one—a short, buxom seventh-grader named Penny. I even gave her a ring so we could say we were going steady.

Penny and I made-out a few times, and once I even got aroused. That, I told myself, was proof the man outside the movie theater had read me wrong. Sure, I might walk and talk funny but that didn't make me queer. Indeed, until Penny dropped me, she made me feel like I was all-boy. One of the guys. Normal. I even started laughing at the jokes the other boys made about pussy. After all, why not? I liked pussy too.

It didn't take long to realize my erection had nothing to do with kissing Penny. In seventh grade, I got hard-ons at the drop of a hat. All the boys did. Once, Lars, a classmate who regularly taunted me, got one in the boys' locker room. He wanted everyone to admire it—he was very well-endowed—but even though nearly all the other boys gave it at least an envious glance, I refused to look for fear my façade would crack and I'd get an erection too.

I told myself all that homo-fruit-queer-pansy locker room banter was about other guys, not me. I even started attending school football games and pretending I cared about what happened. I never had the foggiest notion what was going on, although I made sure I kept my eyes on the cheerleaders, who'd signal it was time to leap up from my seat and, along with everyone else on our side, let loose. I was always careful to use a lower register than the time I screamed my way through *Psycho* but the yelling still felt cathartic—and no one once made fun of me.

Best of all was when our side won and the cheerleaders would lead us in our victory chant: *M with an O, with an M, O, U, with an M, O, U, N, T. P with an L, with a P, L, E, with a P, L, E, A, S. A with an S, with an A, S, A, with an A, S, A, N, T. That's how you spell it. Here's how you yell it! MOUNT PLEASANT!* If only for that moment, I was part of the crowd, another normal kid out for a Saturday afternoon football game. Once or twice, I even ventured behind the bleachers where the coolest kids hung out, smoking cigarettes and making out, and pretended I was cool too.

Thud! Thud! Two more apples fell onto the sundeck. That time, I was sure they were footsteps. My parents had gone to another DuPont Country Club dinner-dance and the house was dark and eerily quiet. Petrified, I glanced at the screen door, crawling with moths, and realized I'd forgotten to latch it. All he had to do was walk in. Like I was expecting him.

My eyes darted nervously about my bedroom. A charcoal portrait of me at age eleven stared dully from the opposite wall. Done by a sidewalk artist on a car trip to Cape Cod, my eyes were as blank and listless as a prisoner of war's and my short-cropped hair swirled around a cowlick into two devilish horns. Next to my bed, on the top shelf of a bookcase, my toy horses reared up against a pack of snarling porcelain dogs.

I was thirteen. My voice had deepened and hair had appeared on my legs and under my arms. And although I'd started to masturbate, I beat off as little as possible—not so much because I thought it was a sin, but because of the thoughts it provoked. No matter how hard I tried to think about girls, every time, I fantasized about some guy—mostly kids from school but sometimes others, older guys. I seemed to like guys older than me, although not too old—guys who knew what they were doing, experienced in being pleasured by another guy.

I knew going down on guys was a sin, although I told myself it was okay as long as I never ended up kissing one. That was the dividing line. Kissing meant falling in love and only real homos—the hardcore types, not the fake kind who were just going through a phase like me—fell in love with other guys. Yes, I'd resorted to even that. As my mother had when I'd started playing with dolls, I'd started telling myself my desire for other men was merely a phase—a shameful but thankfully passing moment in my sexual development that I'd never reveal to anyone, ever.

Bonanza flickered from the portable TV, a Christmas present my parents hoped would put an end to our bickering over what shows to watch, that I'd wheeled up to the end of my bed. Little Joe stood on the Ponderosa's porch, smiling. His strong, smooth chest gleamed through his half-open shirt, and his low-slung gun belt gathered his crotch into a fetching mound. Suddenly, his shaft rose against the tight fit of his pants. Smiling, he stood facing me, fully erect.

Another, then another apple fell onto the sundeck. As if in a trance, I tossed off my sheet and crawled to the end of my bed. Moaning, I licked the TV screen.

Yes, that's it, I heard Little Joe say. Or was it him, the man coming for me, the one on the sundeck?

The hinges of the sundeck's screen door creaked open. Flushed, I turned to face my intruder. He was a multitude of men I had crushes on: Little Joe; the lifeguard at our swimming pool; Dr. Kildare; the guys in peg leg pants and greasy pompadours on Jerry Blavat's TV dance show. He was Lars, the classmate who, waving his dick at me from across the locker room, had tried to seduce me with a rhyme: *for a nickel or a dime/Dale will blow me anytime.* He was Perry, the star of the swim team, who'd grabbed my head one day in the school cafeteria and shoved it into his crotch. "You liked that, didn't you?" he'd sneered before swaggering off.

The intruder lay down beside me. As with all the other times, I slunk down the bed and did what he assured me lots of guys did, nothing to worry about. Just because you put a dick in your mouth doesn't mean you're queer. That time, though, he whispered softly *no, not tonight* and pulled me back to him. He smiled, took my head in his hands and kissed me, at first gently, then hard and deep. Squirming against the thrust of his tongue, I whimpered *No! Let me go. This is wrong. Men don't kiss other men. Homos do!*

He pulled back, stared deeply into my eyes, and smiled. *It's time,* he murmured. *You're ready.* Wrapping me in his arms, he plunged his tongue into me, deeper and deeper. An unbearable heat surged through me and then suddenly I came. A thick glob of semen covered my belly.

In a panic, I raced to the bathroom and cleaned myself up. Returning to bed, I pounded the pillow with my fists and begged God to burn this new horror out of me. I flashed on the man who'd beckoned me after seeing *Psycho. Please God, don't let me be him! Please, not a homo! No!*

A gust of wind rattled the apple tree, unleashing a torrent of fruit. The house groaned and creaked. Penned up in the downstairs kitchen, Jeff growled menacingly. On TV, Little Joe drew his gun and fired. *Good shot*! his older brother, Adam, cried.

Whimpering, I glanced imploringly at the print of *Christina's World* hanging over my bed. I'd seen the original at an Andrew Wyeth retrospective in Philadelphia my parents had taken me to, my first visit to an art museum. Planting myself in front of it, I'd held my own against a shoving, jostling tide of gawkers, transfixed. On my way out, I'd spent my monthly allowance on the print and used all my savings from a summer of mowing lawns getting it matted and framed.

Claiming the picture depressed her, my mother had asked what I saw in it. Unable to answer her, I'd scoured it every night before I went to sleep for clues.

Suddenly, I saw it, a detail I'd never before noticed. There, in the upper right corner, next to the weather-beaten house the crippled Christina was trying to claw her way back to, a tiny black shirt on a clothesline waved menacingly at her. *Go away, you cripple*, it seemed to say, *you are not fit to be among us. We don't want you! Go!*

I buried my face in the pillow and broke into long, anguished sobs. What was to become of me? I didn't want to be that man outside the movie theater. I wanted to be good. To fit in. To make my parents proud. *No, God, please, not me. Please, no!*

That night, a new nightmare rattled my sleep. I lay curled up at the foot of my bed, watching my portable TV. The air was sweet with the perfume of apple blossoms and birds sang from the limbs of a neighboring peach. A morning breeze rustled the soft downy hair on my back and cooled my bed's crisp white sheets. Hearing a far-off rumble, I peered out the sundeck's screen door. Suddenly, the horizon pulsed bright orange, then turned blood red and finally dissolved into a putrid soup of swirling pea green.

Boom! The tell-tale sign of an atomic bomb blast—a roiling, gray mushroom cloud crackling with streaks of lightning—arose over downtown Wilmington. Then, the cedar hedge separating us from the vacant, weed-infested next-door lot where I'd tossed my mother's aquamarine bracelet burst into flames. The apple tree quickly followed suit, dropping tracers of red onto the sundeck's white clapboard railing. A line of fire darted across its tar floor to the screen door, engulfing it in a hoop of flame. I tried to cry out but was mute and helpless.

I took a deep breath and slumped into my chair at the glass-topped table on the back porch where we ate our summer meals. I knew I was in store for trouble. An hour earlier, while shucking corn on the patio, my father had started in on me again. I'd come in late from playing kickball with my girlfriends. Complaining the whole neighborhood could hear me, he'd snarled my screaming sounded just like a girl's. "I'm losing patience," he'd warned me. "Your fourteen. Soon, you'll be in high school."

I'd fled to the den to watch *College Bowl* as quickly as I could. Over its din, I'd overheard my parents whispering in the kitchen. A few minutes later, my mother had come in and told me, much too cheerfully, dinner was ready. She'd even said we were having family favorites: barbequed chicken, potato salad, corn-on-the-cob, home-made apple sauce and, for dessert, cherry pie—what she called a "happy meal."

It was then that I knew something was up. She and I had also been bickering. All week, in fact. About girls. When, she'd wanted to know, was I going to start dating? Penny, my seventh-grade "steady," she'd claimed, didn't count. A Jew, she wasn't the kind of girl my mother thought "appropriate."

Immediately after grace, my father lit into me with a furious barrage. "In case you've forgotten, you're a man. It's time you started acting like one." He demanded I stop playing with girls. "Right now, do you hear?" He looked at me for a terrifying few seconds and shouted, "I'm not taking any more guff about this, understand? I'm sick and tired of your whining and bellyaching." He glared at my mother as his right hand curled into a fist. "It's got to stop."

He warned that if I didn't straighten up and fly right, he was shipping me off to military school. He smiled at the prospect. "They'll give you a kick in the pants so fast you won't know what hit you. Yessirree Bob, your head'll spin." He wiped his mouth with his napkin and chuckled. "That's what you need—a good, swift kick in the butt. I should've done it long ago."

I glanced at my brother across the table from me. Refusing to look at me, he stared at his plate and sullenly poked at his chicken. I turned to my mother and mutely implored her to intervene. Looking instead at my father, she merely urged him to lower his voice. He was shouting. The neighbors could hear.

"I don't care!" my father bellowed, banging the table so hard the silverware rattled. "The whole world should hear me." He pointed at me and asked how she thought it looked with me running around the neighborhood, screaming like a stuck pig. "I can hardly look our neighbors in the eye."

He leaned forward, thrust his face into mine, and snarled, "It's not right, you hear me?" The muscles in his face were taut and his thin brown hair was matted with sweat. He paused and took a sip of iced tea. "You act like a goddamned sissy."

I froze and caught my reflection in the glass tabletop. My eyes were hard; my cheeks were flushed pink. My lips were contorted into a grimace and a thin string of spit hung between the two rows of braces I'd been fitted with to straighten my teeth. Claiming I liked them the way they were, I'd fought that intervention too.

I heard a far-off rumble, like at the start of my A-bomb nightmare. Alarmed, I looked up. The porch sparkled from the glint of cutlery and glass. The house's wall of Brandywine stone pulsed with a dark, inner glow. I wrapped my right fist around my glass of milk. I tapped it lightly—once, twice, three times—on the glass tabletop, my signal that this must stop.

Heedless, my father continued his assault. "I've put up with this too long!" he bellowed. "You should've grown out of it years ago."

The roaring inside my head crashed over me. I stiffened against its pull, but it was no use; the tide was too strong. My neck snapped backwards and I became one with it. "Shut up!" I screamed. "I'm not taking it anymore. Do you hear me?"

My father smirked.

Another wave crashed over me. "You're making my life miserable. I can't stand it." I bared my teeth; licks of fire roared up from my belly and seared my throat. "Why can't you just leave me alone?"

"Because I don't want to," he replied coolly. "You need this."

I raised my glass of milk. "I hate you. Do you hear me?! I hate you!" I shrieked and hurled its contents into his face.

Stunned, my father stared at his plate as droplets of milk dripped off his chin. Then bolting up from the table, he grabbed my arm and yanked me from my chair. Screaming, I swept the contents of my place onto the porch's painted concrete floor. The plate, one of a set of eight from Hadley Pottery that my mother had picked up on one of our many trips back to Indiana, shattered into thick, jagged shards; my blue milk glass exploded into a burst of razor-thin diamonds. My chair flew back, tearing a hole in the screen.

My father hurled me onto a chaise lounge at the end of the porch. Jumping up, my mother screamed, "Please, the neighbors! The neighbors will hear!" My brother mutely cowered in the doorway to the breakfast nook where, in a corner, the parakeet I'd named Tinkerbell flitted about its cage, tweeting, *Pretty bird! Pretty bird!* In the kitchen, Jeff rose from his cushion and whined shrilly, his signal that he wanted to be let out.

Straddling me, my father put his hands around my neck. His eyes were swirling pools of fury and his breath was hot and labored. A purple vein throbbed along the side of his neck and globs of sweat dripped from his brow. A droplet of milk clung to his chin.

"Go ahead, strangle me," I cried. "I don't care. Show her how much you hate me." When he raised his fist instead, I looked him in the eye and, smirking, asked if he wouldn't prefer his gun. "Top drawer of your dresser," I sneered. "Underneath the socks."

"Why you rotten little no-good..." my father growled and slapped me across the face.

Refusing to give him the satisfaction of tears, I continued to taunt him. "Oh, come on, you can do better than that."

From across the porch, my mother shrieked she couldn't take it anymore and ran into the den for her car keys. Returning, she waved them at us and announced she was leaving—for good. "Maybe without me, you two can learn to live together," she whimpered before storming out. As my father and I coldly eyed one another, her Buick barreled out of the driveway, headed for who-knows-where.

Once my mother disappeared, my brother retreated to his upstairs bedroom, while my father stumbled mutely into the den and turned on the TV. Panting, I lay on the chaise lounge and listened to a chorus of crickets herald the onset of night.

Two hours later, my mother returned. Standing in the doorway to the garage, she rebuked me with a wild, hunted look. Her eyes were red and puffy and her hair, always perfectly coifed, was a windblown mess.

Separately, my father and I went to her and begged her to forgive us. Weepily, she berated each of us. "We're a family. We're not supposed to treat each other like this."

Fearing she'd returned only to pack her bags, we each promised her everything would be fine. Weighing in first, my father claimed it was just one of those things while, refusing to be upstaged, I lied and told her no real damage had been done. "These things happen," I even said, as if a fourteen-year-old could possibly know such things. Then, together, we assured her our love for her would keep both of us in line.

At that, she blotted the tears from her eyes and, smiling bravely, relented. "Okay, I'll stay." She stuffed a crumpled tissue in her skirt pocket and asked if anyone wanted dessert. "It's cherry pie. I made it fresh today." When no one expressed any interest, she cleared the table and, after cleaning up the mess on the porch floor, washed the dinner dishes between sobs so anguished I wondered if maybe my father hadn't been right about where I belonged. At least in military school, I'd be the only one in tears.

Later, my mother took me aside and reproached me for provoking my father. I tried to express my fury over being called names but my mother made it clear I'd had my say; it was her turn now. "I can't bear it when you two fight like this." Sobbing, she took me by the hands and again pleaded with me to try to understand my father. "You're all I've got. I'd die without the two of you."

Staring at my feet, I didn't bother asking why she was saying all this to me and not my father. After all, he was the adult. I was just a kid. Nor did I ask who was going to try to understand me. We'd been through all that. What I thought or felt didn't matter.

Fuming, I instead retreated to my bedroom where, playing with my toy horses, I vowed to continue the fight. My father could beat me, ground me, take away my allowance or even send me off to military school; I was not giving up my girlfriends. I was a dog, and they were my bones.

"Stupid dog," my father grumbled, rising from his knees. He kicked the sheet metal patch he'd nailed over the screen that my chair had punctured. It sang dully.

Two days earlier, Jeff had ripped through the tear in an assault on the garbage men, whose twice-weekly visits to the back of our house sent him into paroxysms of rage. Too fat to wedge through the opening, he'd whipped himself into a frenzy that caused one of the men to throw a trash can at him. That evening, my father got a call from the sanitation department: no more garbage pick-ups unless we did something about the dog.

True to form, my mother blamed herself for the trouble. She'd neglected to wrap the bones from the previous night's dinner before tossing them out. But I'd suspected something more sinister. The garbage men were different from us: their skin was dark; their sweat, thick and pungent; their banter, loud and, as my mother complained, "uncouth." Jeff sensed the hostility their arrival provoked. He needed to protect us. He needed to scare them away.

After that, I was assigned the task of keeping Jeff off the back porch until the garbage men left. Nothing I did, however, calmed or even restrained his lunacy. After a while, I just stood back and watched as he threw himself at the back door, teeth bared, mouth foaming, barking rabidly. Once, when he got caught up in my legs, he took a chunk out of me, although that time I didn't bother running to my mother. By then, I knew all about dogs and their bones. You either got out of their way or they got in yours.

After a while, Jeff's outbursts became just more background noise, like Tinkerbell chirping "pretty bird," my father shouting at me across the dinner table or apples thumping out a warning on the sundeck floor: *beware, there's something out there! It's coming, closer and closer!* Some nights, I let the intruder in, although after he'd had his way with me, the fantasy almost always morphed into the far-off rumble of another A-bomb nightmare that blew me and everything I loved to smithereens—my family; the dresses and shoes in my mother's closet; her jewelry box; the sterling silver tea set my father had given her for her fiftieth birthday; Jeff; my girlfriends and their houses, almost all built of glistening Brandywine stone; the Shellpot where we ice-skated every winter;

the private pool beside it where we swam every summer; the vacant lot next door where, on a granite slab perched on the crest of a small hillock, we'd played walk the gangplank; the abandoned Queen Anne mansion across Shipley Road we were sure was haunted; the B&O railroad tracks further down where we played chicken with approaching trains; and the woods abutting them where we found a tree house in which we pretended we were whatever we wanted to be: prince or princess; cowboy or Injun; King Kong or Fay Wray. Even the Presbyterian church where every Sunday I begged God to make me right and, across the street, the junior high school where I desperately tried to prove I already was, were incinerated. Nothing remained, not even the weed-choked gravel pullover off Shipley Road where, amidst the litter of used condoms and sticky girly magazines, I first beat off to a photo of a man's fully erect penis.

4
Things Like This

I flicked on the light overhanging the den's Naugahyde sectional and recalled my mother's complaint: the Liftwood house was too dark; the lack of light was starting to depress her. I peered out the window and sighed. Under the thick shade of an apple tree was a patch of bare earth that drove my mother crazy. Every spring, she'd have my father try something new but nothing took—not grass, ivy, pachysandra, vinca, or even hostas, which were supposed to thrive in shade. Even the cedar border between us and the neighbor's house struggled, giving us full view of their garbage cans. That depressed my mother too. She didn't like having to look at other's people's trash.

My mother had started talking about wanting to move. She said she wanted a bigger, sunnier house; she'd feel better with more light. I'd never heard my mother complain about the lack of light or, for that matter, being depressed. In fact, once she'd even described depression as a "cop-out"—a shameful giving-in to the middle-class sin of self-pity. Instead, I sensed something else brewing, darker and more dangerous, like a volcano erupting way down on the ocean floor, with nary a ripple disturbing the surface. Indeed, few things managed to break through the quiet contentment of my family's middle-class facade. No, the Mitchells were picture-postcard perfect: loving, respectable, God-fearing, *normal*.

I watched a swarm of flies buzz around a half-dozen apples rotting on the ground and told myself I'd get to them later—before my mother complained of them, of course. I was in no mood for any more of her nagging. She'd been on me a lot lately, mostly about when I was going to start dating. Other boys had started. Why hadn't I? After all, I *was* fifteen.

Bored, I slumped onto the sectional and idly picked up the latest issue of *Life* from the magazine rack my mother and I had antiqued the summer before. Above the date line—June 26, 1964—the Republican Governor of Pennsylvania, Bill Scranton, looking like a buttoned-down Burt Lahr, grinned from the cover as his teenage son fastened an American flag pin on his mother's gray woolen suit. Scranton had recently announced his candidacy for president.

I chuckled; my parents would not be happy. Ardent Goldwater fans, they believed liberals like Scranton were ruining the Republican Party. I wasn't sure why that was but I'd started wondering if I might be a liberal too. I certainly couldn't be a conservative. My mother said conservatives liked things the way they were and, God knows, I didn't. The way things were meant being harassed and called names. No, I wanted things to be different. Radically so. I wanted to be who I was and not have to be bullied and made fun of. I wanted to be thought of as normal too.

The day before, I'd watched the movie version of *Anna Karenina* with Greta Garbo on TV with my mother. I'd been outraged by the social restrictions that led to Anna's suicide, but my mother had insisted she only got what she deserved. "There are consequences for breaking society's rules," she'd clucked. When, in turn, I'd called her a Babbitt, after the Sinclair Lewis novel I'd just finished reading, she'd retaliated by complaining to my father that I'd been giving her lip.

That night, my father had relentlessly picked on me during dinner. First, I'd raised my fork before my mother, then I'd put my elbows on the table and finally, I'd failed to fold my napkin before being excused. By the end of the meal, I wasn't speaking to my parents and they weren't speaking to me.

Scenes like that were happening more and more. Dinners had become particularly fraught, with my father laying into me with a sarcasm so withering that had it been a more enlightened time, it would have been deemed abusive. I tried standing up for myself or at least not crying, although, mindful of the gun hidden in his dresser, I knew better than to physically provoke him. After a while, our nightly tensions got so bad, my mother finally acceded and let me eat alone, on a tray in front of the den TV. While I was furious with her for not putting a stop to my father's tirades, by then I knew I was pretty much on my own. After all, I'd made my mother look bad. I was supposed to have outgrown my sissy ways. I hadn't and, if there was one thing my mother hated, it was looking bad.

Politics was the latest irritant in my family's increasingly tense dynamic. A few weeks earlier, when I'd announced I was supporting Lyndon Johnson for president, my father had been appalled. "No Mitchell's been for a Democrat since Roosevelt tried to pack the Supreme Court," he'd harrumphed. I hadn't known what that meant or even which Roosevelt he'd been referring to, but I didn't care. I wasn't for LBJ because he was a Democrat, or even a liberal. I supported him because my parents didn't. Whoever they were against, I was for. That was why I also secretly rooted for Martin Luther King. My parents said he was an uppity Negro and needed to be put back in his place. Like King, I didn't like my place either.

Thumbing through *Life*, I came across a headline that took my breath away. Against a backdrop of pitch black, "HOMOSEXUALITY IN AMERICA" screamed at me in a large gray font. Below it, a large photo showed a knot of men in dark sunglasses and leather jackets milling about a dimly lit room. Behind them, a mural of tough he-men in tight-fitting t-shirts spanned a long wall. At the far right, a burst of blinding white light announced a new arrival: a leather-clad man with a beak nose and bleached slicked-back hair. The caption explained they were patrons of a bar run by and for homosexuals who "make a show of masculinity and scorn effeminate members of their world."

What? I gasped. *They hate me too*? I slammed the magazine shut and tossed it back onto the rack.

"Mom?" I cried. I waited a few seconds and tried again. "Anyone home?" No one answered. The house was eerily quiet.

Returning to the article, I lingered over every photo in search of a likeness. *There has to be someone*, I thought, but page after page, I found only gargoyles. One photo filled an entire page. Two men in fluffy sweaters, tight jeans and teased-out hair strolled through Greenwich Village's Washington Square. Walking past them, a middle-aged "straight" couple glared at them. The caption stated: "Flagrant homosexuals are unabashed by reactions of shock, perplexity, disgust."

On the following page, a bald bartender with a pug nose and horn-rimmed glasses glared into the camera. Over his right shoulder, a misspelled sign in front of a row of liquor bottles warned against funny business: "FAGOTS—STAY OUT." The caption explained that he hated homosexuals and ended with his quote: "I say shoot 'em. Who cares?"

Two other photos were spread across the bottom of a pair of facing pages. On the left, a shadowy profile leaned against a lamppost as a car cruised by. The caption said he was an undercover cop waiting to be solicited. Apparently, the ploy worked. On the right, two police decoys escorted their prey, a short, pudgy man in business attire, to a waiting paddy wagon. The caption observed that, when handcuffed, the man had burst into tears.

When I heard my mother's Buick turn into the driveway, I fled to my room and slid the magazine under a rug. That night, I devoured the article under the glare of a flashlight. Torturing myself with its litany of bad news, I learned about police raids, arrests, firings, blackmailers, and suicides. In a side article, heralded by a big, blocky "WHY?" I read about Dr. Irving Bieber, a psychoanalyst *Life* identified as a nationally recognized expert on sexual perversions. He claimed that homosexual men were mentally ill, the emotionally disturbed offspring of emotionally disturbed parents. He said their mothers babied and demasculinized them and made them the most important love object in their lives. Their fathers grew jealous and were given to disparagement and ridicule.

My heart sank. There, I thought, was the likeness I'd been looking for. Bieber even said homosexual boys feared their fathers and often intensely hated them. *Just like me,* I shuddered.

Over and over, I returned to the article, scouring it for glimmers of hope. I learned that homosexuals congregated in big cities where, taking advantage of their anonymity, they'd created their own institutions. They met in "cruising bars" and "gay cocktail lounges" where performers in "full drag" entertained them with imitations of their favorite movie stars: Judy Garland, Marlene Dietrich, and Mae West. At night, they took over whole sections of cities: Chicago's Lincoln Park, LA's Pershing Square, San Francisco's Tenderloin, and New York's 42nd Street.

I learned that Greenwich Village was their capital, the place where, by sheer numbers, "they say the streets are theirs." Under a photo of a mannequin dressed in a high hat, a kimono, and a checked silk scarf, a caption explained that Christopher Street shops catered to a homosexual clientele with "colorful, off-beat, attention-calling clothes that the 'gay world' likes." I found out their favorite fashion statement—"the gay uniform," *Life* called it—consisted of tennis shoes, baggy sweaters and tight khaki pants.

Two weeks later, my parents took me to New York to see the 1964 World's Fair. After they went to bed, I snuck out of the hotel and hung out on the street corner. I scoured the passing crowds for signs of a shared identity, proudly sporting the baggy mohair sweater I'd harassed my mother into buying for me. On my feet, a brand-new pair of bright red tennis shoes shouted out my signal.

No one noticed.

When grown-ups asked, as they often did, I always said I wanted to be an architect. While other boys played touch football or ambushed Injuns from behind tree trunks, I huddled over a T-square and the silver-plated drafting set my parents had given me for my twelfth birthday. Boxed in plush purple velvet, it was the first gift that had matched the magic of dolls. With its array of sharp and shiny instruments, I carefully designed my dream house, a vast expanse of glass and light for a family with nothing to hide.

After the article in *Life*, I gave up designing dream houses. Instead, I dreamed of moving to Greenwich Village and being a full-time homosexual. I didn't care what Dr. Bieber said—that gay men were "psychologically sick" and suffering from "deep and chronic feelings of pathological depression." For all I cared, they could be foaming at the mouth. They were just like me and all I wanted was to be around them.

One day, I wandered into a paperback bookstore next-door to the A&P where my mother was grocery shopping. Scanning the rack of new fiction, a collection of short stories caught my eye: *Last Exit to Brooklyn* by an author I'd never heard of, Hubert Selby, Jr. Wondering if it might have something to do with homosexuals, I scanned the blurbs on the back cover. Allen Ginsberg called it a "rusty hellish bombshell exploding over America," and *Newsweek* claimed it shed "a scorching light on a limited area of human existence."

Sensing pay dirt, I flipped through it and came upon a story, "The Queen is Dead," which opened with the line "Georgette was a hip queer." Slamming the book shut, I slipped it under my jacket and casually strolled out of the store to my mother's Buick. When I caught sight of my mother leaving the A&P, I slid the book under my car seat and glanced in the rearview mirror to make sure my cheeks weren't still flushed. I'd never stolen anything in my life.

"Here, let me," I said, rushing to help my mother load the car's trunk with groceries.

"Why, aren't you the gentleman today!" she cried, startled by my sudden change of mood. For weeks she'd been complaining that I was sullen and withdrawn. "I don't know what's gotten into you," she'd repeatedly snipped. "You used to be such a happy child."

That night, alone in my bedroom, I devoured Selby's story. Like Dr. Bieber, who explained the dynamics of the homosexual psyche, Selby taught me the how-to's of gay sex. Like how to give a blow job. (No, you don't blow on it, stupid.) *Sals legs shook and he bent at the knees and Camille grunted and gurgled, moving her head fantastically, digging her nails into his ass, trying to get every inch of his cock in her mouth. Soon. Soon...*

Or how to take a cock up my ass. *Lee stopped as Vinnie and Malfie held her and Harry mounted her. Vaseline. Vaseline! Please not without Vaseline. Vinnie handed her the jar, then Lee said alright then closed her eyes and cringed as Harry lunged viciously then put her arms around him and her legs around his waist.*

Foretelling a future harsher than even *Life*'s, "The Queen Is Dead" frightened and repulsed me. Yet, as with *Life*'s exposé, I was unable to put it down. Night after night, I returned to it, intoxicated by its lurid depiction of sex between men. While *Life* may have told me what to wear and where to look for gay men, *Last Exit to Brooklyn* taught me what to do when I finally found one. I studied it as if it were the Bible. I wanted to be prepared for when I finally met my Sal. Or would that be Harry? *Harrys sweat fell on Lees face and she smiled and sucked his neck and groaned, hoping he would never come, that he would continue to lunge and lunge and lunge....*

That August, I spent two weeks in Ocean City, New Jersey, where my parents had rented the top floor of a house with a view of the water. Away from my girlfriends, I'd been lonely and, although my mother kept pestering me to befriend the other kids on the beach, I was afraid they'd make fun of me and call me names and so, thinking it better to be called a snob than a queer in front of my very own mother, I stayed stubbornly aloof.

I let my guard down only when I was alone, on my evening strolls along Ocean City's bustling boardwalk. Then, hidden behind dark shades, I ogled the boys in their swim trunks. The best were the ones in Speedos, a new skimpy, skin-tight bathing suit that showed off—sometimes in graphic detail—what my girlfriends back home gigglingly called their "beach bundles."

I liked to count the number of guys I'd find wearing Speedos. Some nights, I'd find more than a dozen. Those evenings, I'd get so aroused I had to put my hands in my pockets and then race back to our apartment to masturbate. A few times, I went back out to ogle even more boys. Thinking I'd finally made some friends, my mother was thrilled.

One night, a boy figured out what I was up to. "Hi," he said, sidling up next to me while I stood under the awning of a trinket vendor, gawking at a crowd of shirtless, older boys. "You like guys too, don't you?"

"Hey, youse guys want some cotton candy?" the vendor suddenly hollered over the din of whirring pinwheels. "Or how 'bout a kewpie doll for youse girlfriends?" He shook one at us. "They're only a quaddah."

Mumbling a terse no thank you, I turned and warily checked out my interloper. He was about my age, fifteen, but shorter, with darker, wavy hair, fuller lips, and a stronger build. I glanced at the crotch of his shorts. There was definitely a bulge. "*Excuse me?*" I cried.

"I saw you looking," the boy replied, pointing at the lifeguard straddling the boardwalk's railing. His left testicle had slipped out of his trunks and dangled between his thighs like a fat, hairy sputnik. Spying it ten yards away, I'd stopped dead in my tracks. "Pretty hot, huh?" he asked.

"I don't know what you're talking about," I stammered. "Just please leave me alone, okay?"

He suggested a walk instead.

I felt my face flush. "But where? There're people everywhere."

He pointed toward the ocean and said we'd be safe "out there."

I told him I didn't understand.

"Under the boardwalk," he explained. "Nobody will know."

The blood drained from my face as I pointed out the sign warning of undertow. "No one's supposed to go down there when the lifeguard's off-duty. It's not safe."

Ignoring me, he pointed at my crotch and asked if I was hard.

"No!" I cried and, turning scarlet, slammed my fists into the pockets of my Bermuda shorts.

"Yeah, you are, I can tell," he smiled and turned toward the beach. "Come on, follow me."

The air was cool and dry, and the light from the boardwalk crisscrossed our space like drawn swords. He leaned against a post and eyed me coldly. "Ready?" he asked. Then, without waiting for a reply, he grabbed my crotch, unzipped my shorts and dropped to his knees.

"But wait..." I murmured as he took me in his mouth. I didn't know his name or where he came from, what he thought God might think, or how what he was doing might affect his chances in life. Above us, a young couple pushing a baby carriage admired the ocean breeze, oblivious to the outrage going on below them. I pulled the boy up from his knees and, holding his face in my hands, told him I first wanted a kiss.

Grimacing, the boy murmured *faggot* under his breath and pushed me away so hard I fell into the sand. By the time I got up and brushed myself off, he'd disappeared. Crawling out onto the beach, I sat alone and watched the moon rise over a sea as black as tar. I waited and waited for the boy to return but he never did. As he'd said, kissing was for faggots; the only thing he let his lips touch was cock. I was the queer. He was just messing around.

The next boy, I approached. I was still only fifteen but had just entered the tenth grade. The boy was a year ahead of me, a student at Mount Pleasant, the suburban Wilmington high school where nearly everyone was what my mother proudly referred to as "college material." This boy was not. He was what the good, middle-class kids at school called a "hood"—one of about a score of tough, working-class types who allegedly fucked like bunnies.

"There isn't anything they won't stick their dicks in," David, the friend I'd seen *Psycho* with, claimed. And so, hoping he might be like one of the men in Selby's "The Queen is Dead"—rough but available—I phoned him late one Saturday night when my parents were out to see if he'd talk. He played along and so every Saturday night I called him back to hear how his sex life was going.

He never asked my name nor I his, although I knew from school he was called Junior, a business student who'd already been held back two years. He answered all my questions, no matter how smutty, matter-of-factly, without a hint of disdain or trace of disgust. He even claimed to enjoy my calls, especially when I asked about his cock. Most guys, he said, didn't like to talk about dick. I was different.

He was proud of his—its size and girth. His balls too. He said they were big and hairy, although he made it clear he wasn't the least bit interested in what other guys had. Indeed, although I asked a lot about his cock, he never asked about mine. As he once explained, he wasn't no fairy.

He claimed he drove girls crazy and that he nearly always scored, even on first dates. He said that while he enjoyed fucking, what he liked best were blow jobs. With a blow job, he could just lie back and let the girl do all the work. He liked that—girls doing all the work, that is. He said he didn't care what they looked like. If they were ugly, he'd just put a paper bag over their heads. As long as they had lips and a tongue, he said he was happy.

I sensed an opening. I recalled Mr. Selby's instructions: *Camille grunted and gurgled, moving her head fantastically, digging her nails into his ass, trying to get every inch of his cock in her mouth. Soon. Soon...*I too wanted to dig my nails into a man's ass—Junior's ass.

I asked if I could give him a blow job. Junior paused, but only briefly, and then said yes, but only for money. I told him I would pay him the seven silver dollars my grandmother, Mo, had given me as birthday presents. The last one she'd sent only weeks before her death. I told him they were my only treasure. Quaking, I begged him to promise me he was for real. "Yeah, man," he purred like a big sexy cat. "I'm for real."

He agreed to meet me behind the Catholic church a quarter mile up Shipley Road from my house. I told my parents I was going to see a friend for help with algebra. I was an excellent math student. I left with no books.

His souped-up Chevy, the color of gun metal, with oversized tires and fringe around its rear window, roared into the parking lot. Its headlights caught me standing in a crevice of the church's granite hulk. I smiled warily, worried he might not like what he saw. Trembling, I wondered if I should've put a bag over my head.

The door of his car creaked open. As he strode toward me, the click of the silver taps on his boots echoed off the church walls. He stood in a shadow next to me, bolt upright. Thick waves of dark, greasy hair were combed back from his forehead. His eyes were cold and black, his skin clear and smooth. He wore tight, tapered pants whose sheen glowed in the moonlight. A white t-shirt clung to his chest. His nipples were erect and his belly flat. His boots were black and shiny; their toes sharp and pointy.

He glanced at his surroundings contemptuously, as if looking for a place to spit. Settling into a pose, he spread his legs and thrust his groin forward, like he'd done this before. He asked for his money.

I handed him my seven silver dollars.

He slipped them into his pocket and cleared his throat. "Thanks, man," he mumbled and glanced up at the sliver of a moon, hanging in the sky like a bright, shiny hook. He reached for his zipper.

"No, let me do that," I murmured and dropped to my knees. Slowly parting the teeth of his zipper, I flushed as the white of his cotton briefs appeared in the moonlight. *Soon*, a voice inside me moaned, *soon you will know*...My mouth went dry and I closed my eyes. *Please*, I heard myself whisper.

Suddenly, a fist slammed into my face. I fell backwards and hit my head against the church's granite foundation. Groaning, I looked up at a sky blanketed with stars and wondered if this was the way it always went with things like this. I recalled the photo in *Life* of the man arrested for soliciting an undercover cop. The caption observed that, when handcuffed, he'd burst into tears. So did I. I started bawling like a baby.

I heard the passenger-side door of Junior's hot rod swing open and then two more boots raced toward me. Another pair of hands picked me up and threw me against the side of the church. I looked at my new assailant and realized he was T, Mount Pleasant's star linebacker and ringleader of its small band of hoods. He and I were in the same gym class. His locker was two doors down from mine. In two days, he'd be slipping into a jock strap only a punch's throw away from me. *No*, I cried, *oh God, please, no.*

Together, they beat me mercilessly. My lip burst. Blood splattered and stained my shirt. When I covered my mouth, blood spilled down my arms and onto my pants.

Hysterical, I begged them to stop. "My parents will kill me," I cried. They paused and, in the interruption, I sensed an opening. Perhaps if I groveled, they'd take pity on me. Perhaps if I beat myself up, they'd get bored and go away.

I told them they were right; I disgusted even myself. I told T and Junior I knew what I was doing was wrong but confessed I was unable to stop.

Admitting I needed help, I proposed a deal: if they let me go, I'd seek a cure. I'd heard there were doctors who fixed problems like mine and promised I'd hook up with one. "As soon as I get out on my own," I sobbed. I even mentioned Dr. Bieber, the shrink from *Life* who'd claimed homosexuals were mentally ill, to prove I knew what I was talking about. "He's an expert," I said.

I broke down. I even thanked them. "This was just the warning I needed." I begged them to not hit me again and repeated my promise to seek help. "You can even check up on me."

T shook his head. He didn't believe in cures. "Once a queer, always a queer," he declared.

"Yeah, you fuckin' weirdo pervert," Junior growled before kicking me with his boot. "And don't call me anymore. Understand, you disgusting piece of cocksucking shit?"

They chuckled as I collapsed onto the asphalt in a howling heap. "Oh my God, my parents," I wailed. "What am I gonna tell my parents?"

"Come on," T snarled, pulling Junior away. "Let's get outta here. Another minute of this and I'm gonna puke."

As Junior's Chevy roared off, I stared numbly into a scrub forest at the edge of the church's parking lot and wondered how long I could hide out there. My chest felt like it was in a vise. Way down inside me, door after door slammed shut. Soon, everyone would know. *Everyone.*

Back home, my parents asked why I was bleeding. I told them I'd walked into a tree and ran to my room. I threw myself across my bed and shook uncontrollably.

My mother yelled up the stairs, "Is everything all right, honey?"

I gathered up all my strength and replied as calmly as I could that, yes, everything was fine. "Why?" I added feebly.

Within an hour, the phone started ringing. Other boys from high school called to ask for silver dollars. They called me queer and cocksucker and hung up laughing. On the fourth call, my father grabbed the receiver from me and told whoever it was to leave me alone. "This is his father," he snarled when the caller challenged him. "Who are you?"

I waited for my father to start up on me, knowing that if he did, I'd go to the bathroom and drag one of my brother's rusty razor blades across my wrist. I didn't care about the disgrace my suicide would bring. I just didn't want to be told one more time how disgusting I was, especially by my father.

He glanced at me. As our eyes met, I was sure he knew. I braced for the assault that would undo me but, without a word, a shake of his head, or even a sneer, he just turned and walked away. Stunned, I stared at the pale blue princess phone I'd taken the bullies' calls on and wondered if maybe my father really did love me. As my mother had said, I just needed to understand him better.

The next morning, I arrived at school to a crowd of bullies waiting for my bus. As my girlfriends tried to distract them, I ran like hell for the safety of homeroom. Making it, I repeated over and over my mother's mantra—things like this don't happen to people like us—hoping I'd wake up to discover it was all just a dream.

It wasn't. My mother was wrong. Things like this really did happen, although if not to people like us, certainly to people like me. As the squawk box at the head of the room announced the start of a brand-new school day, I recalled Junior's assurances the night he'd agreed to meet me. *Sure, man,* he'd cooed, *I'm for real.* I'd had no idea what a threat that made him. Life as I knew it was over.

The room tittered when our two 10th-grade gym teachers announced the start of Mount Pleasant's first-ever sex education class. We'd needed parental permission to attend and, sensing danger, I'd tried to get excused. But my mother, alarmed by my disinterest in dating, had insisted. "It'll be good for you," she'd said in the same stern way she'd demanded I join the Boy Scouts and take golf and tennis lessons. "Boys need to know how to be with girls."

Both teachers confessed they were unprepared for the assignment. With no course outline and little advance notice, neither knew what was expected of them. However, never one to admit defeat, Mr. Wylie, a bald, blustery ex-wrestler who'd been Mt. Pleasant's gym teacher for over a decade, boasted his knowledge of human anatomy would carry the day. Miss Daniels, the tall, slim, mannishly fit girl's gym teacher who was last year's Teacher of the Year, offered no such assurances. Instead, she simply asked the girls to rise and quietly convene in the hall. "We will need to find our own space," she declared.

As the girls slowly filed out of the room, I desperately tried to conceal my panic. While I avoided all-male settings as much as possible, for the ones I couldn't, I made sure I was as inconspicuous as possible. Here, that would be impossible. Although I'd positioned myself in the back of the classroom—safe, at least, from spitballs—four rows ahead of me on the opposite side of the room sat T, loudly horsing around with his buddies. And while he'd blessedly let me be since that night behind the Catholic church, he quickly let me know that, this time, he was aware of my presence. As the last girl left the room, he pointed at me and yelled out, "Hey, wait a minute, one's still here." Every boy in the room laughed but me.

Mr. Wylie, a crude and hateful bully in a t-shirt stretched thin over an enormous beer belly, smiled but said nothing. The day before, he'd reduced two classmates to tears after accusing them of being homos for spending too much time together in the showers. Such humiliations were a regular feature of his gym class, although strangely he'd never once lit into me, even when I'd burst into tears in the middle of a wrestling match. Hopeless, I suspected he found me—beyond the reach of even his searing taunts.

"Okay, guys, it's time to settle down," Mr. Wylie proclaimed from the front of the class. When T refused, he walked over and twisted his ear. "Ouch, Coach, that hurts!" T cried. Mr. Wylie smiled. "Good, it was supposed to. Now maybe you'll sit up and start acting like a man." T glared at the guys snickering around him, as if to say someone was going to have to pay for that. When he turned and scowled at me, I knew who that someone was.

Returning to the front of the room, Mr. Wylie folded his arms across his chest and announced he had a question for us. He said it was a rather delicate one and he'd only proceed if we agreed to be truthful. "Okay," he said after we murmured our assent, "now I want everyone who sleeps with their hands under the covers to raise his hand." When a couple of boys said they didn't understand, he explained he wanted to know how many of us played with ourselves at night.

Leaning against the front desk, he nodded as he surveyed the sea of hands that slowly appeared in response to his query. "Just as I thought," he clucked, shaking his head. Stepping back toward the blackboard, he picked two erasers from the chalk tray and smiled menacingly. "Guess I have my work cut out for me, huh?" Loudly whacking the erasers together, he chuckled softly as a cloud of chalk dust coated the thick, black bristles on his forearms and turned the ring of sweat where his t-shirt strained to cover his belly button into a scary bull's eye. "Okay, the first thing we're gonna do today is talk about masturbation." He paused and arched his left brow. "Ready, girls?"

I froze as the other boys in the room shifted nervously in their chairs. Recalling his taunts from the previous day, I closed my eyes, clasped my hands together and silently begged God to intercede. *Please, don't let him call anyone a homo. Please not here, not today.* I assured God I'd taken His warning that night behind the Catholic church to heart. *I've been good, Lord, so very, very good.* As I noted, I'd even stopped masturbating. *Just please, don't let him say anything bad. Please, God, please.*

God was either asleep at the wheel or unmoved by the plight of sissies like me. "All right, faggots, listen up," Mr. Wylie continued. "Real men don't play with themselves. They save themselves for their wives." He stopped and smiled darkly at the stunned faces staring back at him. Well into his forties, Mr. Wylie had never married.

"You want to know what'll happen if you keep on playing with yourselves?" He held up a limp wrist and, mincing across the front of the room, feyly tickled the chins of the boys in the front row. "That's what, you'll turn into a bunch of swishes!!" he shouted, again banging his erasers together. For a moment, he disappeared behind a cloud of chalk dust and then re-emerged, a ghostly demon in white face. "*Homos*!" he bellowed so loudly I was sure the girls, wherever they were, heard him too.

The color drained from my face and my breath grew labored. Fearing an asthma attack, I watched T whisper something to his buddies and then, smirking, nod toward me. It was then I realized just how pointless prayer was. As T had said that night behind the Catholic church, once a queer, always a queer—a truth not even God could undo.

Certain another beating was in my future, I prayed the bell announcing the end of class would never sound but God ignored that plea too. When it rang, T and his buddies waited for me outside the classroom and, in full view of Mr. Wylie, dragged me into the boy's bathroom across the hall, where they proceeded to beat the shit out of me. I tried to maintain my dignity by not crying but when they threatened to shove my face in the urinal, I succumbed. Sobbing, I begged them to let me be. Laughing, they left me in a heap on the floor. Thankfully, no one pissed on me, although one of them pulled out his cock on the way out and challenged me to suck it. When I refused, he spat on me and called me a cocksucker anyway.

I pulled myself up off the bathroom floor and examined myself in a hand sink mirror. My eyes were red and puffy, my shirt ripped, and my nose, bloody. I splashed some water on my face, cleaned off the blood, tucked in my shirt, and emerged to face my classmates, all of whom were outside the cafeteria, awaiting the lunch bell. I made a beeline for a group of girls who'd always stood by me but, seeing my approach, they turned their backs on me. During lunch, I sat by myself, enduring as best I could a barrage of spitballs.

Suddenly a known homosexual, I'd never even had sex. The only male flesh I'd kissed were the knuckles at the end of a fist. Two months shy of my sixteenth birthday, I knew much too much about hate and nothing at all about love.

Holding my head up high, I tried to convince myself this was the way things were: a homo's sorry lot. Somehow that was more comforting than the thought that I'd brought it all on myself, although that too occurred to me, late at night, when, wracked with guilt, I recalled the seven silver dollars I'd squandered for the privilege of sucking Junior's cock. "Because we're so very, very proud of you," Mo had penned inside each of the birthday cards that accompanied her gifts. I still had them, tied up in a ribbon and stored at the bottom of my sock drawer—a daily reminder of the ruin I'd made of my life. *D'ja hear that Mitchell kid's a cocksucker? Yeah, a real-live queer!*

The next guy approached me, although he was older, too old really—a lech. A business teacher from Mount Pleasant who had T, Junior, and a number of other bullies in his class, he called out of the blue one afternoon after school. He said he'd waited until my mother was out so, as he said, we could talk freely.

Alarmed, I asked how he knew I was alone.

He told me he sometimes played in my mother's bridge club, which was meeting that afternoon. "She's a good player. A sharp dresser, too." He paused and added, "Like you." He said he was drawn to people who dressed well.

I considered terminating the call right then and there but the connection to T and Junior frightened me. Instead, I asked how he'd gotten my name.

He wouldn't say but acknowledged he'd had his eye on me for a while. As proof, he complimented the shirt I'd worn to school that day. "Those purple and green stripes were a real stand-out."

That was it; I told him I had a paper to write and would have to get off the phone soon. "What is it you're calling about?"

He said he had some movies he thought I might like and invited me over to watch a few. He made a point of saying he lived alone, in a cottage in Arden, an art colony north of Wilmington that my mother had declared off-limits. "Too many beatniks," she'd explained before noting other undesirables lived there as well. When I'd asked what kind, she'd mumbled something about Reds and swishes and then noted her hairdresser had just moved there.

When I asked what kind of movies he wanted to show me, he suggested I come over and find out for myself. "I'm sure you'll like them. Everyone does." When I asked who "everyone" was, he refused to name names but assured me I knew many of them. "They say you're fun." When I asked what that meant, he laughed nervously and murmured, "Oh, you know."

I knew better than to ask if T or Junior had put him up to this, although I was certain they had. I glared out the den window into the thick shade of the apple tree and imagined the good laugh they'd had telling him about me—you know, cocksucker to cocksucker. My face flushed and my cheeks burned. Would they never let up?

I again considered hanging up on him but worried he'd only persist. And what if, on a subsequent call, one of my parents picked up? How would I explain a call from a teacher I didn't have—a *business* teacher? *An older man*!

Or what if he'd threaten to tell the other teachers at school what he'd learned—that I'd paid one of his students for sex. Junior, of course, would be more than happy to confirm his story, especially if the teacher forked over some cash or promised to go easy on his grades. It'd then be only a matter of time before the principal called my parents in. "I'm sorry to have to tell you this, Mr. and Mrs. Mitchell, but your son is being expelled," he'd stiffly inform them. He'd wait for my mother to regain her composure and my father's blood pressure to stabilize. I was, he'd explain, unfit to be around other students. "A sexual deviant," he'd call me. *A pervert.*

"So, whaddyasay?" the teacher asked a bit too gamely. "Up for a show?"

I noted I was only fifteen. "I mean, what if someone calls the police?"

He assured me none of his neighbors would care. Arden, he said, was a very "live and let live" place.

I noted I was too young to drive. "And there's no way my parents would take me to a place like Arden." My mother, I explained, said it was godless.

He chuckled and said he'd heard that from some of his other "guests," as he called his prey, most of whom, he noted, also lacked driver's licenses. "I assumed I'd come and get you," he said before assuring me I'd find his car, a brand-new Thunderbird coupe, impressive. "Red," he purred, "with a red leather interior."

I persisted. "And what about getting back?"

"Yes, that too." He paused. "Whenever you want."

"No matter what?"

He again chuckled. "Yes, of course, but I can assure you you'll have a good time. Everyone always does."

I didn't bother asking what he meant by that. By then, it was obvious what he was after. And while I found the prospect of an older man pawing me revolting, I was intrigued with the idea of meeting a real-live homosexual. After hearing so many horrible things about them, I needed to know what they were really like. And other than that man who'd groped himself outside the movie theater where I'd seen *Psycho*, he was the first one I'd ever come across.

I suggested we meet the next afternoon. As I noted, my mother would be out then too. Wednesdays were bridge club; Thursdays, her church group.

"Great," he said before letting me know just how premeditated his call was. "112 Gibson Avenue, Liftwood, right?" I didn't bother asking how he'd gotten my address, nor did I mention how mortified I'd be if he ever showed up unannounced. By then, I just wanted the call to be over. "It's the house with all the trees," I replied tersely and hung up.

As I'd requested, he parked his T-bird by the next-door vacant lot. I darted into it from our shrub border and slid down in his bucket seat until we were safely out of Liftwood. Much older than his yearbook photo—he appeared to be older than even my parents—he was pale and slight with thinning, badly-dyed brown hair and thick, black-framed glasses. Squirrely and unctuous, he was the exact opposite of Junior, whose taut, slicked-back, haughty indifference I'd found so sexy.

By the time we reached Arden, even his Thunderbird repulsed me. He claimed his cottage was Arts and Crafts but by then I was so nauseous I barely noticed the stenciled walls or its rough-hewn ceiling beams. Ushering me through a living room with a large stone fireplace and an impressive collection of vintage pottery, he led me to a darkened alcove whose main features were a day bed, a tufted ottoman, thick drapes, a pull-down screen and a two-reel projector stocked with a film.

I sat on the edge of the day bed and he on the ottoman next to the projector. "Something to drink?" he asked, lighting a cigarette. He snapped his lighter shut and leered at me. "A beer? Or perhaps something a little stronger?"

"No thank you," I replied a bit stiffly and quickly shifted the conversation to a more suitable topic. I confessed that, while Arden had long intrigued me, this was my first chance to visit. I asked if it was true that he had beatniks for neighbors. When he admitted he did, I confessed I'd never seen one and asked what they looked like. Did they really wear turtlenecks? I'd also heard they eschewed deodorant. Did they smell?

He rolled his eyes and impatiently patted the side of his projector. "Ready for some fun?" he asked, again leering at me.

"Uhm, okay, yeah, I guess," I stammered, not at all sure I was, although I did at least make a point of crossing my legs. Whatever it was he had in mind, I had no intention of making it easy for him.

He flicked off the lights and adjusted the drapes so that not a trace of sunlight entered the room. Returning to his seat, he turned the projector on and then, in the flickering glow of his film, turned to watch me. Staring at my crotch, he waited a few minutes and then, as an engorged penis slid in and out of a garishly pink vagina, he asked how I was feeling—his way, I assumed, of discerning how ready I was for a blow job.

I confessed I felt sick to my stomach.

"Oh really?" he said before turning off the projector. "I've never gotten that reaction before." He reached across the room and flicked on the light. "Why?"

Certain he'd only feign outrage, I didn't bother saying I'd expected a different kind of movie, one featuring people like him and most likely me—two homosexuals making love. I stared at his blank screen and wondered if he even had such a film. After all, they'd hardly appeal to the other boys he entertained—T, Junior, and probably the rest of my tormentors.

I briefly considered asking if he'd kissed any of them, only to realize how absurd the question was. Like the boy under Ocean City's boardwalk, he disgusted himself much too much for that kind of intimacy. I recalled the seven silver dollars I'd used to bait Junior and shuddered. Was that what I'd come here to discover—that being a homosexual was all about paying straight guys for sex or, as with this man, plying underage boys with booze and dirty movies?

My stomach knotted. I stared at the spool of film in his projector and suppressed an urge to scream. I'd rather be anyone but him, anywhere but there.

I rose from his day bed and announced it was time to go. "Now," I said, choking on my own nausea. Like T with me, the mere sight of this man, the first homosexual I'd ever met, made me want to puke. Indeed, it was all I could do to keep from throwing up right then and there.

He got up from the ottoman and escorted me back to his Thunderbird. We drove back to Liftwood in silence and, as requested, he dropped me off at the next-door vacant lot where no one would see me. As I mumbled a terse goodbye, I sensed his relief too. I was no more the prey he'd hoped to catch than he the homosexual I'd hoped to meet.

He never again called and I never told anyone about our time together. I had no desire to get him fired, nor did I want to be implicated in the scandal should he be found out. I just didn't want to end up like him. Not at all certain how that might be assured, I first considered prayer. But, after all the beatings and petty humiliations I'd been through, I decided that God couldn't possibly exist. No one could be that cruel.

So, instead I got back in touch with the girl inside me. Better to be her, I thought, than a homo pervert like that man. Late at night, after my parents went out, I returned to my mother's closet for the solace I could not find elsewhere. Donning a bra and a pair of nylons, I stood in front of her bathroom mirror and watched my cock rise against her girdle's tight, rubbery squeeze. Writhing on the cold tile floor, I fantasized pulling a train with a pack of sweaty, sex-crazed truckers. They called me a whore and a slut, which, under the circumstances, felt almost like flattery. Anything, I thought, as long as it wasn't queer or homo.

I no longer recognized my face in the mirror, a smear of lipstick and rouge topped with a blonde wig. In the back of my head, my mother's rebuke played in an endless loop: *I don't know what's gotten into you, Dale. You were such a happy child.*

Of my family's three cars, my mother's brand-new Oldsmobile was fancier and my brother's Corvette convertible flashier, but my father's Plain-Jane, gunmetal gray Corvair coupe was my favorite. As soon as I obtained my driver's license, I'd wait for everyone to go out, disconnect its odometer and take it out on long joyrides through DuPont country, where, behind the thick walls that surrounded their estates, I imagined myself safe—free of bullies and immune to their insults.

One Saturday night, after my parents had gone to the DuPont Country Club for another dinner dance and my brother had left for a weekend reunion with his old fraternity brothers, I decided to head off in a different direction. As before, I disconnected the Corvair's odometer, but that time I drove downtown where I hoped to find sex, not safety. I wasn't sure where or even if I'd find it but I aimed for Wilmington's main drag, Market Street, at the top of which was a bronze statue of Delaware's Revolutionary War hero, Caesar Rodney, astride a galloping steed, and, at the bottom, the ramshackle, block-long agglomeration of Wilmington Dry Goods, where I bought all my 45s. In between, across the street from the movie theater where I'd seen Hitchcock's *Psycho*, was the vacant storefront in whose doorway a man had once caught my eye and groped himself.

I quickly hit pay dirt. A block south of Rodney Square, I spied two men in tight jeans eyeing each other while, over the next five blocks, at least a dozen others milled about. Some were in pairs, but most were alone, surveying from darkened doorways the cars passing by. Most were too obvious for my taste, but one, a short, well-built man in a sport coat and an open dress shirt, caught my eye.

He noticed me too and, smiling, discreetly signaled his interest. Pulling over, I unlocked the Corvair's passenger door and waited to see if he headed my way. He did and, hopping in, gave me a big toothy grin. "Nice night out, huh?" he asked, reeking of alcohol.

Trying not to stare at the thick crop of chest hair spilling from his open shirt, I followed *Life*'s advice and dutifully asked if he was a cop. He laughed at the notion but acknowledged it was wise to be cautious. As he noted, Market Street was crawling with what he called "vice." When he asked if I knew the street well, I confessed it was my first time. "Or at least this late," I added, glancing at my watch. In a little more than an hour, my curfew would be up.

He placed his hand on my thigh and asked if I liked what I'd found. While I confirmed that I did, I admitted to being nervous. As I noted, I'd never been with a guy before. When he asked if I'd ever been with a girl, I told him I was a virgin "both ways."

"*Sixteen?!*" he gasped when I told him my age, "I didn't know they even made 'em that young." When he noted he hadn't "gone gay" until his late twenties, I instantly corrected him. I wasn't gay; I was just experimenting. "Playing the field," I called it.

"I see," he replied, his hand slowly inching its way up my thigh. When he reached my crotch, he smiled. "You're hard. That's a good sign." When I informed him I didn't like "homo talk," he told me not to worry. "It's gonna be fine." He toyed with the zipper of my Madras shorts. "I promise you."

"Show me," I murmured as I reached over the Corvair's gear shift and discovered he too was hard.

He directed me down a steep hill to the train tracks that followed the Christina River east to the Delaware and then north to the freedom of New York City: Greenwich Village, Washington Square, 42nd Street. We drove through a tunnel glimmering with shards of glass, past the humble stone church the Swedes had built to celebrate their victory over the heathens, to a blasted, burned-out factory at the end of a dark, deserted street. In a parking lot lined with razor wire, we fumbled with zippers and belt buckles and, squirming out of our pants, stroked each other until the windows fogged up and the car reeked of our lust. Then he took me and, for the first time ever, I came inside another man's mouth.

When I was done, he leaned back in his seat and asked me to do the same for him. I stared at his erect penis and felt suddenly sick to my stomach. Pulling up my pants, I told him it was past my curfew. I needed to be getting home.

When I dropped him off on King Street at The Golden Greeks, what he said was Wilmington's only gay bar, he gave me his number and told me to call anytime. As he leaned over to kiss me goodnight, I turned away. He sighed heavily, like he'd been through this before, and patted me on the shoulder. "Good luck," he said. "I hope to see you again. You're cute."

I reminded him I didn't like homo talk and, without bothering to say thanks or even wish him well, sped off. On the ride home, I tried convincing myself the experience was just a fluke. After all, I'd never be doing anything like that again.

Besides, what was the big deal? Straight guys let perverts suck their dicks all the time. Take all those guys the business teacher at school blew, for example. Yeah, no question about it, the man who'd sucked me off was the queer. I was just getting my rocks off.

Two weeks later, I called the man back and met him at a motel south of Wilmington. When I arrived, he pointed to the room's double bed and smiled. Unlike in my father's Corvair, he said we could spread out and take our time. "Have some fun," he added, leering at me.

I told him I wasn't sure how I felt about that. And while I accepted his invitation to lay on the bed next to him, I refused to let him kiss me or remove my shirt. I let him take my pants off and, as before, he was impressed with my erection. He said, generally speaking, only guys who were gay got hard that quickly. I reminded him I didn't like that kind of talk. I also reminded him I wasn't gay.

He sucked me off, but I climaxed so loudly he worried someone might complain. When no one banged on the wall or appeared at our door, he lay back down on the bed next to me and, as before, asked me to return the favor.

"You mean put it in my mouth?" I asked, glancing at his swollen member.

He nodded. "I really need it."

Not wanting to appear selfish, I did what he asked but quickly started to gag. "I can't," I said and started to get up.

"Hey, not so fast. You're not the only one who's entitled to have fun," he griped and, grabbing me by the head, shoved my face into his crotch. "Besides, this is good for you," he added, forcing his cock into my mouth.

"I said no!" I shouted, struggling to free myself of his grip. Back on my feet, I threw on my pants and glared at him. "What's the matter, you deaf?"

"Hey, look, okay, I'm sorry!" he cried as I ran out the door. As I gunned my mother's Olds out of the parking lot, I glimpsed him standing in a terry-cloth bathrobe in the threshold of his motel room, slowly shaking his head. He'd paid for a full-day and I'd been with him a grand total of, what? I glanced at my watch. Less than an hour. Hardly enough time to be called a queer, I smiled.

On the ride home, I berated myself for again indulging in behavior that Dr. Bieber had called "pathological." And, as my mother had once said of fighting what she called the "cop-out" of depression, willpower was key. I just needed to think positively. I could be anything I wanted. All I had to do was set my mind to it.

And so, I started dating girls, although only ones my mother approved of—good, middle-class Protestants whose fathers were fellow DuPonters. They had names like Betsy, Barbara, and Donna. And while I hoped one of them would put an end to the latest phase I seemed to be stuck in, our obligatory end-of-date, suburban make-out sessions—what we called back then "parking"—were profoundly discouraging. While my mind desperately wanted me to be straight, my dick remained stubbornly gay. I didn't get hard once.

I never again saw the man I'd walked out on that day, although he made a powerful impression. Unlike the high school business teacher who'd tried to seduce me with dirty movies, he'd been the antithesis of Dr. Bieber's sad, guilt-ridden homosexual. Other than a penchant for fellatio, he'd seemed so normal—so strait-laced and buttoned-down—he could've been one of my father's colleagues, a fellow DuPonter. "A real guy," he would've called him.

He'd so effectively defied the prevailing gay stereotype that I started questioning all that I'd read about homosexuality. What if the theories of so-called "experts" like Dr. Bieber were wrong? What if all the routine horrors of gay life that *Life* had exposed—the police raids, arrests, blacklistings, firings, and suicides—weren't examples of bad people getting what they deserved but instead injustices society inflicted on them simply because they were different? What if the problem was social, not sexual—man-made, not existential? Might being gay be as natural as being straight?

These questions so unnerved me I had a resurgence of asthma that laid me out for a full week. At one point, my breathing became so labored my mother considered rushing me to the hospital for an adrenaline shot. The next morning, she confessed she was worried. I hadn't had an attack like that in years. What was going on?

I tried my best to assure her everything was fine but I knew that was a lie. And although I desperately tried to keep my sexuality in check, the man I'd walked out on had opened the floodgates. Soon, I was sneaking off to Market Street every chance I got. A few times, I even picked up a man in broad daylight. Once, I rammed the car in front of me while cruising in my mother's brand-new Oldsmobile. She got so upset about that, I wondered if she was on to me. After all, one of my pick-ups had turned out to be her hairdresser, the one who lived in Arden with all the other undesirables. Had he said something?

After a while, I got comfortable getting other men off, although I limited our interactions to hand jobs. Men who put cocks in their mouths were gay and I still stubbornly refused to identify as that. When a pick-up once protested sex wasn't real if he couldn't come in my mouth, I kicked him out of the car. Better to embrace a lie and think of myself as straight than accept the truth and be that beat-up queer behind the Catholic church pleading for mercy or, worse, that dirty old man with a bad dye job and a projector loaded with porn. No, I was still just experimenting around. "Playing the field," I still called it.

My father's revolver re-emerged as a focus of my rampaging guilt and anxiety. I checked on it regularly. And while nothing around it ever seemed disturbed, I could not shake the fear that, at some point, he'd figure things out and shoot me for the crimes I committed in his Corvair. When one terrifying Sunday morning he confronted me with the wad of tissues I'd used to clean up the previous night's spill, he looked at me like that was just what he wanted to do. After that, I scoured the car for every trace of my trysts, certain he was on to me, biding his time until he could finally be rid of me. Like the pug-nosed bartender in *Life*'s exposé had said, "I say shoot 'em. Who cares?"

5
Wild Eyed

I took the news that we were moving out of Liftwood badly, although it wasn't until I learned our new house was two doors away from a bully that I actually freaked out. "I hate it! I won't live here," I shouted as my mother showed me the basement rec-room she claimed would be perfect for sock hops. I glared at her while wheezing through lungs rapidly turning to stone, and quietly cursed our family doctor. He'd said I'd outgrown my asthma. "Merely a phase," he'd called it. I couldn't trust him either. I'd outgrown nothing.

My mother's jaw tightened. "But look, it even has its own refrigerator," she sputtered, opening the door as if it were a prize from *Queen for a Day*. She smiled and pointed at the bulkhead. "And see, you and your friends can come and go as you please."

I ran up the basement stairs, suppressing a scream. I sucked cock, not sock hopped. I had no friends.

"I don't understand," she whimpered, running after me. "You know Carrcroft is so much nicer than Liftwood."

"I don't care. It's hideous," I hissed referring to the white brick, two-story Colonial they'd purchased without even consulting me. If we moved in, I'd be under constant siege. "Tell Dad to pack me off to military school. Anything. You decide. But I'm not moving into this house!"

Storming out, I ran to the back property line where the boulder-strewn Shellpot Creek separated Carrcroft from Normandy Heights, an older suburb that, like Liftwood, lacked the modern amenities my mother craved: a dishwasher; a living room big enough for cocktail parties; and a master suite with a full bath on the first floor. "Your father and I aren't getting any younger, you know," my mother had noted after showing me one of the features she was most excited about: his and her closets. "Someday, the stairs will be too much." I didn't bother noting the steep set of stairs to the back porch or the treeless expanse of crab grass that would need to be cut once-a-week. *And who's gonna do that once I run away, huh, Mom?*

I glumly stared across the creek and cursed my mother for her crassness. I didn't care how light-filled, up-to-date, or age-friendly the new house was. All I wanted was to be safe. And, despite its declining prestige, Liftwood was at least bully-free.

I glanced over my shoulder at the house two doors away where Rory, one of my nastiest tormentors, lived and started to tremble uncontrollably. Certain he was on the phone with T alerting him to my presence, I ran to my mother's Olds, jumped inside and locked all the doors. On the drive back to Liftwood, my mother confessed she was flabbergasted. "I've never seen you like this. What on Earth has gotten into you?"

Too terrified to explain myself, I simply shutdown. While at school I behaved normally, speaking up when called on and raising my hand when I knew the answer to a teacher's question, I clammed up as soon as I got home. I wouldn't even talk to my brother who, though he had nothing to do with the move, agreed one night during dinner that Carrcroft was a much more suitable address for someone in my father's position at DuPont. It was all I could do to keep from throwing my glass of milk in his face.

Six weeks later, on the eve of our Carrcroft move, my mother announced she'd had enough; my silence was driving the family crazy. If I didn't start talking soon, she was sending me to a psychiatrist. Afraid she'd find someone like Dr. Bieber, who'd quickly discover my homosexuality and rat me out to my parents, I muttered my first words—a sullen "no thank you" to her offer of another helping of meatloaf and mashed potatoes.

As my mother smiled triumphantly at my father, I stared at my plate and counted the days to my high school graduation. In the middle of January 1966, I had 4 and 1/2 months left to my junior year and another full year before my May 1967 graduation. My heart sank. I couldn't possibly hold out five hundred days living two doors away from a bully. I'd go stark, raving mad. I just knew it.

By the time we'd settled into our new Carrcroft home, I was a mess. I'd developed a chronic low-grade fever and my asthma had rebounded with a fury. I chewed my fingernails down to stubs and clenched my jaws until they ached. I cried myself to sleep and woke up every morning trembling. Part of me wanted to die, the rest of me simply stayed indoors, terrified I'd run into Rory.

I became a recluse, refusing to leave the house for anything but school and counting down the weeks to graduation from the jumble of periodicals that cascaded through our new Carrcroft mail slot. While my options were vast—

my father had a mania for magazine subscriptions—I relied almost exclusively on *Time*, whose weekly reports of a world in flux offered me hope that, if not in suburban Wilmington, attitudes were at least changing elsewhere. If I could just hold on until I finished high school, maybe I could find a college where bullies didn't roam free, calling people like me queers and beating us up every chance they got.

I took to *Time* the way other teenagers took to comic books and *Mad Magazine*; I devoured it. Every week, it opened my eyes to some startling new event at which I could actually imagine myself safe. Real places like the Manhattan art gallery Andy Warhol filled with floating silver Mylar pillows and whose walls he covered in chartreuse and pink cow wallpaper. Or on the set of the new TV hit, *Batman*, an example of "high camp," a tongue-in-cheek aesthetic *Time* claimed was favored by homosexuals, and which declared everything bad, good. Or in one of the venues that, in an essay called "The Homosexual in America," *Time* said catered to an increasingly visible—and restive—"gay subculture:" mixed bars where both male and female "inverts" gathered; "cuff-linky" bars that catered to college kids and "junior executive types;" "swish" bars for "effeminates and hair fairies;" "TV" bars that catered to "transvestites;" "leather" bars for "tough guy types" with a fondness for chains and belts; and, the latest entry in the series—particularly popular in San Francisco, which *Time* suggested was becoming the new gay capital—"topless boy" discotheques, featuring bare-chested male entertainers.

Every week, a new report, often a dizzying array of them, confirmed old shibboleths were crumbling and new ways of thinking were taking root. The Pill, whose availability the Supreme Court had declared a woman's constitutional right, ushered in an era of unprecedented sexual permissiveness. Nude beaches, wife swapping, interracial dating, free-love parties, and "swinger bars" that specialized in "one-night stands"—the heterosexual equivalent of the "tricking" I engaged in on Market Street—proliferated.

Topless go-go dancing replaced the striptease; "happenings" superseded frat parties; and ultra-chic, anything-goes "discotheques" like New York's Cheetah, at whose opening Andy Warhol's "whip dancers" performed, displaced the night club. Crazed dance-floor gyrations like the Frug, Boogaloo, and Philly Dog killed off the Jitterbug and Foxtrot.

Human Sexual Response, a dry, clinical study of the body's libidinal urges, catapulted to the top of *Time*'s bestseller list. Chapters of a new campus-based advocacy group, the Sexual Freedom League, called for unrestricted sex between consenting adults, including the repeal of all sodomy laws. Attitudes toward homosexuality, it charged, were "hypocritical."

Miniskirts, premarital sex, ecumenism, and the Beatles look became 'in'; modesty, chastity, religious dogma and the gray flannel suit, 'out.' The Volkswagen bug, profanity, experimentation, and protest became 'cool'; the family station wagon, piety, tradition and complacency, 'square.' Women started wearing pants, showing cleavage and baring their backs; men stopped cutting their hair, grew beards and burned their draft cards. Self-determination replaced integration; and militance, non-violence. Urban rioting became, if not exactly fashionable, commonplace, driving whites to the suburbs in droves.

An epidemic of "acid heads" broke out in California. The sage Marshall McLuhan heralded the end of the Mechanical "Gutenberg" Age and the advent of a new Electric "Circuitry" Age. Declaring war on the "Old Order," Chairman Mao announced the start of China's Great Proletarian Cultural Revolution. His *Little Red Book*, a collection of revolutionary quotations, became a worldwide bestseller.

Pop art overtook abstraction; silkscreens, the easel. *Peyton Place* superseded *Ozzie and Harriet*; *Hullabaloo, American Bandstand*. The French New Wave usurped Hollywood; tracking shots supplanted the close-up. Sex scenes became de rigueur.

Even the world order, frozen in place since the end of World War II, fractured. France withdrew from NATO and China split from the Soviet bloc. Albania sided with China, Cuba the Soviet Union, while, breaking with both, the Italian Communist Party invited both believers and homosexuals to join. Among the first was the openly gay film director, Pier Paolo Pasolini, whose *Gospel According to St. Matthew* was the first foreign "arthouse" film I made a point of seeing.

But the most startling developments came from southeast Asia, where the North Vietnamese and their southern allies withstood massive air assaults from the world's greatest superpower, the US. Never before had I seen a victim stand up quite so successfully to a bully, leading to a lifelong sympathy for underdogs: Black Panthers, Palestinians, Haitians, Allende's Chile, Fidel's Cuba, Mandela's ANC, striking farmworkers, protesting welfare mothers and struggling public housing tenants.

In America, the war provoked unprecedented dissent. Draftees burned their draft cards and tens of thousands marched in the streets demanding an end to the carnage. The world heavyweight boxing champion, Cassius Clay declared, "no Vietcong ever called me a nigger" and refused his draft call. Oregon Senator Wayne Morse called for the repeal of the Gulf of Tonkin resolution, while some thirty million viewers tuned in to Senator William Fulbright's hearings against the war, the largest topical TV audience in US history.

In April of 1966, when *Time* published its infamous "Is God Dead?" cover story, I started to think the changes sweeping the rest of the world might finally be penetrating suburban Wilmington's stubbornly closed mindset. However, it wasn't until the following week, when its cover story on "Swinging London" prompted about a dozen girlfriends to defy Mt. Pleasant's dress code by hiking their hemlines above their knees, that I was sure change was in the air. Not a single one was written up or sent home.

It was then that I decided minds had opened up enough for me to emerge from my cocoon and attend a party my classmate Jane threw at her house a few blocks away. Jane had remained a friend despite my reputation, and I was sure her party would be safe. As she'd taken pains to tell everyone she'd invited, which she assured me included neither T nor Rory, there'd be no room for funny business. Her parents, strict Lutherans, were going to be chaperones.

Jane lied. When Rory showed up with T in tow, they dragged me out to the tennis court next to her house and told me in no uncertain terms that I'd better get lost. And just in case I didn't get the picture, T punched me in the gut so hard I doubled over, although I at least managed to keep from crying. When I complained to Jane, she looked at me blankly, as if to say Rory and T were my problems, and then resumed dancing with the other girls, all of whom were far too intent on attracting the attention of a real boy to bother with the likes of me. I slunk home without saying goodbye or, as my mother would've insisted, thanking Jane's parents, who were so awed by the turnout they didn't even object to the underage drinking. Finally, their daughter, who had bird legs and small breasts and who was too brainy for her own good, had made it into the "in" crowd.

I never attended another high school party, although I did try venturing out once more, with equally humiliating results. After a teen dance at a K of C Hall in Claymont, a working-class suburb north of Wilmington, organized by Jerry Blavat, a Philadelphia DJ whose weekly TV show featured white kids from South Philly performing the latest Black dance steps, I went with a carful of girlfriends to the Charcoal Pit, a suburban teenage hangout in whose parking lot kids openly chugged beer from the trunks of their parents' cars. When we arrived, I was greeted by a group of bullies larger than any I'd ever encountered, including a few new faces I'd previously considered friendly. Fleeing to the car, I rolled up the windows, locked all the doors and stayed put for the hour it took my girlfriends to tire of flirting with them. On the way home, Mary even had the gall to gush over how sexy Perry, the star of the swim team and the bully who repeatedly tormented me by pretending to sexually come on to me, looked that night. Two weeks later, they announced they were going steady.

After that, I gave up and devoted myself to cruising Market Street. I made up elaborate lies to get permission to use my father's Corvair, all involving a girl I pretended to be dating. This led my parents to believe I'd finally emerged from my shell and become popular, which my mother, an unabashed social climber, claimed was almost as important as good grades.

Afraid she'd again threaten to send me to a shrink, I didn't dare tell her I was so unpopular I couldn't even show my face at school gatherings. And so, when she suggested I throw a party for the kids who I'd claimed had me to theirs, I had no choice but to go along. And just as I feared, it too was a disaster, although the fact that it occurred at home under my parents' noses made it almost as traumatic as my beating behind the Catholic Church.

T, Rory, and their crew showed up drunk, rowdy, and uninvited. Afraid to confront them, I enlisted two girlfriends to ask them to leave. When, in exchange, they demanded three of the antique English beer steins on display on the rec room's bar, I had no choice but to go along. Getting the bullies out of the house without being beaten up, called names, or otherwise drawing the attention of my parents was all I cared about.

The next morning, my mother reminded me the mugs were priceless heirlooms left to us by Mo, the beloved grandmother whose gift of seven silver dollars I'd squandered on another bully, and informed me she was holding me responsible for their loss. How anyone could steal from a fellow student was beyond her. "Maybe, you need to find new friends," she snipped.

I didn't bother replying that I'd happily find new ones, provided she'd accept the guys I picked up late at night on Market Street. Nor did I bother noting the thieves were bullies, not friends, and if only she hadn't insisted on moving two doors away from one of them—all because of a dishwasher and a living room big enough to throw a cocktail party in—none of this would have happened. Instead, I simply stared at my feet and agreed once again it was all my fault. More and more, it felt like just about everything was.

After that, I sank into a depression that my obsessive cruising of Market Street only deepened. Torn between my duty to my family and the demands of my raging hormones, I turned against my sexuality. If I wasn't a homo, I told myself, everything would be fine. Like my high school classmate Jane, I'd be popular and make my parents proud. More importantly, I'd be safe. There'd be no reason to call me names; I'd be just another guy. It wouldn't even occur to anyone to beat me up.

I revived the notion of seeking a cure. As I had that night behind the Catholic church, I promised myself I'd get help as soon as I went off to college. Until then, I pledged to indulge my sexuality, which I had no capacity to suppress, only as a sinner. Guilt would be the measure of my sincerity—self-loathing, the proof of my intent.

The girl still rattling around inside me re-emerged as my pledge's most vigorous enforcer. Every infraction she met with blistering derision. "If you like guys so much, you should be me, not you," she repeated over and over until I feared she just might be right. And although I agreed whatever changes I needed to undergo had to be drastic, I still wasn't ready to accept a trip to Copenhagen, where Christine Jorgensen, the world's most famous "sex-change" had undergone her transformation, as my only way out. The world was in too much flux. I decided instead to continue scouring *Time* to see what other solutions might turn up.

In March of 1967, two days before my eighteenth birthday, Syracuse University notified me I'd been accepted for admission into its School of Architecture, starting that Fall. Claiming it was one of the best in the country, my mother was elated, although by then I worried I'd made the wrong choice. The girl inside wished I'd applied to Johns Hopkins, which didn't have an architecture school but which had recently opened the nation's first sex-change clinic. And while I'd researched various other cures for homosexuality—lobotomy, electroshock, Freudian psychoanalysis, aversion therapy—the girl inside pushed for surgery. As she noted, after a sex-change operation I'd at least be able to wear a dress with impunity. Unfortunately, *Time* hadn't reported on the clinic's opening until several months after Johns Hopkins' application deadline.

The homosexual in me wished I'd been accepted at Columbia, whose architecture school was considered the best in the country. However, it wasn't its prestige that attracted him; it was its proximity to Andy Warhol, whose *The Chelsea Girls*, a three-hour, split-screen epic featuring S&M lesbians and a flamboyant, drug-shooting gay man who called himself the Pope, had caused *Time* to name him the "Cecil B. DeSade" of underground film. "More fit for a sewer than a theater," it had snipped in its review. Not a single character, it complained, was heterosexual.

With Warhol, I wouldn't need a cure. For him, homosexuality was the norm and heterosexuality the aberration. At his Factory, I wouldn't need surgery to wear a dress. I could just put one on.

Appalled, the girl inside me informed me she had no desire to keep hanging around if I intended to remain a guy. She abhorred what she called my "flirtation" with homosexuality and told me I either went whole hog and opted for surgery or she was giving up the ghost. As she noted, she had dreams and she wasn't going to let me ruin them by turning into something so disgusting as a queer.

As if to underscore her point, a few days later I was bombarded with spitballs and called names at a high school basketball game. At halftime, a girlfriend who was a cheerleader advised me to leave. The guys were planning something far worse after the game. On my way out, Lars, the bully who'd repeatedly taunted me in the boy's locker room, followed me into the bathroom and demanded I suck his cock. When I refused, he punched me and ran out. Fortunately, he left my face alone, so I didn't have to make up another story for my parents. By then, all I seemed to be doing was lying to them about what was really going on in my life.

The next day, I came down with a crippling migraine that kept me confined to my bed, blinds drawn, for four days. Suspecting I was faking it, my mother took me to an optometrist who claimed I was going "wild-eyed" and told me to stare at the end of my nose for thirty seconds three times a day. Later that afternoon, when I read in *Time* about the latest attacks by China's Red Guards, the vanguard of Mao's Great Proletarian Cultural Revolution, on what they called the "Old Order"—wrecking the birthplace of Confucius; parading the mayor of Shanghai around in a dunce cap; and forcing the monks of a Buddhist temple to denounce their scripture as "dog farts"—my migraine suddenly lifted. Finally, I was no longer the only one. Others were going wild-eyed too. Millions even.

After that, I added becoming a Red Guard to my list of options for a cure. While the process of changing sex seemed daunting and the likelihood of getting into Warhol's Factory far-fetched, wrecking things felt very doable. Indeed, it was exactly what my mother complained my obstinacy around not acting like other boys was doing to the family—wrecking it.

My utter inability to be suburban, straight-guy normal didn't just fuel my rampaging guilt and insecurity, it also stoked a budding rage. Over and over, I asked myself why homosexuality was so bad, and the only answer I ever came up with—"because everyone says so"—infuriated me. It made me want to bring down the "Old Order" too. The only problem was, in suburban Wilmington, there were no Red Guards—just smug, middle-class, God-fearing, family-oriented types perfectly content with the way things were.

In this regard, *Time* also proved a godsend. From the start of my seclusion, it brought news of people equally unhappy with the answers they'd been given. Seemingly everywhere, they were up in arms—all different types protesting, breaking rules, and challenging the truths they'd been given: California grape pickers, Alabama sharecroppers, draft resisters, peaceniks, prisoners, welfare mothers, slum dwellers, union members, parents, free speech advocates, ghetto priests, colonial freedom fighters and even Buddhist monks protesting South Vietnam's dictatorship. At the forefront, though, were civil rights leaders like Martin Luther King, who was pelted with eggs while protesting housing discrimination in a Chicago suburb; James Meredith, who was shot by a sniper while marching for voting rights; and Fannie Lou Hamer, whose Mississippi Freedom Democrats had crafted the first integrated slate of Southern electoral candidates since Reconstruction.

But it was Stokely Carmichael and his call for "Black Power" that most caught my eye. Stressing "self-determination," he called for a new go-it-alone strategy aimed at wresting control of Black communities by any means necessary. When, in Mississippi's Klan-infested Delta country, he called for the torching of local courthouses, I wished I'd been there to cheer him on. Stokely was doing what I wanted but was too afraid to do. He was fighting back.

The girl inside belittled my infatuation with Black Power. She noted that, unlike sex, there was no cure for skin color and that, as a white, I'd be as unwelcome in Stokely's movement as the homosexual in me was just about everywhere else. And just in case Black Power had started me thinking about what she called a "closer to home" equivalent, she claimed the notion of homosexuals banding together, let alone standing up for themselves, was patently absurd.

As proof, she pointed to *Time*'s report on the trial of a ring of blackmailers who'd preyed on thousands of gay men for more than a decade. During their sentencing, the judge had commended the prosecution for its perseverance by noting the refusal of nearly all of the victims to come forward. One, an unnamed but famous performer, later rumored to be Liberace, had explained that, while he'd easily managed the payoffs, being known as a homosexual would have ruined his career. Another, a Navy admiral, had so feared exposure he'd blown his brains out in a Maryland motel room. "Pathetic," the girl inside said of their cowardice. As she noted, if you couldn't be proud of who you were, you should be something else.

She suggested I instead consider what she called a more "gestural" outlet for my budding rage. Based on *Time*'s coverage, she noted rioters were popping up practically everywhere and not only in urban ghettoes, where she doubted my presence would be welcome. As evidence, she pointed to the "hippies" who'd rioted a few weeks earlier on LA's Sunset Strip and a Dutch anarchist group called "Provos" who'd torn up Amsterdam for several days, allegedly just for the fun of it. While she acknowledged I was unlikely to encounter Provos in the US, she urged me to look into the growing number of stateside groups constituting what *Time* called the "New Left," many of which she claimed were just as fun-loving.

She was particularly impressed with the eclectic group of "Vietniks," as *Time* called them, who'd disrupted a Congressional hearing investigating communist infiltration of the anti-war movement. One witness, Jerry Rubin, future leader of the Yippies, showed up in Revolutionary War garb; another discoursed on the offerings of New York's "Free University"—courses such as "The Search for the Authentic Sexual Experience" and "Hallucinogenic Drugs"; a third, Arthur Kinoy of the ACLU, was carried out screaming; and a fourth confessed he was so nauseated by the panel's inquiry he threatened to vomit all over the witness table. *Time* called the stand-off a new low in political discourse, but I was secretly thrilled. Finally, the wild-eyed weren't only in China or Amsterdam. There was a homegrown variety too.

Happy we were finally seeing things eye to eye, the girl inside promised that if I got "real," as she called a stay at Johns Hopkins, I could scream at my adversaries and vomit over any table I wanted. Even better, she had me go out and, much to my mother's chagrin, buy a Mao jacket, which, as the girl inside so proudly noted, I could even keep after "the change." Female Red Guards, she said, looked just as good in Mao jackets as guys. "Unisex," she called them. She even promised that, once the surgery was complete, she'd let me take after Jiang Jing, Mao's wife and leader of the Cultural Revolution's much-feared "Gang of Four."

Having never known a woman as fierce as Jiang, I had to admit I was tempted. However, when I read Jiang had called the wife of Mao's biggest foe a whore, I decided to move on. That sounded too much like fag and queer to me and, while I remained committed to finding a cure, I wasn't going about it by calling other people names. I'd had way too much of that already.

The girl inside scoffed I was going soft and urged me to drop what she called my "Golden Rule crap." As she noted, "doing unto others" worked only if others played along. And there was absolutely no evidence to indicate anyone— Red Guard militant, Black Power advocate, New Left crazy—was inclined to treat homosexuals with anything but contempt. As proof, she referred me back to the essay on homosexuality *Time* had published at the start of my seclusion, whose claims of an increasingly visible "gay subculture" I'd found reassuring— but whose conclusion had so upset me I'd come down with my first migraine: *Homosexuality is a pathetic second-rate substitute for reality, a pitiable flight from life. It deserves no encouragement, no glamorization, no fake status as a minority, no sophistry about simple differences in taste–and, above all, no pretense that it is anything but a pernicious sickness.* People hated homos for a reason, the girl inside me sneered. They were sick—as *Time* had said, *perniciously* so. The sooner I stopped being one, the better.

She and I also bickered over the changes sweeping the arts, whose growing sexual frankness *Time* covered with a prurient fervor. And though she was relieved I found Burrough's *Naked Lunch*, whose ban the Supreme Court had just lifted, revolting, and Christopher Isherwood's *A Single Man*, the first book about homosexuals I didn't steal, depressing, she was appalled to see me devour books like Frantz Fanon's *Black Skins, White Masks*, an analysis of self-alienation and shame among colonial Africans, and John Barth's *Giles Goat-Boy*, about a bisexual campus messiah. John Rechy's *City of Night*, which became my new sex manual, nearly sent her packing. As she noted, at least *Last Exit to Brooklyn*, my previous sex manual, had straight sex scenes. Rechy's novel had none.

We bickered over films too. She preferred slick, stylish fare—films like *Darling* with Julie Christie, *Alfie* with Michael Caine, and *A Man and a Woman* with Anouk Aimee—which the increasingly rebellious homosexual growing alongside her dismissed as empty-headed fluff. He wanted meatier stuff—films like Peter Brooks' *Marat/Sade*, which depicted society as a madhouse, and Pier Paolo Pasolini's *The Gospel According to St. Matthew*, which portrayed Jesus as a revolutionary. And while another of his recommendations, Michelangelo Antonioni's *Blow-Up*, was the most sexually explicit film I'd ever seen, Leroi Jones' racially-charged *Dutchman*, whose murderous white prostitute, Lula, embodied all the hatred and violence I'd endured growing up, was the most cathartic. After *Dutchman*, I not only embraced the homosexual rebel within, I gave him a voice.

Two weeks later, in a paper on D.H. Lawrence's *Sons and Lovers* for my senior-year English class, I dared to even write about homosexuality. Espousing the prevailing view, I claimed it had nothing to do with personal weakness, as I'd been taught in sex education class, but was the fault of possessive mothers who turned their sons against their fathers and psychically emasculated them. I even speculated Lawrence was a repressed homosexual.

My teacher, a prim, middle-aged spinster whom I suspected might be a lesbian, called me courageous for tackling taboo subject matter and gave me an A-plus. The girl inside me, on the other hand, was so outraged she claimed I deserved an F. She made no secret of her disdain for the rebel who'd led me to write such drivel and warned me that any more outbursts like that would leave her no choice but to move on.

She announced she'd re-evaluated my whole "rebellion thing," as she called it, and decided I'd be better off pursuing a more feminine path. She pointed to my ongoing fascination with young, hip designers like Betsy Johnson, who'd designed a dress with battery-powered lights, Mary Quant, whose miniskirt soared to eleven inches above the knee, and Paco Rabanne, whose silver 'disc dress' was supposed to be worn only while dancing, as evidence that I took after my mother more than I cared to admit. As she so wryly noted, I was a clotheshorse too.

Glamour, not rebellion, was my calling, the girl inside insisted, and so she embarked on a search for an icon the new chic "post-change" me could emulate. At first, she toyed with Nancy Sinatra, whose "These Boots are Made for Walking" had reached the top of the Billboard charts at the start of my seclusion. Then, after watching *Tender Is the Night* on *Saturday Night at the Movies*, she considered Jennifer Jones, whose svelte figure and Roaring Twenties bob had mesmerized her. But it wasn't until March of 1967, when *Time* covered the US tour of the flat-chested, ninety-pound androgyne, Twiggy, that she actually settled on one. She even intimated that I might be able to remain a boy if I agreed to take after Twiggy. As she noted, I was certainly skinny enough.

I confessed I was tempted although, as I reminded her, *Last Exit to Brooklyn* had made it clear that drag queens led very rough lives. And besides, as even the girl inside me had to acknowledge, "transvestitism," as *Time* at that time called drag, was a half-measure that did not really qualify as a cure. Under all that make-up, the men who dressed up as women were almost always homosexuals.

She and I battled furiously over TV, which by the mid-Sixties seemed to have suddenly become unhinged. While she tolerated the smutty *Peyton Place*, mostly because Mia Farrow reminded her of Twiggy, she disapproved of *Batman*, whose embrace of camp she said made the show gay, and despised Paul Lynde, the outrageously fey comedian who debuted as Uncle Arthur on *Bewitched*. And while we were both thrilled to see Jefferson Airplane sing "Somebody to Love" on *The Bell Telephone Hour*, she refused to let me tune into *CBS Reports'* "The Homosexual," TV's first exploration of the subject. As she so wryly noted, I didn't need to understand the homosexual's "human condition," as *Time* defined the show's purpose. I needed to run away from it.

We also disagreed over *Time's* coverage of Britain's move to decriminalize homosexuality, which I somehow mustered the courage to defend in my Current Events class. However, when it reported on a small group of homosexuals demonstrating against harassment outside Philadelphia's Independence Hall, I agreed with my inner girl that they'd gone too far. People like that were supposed to be too ashamed to show their faces in public. And yet there they were, announcing to the world that they were gay. They even had the audacity to look normal. In broad daylight!

What most upset my inner girl, though, was my decision to secretly start seeing another guy. Larry, a trick I'd picked up one night on Market Street, was a hairy, thick-chested, white man who, in his early thirties, lived in a tiny, cramped two-bedroom suburban apartment with a roommate, Victor. She tormented me endlessly about lying naked in bed with Larry, which I'd never done with a man before, and when one night I put his penis in my mouth, she claimed I was even more disgusting than those protesters outside Philadelphia's Independence Hall. Again, she threatened to pack up and leave.

But it was Victor, Larry's roommate, who really got under her skin. He ridiculed my insistence that homosexuality was a mental illness and tormented me by naming all the famous people he claimed were similarly diseased. Many of them—Socrates, Alexander the Great, DaVinci, Michelangelo, Oscar Wilde, Gertrude Stein, Truman Capote, Tennessee Williams, Gore Vidal—I already knew about but when he named the crooner Johnny Matthis; George Maharis, the star of TV's *Route 66*; and *Dr. Kildare's* Richard Chamberlain—heartthrobs my inner girl had promised I'd be on track to nab once I became "real"—she had me storm out in protest.

After that, she insisted I go back to confining my sexual activity to my father's Corvair—no more beds, apartments, or idle chit-chat with the roommate. When I complained of loneliness, she reminded me that was how homosexuals were supposed to be: sad, pathetic, and guilt-ridden. If I wanted to feel differently, I needed to be different—a girl, not a faggot.

She and I were both mesmerized by the rumblings that gave rise to what *Time* dubbed the "counterculture." First, there were "happenings" which led to "free love," LSD, and the rise of the peace-loving mutants Timothy Leary called hippies. From there, it wasn't long before acid rock, light shows, head shops, vintage clothing, incense, underground newspapers, crash pads and communes joined the scene, all of which fed off each other and eventually flowered in early 1967 into the scene's fullest, most complete manifestation—" human be-ins," gatherings which, in a stunning rejection of the prevailing ethos, were devoted exclusively to the simplest of themes—peace and love—and which attracted thousands.

Local officials were flummoxed. In contrast to the violence engulfing the rest of the world—during my seclusion, four inner cities went up in flames; the US dropped over ten million tons of bombs on North Vietnam; seventy-six nuclear weapons were tested by five different countries; and three mass murderers killed almost sixty Americans—be-ins were entirely peaceful. When ten thousand hippies turned out for one in San Francisco's Golden Gate Park, not a single fight broke out.

Drug use, on the other hand, was reportedly rampant, with LSD a crowd favorite. When, a few weeks later, *Time* covered San Francisco's Haight Ashbury, which it called a center of free love where nearly everyone was high on LSD but hardly any violent crimes were committed, I wanted violence out of my life so badly I nearly dropped out of high school and hitchhiked cross country. Instead, I added becoming a hippie to my growing list of cure options.

For once, the girl inside me concurred, although for a very different reason. As she said, if LSD could rearrange chromosomes, as *Time* claimed, or cure crazies, as TV's *CBS Reports* argued, it could certainly turn a budding faggot like me straight. Indeed, she even suggested a sequencing of cures: an initial visit to Haight Ashbury for what she euphemistically called a "lifestyle correction," by which she meant turning me on to girls via heavy doses of free love and LSD, followed by a trip to Johns Hopkins for what she deemed the "final mutation."

When I noted her plan would leave me a lesbian, she scoffed sex was inconceivable without a penis. And just in case I proved her wrong, she said I'd simply have to return to the Haight for more LSD. When I worried that might send me over the edge—*Time* claimed users who took too much often never came back down—she shrugged. Better to be crazy, she snarled, than gay.

Time's profile of R. D. Laing, a radical British psychiatrist who claimed to have cured the mad by treating them as sane, I also found intriguing. In his clinics, which he termed "households," the goal was to free his patients from their "checkmates," strategies they invented to survive "unlivable situations." He acknowledged many of his discharges remained "a bit queer," but he was okay with that as long as they could live with others and themselves. Most, he claimed, did.

Unable to live with either myself or others, I considered adding Laing's "anti-psychiatry," as *Time* called it, to my list of potential cures. But that time, it wasn't the girl who objected but the homosexual, who stated he was fed up with being deemed a disease. As a Kinsey Institute official had claimed in *Time* nearly six months earlier, he insisted homosexuality was just another form of sexual expression, as natural, if not nearly as prevalent, as heterosexuality. He even went so far as to suggest I start using the word 'gay' instead of what he called the more "archaic" 'homosexual.' Horrified, the girl inside again threatened to pack up and leave. And so, unwilling to be left alone with nothing but the label queer to look forward to, I told him to back off and let the girl handle "intimate matters," as she called my sex life.

While he reluctantly agreed, my inner homosexual continued to press me on politics as another possible cure. In that regard, he cautioned me about the status quo, warning me that the war policies of President Johnson, whom I'd supported in his race against Barry Goldwater, were only creating more bullies.

He suggested I instead consider Bobby Kennedy, the brother of LBJ's assassinated predecessor, who was rumored to be considering his own run for president as a peace candidate. When *Time* reported that, on a visit to apartheid South Africa, Bobby had stood atop a car and sung "We Shall Overcome" to a throng of Black admirers, I had to admit I was intrigued. And then when, a few days later, he'd called for "full human equality" before a racially mixed Cape Town audience, I dared to think he might even be including people like me.

After that, I accepted my inner homosexual's advice and added Bobby Kennedy to my list of possible cures. With him as president, it occurred to me that maybe I wouldn't need to go to Johns Hopkins for a sex change, become a denizen of Andy Warhol's Factory, study the thought of Chairman Mao, run away to the Haight and drop LSD, or move into one of R.D. Laing's "households." Maybe I could just be me.

The girl inside scoffed at the notion that a Roman Catholic with nine kids could ever accept homosexuality as anything but a perversion. And so, she continued her hectoring, warning me time was running out. And while she acknowledged I could obtain a sex-change at any age, my window for becoming glamourous, which was her real goal, was much narrower. If I wanted to wear a Mary Quant miniskirt, do my eyes up like Twiggy, and dance the Philly Dog with a handsome admirer at Cheetah, I needed to move fast. I wasn't going to be young forever.

Ignoring her, I sided with the increasingly strident homosexual inside me and became instead a protest junkie, avidly following discontent's ebb and flow through the pages of *Time*. Hardly a week went by without news of some venting, but it was Martin Luther King's April 1967 speech at New York's Riverside Church a few days before a massive peace march that most grabbed me. In it, he described the country to which I pledged allegiance every school day as the greatest purveyor of violence in the world and compared its use of weapons in Vietnam to Nazi medical experiments.

His speech became a turning point. Suddenly, I was more ashamed of my country than I was of my own sexuality. Then, when North Vietnam's Ho Chi Minh echoed King by threatening to try downed US airmen as war criminals, I began to seriously re-evaluate my place in the world. If bombing North Vietnam was a war crime, what were the beatings I'd endured throughout high school? Was I just getting what I deserved, as nearly everyone else seemed to think, or could it be, as Ho asserted for his country, that I too had a right to live life on my own terms? I recalled the phrase I'd learned from my infatuation with Stokely Carmichael and Black Power: the oppressed had a right to what he called "self-determination." Might I have that right too?

That night, as if on cue, a new set of bullies called to inform me, in case I'd forgotten, that I was still nothing more than a queer and a homo. They persisted until my father again came to my rescue, although by then I knew there'd be no getting away from them. As long as I was in Wilmington, I'd be stuck in the crosshairs of hate.

That weekend, holed up in our basement rec room, I pored through back issues of *Time* for its article on the British painter, Francis Bacon. Entitled "The Coroner's Report," with color prints of several of his portraits, I reread it and realized I'd been right. There, in black and white, Bacon had admitted he was a homosexual.

I stared at his portrait of a friend, Isabel Rawsthorne. Her face was battered and in disarray, as if it'd been run through the spin cycle of my mother's Maytag. Of his vision, which *Time* called "pathological"—the same word Dr. Bieber had used in *Life* to describe the gay psyche—Bacon had said, "Somewhere you have to drive the nail home into fact." Then he asserted that everything in life was violent, even a rose.

Horrified that I had not a shred of evidence to refute him, I ripped the article from the magazine, tore it to shreds, and flushed it down the basement toilet. I didn't care how great an artist Bacon was; there was one nail I was never driving home into fact—the one that defined me as gay. I'd learned my lesson the night I'd paid seven silver dollars to see how the definition fit and returned home with a busted lip, a ripped shirt, and the start of a crippling anxiety disorder. I'd never tell anyone I was that way again. Ever.

In the background, my tinny transistor radio played the Beatles' latest hit, "Strawberry Fields Forever," which warned of living with eyes closed, misunderstanding all I see. Sensing the onset of another migraine, I placed a forefinger on the tip of my nose and the other six inches away, directly in front of me. I crossed my eyes to stare at the tip of my nose and started my countdown: one thousand thirty, one thousand twenty-nine, shifting my gaze at each count from one finger to the other. The optometrist had promised that, if I followed that procedure faithfully three times a day, I'd be cured of my wild-eye.

So far, it hadn't worked. I still had migraines, although my low-grade fever finally went away when my tonsils were removed. The surgeon had been surprised at how ravaged they were. Nothing but nubs, he'd said of them. He'd chastised me for letting them fester and was surprised I'd lived with them for as long as I had. Next time, he said, I needed to act sooner.

That night, I returned to Market Street for another desultory few hours of cruising. In my father's Corvair, I stopped at the corner of 9th Street and waited patiently for the light to turn. Up ahead, a man in peg leg pants and Beatle boots leaned seductively against a lamppost. On the radio, the Four Tops sang their latest hit, "Reach Out, I'll Be There," my new favorite song.

Feeling sorry for myself, I started to sing along when, suddenly, a carful of boys appeared behind me, honking and waving for me to pull over. Afraid they were out looking for a fag to beat up, I rolled up my window, locked the door, and anxiously drummed my fingers on the steering wheel. "Come on, goddammit, turn!" I yelled at the traffic light. Ignoring me, it stayed stubbornly red.

"Hey, we just want to talk!" a plump, pimply, dark-haired guy shouted from the window of a beat-up Chevy Malibu. I pretended not to hear, but when their car started tapping my rear bumper, I stepped on the gas and, without waiting for the light, gunned my father's Corvair around the corner. Thankfully, the Chevy didn't follow.

Rolling my window back down, I gulped in the cool night air and cursed the young toughs who were slowly taking over Market Street. The previous weekend, I'd picked up a guy who'd threatened to bash my face in unless I paid him ten dollars for the handjob I'd just finished giving him. I'd told him I didn't have that kind of money, but it was only when I'd burst into tears and confessed my parents would kill me if I went home with another bloody lip that he'd backed off. "Hey, okay, kid, no sweat. You can drop me off over there," he'd said, pointing to the corner where his buddies, all in tight jeans and muscle shirts, glared at the cars passing them by.

On my next swing down Market, I spotted someone new. He was younger than the rest of the men on the street that night, with a prominent nose, thick wiry hair and a husky build stuffed into a pink polo shirt with a raised collar. We locked eyes and he discretely grabbed his crotch. Pulling over, I waited for him to hop in.

He slid into the Corvair's passenger seat and gave me a big, toothy grin. He introduced himself as Dominic and, from Philadelphia, said he was in town only for the night. I didn't bother telling him my name or where I was from and instead, reaching for his thigh, asked if he wanted to go for a ride. I said I didn't have long. My curfew was up in an hour.

Blocking my hand, he smiled sheepishly and informed me he wasn't looking for sex. He pointed at the car parked on the other side of the street and explained his lover, a guy named Donnie, wanted to meet me.

I looked at the car and realized it was the beat-up Chevy I thought I'd ditched. On the other side of the car was the now-boarded-up movie theater where I'd seen *Psycho*. Directly opposite was the storefront, also vacant, in whose doorway a man had once caught my eye and groped himself—my first sighting of a real-live homosexual. "Meet me?" I asked. "But why?"

Dominic repeated Donnie's name. "Recognize it?"

"No," I replied and again reached for his thigh. Swatting my hand away, Dominic said I should. "You go to the same high school. He's a senior too."

I froze. The other car honked. Dominic waved and laughed.

I gripped the steering wheel and told him to get out of the car. "Right now!" I shouted, turning on the ignition.

Wincing, Dominic turned down the radio, which had suddenly started blaring Mitch Ryder and the Detroit Wheels' "Sock It to Me, Baby." "Hey, look, it's okay. I'm not out to get you. I'm gay too."

"Don't use that word around me," I snapped. "I don't want to hear it. Understand?" I grabbed the car's gear shift to steady my hand and turned to face my intruder. "Just leave me alone, okay? And tell your, uhh, friend not to say anything about seeing me here." I bit my lip to keep it from quivering. "I don't need any more trouble at school."

"Hey, it's okay, really!" Dominic cried. "You're not alone. There's a whole world of people like you out there." He smiled and assured me I'd have a good time if I'd only give it a chance. "You're young. That's a premium in gay life."

"There's nothing gay about it," I retorted. "We're sad and pathetic just like everyone says." I shook my head at a bleach blond a half block away who blew a kiss at a passing Lincoln Continental. His companion, a tall, thin Black man in skin-tight jeans, howled like it was the funniest thing he'd ever seen. "I can't wait till I get out of this hellhole. I'm tired of being beaten up and made fun of." My face flushed. "I want to be like everyone else." I looked at him combatively. "*Normal.*"

Dominic shook his head and sighed. "You'll feel better once you meet other gay people. Why don't we go over and I'll introduce you to Donnie?"

I glanced at the Chevy. Everyone in it was laughing and pointing at a short, dark-haired, apple-cheeked guy squeezed into the middle of the back seat. I flushed slightly, realizing he looked vaguely familiar. "I can't. I just can't."

Dominic asked if I'd wait while he brought Donnie to me.

I tightened my grip on the Corvair's gear shift. "No, absolutely not!"

Dominic slapped his knee. "Oh, come on! You can't be serious. It's an offer of friendship, not a marriage proposal. What's with you, anyway?"

"I don't want to know anyone like me. We're sick and deserve to be lonely," I replied, echoing my inner girl's mantra. I turned beet-red. "It's our punishment for being..." I paused to spit out the word. "*Perverts.*"

Dominic broke into a loud guffaw. "Look, here's Donnie's phone number," he said, handing me a piece of paper with some scribbling on it. "There's a party in Philadelphia next weekend. Call him if you want to go. You can drive up together and talk. It'd be good for both of you."

Later that night, my heart sank as I looked up Donnie's picture in Mount Pleasant's yearbook. He was no one I had any reason to know. A business student, he was one of the kids the middle-class academic crowd called 'retards.' *At least we're not them*, we'd mutter as we worried over SAT scores and which after-school activity most enhanced our chances of getting into the colleges of our choice. Except on the football field, where the pom poms of middle-class girls urged on the sweaty hulks of working-class beef, fraternization between the two worlds was strictly forbidden.

I tossed the yearbook aside and realized from my still-trembling hand Dominic was right. I needed someone to talk to. What Donnie's standing was in school or what social class he came from were irrelevant. This time, I was the one who mattered.

Heaving with panic, I called the number Dominic had given me and brusquely offered Donnie a ride to Philadelphia the following Saturday night. While I appreciated the clipped brevity of his response, in the background, over the laughter of his friends, the Four Tops surprised me by finishing the song that, two hours earlier, a carful of guys, honking and waving for me to pull over, had so rudely interrupted. "Come on, girl," Leo Stubbs, the group's mellifluous lead, commanded, "reach out for me." I could, he assured me, always depend on him.

The next morning, just six weeks shy of my high school graduation, the girl inside me packed up and returned home—to the grave overlooking the mighty Ohio where my twin sisters, Nan and Jane, were buried. I never heard from her again. At eighteen, I'd finally awakened from my mother's dream of a daughter with whom she could giggle and share secrets into the harsh reality of being her gay son.

Although I was wracked with guilt and paralyzed with fear over what lay ahead, I stopped getting migraines and again started carrying my schoolbooks like a girl, clutched against my chest rather than at my side like the other boys.

I even dispensed with the glasses I'd been prescribed for my wild-eye, perhaps the only turn in a long, fraught coming out process that pleased my mother, who complained that my choice of frames—wire-rim "granny glasses" inspired by John Lennon, the Beatle on whom I had the biggest crush—made me look like someone she no longer knew.

6
Fresh Meat

On the drive to Philadelphia, I gripped the steering wheel of my father's Corvair and tried not to squirm as Donnie told me about his new "gay life." He said Dominic, whom he'd met six months earlier in the "tearoom" of Philadelphia's 30th Street train station, had snuck him into a gay bar and gotten him "done up in drag" for the Mummer's Parade. Bragging he'd even done a "three-way," he asked if I'd ever been "lucky Pierre."

I stared at him blankly, trying to figure out why I'd never been to the tearoom at the 30th Street train station. Every December, my mother and I took the train to Philadelphia to Christmas shop at Wanamaker's, the city's poshest department store. When we finished, we'd always met in the store's lobby, by the giant organ and the perfumed fountain illuminated in purple and pink lights. My mother had always insisted it was *the* spot in town to rendezvous. If the train station's tearoom was so lovely, why hadn't we met there?

Donnie asked if I'd seen the movie version of *Who's Afraid of Virginia Woolf*? When I replied it was one of my favorite films, he said he'd done a project for shop class entitled, "A Pictorial Representation of the Order of Martha's Mind." He'd glued a roll of torn, melted film and pieces of frayed electrical wire to a plywood base on which he'd pasted stills from the film. He chuckled. "Dominic warned me not to turn it in. He said only queens did decoupage. He said I'd be wrecked and my beads would drop for days."

Bewildered, I wondered what was all this about queens and decoupage? And who in their right mind wore beads to shop class?

"He was right, you know," Donnie continued. He ran his fingers through his mane of thick, Black Irish hair and sighed. "All the guys in class laughed at me and called me a queer. But you know what? I didn't care. I really liked that piece. It was like a self-portrait. I really identify with Martha. Sometimes I feel like that mess on the plywood, all charred and twisted."

He looked at me and smiled warily. "You ever feel like that?"

I panicked and tightened my grip on the steering wheel. "Umm, I don't know, I mean...." I stammered, not at all sure I wanted to admit to having the same feelings as someone who called himself gay.

"Oh, come on. You can tell me. After all, I'm one too."

"Yeah, alright," I said, reeling, "maybe sometimes..."

Donnie nodded. "You know, the guy who wrote the play—his name's Edward Albee—is gay."

I replied I did, relieved I finally knew something he did.

"I think that's such a hoot," Donnie continued. "I've read the play at least ten times and know most of its lines by heart." He put his hands on his hips and drunkenly rolled his eyes. "I'm loud and I'm vulgar and I wear the pants in this house because somebody's got to," he slurred, grandly mimicking Elizabeth Taylor's Martha. "But I'm not a monster."

Grinning, I chimed in and we both shouted at the top of our lungs: "I'm *not* a monster! I'm *not*! I'm *not*!!"

"That play really dishes straight people," Donnie smirked, toying with his St. Christopher medal. "I think it's Albee's revenge for all the horrible things they say about gays." Laughing at his use of 'dish' as a verb, I let the adjective that I refused to use as a noun—'gay'—slide.

"So, how did you know that I was, uh..." I paused as my mouth went dry. "Um, you know, that way?"

Donnie laughed. "Well, I saw you on Market Street, didn't I? Who else drives around down there that late at night?"

"No, I mean were you surprised?"

"Ah, like, had I ever suspected you were gay?"

"Ummmm," I stammered, grimacing over the word's application to me. "Yeah, I guess," I finally mumbled.

"Well, honey, let's face it. You aren't the butchest thing around."

I wasn't sure what "butch" meant but blushed nevertheless. "No, I mean, has anyone at school ever said anything about me?"

"Uh-uh," Donnie said, shaking his head. "Why? You have some deep dark secret you're hiding?"

"No, of course not," I lied and recalled how swiftly word of my beating behind the Catholic church had spread through school. Ironically, the one who might have come to my aid was the one who'd never heard about it.

Donnie patted me on the shoulder. "Don't worry, dear. Your secrets are safe with me. We all live with them. They're our children, just like George and Martha's little darling." At that, he laughed so hard tears welled up. "Sorry," he said, patting his eyes with a tissue. He blew his nose and smiled warily. "Dominic says I'm too emotional."

I confessed I was nervous about meeting his lover. "He seems very sure of himself." I flushed slightly and added I wasn't. "At least around stuff like this."

Donnie agreed Dominic was a bit overbearing and, like Albee's Martha, a little loud. "But he's a sweetheart, a pussycat really." He suspected much of his bluster came from having to live off the streets. His parents, he said, had kicked him out of the house when he was only sixteen. When I asked why, Donnie chuckled at my naiveté. "For being gay, of course, what else?" As he noted, Dominic had come out very young. "Thirteen," he said when I asked how old. "He seduced his uncle," he added, smiling wryly.

When I noted I lived in terror of my parents finding out about me, Donnie shrugged; Dominic insisted it was the best thing that had ever happened to him. "Toughened him right up," he said, his apple cheeks flaring. "He says there isn't anything he can't handle now."

When I asked if Dominic had at least been able to finish high school, Donnie shook his head. "But don't give him any shit about it. He's very proud." He looked at me and smiled. "Street smart," he called him.

I admitted I'd never met a high school dropout and wasn't sure I approved. "I mean, how's he ever going to get ahead without a diploma?"

Donnie laughed. "Honey, in gay life, it's all about what you got between your legs. And, believe me, Dominic's hung." I wasn't sure what that was but I let Donnie continue anyway. He noted that one of the regulars from Dominic's hustling days, an older guy who ran a restaurant on Rittenhouse Square that was popular with the after-hours gay set, had offered him a job busing tables.

He said it was just the kind of break Dominic needed. With the tips he made off his impersonations of stars like Ethel Merman and Mae West, he'd finally been able to get a place of his own. While Donnie acknowledged it wasn't much—he had no kitchen and shared a bathroom with the rest of his floor— he gushed it was in the part of town he called "gay central." When I asked if that was anywhere near the Wanamaker's my mother and I had shopped at, he shook his head but assured me it was within walking distance of just about everything else—the gay bars on Broad Street, the "cruising block" on Spruce and Rittenhouse Square where, he said, "all the queens" walked their poodles. When I said I'd been to Rittenhouse Square several times with my mother and never once saw a queen, Donnie laughed. "Just wait, you'll see plenty tonight. The host of the party we're going to is one of Philly's biggest."

He said kids too young for the bars frequented Dominic's place, mostly so they could let their hair down and be themselves, although that night he expected there'd be only Mike. "We wanted to go easy on you," Donnie explained before noting that camp, or at least what he called the "street version," was a bit of an acquired taste. "You might not be quite there yet." He added he thought I'd like Mike, a childhood friend of Dominic's from South Philly. "He's going off to college this fall, too." He smiled. "The first in his family."

"NYU," he said when I asked what school Mike would be attending, "a theater major." He laughed and noted Mike was what he called a "show tune queen." When I asked what that was, he said it was a gay man who loves the music of Broadway divas like Ethel Merman, Barbra Streisand, and Judy Garland. When I revealed my musical tastes ran more along the lines of the Beatles, Simon and Garfunkel, and Jefferson Airplane, Donnie grimaced. As he noted, rock was not nearly campy enough to be considered gay. "That's okay, though. Give it time. You'll eventually figure out what kind of queen you are."

He rattled off a bewildering variety I'd have to choose from—size, rim, drag, drama, tearoom, truck stop, chicken, butch, toe, shoe, street, and leather queens. He said size queens liked big dicks, and chicken queens, boys. "But only ones old enough to know what they're doing." The ones who went for still younger guys, he said, were called "sick queens," although he was happy to report he'd never run across one. Of the tearoom variety, he said they only did it in toilets. "Public ones." When I asked about rim queens, Donnie confessed they were, to his way of thinking, the least campy. "They take themselves very seriously. They eat ass."

When I protested that I'd never do anything like that, Donnie replied I'd probably once said the same thing about sucking cock. "And now look at you." When I confessed I had yet to let a man come in my mouth, Donnie got suddenly serious. "You're not really gay until you swallow it, you know." When I admitted I mostly just jerked men off into a tissue in my father's Corvair, he grimaced. The word for that kind of queen, he said, was "closet." "Someone who hasn't yet accepted he's gay," he replied when I asked what that meant. "Who's too guilt-ridden."

Dominic was waiting for us outside his building, a drab, stucco four-story rooming house on 17th Street a few blocks off Market. He barely nodded at me and then, pulling Donnie to him, gave him a big sloppy kiss on the lips. "I missed you, baby," he murmured.

"Faggots!" a bearded man in a Phillies' baseball cap shouted from the driver's seat of a passing pickup truck. He stepped on the gas and, over the squealing of his tires, added, just for emphasis, "Fucking perverts!"

Not to be outdone, Dominic ran to the curb, gave the man the finger and shouted back, "Fuck you! And your motha, too!"

"Hey, watch your language!" a man across the street protested. He grimaced and nodded at his two companions. "There are ladies here."

Dominic drew Donnie in and laughed heartily. "Here too!" he cried.

Mortified, I ran into Dominic's building and cursed him for his recklessness. Kissing in public? Talking back to a straight man? What was he trying to do, get us killed? Cowering in the vestibule, I wondered who this hothead was that Donnie had brought me to. The last thing I needed was more trouble.

"What's the matter, Mary," Dominic bellowed, bounding into the building after me, "freaked out by your own kind?" Rushing to my defense, Donnie tried to calm him down. "Come on, Dominic, give him a break. He's just coming out."

As Dominic led us up the stairs, I wondered what the hell Donnie was talking about. While I may not have known about queens, lucky Pierres, or dropping beads, one thing I knew for sure was that girls came out, not guys. A few weeks earlier, I'd even helped my friend Nancy, a girl I'd pretended I was going steady with, do just that at the Hotel DuPont's annual Cotillion Ball. I'd even worn a tuxedo, a get-up that made my mother tear up. "So handsome," she'd blubbered, dabbing her eyes with a hankie. "And such a gentleman, too!"

"Oh, come on, it's time she faced facts," Dominic sneered from the building's second-floor landing. "She's walking around with her nose stuck up in the air like everyone's shit stinks but hers." He twirled on his heels, marched to the first door on the right and flung it open. "She needs to learn she's just another queen like the rest of us."

Following him inside, I encountered Dominic's friend Mike, a short, pudgy guy with acne scars and a turban he'd fashioned out of a silk scarf. "I heard shouting and thought I'd put on Babs' 'People,' he said, clutching a vinyl record. "It calms all the queens down. Do you mind?"

"Of course, she minds. She probably doesn't even like Streisand," Dominic sneered. "Too gaudy and coarse."

"Oh," Mike muttered. Confused, he looked at me. "Really? You don't like 'la Camp?' I've never met a queen who didn't."

"I guess that means I'm not a queen, huh?" I shot back, glaring at Dominic. Then, turning, I realized I was inside what could only be described as a slum. To my left was a stained, dark blue sofa with stuffing that plumed out of both arms and, in front of it, a pair of milk crates supporting a cracked marble slab scattered with movie magazines, cans of hair spray, and black and white photographs of men in bathing suits vamping on a boardwalk. On the floor was an Oriental rug crisscrossed with tire tracks, while on the wall a ripped poster featured Barbra Streisand from *Funny Girl*. Next to it a red velveteen drape, partially obscured an alcove with an unmade bed littered with clothes, not all of which were men's.

Standing in the middle of the room, Dominic defiantly folded his arms across his barrel chest. "Well, does Her Majesty require an engraved invitation? Make yourself at home." His eyes narrowed. "Or are we too good for this?"

Clearing a space on the sofa, I sat down and told Dominic I didn't appreciate being referred to as a girl. "Besides, you sound just like a cheap homosexual." I crossed my legs and met his stare. "It's bad enough being that way without having to flaunt it."

Breaking into a loud guffaw, Dominic reminded me that the word for 'that way' was 'gay.' "Listen, Mary, you have a lot to learn. Just shut up, sit back, and try to enjoy the ride. You're going to see things tonight you've never thought possible. It'll be hard at first, but you must try. Understand? It's your life now, dearie."

"I'm not your dearie," I haughtily replied.

"Here, Miss Thing, suck on this," he snarled, handing me a brass pipe whose contents he'd just lit.

"Is this marijuana?" I gasped, holding the pipe at arm's length.

"Yes, although we call it pot," Dominic replied, rolling his eyes.

"But that's illegal!" I cried, slamming the pipe down on the marble slab.

"So is sucking dick but that doesn't seem to have stopped you," Dominic sneered. Donnie, standing next to Dominic, snickered, although Mike, sitting in a tattered wingback chair facing me, confessed he didn't approve of drugs either.

"Don't pay any attention to her," Dominic snarled. "Mike's a mama's boy. He had to be rushed to the ER after her very first puff. Thought she was losing her mind." He re-lit the pipe and again handed it to me. "I suspect you're not so delicate. Besides, you need to loosen that board up your ass."

As my head slowly started to spin, Dominic tried to prepare me for the party that lay ahead. He noted the term for men who wore dresses was "drag queen" and, no matter what, I was to always say they looked real. "And never refer to them as a 'he.' A drag queen is always a 'she.'"

He popped a white cross pill he kept in a vial on the marble slab and continued to instruct me on the vagaries of gay life. "Now, Mary, you're from the suburbs, so I need to warn you there'll be dinge at this party. Dinge queens too." He smiled slyly. "You know, white guys into Black men."

At that point, Donnie chimed in. "Dominic's last lover was dinge." He looked at me and smiled proudly. "I stole him away."

"*Dinge*?" I cried. "You mean Blacks?" When Dominic confirmed that was indeed what he meant, I told him I found the term offensive—as insulting as the slurs the guys routinely flung around Mount Pleasant's lily-white locker room: jungle bunny, coon, and monkey. "No, worse," I added, correcting myself, "people like you should know better."

"Well, aren't we Miss Black Power of 1967," Dominic sneered. "Listen, queen, gays have their own language. And nobody gets to judge it but us. If you don't like it, just don't use it."

"I won't," I replied. "Ever."

"Suit yourself, Mary," Dominic snipped before returning to his lecture on the various shocks I was in for. He assured me the leather queens I'd see were, notwithstanding their get-ups, sissies just like the rest of us. From there, he launched into diatribes against "trade," whom he called closet queens posing as straight, and then lesbians, whom he called man-hating "rug munchers." After that, he lit into the Mafia, which he said was milking the gay community dry, and finally the vice squad, which he called our number one enemy, worse, he said, than even the Church.

When he launched into a diatribe against Frank Rizzo, Philadelphia's new police chief, whom he called a "racist Dago-Wop-Guinea," Donnie interrupted him. "The party started an hour ago, dear. It's time to go."

Mike rolled his eyes. "He can go on, can't he?" I rose from the sofa and nodded, happy at least that someone had finally used the correct pronoun.

"Darlings, welcome!" a man in a towering blonde bouffant wig and a white beaded dress bellowed from the doorway of an apartment on the fifth floor of a surprisingly upscale building. "How the hell are youse?"

Coyly batting false eyelashes, he proffered a hand sheathed in a white satin opera glove and smiled maliciously. "Time to kiss Mother's ring," he purred, fluttering an obscenely large rhinestone. Behind us, the doors to the building's elevator slammed shut. Ahead, a man in a fright wig and a leather miniskirt lip-synced to the Supremes' "Stop in the Name of Love."

"Yes, of course, Your Majesty," Dominic said, presenting himself first. He bowed slightly from the waist and gently kissed the ring. "It's gorgeous," he murmured, still holding our host's hand. "Where did you get it?"

"Goodwill," the man coyly replied and burst into a loud, deep guffaw. "It's where every queen gets her jewels."

Mortified, I watched as Mike dutifully followed suit, curtsying rather than bowing and complimenting the wig, not the ring. "You could nest birds in that," he gushed, although I could tell by our host's reaction that he—er, she—was not amused.

"Next!" he roared, at which point Donnie stepped forward. Dropping to a knee, he made a point of congratulating our host on how real "she" looked and then lewdly licked the ring with his tongue.

Our host was clearly impressed. "Thank you, Gertrude," he cooed. "For that, I appoint you my lady-in-waiting. You have free use of the tearoom for the rest of the evening."

"Oh, thank you, your ladyship," Donnie murmured, stepping back.

After that, all eyes turned to me. Terrified, I tried to hide behind Dominic but he would have none of it. "Get your ass out there, right now," he ordered in a stage aside I hoped our host couldn't hear.

"But I can't," I whimpered. "It's demeaning."

Clenching his teeth, Dominic hissed that if I wanted to get into the party, I better do as I was told. Our "hostess," as he insisted on calling the man greeting us, got nasty when crossed. His eyes narrowed and his face reddened. "And no, Miss Thing, no one will walk you back to your car if you don't do as she says. You piss her off and you're on your own. We have to get along in this town, you know. You're just visiting."

Our host fixed me with his heavily-mascaraed gaze, licked his ruby-red lips and cooed, "Come now, don't be afraid, my lovely." He nodded at the ring, shimmering in the lobby's bright fluorescent light, and smiled knowingly. "Don't you want to kiss it?"

"I'm telling you, you better do this," Dominic snarled, shoving me forward. And though I refused to call him a she or tell him how real he looked, I did brush my lips across the rhinestone, an act of fealty he rewarded with a shrill pronouncement. "Marys, wake up, there's fresh meat at the door!"

I wanted to die. Had the elevator not already gone, I would've run into it, mashed on the close door button and fled the building in tears. Instead, Donnie grabbed my arm and whisked me through a small but well-appointed foyer into a large living room. "Everything will be fine," he assured me before pointing to a cluster of extravagantly dressed men standing in the center of the room. "Come on, let me introduce you. You'll love 'em. They're *real* camps!"

Donnie's friends greeted him with piercing screams and grandly-placed pecks on the cheek, while I kept them at a distance by stiffly offering them my hand. When one particularly effeminate man called me Helen, I testily corrected him by noting I didn't go by a girl's name. Arching an eyebrow, he coolly reminded me that the wife of the TV cowboy, Roy Rogers, was also named Dale. "And she's a girl, ain't she?" he asked to titters all around. After that, an exasperated Dominic pulled me aside and again advised me to keep my mouth shut. "Everyone's Helen here, Mary," he explained.

Doing as I was told, I quietly listened as the group engaged in what Donnie called "dish." While I still wasn't sure what that was, I didn't bother asking. What I'd found amusing while alone in the car with him seemed suddenly repulsive among these gargoyles. I actually felt sick to my stomach.

A man with plucked eyebrows and a blousy top crowed, "Oh girls, everyone knows about Rock Hudson. But Tab Hunter, have you heard about him? Well, honey, you just wouldn't believe. Her favorite vacation is staring at mattress buttons."

Appalled, I watched the group nod and wink over their secret solidarity and vowed I'd never stoop so low. Dragging good, wholesome, all-American types like Rock Hudson and Tab Hunter down to their level just so they wouldn't have to feel like freaks was pathetic. I despised them. I wanted to be anywhere but there.

Another man—this one in mascara and leopard-skin slippers—cleared his throat. "Mary, that Sal Mineo is *such* a doll. A friend of a friend claims she did him in an LA tearoom." Placing his hands about a foot apart, he cooed, "Very tasty, if you get my drift."

I wasn't sure I did, although the rest of the group squealed with delight. Across the room, our "hostess" circulated, hawking canapes. "Want some meat?" she inquired in her deepest basso profundo. She smiled knowingly as two guests surveyed her offerings. "Yeah, that's right, honeys, pigs-in-a-blanket."

"Have you heard?" a man sporting a studded dog collar and teased-out, bright orange hair asked. "Marlon Brando and Wally Cox are lovers." When the others expressed disbelief, he got annoyed. "I'm serious, Marys." He prissily held up a heavily ringed hand and smiled lasciviously. "It's l'amour, darlings, l'amour."

Donnie jabbed me with his elbow and gushed, "Ain't it a *hoot?!*"

I smiled wanly and, glancing at my watch, realized I still had an hour-and-a-half left to my curfew. I watched our hostess grope a guest and prayed she didn't come near me. My stomach was in knots.

"And what about Paul Newman?" a man in skin-tight pants and sparkling white tennis shoes cried. "Oops, do we hear beads dropping, Miss Things?"

I didn't, but as the crowd guffawed, I noticed four conservatively dressed Black men talking quietly over by the fireplace. I watched them for signs of discomfort but, seeing none, marveled at the ease with which the partygoers seemed to navigate the color line. Back home, "race-mixing," as my parents called it, was strictly forbidden. Indeed, the only Blacks I'd ever shared a room with before that night was the "help" who were paid to be there: porters, waiters, maids, and cleaning ladies. These guys were not only there of their own accord, they seemed to even be enjoying themselves!

A short, pudgy white man in an ascot and velvet jacket quieted the group with a wave of his arms. "Hold on, girls, hold on. I've got one better." He smiled maliciously and ran bright red nails through thick wavy hair. "You know, of course, that Mae West is a man. I mean, really. Think about it, queens. Oh, and did you see Tallulah Bankhead on *Merv Griffin*? Oh, my God, she was *such* a camp! I nearly died. I mean for days, girlfriends, for days." Even the four Black men, who'd dropped their conversation to listen in, laughed.

Feeling faint, I pulled Dominic aside and asked if he'd guard the bathroom door while I splashed some water on my face. He snarled that I was a big boy now and, pushing me on my way, said it was time I started fending for myself. And although I somehow managed to make it to the bathroom on my own, an older man with a bulbous red nose and thinning hair burst in on me and, reeking of alcohol, announced he wanted to "do" me. While I wasn't quite sure what that was, his wandering hand told me I needed to get away fast. Shoving him onto the toilet, I ran out and slammed the door behind me.

"My, that was fast!" tittered a jowly older man who claimed to be the bathroom monitor. He smiled lewdly. "Was it good?" Glaring, I told him to mind his own business and, over his loud protests—*Oh, baby, why're you being so sensitive? I was just joking around!*—ran off. When I described the incident to Dominic, he groaned, rolled his eyes, and admonished me to loosen up. "Look, honey, you're young. They're chicken hawks. They're everywhere in gay life. Quit acting so fucking uppity and get used to it."

A half hour later, my stomach finally settled down when a tall, good-looking guy with brown, short-cropped hair and an easy smile sauntered up to me and said hi. Dressed in khakis, penny loafers, and a buttoned-down dress shirt, he seemed blessedly normal. Introducing himself as Tom, he asked if I was the one from Wilmington.

"Boy, word gets around fast, huh?" I replied before admitting it was my first gay party. Blushing, I wondered if he'd noticed how my voice cracked over the word 'gay.'

Tom smiled and asked how it was going. I shook my head and fought an urge to cry. "That bad, huh?" he murmured. He looked around the room and confessed it'd been so long since he'd come out that he'd almost forgotten how tough it was. "You'll get used to it, though. I promise." He pointed to a sofa and smiled. "Come on," he said, steadying me with a hand to my back, "let's sit down and talk."

He didn't once mention Rock Hudson or Tab Hunter or discuss the alleged love affair between Marlon Brando and Wally Cox. Instead, he asked about my plans for college and seemed impressed when I told him I'd be studying architecture. "So, I guess that means you're not just another pretty face, huh?"

I tried not to blush but, a little later, when he said he found me sexy, I started to tremble. "I don't know," I muttered by way of explanation, "this is all so new." I felt the heat from his thigh as he inched in closer. "I'm very nervous." It was then that he put his arm around me and apologized if he was moving too fast. "I just happen to think I like you, that's all." He smiled. "Is that okay?"

"Oh no, I mean, er, yes, it's fine," I stammered before saying it was also okay to keep his arm around me. However, a few minutes later when I glanced at my watch, I had to jump up. "Oh my God, I'm late. My curfew was up twenty minutes ago." Following me to the door, Tom kissed me on the lips and said he hoped to see me again. "Soon," he whispered, standing so close I felt his breath on my cheek. Clutching the slip of paper on which he'd written his phone number, I floated out the door and somehow managed to find my father's Corvair a few blocks away.

Two days later, under the nose of my mother, I called Tom collect and made a date for that Saturday night. We agreed to meet at his place, a first-floor apartment on Queen Street. I surprised myself by actually commenting on the irony: "Queen Street?" I asked. He laughed and assured me it was easy to find. "Only a few blocks over from South," he murmured. "Yeah," he said in response to my query, "just like in the song," I asked if he understood I couldn't stay the night, to which he replied in a voice so sultry I nearly melted, "I'll try to get used to the idea."

I hung up and put on my portable stereo a 45 of the Orlons' hit, "South Street." Jumping around my room, I whooped out its lyrics until my mother yelled from the bottom of the stairs, "Hey, what's going on up there? Sounds like an army of elephants on the loose. The whole house is shaking!" Collapsing onto my bed, I muttered, "If only you knew, Mother, if only you knew."

Donnie and I quickly became fast friends, although he insisted that we avoid each other while at school. As he said, one of us would slip up and "drop our beads" and then all hell would break loose. And so, when we passed in the halls or shared the same lunch period, we pretended we'd never met.

When I complained this felt dishonest, Donnie assured me it was the way gay people survived. "No one's who they say they are," he said of gay life. Lying, he claimed, was standard practice—sometimes even to each other. And, after a while, we managed to turn our ruse into a game to see who could come closest to crossing the line without raising suspicion. In this, Donnie agreed that the time I retrieved the hanky he'd campily dropped in the hall between classes was the best, although Nancy, the friend I'd taken to Cotillion, sensed something was amiss. "You don't know him, do you?" she asked, incredulous. "I mean, he's a business student."

"Oh no," I replied, reassuringly. "Never seen him before in my life." Later, Donnie congratulated me. My lying, he said, was "flawless."

Two weeks before graduation, Donnie got careless about what he was up to in Philadelphia and rumors started circulating at school that he too was gay. On the day of our graduation, we were so worried about trouble we sat at the back of Mount Pleasant's auditorium in case we had to get our parents out fast. Fortunately, the bullies let us be and our parents were able to be as proud of us as the others were of their kids. As Donnie later quipped, graduation went so smoothly he almost forgot he was gay.

On the drive home, my mother asked why I hadn't lingered outside the auditorium to hug my friends goodbye like the others had done. Rather than confess I never wanted to see any of them again, I simply shrugged and told her I'd said all my goodbyes the night before at a party my friend Mary had thrown in Normandy Heights. It was a lie, of course. That night I'd spent on Queen Street in Philadelphia with Tom, who'd generously offered me tips on how to give a better blow job. I hadn't been invited to Mary's in over a year.

But I had survived. After more than two years of regular, near-daily harassment, my parents still thought me respected and well-liked, a member in good standing of Mount Pleasant's cliquish 'in crowd.' All those lonely nights I'd spent cruising Market Street, my parents actually believed I'd been with a girl, partying with friends, being a well-rounded, suburban, middle-class, white-bread teenager—the epitome of normal.

As my mother prattled on about how proud she was of me, I toyed with the ribbon around my National Honor Society certificate and smiled darkly. The one course I'd taken that no one but Donnie knew about—how to live a lie—I'd also aced. The toll it had taken—the assault on my dignity, my growing guilt and anxiety, the breach it threatened with my parents—no longer mattered. I'd made it through. I'd beaten them at their own game, the one they called "maintaining appearances" and the one Donnie simply called "passing," the game of pretend every homosexual needed to master in order to survive.

Tom and I saw each other for about two months. Although my curfew kept us from spending a night together, he quickly claimed he was in love with me. That was pretty heady for an eighteen-year-old just entering gay life. However, when Tom suggested we show the depth of our feelings by playing with each other's feces, I called it quits. While by then I'd at least learned to swallow his cum, I wasn't about to start messing around with his bowel movements.

When I told Donnie about Tom's request, he explained gay men like that were "scat queens." Like the other varieties he'd told me about, Donnie said they were a part of gay life that I just had to get used to, although I admitted I was finding that increasingly difficult. Surely something was off-limits.

While Donnie acknowledged our public lives were highly proscribed, he contended the situation was very different behind closed doors. Gays, he claimed, were much freer than straights to express themselves sexually. It was, he said, one of the reasons why he thought we were actually superior to straights. We at least had the freedom to get over our sexual hang-ups, while most straights just had to live with theirs. Nothing, he thought, was more constraining than that.

I knew better than to contend that I thought there were more pressing issues to deal with than the exploration of our sexual limits. Every time I'd tried to talk about the Vietnam War, the arms race, our country's seemingly intractable racial divide, or even our own sorry legal state, I was met with blank stares. Even books and film—except, of course, for the Hollywood camp classics Dominic and his crowd relentlessly quoted—were off-limits. After a while, I learned to just clam up and try to endure as best I could the manic hilarity by which they lived their lives—an endless round of camping, vamping, and dishing interrupted only by the near-nightly need to "trick." While they knew as well as

I how hostile the straight world was, their revenge was to ignore it. Mine, on the other hand, was to want to change it. After a while, I started to worry I was the only one.

After Tom, I took up with Dominic's pot dealer, Cliff. He was a short, brash, well-built blond who, like Tom, was about ten years older than me, but who lived not a few blocks off but on South Street, the heart of Philadelphia's Black ghetto. The only white in the area, he said his neighbors, all devout churchgoers, remained friendly even after he'd told them he was gay, although he acknowledged they'd probably feel differently if they knew the whole story.

"I'm a chicken hawk," he explained. "If they knew, they'd have me firebombed, no questions asked." That was why, he added, he'd blackened his windows and, except for the Saturday afternoon Donnie and I went over to taste-test a new shipment of marijuana, he never let me visit during the day. As for my curfew, which precluded overnights, Cliff was, unlike Tom, happy my parents kept me on a short leash. That way, he could go out and pick up more guys. Some nights, he'd claim he had three or four more after me. "A sex fiend," he called himself with a matter-of-factness that I found off-putting.

Unlike Tom, who claimed to be in love with me after only a week, Cliff eschewed any hint of a romantic entanglement. The most loving he'd ever get would be to pull me to him, slip his hand down the back of my pants and ask if it was time for another "roll in the hay," as he called sticking his dick up my ass. I had to admit, for someone learning his way around gay sex, I found Cliff's come-ons every bit as heady as Tom's professions of love.

I'd never had anal sex before Cliff and, while I was at first dubious, he made buttfucking so exciting it was just about all we did. He'd throw my legs over his shoulders and enter me until, drenched in sweat, we both exploded. Sometimes, we'd do it two or three times before calling it a night. Once, he even made me come through my prostate, a rare, hands-free orgasm he took great pride in provoking. "Only experts are able to pull stuff like that off," he boasted before claiming to be my sex educator.

Donnie said our fondness for anal sex made Cliff and I "Greek" as opposed to the gay men who preferred oral sex, whom he called "French." He noted Cliff, like Dominic, was Greek "active" and I, like Donnie, was Greek "passive," although he acknowledged both terms were quickly going out of style. He said "butch" and "fem," the former being the fucker and the latter the fuckee, were more au courant, although "fem" sounded too much like "sissy" to me. After that, I stopped saying what I did in bed. If someone wanted to know, they'd just have to take me for a spin and find out.

In late July, Cliff invited me to a gay pool party at a client's house out on Philadelphia's Main Line. Since he didn't have a car, I picked him up in my father's Corvair and he directed me. When, after about an hour, we finally arrived at the house, I was so turned around I had no idea how to get either of us back home. Afraid I might again miss my curfew, I asked Cliff to promise he wouldn't desert me for someone new. "Don't worry, baby. I'll be there for you," he purred.

That night, Cliff smoked a lot of pot and got eerily quiet. When we got into the pool, he pulled me to him and told me he wanted to fuck me. Noting all the people around, I suggested we save it for later—perhaps on the side of the road on the ride back to town or in his apartment or, pointing to an upstairs window, in one of our host's many bedrooms. Unmoved, Cliff ground himself into my backside and confessed the crowd was what turned him on. He wanted the others to see him fuck the "eighteen-year-old," as I'd quickly become known to the other guests, all gay men older than Cliff. As one had remarked upon meeting me, he'd never met a gay guy so young. "Jailbait," another had quipped, only half-mockingly. "How about precocious?" a third had more generously offered.

When I tried to squirm out of Cliff's grip, he tightened his hold on me and told me that if I didn't do as he wanted, I'd have to find my own way home. When I reminded him of his promise, he growled, "Yeah, but that was then and this is now."

Trapped, I let him pull down my trunks and enter me. Fortunately, he was either too nervous or too high and came after only a few thrusts. He grunted loudly but the crowd around the pool was having too much fun to notice. "Happy now?" I snarled as I pulled my trunks back up. Bleary-eyed, Cliff couldn't believe no one had gathered around to admire his prowess. "What a bunch of nelly queens," he groused.

Shortly after that, Cliff agreed it was time to go and sullenly directed me back to his apartment, where I begged off his invitation for another fuck by noting the hour. My curfew was almost up and, as I said, I didn't want to have to endure another upbraiding from my father. I never raised my voice or accused Cliff of anything untoward, let alone rape. As I'd already learned from Donnie, there was no such word in gay life. According to him, saying no to sex with a good-looking guy like Cliff was like refusing to kiss or swallow cum. No self-respecting gay man would ever do that.

My only consolation was cutting off all contact with Cliff, although I was shocked to learn he'd quickly found someone even younger to replace me. After explaining chicken hawks always came out on top, Dominic once again grumbled about how green I was. As the hostess of my first gay party had said, I was still fresh meat. I had to learn the ropes of gay life one wrenching lift at a time.

It didn't matter that, in the learning, I often felt like I lost as much as I gained. I was gay now and, as Dominic repeatedly reminded me, that meant I had to get over myself. And while I gave it my best, I was surprised by how resistant I was to giving up values which, according to Dominic, made me a lousy gay man.

Like compassion. I didn't like the biting wit gay men used on each other, belittling each other based on revelations they'd secured either directly or, more often, on the sly, with the clear intent to hurt or harm. Or engagement. I didn't like the haughty indifference with which they dismissed the straight world, convinced they could build a cocoon that insulated them from the hatred that otherwise confined and distorted their lives. Or honesty. I hated the lying, the determination to make a go of it, to find contentment in the margins—to appear, if not to each other, at least to the rest of the world, straight.

But what bothered me the most about gay life was the sexual promiscuity. Every gay man I knew was on the make, morning, noon and night—even Dominic and Donnie, who were a couple. As Cliff had once contended, the number of tricks you had in the course of a day was the measure of how successful you were as a homosexual. By that measure, I was indeed a failure. When I fell in love, I wanted it to be just him and me.

No, no matter how many times Dominic berated me for not getting over myself, for not joining in the festivities more enthusiastically, more *gayly*, I refused to give in. I'd grown up believing in the middle-class dream. In that world, people were supposed to succeed on their merits, and I saw no reason why being gay should in any way diminish that. I didn't care how searing Dominic's critiques were. I refused to give up my pride or self-respect just because I was gay.

After Cliff, I mostly just hung around Donnie as his "gay sister," the first "camp" term I embraced. We did everything together. This was greatly reassuring, since I found gay life deeply unsatisfying—more a perverse reflection of the status quo than the robust rejection I longed for.

Donnie, on the other hand, loved everything about gay life. "The tackier, the better," he'd say, although, as he once warned, 'tacky' was a gay word that I must never use around straights. "It will immediately wreck you," he explained. By then, I'd learned to be "wrecked" was the same as having your "beads drop," both of which meant you were "outed" not just to other gays but to the whole world, a fate Donnie described as worse than death.

While being out to other gays was required, letting straights in on the secret was to be avoided at all costs. "Only a madman would come out to the whole world," Dominic insisted. This was not simply because of the personal risks involved. Coming out to straights also put one's gay friends at risk too.

Advance notice, Donnie said, was always expected. "So we can take precautionary measures," he explained. When I asked what kind, he smiled and said, "Like pretend we never knew you." Removing people from address books and tossing their mementos into the trash were two examples he cited. When I complained that those seemed rather cold-blooded, Donnie shrugged. In gay life, he said, one always had to be prepared for trouble. And there was no bigger trouble than being wrecked.

After that, my anxieties over exposure escalated, although I was at least able to keep them in check while under the cover of night. However, when I tagged along for a weekend tryst Donnie had set up in Atlantic City with a tall, good-looking grad student with whom he was havings a secret affair, my anxieties came suddenly to a head.

Donnie had explained in advance why he'd chosen Atlantic City. As he'd noted, it wasn't, as I'd imagined, because the Miss America pageant's opening parade—a cavalcade of convertibles featuring the contestants in strapless bathing suits—was scheduled for our second day in town. No, it was because of its "gay beach," a two-hundred-foot stretch of sand right off the boardwalk that he said attracted the largest daytime crowd of homosexuals ever assembled in any one place anywhere on the planet. "It'll blow your mind," he'd promised.

Donnie was right. I'd never seen such a raucous spectacle, hundreds of gay people crammed blanket-to-blanket on a stretch of sand bounded on one side by the ocean and the other, Atlantic City's bustling boardwalk. Most were men but there was also a smattering of women, whom Donnie differentiated by referring to one set as "fag hags"—straight women who preferred the company of gay men—and the other as "bull dykes"—man-hating lesbians who hung out only with each other. The men, he said, were all "flamers," meaning they were so obvious even the hot dog vendors had to camp it up to secure a purchase. "OK, Marys, I got six inches for you," one shouted while a competitor several yards away promised a "mouthful." The scene was so campy even the cops got into the act—mostly through the lewd use of their billy clubs—although the families on the adjoining beach kept close watch over their children, who were forbidden to cross the invisible Maginot line separating us to join in on the fun.

"They think we're all child molesters," Donnie grumbled of the parents, although, as he noted, no one he knew had ever encountered a gay man that sick. He ran his hand through the sand and sighed. "You know you really have to watch yourself around kids. Someone accuses you of something and then–bam!–you're in prison. Personally, I steer clear of them." He shook his head over all the lies gay people had to skirt. "It's amazing we haven't all gone stark raving mad."

When, later, he marveled that the beach was so out in the open even our mothers could see what we were up to, my anxieties over being discovered went into overdrive. What if a friend—or, worse, one of my parents' friends—spotted me? After all, the Jersey shore was a popular vacation spot for Wilmingtonians, with a day trip to Atlantic City for the Miss America parade always a must. How would I explain my whereabouts? I quickly became so overwrought, I even thought I spotted my mother on the boardwalk, scanning the beach through binoculars. Fearing I was about to lose it, I told Donnie and his trick I was splitting and took the next bus back to Wilmington.

When I got home, I was so relieved my mother didn't grill me about my aborted weekend—I'd told her I was spending it in Rehoboth Beach with girlfriends—I even vowed to stop seeing Donnie. I told myself the risks of exposure were too great. I couldn't handle the anxiety. Better to play it safe and go back to cruising Market Street. At least there no one knew what I was up to.

Besides, I'd decided gay life wasn't worth being wrecked over. The banter was too catty, the sex too predatory, the culture too vapid. I wanted something deeper and more meaningful than what I'd grown up with, not something even more superficial and materialistic. And so, I'd decided to be a hippie instead. While I was sure most were straight, I was equally sure they'd be okay with me being gay. After all, wasn't their favorite slogan "Do your own thing?" What could possibly be gayer than that?

My vow to ditch Donnie lasted only a few days, although my misgivings about gay life continued to mount. These reached a peak when, a few weeks before I was to go off to Syracuse, Dominic invited me to join him, Donnie and Mike for an open-air Judy Garland concert. Although I'd adored Judy in *The Wizard of Oz*, I'd never much cared for her since and her long, slow decline through drugs and booze had appalled me. How could someone sink so low? I'd wondered while watching her TV show. And in front of *millions*! I had no idea that gay men worshiped her for the very reasons I found her so repellant: her shamelessness, her lack of restraint, and her self-abasement. Had the woman no pride?

Assembled under a large tent on the industrial outskirts of South Philly, the crowd for Judy's concert was large, boisterous, and almost entirely gay. Like the beach crowd in Atlantic City, almost all were men, although this time they were nattily decked out in sport coats and dress pants rather than swimming trunks and flip flops. As in Atlantic City, there was also a smattering of women, although Donnie insisted only fag hags turned out for Judy. As he noted, "bulldaggers," his new word for lesbians, hated camp. "Mud wrestling," he sneered when I asked what they were into.

That was something else I disliked about gay life—the disdain gay men had for women who didn't fawn all over them, lesbians in particular. Perversely, the most effeminate, the ones who called each other "girls," were often the vilest. "Fish," they liked to call women, although I once again had to rely on Donnie for a translation. "What, don't you know what a vagina smells like?" he asked. Donnie was shocked when I confessed I'd never been with a woman. "A Kinsey six," he called me, although I'd again had to ask what he meant. "A total faggot," he explained. "Hopeless."

The four of us dressed for the concert, although, as the youngest of Judy's fans, we still stood out, a distinction Dominic claimed added considerable heft to the evening. Calling us "acolytes," he said it was our duty to absorb every nuance of Judy's performance so we could carry on "gay culture," at whose apogee "Miss Garland," as he insisted on calling her, stood and without which he contended we'd still be a bunch of tearoom queens sucking off trade for five bucks a pop.

I was skeptical, although when I commented on the paucity of young people in the audience by noting most kids our age considered Garland a has-been, Dominic got indignant. "Oh, you mean the hippies. Well, what do they know? They wouldn't recognize a star if one hit them in the head." Besides, Judy was "ours," an icon he called the "patron saint of gay suffering." Hippies, he snarled, could go fuck themselves if they disapproved.

Stunned by the ferocity of his rant, I asked if he'd been dipping into his vial of white-crossed pills. "Well, of course, darling!" Dominic replied. "This *is* a Judy Garland concert. We want her to feel at home, don't we?"

The crowd wanted their goddess late, perilously so, and in this regard Judy did not disappoint. When we arrived, rumors were already circulating that she'd overdosed and, as at many of her recent concerts, would be a no-show. As the clock ticked on, these rumors intensified until, right before her arrival, she was supposedly comatose and in the hospital on a respirator.

Speculation raged as to what drugs she'd taken, with people rattling off a list of possibilities, few of which I'd ever heard of. Dominic assumed she'd done too many "uppers," like the "dexies" he'd popped for the occasion, while others were certain she was on "downers," like the "two-ees" an older man in an ascot in front us confessed he was fond of. Someone even mentioned mainlining, which I knew meant using a hypodermic needle, although the mere thought of doing something like that made my stomach turn.

Whatever she'd taken, they were sure she'd mixed it with booze, lots of it. On that point, they were in agreement—Judy was a lush. A big one. I gathered from their snickering that many of her admirers were too. Certainly, the two men behind us, both of whom reeked of alcohol, were.

"Miss Garland! Miss Garland!" the audience cried when she finally appeared, an hour-and-a-half late and so out-of-it two bodyguards had to help her onto the stage. "Thank you," she woozily replied, bowing so deeply one of them had to spot her. She straightened up and, leaning into his shoulder, wrapped herself in her mic's cord. "We'll sing 'em all and stay all night," she cried, a line from her Carnegie Hall concert album that Mike called the ultimate camp line. "Just watch," he whispered, "the queens'll go crazy." He was right. "Judy, we love you! We love you!" they screamed as if we were at a Beatles concert, except Judy's fans were middle-aged gay men, not teenage straight girls.

Judy proceeded to sing, although often against the beat and hopelessly off-key. The worse she was, the more frenzied her admirers became. When she forgot her lyrics, as she often did, they happily joined in, finishing the song for her. When she teetered on collapse, her bodyguards came to her rescue, a charitable act the crowd lustily cheered on. "Can they do that for me too, Miss Garland?" a man in the front row shouted. "Well, of course, darling," Judy slurred. "You just have to drink as much as me." The crowd again roared its approval. When she was no longer able to stand on her own, her bodyguards finally escorted her off the stage, at which point everyone—or at least everyone but me—jumped to their feet and broke into a thunderous roar: "Come back, Miss Garland! Miss Garland, come back!"

She didn't and, after a performance of less than forty minutes, the crowd began to feel cheated. However, when rumors again swirled about an overdose and that this time she really was on death's doorstep, her fans seemed suddenly satiated, as if it wasn't her performance they'd come to witness. It was her demise. Some even gloated that they were among the last to see her alive, a very special night indeed.

On the way out, Dominic, sweaty and hoarse from shouting her name, asked what I thought. "I hated it," I snipped. "The whole thing was pathetic. I don't know which was worse: Judy or the crowd." Turning beet-red, Dominic refused to say another word to me. I was, he later told Donnie, "self-loathing" and he wanted nothing more to do with me.

A few days later, I sought Donnie's help in patching things up with Dominic. While I acknowledged he and I were often at loggerheads, I admitted adjusting to gay life was much harder than I'd imagined. Maybe more of Dominic's browbeating would help.

Donnie agreed but warned me Dominic's patience was wearing thin. Any further attacks on gay life would only lead to his rejection. And hadn't I already had too much of that? What would I have if not for other gay people?

It was then I blurted out my intent to become a hippie. I was sure Syracuse, a sprawling inner-city campus in a liberal state like New York, would have plenty. Donnie, who, like Dominic, thought hippies were dirty, was appalled and two days later, Dominic broke his silence by inviting me to go with him for a visit with his "gay mother," a mentor who'd helped him when he struggled with his own coming out. He thought I might find the encounter "inspirational."

I wasn't sure what he meant by that, although when we arrived at the West Philadelphia address, Dominic warned me I should prepare myself for a shock. After twenty years as a gay man, his mentor had undergone a sex change and was now a woman. "A lesbian," he added, staring coolly at me.

"What?" I gasped. "You mean he went through all that only to remain gay?"

"Yes," Dominic replied and confessed that was why he'd brought me along. "To show you your heritage."

"My *what*?"

Dominic exited my father's Corvair and told me to follow him. "You'll see."

Lee raised parakeets and her apartment was dark, musty, and littered with doilies. She had a fondness for fake Tiffany lamps, which she said she got at Woolworth's along with her parakeets, one of which chirped in my ear as we chatted over tea. Dressed in slacks and a dress shirt with a button-down collar, only her tits indicated she was no longer a man, although she still screamed gay. She even spoke with a lisp.

Lee said she'd been happy being gay but could never quite shake the feeling that she was really a woman. She said it was more than just being a sissy, which she readily acknowledged she'd been, or liking to get fucked, which she confessed she really hadn't. It was deeper and more mysterious, an urge she defined more as a calling than an obsession. "Like the apparition in *Song of Bernadette*," she said. "Something you just can't shake and keep going back to, despite yourself."

"Like being gay," Dominic interjected after confessing the Jennifer Jones flick was one of his favorites too.

"Yes," Lee said, pouring herself another cup of tea. "Very much like that."

She said she was among the first to sign up when Johns Hopkins opened up what she called its "sexual reassignment" clinic. She loved her new body but admitted she hated straight life. She missed the camaraderie and openness she'd enjoyed as a gay man. Straight people were close-minded and judgmental and straight men, she added, were pigs. Sex with them was degrading.

After a while, she'd turned to women. "Best decision I ever made," she said of what she called her "second coming out." She admitted she had to learn to appreciate the sex but the rest—the feelings of belonging and the sense of a community she got from being gay—came naturally. "And, you know, when you get right down to it, sex isn't all that important. What's important is being part of something bigger than yourself." She turned and smiled at one of her parakeets. "A community."

When Dominic asked if she thought there was a spiritual element to being gay, she took a sip of tea and nodded. "Absolutely. No question about it. Being gay is a calling." She put down her teacup and giggled. "Like Bernadette's."

At that, Dominic stood up and announced it was time to go. He was already late for a date with Donnie. And after I politely shook her hand and Dominic gave her a bear hug and a kiss on the cheek, we bade Lee farewell.

"I assume Donnie told you what I said about becoming a hippie," I remarked as we walked back to the car. "I mean, that is what this was all about, right?"

Dominic grimaced. "Don't tell me you've actually fallen for that 'do your own thing' shit?"

When I said I needed to be something other than a queen or a camp, he exploded. "Oh, so it's the life, is it? Little Miss Sunshine thinks she's too good for it." I tried to protest but, in high dudgeon, Dominic would not let me get a word in edgewise. "Listen, I know straight people. I don't care how long they grow their hair or what drugs they take, hippies are still straight. And as far as straight people are concerned, you're just another queer." His face hardened. "Always have been and always will be."

When I insisted hippies were a different breed, he became even more agitated. "Listen, Mary, I'll tell you this. You become one of those dirty, disgusting vagabonds and you'll be a traitor to your own kind. Understand? A traitor. I'll never speak to you again."

Stunned, I asked Dominic if he was serious and he assured me he was. Hippies, he said, were a threat to everything gay life stood for, and he would not tolerate any desertions. When I asked if he was high on "dexies," the white-crossed pills he'd started popping on a regular basis, he told me to mind my own business. Hippies, he said, were in no position to judge anyone's drug-taking.

My last week in Wilmington, Donnie and I agreed to test Dominic's theory about straight people by coming out to one. We chose as our guinea pig Angie, a Mount Pleasant business-track student who, mostly because she was a great dancer, was also popular with the academic crowd. Because she was also what my father called "horsey" and rarely dated, Donnie thought she had great "fag hag" potential and might become a companion to replace me when I went off to college.

Knowing her to be unusually open-minded, I was certain she was the perfect choice. Next to me, no one at Mt. Pleasant seemed more unhappy with suburban life than Angie. As she'd confessed shortly before graduation, she hoped to become a hippie too. Unfortunately, with no college prospects, she was stuck. Neither of us had ever seen a hippie in Wilmington.

That summer, when I wasn't hanging around Donnie, Angie and I became renegades together, getting high on pot and grooving to the psychedelic sounds of bands like Jefferson Airplane, the Doors and Big Brother and the Holding Company. Once we even put flowers in our hair and danced in her backyard to Scott McKenzie's *San Francisco*. When the neighbors complained about the sissy she was hanging around, her parents suggested Angie drop me, which she refused to do. We were "buddies," she told them. We saw things the same way.

The coming-out experiment Donnie and I devised for Angie did not go well. As planned, we got her stoned on pot, went to the swim club she and I belonged to and then, after a few obligatory giggles and the consumption of an entire bag of M&M's, Donnie abruptly got to the point. "We're gay, Angie."

She immediately stiffened. "You're what?"

Donnie repeated himself. "You know, homosexual."

"You're joking," Angie replied, gripping the arms of her pool chair. She looked around her—at the freshly-mowed grass, the pool's lapping water and then up at the sky, a soft pale blue. From the parking lot, an ice cream truck announced its fare: creamsicles for only a quarter, ice cream sandwiches for two. "I mean, you're playing some kind of mind game on me, right?"

Donnie shook his head. "No, Angie, we're serious." He fumbled with a button on his dark blue polo shirt. "I even have a lover. His name is Dominic. I'd like you to meet him." He laughed nervously. "He's a Goombah too."

Angie glared at me and asked if what Donnie had said was true.

"Yes, Angie, it is," I replied and started to tremble. Around us, children frolicked. Mothers laughed. The lifeguard settled into a pose—a Greek god attired in a Speedo, resting on his plinth. "We wanted you to know," I continued, fighting an urge to flee. "You're a friend. We don't like lying to you."

"Gee, thanks," Angie sneered before bursting into tears. Devastated, Donnie and I took her by the hands until, composing herself, she rose from her chair and informed us she didn't appreciate being dragged into what she called our "little secret." While she was willing to continue to be our friend, she never wanted to discuss the topic again. "What you do in bed is your business. It has nothing to do with me." We tried to argue the point but she was adamant. And, no, she did not want to meet Donnie's "Goombah."

Mortified, we agreed to never talk about who we really were in front of her again, although later Donnie vowed to drop her as a friend. "Dominic was right. Straight people can't be trusted." He fought back tears. "And to think Angie's supposed to be one of the better ones."

He said he was giving up on straight people. "They can just go fuck themselves for all I care." As for him, he was going "full-time," living and working only around other gay people. He'd heard the Strawbridge & Clothiers that was a short drive from his house was looking for what he called "window queens." "Oh, you know, the fairies who dress the mannequins and arrange the displays," he explained when I asked what they were. He was sure his high school shop project, "A Pictorial Representation of the State of Martha's Mind," would clinch the job for him. Like Dominic had said, only queens do decoupage.

Having already endured more than my fair share of abuse, I was less outraged by Angie's reaction. Besides, I still felt like a fish out of water in gay life. I was terrible at camp, disliked dishing, and refused to call myself a queen. I preferred foreign arthouse films to Hollywood camp classics and listened to rock 'n' roll, not Broadway show tunes. Ethel Merman left me cold; I couldn't stand Barbra Streisand; and, as I'd made abundantly clear, Judy Garland offended me.

I wanted a warrior to look up to—someone like Fannie Lou Hamer of Mississippi's Freedom Democrats, Bettina Aptheker of Berkeley's Free Speech Movement, Jiang Jing of China's Gang of Four or even the boozy, hard-living Janis Joplin from Big Brother and the Holding Company—not a train wreck like Judy Garland. And, as far as I could tell, at least in gay life anyway, warriors were few and far between. The few who managed to survive ended up cranks, raising parakeets amidst musty old furniture covered in doilies, lost in reveries over their "calling." *The Song of Bernadette*, my ass...

7
One of Them

"Well, Mother, we better be going," my father said, tapping his watch. After two hours of helping me carry my belongings up three flights of stairs, my parents were finally ready to head back to Wilmington. He wiped his brow with the monogrammed hanky he kept in his back pocket and pulled out his car keys. "We have a long drive ahead of us."

Bursting into tears, my mother hugged me and made me promise to call the very next day. I hung limply in her arms and wondered if she too felt the vertigo of our release. Soon, she'd have no one to lose sleep over. Soon, I'd have no one to lie to.

My father stiffly held out his hand. Wincing against his grip, I dutifully assented to his list of demands: be good, watch my money, study hard, and write once in a while. "Good luck, you're getting something I never had," he said of the college education the Depression had forced him to abandon. "Don't waste it."

"Yes, sir," I said, chewing on a fingernail.

Pulling me in closer, he tightened his grip. "And don't worry your mother." He looked at me sternly. "And take that finger out of your mouth."

"Oh no, never. I mean, yes, of course," I stammered. I grimaced and shoved my hands into the pockets of the Bermuda shorts I'd worn for the trip to Syracuse. Soon, I'd be free of him too—his carping and incessant, cuttingly cruel sarcasm. The last of my bullies, I thought. Freedom.

My father patted me on the shoulder and climbed into the driver's seat of the family Olds, the one my mother used for errands but which we always took on car trips. "Don't forget to check out the Kappa Sig house," he advised of the fraternity he'd joined while at Indiana University, his would-be alma mater. He still didn't understand why I hadn't also wanted to go there, situated as it was in what he called "God's country." "They'll treat you just like family."

I waved as their car headed down the hill for the southbound ramp of the recently-completed I-81. When it finally disappeared, I turned and examined the façade of my dorm, Sibley Hall, a rickety, three-story Victorian with rotting clapboards and a teetering turret high up on a hill overlooking the city. Five hours by car from anyone I knew, I'd arrived for the start of my first year at Syracuse University's School of Architecture. Taking my first big step toward fulfilling a dream, I was the only one who knew it no longer had anything to do with T-squares, slide rules, and floorplans. I was instead intent on designing the new me: a gay man, unafraid of the truth.

I bounded up the stairs to the room I'd been assigned to share with another incoming architectural freshman and smiled at my good fortune. Snoring loudly, Jim, a working-class kid from Youngstown, Ohio, had passed out after polishing off his first six-pack of beer. Just as I'd hoped, I was free to do as I pleased. Rummaging through my trunk for just the right outfit—a pair of dark gray Farrah slacks, a short-sleeve Madras print shirt, and my Bass Weejuns—I raced to the bathroom to shower, shave, and make myself presentable. Night approached and somewhere out there in Syracuse's recesses my new gay life awaited. I wanted to look just right.

The moon was full and the night warm—good cruising weather, I told myself, as I left Sibley Hall and headed down Irving Street. I turned left at the first intersection and, descending a steep hill, walked under an overpass for the interstate onto which my parents had disappeared and suddenly emerged into a vast expanse of broken bricks, straggly weeds, and shards of glass that shimmered in the moonlight. I recalled a similar stretch in downtown Wilmington and surmised I'd come upon Syracuse's former Black ghetto, razed in retaliation for the riots that had sent the city's whites fleeing to the suburbs. As I wandered through, a dozen or so people partying outside a run-down housing project the wrecking ball had somehow neglected to raze warily sized me up.

Suddenly, a boy of about ten ran up to me and asked if I knew where I was. "Not too many people like you come by here this time of night," he shyly noted. He turned and looked back at the man in a brightly-colored dashiki who'd sent him. "That's right, son," the man shouted. "Find out what he's up to."

"You need directions?" the boy dutifully asked.

Recalling Dominic's claim that where there were Blacks there were also often gays, I considered revealing my aim—new in town, I was looking for a gay bar; did they know of one? But as the boy had indicated, I was an intruder, a white one, and perhaps as unwelcome there as he and the project's other residents would be had they wandered into any of Wilmington's lily-white suburbs. Besides, with no streetlights and the area's only other structure, an I.M. Pei-designed art museum intended to lure whites back to the city, still under construction, I was a sitting duck for anyone looking for trouble.

Lying, I told the crowd I was a returning SU student on my way across town to spend the night with my girlfriend. "Over there," I added, pointing in a direction that I hoped meant she too was white. As Dominic had also noted, Blacks disapproved of "race-mixing," as my parents called it, almost as much as whites, although he'd been careful to exempt gays from that prejudice. As he noted, "dinge" and "snow" queens, the latter being Black men who went for white guys, were nearly as common in gay life as chicken hawks.

"Right on, brother!" the man in the dashiki cried. "Don't do anything I wouldn't do," the man flipping burgers added. The women in the group rolled their eyes but when another man, this one in a fedora and pink pants, asked if I'd brought along all the right precautions, they squealed with delight, and the men noisily high-fived each other. "What you give up in pleasure," he advised, "you get back in peace of mind."

I feigned a smile and, after assuring them I was all set, resumed my search, although once out of their sight, I stopped and cursed myself for my cowardice. The start of the first night of my new gay life and I'd already lied about who I was. I listened to the wail of a far-off police siren and promised myself that, next time, things would be different. Once I found that gay bar, I'd be doing nothing but telling the truth.

Five blocks on, I came upon downtown Syracuse, a hapless stretch of commercial tedium more forlorn than even Wilmington's Market Street. I walked the main drag looking for action but hardly a car passed and, of the few that did, none blinked their lights or paused to check me out. About to give up and return to campus, I turned onto a side street—Adams, the sign read—and, lingering in a dimly lit bank plaza to smoke a cigarette, spotted three men in tight white jeans and tennis shoes sashaying toward a pub tucked between a haberdashery and a used furniture store. Three doors away, a gaping hole in the streetscape led to a parking lot that charged fifty cents an hour. At night it was free and, that evening, full.

Sensing a turn in my luck, I sat on a bench and scoured the pub's exterior for confirmation of my suspicions. Its faux-Tudor facade of white stucco and darkly-stained beams was much too prim although, dangling from a shingled overhang, a flickering Genesee beer sign conveyed the right amount of neglect. The door of heavy oak was aptly forbidding but its small window of beveled glass was much too revealing. I could even see the faces of the patrons inside. To the left, a large oval window was appropriately blackened although, below it, a planter of red geraniums was much too cheerful. The furtive glances of the men who kept slinking toward it helped, as did their squeals of delight upon opening the door, but it was the blast of music that came pouring out—Smokey Robinson and the Miracles, Aretha Franklin, Marvin Gaye, Martha and the Vandellas, the Supremes—that clinched it. I'd found it, my "Goin' to a Go-Go:" the Continental Room, Syracuse's only gay bar.

To the Mafia, it was just one more cash cow, one of a hundred seedy joints around the country it milked for every penny of its worth. To its suppliers, it was just another stop on a long day on the road. To the city, it was just another blighted parcel, a small section of a larger district slated for renewal. To the downtown lunch crowd, it was just another place to down a beer along with a sandwich; the roast beef was rumored to be the best in town. To unsuspecting straights out for a night on the town, it was just another watering hole, one which they entered and, shocked by what they found, immediately fled.

To those who stayed, it was their home away from home, the only place around where they could be themselves. A few even claimed it was a place to find the love of one's life but, back then, love generally took a backseat to companionship. In the fall of 1967, two years before the denizens of another Mafia dive in a city far bigger and gayer than Syracuse rose up and said no more, that was about the best one could hope for from places like the Continental Room.

The bar's small band of regulars gave it the squalid fervor typical of its time. For my first two months in Syracuse, these people were my only friends, although I never met them for a movie, joined them for dinner or called them on the phone just to chat. I knew most of them only by their first names, some of which were fake and a few female, although no one was a drag queen. They expected nothing from me except to show up as often as possible, laugh at their hijinks and dance until the bar rocked. Oh, how those queens loved to dance.

Of all of them, I got closest to Larry. A year ahead of me, he was nineteen and, astonishingly for a college town, the Continental Room's only other SU student. Indeed, Larry and I were the only gay students either of us befriended while at Syracuse, although he insisted there were lots to be had in the tearoom in the basement of Maxwell Hall. I went once to find out if what he said was true, only to flee when a man much too old to be a student stuck his finger through a hole in the panel between our stalls and beckoned me to join him. "Oh, those are called 'glory holes,'" Larry later explained. "All tearooms have them. The queens make them with their nail files."

Larry grew up in Jacksonville, Florida, and was what the other regulars called "experienced." He'd been out since he was fourteen and, unlike me, took most of gay life in stride. Indeed, he'd been at it for so long, being gay was his version

112

of normal. The straight world was where he felt like a freak. Short and pudgy, he wore mascara and dyed his hair bright orange. When I advised him to tone it down—what went over in a gay bar wasn't necessarily safe on a college campus—he stroked a finely sculpted eyebrow and stared defiantly into his dorm room mirror. "What's wrong with the way I look?" he cried. "I think I'm beautiful."

Randy, another regular even shorter than Larry, was a teller in the bank across the street from the Continental Room. A slight, high-strung queen with a shrill giddy laugh, he liked to get out on the dance floor and twirl around in a haze of brightly colored scarves. While the other regulars loved it, they agreed Randy was odd. Several worried he might even be crazy.

One afternoon, when I stopped by the bank where Randy worked to say hi, he looked at me blankly and, in a register far lower than the one I knew, inquired how he might be of help. "Very convincing, dear," I replied from the other side of his teller's window. "Now, let's be Randy. Wanna meet me after work for a beer?" Glancing nervously at his co-workers, he replied in the same deep baritone that he was sorry but I must be mistaken, his name was Bob. On his left hand, a gold wedding band glinted in the late afternoon light.

"I don't want anyone to know," Randy explained when I confronted him that night in the bar. Incredulous, I asked what made him think they didn't already. "I mean, you're not exactly the butchest number around." Indignant, Randy informed me he was only going through a phase. Someday, he intended to turn straight. When I asked why, he looked puzzled. "Because being gay is sick. Everybody knows that." When I asked if his real name was Randy or Bob, he refused to answer.

After that, I tried limiting our interactions to the dance floor, although it proved difficult. Crazy or not, Randy was always good for a laugh and, in the Continental Room, laughter often came at a premium.

Trudy was the bar's resident "fag hag." A tall, obese blonde, she arrived every night after work in a black hairdresser's smock. Cooing like Betty Boop and waving at her fans like a beauty queen working a runway, she waddled past the bar and slid into a red vinyl booth off the dance floor where, sipping Cape Codders, she held court with all her "boys." Nestling them in her mammoth breasts, she stroked their brows as they recounted the latest twists to their love's sad travails. "Oh, poor baby," she purred consolingly while waiting for them to dutifully light her cigarettes.

Trudy was the regular who took me under her wing, offering me advice on how to adjust to my new life as a gay barfly. Stay away from the bull dykes in the front room—they like to brawl, she warned—and never give the bartender lip.

If I got thrown out, I'd never get back in. Keep up with the latest dance steps and always be deferential to the regulars—laugh at their jokes, compliment their outfits, and every now and then drop a few quarters in the jukebox. They kept track. "You'll be expected to do your part."

And, she warned, I must always look my best. People dressed for the Continental Room. "Nothing too freakish or flamboyant though. The look here is clean-cut. You know, like you're normal."

A few weeks into my tenure at the Continental Room, Trudy pulled me aside and told me people were starting to talk. "It's your hair," she said. "You're starting to look like a hippie." When I replied that was my aim, Trudy warned me the crowd at the Continental Room looked down on hippies as crab-infested sex fiends. When I told her that was as crazy as some of the things straight people said about gays, she shrugged. If I wanted to fit in, I needed to do something about my hair. She even offered to cut it.

The next weekend, Trudy pressed me further on my emerging hippie look. Hippies, she contended, were drug-crazed zombies who, along with the Black Panthers and SDS, were intent on destroying everything that was good and decent about America. When I explained that was my goal too, Trudy grimaced. "Everyone says things have never been better." No one in the Continental Room, she complained, thought like me.

I thanked her for noticing but, as she quickly pointed out, she hadn't intended to be complimentary. "You're too serious," she grumbled before listing the litany of complaints I'd brought into the bar's walled-off cocoon: the Vietnam War, the Bomb, the cops and the way they treat Blacks, the FBI, and that "military whatever-it-is-you-call-it thing."

"You mean, the military-industrial complex?" I asked. "Yeah, that," she sneered before stabbing the lime in her Cape Codder with her swizzle stick. "I mean, can't you ever be happy with the way things are?"

I shook my head and confessed no, I couldn't; it was one of the reasons why I wanted to be a hippie. Hippies didn't like things the way they were either.

A tall, regal presence, Paul was the leader of the Continental Room's small coterie of Blacks. He wore sky-blue contacts and muted his purple-black hue with multiple applications of base. Every Friday at eleven, he draped an arm over the jukebox and performed a plaintive sing-along to Aretha Franklin's "Ain't No Way." When I worked up the courage to tell him it was my favorite Aretha song, he smiled and told me if I put a quarter in the jukebox, he'd sing it again. As he noted, while Aretha was the Queen of Soul, he was, at least in the Continental Room, the Queen of Dinge.

Appalled, I slunk back to Trudy's booth and complained about how little people in the Continental Room seemed to think of themselves. "I mean, a Black man calling himself *dinge*?"

"Oh, there you go again," Trudy huffed. "Always finding fault." She took another sip of her Cape Codder and smiled. "Besides, everybody uses that word here. They're just having fun."

One night, Paul strolled up to me, planted hands on both hips, and fixed me with his sky-blue gaze. "Mirror, mirror on the wall, who's the fairest of them all?" he demanded.

"Excuse me?" I asked.

Paul repeated his question.

I instantly knew from the smirks on the faces of the small crowd gathering around that this was a prank they'd seen many times before. "Okay, Paul, I give up. Who?"

"Not you, you black bitch!" he shrieked before cackling madly. Snapping his fingers, he twirled on his heels and swept back onto the dance floor. The crowd roared with delight.

Later that night, Trudy explained that was Paul's way of initiating me into the bar's inner circle. "You're one of them now," she cooed, her vintage pink Cadillac idling in the driveway behind Sibley Hall. As she noted, "black" had little to do with race—Paul's terms for that were "dinge," "snow," and "rice"—and everything to do with social standing—with gays being the lowest of the low.

"But I thought you said I'm too serious," I countered, not at all certain the Continental Room's inner circle was where I wanted to be. "Like something's always bothering me."

"Oh, there you go again, silly," she chided. "Complaining about what you've got. Don't you see? They *like* you."

A raccoon caught in her Caddy's headlights looked up from the trash barrel it was rummaging through and stared directly into my eyes. No, I thought, I didn't want to be one of them. I wanted to be somebody else. Someone so out there the Continental Room crowd would have nothing to do with me.

Walter was a tall, razor-thin Black who was the first gay man I knew who also considered himself a rebel, although, unlike me, he refused to hang out in gay bars. "I can't be bothered with those screaming meemies," he once sneered when I suggested we go to the Continental Room to dance. Besides, the last time he'd gone, he and Paul had gotten into a bitch fight the others still talked about. "Nearly cleared the place out," Trudy recalled. When I asked what they'd fought over, she murmured, "Paul's contacts." Walter, she said, had accused Paul of trying to pass.

Trudy asked if Walter and I had gotten it on. When I told her no, she expressed surprise. After all, everyone in the Continental Room knew Walter was into white guys. What she didn't know, and what I didn't tell her, was that he also liked his men straight. Attracted by his Jimi Hendrix look—a large Afro, tinted granny glasses, spangled vests, silver bracelets and velvet bell bottoms that, with no underwear, showed off his considerable endowment—they'd spot Walter hanging out on Marshall Street, SU's tiny commercial strip, ask for his autograph and—nine times out of ten, according to Walter—end up in his bed.

"It's amazing how easy straight guys are," Walter said over beers at The Orange, an off-campus bar where he found much of his prey. He claimed "frat rats," whom he said liked to just lie back and let him do them, were the easiest. He said he was happiest when he was with them, although he admitted he never saw any of them twice.

I didn't want to go to town on a straight guy or even hang out at The Orange, whose preppy vibe reminded me too much of high school. At least at the Continental Room, I could be myself without fear of being beaten up or called names. Besides, at The Orange, dancing was forbidden, while at the Continental Room, it was just about all anyone did. And at dancing, even Paul had to acknowledge that, for a white guy, I was pretty good. On the Continental Room's dance floor, there was no question: I was one of them.

Arnold was the Continental Room's doyenne, the regular who was also its most outrageous queen. A hairdresser in Trudy's salon, he minced and pranced about in white jeans, a baggy SU sweatshirt, and spotless white tennis shoes. Pale, barrel-chested, and badly scarred from acne, he bleached his thinning hair platinum and plucked his eyebrows into long sleek lines.

Archie, his roommate, was always at Arnold's side, mostly because Arnold made him look butch. Shorter and swarthier, he had a hairy chest which he went out of his way to show off. Archie laughed at all of Arnold's antics but never joined him on the dance floor, over which Arnold graciously ruled. I later learned from Trudy this was because Archie feared dancing would ruin his reputation. He claimed only fems danced with other men and, as he ceaselessly reminded everyone, he was butch. He once bragged he didn't even swallow cum, although I suspected he was lying. At the Continental Room, everyone seemed to lie about something.

One night, Arnold and Archie invited all the regulars to an after-hours bash at their house, a dingy, vinyl-sided, two-story box with a black-topped backyard on the city's northside. Being new to the inner circle, I didn't understand this was mostly to showcase Arnold's favorite drag routine, the final aria of Puccini's *Madama Butterfly,* for which he donned a red silk kimono and a black wig pinned into a giant bun with a half-dozen brightly-colored chopsticks. I was dubious about going but, on the drive out, Trudy said Arnold had done his routine a million times and assured me I'd find it a "scream."

I had no idea just how right she was. At the aria's climax, Arnold pulled a carving knife from the sleeve of his kimono and, with three swift strokes, shredded the front of his robe. Pressing the blade against his pale, hairless chest, he announced this was to be his final performance. Madama Butterfly was about to die. "For real!" he shrieked as blood slowly trickled down his chest.

As everyone else froze, Archie and Trudy wrestled the knife from Arnold and pinned him to the floor. Reduced to a blubbering heap, he screamed we were all a bunch of sick fucking queens who'd be better off dead. "Dead, do you hear me?" he ranted as Archie and Trudy carried him up the stairs to his bedroom. "*Dead!*"

I was horrified, although everyone else seemed to take Arnold's breakdown in stride. Days later, when I finally inquired about his whereabouts, Trudy said he'd been admitted to a state mental ward up near Rochester. No one knew when, or even if, he'd be back. She said that when the men in white coats had come to take him away, he'd still been ranting about how we were all a bunch of sick fucking queens who'd be better off dead.

The Continental Room's biggest gargoyle was its bartender, Karl, a petty Mafioso whose wife, Mary, worked as the barmaid. Big and fat with a bulbous red nose and greasy gray hair plastered across a spreading bald spot, Karl gruffly taunted the bar's patrons by grabbing his crotch and bellowing from behind the bar: "Suck on this, you fucking cocksuckers!" Or "Bend over, faggot, while I show you what a real man feels like." Lapping it up, the crowd in the front room raised their glasses and slipped him dollar bills as he poured them all another round.

The half-dozen swaggering, duck-tailed bull dykes who sat at the bar were Karl's biggest fans. The more insulting he got, the more raucous they became. More than once, he got them so worked up they broke out into fist fights which Paul and Randy, who both despised lesbians, claimed was their favorite pastime. "It's their way of making love," Randy sneered after two had been kicked out for threatening each other with broken beer bottles.

Having never been around lesbians, I hoped that Paul and Randy were, as Donnie would've said, just "dishing." Yet while all of the Continental Room's lesbians were indeed crude caricatures of straight men, most of its male patrons were also grotesque parodies of straight women. After a while, I began to wonder what gay life was outside of the garish burlesque everyone called "camp." And, as I'd told Trudy the night she'd worried I'd never fit in, the one thing about the Continental Room I truly despised was the camp.

The rudest insult of all came not from within the bar, but without. Every Saturday night, the cops arrived at 1 a.m. like clockwork. Flicking on the lights and pulling the plug on the jukebox, Karl heralded their arrival by barking at the back room that, just in case we'd forgotten, it was a crime in the state of New York for men to dance with men. Smiling obsequiously and muttering about goddamned queers, he rang open the till and quietly slipped the cops a roll of twenties. Locked in a tableau of frozen dance steps, the regulars in the back room anxiously waited for the cops to leave while quietly muttering thanks to Karl. Between them and the law, he was all they had.

I tried arguing they were too good for the likes of a loathsome creature like Karl, but none would listen. After all, I was just a kid, an eighteen-year-old still wet behind the ears. I'd never even been to a gay bar before the Continental Room. Besides, before Karl, the nearest gay bar was a two-hour drive way up in Rochester. And while everyone agreed the bars there were a gas, few could manage the trip with anywhere near the regularity they wanted. They needed something closer to home and Karl was the first to come along and provide it.

Oh sure, before the Continental Room, Syracuse had its requisite tearooms, parks, and truck stops. But after a while the locals grew weary of the dangers associated with such venues. They wanted other options—ones where they could sit down and drink a beer, swap stories, and maybe even camp it up or make a move on a guy without worrying about being beaten up or thrown in jail. They wanted what everyone else took for granted: to feel like they belonged, had a refuge—that someone other than the vice squad cared about what they were up to.

And so along came the Mafia with a string of gay bars that, despite the rules against their establishment, it bribed the local authorities to ignore. And while the arrangement didn't always hold, the bars quickly developed a reputation as safe havens, the first outside the big city meccas—New York, San Francisco, LA, Philly, Chicago—to which gays had always flocked. Soon the Mafia was running gay bars in nearly every medium-sized city in the country. Even Wilmington had one, The Golden Greeks, although I'd been too young to get in. Not so for the Continental Room. The year before I'd applied to SU, New York had lowered its drinking age to eighteen.

Of course, Mafia protection came at a price—seedy dives staffed by contemptuous, petty thugs who served watered-down drinks at rip-off prices. But who cared? The music was hot, the dancing sweaty and, on a good night, when everyone's guard was down, you might even forget you were an affront to everything decent in life. God knows, nothing like that ever happened in a tearoom or at a truck stop.

Nevertheless, I couldn't shake my disgust over the indignities the Continental Room routinely meted out. And so, when the old-timers noted how, in the days before Syracuse had its own gay bar, so-and-so had so despaired of his loneliness that he'd killed himself, I nodded sympathetically, certain that if the Continental Room was all that gay life offered me, I'd end up a suicide too.

Late one Saturday night, Randy, Larry, and I drunkenly stumbled out of the Continental Room into the cool autumnal air. "Damsels of the night!" Randy cried. "Les belles de nuit," I haughtily retorted. "Bitches in heat," Larry corrected.

Giggling, we turned left onto Warren, a dark and deserted thoroughfare that Larry assured us we'd find promising. He pointed out the streetlight under which he regularly stood and claimed he was rarely disappointed. "Gentlemen callers," as he called his tricks, almost always stopped to inquire about his availability. "Oh, yes, Miss Things!" he squealed. "We're definitely *there*."

As if on cue, a red Corvette swerved around the corner and pulled up next to us. From behind the wheel, a handsome, well-built man with a dimpled chin and wavy brown hair combed back from his forehead smiled alluringly. "See, what did I tell you?" Larry crowed.

"Oh my God," I gasped, stunned by the man's good looks.

"What do you think he wants?" asked Randy, a newcomer to street cruising.

"It's not a question of what, dearie," Larry drolly replied, "but who." He stepped forward and, raising a ringed forefinger, inquired which of us he wanted.

"Yeah, him," the man murmured when Larry's finger rested on me.

I froze.

"Are you sure, Mary?" Larry inquired before lewdly licking his lips. "After all, I'm much more experienced."

"Yeah, that one," the man confirmed.

After Larry shoved me forward, I warily approached the man's Corvette. "Nice night, huh?" I muttered and pulled out a cigarette, hoping he'd offer me a light. "Leaves'll be turning soon."

"Wanna go for a ride?" the man asked, ignoring my cigarette.

I laughed nervously and informed him I lived in a dorm with a straight guy. "How about you? You got a place?"

"Just the car, man," he replied.

I noted his Corvette's cramped interior and said I'd prefer something a bit roomier. "You know, where we could spread out."

He continued to stare straight ahead, although his right hand slowly slid from the car's gear shift to his crotch. "What you see is what you get," he murmured, thrusting his groin slightly forward.

"I don't know, I mean..." I stammered and leaned in closer to get a better look. His chin was covered with stubble and his forearms were knotted with veins. Tufts of silky chest hair poked through a long tear across the torso of a sweat-stained t-shirt, while his left nipple gleamed in the streetlight like a pink full moon.

"What you afraid of, the fuzz?" he mumbled, lifting his hips so I could get a better look. "Or this?" he asked as the fullness of his bundle emerged into the light.

Trembling, I took a long drag of my cigarette and recalled Larry saying his dorm mate had left to spend the weekend with a girlfriend in Elmira. Sheepishly, I turned and asked if we could use his room. "Just for an hour or so," I promised.

"Take your time, Mary," Larry replied, waving at a passing car. "I'm sure I won't be needing it."

"Thanks," I murmured and darted around the back of the man's car. I stopped to bid my friends goodbye and then, over the roaring of its engine, jumped into the Corvette's passenger seat. Pointing out the way, I tried not to stare as he spread his legs and, without uttering so much as a word, kneaded the bulge in his jeans.

On the dorm's elevator, he pretended not to know me, although once inside Larry's room he headed straight for the bed. When he started to unzip his jeans, I sat down next to him and suggested we get to know each other first.

"Whatever you say, man," he replied.

I told him my name and asked him his. "Joe," he mumbled. I told him I was an SU student studying architecture and asked what he did. "You know, for a living," I added, blushing slightly.

"Construction," he replied. When I noted I'd never met anyone in that line of work, he shrugged. "Guess there's a first time for everything, huh?" When I asked if he enjoyed the work, he grunted the pay was good. When I followed that up with a question about his co-workers, he replied, "Yeah, they're okay."

When I explained I thought most construction workers hated gays, he muttered, "Yeah, so?" When I inquired if that meant he wasn't gay, he said he liked to get blown. "Guys do it better than girls," he explained.

After that, I gave up on small talk and, sliding over next to him, placed my hand on his thigh. When he made no effort to reciprocate, I leaned over to kiss him. Turning away, he shook his head and grumbled he wasn't into that.

"What, you don't kiss?" I gasped.

"That's what I said, man." When I asked if he kissed girls, he said it depended. When I asked on what, he said their breasts. He was, he noted, a "tit man."

Stymied, I leaned back against the cinder block wall of Larry's room and weighed my options. I could either honor my sense of pride and walk out on him or indulge my lust and stay. I watched him stroke the bulge in his jeans and decided he was much too sexy to pass up. Besides, I hadn't had sex once in Syracuse. I cleared my throat. "So, what do you want from me?"

He flicked his head downward and smiled slightly.

I turned and stared numbly out Larry's sixth-floor window. Since Tom from Queen Street, I'd made it a point of pride to kiss every man I'd been with. It was, I told myself, a gesture of solidarity—an acknowledgment that, no matter what position we took in bed or how brief our encounter, we were both in this together, each equally gay. "I see," I murmured, turning back toward him. "Just that, nothing more?"

"That's it, man."

Swallowing my pride, I slid onto my knees, unzipped his jeans, and pulled out his cock. It was satiny pink and hard as a rock. Releasing it, I watched it flop against his belly and gently bob up and down. I cupped his balls in the palm of my hand. They were fat and hairy and smelled of musk and soap. I raised his t-shirt and ran my hand through a swirl of dark curly hair that swept up a taut belly and swarmed across a perfectly chiseled chest.

The blood seeped from my face and my mouth went dry. I trembled from head to toe. I thought of Junior that night behind the Catholic church: the echo of his cleats, the sheen of his peg leg pants, the teeth of his zipper slowly opening. "Yeah man," he'd said of my offer to blow him, "but only for money." *This time, you will have to pay more*, a voice inside me warned. I closed my eyes and frantically tried to work up some spit. *Much more.*

The man adjusted the pillow behind him and thrust his crotch slightly forward. "Come on, man, suck it."

I bent over and lightly licked his shaft.

"I said suck it," he growled.

I wrapped my mouth around his cock and plunged headlong into a pit of blind, heedless lust.

Just as my jaw was starting to ache, he told me to stop and, wrapping a fist around his shaft, smiled at its girth. "You like that big dick, don't you?"

I stared at the long string of spit connecting my lips with the tip of his meat and replied I'd like it better if we both got undressed. "You know, like we're in this together," I added, trying to shake out a cramp in my right leg.

"Sure, man," the man shrugged, "but I gotta warn you I'll have to fuck you if you show me your ass." When I asked why, he said that was just the way things were. "With fags, anyway." When I asked if he had any lubricant, he spit into the palm of his hand and smirked. "Yeah, this," he said, showing me a thick glob of sputum. When I told him he was too big for just spit, he'd rip me to shreds, he shrugged. "It's up to you, man. All I know is, if you take your clothes off, I'm gonna have to fuck you."

I asked if I could at least remove his jeans.

"Sure, be my guest," he said, lifting his hips, although he got impatient when I also tried to unlace his boots. "Come on, man," he snarled, grabbing his cock. "You're wasting time."

Dutifully, I returned to my task. He let me work on it until he said he was close and then, gripping the back of my head, shoved himself so far down my throat I gagged. Gargling on vomit, I squirmed out of his grip and, gasping for air, told him I needed a kiss to go on.

"How about this instead?" he replied and rammed a thumb down my throat. I let it root around the back of my mouth until I felt violated enough to pull it out and asked what the hell he thought he was up to.

"It's to keep you focused on sucking my cock," he replied. He looked at me blankly and added, "What you faggots are good for."

"I see," I murmured. Patting him on the thigh, I got up off my knees and told him I'd had enough. I smiled sheepishly. "I need to be going."

"Come on, man, you're not finished," he grumbled and flicked his head in the direction of his crotch. Supremely confident, he'd clearly never been walked out on before.

I considered asking how many others he'd demeaned in just this way but, afraid he'd say all of them, I instead just smiled and repeated myself—I'd had enough; I needed to be going. When I reached Larry's door, I turned to admire him one last time. Propped up against a pillow, with his jeans pulled down around his ankles and his t-shirt tossed upwards to show off his chiseled chest, he was still hard as a rock—a Greek god awaiting a supplicant. Fighting an urge to drop to my knees and crawl on all fours back to him, I ran into the hall and raced down the dorm's six flights of stairs, although it wasn't until I was outside that I was able to breathe free. I'd escaped. I was still different from the rest. Pride had won out over lust.

The next night, I encountered Larry on the dance floor of the Continental Room. He told me he'd returned to his room to find the man, rock-hard, still on his bed. Boasting he'd finished him off, Larry gloated the man, whose name he insisted was Jack, not Joe, had "come buckets."

When I hesitantly asked if they'd kissed, a look of disgust swept over Larry's face. "Of course not, Mary," he snipped. "Honey, last night I did a *real* man."

A few days later, Larry called, hysterical. "I've been wrecked," he shrieked. "*Wrecked*!" The night before, his roommate had discovered a letter from an old lover and, in disgust, packed up and moved out. Word had quickly spread through the dorm and, all night long, guys had banged on his door, shouting obscenities. Terrified, he said he was thinking of dropping out of Syracuse and returning to Florida.

I assured him everything would blow over. "You'll see," I added before reminding him a college degree was his key to success—the only thing between him and a lifetime of Continental Rooms.

Larry reminded me he liked gay bars. It was the straight world he loathed. "Besides, college doesn't make a damn bit of difference. We'll never be anything more than just faggots."

The next morning, he called to say he was leaving Syracuse for good. The night before, egged on by the proctor, his dorm mates had cornered him in the showers and beaten him up. He'd managed to cover up his black eye with foundation but there was nothing he could do about the busted lip. People on the flight back to Florida his ex-lover had booked for him would just have to stare.

I asked if his parents knew what had happened. He paused briefly to compose himself and said his ex-roommate had called them and read them the letter. "They never want to see me again."

He said he was leaving me his portable typewriter but told me I had to come get it right away. A cab was on its way to take him to the airport. He warned me to come prepared. The scene at his dorm was ugly.

I had no idea just how. When I arrived, Larry was already at his cab's side, curtsying and blowing kisses to the scores of men chanting from the dorm's open windows: *Two, four, six, eight, who do we obliterate? Queers!* He handed me the typewriter and, as we embraced, a roar of disgust swept over us: *Oh look, two!!* Feyly waving a frilly pink hanky at his tormentors, Larry got into his cab and told the driver to step on it. "Be careful, sweetie," he said to me, welling up.

"You too," I replied feebly, clutching the typewriter on whose carrying case he'd proudly embossed SU's logo, his ticket to a better life. As Larry's cab sped off and his tormentors shifted their focus to me, I recalled his claim—that all any of us were ever gonna be was faggots—and ran like hell for the safety of Sibley Hall.

At the Continental Room, everyone took the news about Larry in stride. As Paul said, things like that were the price we paid for being gay. Randy, on the other hand, blamed Larry, who he claimed was too obvious. "I mean, couldn't she have just done without the mascara?"

I wrote Larry several times at the address he'd given me but never got a response. When my last letter was returned 'addressee unknown,' I was so afraid my roommate would discover it, I tore it to shreds and buried it under the cover of night in one of the trash barrels behind the dorm. After that, I was terrified that what had happened to Larry would also happen to me. I had nightmares; I had difficulty sitting through my classes; and my first semester grades started to plummet.

A voice in the back of my head kept asking who I'd run to if I was ever wrecked like Larry. Unlike him, I didn't have an ex-lover in Florida. All I had was Donnie, who still lived with his parents, and the crowd in the Continental Room, none of whom had ever given me so much as a phone number. I didn't even know Randy's real name. The image of Arnold being carried up the stairs in his shredded kimono came back to haunt me. *You're a bunch of sick fucking queens who'd be better off dead*, he'd screamed. *Dead, do you hear me? Dead!!*

Valerie sidled up next to me as we exited our English Lit class and, after introducing herself, confessed she'd had her eyes on me for a while. "Your shirts are groovy," she said by way of explanation, adding that the blue, green, and purple stripes on the Eagle dress shirt I wore that day were particularly "trippy."

I shyly thanked her and fought an urge to flee. I'd noticed her checking me out and, afraid she might be coming on to me, studiously ignored her. That day, she'd even taken the desk next to mine, although short of vaguely smiling at her, I'd pretended she wasn't there.

She did stand out, though. Short, round, and buxom, with hairy legs and a shrill, high-pitched giggle that made other girls stare, she was unlike any woman I'd ever encountered. She refused to shave even her armpits, while the outline of her nipples on her hippie peasant dress indicated she also eschewed bras. Her long frizzy hair was what my mother would have called a "fright," while the boldness of her approach indicated she was what my father would have deemed "uncouth." Intrigued, I wondered if she might be the one to show me the ropes of the counterculture I longed to be a part of—the hippie equivalent of Dominic's "gay mother."

She waited until we were in a small courtyard outside the lecture hall and asked if I smoked marijuana, although she called it "dope," not "pot," as Dominic and Donnie did. When I admitted I did, she giggled and said she thought so; I had what she called "the look." When I asked what that might be, she replied, "Oh, you know, like you don't fit in either."

When I asked what set her apart, she said in suburban St. Louis, where she'd grown up, "chicks" were supposed to be blonde and pert. "I'm fat and loud. Besides, out there, Jews are supposed to have horns." She ran her fingers through her auburn frizz and again giggled, although that time so shrilly the girls next to us, all of them primly attired in Villager outfits, noisily huffed off. "Still can't find them," she said before telling our departing neighbors to go fuck themselves.

I told her growing up in suburban Wilmington had been hard too, although I avoided mentioning the reason why, except to note it had nothing to do with my ethnicity. I was, I told her, a WASP. I also said I'd always been thin and, as a kid at least, blond, an admission she greeted with a loud shriek. "Oh my God, you're one of the kids who used to make me cry."

I didn't dare say straights like her were the ones who'd made me cry and instead noted I'd gone through the pot—er, dope—I'd brought with me from Wilmington. "Know where I might get some more?"

"Yeah, me," she replied before asking if I might also be interested in LSD. She said she had some really good stuff—"very visual," she said—that she was sure I'd find mind-blowing. When I replied I didn't think I was ready for a high quite that rigorous, she assured me I was. She could tell from my shirts. "Oh, yeah, you're a head alright!"

"Blue Cheer," Valerie called the pretty, pale-blue tab of LSD she sold me for a buck. Being my first time, she recommended a "trip guide," someone I could trust to make the experience as positive as possible. But the only people I knew were Continental Room regulars, people I'd never entrust my well-being to while high on something like LSD. After all, Arnold was still locked up in the loony bin; Archie was still refusing to dance with other men; Randy was still insisting he was going to turn straight; and Paul was still pulling his Evil Queen routine on every unsuspecting newcomer who ventured into the bar. And then there was Karl, whose insults and name-calling cast a pall over all the bar's proceedings: *Bend over, faggots, and let me show you what a real man feels like.*

I briefly considered Trudy but her misgivings about hippies gave me pause. And then when, a few days after I'd purchased the Blue Cheer, she refused to give me her home phone number because she didn't want her father to know she hung out with gays, I thought better of it. Anyone who claimed I gave myself away every time I opened my mouth couldn't possibly be a good fit for LSD.

After that, I decided to be my own trip guide, although I still worried that I wasn't up for the psychedelic challenge. The media was full of stories of trippers who'd fallen to their deaths thinking they could fly or who'd landed in emergency rooms raving like lunatics and, although Valerie dismissed them as scare tactics intended to keep us sheep, I was afraid gays were prime candidates for a bum trip. As Mike, the South Philly show tune queen who'd freaked out on his first puff of pot, had said, "There's a reason we're called Nervous Nellies. Everything scares us."

Valerie, on the other hand, pointed to herself as proof that LSD was the perfect corrective for misfits like me. After more than a dozen trips, she'd learned to flaunt what she'd once been ridiculed for—her shape, her loud and raucous vulgarity, even her innate hairiness—and claimed one of her favorite activities was freaking out "straights"—her term for people who didn't do drugs—with the outlandish behavior she called "goofing." She even took it as a matter of pride that she intimidated other women, most of whom complained she was too "ballsy"—a word I'd never heard used on a woman before. Indeed, she was the only woman I'd ever run across who actually liked being called names. Slut, whore, cunt, ballbuster—even lesbo and queer—were to her compliments on the progress she'd made transforming herself into a loud, proud, in-your-face non-conformist—or, as she preferred to call herself, a "freak."

My first acid trip far exceeded Valerie's hype, although in ways different from what she'd predicted. While I was dazzled by the colors and the way the walls of my dorm room danced to my 45 of "Love is Blue"—the theme song for *A Man and a Woman*, one of my inner girl's favorite films—it was the acid's effects on my world-view that most blew me away. High, all the boundaries that had previously defined my life—gay, straight; butch, fem; boy, girl; Black, white; rich, poor; good, bad; right, wrong—dissolved, replaced by a universality that I could only describe as cosmic. The perverse, gutter equality that Dominic had declared upon my entry into gay life—that everyone's shit stank—the LSD turned on its head. It was our beauty, it declared, that united us, not our ugliness.

While I was "peaking"—the point at which Valerie said the LSD's effects would be strongest—I asked my dorm room mirror Paul's Evil Queen query: *Mirror, mirror, on the wall, who's the fairest of them all*? The face staring back at me—a fractured, rainbow-hued version of my own with sunbursts for eyes and clusters of stars for earrings—burst out laughing. "Fairest?" it howled. "People, simply are." The LSD was even more direct about the mirror's response—*Not you, you black bitch*: "Oh, no, that's self-hatred." Of Joe, the man in the red Corvette who'd tried to make me his cocksucker, it railed against what it called the "eroticization of shame." I'd been right to walk out on him. Everyone should. The time for putting ourselves down, it declared, was over.

The LSD warned a gay's biggest enemy was internal. With the full weight of history and tradition against us, too many were mired in guilt and shame. Rebellion, it said, was our only cure. We needed to rise up and give birth to a new kind of homosexual, one never before seen—one built on affirmation, not fear; pride, not shame.

The acid's assertions were nothing short of mind-bending. Rejecting the liberal consensus that gays were guilty only of "victimless crimes," the drug instead asserted we were revolutionaries—the natural-born leaders of a growing movement against sexual repression and sin. No other group, it said, had the focus, experience, or drive to liberate our collective libido. But, it cautioned, we needed to believe in ourselves first. Without pride, we'd remain ciphers. "Shadows," it warned.

My first acid trip transformed me. Before it, I was on a quest for validation; after it, I was on a mission for liberation. Before it, I questioned; after it, I asserted. I started using words like "oppression," "repression," "liberation," and "alienation," words I'd been raised to think of as alien, communist even. I started referring to cops as "pigs;" conformists as "straights:" drug-users as "heads;" our president, a "warmonger." I read Wilhelm Reich, Herbert Marcuse, Nietzsche. I reconnected with Frantz Fanon. I fell in love with the 'abnormal'—the photography of Diane Arbus, the paintings of Francis Bacon, the poetry of Sylvia Plath. I started shopping at thrift stores. I let my hair grow longer and longer.

I even decided to tell Valerie I was gay—my first coming out since the debacle with Angie, the high school friend with whom Donnie and I tried to be open. I told myself if Valerie accepted me, I'd know Timothy Leary's claim was true—that LSD really was giving birth to a new more harmonious, peace-loving race of mutants. If Valerie accepted me, I promised myself I'd follow Leary's lead and become a mutant too—the rebel Valerie called a "freak."

To say that Valerie was nonplussed by my revelation would be an understatement. "Oh, yeah, that's cool" was all she had to say, although a few tokes of a hash pipe later she admitted she'd suspected from the start that I was gay. "Well, for one, you show your feelings," she replied when I asked why. Most straight men, she said, went out of their way to hide theirs. "And you didn't try to ball me." She said that, while straight guys almost always tried to get into her pants, I was content to just hang out and laugh. "You have a great giggle," she confided.

Later, after even more hash, Valerie asked if I'd take her to a gay bar sometime. She said she'd always wanted to see what one was like but had never had anyone to go with. She said she imagined it would be a cross somewhere between an Andy Warhol underground film and an Allen Ginsberg poetry reading. "You know, really cool people dressed in black, smoking joints, goofing on things and dancing to acid rock." She giggled. "A gas!"

I didn't have the heart to tell her otherwise and so, when she suggested we drop acid and trip out at the Continental Room, I warily agreed. Maybe, I thought, LSD could do for a Mafia-run dive what it had done for my rickety dorm room—make the walls dance to music and the floor roll like I was out to sea. Or maybe, through Valerie, I could see the Continental Room in a more forgiving light. Maybe we could even turn the rest of the crowd on. I chuckled at the prospect. Maybe Paul would drop his Evil Queen routine and Randy would stop wanting to be straight. Maybe Archie would even dance with another man!

At first, Valerie's introduction to gay bar life went smoothly. She marveled at the brightly colored cocktails the dykes at the bar glumly nursed and even held her own with Karl, a type she claimed to know well. As she noted, her father owned a construction firm back in St. Louis and she'd grown up sparring with petty thugs who liked proving their manhood by putting other people down. "I tell 'em their dick's so small I couldn't find it with tweezers," she giggled. "Shuts 'em up every time."

Her mood, however, soured once we made our way to the back dance floor. She visibly blanched over Paul's lightened hue and blue contacts and called Randy's antics on the dance floor grotesque. As she grumbled, she'd seen men act like thugs lots of times but never women. She even hated the music.

Motown, she complained, was too "Top 40," while the line-dancing then all the rage, too "straight." But it was Trudy who, introducing herself as the Continental Room's resident "fag hag," sent Valerie over the edge. "I don't think I'm going to be able to handle this," she whispered after Trudy returned to her booth full of adoring boys.

Imagining the regulars as characters from *Animal Farm*, I told her to give the place time; I was sure she'd come around. But I was wrong. Within seconds of Paul starting his singalong to Aretha's "Ain't No Way," she was dragging me toward the door. "We gotta get outta here," she whimpered. I tried to assure her Paul's performance was harmless but she said she'd seen enough. She was, she informed me, starting to freak out. "For real, man, *for real*!"

Once outside, she said she was so turned off by what she'd seen she vowed never to darken the doors of a gay bar again. And although she complained bitterly about the lurid effeminacy of the men and the drunken sullenness of the women, Trudy was the one who bothered her the most. "How can anyone call themselves that?" she shrieked. "*A fag hag*!"

I tried to explain words had different meanings in gay life but she insisted fag hag was an insult. "I mean, what does that make me?" she demanded. "Or you?" she asked, her eyes narrowing. When I replied it depended on who was doing the talking, she shook her head. No, some words were hateful no matter whose mouth they came out of.

As we trudged across the vast bulldozed wasteland separating downtown Syracuse from SU, Valerie continued to sputter about how freaky her visit to a gay bar had been. "I can't believe how straight they all were!" she cried. "Not the least bit cool." When I suggested she might have been expecting too much, she asked if it was true what I'd once said—that the Continental Room was the only place in town for gay people to meet. When I noted there was also the men's restroom in the basement of Maxwell Hall and the dive on the other side of the railroad tracks that specialized in rough trade, she shook her head and said she had no idea gay life was so grim. "I mean, not even a coffee house?" When I assured her that was it, she asked for a cigarette, even though she didn't smoke. "You deserve better," she said as I lit a match. She guided my hand as it struggled to connect with her cigarette and met my gaze; her eyes were blazing. "*Much* better," she added for emphasis. "*Much*."

Stunned, I looked up at a sky littered with stars. Except for the angry voice inside my own head—the one Trudy insisted I needed to turn off—no one had ever said anything like that to me. In fact, if asked, most people would say even Mafia-run dives like the Continental Room were too good for people like me. "But you don't understand," I stammered. "We're hated."

"That's no excuse for acting like freaks," she shot back. When I reminded her that was a word she proudly applied to herself, she snipped that was different. "We're leaving the shit behind. They're wallowing in it." She stopped in the midst of the rubble and looked at me sternly. "You're not gonna be able to be both, you know. Someday you're gonna have to choose."

"Choose?" I asked.

Valerie nodded. "Yes, between being one of them and one of us. There's no way you can be both. Gay and hip don't mix. At least not that kind of gay." She took a puff of her cigarette and, grimacing, instantly tossed it aside. "And don't you ever call me a fag hag, understand?" she snarled, marching off toward the hill up to SU.

The next night, the Continental Room's regulars road me mercilessly for bringing someone like Valerie into their midst. Everything about her had bothered them: her hairy legs, her refusal to wear a bra, her granny dress, her unruly hair, her beads, her shapelessness, even her free-form dancing. "Does she even know what a beat is?" Paul cried, rolling his blue-tinted eyes. Randy chimed in by holding his nose and noting she hadn't worn deodorant. Trudy was even cruder. "A rich bitch," she snarled between sips of her Cape Codder. "I bet she's a Jew."

The next time I saw Valerie, she suggested we spend the summer together in New York. Her father had agreed to pay for an apartment in the East Village and she thought it might be good place to work on my hip bona fides. "And wean yourself off all that gay bar shit. I'm warning you, it's ruining your head."

That time, I didn't bother feigning insult or claim she didn't understand. Instead, I just smiled and replied, "far out," a hip term that, unlike the gay "fag hag," we both embraced. Finally, I'd found my escape. The Florida I'd run off to if I ever got wrecked like Larry was a hippie chick named Valerie.

A message from my father demanding that I call right away greeted my return from my architectural drawing class. Since my mother had always been the one to leave messages, I assumed it was serious. Was someone sick?

"What the hell you doing up there?" my father bellowed after a few opening pleasantries. When I asked what he was referring to, he told me "National" had informed him that I'd refused to rush Kappa Sigma, his old fraternity. When I confirmed that was true, he claimed I was making the biggest mistake of my life. "Those guys will always be there for you," he said of my would-be fraternity brothers. "Just like family."

I knew better than to say the mistake was all his. As the unhappy ending to Larry's brief SU tenure had shown, guys like that didn't countenance guys like me. Besides, I'd already been rushed by the crowd at the Continental Room. And while I'd tentatively accepted their offer to be one of them—a full-fledged gay barfly—I'd decided instead to join the ranks of the psychedelic tribe Valerie called "heads."

I'd already passed their acid test—two LSD trips without even a hint of a freak-out. Indeed, I'd come through both so strongly I'd started to think Larry had it all wrong. We actually could be something more than just faggots. As Valerie had said, we deserved better, much better—a mind-blowing notion the LSD reinforced with a messianic fervor.

With the drug's guidance, I intended to unveil a new and, like Valerie, more ballsy me, one blending the two worlds she contended were hopelessly at odds: the hip and the gay. I imagined someone like Arnold, an excellent dancer with an inherent sense of the beat, but with long hair and high on LSD instead of locked up in a loony bin, and espousing peace and love rather than foaming at the mouth about how better off we'd be if only we were dead. *Dead, did you hear me? Dead!*

8
A Grain of Sand

He sat alone in a booth off the dance floor, anxiously stroking a bushy moustache and puffing on a cigarette he'd rolled from a tobacco pouch tucked between his legs. Long wisps of curly brown hair cascaded from the edges of a small bald spot and brushed against soft, sloping shoulders. He wore baggy, olive-drab Army pants and a threadbare denim shirt whose top three buttons were undone, exposing a pale chest speckled with tufts of baby-fine hair. A safety pin held his wire-rim glasses together and two strings of brightly colored beads hung from his neck.

No one in the Continental Room looked like him. Indeed, for a newcomer, he attracted surprisingly little notice—no doubt a consequence of his disregard for the bar's strict sartorial standards. Intrigued, I caught his eye and, angling toward him, wondered if he was the melding of opposites that Valerie had claimed were incompatible—my first sighting of a gay freak.

He cleared his throat and returned my smile. His teeth were bad but his cheeks were flushed a bright pretty pink. He placed his tobacco pouch on the booth's Formica tabletop and shifted nervously in his seat. "Hey man, wanna smoke?" he asked, the dark circles under his eyes lightening slightly.

"Yeah, sure," I replied and slid into the other side of his booth. Never having seen a gay man roll a cigarette before, I wondered if, as straights often did, he'd wandered into the bar by mistake. I smiled warily. "You do know this place is gay, right?"

He sealed the cigarette with his tongue and, handing it to me, whinnied like a horse. "Shit, man," he cried, "I met my first dude in this dive."

Intrigued, I accepted his offer of a light and, in response to his query, told him I was a student at SU studying architecture, although I professed what I really wanted to do was freak out. "I hate the way things are," I added, just in case he was more like the others than he looked.

"Yeah, me too," he smiled and introduced himself as Sal, although he noted he also went by Sallie, sometimes even Salvatore, with an emphasis on the final vowel. He said he'd grown up on Syracuse's West Side, the only son of Italian and Irish immigrants. When he'd gone off to college, he'd been the first in his family to make it past high school. However, near the end of his junior year, he'd broken his parents' hearts and followed the call of Flower Power first to New York, where he'd mostly hung out at Beat poetry readings, and then, via New Mexico, where he'd dropped lots of acid, to San Francisco for the Summer of Love.

"Thomas Merton," he said when I asked about the influences that had led him to drop out. He smiled shyly and flushed another shade of pink. Having grown up in the Church, he said asceticism had always attracted him; he'd even toyed with the idea of becoming a monk.

When pressed, he acknowledged coming out had also played a part. Being gay at a small Jesuit college had been hard and toward the end, before he'd finally had enough and dropped out, he'd had what he was sure was a nervous breakdown. Once, he'd even contemplated suicide. Then, one evening, he'd attended a poetry reading by a radical priest named Daniel Berrigan. It was Berrigan, Sal said, who gave him the courage to leave the Church and be himself. "The cat fucking saved my life, man."

When I asked if drugs had also played a role, he shook his head. "No, dropping out was mostly a head trip. You know, from protesting the war and doing the civil rights thing." The drugs, he said, came later, after he'd dropped out. He rolled his eyes. By the time he'd fled San Francisco, they were just about all he and everyone else around him were doing.

"Hepatitis," he said when I asked what had prompted him to leave San Francisco. He said he'd first fled back to New York but got too sick for the ex-lover who'd put him up. "Yeah, with my folks," he said when I asked where in town he was staying. He said they were getting up there in years and could use his help around the house. "Oh God no," he replied when I asked if they knew he was gay. "Dropping out and becoming a hippie was bad enough. No way I'm gonna break their hearts twice."

I asked about the Summer of Love. "The Be-Ins sounded really cool. I mean, thousands of people and not a single fight!"

"Yeah, but the scene got really bad toward the end," Sal grumbled. He lowered his voice and looked nervously around to make sure no one was listening. "Lots of speed." He took a long drag off his cigarette and pulled a shred of tobacco from his tongue. "Weird, fucking shit, that speed. You ever tried it? I mean crystal, not pills."

"Oh, no," I said, not at all sure what crystal or even speed were. "But I love LSD," I said, determined to impress him.

Sal warned me to stay away from speed. "I even let a cat shoot me up once. Said he loved me but he was just a fucking junkie. All I got out of it was the hepatitis." He grimaced. "Turned my piss the color of mud, man." He put his cigarette out and confessed he was worried about his liver. "It hurts, man. Sometimes bad. Real bad."

He told me to watch out for junkies. "The only thing they love is the needle. They'll eat you up, man, make you sick, kill ya."

I assured him I'd never stoop so low. "Needles have always freaked me out."

Sal smiled. "Yeah, good, man. Keep it that way. They're a death trip—a bad, really bad scene."

Before I could ask what a "death trip" was, Sal launched into a rap about the English poet, William Blake. "Ever read him?" he asked. When I said I'd read *Tyger! Tyger! burning bright* in high school but had failed to understand what all the fuss was about, Sal cried, "Oh, man, the cat's a fucking prophet. You've got to check out *The Marriage of Heaven and Hell*. It'll blow your mind!"

When I asked how, Sal explained Blake turned the traditional Heaven and Hell dichotomy on its head. Hell was a liberated zone, while Heaven was uptight and sexually repressed. He rattled on about a place called the "New Jerusalem," where he said right and wrong no longer mattered and which came about only through a violent revolution, but when he got to "epiphany," a word I'd never heard before, I finally had to interrupt. "Does that have anything to do with infamy?" I asked.

Sal chuckled and explained that an epiphany was when what he called the "doors of perception" were suddenly thrown wide open. "You know, like when you're on LSD." He took a sip of beer and leaned in closer. "Like when Blake said you can hold infinity in the palm of your hand. Or see the universe in a grain of sand."

Over his shoulder, I spied the pool of piss outside the ladies' room that Karl blamed on us regulars. "When you pussies stop flushing your tampons down the loo, the problem will disappear," he'd snarled after Randy had finally worked up the courage to complain. Paul, who used the ladies' room because the men's room was so filthy, had nearly lost it over that one. "Why, you motherfuckin' honky!" he'd shrieked before being dragged back onto the dance floor. In retaliation, Karl had let the puddle grow until Trudy started carrying a roll of toilet paper in her purse so she could take a leak in the parking lot. After a while, she simply stopped coming to the Continental Room. I hadn't seen her in weeks.

From behind the bar, Karl hollered for his barmaid-wife Mary to get a move on; he didn't have all night. As she stood bravely in the puddle of piss and dutifully shoveled ice from the ice machine into two blue plastic buckets, I noticed she had another black eye. I'd seen one before and, while the regulars insisted she was dizzy and had probably just walked into something, I was certain Karl was beating her. I turned back to Sal and smiled; a pool of piss and a black eye were perfect metaphors for a gay bar dive like the Continental Room. "I like that—the universe in a grain of sand."

Sal's cheeks burned bright as he returned my smile. "Maybe we can groove together sometime. Whaddya say?"

"Far-out," I replied and suggested the very next day. "My last class is out at two."

"Cool," he said and suggested we meet at the bookstore on Marshall Street around the corner from my dorm, Sibley Hall. He said he knew of some writers he thought I might like.

I offered to bring along some pot. "Maybe we can get high and take it from there."

"Yeah, man," he replied before admitting it'd been a while since he'd gotten stoned. "You know, the hepatitis," he said by way of explanation. Besides, he thought a good high would help his mood. As he noted, he'd been a bit down since ending up back in Syracuse, the hometown he thought he'd finally left behind.

"Yeah, must be a drag," I murmured, hoping he couldn't tell it was the first time I'd used that word in just that way.

The next afternoon, Sal met me outside the bookstore on Marshall Street and immediately started grumbling about the state of what he called the "scene." First, it was the two strung-out teenyboppers panhandling by the curb—a hippie chick in a grimy granny dress with leaves in her hair and an unshaven, bare-chested cat smoking a butt he'd picked out of the gutter. "Fucking runaways, they're everywhere, man. All they want is to get high." Then, it was the drug-dealing going on across the street on a grassy berm known around campus as "the beach." "Goddamn smack, it's everywhere too." When I noted the head shop that had opened a few doors down from the bookstore, he even complained about that, although then the problem was "hip capitalism." "Everything's about bread now," he groused. "Cash. Filthy lucre." When I said I wasn't familiar with the term 'filthy lucre,' he told me to follow him. He had a book he wanted to show me.

He led me to the back of the bookstore where the religion/philosophy section was located. "Here," he said, handing me a copy of Norman O. Brown's *Life Against Death*. "If there's one book you gotta read, it's this. The cat will tell you all you need to know about 'filthy lucre.'" He pointed to a copy of the *New Testament* and asked if I'd recently checked it out. "Brown says the revolution has to be as much about Jesus and Freud as Marx." When I assured him I'd had my fill of the Bible, he asked what I knew about Buddhism. When I told him nothing, he handed me two books he called "classics:" *The Tibetan Book of the Dead* and D.T. Suzuki's *Introduction to Zen*. Both, he promised, would blow my mind. He chuckled. "Leary says *The Book of the Dead* is really a trip guide."

"You mean for LSD?"

"Yeah, man, but for dying too," he replied. "Takes you to the clear, white light."

"The what?"

"Oh, you know," Sal replied. "Ego loss. Enlightenment. Nothingness."

"Far out," I murmured, afraid to once again admit I had no idea what he was talking about.

After that, he took me one aisle over to the poetry section and handed me an anthology of Blake's poetry. "Nobody's hip unless they know this cat." He pulled out Allen Ginsburg's *Howl*, Lawrence Ferlinghetti's *A Coney Island of the Mind*, Whitman's *Leaves of Grass* and, for good measure, Shakespeare's sonnets, some of which he claimed were written for a male lover. "Poetry's my thing, man," Sal said and tapped the Whitman volume. "Blake's good but Whitman's my man. He has balls." He looked at me and, in almost a whisper, noted Whitman was also gay.

"Yeah, so I've heard," I mumbled, although I admitted I found him hard to stick with. "A little too ballsy," I conceded.

In criticism, Sal pointed to Susan Sontag's *Against Interpretation* and told me it too was a must. Her "Notes on Camp" was *the* take on the subject. He blanched when I told him I hadn't been impressed, although I "dug"—it was my first time using that word—her novel, *Death Kit*. "Oh, yeah?" he mumbled before admitting he didn't know she "did" novels.

That prompted a visit to the fiction section, where I was pretty much able to hold my own. I noted I was familiar with Dostoyevsky, D.H. Lawrence, and Burroughs, although when he asked about Norman Mailer, I had to admit that, thinking him a bit too straight, I'd steered clear of him. "Here," he said, adding *Why Are We in Vietnam?* to my stack. "It's the best thing that's been written about modern-day America." He'd also tried to turn me on to Kerouac, although I told him I had limited patience for stream of consciousness and pointed instead at a selection of works by Jean Genet, an ex-convict who, in prison, supposedly had written his novels on toilet paper. Recalling *Time* had once called him a "practicing pervert," I asked Sal if he'd read anything by him. "Nah, man," he said, "too effete. I like cats with balls."

On the way out, as we passed Psychology, I stopped and, mostly to redeem myself, pointed out Frantz Fanon's *Black Skins, White Masks*. It was, I claimed, a book that had blown my mind when I'd read it in high school. I even ventured an opinion: I thought Fanon's theory of self-alienation was as applicable to gays as it was to colonial Blacks.

Sal grimaced. Identity, he said, was "ego" and, as such, wasn't cool. Adding a copy of Aldous Huxley's *The Doors of Perception* to my stack, he noted the point of being hip was to transcend the world, not find oneself in it. When I asked how that happened, he offered up a quote from Blake: *The road of excess leads to the palace of wisdom*. "Come on, man," he crowed, "let's go smoke that joint. It's been weeks since I've been high."

I hoped that would be a prelude to sex but, once we got stoned, Sal wanted to check out the record store at the other end of Marshall Street. He hadn't listened to "tunes," as he called music, since he'd gotten sick. There, he turned me on to albums by Odetta, Taj Mahal, and Canned Heat and, in turn, I introduced him to a group that was one of my favorites, right up there with Aretha and the Beatles—The Velvet Underground. As I noted, the banana on their album cover was by Andy Warhol. The skin even peeled off, revealing what looked just like an erect penis. He thought that was hilarious, especially when he imagined straight guys doing the peeling. Their look of shock and embarrassment, he said, had to be priceless.

I was sure after that we'd get it on, but Sal wanted to return to the bookstore. He had something else he wanted to show me. Heading again for the fiction section, he asked if I'd ever read Flannery O'Connor. When I admitted I'd never even heard of her, he handed me her collection of short stories, *Everything That Rises Must Converge*. "Check out 'Revelation' and next time we meet tell me what you think." He suspected I'd like its perversity, although I was just relieved he wanted to see me again.

A few days later, I was pleased to inform him over beers at the Continental Room that he'd been right; "Revelation" had indeed blown my mind. I told him I particularly liked how O'Connor had used an angry teenage girl to lay low the smug, self-righteous white Southern Baptist lady, a type I professed to know well. I called the girl's "warthog from Hell" comment so priceless I intended to use it on a few choice targets. "Like that pig over there," I said, nodding at Karl, the bar's resident Mafioso. Sal laughed so hard at that I thought we'd surely get it on. But, later, when leaving the bar, he headed west, for his parents' house, and I, east, for Sibley Hall. We hadn't so much as even touched, although I had to admit talking with Sal—what he called "rapping"—was almost as mind-blowing as sex. Maybe even more.

Sal and I never did get it on. We both ended up blaming logistics—neither of us had our own place—although I suspected the problem was more aesthetic; I was too gay for someone as hip as Sal. And so, after a few "dates," we settled into being friends—or what I once made the mistake of calling "sisters." Sal immediately objected. As he noted, he hated anything that smacked of "gay talk." Indeed, it made him so uptight that, after being subjected to it for too long, he'd just get up and walk away. He did that enough with me that, after a while, I just expected him to, at some point, disappear. It was his signal I was being too "queenie," a particularly theatrical form of gay male effeminacy that he called "plastic."

"Plastic" was Sal's putdown for anything he deemed phony, pompous, superficial, affected, or otherwise lacking in soul, a category that included just about anything made by a machine, commercially marketed, or otherwise embraced by a mostly white, conformist middle class. There were, however, exceptions. For example, the mass production of LSD pioneered by Owsley Stanley he called revolutionary, while the advertisements needed to sustain underground "rags" like the *East Village Other* and *Berkeley Barb*, both of which were sold on Marshall Street, were necessary evils. As Sal noted, acid and the underground press were the only ways we got past the "Big Lie" promoted by an oppressive system run by what he called "the Man." Regular doses of both, he said, were necessary to remain cool, the opposite of plastic.

When I asked if all the horrible things said about gay people were part of his "Big Lie," Sal equivocated. He pointed to Allen Ginsberg and William Burroughs as proof that the counterculture was "hip" toward gays, but acknowledged this was mostly because neither were particularly obvious. Swishes like Andy Warhol and Truman Capote, on the other hand, were generally looked down upon. "Embarrassments," he even called them. As for drag, Sal rolled his eyes. Fetishes like that, he called "totally plastic"—much worse than swish. Men who acted like chicks, he said, degraded themselves.

Mostly, Sal's "plastic" was similar to Valerie's "straight," although he was not averse to calling things Valerie deemed hip plastic. For example, at a Big Brother and the Holding Company concert he and I attended at Syracuse's War Memorial, he stormed out after becoming incensed over the preponderance of attendees who were teenyboppers and "daytrippers," suburban middle-class types who only played at being hip. Not even Janis Joplin's riveting performance mollified him. Indeed, her boozy, ball-busting stage persona, which he claimed was fast becoming a "schtick," put her at risk of becoming plastic too.

Sal even called Valerie plastic. When I suggested he go easy on her—she was, after all, the source for the drugs I shared with him—he relented but neither one had much time for the other. Valerie complained Sal's poetry riffs bored her, while Sal found her incessant "goofing" sophomoric. They couldn't even agree on what hip was. For Sal, it meant being a rebel, or what he called "right-on." For Valerie, it meant being fun-loving, or what she called a "goof." Trying to keep the peace, I suggested we be both, an assertion which at least allowed us to get high together.

Sal also considered gay life plastic and tried to limit his exposure to those times required to satisfy his sexual needs. The rest of the time he preferred hanging out with like-minded straight people who, like Valerie, he called "heads" and "freaks." Like me, he detested the Continental Room and claimed he only went there to see me. He said he enjoyed "grooving" with me. He even said I was "cool."

Although Sal never introduced me to his straight friends, he treated me pretty much as if I were one. Although he repeatedly went on long raps about the abstraction he called "love," for the six weeks we hung out together, he never once embraced me or greeted me with so much as a peck on the cheek, as Donnie had done with his gay Philadelphia friends. And while he assured me he was out to nearly all his straight friends, he admitted he was reluctant to "rub their noses in it," as he called being "too gay."

I also never saw Sal pick up a man, although he insisted that was because, as Valerie had already noted, Syracuse gays were hopelessly straight. However, Walter, the Jimi Hendrix lookalike into "frat rats," claimed he'd seen Sal cruising the men's room in the basement of SU's Maxwell Hall. At the time, I'd dismissed Walter's allegation as "dish"—after all, Sal was much too high-minded for degraded, low-life stuff like that—although later I feared Sal was more like the rest of us than I'd thought. Guilt over who he was had him settling for too little too.

One night after I'd again complained about the pool of piss outside the Continental Room's ladies' room, Sal suggested we catch some air. The night sky, he said, was beautiful. We ended up in the blasted buffer between downtown and SU's hilltop campus, the thriving Black ghetto the city had bulldozed into acres of rubble. Deciding to get stoned, we sat down in the shadow of the Everson, the new modernist art museum intended to lure whites back to the city, and smoked a joint. The conversation meandered until I launched into a riff attacking the half-finished I.M. Pei structure, the centerpiece of the city's revitalization plan. I didn't care how dramatic its design or renowned its architect, the museum was, I insisted, an insult to a once-thriving community driven out in the name of a racist plot euphemistically called "slum clearance."

Sal took the joint from me and murmured, "Right-on, brother."

Stunned, I asked if he was goofing on me. As I noted, no one had ever called me "brother" before. Reminding me he didn't do the "fag sister thing," he insisted he'd been serious. "What, are you insulted?"

I assured him I was not. In fact, it was all I could do to keep from hugging him. And so, not knowing how else to thank him, I asked if he wanted to join Valerie and me for the local premiere of *Bonnie and Clyde*. According to the buzz on Marshall Street, the premiere was expected to be a real freak show.

"Sure, man," Sal murmured before saying he'd also heard the film was "right-on"—a searing take on the violence tearing our country apart. I watched the moonlight light up the rubble's carpet of glass shards and repeated his phrase over and over inside my head. My ticket out of the Continental Room, "right-on" was what I wanted to be too.

A thick cloud of pot smoke hung over the crowd outside the former burlesque house where *Bonnie and Clyde* was having its Syracuse premier. Off to the side, Sal, Valerie, and I waited patiently for the doors to open. In preparation, Valerie and I had dressed up in our hippest finery—she in a bright red flapper dress with fringe and me in a top hat and Red Army coat I'd picked up at a second-hand store. Refusing to play along, Sal had shown up in rumpled jeans and a wrinkled brown tee.

A determined impresario, Valerie insisted we wait outside until everyone else was seated. "That way," she gushed, "we'll have maximum effect." And so, with Sal reluctantly in tow, Valerie and I paraded at the last minute down the theater's center aisle to a chorus of *oohs* and *aahs*. Settling into the front row, we giggled like schoolgirls while tossing popcorn at the previews. Mortified, Sal slunk down in his seat and scowled at a glob of Juju fruit on the floor until the film swept everyone—including Valerie who'd dropped acid for the occasion—into a stunned silence.

Afterwards, Sal and I agreed the film was a hard-hitting indictment of America, although Valerie complained its violence had nearly bummed her out. She'd even had to close her eyes and cover her ears for its bloody climax—the slaughter of Bonnie and Clyde. Sal just rolled his eyes. As he'd grumbled on the way into the theater, only a teenybopper would be so reckless as to drop LSD for a film like the one we'd just seen.

The next night, when he and I again met over beers at the Continental Room, Sal chastised me for what he called my "performance" at *Bonnie and Clyde*. "Hip isn't about the outrageous gesture. It's spiritual, man. You've got to find the center. It's a place devoid of all things."

I replied by doubting I could ever be that hip. While I acknowledged Valerie was often silly, I admitted I liked blowing minds, especially straight ones— "goofing," as Valerie called it. "Besides, I don't want to transcend the bad stuff. I want to confront it." I even quoted Valerie, although I knew better than to use her name. "We deserve better than all this, Sal," I said, my hand sweeping the Continental Room's dance floor. "Much better."

His face suddenly darkening, Sal countered we needed to first change ourselves. Being gay—or at least exclusively so—was as much a problem as other people's attitudes toward us. Citing Freud, he claimed bisexuality—what he and his straight friends called the "hip ideal"—should be our goal, not acceptance. Indeed, he even claimed shame was a positive element in our lives. It kept us honest, focused on the changes we needed to make in order for us to be what he called "whole."

I nearly lost it over that. "*Whole*?" I blurted out so loudly Paul rushed over to see what was brewing. I told Sal I didn't give a shit about what Freud said or how hip he and his friends thought bisexuality was, I hadn't gone through what I had to sit there and be told I was sexually stunted. "Especially," I sneered, "from another faggot." I said Sal could be whatever he wanted, that was his business, but I was staying me. "You got it?" I spat. "*Gay*!"

"Well, all right, girlfriend!" Paul shrieked so loudly it brought even Sal to his senses.

"Okay, let's drop it," he grumbled before getting up for another beer.

Later that night, he made amends by agreeing to join me for an SU protest against on-campus recruiting by Dow Chemical, whose defoliant, Agent Orange, was being used to horrifying effect in Vietnam. I'd never protested anything before and hoped a veteran like Sal would make me at least look like I belonged.

"Sure," Sal said, although he warned me he drew the line at violence. If things got out of hand, as antiwar protests had recently started to do, he was splitting.

"Okay," I said, not at all sure violence wasn't exactly what I wanted.

Hey, hey, ho, ho, Dow Chemical has got to go! a large, boisterous crowd shouted as it pressed against a wall of cops blocking access to the Quonset hut where Dow's SU recruiters were housed. Placards with peace signs and others demanding *Out Now!* bobbed above a sea of protesters. *Shut it down!* a voice shouted into a bullhorn. Whistles screeched, banners flapped, voices rang out *Right-on!* Off to the side, a small group of Black men in berets and leather jackets raised their fists and shouted in unison: *Seize the time, brothers and sisters! Seize the time!*

At the other end of the block, Sal and I watched the action from the safety of the grassy berm at the back of SU's Fine Arts building. Chain-smoking Camels, Sal was worried. The word on the street was that SDS, or Students for a Democratic Society, a New Left group known for its militance, had come to town. "Not good, man," he groaned. "SDS means trouble."

Secretly thrilled, I didn't care how worried Sal was or how uptight the vibe on Marshall Street had gotten. I wasn't even sure how much I cared that, like Sal, SDS believed being exclusively gay was a cop-out, although I'd heard they preceded that putdown with the word "bourgeois," which, shortening it to "bourgie," Sal claimed was the very essence of plastic. All I knew was that I wanted to raise hell too. And if SDS was in town, the least they could do was show me how it was done.

Suddenly, a hail of rocks and rotten eggs descended on the Quonset hut. Cheering the tinkling of broken glass, the crowd surged forward. A line of burly cops linked arms against the onslaught while others stepped back and slipped on gas masks. Dropping to their knees, they aimed their rifles into the air and fired. A loud boom rattled the street and a puff of white smoke rose from its midst. Coughing and screaming, people fell on top of each other as more fusillades—*pop! pop! pop!*—exploded into the crowd.

The cops barreled into the throng, swinging their clubs. Like a stirring leviathan, the melee's tentacles quickly spread down the street, heading directly for us. Descending the berm, Sal yelled for me to follow. "The pigs are coming!" he shouted. "*The pigs!*"

I stood on my perch, transfixed. I wanted to run into the street shouting, *It's time! Time to bring the whole motherfucking mess down!* and incite the mob to head downtown and burn the Continental Room to the ground. I turned to Sal, certain he'd want to join in, and cackled madly.

"Hey, man, I'm serious," he shouted. "We don't belong here!"

I looked longingly back at the tumult. A cop dragged a bleeding protester into the hull of a paddy wagon. A man hurled a rock through a store's plate glass window. A woman stood in the middle of the street and wailed. I swung around and confronted my friend. "So, where *do* we belong, Sal?"

"Nowhere, man," he snapped. "Nowhere at all. Now, come on. It's getting too hot."

I hesitated until the popping of tear gas canisters got perilously close and then joined Sal for a run that took us nowhere in particular. When I later complained I felt like a cop-out, Sal got angry. Violence, he said, was the cop-out, not us, and stormed off.

That night, when I told the regulars at the Continental Room about the protest, they looked at me like I'd gone mad. "You wanted to do what?" Randy gasped, fidgeting with his scarves. "And with whom?"

"Oh, no, honey, those protest people are *dirty*!" Paul snorted, powdering his nose. "Besides, they hate you." He paused and looked at me through his hand mirror. "Everyone does," he smirked. "Except for us, of course."

I met him in the Continental Room one early November evening. Hardly anyone else was there and nervously sipping a beer, he looked like he could use some company. I sat down next to him and, after ordering my own beer, noted I'd never seen him before. Was that his first time in the Continental Room? He nodded shyly and confessed it was. His name, he said, was Mack.

Built like a linebacker, he had steel-gray eyes, a voice as smooth as silk and curly blond locks that fell to his shoulders. When I noted he was one of only a few patrons in the Continental Room with long hair, he asked if that was bad. When I assured him it wasn't, at least with me, he rubbed his knee against mine and said he liked my look too. "I think we might have a few things in common," he murmured. When a few minutes later, we left to find out exactly what, I noticed I'd barely touched my beer. His was still half-full.

On the way out, Mack admitted he'd never picked anyone up so quickly. "But then I'm still new at this," he said before noting it was his first time in a gay bar. "Are things always so easy?"

"Hardly," I replied before noting in the two plus months since I'd been a Continental Room regular, he was my first pick-up. "People go there to not be alone," I said.

"Hmmm," he murmured, sidling up next to me. "Guess I lucked out, huh?"

We arrived at an olive drab VW bus with Day-Glo peace signs on both sides that Mack said he'd gotten in San Francisco. Like Sal, he said he'd been there for the Summer of Love, although he didn't mention anything about dirty syringes or coming down with hepatitis. All he said was that he liked the vibe. "You know, peace and love, stuff like that." He laughed. It was during the Summer of Love that he'd first had sex with a guy.

On the drive out of town, he lit a joint and told me he lived with a couple of straight hippies on a farm out near Skaneateles. "But don't worry. They know I'm into guys," he said, handing me the joint.

"Cool," I said, sliding over next to him. I nibbled on his neck and then kissed him so hard on the lips he had to pull over. "Wow, you're a good kisser," he murmured. "Not every guy is." I recalled the man in the red Corvette I'd walked out on for wanting nothing more than a blow job and nodded. "Yeah, you can learn a lot from the way guys kiss."

"There's only one problem," he sighed of our upcoming tryst. "I share a bedroom with two kids." One, he explained, was his roommates' four-year-old son and the other their daughter, a six-year-old he described as a "real terror." He smiled and said he loved them like they were his own. As he noted, he and his wife had known them since they were born.

"Your wife?" I gasped.

"Yeah, I'm married," Mack sighed, "and happily too—or at least we used to be." He said after he'd returned to Syracuse from the Summer of Love, he'd told his wife he was getting into guys and, before he could say another word, she'd kicked him out of the house. If it wasn't for the couple whose farm we were headed for, he said he'd still be living out of his VW bus.

When we finally pulled up to their place, a ramshackle ranch house with a rusty washing machine and two goats in the front yard, he admitted he was nervous. "I mean, it's one thing to be cool about two guys getting it on. But to let them do it in the same room with your kids? I don't know." He stepped out of his VW bus and peered back at me. "Wish me luck."

Inside, Mack had me wait in the kitchen while he talked the situation over with his roommates. After a few minutes, he returned smiling and grabbed my hand. "Come on," he said, leading me to the bedroom he shared with the couple's kids. "We're all set. Everything's cool."

We made love so quietly we were sure the kids slept through everything, although when, the next morning, they woke us up by jumping on our bed and asking if we both had penises, we knew the gig was up. A few minutes later when, giggling, they asked to see us kiss, I was sure we were headed for trouble but, unperturbed, Mack pulled me to him. "Just like Mommy and Daddy!" they cried when we were finished.

Sipping coffee, Mack's roommates laughed over their kids' reaction like it was the cutest thing they'd ever heard. The mother even patted Mack on the back and said she wanted them to feel good about themselves no matter how they turned out. "Even gay," she said without the slightest stumble. I stared into my bowl of berries sweetened with honey from a hive she kept out back by the barn and waited for her husband to correct her, but he just smiled and murmured, "Right-on." It was then I decided there was no greater calling in life than to drop out, move to the country and be a hippie.

The next night when I met Sal in the Continental Room and told him about my new-found conviction, he explained the difference between hippies and freaks. He said the former were almost always pacifists, while the latter tended to be more confrontational. While hippies often lived on farms, like Mack's roommates, or in communes, freaks preferred "crash pads" in or near the urban ghettoes where "spades," as he called Blacks, lived. While both smoked grass and dropped acid, freaks took other drugs hippies eschewed, like speed and smack. Some freaks even shot up. Hippies, he said, never used needles. "They say the body is their temple," Sal explained. "They treat it with respect. Freaks say it's just there for sex." He giggled. "They tend to abuse it."

He said the biggest freak he'd ever met was Forrest, the cat from the Haight who'd shot him up and given him hepatitis. Freaks, he said, were into what he called "flash" and were also more likely to be gay. Hippies, on the other hand, hated anything showy and, Mack aside, were almost never gay.

Sal acknowledged freaks were often too fast for him and said he had a hard time keeping up. Hippies tended to be more his speed. As for me, he said he really couldn't see me as a hippie, although he thought I'd make a very good freak. "You like to blow minds." That, he explained, was a freak specialty.

When I said I'd never stoop so low as to stick a needle in my arm, Sal smiled wryly. Recalling "Revelation," the Flannery O'Connor story that had sealed our bond, he warned me against smugness. As he noted, he'd always been appalled by needles and then along came Forrest. Thinking he was in love, he'd let Forrest shoot him up, although all he ended up with was a bad case of hepatitis and a liver that still gave him trouble.

"You never know how far you're gonna fall until you hit rock bottom," he advised. That, he noted, was another thing about freaks. Unlike hippies, sooner or later freaks always seemed to bottom out. "Death trips," he called their trajectories.

Climbing out of Mack's VW bus, Sal called Luis Buñuel, the Spanish surrealist whose latest film we were about to see, a "head trip with balls." Stoned, Mack giggled nervously. Racing ahead, I noted the riot that had broken out after the Paris premiere of Buñuel's 1929 directorial debut, an experimental short he'd done with Salvador Dali called *Un Chien Andalou*. I pointed across the parking lot at the nondescript strip mall cinema we were heading for and cried, "Do you think one might break out here?"

Mack clucked he certainly hoped not. As he noted, riots were uptight and he preferred his scenes mellow. I glanced at Sal, who, after the latest atrocity in Vietnam, had finally agreed fleeing the Dow Chemical protest had been a cop-out, and rolled my eyes. While I'd tried, things were not working out with Mack. I hated mellow.

I'd cut my two afternoon classes to catch a matinee of Buñuel's *Belle de Jour*. Promising a wild ride, it starred Catherine Deneuve as a bored, sexually repressed society matron who takes a day job whoring in a high-end brothel. A local reviewer had warned its tongue-in-cheek take on sexual perversity was not for the squeamish.

Instantly calling Sal, I'd said we had to see it. "Says here it's a shocking portrayal of female masochism. Sounds right up our alley." Sal had groaned as if to say there you go, Dale, talking gay again, but he agreed Buñuel was too good to pass up. His *Exterminating Angel*, a film about wealthy revelers unable to get up from a dinner table, was a favorite. "A real mindfuck," he'd called it.

A hilarious blend of fact and fantasy, *Belle de Jour* did not disappoint. The opening scene, during which Deneuve imagines herself being whipped and then ravaged from behind by a manservant, left me shrieking with laughter. Later, when she fantasizes her husband slinging mud at her while his best friend calls her a sodomite and shit-eater, Sal finally joined in. Still later, when she lay in a coffin dressed as a little girl while her john masturbates on the floor beneath her, we howled so loudly the woman behind us got up and moved to another part of the theater. "Perverts," she clucked before storming off.

On the way out, Mack called the film a disgusting sick joke. I didn't bother saying that's precisely why I'd loved it. Instead, I called him the next day and told him we weren't right for each other. And although he claimed to still be in love with me, I could tell he was relieved to be rid of me. As he'd said after the film, he was worried I might be a little too freaky for him. "Angry," he'd even called me.

After that, I was content to just hang out with Sal and laugh. Sputtering out of him like gunfire, Sal's laugh riddled the air and turned his cheeks rosy pink. After *Belle de Jour*, laughter with Sal was better than sex with a thousand Macks.

A few days later, Sal and I attended an evening screening of Ingmar Bergman's *Persona* at SU's Film Club. Several weeks earlier, we'd gotten hooked on its fare after seeing Alain Resnais's *Last Year at Marienbad*, about a man who tries to convince a woman they'd had an affair the previous summer. Stumbling out of the screening, we'd looked at each other and, after admitting we'd both loved the film, wondered what the hell it was all about. Interrupting Sal's rap on the paradox of time and memory, I'd blurted out that I thought *Marienbad* was about homosexual panic.

"What?!" he'd cried. "It stars a man and a woman, for God's sake." "So?" I'd replied. "Anything that decadent has got to be gay. Oh my God, did you notice the gowns?" Sal had looked at me like I'd sprouted a second head. "You sound like those gays who claim Albee wrote *Who's Afraid of Virginia Woolf?* for an all-male cast." I'd looked at him sardonically. "You mean, he didn't?"

Like *Belle de Jour*, *Persona* radically demolished the line between dream and reality. And, like Buñuel, Bergman used women as his protagonists—in this case, Liv Ullman, who played Elisabet, an acclaimed actress who is hospitalized after willing herself mute, and Bibi Andersson who portrayed Alma, her shy, star-struck nurse. But, unlike Buñuel, Bergman was no social critic. A hallucinatory slide into the hidden corners of the psyche, *Persona* gave sex no power to subvert convention or ridicule bourgeois pieties. For Bergman, sex was merely the stage on which we stood, alone and naked, shivering in the glare of our own self-disgust. Spiritual rot was what Bergman was into, not sexual hypocrisy.

Sal and I didn't laugh once during *Persona*. Leaving the screening, he asked if I knew the title was Latin for mask. I shook my head and confessed I didn't. Although I'd taken three years of high school Latin, the only phrase I remembered was Caesar's *Veni, vidi, vici*: I came, I saw, I conquered. There was no conquest in *Persona*, only conflict.

After *Persona*, we agreed we couldn't face another night of the Continental Room and parted ways early. I slept poorly and when I saw Sal the next night, I contended I'd never felt a film so intensely as *Persona*. My jaw had dropped the moment the projector flashed its first image on the screen and stayed on the floor until the film's exasperatingly ambiguous close. And while there had been several scenes so intense I'd found them hard to sit through, there had been one for which I'd nearly stood up and cheered. A turning point in the battle of wills that was at the film's core, it featured Elisabet and Alma meeting in the middle of the night and, to the mournful blare of a far-off foghorn, wordlessly embracing. While the two never kissed and not a stitch of clothing was shed, the atmosphere was so erotically charged I could not help but gasp. Finally, our kind of love had made it onto the silver screen.

Sal argued I'd read too much into the scene, but I insisted it was a breakthrough, the first depiction of same-sex love in a modern film. Nor did I stop there. Noting *Persona* dealt largely with guilt and shame, afflictions I claimed were particularly relevant for gays, I said I'd found one of Alma's most anguished outbursts to be almost unbearably resonant: "You mustn't touch me...I'm poisonous, bad, cold, and rotten. Why can't I be allowed to just die away?" That, I contended, could have come out of the mouth of almost any gay man.

Indeed, hadn't Arnold already said as much the night he'd tried to kill himself? *You're a bunch of sick fucking queens who'd be better off dead. Dead, do you hear me? Dead!* As I told Sal, the image of him holding the knife to his chest still haunted me.

Sal agreed *Persona*'s sense of shame was crushing, although I argued the film also posited a way out. "Through standing up for ourselves," I said before noting the scene in which Alma, seething over the mockery to which Elisabet had subjected her, left a shard of glass for her to step on. We agreed Alma's revenge was the film's most shocking moment, although Sal contended the chaos following her act was Bergman critiquing violence. I argued the opposite. The moment Elisabet had sliced her foot open, Alma ceased being her subordinate. Only a few scenes later, the two became, at least psychically, lovers—equals.

I claimed *Persona* showed us that ends did sometimes justify means, violence included. "Take Alma's shard of glass," I said. "Nothing would have changed had she not purposefully left it behind." I told Sal that was what I wanted—"A shard so sharp it disrupts the entire story line."

Sal looked at me quizzically. "The story line?"

"Yes, this one," I continued, my hand sweeping the Continental Room. "The whole fucked-up, twisted, dirty mess." I reached across the booth and, lightly touching Sal's hand, reopened an old wound: our disagreement over the importance of coming out. "Someday, I'm going to chuck it all and tell everyone." I took a sip of beer and nodded. "I can feel it building up inside me, Sal. Like Alma sweeping up her shards of glass and suddenly deciding to leave one behind."

"But what about your parents? You know you'll break their hearts."

"Maybe," I replied, glaring at the increasingly pungent pool of piss outside the ladies' room. "But I can't go on like this." I took another Camel from Sal's pack and flashed on Alma's lament: *I'm poisonous, cold and rotten. Why can't I be allowed to just die away?* "Sometimes, I don't know which is worse—the hatred the straight world has for us or the disgust we have for ourselves." Coming clean, I insisted, was the cure for both.

Sal disagreed. Nothing, he said, warranted the hurt our coming out would cause those we loved. He wouldn't do it. It wasn't right. "Selfish" and "self-indulgent," he even called it.

Undaunted, I argued violence was sometimes necessary. As with Bergman's Alma, for us to be free, others necessarily would have to be hurt.

"Look!" I squealed, kneeling beside a mud puddle on the edge of a large park at the far end of Marshall Street. I poked it with my finger and let out a scream so piercing the people milling around me stopped and stared. "It's primordial! Our primordial ooze!" I cried before motioning for Sal and Valerie, both of whom had also dropped acid, to come over; they simply had to see. "It's where we started," I shouted, flailing my arms. "The beginning!"

Valerie giggled and ran over but, mortified, Sal stood his ground. "Get up," he growled, nervously lighting a Camel. "People are staring."

"But, Sal, it's Blake, remember? He was right!" I replied, pressing my palm into the muck. I held my hand up and beamed. "See! Infinity in the palm of my hand!" I squealed as I pointed at a speck of sand in the crease of my thumb. "Can you see? There! It's all there. Everything!!" I got off my haunches and, laughing at the absurdity of it all, ran to him. "The universe in a grain of sand!!"

Sal glanced at a group of snickering hippies passing by and grimaced. "Stop it," he demanded. "You're making a scene."

"So?" I replied, giddily waving at the group as they sauntered off. "I'm just goofing. What's wrong with that?"

"It isn't cool," Sal grumbled, shaking his head. His lips quivered as he took a long drag of his Camel.

"Ah, I see," I said. "I'm making you uptight."

Sal suddenly turned ashen. "Yes," he hissed.

"I'm being too gay, is that it?" I asked. My scalp tingled and my cheeks burned. I'd never been so direct with him. "I'm embarrassing you."

Sal's face turned grayer still and lines furrowed his brow. "Yes," he whispered.

I placed my hand on his shoulder and asked if he remembered the night in the Continental Room when he'd taught me the meaning of the word 'epiphany.' "We'd just met. You were sitting in that booth off the dance floor, Trudy's booth, rolling cigarettes." I smiled wistfully. "I'd never seen a gay guy roll his own cigarette before."

Sal brushed my hand away and grumbled he had no idea what I was talking about.

I persisted. "You said an epiphany was what we sometimes feel when we're tripping." I smiled. "Well, I've had one, Sal. An epiphany!" I twirled on my toes like the diva ballerina I'd been as a young child. "And you know what?"

He stepped away and wiped the sweat from his forehead. He was perspiring heavily. "What?"

I held out my arms. "It doesn't matter what anyone thinks!" I threw my head back and cackled. "I'm a sissy, Sal! And it's good!" I even danced a little jig. "I used to hate the word. Now I love it. It's mine. I own it!" I let the slur roll lispingly off my tongue: *s-s-s-i-i-s-s-s-e-e-e*. Finally, I was the unafraid, upfront gay man that, on my first night in town, I'd promised myself I'd be.

Sal looked nervously around to make sure no one had heard me and shook his head. "I'm splitting," he mumbled and suddenly raced off, disappearing into the sea of plastic people he complained were taking over Marshall Street.

Valerie came running over and asked what had happened. "Oh, you know," I grumbled, "Sal did another one of his disappearing acts." I shrugged and told her he was prone to them. "Things sometimes set him off." Knowing she wouldn't understand, I didn't bother noting being "too gay" was one of them. "Bummer," she groused. "And we were just starting to trip out."

"Come on," I said, grabbing her hand and pointing at a patch of trees on the crest of a hill. "Let's groove." We wandered the park until sunset and though I continued to shriek and flail my arms, Valerie didn't once complain that I embarrassed her. Indeed, she seemed to enjoy the attention that being around a screaming meemie like me brought.

Later, when I confessed that I'd never felt so free, she nodded knowingly. "It's the acid," she intoned, suddenly serious. "It breaks down inhibitions."

Two days later, Sal disappeared. "He no here no more," his nearly deaf, immigrant Italian father shouted into the phone. "No know," he replied when I asked where he'd gone. "Maybe New York, maybe not. He no say." He chuckled. "You know Sallie."

"Yes," I replied and confessed I'd miss him.

"Sorry he no say goodbye. But Sallie's a good boy," his father said before hanging up.

After that, I hung out mostly with Valerie, getting high at the hippie pad off Marshall Street she'd moved into as soon as Syracuse lifted its ban on female students living off-campus. I let my studies slide and, while I knew I was heading for probation, I didn't really care. Architecture had lost its allure and, while college itself seemed increasingly irrelevant, my academic advisor assured me I could keep my draft deferment by simply transferring to Liberal Arts. And if there was one place where I belonged even less than the Continental Room, it was Vietnam. It was not even up for discussion. I wouldn't last a week. I would not go.

It wasn't so much the Viet Cong I feared. It was our side. "Friendly fire" was what they called the killings by which we mistakenly took out our own, although in my case that would just be how they covered up my murder. As the guys in the dorm had shouted as Larry fled SU for an ex-lover in Florida, *Two, four, six, eight, who do we obliterate? QUEERS!*

9
War

"But I don't understand," my mother said, staring at the probation notice at the bottom of my first-semester transcript. "You've wanted to be an architect your whole life." She scanned its string of D's and F's and shook her head. "We came to expect things like this from your brother but never you." Her jaw stiffened. "You've always been such a good student."

I was tempted to tell her all that was behind me now. As the LSD had shown me, college didn't mean anything anymore; being honest about who I was was where things were at. Instead, I just shrugged and, glancing at the joint in my shirt pocket, wondered how much longer this was going to take. It had been hours since I'd gotten high.

"It's as if you're throwing your whole life away," my mother persisted. She brushed a strand of hair from my face and, after again noting how badly I needed a haircut, asked what was going on. Something, she said, seemed to be bothering me. She smiled sweetly. "We've always been so close. You know you can tell me anything."

"Oh really?" I replied, recalling the time I'd gone to her after my father had said he hated me—a scene I'd been brooding over for weeks. "That's news to me."

My mother flinched. "What did you just say?"

"I went to you once looking for understanding. But all you did was walk away."

"What are you talking about? I've never once walked away from you!"

I shook my head. She couldn't possibly want me to spell it out.

"Well, I'm waiting. Tell me when I failed you."

"Dad and me in the driveway?" I said, hoping clues would be enough.

She shrugged.

"In Liftwood?"

She stared at me blankly.

"With the baseball mitts?"

She still showed no sign of recognition.

I paused and sighed; the regulars in the Continental Room loved it when I got to this part. "You were deadheading pansies." Although she claimed she still had no idea what I was talking about, I knew from the flush of her cheeks and the clench of her jaw that I'd finally struck a nerve. I persisted, "Dad said he hated me."

"Your father did no such thing!" my mother fumed. "How dare you say something so vile!"

I glanced at the charcoal portrait of me hanging over a bookcase. Done later that same summer on a car trip through New England, my gaze was hard, my jaw set, and my hair a swirl of devilish horns. "I was crying and went to you for support but all you did was tell me I needed to understand my father better." I paused; was she really going to pretend this never happened? "Then you turned and walked away."

Downstairs, the mailman's weekly delivery of magazines loudly tumbled through the mail slot, the promise of more news from my generation's war on the "Old Order." "You didn't hug me or anything. You just followed Dad into the house." I started to tremble. Never before had I confronted her about this. "I was eleven, Mother. I mean, shouldn't it have been the other way around? Isn't understanding a parent's job?"

"Oh, I see, this is all my fault, is that it? Your failing grades, your refusal to get a haircut, that alienation or whatever it is you've been whining about since you went off to college, it's all because I don't love you enough."

I noted I hadn't said that but she was off and running. "Look, mister, I've been your slave your whole life. I cook your meals, wash your dishes, iron your shirts, and make your bed. I even take care of your dog. You have a car at your disposal whenever you want, your own TV and stereo so you don't have to act like you're a member of this family, a very expensive college education that is fully paid for and, I might add, a rather generous monthly allowance. When have you ever been denied anything?"

I groaned and rolled my eyes. "I'm not talking about material things. I'm talking about..."

She wouldn't let me finish. "Don't you accuse me of not doing enough for you ever again, do you hear?!" She stepped within striking distance. *Ever*!!"

"Don't, I'm warning you, Mother," I snapped, grabbing her arm. "You hit me and you'll be sorry."

"Are you threatening me?"

"No, I'm telling you. If you hit me, I will hit you back," I replied so coldly I startled even myself. "I'm not going to be pushed around by this family any longer."

"*Pushed around*?!" she shrieked. "Why, you're so self-centered you can't see beyond the end of your own nose." Her face was red and her eyes were narrow slits. "You've had it too easy—way, way too easy, young man."

I recalled the years of bullying I'd protected her from so she wouldn't have to bear the shame of having a son like me and burst out laughing. "Oh, that's right. I forgot. How thoughtless of me. I've had it so, so easy..."

I stopped and glared at her. "You don't know the first thing about me or what I've gone through, Mother. Nothing. Nada. So, why don't you just go back downstairs and iron some shirts or something. Surely there're more sacrifices you can make that I won't appreciate." I paused to look at myself in my dresser mirror. My face was flushed and I was visibly shaking. "Yes, go and make me feel guilty about something else. I mean, isn't that what you do best?"

At that, her eyes welled up and she stormed out of my bedroom warning me I'd be sorry. She was telling my father everything.

"Be my guest!" I yelled as she disappeared down the stairs. "Let's get this out in the open and discuss it like a real family." I cackled. "I can just see it now," I shouted before slamming my door so hard my print of *Christina's World* crashed onto the floor, sending shards of glass everywhere.

My father scowled at me from his seat at the head of the table. He was still dressed for work, although he'd loosened his tie and rolled up the sleeves of a starched white shirt, part of a batch my mother had spent the previous day ironing. "Go ahead, get kicked out of school. You're only biting off your nose to spite your face. The Army'll whip you into shape so fast your head'll spin." He glanced at my mother, whose smudged plaid apron was in stark contrast to the navy-blue suit and pop beads she'd had on for our encounter earlier that day.

"Isn't that what I've always said, Mother? Frankly, I think it'd be the best thing for him."

I reminded my father we were at war. If I got drafted, I'd be shipped off to Vietnam. "Or perhaps that's what you want." I straightened the fringed blue linen napkin in my lap and smiled sweetly. "Me shot in some southeast Asian jungle?"

Turning beet-red, my father shifted menacingly in his chair. I chuckled, imagining the look on his face as he threw me against the dining room wall and I screamed out the news, *Look, you fool, don't you know? The Army doesn't take people like me. I'm a faggot, Dad. A homo!*

"Okay," my mother interjected, "I want the two of you to stop. Right this minute. I won't tolerate any shouting at the dinner table."

"About eighteen years too late, wouldn't you say, Mom?" I sneered.

"Okay, that's it," my father snarled, throwing his napkin onto the table. "I've had just about all the lip I'm going to take from the likes of you."

As he pulled back from the table, I imagined vaulting onto it and diving head-first into the mirror on the wall opposite me. Instead, I grabbed the seat of my chair and glanced up at the chandelier. God, I hate that thing, I thought; brass is so tacky. I smiled as I recalled Donnie's warning. Only gay people called things tacky.

"Honey!" my mother bellowed, banging the table so hard water spilled from my pewter goblet. I watched the stain spread across the table's gleaming mahogany surface and thought about how much I hated the goblets too. "Piss-elegant" was the term Donnie said we used for things like that, although he'd also advised me to never use it around straights. "You'll be instantly wrecked," he'd explained before adding pretentiousness was a luxury few gays could afford.

"Hardin!" my mother again shouted at my father, standing with clenched fists at his end of the table. "Sit down!"

Fuming, my father slumped back into his chair.

Glowering as I guiltily dabbed the water spill with my napkin, my mother told me to leave the stain alone. "You'll only make it worse," she snarled. Then, she looked across the table at my father and complained she hadn't had a moment's peace since I'd returned home from Syracuse. "There's always something, always some goddamned..." Then, catching herself, she apologized. As she noted, it wasn't like her to swear.

Stunned, I stared at our reflection in the mirror across from me—a seething tableau of bitterness, rage, and recrimination. We're killing each other, I thought, before turning to my mother and begging her with my eyes to bring us back from the brink. Ignoring me, she merely pulled a crumpled Kleenex from her apron and dabbed her nose. "Well," she sighed, biting her lower lip, "can I interest anyone in dessert?" She rose and looked at my father. "Honey, how about a piece of chocolate fudge pie?" She smiled bravely. "I made it fresh today."

She was in the kitchen doorway before she turned and asked, almost as an afterthought, if I wanted anything. When I replied I only wanted to be excused from the table, she nodded and waved me off. "Yes, please," she mumbled. She turned back to my father, tears streaming down her cheeks. "I think he's done quite enough for one night, don't you, honey?"

He nodded. "Frankly, it'll be a relief to be rid of him."

A few days later, my mother cornered me in the living room. Smoothing the wrinkles from our Christmas tree's red felt skirt, she asked how long I'd known this new friend, Donnie, with whom I'd been spending most of my semester break. "Oh, really?" she replied when I said we'd met a month or so before high school graduation. "Funny, you've never mentioned him before."

When I said we'd met through Angie, the high school swim star my father called "horsey," she picked an errant tinsel from the carpet and frowned slightly. "Are they dating?" Compounding the lie, I told her yes, although I knew better than to say they were going steady. The next time she'd see Angie she'd check for a ring and then all hell would break loose. *And how many of your other stories are lies?* my mother would demand to know.

"And who does Donnie know there?" she asked when I acknowledged we'd been going to parties in Philadelphia. "Dominic, huh? Sounds Italian. Is he Catholic?" When I told her yes, she asked what Donnie's father did for a living. When I replied he was an electrician, she complained my taste in friends was almost as bad as my grades. Then, heading back into the kitchen, she stopped, looked at me sternly and informed me she wasn't at all sure she approved of the company I was keeping. When I asked why that should matter—after all, at eighteen, I was more than capable of choosing my own friends—she growled, "Because I control the keys to the car you use for all your little excursions. Got it?"

That evening, I sat quietly in the living room and listened as my parents complained over cocktails about my brother's fiancée, Kathi. "The woman's never even been to college," my father snipped before noting that Kathi's father, who was a plumber, "worked with his hands." But what seemed to bother him most was Kathi's aversion to the shrimp cocktail my mother had put out for the party they'd thrown to announce my brother's engagement. "What kind of wife will a woman like that make?" my father wondered. "I certainly don't see her helping Dean's career at DuPont." Poking the onion of her vodka gimlet with a sterling silver swizzle stick—a set of which my father had given her for Christmas—my mother shook her head. "I just don't understand it," she clucked. "Dean used to have such good taste in women."

I knew better than to point out that my father, the son of a newspaper editor, had crossed class lines to marry my mother, the daughter of a mere meter reader. Or that, like Kathi, my mother had never attended college or worked as anything more than a secretary. Instead, I mutely sampled my mother's array of Christmas cookies and quietly seethed as my parents continued to question Kathi's qualifications as their future daughter-in-law. However, it wasn't until my father called her the "dumbest white woman" he'd ever met, and my mother said she couldn't imagine Kathi ever making it in what she called "polite society," that I realized just how hopeless my own case was. While Kathi and the family name might someday co-exist, gay and Mitchell never would.

The next time I saw Donnie, I confessed I was getting worried. "My mother suspects something. I can tell. I think she might be on to us."

"Us?" he cried, maneuvering his battered Chevy Malibu onto the northbound lane of the still-unfinished I-95 to Philadelphia. "She's never even laid eyes on me."

"I know, I know," I murmured before confessing my mother was a terrible snob. "You're from the wrong side of the tracks. I'm not supposed to have friends like you."

"Well, excuse me, Mary," he replied before reminding me I was the one who cruised Market Street. "And you can't get much more low-life than that."

"I said you were dating Angie," I replied when Donnie grilled me on how I'd told her we'd met.

"Yeah, but what about Dominic? How'd you explain him?" When I replied I'd said he was Angie's cousin, Donnie congratulated me. "You're getting very good at lying." He smiled at me. "That's very gay."

I confessed the lies were taking a toll. "I'm constantly on guard. Sometimes, I think my mother's trying to trip me up." I told him about Randy, one of the regulars from Syracuse's Continental Room, who wore a wedding ring to work so people would think him straight. "I don't want to live like that. Always hiding and worrying who might know or find out." I said I was thinking about coming clean and telling my parents everything.

"What, are you *crazy*?!"

"Maybe," I shrugged. I told him about my arguments with Sal, the Syracuse freak who'd recently fled for parts unknown. "He says we mustn't ever come out to our parents. He says they don't deserve that kind of shame." At a sign announcing a detour, Donnie turned off the Interstate and headed into Chester, a dirt-poor ghetto abutting a string of smelly refineries. "But why isn't lying the shameful part? I thought we were supposed to always tell the truth!"

Donnie looked at me sardonically. "What, you missed the lesson about not kissing other boys?"

I laughed. "Of course not, but kissing boys doesn't make me feel dirty. Lying does." I glared at the burning gas stacks that made the drive through Chester feel like a descent into hell. "I've started trembling," I complained. "I can't seem to make it stop."

"Look, it's the hand we've been dealt. We just gotta make the best of it," Donnie sighed. Then, noting the stench, he turned off the car heater, although he promised that once we got out of Chester's range, he'd turn it back on. "I don't know how they do it," he grumbled of the town's poor, mostly Black residents. "You know, living like this." I didn't bother saying I wondered the same about us.

When we got to Philadelphia, Dominic lit into me when Donnie told him what I was thinking. "Listen, you fucking douche bag, take it from someone who knows. You do not want to tell your parents. They'll kick you out. They'll disown you."

"You'll be wrecked," added Mike, who was also home from his first semester at NYU's Drama School. He strode to the middle of Dominic's room, put both hands on his hips and, announcing a need to lighten the mood, belted out a few lines from Ethel Merman's "There's No Business, Like Show Business." "There, don't we all feel better?" he murmured before returning to the couch.

"I think knowing will be good for them," I persisted. I confessed how horrified I was by what my parents had said about Kathi, my brother's fiancée. I suggested that if they knew about me, maybe they'd change. "You know, be more open-minded, less bigoted." I looked guiltily at Donnie. "Not such snobs."

"Like love conquers all?" Dominic scoffed.

"Yeah, something like that," I replied.

"So, go ahead, Mary, see what happens. But don't say I didn't warn you. I don't care who they are or how much they say they love you. Straight people cannot be trusted." Dominic picked up a hash pipe, handed it to me and lit it. He watched me inhale deeply and smiled wickedly. "You know, if you really want to do something for your parents, why don't you get a haircut? You're starting to look like a hippie."

"Freak," I said, blowing a thick cloud of smoke back at him. "Nobody's a hippie anymore."

"Freak?!" Mike gasped. "What self-respecting gay would call himself that?"

"Me," I murmured before taking another puff. I handed the hash pipe to Donnie and announced I'd even dropped LSD. "Several times," I boasted.

"No!" Mike gasped, clutching the beads he claimed made him a hippie too. "You wouldn't!" When I confirmed I indeed had, he insisted I had to be under the influence of straights. Gays, he claimed, would never do anything like that. "It's against the law!"

When I noted being gay was also illegal, Dominic flew into a rage. "Talk about being wrecked. If you call yourself a freak one more time, I'll be the one who disowns you." He looked at Donnie and grimaced. "What is it with your college friend anyway? Is he a fucking idiot or what?"

Shadows from the front yard's only tree, a stunted, leafless crabapple, flickered across the foyer's wall and sent me reeling. I stopped and grabbed the banister to steady myself. I'd come home late from another party in Philadelphia and slept until three. Although the house was quiet, I knew my mother was home. I could feel her.

I ventured further down the stairs but hesitated at the step where, two nights earlier, I'd eavesdropped on my parents talking after dinner. "But, honey, you don't think... He can't be. I've read they're deformed. You know, from books in the library. One of them said homosexuals only have one testicle." Sitting across the dining room table from my mother, my father had replied so softly I had to go one step further to hear him. "I don't know, Jane. I think we may have to prepare for the worst." After that, all I heard was my mother's sobs.

My mother called for me from the den. Her voice was sharp and her tone shrill. "I have something I want to discuss with you."

"Can't it wait until I've had something to eat? I just woke up."

"No," she replied, she'd waited long enough. "All day, in fact."

I made my way as far as the den's doorway and stopped. My mother was seated on the creamy Naugahyde sectional closest to me, sheathed in a circle of light from an overhead lamp hanging from a large hook screwed into the ceiling. In her lap was the stack of eight dining room seat covers she'd been needlepointing for almost as long as I could remember, the gift she intended to give herself when the family was finally complete: she and my father; Dean, Kathi and their first born; and me, my wife and mine.

Her eyes were red and puffy, like she'd been crying all day. Probably all night too. As she'd complained the day before, crying seemed to be just about all she did anymore.

Across the room, a wall of shelves held rows of books I'd never seen either of my parents read. "Oh, I don't know," she'd once dreamily replied when I'd asked her about them. "I just like the way they look." I tried to imagine my mother in the library asking for books on homosexuality. She must have gone to the main branch, downtown in Rodney Square, where nobody'd know her. I wondered if the librarian I'd tricked with had been the one to help her find what she was looking for or if, on her way back to the car, she'd passed the corner of 9th and Market where I'd picked him up.

My mother's feet, sheathed in red leather slippers with gold arabesques, slid off a tufted faux leather ottoman and dropped to the floor. Her back stiffened and her tiny hands curled into fists. The thin circle of diamonds on her wedding band blazed. She announced she had a question she wanted me to answer. "Truthfully," she added, arching the delicate sliver of her right eyebrow.

"Yes?" I responded, my voice quavering.

My mother stared at me and slowly bared her teeth. The silver hook of her bridge glistened against the soft pink of her gums. "Is that friend of yours..." She paused and swallowed hard, as if about to say something distasteful. "Donnie..." She cleared her throat and grimaced. "Is that Donnie friend of yours a homosexual?"

I lifted my right arm to steady myself against the door frame and then, giving up, let it drop to my side. I took a deep breath and listened to the air hiss out of me. As Donnie had said, she'd never even laid eyes on him. All she knew was that his father was an electrician—as my father had said, someone who "works with his hands."

Her eyes narrowed. "Well? I'm waiting."

I looked out the den's front-facing window and watched a car head up the street on its way out of Carrcroft. "Yes, Mother," I answered coolly. Then, checking for just an instant the accuracy of my aim, I lobbed the bomb I knew would blow both of us away. "And so am I."

She froze for a moment and then her jaw went slack. Outside, a neighbor's dog went berserk as the maws of a garbage truck slammed shut. "No, you're lying to me," she whimpered, her voice suddenly coarse and raspy. "Tell me you are."

I paused to catch my breath and then uttered the words that only six months earlier I'd refused to put into the same sentence: "It's true, Mother. I'm a homosexual. I have been for a while." I smiled feebly. "For the past two years, actually." Then, stepping tentatively toward her, I tried to bring us both back from the brink. "Those books you've read are lies. You're not to blame." I smiled slightly. "No one is." I held my arm out for her.

"Don't come near me! You disgust me!" she shrieked, bursting up from her seat in an explosion of hooks, needlepoint, and yarn. When she got to the doorway, she stopped and demanded I move aside, although her exact words were, "Get the hell out of my way." When I noted mothers weren't supposed to call children disgusting any more than fathers were supposed to say they were hated, she yelped like I'd slapped her, shoved me aside and, retching into her hand, raced down the hall to her bathroom.

As she bent over the toilet and heaved out her disgust, I turned and stared numbly into the foyer. A step up from the dark, cramped bottleneck of Liftwood's entry, it was one of the features my mother liked most about the Carrcroft house. Finally, she could greet her guests graciously—"like refined people," she'd once murmured. I listened to her retch into the toilet and considered announcing her latest arrival. *Come, Jane, where are your manners? He's here. Your son, the homosexual! Don't you want to say hello?*

Suddenly, the grandfather clock at the base of the stairs sounded an alarm. In an hour, my brother would be returning home from work. And shortly after him, my father. I'd have to go through all this again. And again. Meanwhile, in the bathroom at the end of the hall, my mother continued her retching. I could even smell the vomit.

Panicking, I raced to my parents' bedroom, grabbed my mother's purse from her nightstand and dumped its contents onto the bed. "Where are your fucking car keys?" I yelled, rifling through its spillage. I'd never once sworn in front of my mother, not even a 'damn' or a 'Jeez.'

I heaved a tube of lipstick at the family photo over the bed and a compact at the closet whose contents I'd once modeled to the delight of the women in my life: my mother; my great aunt Kitno; my two grandmothers, Mo and Nanny; and Katie, the hard-drinking wife of my father's best friend, Norm. Now, there were no more closets—no more petticoats, polka-dot sundresses, aquamarine bracelets, or sling-back pumps with rhinestone-studded straps—just a suburban mom and her homosexual son trapped in the headlights of a roaring, blaring, barreling tractor-trailer of truth. "I'm leaving. Getting the fuck out of this suffocating, guilt-ridden"—I covered my ears to block out her retching—"*Hell*!"

"No God, please, no!" my mother wailed.

"Stop it! You're driving me..." I kicked the side of her bed, dropped to my knees and clawed the carpet as a torrent of obscenities gushed out of me. "I'm going fucking mad. Do you hear me?" I screamed at the top of my lungs. "Goddamned motherfucking *insane*!!"

I grabbed her car keys and a checkbook and ran to her bathroom doorway. "Are you happy now, Mother? Got what you wanted? I've destroyed your precious little dream, our goddamn happy family. It's all out in the open now. You've raised a horror." My fury soared. "An abomination!"

I taunted her as she squatted on a fringed baby-blue bathmat and dry-heaved into the toilet. "Oh, come now, you can do better than that. Surely, you're not finished. Show me again how disgusting you think I am!"

Sobbing, she looked up from the toilet bowl. Her hair had globs of vomit in it and her face was streaked with mascara. "Oh please, God, not this," she whimpered. "Please, not me. I've been so good..."

"*You!?*" I shouted so loudly Jeff growled at me. "No, Mother, this one's about me. Sorry, but this time it's your turn to understand." I cackled madly. "Ha! That'll be something!"

I ran to the back door and stopped for one last rejoinder. "Oh, and by the way, Mother, just in case you're interested, the word is *gay*." The dog went wild.

I ran to her Olds and gunned it, tires squealing, until I was safely out of Carrcroft. Heading east on Marsh Road, I cursed myself for my recklessness. Dominic had been right. Only a douche bag would think love could conquer something like this. Pulling over, I stared at the railroad overpass ahead and tried to sort through my options. I could lay on the tracks and wait for a train; drop out of school and spend the rest of the war dodging the draft; or return to Syracuse and hope for the best. For a moment, I even considered banging on the doors of the church off to my right and begging for refuge.

Not yet ready to give up on my parents, I settled on a hybrid. I'd fly back to Syracuse, swallow a bottle of aspirin and tell my roommate what I'd done. Yeah, I thought, just wait till she gets the call. *Yes, Mrs. Mitchell, this is the hospital up in Syracuse. I'm terribly sorry to have to say this. But your son has tried to kill himself.*

I turned onto the Interstate and headed for the Philadelphia airport. Yeah, then they'll be sorry. I watched the speedometer shoot up to 90, then 100. *Yeah, that's right. Go ahead, Mom, vomit some more. Tell me how disgusting I am. Fuck you, fuck Dad, fuck the whole goddamn motherfucking family.*

I sat huddled in a bright fluorescent-lit hallway outside the boarding area for my flight back to Syracuse when an announcer requested my presence in the baggage claim area. A half-hour later, my father strode up to me with a state trooper in tow and told me to get up. It was time to be heading home.

When I turned to the cop for confirmation, he put his hand on his revolver and said, yup, that's right, son, I needed to do as my father said. "Thank you, officer," my father replied, shaking his hand. "I think we're all set now."

"Glad to be of help," the trooper murmured. "You wouldn't believe how many calls like this we get nowadays." He shook his head. "From nice, wholesome families like yours too." He shot me a look of contempt. "Kids getting caught up in all kinds of bad stuff—drugs, prostitution, crime. The world's going to hell in a handbasket, if you ask me," he added before sauntering off.

My father held me by the arm while I led him to the Olds, then opened the passenger door and brusquely told me to get in. As he said, he wasn't putting up with anymore "funny business." I mumbled I didn't think any of it was the least bit funny, but he just shrugged. "You've made your bed."

When we got to Chester, the hyper-polluted ghetto that felt like a stop on the way to hell, he pulled into an abandoned gas station and asked for my mother's checkbook. As I handed it to him, I steeled myself for some rough stuff, but my father just slipped the checkbook into his suit pocket and resumed the drive back to Carrcroft. He didn't say another word the entire trip, a restraint which, given what I'd gone through with my mother, I almost mistook, if not for love, at least resignation.

When we got home, my mother's eyes were redder and her glare even angrier than before. When she announced dinner would be ready any minute, I mumbled I wasn't hungry and hurried off to the den, where I threw myself into a recliner and tried to keep from crying. As the voice inside my head kept reminding me, all I'd done wrong was tell the truth.

A few minutes later, my brother came in and sat at the very spot where my mother had heard me tell her I was gay. Too ashamed to look him in the face, I stared out the window into a night so black the neighbor's lamppost seemed suspended in tar. "Just please don't call me a faggot. It's all I ask," I whimpered, struggling to hold back a flood of tears.

He recoiled like I'd sucker-punched him. However, when, after what seemed like an eternity, he finally mumbled his assent, I broke into wails so anguished he asked if he should call an ambulance. When I begged him please, no, I didn't want to go through this with anyone else, he leaned forward and, slowly rubbing his palms together, whispered over and over that everything was going to be okay. *I promise you*, he even managed to say.

His voice was so calm and his manner so measured that, after a while, I actually believed him. However, when he got up and left the room without so much as a pat on the back—just an empty, stupid "hang in there, tiger"—I realized just how radioactive I'd become. The only physical contact I'd had that night was my father's, whose grip on our way out of the airport had been so tight my upper arm was bruised. That and the image of my mother vomiting into the toilet bowl and begging God to please spare her this shame were what I took to bed with me that night.

Neither parent said another word to me. I just got up and silently trudged up the stairs to my room while an air raid siren inside my head warned me this was far from over. The A-bomb blast that had rattled my childhood dreams had finally detonated. The only remaining question was how extensive the carnage was. And, as with Hiroshima, would there be a Nagasaki too?

Donnie was the first gay person to tell me how appalled he was at what I'd done. After insisting I had to be out of my mind, he quickly turned to worries about his own cover. Would my mother tell his? How likely was it that word would get out? As he said, he wasn't ready for the whole world to know. "You don't live in a vacuum," he reminded me. "Other people's reputations are at stake too."

Dominic was more indignant. "How dare you! Sure, you can throw your own life away but what about his?" he asked, pointing at Donnie. Wilmington, after all, was a small town. People talked.

I was still too traumatized by my mother's reaction to absorb theirs. Of my gay friends, only Mike, the showtune queen, offered any support. He said gay men and their mothers often shared a unique bond and suspected the breach with mine would hurt for a very long time. If the same thing ever happened to him, he wasn't sure he'd survive. I was too frightened to admit I wasn't sure I would either.

Two days later, my mother broke our silence by cornering me in the foyer. "I have some very good news," she announced. "I think I've found the solution."

"Oh?" I muttered, bracing myself. "Solution for what?"

"For setting you straight," she replied darkly. She said she'd consulted Dr. Connolly, our Presbyterian minister, who'd given her the name of a local psychiatrist who, in turn, had referred her to a colleague in Syracuse who specialized in curing what she insisted on calling "things like this."

I bit my tongue. I didn't dare remind her the term was "gay." I could tell from the look in her eyes that she was possessed.

She smiled brightly and handed me a folded piece of pale blue stationary containing the psychiatrist's contact information. "He was very reassuring. He says things like this are very treatable, especially with someone as young and impressionable as you."

I unfolded her note and mutely stared at her stamp, a dark blue desk floating in its upper left-hand corner. Beside it, a straight no-nonsense font proclaimed it a message from her, my mother, Mrs. Jane P. Mitchell, once my only solace and now my most implacable foe. Below it, she'd written in her neat lilting script the doctor's name and address. Yes, I mumbled, I knew where the office was—just a short walk from my dorm, Sibley Hall.

"Good. I've made an appointment for you the day after you get back. 4 o'clock. I want you there."

"I see," I stammered, stunned at how far she'd gone without consulting me. "And if I refuse?"

"Then you're on your own," she said flatly. "Your father and I have discussed this and we are in complete agreement. We will not subsidize this illicit lifestyle of yours."

Incredulous, I didn't waste time debating what homosexuality was: a crime, a sickness, a choice, or simply a fact of life. Instead, I cut right to the chase. "You'd stop paying my tuition?"

"That's right."

"You know, of course, I'll be drafted if I'm no longer in college."

She replied Vietnam was my problem. Getting me back to normal was hers.

I protested there was nothing wrong with me but my mother would hear none of it. "That's that friend of yours, that Donnie, talking. He controls you. He's taken over your mind." At that, she issued a new order. I was to stop seeing him or any of his friends including, as she put it, "that wop Dominic or whatever his name is."

"But you've never met any of them!"

She shrugged and said she didn't need to. She and my father knew all they needed to know about people like that. "Perverts," she called them.

I didn't bother arguing that point either and instead simply refused to comply. "I will see who I damn well please."

"Oh no, you won't," she snapped after warning me about my language. "You're under our care now. You do as we say."

"Under your care?!" I cried. "What is this, prison?"

"Yes," my mother coolly replied. "Until you're cured, that is exactly what this is."

At that, I stuffed her note in the same jeans pocket where I kept a nickel bag of pot and smiled darkly. I didn't care how long it took or what it cost. She was going to regret this. The whole family was. This was war.

The Continental Room crowd was as appalled by what I'd done as Donnie, although my harshest critic was Arnold, who'd been released from the loony bin while I was in Wilmington coming out to my parents. He said he'd seen lots of types like me in the hospital—fucked-up kids from what he called "good families" whom he said were hellbent on self-destruction. When I countered that I thought of myself more as a guerilla fighting for my right to self-determination, he scoffed. "You mean like the Viet Cong?" When I admitted the Tet Offensive, then in full swing, had given me hope that underdogs could indeed beat back bullies, he shook his head and confessed that while he'd always found me odd, he'd never thought me un-American. He even called me a "pinko."

I tried to act insulted but, with everyone reacting so negatively, I secretly feared Arnold might be right; I'd gone too far. Unfortunately, there was no turning back. I'd just have to face the music and see where my time with the shrink took me. All I knew was that I didn't want to be straight, although, on that point, nearly everyone in the Continental Room agreed I should give it a try. After all, what did I have to lose? *My dignity*? they laughed. Besides, as Paul so wisely pointed out, anything was better than Vietnam.

On my way back to Sibley Hall, I wandered aimlessly around the acres of broken bricks and glass shards where Syracuse's once bustling Black ghetto had stood. Ending up in the courtyard of the partially completed I.M. Pei-designed art museum, I dropped to my knees and howled so loudly lights went on in the nearby housing project. "Hey, everything alright out there?" a man shouted into the darkness.

I waited for the young boy who'd offered to give me directions on my first night in town to show me the way out, but he never appeared. No one did. I was in this all on my own.

10
Gay on the Brain

The black leather of his swivel-back chair squished as he leaned forward and folded his hands on top of an oversized mahogany desk. He glanced at his calendar and then his watch and mumbled, "Oh, yes, you must be, uhmmm ..." He fumbled through his desk's clutter and pulled out a file folder. "Yes, here it is..." He paused to peer at me over his bifocals and uttered my name. Then without the slightest trace of a smile, he told me his. "I'm Dr. Radin, your psychiatrist."

I smiled and said, yes, I knew. "I talked to you on the phone, remember?" Arching an eyebrow, I noted he'd also been in touch with my mother.

His chair sighed.

I scanned his office. Rows of books and an array of primitive masks—some Oceanic, others African—spanned the wall behind him. At the edge of his desk, a triptych of framed photos—his wife laughing in an Adirondack chair and two strapping sons, one clutching a football, the other a tennis racket—faced me. Behind them, twin stacks of manuscripts teetered precariously. With a sweep of his hand, he pointed out my seating options: a small captain's chair facing his desk or a dark blue sectional tucked into a corner lined with diplomas. His gold wedding band glinted in the late afternoon light.

Laughing nervously, I chose the chair and, lighting a cigarette, peered at him over my match's flame. He met my gaze head-on. His eyes were dark and impenetrable.

I blew a thick cloud of blue smoke at him and smiled haughtily. Randy from the Continental Room once said I smoked like Bette Davis. I liked that. No one fucked with her. Bette was almost as tough as Janis Joplin, whose photo was the first thing my dorm mates saw when they entered my room. A small, puckish breast peeked through her thick drapery of beads while a mane of wild frizzy hair obscured half her face. Her one visible pupil was so dilated she looked like she'd been wired directly into my wall socket. *Fuck you*, she seemed to sneer. *Fuck you all.*

"Well, isn't this cozy," I gushed, slapping a knee. "Now what, Doctor?"

He looked at me sternly and suggested I start at the beginning.

I touched on most everything. I told him about the deaths of my twin sisters, Nan and Jane; dressing up in my mother's clothes; dancing 'The Dying Swan' in a tutu; the time my father had said he hated me and the other time I'd thrown a glass of milk in his face; picking up guys in his Corvair; being bullied in high school; meeting Dominic and Donnie and learning the ropes of gay life in Philadelphia; coming to Syracuse to enroll in architecture school; and watching my mother vomit into a toilet bowl after I'd told her I was gay. I even mentioned the gargoyles from the Continental Room and my desire to chuck it all and become a hippie. "Yes," I said when he asked if I took drugs, although I refused to admit to anything stronger than marijuana. "I'm sure," I mumbled when he said he'd be very concerned if I also took LSD.

The only thing I didn't mention was my beating behind the Catholic Church. I hadn't told anyone about that. I was too ashamed, especially of my confession that I was sick and my promise to seek a cure. In that story, I wasn't Janis Joplin. Or even Bette Davis. I was Alma, the nurse in Bergman's *Persona*: *Just leave me alone; I'm poisonous, bad, cold, rotten. Why can't I be allowed to just die away?*

Listening quietly, Dr. Radin fixed me with a firm gaze and pensively stroked a salt and pepper goatee. He filled all my pauses with a studied *mmmm* and met all my questions with a flat *and how do you feel about that?* When I admitted I roiled with anger, he again leaned forward in his chair, placed his elbows on his desk and stared at a yellow pencil he twirled between his fingers. "And what do you think about your homosexuality?"

"What about it?" I replied testily. "I've been sexually active since I was sixteen. What else would you like to know?" I aimed a smoke ring at a ceiling tile. "Oh, and, no, I've never been with a woman nor have I ever wanted to be." I crossed my legs and batted my right foot into the space between us. "And just in case you're wondering, I don't molest children either." I returned his gaze and smiled sweetly. "Contrary to popular opinion, Doctor, I'm not a pervert."

I reached down to straighten a sock and wondered what he thought of the story of me dressing up in my mother's clothes. My gay friends called that one a "hoot." I smiled. I loved that word. It was gayer even than "tacky," although not nearly as gay as "piss-elegant." I noticed the fluted scrolls on the corners of his desk and rolled my eyes. They were definitely piss-elegant.

"Are you happy with your choice?" the doctor asked.

Stubbing my cigarette out, I noticed the box of tissues on the molded, white plastic side table next to my chair. "I can't remember a time when I wasn't gay,

Doctor. Not one. Frankly, I consider that a fact, not a choice." I nodded at his pencil. "Like you being left-handed."

He smiled faintly. "You haven't answered my question."

I sighed and stared at the floor. Shreds of tissue littered the carpet around me, detritus from his previous patients' long litany of woes. "Yeah, okay, it's taken some getting used to." I paused. "I'd be a lot happier if people would leave me the fuck alone about it." Our eyes locked. "Of course, no one will." I clenched my teeth. "No one straight, that is. When I graduated from high school, I watched the other kids hug each other and thought, thank God, I've survived. I'd beaten them. Finally, I could be me—the real one. Then ..." I glared at the masks on the wall behind him. "This."

He cleared his throat and stared at his pencil's perfectly proportioned point. "Would you consider a cure?"

"Absolutely not," I snapped. I leaned back in my chair and asked in return if he was doing my parents' bidding. "After all, that is what they're paying you for, isn't it?"

He smiled and asked me to please keep the legs of my chair on the floor. "I don't want you to injure yourself."

"Oh sorry," I muttered before noting he still hadn't answered my question. "Who are you working for?"

He assured me I was his client. He did not work for my parents.

"Even though they're footing the bill?"

"Absolutely," he replied. "It's a matter of ethics." When I asked about the ethics of being coerced into treatment, he shrugged. If I didn't want to see him, I was free to leave. "Anytime you wish."

"Even if that means being shipped off to Vietnam?"

He said the draft was entirely outside of his control. "You're the patient here, not our president." When I asked, ethically speaking, who'd be responsible for the damages if I hurled my chair through his window, his gaze suddenly hardened. "You would be, of course."

"Not my parents?"

His eyes narrowed. "No, you."

I leaned forward. "Look, Doctor, let's get something straight. I'll admit I'm confused and unhappy. There are a lot of things I need to sort out. But being gay isn't one of them."

I bit my lip and looked out his office window at a row of Norway maples, their bark as gray and rumpled as the hides of old elephants. In a muddy park across the street, a man played catch with a small boy. I recalled the last time my father and I had done that—the time he'd told me he hated me—and waited until the urge to cry had passed. Turning to face him, I felt suddenly cold and started to shiver. "Everything has fallen apart. Everything." I held myself tightly. "I'm scared, Doctor."

He asked if I had anyone to confide in.

Shaking my head, I broke down. "No one." I told him even the crowd at the Continental Room thought I was nuts to have come out.

"What about your parents?"

Reaching for a tissue, I groaned and rolled my eyes. "My father says what I need is a good kick in the butt. My mother says I'm wallowing in self-pity." I again welled up. "They refuse to talk about what's happened. Other than my mother vomiting when I told her I was gay and, of course, this..." I glanced at the trio of family photos staring at me from the edge of his desk. "You'd think everything was fine."

I took a deep breath. My heart was pounding. "My parents refuse to even utter the word 'gay.' I can't tell you how much..." I squeezed the fingers of my left hand, hoping the pain would keep my tears at bay. "Their silence makes me feel ..." I tried staring at a ceiling tile. It didn't work either. "Dirty, ashamed..." I covered my face with my hands and again broke down. "*Disgusting.*"

Grabbing a fistful of tissues, I apologized for my tears.

He looked at me puzzled.

"Because I've been a crybaby my whole life, that's why." I paused to light another cigarette and grimaced. "I thought tears would make everyone back off—you know, feel sorry for me. But they only made everything worse." I furiously tapped the floor with my foot. "I'm too weak. I can't stand up for myself." I looked at him plaintively. "I don't want to be straight, Doctor. I want to be strong."

Tapping his watch, he assured me there'd be plenty of time to talk about that. For our next session, he suggested we discuss one of my dreams. "I've found them useful for treating problems like yours."

I agreed on one condition—I refused to have my dreams used against me. "I need to know I can trust you," I said, my voice quaking. "That you really do work for me." I reminded him I did not want to be straight.

"Mmmm," he purred. "So you've said."

"I mean, it shit on my head!" I cried, staring at the shrink. "I took refuge under it, and it just dumped a big load on me." I chuckled. My dreams were so bizarre they were almost fun—like being in a Buñuel film. Catherine Deneuve in *Belle de Jour*, I thought.

The night before, I'd dreamed I was at the circus with my grandmother, Mo. She was the one who'd given me the silver dollars I'd used to lure Junior into meeting me behind the Catholic church. Clowns with hideously painted faces ran about the ring, brandishing long knives. Suddenly, they darted into the bleachers after me. No one came to my aid, not even Mo. Indeed, she even laughed at me. Everyone did. Even the clowns.

Terrified, I ran and hid inside a herd of elephants standing off to the side of the circus ring. As the clowns ran off, one of the beasts raised its trunk, heralded its moment, and shat on my head. The crowd in the bleachers broke into applause as I burst into tears. Someone started a chant and then everyone chimed in, *crybaby, waaaaaaaa*. Even Mo.

I looked anxiously at the doctor. "What do you think? Pretty weird, huh? Do you think I'm crazy?"

The doctor leaned back in his chair. Scowling, he tapped his pencil on the tip of his nose and inquired if I had access to my own funds.

Confused, I asked what money had to do with an elephant shitting on my head.

He explained my father hadn't paid his bill. "When I called him about it, he got very defensive." The doctor shook his head. "He demanded to know how much longer this was going to take. When I replied psychoanalysis doesn't work that way, he shouted money doesn't grow on trees either and hung up on me." He tossed the pencil onto his desk and clasped his hands in front of him. "Your father is a very belligerent man."

I numbly stared at the street salt my boots had picked up on the frigid, wind-blown walk over from Sibley Hall. All my life, people had told me how lucky I was to have a father like mine: so kind and gentle and generous. "A real family man," they'd called him. After a while, I just assumed the problem was me. I brought out the devil in my father.

"I believe your parents are trying to interfere with our work together," the doctor intoned. "They are clearly upset about your situation. But I think it goes deeper than that. They're afraid of something." He paused and looked at me intently. "I think they may be mentally ill."

I gripped the arms of my captain's chair. "I'm sorry, what did you just say?"

"I said I think your parents are emotionally disturbed."

I didn't bother asking in what way that was relevant to my "situation," as he'd called it. I didn't even object to his term "mentally ill," a classification the radical British psychiatrist R.D. Laing, whose *The Politics of Experience* I'd just finished reading, had decried as needlessly pejorative. I was too elated. Someone had finally sided with me. A straight man!

He'd even said the problem wasn't me. It was my parents!

That evening, Valerie called to ask if I wanted some really dynamite blotter acid. "Great visuals, very trippy," she gushed. "And only two bucks a hit." I thanked her but begged off by noting my mind was already blown. "Dream therapy," I replied when she asked what I was high on. I advised her I wouldn't be tripping for a while, maybe ever again. Instead, I'd decided to give the shrink a chance. I even said I thought I could trust him. A straight man!

Confused, Valerie asked if I'd changed my mind about a cure. When I assured her I was in therapy to regain the self-confidence I'd lost coming out to my parents, she informed me there was a drug for that too. "Speed," she said, noting she had it in pill form for only fifty cents a pop. "They're called black beauties. You'll never feel more in control. Nobody gets to you on them."

I begged off that offer too, although I left the door open to a possible change of heart. After all, I'd never opened up to a straight man before. And while he hadn't brought up a cure since our first session together, his query about being open to it still haunted me. If it came up again, I told her, she'd be the first to know.

"Cool," she said before acknowledging she'd miss tripping out with me. I was, she acknowledged, a much better head than her straight freak friends. A "real goof," she called our times together.

February 11, 1968

Mom and Dad—

Last night there was a dance with Wilson Pickett and Sam and Dave at Syracuse's War Memorial. A friend of mine, Walter, went up on stage and started dancing while Pickett was singing. It was pretty wild.

I start seeing Dr. Radin twice a week at the beginning of March. I know this is going to be a financial strain. Please sell my stocks.

As for 'miracles,' I don't hold much faith in them. You have got to realize I am not going to change. I know I can achieve a happy life the way I am. My greatest problem right now is to adjust to our altered family situation. Sometimes I wonder if I will make it.

I'm sure the fact of my life has made yours very difficult. Your whole value system runs counter to accepting it. I'm asking that you somehow change....

Sometimes I fear your overpowering morality will destroy me. I've had quite a few dreams to that effect.

The thought of coming home absolutely terrifies me and I become severely depressed. It's very scary and I suppose I am begging for my life. I hope you understand but I doubt that you do.

I'm sorry for this but at least now you aren't in the dark so much.

Love, Dale
P.S. Thanks for the Valentine's Day card. It was very nice.

I dutifully recorded my dreams and recounted as many as I could during my new, "enhanced" twice-weekly schedule with Dr. Radin. And while I remained wary of his intentions, over time I felt increasingly comfortable using our sessions to explore the conflict with my parents, which Radin seemed content to let me focus on. My homosexuality came up, of course, although merely as a fact, never, as I'd initially feared, a disease. After a while, I even started to think I'd won him over—that he'd dropped the notion of a cure in favor of what I'd told him I wanted—the strength to stand up to a hostile world and live my life as I saw fit.

Yes, I was that naive. But Stonewall was, after all, still a year-and-a-half away and I was only eighteen—a virgin to the hateful, anti-gay mindfuck known back then as Freudian psychoanalysis. But there was also something else at play. Radin was the first person in my life who let me open up—to tell my side of the story and explore just how deeply wronged I felt, not by fate or bad luck but by real human beings—my family, my peers, and society-at-large.

Before Radin, I was merely another unhappy homosexual, one among hundreds of thousands. After him, I became something altogether different, seemingly unique, at least to him and me—an angry gay man. Through my time with him, I learned what other rebels—the Black Panthers, Freedom Riders, SDSers, the Viet Cong—already knew. The cure wasn't in the capitulation. It was in the fighting—the doing, not the caving in.

Through Radin, I stopped being a crybaby. In place of my tears, came fury.

"I think you'll like this one. It's fresh. I had it just this morning," I said of my dream. I sighed and shook my head. Since starting my twice-weekly sessions with Dr. Radin, my dreams seemed to have taken on a new intensity. "It even woke me up," I added.

The doctor looked at me blankly, leaned back in his chair and, folding his hands over a barrel chest, instructed me to proceed.

I told him I was sleeping over at Donnie's house, where I'd fled to escape my parents. Donnie, I reminded him, was my first gay friend, the one who'd introduced me to gay life—to pot, drag queens, and words like "wrecked," "tacky," "dish," and "piss-elegant." Thanking him for taking me in, I confessed I finally felt safe. Then, just as Donnie drifted off to sleep, my mother crashed through his bedroom window and came after me with a pair of hedge clippers. I'd awakened screaming.

"Mmmm," the doctor murmured, stifling a yawn. "And what do you think this dream means?"

I said it clearly showed how terrified I was of my parents, especially my mother. "I really do think she's out to get me."

"Hmmm," the doctor purred. He stifled another yawn and closed his eyes. "I believe you've expressed this fear before, no?" Before I could reply, he asked about the hedge clippers. "Where do you think they might have come from?" He adjusted his position in the chair. "First thing that comes to mind. No censoring."

I lit a cigarette and told him about the time my mother had goaded my father into cutting down a backyard forsythia hedge. For years, she'd complained about it, arguing it was a gaudy, unkempt, embarrassing eyesore. However, it wasn't until she was recuperating from a hernia operation that she was able to overcome my father's resistance. "I don't care how damn bad the forsythia looks. Somebody put it there," he'd repeatedly argued. "We should respect that."

I said it was one of the few times I'd sided with my father. "The forsythia was the first thing in all of Liftwood to bloom." Liftwood, I reminded him, was where all the kids my age were girls—my first refuge away from bullies. "I remember once snow was still on the ground." I smiled. "I'd never seen a flower open through snow before."

"Mmmm, yes," the doctor murmured, his eyes still shut. "And how old did you say you were?"

"I didn't," I replied tartly before asking if I was boring him. "You seem to be falling asleep."

He roused himself long enough to remind me the session was about me, not him, and then, settling back into his chair, instructed me to continue.

Guessing I was around ten, I said that, of our yard's many flowering options, the forsythia was my favorite. I acknowledged it was an odd choice. Struggling under the thick shade of a tulip tree and battered by the falling fruit of a nearby apple, its early spring bloom was anemic and its summer greenery spare and sallow. "It never did amount to much," I sighed, smiling warily. "That's what my father says about me too—you know, that I'll never amount to much." I told him that, after a while, the forsythia appeared in one of my dreams. "One I had over and over," I added.

"Mmmmm," Radin murmured sleepily. "Yes, a recurring dream. Very significant."

I described the dream. Crawling around inside the forsythia's tangle, I discovered a rabbit hole that, burrowing under our property line, led to a secret garden with flowers, songbirds and, beside a small pond teaming with koi, a granite bench inscribed with my name. I said it was my favorite dream, one of the few I had where I wasn't chased by demons, incinerated in A-bomb blasts, or laughed at by strangers. "No one was around—just me, the songbirds, and the fish. No bullies beating me up. No father calling me a sissy. No mother trying to appease him by claiming I was going through a phase." I chuckled. "There was even a caterpillar living inside an iris that kept telling me I was beautiful just the way I was."

The doctor emerged from his stupor and smiled vaguely. "You must've been very upset when your father cut the hedge down."

"Horrified," I replied before confessing I could remember even minor details from that day. I recalled it was hot and oppressively humid and my mother sat in a winged-back wicker chair in a robe and a wide-brimmed hat that hid her face, directing my father's every move. At first, he'd gone at his chore hesitantly but when she'd accused him of being a namby-pamby, he'd gotten the hedge clippers from the garage and really lit into it. I'd begged him to stop but my mother kept demanding more and more until nothing was left of the forsythia but stubble. I paused and sighed. "Nothing ever grew there again—not even weeds."

"So, that's where you think the hedge clippers come from?" the doctor asked.

I nodded. "I'd always looked to my mother for support. But that day I saw she was just as scary as my father. If she didn't like something, she went after it tooth and nail."

"Hmmm, interesting," he murmured, pensively stroking his goatee. When I informed him my mother believed Donnie had brainwashed me into being gay, he seemed even more impressed. "Yes, very interesting indeed." He toyed with his pencil as he stared at me and then asked if Donnie and I were lovers. When I assured him we'd never been more than just friends, he leaned back in his chair and coldly eyed me. "What position do you take in bed?"

Stunned, I asked what my sex life had to do with what we'd been discussing but he just smiled and reminded me it was his job to ask the questions. Mine was to answer them as truthfully as I could.

"You mean, am I active or passive?"

He nodded.

Stalling for time, I informed him that in gay life we called the active partner 'butch' and the passive one 'fem.'

"I'm aware," he replied, a bit too archly. "As you know, you're not my only homosexual patient."

"Yes, I remember my mother saying you're a specialist in..." I paused and tried to recall her exact wording. "Oh, yes, I remember now. She said you specialize in treating 'this kind of thing.'" I took a long drag of my Marlboro and smiled. "You know, I prefer the word 'gay,' Doctor. 'Homosexual' sounds, well, I don't know, almost hostile, like it's a disease or something."

His eyes narrowed as he asked me to stick to the question. I was, he said, wasting time.

I didn't bother noting another man had once accused me of the same thing, although then I was supposed to be sucking his cock not analyzing my dreams. Fidgeting with a shirt button, I told him I didn't like talking about what I did in bed, even with other gays. "People cop attitudes. They pigeonhole you."

The doctor persisted. "You still haven't answered my question."

I shook my head and warned him this was a topic we needed to avoid. "It's impossible. Straight men cannot understand gay sex. They just can't."

"But this is important," he said. "We're getting at something here."

I looked at him imploringly. "If I tell you, will you promise not to use it against me?"

"Of course," he murmured, his gaze intensifying. "I'm here for you." A smile crept across his face. "Only you."

I again reminded him of my limits—I did not want to be straight.

He nodded. "So you've said."

"Okay," I replied, "I'm passive." I stubbed my cigarette out in the ashtray on the molded plastic table next to me and re-crossed my legs. "You know…" My face flushed. "A fem."

He squirmed ever so slightly in his chair. "I see," he said over the hissing of its cushion. His eyes narrowed. "Do you think of yourself as a girl?"

I laughed nervously and told him I'd grown up convinced I was the reincarnation of my mother's stillborn twins, Nan and Jane. "I mean, what else was I supposed to think? She bought me dolls to play with, let me wear a tutu and dance 'The Dying Swan' for family get-togethers. She even watched me put on fashion shows with clothes from her closet." I looked up from the carpet, my face still red. "My mother wanted a girl. I was what she got instead."

"So, you blame your mother?"

"You mean for being gay?"

He nodded.

I admitted I wished I could. "Nothing would please me more than to get back at her by saying, look, Mom, this is all your fault. You made me gay. But, no, I don't think my mother's to blame. I don't think anyone is. Like I've said, I've always been like this. It just showed up sooner in me because I had a mother who tolerated my girly ways." I smiled warily. "She protected me."

"But, as you just said, she dressed you in her clothes. She put you in a tutu."

I corrected him. "No, I dressed myself. And I begged and begged for that tutu long before she finally got it for me. Same with the dolls—which, by the way, drove my father insane."

He countered children were like sponges and could not possibly comprehend a parent's subconscious messages. "You have repeatedly said your mother wanted a girl."

"She did. And she almost got one!" I laughed. "What is the saying? Beware of what you ask for; you just might get it? Once she understood the full picture—you know, that sex was involved—she ran for the hills." I turned and stared at his wall of diplomas. "What I blame my mother for is her betrayal. When she realized I wasn't just going through a phase and was never going to be anything more than…" I waved a hand in front of me as if swatting away flies. "A queer…" I paused to compose myself. "She dropped me."

I numbly stared at my shoes. "I don't blame my mother for making me gay. I blame her for turning on me. For making me feel sick and ugly." I paused and glared at him. "For making me go through this."

My chin started to quiver and I grabbed a tissue. "But she's my mother, Doctor." My eyes again welled up. "I need to know she still loves me. I'm not sure I can make it without her."

"Well, you're certainly getting at something very important," he said, pointing at the clock. "Unfortunately, it will have to wait until next session." He glanced at his calendar. "Thursday at three?"

Radin started off our next session by announcing he'd arrived at a diagnosis. He sat stiffly in his chair, his hands folded atop his desk, his eyes fixed on me. He watched me light a cigarette and nodded gravely. "Yes," he intoned, "I've given it much thought. Careful thought." His gaze hardening, he informed me I had what he called a 'castration complex.' "Yes very," he replied when I asked if that was serious. "Unless it's treated, you will be crippled for the rest of your life."

The blood drained from my face. "Crippled?"

He nodded. "You will never have a meaningful, loving relationship. You will forever be alone and unhappy. You will be in constant search for the kind of fleeting, degraded sexual gratification we've discussed."

I objected. "I never once used those words. I simply told you I was passive in bed." I stared out his office window and cursed myself for confiding in him. Like I'd feared, I was paying the price for talking gay sex with a straight man. I asked if his diagnosis was based on my homosexuality or the hatred I'd experienced because of it.

"The former," he replied curtly.

"I see," I said, stunned. "But I've said over and over I don't want to be straight. I've been clear about that since day one."

He countered he was professionally bound to treat the source of my distress. "And that hinges entirely on your sexual choice."

"*Choice*? What choice?!" I cried. "No sane person would ever choose to go through what I have."

"Ah, but that is at the very heart of your perversity." He looked at me coldly. "Your need to be unhappy. To be self-punishing." His gaze softened slightly as he acknowledged the pain I'd endured as a result of my "lifestyle choice" but insisted society had every right to protect itself against what he called "deviance."

Bristling at his use of that word, I changed tack and asked what connection there was between my homosexuality and his diagnosis.

"Oh, yes, it's causative," he intoned. "Every male homosexual I see suffers from it." A castration complex, he explained, was a neurosis caused by a "psychic mutilation" intended to make sons more attractive to their fathers.

"You mean for sex?"

Radin nodded. "Yes, I'm afraid so."

I protested I'd never felt even remotely sexual toward my father, even in a dream. And while I acknowledged I'd once been fascinated by his penis, I insisted that was just childish curiosity. Indeed, I contended the mere thought of having sex with him was repugnant.

The doctor contended the unconscious works in mysterious ways. "Your ego often doesn't know what your id is up to because your superego censors it." The superego and id, he explained, were locked in a never-ending battle for control of the ego.

"Your mother," he said when I asked who'd performed this so-called "psychic mutilation." He said she wanted a surrogate to satisfy my father's sexual needs. "That's why your father hates you. He doesn't want you. He wants your mother." He even said he thought my mother might be a lesbian.

Shaking my head, I stared at one of the masks on the wall behind him. On some South Pacific island it had once cured illnesses and warded off evil spirits while worn by a shaman who most likely lived his life as a woman. I looked at his modern-day stand-in, a psychiatrist, as he slowly rocked in his black leather chair and smugly smiled over the cleverness of his diagnosis. Here, in the soundproofed confines of his chamber, he was master: omniscient and infallible, his every pronouncement beyond dispute; every challenge, "resistance." I wondered how he'd react if I told him his mask's original owner had probably also taken it up the ass. Our only difference was context. In the shaman's world, he could do no wrong. In mine, I could do no right.

I refused to say another word for the rest of our session, although the doctor still professed to be pleased with my progress. "Our work together seems to be going very well," he said after announcing our time was up, although by then I was certain he was talking more about his work than mine. He'd just nailed another homo, his specialty. All I'd done was sit there and once again let someone vomit in front of me. I was furious.

When I got back to Sibley Hall, I immediately called Valerie to see if she still had some acid. I was ready to start tripping again. When she replied she only had black beauties, I said I'd be right over.

We each took one and stayed up all night talking or, as she called it, "speed rapping." As I told her the next morning, before popping another black beauty and heading off to anthropology class, where I hoped to learn more about

Margaret Mead's pioneering work on Polynesian androgyny, I'd never felt so powerful. I even said I thought I could change the shrink's mind about homosexuality. "That motherfucker's going to eat his words," I vowed.

Two sessions later, I asked Radin if we could shift from his focus on my unconscious and talk instead about the day-to-day realities of my life. As I noted, the night before, I'd called home to tell my mother I wasn't ready to face the family and would be staying in Syracuse for spring break. She'd burst into tears and handed the phone to my father who'd told me, in no uncertain terms, that I was to stop upsetting my mother. I either came home or started packing for Vietnam. "There're no ifs, ands, ors, or buts to this, understand?" I'd hung up the phone shaking. I shuddered as my hand struggled to light a cigarette. "See, I'm still trembling." I told him I feared I was on the verge of a nervous breakdown.

Radin agreed. "I've seen it coming for a while. If your parents can't guarantee you peace and quiet, then in my professional capacity I must urge you to stay away from them."

I nearly fell off my chair; no one had ever been so directive about my problems with my parents. "Are you serious, just break ties with them?" When he assured me he was, I spent the rest of our session talking about how terrified I was of my family. Castration, thank God, didn't come up once, but suicide did. I told him killing myself had crossed my mind several times, although I assured him I had no intention of going through with it. "I wouldn't give them the satisfaction."

"Them?" the doctor asked, peering over his bifocals. "You mean your parents?"

"No, I mean all of you. I'm gonna beat you at your game, too, Dr. Radin." I smiled sweetly. "I'm gonna show you gays can be happy too." I also said I wished all of our sessions were like this one. "I don't need a cure, Doctor. I need someone to talk to."

"Mmmm," he murmured. He thumbed through his calendar. "Next Tuesday at noon?"

That evening, Sal, whom I hadn't heard from since he'd disappeared four months earlier, phoned. Having finally found what he called his "groove" in New York City, he said he wanted me to come down for a visit. "Yeah, man, I'm set up in this pad in the East Village. You could crash here with me."

"Wow, the East Village!"

"Yeah, I hooked up with this cat named Otto. Met him in Julius's, a gay bar over in the West Village. He's older and sorta straight. You know, he worries about his career. And keeping up with trends, fashion and shit like that. But he's really sweet." He snickered. "I think he kinda digs me. He's always asking me to read Whitman to him. Says it gives him goose bumps."

We burst into giggles, but Sal turned serious when I informed him that I'd finally followed through on my threats and come out to my parents. When I told him they had retaliated by demanding I see a shrink, he sighed and told me he'd often thought about seeing one but had been afraid of how the "gay thing," as he called it, would be handled. He asked how it was going.

"It's a real rollercoaster but I've made it clear I don't want to be straight." I struggled to clear my throat. "Not sure how much he hears me though. Lately, he's started in on this trip about my mother. Insists she made me gay." I took a deep breath. "Why does someone always have to be blamed?"

Sal chuckled. "That reminds me of some graffiti Otto told me about. Said he saw it in a subway tearoom. Someone had scrawled in black caps: *MY MOTHER MADE ME A HOMOSEXUAL!* Below it, someone had replied in red: *If I buy her the yarn, will she make me one too?*"

We both howled.

When I mentioned the shrink thought I was on the verge of a nervous breakdown, Sal asked if I was still doing drugs. "Lots," I said proudly. When I told him I'd just discovered black beauties, he asked if I could bring some with me when I visited. He admitted he missed the high.

"Yeah," I murmured. "Speed's great. Like being on top of the world." I didn't mention that, without it, my depression sometimes got so bad I barely made it to class, although I did note I was well on my way to flunking out of architecture school.

Sal said it was probably for the best. He never could see me in that line of work. "Talk about straight! Those architects, man, they think they're God."

When he asked what I'd major in next, I replied only half-jokingly, "drugs." I said I'd tried just about everything out there—except for heroin, of course—and still hadn't met my match. "Oh God no," I replied when Sal asked about needles. "They terrify me. I'd never do anything like that."

Sal closed the conversation by noting it seemed like just about everyone in New York was shooting up. "Present company excluded, of course."

"Whitman's Mannahatta!" Sal crowed while fumbling with the police locks to Otto's flat. I looked around me in abject wonder. Walking up the three flights of stairs of his E. 10th Street townhouse, I'd asked Sal over and over if the neighbors knew he and Otto were gay. While he'd assured me they did, I simply could not believe no one cared.

"Oh my God, the place is beautiful!" I gushed after Sal ushered me into a small, sunny living room. "Not at all like the hippie pads you see in Syracuse." The walls were stark white, and the sofa and chairs, chrome and black leather. A vase of white tulips and a brass hookah sat on a glass coffee table shaped like a boomerang, while a *Playbill* for the new Broadway musical, *Hair*, was displayed next to the telephone. "It's Otto's," Sal groaned. "He keeps it there so people'll think he's hip." He sighed and shook his head. Otto, he said, was a tad plastic.

I asked what the grates on the windows were for. "To keep the junkies out," Sal replied. "The West Village has gays, the East, junkies." He rolled his eyes and warned me to watch out for bugs too. Cockroaches were everywhere. The other day he'd found one in his coffee mug.

I pointed to the Aubrey Beardsley print, *The Dream*, over the sofa. "We studied that in drawing class. It's part of his series for Pope's *Rape of the Lock*, which we read in English Lit." Smiling, Sal quoted a verse: *Belinda still her downy pillow pressed/ Her guardian sylph prolonged the balmy rest/ 'Twas he had summoned to her silent bed/ The morning dream that hovered o'er her head.* Pope, he said, was one of his favorite poets.

"And voila!" he cried, pointing out Otto's stereo. "I finally have sounds! It's been since San Francisco. I can't tell you what this has done for my soul." He knelt down and pulled out an album. "Come on, man, sit down," he said, patting the spot on the floor across from him. "I'm dying to play some tunes for you." When, lighting a joint, he asked if I'd heard *Blonde on Blonde*, I shook my head and said I thought only straight people listened to Dylan. Sal groaned and, rolling his eyes like he did when he thought I was being too gay, said he'd play Dylan's vicious songs first. "I know you'll dig them," he murmured, smiling maliciously.

We listened to "Leopard Skin Pillbox Hat," "Just Like a Woman," and "Most Likely You Go Your Way and I Go Mine," all of which were so nasty I said Dylan sounded just like an evil queen. Laughing, Sal acknowledged there were rumors; Dylan, after all, had once hung out at Warhol's Factory. Then, picking up the needle, he said he wanted to play me a more serious song, one he said nearly always blew him away. "It's "Visions of Johanna,"" he said, folding his legs under him like a yogi. "I think you'll dig it too."

Sal was right. Dylan's long, bitter lament so moved me I had him play it two more times. By the third, I was in tears. "I don't know, that line about his visions making everything seem so cruel, it just got to me," I mumbled, trying to explain myself. I apologized for tearing up and admitted I was going through a difficult time. "It's my parents. They're really getting to me. I never should've come out to them. I thought it would clear the air. But it only made things worse."

Sal commented on how much my hand trembled as I reached for the joint.

"Yeah, I thought love would pull us through." I wiped away a tear and shuddered. "My own vision of Johanna, huh?"

That night, Sal took me uptown to check-out the student takeover of Columbia. It was my first time on a subway and my first glimpse of what people were starting to call 'the revolution.' Huddled in front of a campus gate draped in red and black banners, a group of bleary-eyed rebels greeted our arrival by calling us brothers. Giggling shyly, I hid behind Sal as he returned the favor by handing them a joint.

"Thanks, man," a guy with long sexy eyelashes and a full beard said before lighting the joint and passing it on to his comrades. As we sauntered off, they raised their fists and bid us a husky farewell: "Power to the people! All power to all the people!" Feeling only slightly silly, I followed Sal's lead and returned their salute with my own raised fist and a hearty *Right-On!*

On the train back downtown, I asked Sal if he thought the strikers knew we were gay. He replied he didn't know, nor did he think it even mattered. Sometimes, he said, people were just people. When I persisted by asking if the 'all' of the 'all the people' part of their chant was meant to include people like us, he shook his head and said he sometimes felt sorry for me. "Cuz, you have this disease called 'gay on the brain.' You need to get over it. It's uptight, not cool. Nobody cares what you do in bed."

Fearing I'd only prove his point, I didn't bother noting being gay was about more than just what we did in bed. It involved everything: the way we talked, moved our bodies, saw the world, expressed ourselves. I recalled my last session with Dr. Radin and grimaced. Although he'd strenuously disagreed, it even influenced our dreams. Indeed, as I'd noted, I was gay in one way or another in nearly every dream I'd ever had.

Back downtown, Sal took me to a "bourgie" gay bar on West 10th Street called Julius's. He apologized in advance for its buttoned-down vibe but said, after our brush with the revolution up at Columbia, he wasn't in the mood for the drag queens who frequented the Stonewall, the Village's more raucous dancing venue. While I quickly grew bored with Julius's crowd, I nearly lost it when Edward Albee strolled in wearing a leather bomber jacket and quietly stationed himself about fifteen feet away from us. As I explained to Sal, Albee was an icon—one of only a few examples we had of gays who'd come out to the world and not ended up wrecks.

Sal again scoffed that I had gay on the brain, although later, when we got stoned at Otto's listening to the Chambers Brothers' "Time Has Come Today," and I reprieved the line from *Who's Afraid of Virginia Woolf?* over which Donnie, my first gay friend, and I had bonded—*I'm not a monster. I'm not! I'm not!*—Sal at least laughed. It was then I confessed that, while I thought being called "brother" by a bunch of straight revolutionaries up at Columbia had been cool, seeing a real-live, in-the-flesh Edward Albee casually sipping a beer in a Greenwich Village gay bar had blown my mind. "I now know I can make it, too," I said and held up my hand to prove it. "See, it's stopped shaking."

The next afternoon, Sal took me to my first Be-In, a Sheep Meadow gathering of ninety thousand peaceniks where Allen Ginsburg blew into a conch shell, men in saffron robes sang "Hare Krishna," and Coretta Scott King read from her husband's "Ten Commandments on Vietnam." *Thou shalt not believe in a military victory. Thou shalt not believe the generals know best.* Behind us, a group of women bared their breasts while, in front of us, two bearded men in beads burned their draft cards.

From there, Sal took me back downtown to St. Mark's Place, where strung-out runaways in beads and tattered jeans spare-changed outside hip boutiques selling velvet bellbottoms and leather miniskirts at what Sal called rip-off prices. In the middle of the block, a crowd formed outside the Electric Circus for a Velvet Underground concert, while around the corner the Fillmore East announced upcoming performances by psychedelic groups like Jefferson Airplane, Big Brother and the Holding Company, and Moby Grape. Under the marquee advertising the Negro Ensemble Company's latest production, *Song of the Lusitanian Bogey*, a tall, gaunt hippie hawked copies of the *East Village Other*, while across the street, another in a fringed vest offered tabs of Blue Cheer for three bucks a pop. "Best shit in town," he murmured as a crowd quickly formed.

"Well, here we are, freak central!" Sal crowed as we climbed the steps of the tenement building, where his friends, Karen and Murchoch, lived. I gaped at the scene unfolding around us and recalled the night Donnie had called Dominic's Philadelphia neighborhood "gay central." In less than a year, I'd gone from middle-class queens walking their poodles in Rittenhouse Square to strung-out hippies queuing up for LSD on Saint Mark's Place. "Wow" was all I could say.

Struggling over chopsticks, I listened to Sal and his friends debate the blues versus soul; Christ over the Buddha; and Haight Ashbury as opposed to the East Village. They rapped about the ego and id; karma, nirvana and the clear white light; polymorphous perversity; revolutionary violence; the theft that was property; and all types of trips, both good and bad, although when they got to death trips, my head started to spin. There was talk of bonecrushers, needle tracks, cooking up elixirs in a spoon, and speed freaks, who they complained were ruining the scene. When Murdoch said a group called the Diggers had posted flyers on Saint Mark's Place warning speed kills, I glanced guiltily at Sal. That afternoon, after we'd each popped our second black beauty, we'd agreed speed was becoming our favorite high.

Meanwhile, in the front room, where tie-dyed sheets covered both windows, Karen and Murdoch's five-year-old daughter giggled as she smeared globs of Day Glo paint all over her naked body. When, later, she stuck her finger up her vagina and started to masturbate, Karen nodded approvingly. "We want her to feel good about her body," she murmured, smiling first at Sal and then at me. "I mean, sexual guilt is such a mindfuck, don't you agree?" I wanted to jump up and hug her but, fearing I'd appear uncool, I merely nodded and, along with Sal, mumbled a stifled right on.

On Sunday, Sal took me for a stroll through Washington Square, which he called the Village's "heart and soul." On the backs of park benches, smiling hippies with long, stringy hair passed joints to haughty queens with plucked eyebrows and teased-out bouffants. On a milk crate, a dashiki-clad man with an Afro and dark shades denounced the FBI's war on the Black Panthers, while a line of tripping teenyboppers snake-danced through the arch singing "Lucy in the Sky with Diamonds." Next to a gaggle of chess players arguing in Yiddish, a quartet of bare-chested Jamaicans banged on bongos and laughed heartily. Dazzled by the glint of gold in their teeth, I turned to Sal and said I felt suddenly at peace. "Like I'm home."

"Yeah," Sal replied. "If you want to be gay and hip, the Village is where you want to be." He looked around the Square and smiled. "No place like it on earth."

Later, as I waited in line to board my bus back to Syracuse, Sal pulled a paperback from his hip pocket and handed it to me. It was a meditation on apocalypse called *Love's Body* by Norman O. Brown, the classics professor whose *Life Against Death* he'd introduced me to when we'd first met. "Watch out for the shrink, man," he said. "You don't want to end up straight."

"Fat chance of that," I replied, stepping into the bus. I turned back to him and smiled mischievously. "Like you said, I have gay on the brain."

"I'm serious, man," Sal protested. "You gotta be careful. Shrinks work for the 'Man.'"

On the bus ride back to Syracuse, I pondered a string of *Love's Body's* aphorisms. In his tenth chapter "Fire," Brown wrote: *To heal, to cauterize. Therapy as apocalypse, conflagration, error burned up.* And later: *Violent eruption, vulcanism: the patient becomes violent as he wakes up. The madness of the millennium breaks out...* And finally: *The final judgment, the everlasting bonfire, is here. Truth is error burned up...*

I stared out the bus window at the evening sky. A vast, luminous mirror, it was smudged with puffs of dirty-white clouds and glowed around the edges as if lit from inside. As I noticed Venus flickering bravely above the spectacle, I recalled a story entitled "A Baffling Burning Death" that I'd found in *True*, one of the many "men's magazines" I tore through every time I went to the barber, across the street from the donut shop my parents stopped at every Sunday after church. Above the title was a sketch of a man in a suit watching in horror as his dance partner, a pert blonde in a pleated skirt, form-fitting sweater, and pearls, suddenly burst into flames.

She was, the story claimed, a victim of "spontaneous combustion." According to the article, the phenomenon was a medical mystery, affecting all races and creeds and people from all walks of life. Burned to a crisp, they left behind just a trace of ash. With some alarm, the article stated that combustion almost always occurred while dancing.

Oh, how I loved to dance.

Two weeks later, I told Dr. Radin I was starting to feel better—less anxious and fearful and more comfortable being me. As evidence, I told him about the dream I'd had the night before. It was late at night and I was in my father's Corvair, the car in which I'd first had sex with a man, racing it along the tracks of a roller coaster. The car swerved and swooped, rattled, and shook. I rode it up a long, steep slope, my left foot pumping the clutch, my right arm cranking the gear shift. *Come on. Come on, you can do it. Come on, girl!* Slowly, slowly the car chugged up the incline.

I reached the crest. The air was cold and thin. I looked down. The Earth was a mottled blue marble. The car tilted and—*whoosh!*—dropped into a long steep dive. I struggled to control the wheel but the car was going too fast. At the first curve, it careened off the tracks and sailed into the night sky. Caught in an updraft, it floated like a feather, higher and higher.

I turned to Dr. Radin and smiled. "I love that dream. It's the first one I've had in a long time where I felt free." I attributed it to my visit to New York, where I said I finally felt at peace.

Mmmm, he purred and removed his bifocals. "We need to talk. I'm concerned. Very concerned."

I felt the muscles in my neck tighten. We'd spent the previous two sessions arguing—first about drugs, then about Sal and New York. He hadn't approved. He said I shouldn't have gone. He hadn't even been impressed that I'd encountered Edward Albee quietly sipping a beer in a Greenwich Village gay bar. "He's not the kind of man someone in your situation should be looking up to," he'd clucked.

Radin's eyes hardened. "I'm concerned you're becoming a confirmed homosexual." Folding his hands across the top of his desk, he leaned forward in his chair. "You're at a very precarious moment in your treatment. I think we need to spend more time together."

My back stiffened. "Oh?"

"Yes, I suggest three, maybe four times a week. Homosexuality, you know, is a serious mental illness. In your case, it's quite clear. You're the product of an overbearing mother and a distant father."

I froze. It was virtually a direct quote from Dr. Irving Bieber, the nemesis from *Life*'s 1964 exposé, "Homosexuality in America." "But we've been through this. I thought I'd made it clear. I do not want to be straight. I thought I could trust you."

He looked at me sternly. "As my patient, I have an obligation to be truthful with you. I must warn you life will be harsh if you persist in this lifestyle." He demanded I relent. "You're still young. I can cure you but you must commit yourself fully to my care."

"*What*?!" I shrieked. "Look, I've been sexually active since I was sixteen. I hang out in gay bars. My closest friends are gay. I *like* being gay." I shook my head and stared out the window. The Norway maples outside his office were ablaze with chartreuse buds. A band of hippies played frisbee in the park across the street. "No," I said, folding my arms across my chest. I looked him in the eye and repeated myself, "no, no, no."

He smiled and, glancing at his watch, said our time was up. "We'll talk more about this on Friday."

"We'll see about that," I hissed and stormed out of his office.

After that, I simply stopped cooperating. For our next four sessions, whenever Radin inquired about my dreams, I told him I hadn't had any. When he asked about my parents, I simply stared stonily ahead, as I did when he inquired about my drug use, my failing grades, or my sex life. For fifty interminably long minutes, I sat in the captain's chair facing him, glaring at the photos of his wife and two sons, and saying absolutely nothing.

When I arrived, I refused to return his greeting and, when I left, I simply stormed out. What I wanted to do was tell him to fuck off but, fearing my parents would retaliate by pulling me out of college, I didn't dare. To keep my draft deferment, the shrink had to be the one who called it quits, not the patient.

At the start of our fifth session, he finally gave me what I wanted. "There's no point in continuing," he murmured as he pierced me with a dark, foreboding stare. "I suggest we terminate."

I wanted to leap up and cheer but instead I merely thanked him. "It's been quite a strain. Fifty minutes is a long time to say nothing."

He nodded and congratulated me on my willpower. "It's impressive, although I must admit I wish you had applied it in a more constructive manner."

I reminded him I'd never agreed to a cure. "You've played games with me, Doctor. I trusted you."

Fondling a freshly sharpened pencil, he leaned back in his chair and asked what I planned to do next.

I told him I hoped to move to New York for the summer. "I may just stay there. I don't know. I need to get away from my parents."

"I think that's a very good idea," he replied before informing me of their last conversation. When he'd told them his intervention had failed and I remained what he called "hopelessly resistant," my mother had burst into tears. When he'd suggested they instead try to accept me as I was, my father had exploded and accused him of siding with me. When he'd offered them the name of a

Wilmington psychiatrist to help them adjust to what he called their "new reality," my father had snarled that he was the man of the house and he'd decide whose reality they lived by. Then, he slammed down the phone. Shaking his head, he said my father had even called him a dirty Jew bastard. "Several hundred dollars," he said when I asked how much my father owed him. "But I doubt I'll ever see it."

I looked at him and shook my head. "Never in my wildest dreams..." I stopped to catch my breath. "They're out of their minds." I glanced at the doctor.

He nodded. "I believe you are correct."

My face flushed bright red. "I won't let them get me. I won't." I bit my lip and cleared my throat. "I'm going to wipe the slate clean." I recalled the quote from *Love's Body—truth was error burned up* – and felt my jaws clench. "I'm going to burn every trace of them out of me."

The doctor's eyes narrowed as he asked if I was referring to drugs.

"Yes," I snarled. "Lots of them. I'm going to become their worst nightmare." I paused for emphasis. "A hippie faggot freak."

His chair swung forward. "I must warn you. Drugs will only make matters worse."

"Worse than what?" I cried. "This?" I stiffened my back and glared at him. "You want to know something, Doctor? No one who takes drugs has once told me I need to be straight. Not one. And you want to know something else? When I'm high, I feel whole. You make me feel sick."

"You are," he replied. "You're going to be unhappy as long as you persist in this choice."

"Here we go again," I sighed and slowly rose from my chair. I strode up to his desk and, breaching the so-called "therapeutic distance" he'd demanded of me, leaned over his stacks of manuscripts and looked him directly in the eye. I told him I really didn't care what he or my parents or *Life* magazine or the books in the library my mother had researched or even God, whoever or whatever the fuck that was, thought about what I was, or what I should or shouldn't be doing about it. I no longer even cared what other gay people thought, not Donnie or Dominic or, God knows, that band of gargoyles in the Continental Room. I wanted out. Of it, them, everything. From there on out, I was calling the shots. I stood up straight and told him I hoped he'd try to understand his other gay patients better. "No one deserves this shit," I spat.

He smirked and leaned so far back in his chair it almost tipped over. As I walked to the door and turned to mutter a terse goodbye, he peered at me over his bifocals. "Good luck, son," he murmured.

I didn't bother telling him I didn't want or need his luck nor did I, as I thought for a moment I might, rip his door off its hinges. Instead, I just nodded and walked out.

In the small, windowless anteroom outside his office, his next patient, a scrawny-looking guy about my age with beady eyes and a sweaty demeanor sat in the corner, nervously petting a plucked plastic chicken. Locking eyes with him, I instantly knew he was the sick, guilt-ridden homosexual I'd be if I'd done as I was told or, as the doctor had put it, committed myself fully to his care. Shuddering, I rushed outside and, savoring my victory, took a long walk on my way back to Sibley Hall. The disease Sal had called "gay on the brain" had ended up my salvation. I'd done it. I'd survived the 'Man.'

I danced a little jig and gave myself one of those 'power salutes' the rebels at Columbia had introduced me to. "Hopelessly resistant," Radin had even called me.

That night, Valerie and I celebrated my new-found freedom with psilocybin and hashish. When I asked if her invitation to live with her in the East Village for the summer was still good, she assured me it was, although she warned me that, during my hiatus with the shrink, she'd only gotten more deeply involved with drugs. I'd have to commit to being what she called a "full-time" head. "We'll smoke dope every day and do acid three or four times a week. Speed too. I hear everyone's doing it in New York." She giggled. "We'll be so cool everyone will want to hang out with us."

"Far out," I murmured as the walls of her pad swayed to the Jefferson Airplane's "Comin' Back to Me." My parents' worst nightmare, a hippie faggot freak, was about to be make his official debut.

May 1, 1968

Mom and Dad—,

I really want to be living in New York this summer. I know I have to earn some money for next year at school but please don't expect me to live my whole life for college. If you think Syracuse costs too much, I will transfer after next year.

I am not ready to come home for a whole summer. Although you may think I am feeling sorry for myself, this semester has been very rough on me and a lot of people and things and situations I have depended on have collapsed. I really have been miserable.

I hope you aren't being blinded by one thing about me.

Love, Dale

My mother called as soon as she got the letter. She informed me that, under no circumstances, was I to spend a summer in New York. When I demanded a reason why, she said I'd get involved with what she called the "wrong types." When I asked her to name one, she handed the phone to my father.

"Look, we're not taking any more guff about this," he growled. "You're upsetting your mother. You're coming home for the summer and that's that. If not, you can plan on being drafted and shipped off to Vietnam. Does that get through that thick numbskull of yours?"

I hung up and fired off an outraged response: *All right. All right. One more disappointment doesn't mean a thing to me anymore. My life's becoming one long string of them. Pick me up on the 21st at Sibley. My last exam is the 20th.*

The night of the 19th, Valerie and I split a hit of windowpane acid. The next day, she moved to the East Village and I flunked my last two architectural finals.

On the drive back to Wilmington, my mother turned to me in the backseat of the Olds and announced she'd landed me a job working the grounds at Hagley Museum, the sprawling estate along the banks of the Brandywine River that commemorated the founding of E.I. DuPont de Nemours and Company. Claiming the competition had been fierce, she described it as a "real coup."

My father suggested it might be the start of something bigger. "If you mind your p's and q's," he said, peering at me through the car's rearview mirror, "you might even move up to a job with the Company."

Fiddling with the Olds' rear door latch, I stared into a forest of larch off to the side of the Interstate. While student revolutionaries were taking over the streets of Paris and throngs of dissidents were demanding "socialism with a human face" in Prague, I was heading back to suburban Wilmington to cut grass. Even the word 'gay' would be verboten.

I quietly pushed down on the handle and opened the door just a crack. I slid over to the edge of the seat. Gravel, possum guts, crushed soda cans, tiny shards of glass, and the blown-out remains of a tire whizzed by. Air fired by the car's roaring engine, its spinning tires and the sizzling asphalt scorched my face.

I needed water. I was on fire.

11
The Mass Production of Gunpowder

I stared into Hagley's murky canal and imagined myself floating face down, like Ophelia. The previous night, I'd watched in horror as my idol, Bobby Kennedy, had been shot and killed on TV only minutes after winning California's Democratic Presidential primary. His assassin, Sirhan Sirhan, a Palestinian allegedly protesting the sale of US bombers to Israel, said he'd been brainwashed by unknown conspirators. He couldn't even remember pulling the trigger.

Two days earlier, another icon, Andy Warhol, had been shot at point-blank range and lay near death in a New York hospital. Caught hours later, the shooter, Valerie Solanas, a deranged lesbian and Factory hanger-on, had said she'd done it on behalf of the Society for Cutting-Up Men or SCUM, whose manifesto she'd written. Like Kennedy's assassin, she'd also alleged she was the victim of a conspiracy. However, unlike Sirhan, she knew exactly who the culprit was—her victim, Andy Warhol. She'd said he'd stolen her play, *Up Your Ass*, and intended to make off with its royalties.

Two months earlier, yet another hero, Martin Luther King, had been killed after leading a strike of Memphis sanitation workers. On the eve of his death, he'd said to the strikers: "Up to now, only garbage men have been feeling the pain. Now we must redistribute the pain."

Apparently, others agreed. Outraged by his killing, Blacks rose up across the country and burned dozens of inner cities, including Wilmington's. In retaliation, Delaware's Republican Governor called out the National Guard with orders to shoot to kill. On Market Street, machine-gun-toting soldiers in camouflage and gunmetal gray Jeeps replaced tight-jeaned men in fluffy sweaters and tennis shoes cruising for sex. Two blocks east, bulldozers were already busy razing the ghetto where the rebellion had broken out.

Ten miles north, in the lily-white suburbs my parents called home, life went on as usual. The shopping centers were full and the beauty parlors busy, while golfers at the all-white DuPont Country Club continued to call their caddies, all Black, "boys." At home, oblivious to King's call for redistributive justice, Jeff, the family dog, still went berserk every time the garbage men, also all Black, appeared.

The lawnmower Hagley had assigned me idled quietly by my side. Behind me, the ruins of a stone shed hugged the banks of the boulder-strewn Brandywine River. On the other side of the canal, a blue-haired docent explained the shed's design to a jitney full of tourists. "It's almost two hundred years old so you can see it was built to last. Three of its walls were constructed of stones hauled from the river. The other was made of wood." She smiled vaguely. "It no longer survives."

A woman holding a squirming child asked if they could walk around. The guide shook her head and told her the museum's grounds were off-limits; once a child had fallen into the canal and nearly drowned. A friend of my mother's, the docent noticed me standing a few yards away and waved. Fidgeting with my lawnmower, I pretended not to see her.

"Besides," she said, glancing anxiously at her watch, "we're behind schedule." By this, she meant my mother, the docent for the one-room building at the end of the road, had been kept waiting. Recently restored to its condition the day General Henry DuPont had died in 1889, the office was my mother's favorite place at Hagley. Ruthlessly ambitious, the General had plotted the Powder Trust that had transformed DuPont, flush with profits from the Civil War, into the nation's first manufacturing giant, an industrial monopoly.

"Also please note," the guide said, pointing over my head, "the single plane of the shed's roof. It slopes steeply from its peak on the wall facing the canal down to the river. Eleuthere Irenee, DuPont's founder, devised this design after coming here from France."

She acknowledged a question from her audience. "Yes, that's right. The DuPonts were Protestants, what they called in France 'Huguenots.' Like so many others, they had to flee religious persecution for the freedoms we enjoy. The DuPont family has always felt a deep debt of gratitude to this great country of ours."

She asked how many people had seen the dioramas in the museum's main hall. "Good," she smiled, surveying a sea of hands. "Then you know that DuPont gunpowder was fired from American guns in our war against the Barbary pirates." Tousling a boy's curly red locks, she asked if he'd rather be a pirate or a cowboy. He giggled and shyly buried his head in his mother's shoulder. "That was our country's first naval victory," she announced, her voice full of pride.

"But," she went on, moving in closer as a baby's wails threatened to drown her out, "the manufacture of gunpowder was very dangerous. Explosions were common." She paused and stared admiringly at a large diamond in her wedding ring while she waited for the baby to quiet down. "Many people were killed. As a result, gunpowder was only made in very small, out-of-the-way places. The supply was limited. This, of course, made the waging of wars difficult."

The crowd tittered.

She nodded and smiled knowingly. "Mr. DuPont's design solved this problem. Hemmed in by thick stone walls, the force of the explosion would be directed by the roof out over the river. The other sheds were safe. And, for the first time in history, gunpowder could be safely mass-produced."

I was in the belly of the beast, the birthplace of the military-industrial-complex, the engine fueling the Vietnam War and the occupation of scores of inner cities across the country. I stared at the sun and fluttered my eyes in hopes of inducing an acid flashback. "DuPont is like one big happy family," my father had gushed on the eve of my first day behind Hagley's lawnmowers. "You play your cards right, it'll take care of you for the rest of your life." At the start of my second week, a co-worker had told me over lunch that he and his buddies from the grounds crew had started to talk. "We've noticed that curl over your right ear. You a kike?"

I'd wanted to say yes, if only to fuck with their bigoted little minds but, afraid of what they'd do in return, I mumbled a cowardly no and trudged off to eat my sandwich alone under a stand of ancient oaks. After that, I kept to myself, speaking mostly just to my mother, who'd been a Hagley docent for over a year. She'd failed the qualifying test twice, but my father had pulled strings and finally gotten her the position, her first job in over thirty years.

Unlike my mother, an empty-nester thrilled to finally be doing something outside the home, I was miserable at Hagley, a fish out of water. I was a skinny, nineteen-year-old, bookish, long-haired hippie on a crew of beer-bellied, middle-aged, working-class yahoos. When I'd stupidly revealed I supported Bobby Kennedy for president, they'd asked why I hated America so much. The Kennedys, they said, were a bunch of dirty Reds. They even said JFK got what he deserved. In their minds, Lee Harvey Oswald was a hero.

I was terrified my co-workers would ask about girlfriends, certain that if they suspected I was gay, I'd be a goner. Indeed, violence lurked in the background of nearly all of their grievances. When they called Hagley's docents a bunch of rich bitches who needed to be taken into one of Eleuthere Irenee's sheds and shown who the real bosses were, I was so afraid they'd find out my mother was one, I told her to ignore me while at work. I refused to even enter the pump house, where our lockers were located, mostly because of the nude girlie calendar I was expected to ogle every time I ventured in. When one of them noticed I was reading Eldridge Cleaver's *Soul on Ice*, he asked if I was a nigger-lover like that fag Gore Vidal, whom he'd seen a few nights earlier on *Jack Paar*. After that, I spent my lunch hours alone on the banks of the Brandywine, getting high on pot and reading books—*The Communist Manifesto*, Marcuse's *Eros and Civilization* (no, I couldn't finish it), Richard Wright's *Black Boy*, John Rechy's *Numbers*, Tom Wolfe's *Kandy-Kolored Tangerine Flaked Streamline Baby*—all of which I'd covered in brown wrapping paper.

And now Bobby Kennedy, the underdog's friend—the man who used Black Panthers as bodyguards, had marched with Cesar Chavez and his striking farm workers, and chanted Om with the gay poet Allen Ginsberg—was dead. Murdered. While I was beside myself with grief, my co-workers had arrived at work rejoicing. Finally, we were rid of the Red menace. Like his brother before him—and, of course, Martin Luther King too—Bobby had gotten just what he deserved.

It was almost as bad at home, although at least there no one called me a kike or asked about girlfriends. My brother, who railed about the Kennedys even more than the Hagley crew, had joined the John Birch Society and, in anticipation of an impending class war, purchased a gun in case of trouble. "Hell, if I'm gonna let a bunch of Commies roll over me," he'd snarled. As he noted, unlike me, he'd much rather be dead than Red.

My parents also loathed Bobby Kennedy, although they were much more appalled by his support of the "Coloreds" than his alleged ties to Reds. When my mother heard he'd met with welfare rights leaders in New York, she went apoplectic. "Why, those people eat better than we do," she cried before launching into a tirade about the "girl"—her term for grown Black women—in line ahead of her at the A&P. "I couldn't believe it. Her cart was full of London broil, shrimp, and cocktail sauce." She said the woman had paid for it all with food stamps and then carted the haul off to a Cadillac where her "pimp" had helped her put it in the trunk. "And where," her voice rising, "did she get the money for that car?" As she'd bitterly noted, we couldn't afford anything fancier than an Oldsmobile.

I hadn't bothered asking how old or beaten up the woman's Cadillac was, nor had I wasted my breath noting the usurious loans that ghetto car dealers extended to people like her. Nor did I mention the reparations plan I'd concocted one night while high on hashish—one in which Blacks would be given brand-new cars, paid for by our tax dollars, while whites would be forced to give theirs up and ride the bus, where they'd be required to sit in the back—although I was sure a comeuppance like that would do my mother a world of good. After all, it had certainly opened up my eyes. Indeed, once I'd come out, I saw people in an entirely different light. Those I'd formerly considered "our kind"—the respectable, law-abiding, God-fearing, white bread, family types I'd grown up with—were now enemies while those I'd been raised to fear—Blacks and other dark-skinned people as well as the prostitutes, drug addicts, and bums "our kind" called trash—were now allies.

Even Donnie and Dominic had ended up foes. One night when my parents went out and I snuck up to Philadelphia to see them—my mother had forbidden all contact—Dominic instantly lit into me about my appearance, complaining my second-hand clothes were better suited on a bum, while my hair made me look like a drag queen. Later, when I told him I'd visited the East Village and dropped acid with my college friend Valerie and two of her neighbors, he exploded. It didn't matter that one of them, Gino, had starred opposite Edie Sedgwick in an early Andy Warhol film or that his girlfriend, Sandrine, was a chic Carnaby Street fashion designer visiting from London. All that mattered was that I'd taken LSD, called myself a freak and, worse, looked like one too.

Once again, Dominic accused me of being a traitor to my own kind and threatened to never speak to me again. That time, sick of his hectoring, I said fine, I'd had it with him too and stormed out. That night, I realized there were two kinds of gay men: mine—the restless, risk-everything, in-your-face, Janis Joplin kind—and Dominic and Donnie's—the safe, go-along-to-get-along, Judy Garland kind. We never spoke again.

Alone, isolated, and depressed, I feared I wouldn't make it through an entire summer in Wilmington. And so, when, two days after Bobby's assassination, Syracuse notified me that my transfer from Architecture to Liberal Arts had been approved on the condition that I do six weeks of summer school, I was elated. That was six weeks less of my family, the grounds crew at Hagley, and the whole fucking smug, straight, uptight suburban thing that made my head want to explode like it was one of Eleuthere Irenee's gunpowder sheds.

Draped in black bunting, the funeral train slowed as it entered Wilmington's decrepit train station. Inside the last car lay the corpse of Bobby Kennedy, on his way from New York to Washington, where he was to be buried next to his brother, the former president, in Arlington National Cemetery. I'd gone to pay my respects not just to the man but also to my own dashed hopes for a peaceful redress of grievances. After Martin Luther King and Bobby, the only way out was through fire. Revolution and riot. *Burn, baby, burn.*

Clumps of mourners were scattered about the platform. Next to me, a group of older Black women in feathered hats rocked on scuffed heels and, moaning, dabbed their eyes with starched hankies. Standing at the edge of the platform, a half-dozen grizzled veterans, all white, clutched olive-green caps to breasts laden with medals. At the far end, standing outside the rotting canopy in the sunshine, a mixed band of hippies in beads and rawhide sandals flashed peace signs and quietly sang the Beatles song "Hello Goodbye." Behind me, by the piss-stained stairs leading down to a street littered with empty nips and broken beer bottles, a dozen stern, dark-skinned men stood stiffly at attention, their Afros neatly tucked into somber black berets. As the train rumbled past, they raised their fists and chanted in unison, "Right on, Brother Bobby."

The train returned their tribute with a long mournful whistle. Turning a sharp corner on its way south, it slowed and let out a plume of black smoke that lingered on the horizon. Under its cloud, we shuffled aimlessly about until, one by one, we each departed. Outside, on a street corner, the Panthers regrouped and chanted slogans until a Jeep with a mounted machine gun arrived and two National Guardsmen, both white, ordered them to disperse.

"Was it fun?" my mother asked when I returned home from paying homage to my last hope for America. She noted my astonishment and sighed. "No, seriously, did you have a good time?"

"It was a funeral train, Mother. For another leader gunned down in cold blood. One I happened to admire..." I stopped and glared at her. What did it take to get through to her?

"Well, I just thought..." she said and shrugged. As she resumed chopping celery, her charm bracelet clanged loudly against the edge of the kitchen counter. She wore a red and white checked apron, and her hair, sprayed into a stiff helmet, was dyed a hideous orange. When I'd asked what was wrong with her natural color, she'd gotten instantly defensive. "What?" she'd cried, "I've done that wrong too?" On her feet were the same red leather slippers with gold arabesques she'd worn the day I'd told her I was gay.

Panting at her side, Jeff wagged his tail in anticipation of a handout. "Go on, now, boy," she demanded as they did a little dance on her way to the refrigerator. "You're in the way. I'm not giving you a thing."

"It's all over now, Mother," I muttered, corralling the dog. "Nothing's ever going to change."

"Oh, you don't mean that. You're just upset," she murmured as she started dicing carrots. "It's never too late to change." She looked across the room at me and frowned slightly. "I mean, take your hair. Why don't you let me trim it? Just an inch or so, I promise."

I shook my head. "No, I'm giving up, Mother. It's kaput, finished." I stared at the yellow ruffled curtains obscuring a view of the house next door and imagined Carrcroft engulfed in flames. I smiled wanly. "I'm not playing this game anymore."

"Game?" she asked. "What game?"

"I mean this, the silence, the guilt and shame, the obsession with respectability, Carrcroft, all of it."

"Well, young man, you certainly seem to have done alright by everything, if I do say so myself." She wiped her hands on a dish towel and grimaced. "When have you ever lacked anything?"

"Mother, please, can we just this once forget about material things?" I reached down to pet Jeff. "Yes, I'm privileged."

She nodded. "You should be more grateful. You're a very blessed young man. I just don't understand why you can't see that."

"Yes, mother, you're correct. I'm selfish and self-centered. I can't see beyond the end of my own nose."

She tossed her dish towel onto the counter and smiled as if I was complaining about the weather or the lack of a party to go to that night. "I'm sure you'll feel better after dinner. I'm making one of your favorite meals—home-made vegetable soup with cornbread." Next to the oven was the cast-iron mold that shaped the cornbread into miniature ears of corn. As a child, I'd been so enchanted by it I'd asked her to leave it to me in her will. Now, I wanted nothing from her but to be cut loose.

"I think I'll pass," I mumbled, turning to head up to my bedroom. "I'm too upset to eat."

"But I've been slaving over this meal all day. I've made it just for you." Her jaw stiffened and her eyes welled up with tears. "I wanted to do something nice for you. To make you feel better."

"Mother, can't you see I'm beyond all that?" I felt myself start to tremble. "I feel like a wave has crashed over me and I can't get back up." I clenched my teeth. "I'm miserable. I have been for a while. Can't, just this once, we talk about what it feels like to be me?"

My mother grimaced like I'd just slapped her. "Well, Mister, let me tell you something. You certainly don't have a monopoly on misery, that's for sure. I can't tell you how many nights I've cried myself to sleep over what you're putting this family through."

"Putting *you* through?!" I cried.

"That's what I said," she retorted. "You need to start thinking of someone other than yourself for a change. And let me tell you something else, young man. When I call you for dinner, I want you down here with a smile on your face, a demeanor that says you're a part of this family and a healthy, respectful appetite, do you understand?" She glared at me. "Enough of this feeling sorry for yourself. It's time you stood up straight and faced things like a man."

Suppressing a scream, I ran up the stairs and threw myself across my bed. My chest was tight. I couldn't breathe. I felt like I was suffocating.

The next weekend, my parents flew to Myrtle Beach for four days of golf and cocktails, while I drove my father's Corvair up to the East Village for air. There, I picked up the trio I'd tripped out with earlier that summer—Valerie, my friend from SU, and her upstairs neighbors, the former Warhol protégé, Gino, and his fashion designer girlfriend, Sandrine—and drove them down to Longwood Gardens, a former DuPont estate on the outskirts of Wilmington whose Beaux-Arts excesses I'd promised would be the perfect setting for an LSD trip.

They were psyched—as much by the prospect of blowing uptight suburban minds as sampling the special stash of Purple Haze Gino had brought along. A "guerrilla attack," I'd called our caper, and, always up for a goof, the three had done themselves up in their freakiest finery. In cowboy boots and a fringed vest over a tight bra-less t-shirt and a pair of frayed denim hot pants, Valerie was the most cartoonish—a take-off on R. Crumb's bodacious, blissed-out *Zap Comix* slum-goddesses. Sandrine, on the other hand, fresh off a month-long Dexedrine diet, was thin as a rail, pale and, in a tie-died tunic, sandals and wide-brimmed hat with a red cabbage rose, the epitome of Carnaby Street chic.

But it was Gino who was the real stand-out. With a thick mane of straight, shoulder-length, dirty-blond hair and dressed in a white linen Nehru shirt, beads, and loose-fitting red, green, and gold-striped pants, he could have been mistaken for a rock star. Instead, he was a debauched, tripped-out, aspiring composer on the Moog synthesizer who paid for his drugs by modeling—a chiseled, high cheek-boned, pouty-lipped glamour-puss who turned heads even in the East Village. From a distance, you couldn't tell what he was—boy, girl or, more likely, something in-between.

Dressed much more sedately in a t-shirt and shorts, I was anointed the day's "trip guide" and, after we got off on Gino's Purple Haze, I took them on a tour of my favorite Longwood spots. I led them to a lake where swans drifted among waterlily pads so huge Gino was sure we could dance on them, through a forest teaming with bamboo, up a hillside covered in blooming rhododendron and onto a long greensward lined with tulip poplars so tall they had to be supported by guide wires. From there, I led them to a field glittering with wildflowers and, looping back through a grove of dogwood, let them loose in a topiary of giant birds and towering beasts.

Blitzed out on Purple Haze, they wondered if the creatures were real. *Yes, more than anything*, I replied, certain I'd never been higher. Squealing with delight, they ran onto a carriage path and pointed to a towering glass enclosure. "What's that?" they cried. "A spaceship?"

"No," I whispered, "it's the Grand Conservatory." I smiled. "Inside is the whole, entire world."

Their eyes got as big as saucers. "Oh, show us, please," they begged. "*Please*!"

"Come," I said, leading the way. Inside, I led them across a desert, through a jungle, up a mountain and over a plain, through a thicket of oranges, past walls of ferns and carpets of moss, to a mirrored banquet hall of parquet floors and velvet drapes where the DuPonts had once toasted their family's triumphs—the take-over of General Motors; the invention of nylon; and the production of plutonium. There, we hailed the light streaming from our pores, the wisdom of the air, and the hilarity of our flesh and, with purloined orchids tucked behind our ears, danced to music only our feet could hear. At one point, we even talked in tongues, although we knew exactly what each other was saying.

I took them back outside and led them by the hand down a grand staircase to a vast formal water garden. I told them that, every Thursday night, its fountains, lit in the colors of the rainbow, danced to the command of a huge underground organ. Pulling them in close, I whispered that all of it—the electric pumps, the colored lights, the tiled pools, the urns, the statues and friezes, the pleached and pollarded trees, and even the organ, second only in grandeur to the one at Wanamaker's in Philadelphia, the one where my mother and I rendezvoused after our annual Christmas shopping sprees—was borne of Pierre Samuel DuPont's grief over the death of his chauffeur, Lewes Mason, in the flu epidemic of 1918.

You mean he was gay? they gasped.

"Yes," I whispered, "but what does it matter?" And then we all burst into hysterical, gut-splitting laughter.

My voice trembling, I told them we were now the fountains, the flowers, and the trees. I said that, like the couple in *Last Year at Marienbad*, we too had to break free of symmetry and order, reason and perspective, and rekindle a love we may have only imagined. Sandrine squealed with delight and Gino clapped. Valerie, brimming with pride, noted she was the one who'd first turned me on. "What a great trip guide!" they cried in unison. I beamed, certain I could never be anything better.

And then, gathering us under an espaliered sycamore, Gino handed us each another tab of Purple Haze. Again, we put it on the tips of our tongues and waited until the sun swelled into a fireball. When the sky melted into a swirl of mercury and the grass under us hummed in a chord no one knew, they looked at me and pled: *Oh please, show us more, Master Trip Guide. More! More!*

I led them up another grand staircase to a long, ornate arcade overlooking the fountains. It was there where I professed, amidst the potted palms and ancient ferns growing out of sculpted clam shells, that Longwood's legion of fairies and elves held their nocturnal balls. At that, they cheered and started dancing until, pointing at the two burly security guards who were descending the stairs on the opposite side of the water garden, I suggested we cool it. I recalled the time Gino had taken off his shirt. As I'd noted then, it was against the rules. "Somebody must've complained," I whispered.

"What are rules to people like us?" Gino scoffed, ignoring the security guards' approach.

I reminded him we weren't in the East Village anymore. "This is Delaware. The South. Rules matter down here."

Gino again scoffed. Location, he charged, was merely a state of mind. "An illusion."

I pointed at the black leather trip pouch he carried around his waist and asked if his stash of Purple Haze was also an illusion. As I noted, if busted, we'd all be locked up for years.

At that, a look of terror swept across Sandrine's face. She pointed into a nearby tree at what she insisted was a camera and started to tremble. "They're going to do horrible things to us, aren't they?" She nodded at me and turned suddenly ashen. "Like he said, it's the South. The *American* South." Running for the cover of an archway, she cowered behind the fronds of a giant fern and pointed up at the sky. "Why is it so dark? What have they done to the sun?"

Rushing to her, we trundled her out of the park as the two security guards, their walkie-talkies squawking madly, followed twenty paces behind. We tried to be as nonchalant as possible, given we were tripping on two hits of Purple Haze and facing possible prison time, but, at one point, when Sandrine started to scream, Gino had to put his hand over her mouth. When we finally made it back to my mother's Olds, our nerves were shot and our trip ruined, but at least we hadn't been busted. "Some guerilla attack, huh?" I grumbled. Once again, Wilmington had won out; the only minds we'd blown that day were our own.

By the time we made it back to my parents' house, all any of us wanted was to come down. And while I volunteered the contents of my parents' liquor cabinet, Gino pulled a syringe from his trip pouch and suggested instead a "poke" of Seconal. "Just to take the edge off things," he said, smiling alluringly.

Although I begged off, I watched his every move as he slipped the needle first into the taut pink flesh of Sandrine's ass and next into Valerie's fat, puckered behind. Then, bending over the same toilet to which my mother had fled the day I'd told her I was gay, Gino poked himself in his own firm, round buttock. "There," he murmured, while cleaning out the syringe in her bathroom sink, "all done." I nodded and smiled warily, certain I'd finally found an outrage worthy of my mother's vomit.

Sandrine instantly passed out, but Gino and Valerie quickly resumed the silly banter of our trip's brimming start. Although I tried to get them to talk about the tumult engulfing us—Warhol's shooting, Kennedy and King's assassinations, Tet, the Cultural Revolution, the uprisings in Paris, Detroit, and Prague—but they refused to indulge me. Assassinations, riots, and war, they insisted, were the province of bores. For Valerie, the daughter of a St. Louis real-estate tycoon, and Gino, a promising young composer on the Moog synthesizer, only the moment was real. Loaded with opportunities, one from money, the other, talent, they were gladly, giddily throwing their lives away for drugs.

When my parents returned from their South Carolina golf trip, my mother confronted me about what I'd been up to while they were away. She said the neighbors had complained about "weird types" wandering about and she'd noticed that their bed looked like it had been slept in. "Did you have strangers in our house?"

For once, I told her the truth, although I didn't need to say I'd actually driven Valerie and the others down from New York. My father had already figured that out when he realized I'd burned out the Corvair's clutch. Nor did I mention that drugs were involved, although my mother suspected from the number of spent matches in the fireplace that something was up.

What everyone agreed on was that I'd crossed a line, although only I understood exactly how far I was prepared to go. LSD was no longer freaky enough. I needed bigger guns. The next time I saw Gino, I was going to have him give me a poke too.

I never got a chance to make good on my resolve. At the start of July, Valerie wrote to say she'd left New York. She'd contracted hepatitis from one of Gino's pokes and after he'd refused to help with her medical bills, she'd packed up and gone home to St. Louis. She ended her letter by saying she regretted the way things had ended. Gino was by far the coolest guy she'd ever known. She even called him a soulmate. She doubted, though, they'd ever see each other again.

Two weeks later, I returned to Syracuse for the start of summer school, the precondition for my switch to liberal arts. While I'd finally put architecture behind me, I was still dragging around the baggage from the rest of my life: my fury over my mother's rejection, my parents' refusal to utter the word 'gay,' the shambles my coming out had made of our family.

I knew I needed to make a clean break but I was paralyzed with fear: afraid of the draft, of being shipped off to Vietnam, of further ripping apart the family, of hearing one more time of how I was breaking my mother's heart. Instead, I told myself things would work out: my mother would eventually come around; another Bobby Kennedy or Martin Luther King would emerge to lead us to the Promised Land; love would conquer all. The middle-class dream still beckoned. Stay the course, it urged. It doesn't matter who you sleep with; the world is your oyster. All will be well.

Vulcan had not come knocking, demanding his due. Fire had not yet consumed me.

12
Click

Furry and with little in the way of muscle tone, Ben lacked the rugged good looks I usually fell for, although his "Art Garfunkel," as he called the wiry brown frizz that set him apart from everyone else in the Continental Room, drew me in. He felt the same way about my hair—long, wispy and, except for that curl over my right ear, straight as an arrow—what he called a "WASP look." And so, within a week of meeting each other, we were what we called "going steady," by which we meant we no longer had to hang out at the Continental Room, cruising for tricks and putting up with Karl's insults, both of which we found degrading. We also balled multiple times a day, almost always in the suburban split-level Ben had the run of while his parents summered in the Adirondacks, although he also liked doing it at the drive-in, in the back seat of his parents' brand-new Chrysler Imperial.

As Ben noted, he liked his sex "transgressive," by which he meant done in venues traditionally reserved for straights. At home, he always wanted to do it in his parents' bed, which I thought creepy but he, a turn-on. He also liked what he called "kink," which he thought decadent, but which I found mostly just silly, especially the time he wanted to get done up in leather and have his way with me while I was tied to his parents' headboard.

A self-described neurotic, Ben also used sex to manage his many panic attacks. These came on with little notice and were seemingly randomly provoked, although protests—he'd had to flee his one and only anti-war march; drugs—he couldn't even tolerate marijuana highs; and antisemitism—he hadn't been able to hold down a job since a co-worker on one of his father's construction crews called him a kike—were frequently mentioned culprits. But guilt was his biggest bugaboo; anything that made him feel bad about himself was guaranteed to bring on an attack. As a result, Ben was a chronic masturbator, beating off multiple times a day, sometimes even right after sex. "Guilt-ridden," he called himself.

Ben tried to blame his guilt on being Jewish but when I insisted Protestants were equally hard on themselves, he acknowledged guilt was universal.

"Existential," he called it—like accommodating the needs of other people, another social expectation he had difficulty with, guilt was the price we paid for being human.

Curiously, given the times—and in striking contrast with nearly everyone else I'd run across—Ben felt not one iota of guilt over being gay. Indeed, citing the work of Evelyn Hooker, a trailblazing American psychologist I'd never heard of, he was the first gay man I knew who insisted homosexuality was as natural as heterosexuality. He even said shrinks like Dr. Radin who peddled so-called cures were quacks. No one I knew had ever gone quite that far and sometimes I'd ask him to tell me again what he thought of Radin just so I could hear him say that word 'quack' again: *Quack, quack, quack, quack.*

Even better, Ben the first gay man I knew who refused to be in the closet. He was out to everyone he knew, even his parents. He even wanted me to meet them when they returned from the Adirondacks, although I had to decline his offer. As I noted, the family I had was already more than I could handle; another one, I feared, would send me right over the edge.

Home from his junior year at SUNY Binghamton where he was studying French and European literature, Ben was also the first gay man since Sal with whom I could have a serious conversation. At one point, he even said he liked me for my mind almost as much as my body, although, except for the importance of coming out, the quackery of various cures, and the vacuity of gay bar life, we rarely agreed on anything. We argued incessantly.

It was almost as if Ben and I came from different planets. He dismissed the counterculture as anti-intellectual; I found it liberating. He prided himself on being strictly highbrow; I was an unapologetic magpie. He sought transcendence through art; I, drugs. He thought radicals prosaic; I, heroic. He was chronically ambivalent; I, impudently brash. His favorite book was Goethe's *The Sorrows of Young Werther*, which he called the neurotic's bible; mine was *Love's Body*, which I called a revolutionary manual.

Like Sal, Ben made a point of turning me on to the writers he loved. Baudelaire, Kafka, and Sartre were highlights but Jean Genet, the French novelist and petty criminal *Time* had once dismissed as a "practicing pervert," was the real mindblower. In Genet's world, everything was sexual but nothing neurotic. In fact, the more sexually debased his characters got, the more transcendent they became. Through Genet, I could inhabit a world that, while utterly perverse, was also unabashedly, even lyrically gay. When Ben and I caught a rare screening of his homoerotic short, *Un Chant D'Amour*, at SU's Film Club, I was sure I never needed to see another movie.

Of course, I did; film was one of the few things Ben and I saw eye to eye on. At SU's Film Club, we also saw Cocteau's *Beauty and the Beast*, Fellini's *Nights of Cabiria*, Buñuel's *Land Without Bread,* and Joseph Losey's *The Servant*. We even caught the local premieres of Bergman's *Hour of the Wolf*, a film so psychically fraught we both had to resort to the round-the-clock, drapes-drawn escapes Ben called "sleep cures," and Paul Newman's directorial debut, *Rachel, Rachel*, a film in which Estelle Parsons plays a closet lesbian secretly in love with a spinster schoolteacher played by Joanne Woodward. Although Ben dismissed it as prosaic, I thought it significant—the first film I'd seen in which the gay character didn't end up dead, suicidal, locked-up or otherwise ruined after being outed. She just kept on living.

In late August, Ben had me over to watch the TV coverage of the Democratic Party's 1968 Chicago convention. I brought hash and he raided his parent's liquor cabinet for a bottle of Mogen David, which he called fine wine. I had no idea. I'd never drunk wine before, just beer and Sloe Gin. I thought we were being fancy.

That night, we watched the police brutally attack the thousands of anti-war protesters who'd massed outside Chicago's convention hall. They waded into crowds who were chanting, "The whole world is watching!" and, in full view of TV cameras, billy-clubbed everyone in sight: protesters, journalists, innocent bystanders, even children and the elderly. We watched as a panicked crowd crashed through a plate glass window to escape the melee, only to have the police chase after them, clubs swinging. Then, inside the convention hall, we watched Chicago's Mayor Daley shout obscenities at Abraham Ribicoff, the Senator from New York, as he nominated George McGovern, the peace candidate, for president.

It was such a repulsive spectacle we both ended up getting sick, although for Ben that meant another panic attack. My reaction was more physical. After chugging Mogen David and puffing on a hash pipe all night, I simply let loose and vomited all over one of his mother's prized Persian rugs, after which I passed out and Ben had to carry me to the bathtub, where I spent the night.

Ben said he found what he called my "sensitivity" touching but I sensed his ardor cooling after that night. He called less often and when we did get together, we mostly just cuddled or took the day-long "sleep cures" he resorted to when trying to avoid something painful. We also started arguing about current events, culminating in a big blow-up over the "women's lib" protests outside the Miss America Pageant in Atlantic City that September. He called the women who tossed girdles, bras, and various beauty products into trash barrels they'd renamed "freedom cans" silly. I, on the other hand, praised them as radicals challenging their "oppression," a word Ben deemed "prosaic." By the next morning, when he'd split for Binghamton for his last year of college and I'd moved into a new dorm for the start of my sophomore year as a Syracuse liberal arts major, we were barely speaking. Then, a week later, he broke up with me after I said I'd loved Stanley Kubrick's *2001: A Space Odyssey*, whose local premiere I'd gone down to Binghamton to see with him.

He explained it wasn't so much because he'd hated the film's New Age pretensions as it was our minds worked on different levels. He was an intellectual and, well, he couldn't quite figure out what to call me. When I guessed "prosaic," a word he tossed around much too promiscuously, he accused me of sounding bitter. Knowing I'd only confirm his assessment, I didn't bother telling him to go fuck himself, although I did at least refuse to do what he asked, which was to forgive him for the breakup. As Ben had repeatedly noted, guilt provoked panic attacks and he needed to know I didn't harbor any grudges. That, I said before catching a bus back to Syracuse, was one thing I couldn't promise.

Afterward, I pretended I didn't care what Ben thought about my intellectual capabilities but, in truth, his dismissal had cut deeply into my rapidly depleting reserves of self-confidence. And so, although I was doing well enough in my literature courses to think I might have a future in academia, I decided to forego a career and focus all my energies on drugs. Like Genet, I was going to find my way up by going down, as far down as I could go. I was going to break rules for a living—be a hippie faggot freak, everyone's worst nightmare.

In late October, I took a week off from Syracuse and returned home to be the best man for my brother's wedding. I thought I was an odd choice—with ten years between us, Dean and I were hardly close—although I sensed he was doing what he could to patch things up between my parents and me. In return, I'd agreed to trim my hair and, as my mother had said, behave myself, by which she'd meant act like I was normal—or, as she preferred to call it, a part of the family.

It was a tall order. I hadn't been home since I'd left for summer school and, in the interim, tensions between my mother and I had grown to a fever pitch. So had my drug-taking. The day I arrived, my mother found a baggie of marijuana in a pocket of my Red Army coat and demanded I flush it down the toilet. While she wasn't looking, I filled another baggie with oregano and, waving it in her face, asked if she wanted to witness its disposal. Shaking her head, she said she couldn't. It made her want to vomit.

We'd developed an elaborate code to express our rage. "Vomit" was my mother's synonym for homosexuality. It was also her code for drugs, long hair, and secondhand clothes. Such economy was not merely a measure of her fury. Almost overnight, I'd exploded into someone she no longer knew—a long-haired, pot-smoking, directionless, street-urchin queer.

I got a perverse rush each time I heard her use that word, 'vomit.' It hardened me. I heard it and ran deeper into the arms of a vengeful rebelliousness. I heard it and went deliriously, uncontrollably mad.

From Syracuse, I'd scared her with dark, foreboding letters. *My English course is my favorite... The books are very depressing and their moods always seem to rub off on me. I just finished one about a girl who freaks out and kills herself. I went into the depths of depression. It's really strange. I don't identify with the characters; it's just that the books make everything seem so hopeless and messed up that it is just sometimes too much.*

She'd written back, urging me to resume therapy, her code for seeking a cure. I'd responded indignantly. *As far as I am concerned, there are worse things than neuroses—or for that matter, insanity.* "Neurosis" was my concession to her demand for discretion, an encoded response to her "vomit"—my way of informing her that, no, I still didn't care how sick she thought me, I was staying gay.

"Insanity" was my euphemism for drugs. In another long rambling letter, I'd dropped even bolder hints. *I wrote Dean and Kathi. I started to write about 5 a.m. (my hours are very strange up here). I didn't finish until noon.* "Strange hours" was code for the uppers, mostly black beauties, that I ravenously popped. They made me feel powerful and in control of things. I had no idea that was a sham. I was too scared. In the same letter, I'd hinted at even this. *After all that work, I chickened out and never sent it. It was very personal.* "Personal" was my code for the demons that had started to devour me, the desire for revenge that was taking over my life.

After that, no rebellion was too petty or trite to rub in my mother's face. I'd written saying I'd joined the Peace and Freedom Party and was supporting Eldridge Cleaver, a Black Panther, for president. Later, I'd told them I'd switched loyalties to the Yippies' pig. Another time, I'd written I'd gone vegetarian and was living off seaweed and brown rice. That was an outright lie, intended merely to explain the weight I'd lost from popping black beauties.

In two other letters, I'd been more straightforward. In one, I'd told them I'd gone to New York for a peace march; in the other, for a screening of Godard's *Weekend,* a "cathartic" film about a gang of murderous hippies who terrorize a traffic jam of bourgeois family-types on their way to weekend homes. I hadn't needed to say I'd also gone to Julius's, the Greenwich Village gay bar where I again saw Edward Albee, or the Garrick Theater, where I saw Andy Warhol's *Flesh*, over which Sal and I had bitterly fought. He'd said it was a mindless rip-off in which nothing happened, and I'd insisted it was a breakthrough, the first film to show gays as we actually were—not as freaks, but as ordinary, everyday people. "New York," code for "confirmed homosexuals," was more than sufficient to get my point across. It told my mother that no, I'd live my life as I wanted, with the people I chose for friends—*gay* people.

At the close of another letter, I'd sneered I'd heard a rumor. *Perhaps you can confirm it. Is it true Nixon is Rosemary's Baby?* An ardent supporter, my mother even had a Nixon for President charm bracelet. In another letter, I'd called her a racist. Responding to her tale of my brother's emergency appendectomy, I'd written: *It sounds like the whole mess was pretty harrowing—especially when you thought a Negro was going to operate on Dean. How horrible... I am sure it was a relief to know the surgeon was Puerto Rican—shades of color make such a difference in matters like that. His lighter skin made him so much more qualified and expert.*

For once, my father ignored my taunts. He sent no letters, only my monthly allowance stuffed into a white security envelope. As the home fires he'd stoked raged out of control, he simply watched from the sidelines as his wife and second son ate each other alive.

"I don't understand," I started out, staring out the passenger window of my mother's Olds. We were heading down Marsh Road to the shopping mall off Governor Printz Boulevard, with its acres of free parking and its own security patrol. My mother wanted nylons; I wanted truth. "Surely, you've always known," I said as we passed a boulder-strewn park where she and I had once gone for picnics—just me, Jeff, my girlfriends, and her.

My mother's brow furrowed as if to warn me: don't go there, Dale. On the radio, James Brown sang, "Say It Loud: I'm Black and I'm Proud."

"Look, we have to talk about this," I persisted.

She flicked off the radio and glowered at the road ahead.

I felt my face flush and swallowed hard. "What about those times you watched me dress up in clothes from your closet?"

She turned to me and hissed she'd never, ever seen me in her clothes. "How could you even say such a thing?"

"What, you think I'd invent something like that?"

She swerved onto the road's shoulder and headed for a tree. I grabbed the wheel. *Mother!!*

"Yes," she shrieked, slamming on the brakes. "That's exactly what I think. You're so sick you can't tell fact from fiction any better than you can right from wrong. You need help, young man. You're mentally ill."

Stunned, I stared at her and numbly noted the escalation in her rhetoric. "Are you threatening me, Mother?"

She leaned in closer, her face a wild contortion of fear and fury. "Consider it a warning. If you ever say anything like that again..." Her jaw tightened and her eyes narrowed. "To anyone..." Her back stiffened. "Do you understand?"

I tried to reason with her. "This is not about blame, Mother. Can't we just talk?" I paused to gather my thoughts. "Rationally?"

She'd have none of it. "I'll have you locked up, that's what. Put away." As she noted, I was only nineteen. She could do anything she wanted with me.

I laughed nervously. I'd never seen her like this, even that horrible afternoon when I'd told her I was gay.

"Think I'm joking around, buster?" she asked before outlining the scenario for me. "I'll say you've been seduced with drugs and brainwashed into thinking you're one of them." She paused for emphasis. "*A pervert.*" She then proceeded to describe her next steps. "I'll tell them I tried rescuing you but you were too far gone." She smirked. "Content with what you are," she sneered, the tell-tale sign of what she called "true madness." She even promised, if need be, to call on Dr. Radin, who'd confirm I required far more aggressive treatment than what he'd been able to offer. And, just in case that wasn't enough, she'd pull out my letters—saved, she said, for just such a moment—that showed I'd even been contemplating suicide. "Shall I go on?" she snarled.

Reeling, I searched for a trace of softness in her face but found only fury: Jeff going after the garbage men. "You wouldn't," I stammered.

Her jaw stiffened. "Just try me, young man. Just try me."

"Ouch," I muttered and yanked my hand away from the hem of the drapes I'd been nervously fondling. Moments earlier, my mother had called me into the den saying she had something she wanted to discuss. "Something important," she'd added ominously. Her tone had been cold and flat, her expression severe. I glanced at my thumb; it was red and throbbing. "Jeez, that hurts."

"What's the matter?" my mother asked, looking up from her needlepoint. "Got stuck again?" She sucked on the end of a string of white yarn and shrugged. "Serves you right. You should've known better." She pulled the string through the head of her needle.

She was right. I never learned. I kept going back, as if the fabric's taming was merely a matter of persistence. "It's fiberglass," my mother had warned the first time I'd been stuck. "Hurts, huh? I did it yesterday. Took me hours to get all the shards out." She'd explained the drapes were my father's idea. "A safety feature. He says fiberglass doesn't burn. It just melts."

In their bedroom, on my mother's sewing cabinet, my father proudly displayed a small plaque that read *Think Safety*. It was an award he'd received for a perfect safety record at Carneys Point, the DuPont explosives plant he helped manage in the marshlands of southern New Jersey. At home, things had been different. I was an explosion that wouldn't stop.

My mother squinted at her needlepoint through flared, silver-framed glasses. In their corners, a cluster of rhinestones sparkled brightly. Turning to the side window, she stared at the fiery red leaves of a crepe myrtle and sighed it'd soon be cold. "I'll miss it when it goes," she sighed. "The light, I mean." Winters, she confessed, were becoming hard. In a year, she'd be sixty—time, she said, a bit too bitterly, for life to be getting easier.

She shoved the needle through a canvas square with a sterling silver thimble. A long thread spun out of a skein of yarn nestled at her side. She let the needle drop. As it dangled perilously close to her nylon, she gently smoothed out a tiny ripple in the square. She cocked her head and quietly surveyed her work. Against a partially completed field of pale white, a large blue flower rose out of a nest of bright green leaves. She smiled. Blue was her favorite color.

She counted the rows to go; she was almost done. The last time we'd had it out—the time I'd come out to her—she'd just completed the flower's outline. Eight years earlier, when she'd started the project, she'd sighed I'd be off on my own by the time she finished the set.

I'd laughed. Back then, the notion of us parting ways had seemed unthinkable. Now, I wished we'd never met.

Year after year, she'd worked on her needlepoint. She'd labored over it during summer car trips to calm her nerves over my father's driving and on week nights when she couldn't sleep. But her favorite time to stitch was on Sunday afternoons, when the house was quiet and she could gather her thoughts after another round of shouting at the supper table. She'd completed one seat cover a year. Soon, the last would be done. Eight, she sighed: one for each member of the family and four more—two for each of her sons' wives and the others for her first two grandkids. Once, she'd fretted the arrangement wouldn't be fair to me. Given our age gap, Dean's kids would probably be the ones to sit with the grown-ups. Mine, she'd have to put at a card table in the living room.

She suddenly frowned. I'd killed that dream too.

Following her instructions, I sat on the edge of the recliner next to the window—the same one where, ten months earlier, I'd listened as my brother assured me the shock of my coming out would eventually blow over. "Everything will be fine," he'd promised. "You'll see." He'd lied. Nothing had been right since. But the worst had been with her. My mother would not budge. I'd become a horror she simply would not abide.

Piercing her canvas with another thrust of her needle, my mother asked me to promise her something.

"Yes?" I replied, digging my fingernails into the recliner's plush dark blue Naugahyde.

"I don't want to hear anything more about that," she said sternly. I understood her clearly. "That" was more code for my homosexuality, the times I'd dressed up in her clothes and danced 'The Dying Swan' in the tutu she'd purchased for me. It was also code for me; she wanted to hear no more about me.

"About yesterday," my mother said, continuing her needlepoint. She stopped and reached for her cigarette—she'd recently switched from Newports to Virginia Slims—in the large ceramic ashtray on the Parsons table to her right. Beside it, atop a stack of that week's periodicals, was the latest issue of *Ladies' Home Journal*, open to an article on twenty of the newest hairdos. She blew a thick cloud of smoke at the overhead lamp and reiterated she had no intention of putting up with any more of my hateful lies or crazy, made-up stories. If I chose to live in the gutter that was my business but she refused to let me drag her down into it with me.

After all, she had a reputation to uphold. People looked up to her. She was the leader of her church group, president of the bridge club, a docent at Hagley Museum, Winterthur too. "None of that is to be talked about again," she instructed. She patted the edge of her needlepoint and looked coolly at me. "Am I making myself clear?"

I again reached for the hem of the drape but stopped mid-air. As she said, some things were just meant to be painful. This was one. I clenched my teeth and, staring stonily at her needlework, mumbled yes, she was clear; I'd never mention any of "that" again, although what I really meant was that I'd never be myself around her again, never try to talk things through. From that moment on, we'd be strangers. I looked up and glared at her. I asked if that was all.

She stared at her lap and nodded. She bit her lower lip and pulled from her skirt pocket a crumpled Kleenex. She blew her nose and returned my stare. Her eyes swam with tears.

I pushed off from the recliner and slowly walked out of the room. My legs wobbled slightly. In my ears, I heard a buzzing, like the lonely, late-night moan of a TV test pattern or the far-off wail of an air-raid siren, angry and wild with hysteria.

My mother and I didn't speak again until the next morning when she dropped me off at the bus station for my return to Syracuse. And even then, all we exchanged was a clipped goodbye and a half-hearted kiss on the cheek. "Don't forget to write," she said bitterly, almost as an afterthought, just before I slammed the passenger door of her Olds.

After that, my letters home assumed an off-hand, perfunctory air. I said little about what was going on with me and focused almost entirely on my studies, which despite my escalating drug use, went well, and the weather, which, given I was in Syracuse, always offered something to complain about. Otherwise, I became an empty shell to which she could continue to profess the maternal love expected of her but which demanded nothing more than material support: meals, clean clothes, and access to a car when home and well-wishes on holidays and birthdays when not. In all respects but one—my hair, which I let grow back after my brother's wedding—we dropped the code we'd used to dance around my gayness. For my mother, "long, straggly hair" continued to be a stand-in for homosexuality, although to me it simply meant fuck you.

Meanwhile, my rage, deprived of an outlet, turned inward, festering into a toxic brew of despair and self-destruction. I became consumed with the need for revenge. As with Genet, who I'd turned to with a frightful intensity, I would turn defeat into glory, pity into valor: *Eyes blackened by fists are the pimp's shame but of them Darling says: "My two bouquets of violets."*

My first bouquet of violets appeared in the guise of sex. I'd been back in Syracuse a week and, bored, left the Sunday tea dance that a new gay bar around the corner from the Continental Room had organized to drum up business. He appeared in his car shortly thereafter and, although he didn't seem to recognize me, I knew who he was as soon as he signaled his interest. He was the guy in the red Corvette I'd taken to Larry's dorm room a year before and, in a prideful outburst, walked out on because he wouldn't kiss me.

I'd told myself then that I was too good for the fag cocksucker routine he peddled. A year later, I wasn't so sure what I was too good for. After all, my own mother had spurned me. And as even the regulars in the Continental Room had noted, one had to be pretty bad for something like that. Even someone as nelly as Paul claimed his mother as his best friend, although, when pressed, he had to admit he'd never tested her by actually coming out to her. That, he said, he'd leave up to crazy-ass honkies like me. He and his mom had their hands full just being Black.

That time, the man drove a silver Cadillac rather than a red Corvette and called himself Paul, not Joe or, as he'd told Larry, Jack. As before, he was big and strong with a sweet, sexy smile and thick, curly hair swept back from his forehead, although he wore a polo shirt with an upturned color rather than a torn, sweat-stained tee. That time, no one was around to shove me forward or offer me their room, although he again stroked his crotch to entice me. As before, he asked if I wanted to go for a ride. Unlike before, I didn't bother saying I'd prefer somewhere we could spread out. Instead, I just smiled and said sure, why not.

We headed out of town on East Genesee. As before, one of his hands held the steering wheel while the other kneaded his crotch. Unlike before, I didn't hesitate or try to make small talk. I just reached over and groped him. As before, he spread his legs but that time he ordered me to get down and suck on it. "Yeah, man, that's right," he said in the same sexy baritone as before. "Right here in the car."

As I scrunched down on the floor and slid over next to him, he waved at two young women passing us. He even called them "foxes." I didn't bother saying if he'd wanted a woman so much, he should've gotten one; he was certainly sexy enough. Instead, I just unzipped his jeans and, encountering no underwear, swallowed him whole. He sighed and held my head while he slowly fucked my mouth. I tingled as I controlled my gag reflex. My head banged against the steering wheel. *Thud! Thud!*

That time, it was his turn to say he wanted to spread out and, after a few minutes, he turned onto a dirt road and drove to the edge of a deserted gravel pit. "Follow me," he grumbled, opening the driver's door without bothering to zip up. It was warm for November and the sun was still bright and, although I saw there was nowhere to run, I wasn't concerned. Unlike before, I had no intention of feigning pride. That time, I was going to finish him off.

He walked to the front of his Caddie and hoisted himself onto its hood. The pink satin of his shaft bobbed in the afternoon light. Staring at it, he smiled admiringly and then ordered me back to work.

I did as I was told. I sucked and sucked until my jaws ached and my throat was raw. His thighs tensed, his breath quickened and his bark—*yeah, faggot, that's it, suck on that cock*—grew labored. But when he came, he uttered not a sound—not a groan, a moan, not even a short perfunctory ugh. He just shot his wad. I could've been anyone. Or no one at all.

He quickly zipped himself up and slid off the hood. On the drive back to town, I knew better than to try to make conversation and instead tried to cough up the sticky glob of jizz stuck in my craw. Larry had been right. Joe, Jack, Paul, or whoever the fuck he was, had come buckets. I'd nearly drowned on the stuff.

When I returned to the Continental Room a few nights later, Randy told me about a man who regularly stopped by his house on his way home from work. He was wildly handsome, with a strong, hairy chest and brown curly hair brushed back from his forehead. Each time, he'd sit in a chair, spread his legs and wait for Randy to drop to all fours and crawl to him.

Randy said he loved it. It was the best sex he'd ever had, although he confessed the man never touched him. No messy emotions; no talk; just a big, fat dick and plump, hairy balls to suck on until he thought he couldn't suck anymore. When I asked what the man's name was, Randy just shrugged. "Tom, Dick, Harry, what do I care?" He moaned and lewdly licked his lips. As Larry also had, he noted the guy came buckets.

I recalled the guy's insult the night I'd walked out on him—that sucking cock was the only thing a faggot was good for—and warily glanced around the bar. The dance floor was crowded with queens, screaming and strutting their stuff to Aretha's "Chain of Fools." On the sidelines, a half-circle of butches held themselves stiffly in check and anxiously sized each other up. In the front room, a line of old men slumped over the bar, glumly staring into amber-colored drinks. By the window, our man stood a head above all the rest and arrogantly swigged a beer. Framed in a halo of orange neon, he stared at the clock, supremely indifferent to the stir he was causing. A "real man," he could have whomever he wanted, or no one at all.

When Randy spotted him, he acknowledged he was the guy. And although I didn't let on I knew him too, I did quietly try to get his attention. However, the one time he glanced my way and looked right through me, it wasn't his indifference that upset me; it was my disappointment. I'd actually wanted more of his contempt. Maybe like Randy, he'd even make me crawl on all fours just for the honor of pleasing him—as he'd said, the only thing a faggot was good for.

That night was the second time in my life I cried myself to sleep over sex. The first time I'd been thirteen and I'd freaked out over a fantasy of kissing a man. The second, I was nineteen and I'd fantasized about not being worth even that. I tried telling myself the intervening years had been tough—a "rude awakening," as my father would've said. After all, who could have possibly gone through what I had unscathed? Besides, wasn't every gay man in some way damaged goods? I mean, how could we not be?

After my encounter with the guy in the Cadillac, it occurred to me I needed professional help. But after Dr. Radin, I knew that was impossible. Help for people like me simply didn't exist—at least in the way we needed it. What was available was an array of interventions so abhorrent—electroshock, lobotomy, castration, aversion therapy, solitary confinement—as to constitute real torture. No one in their right mind would put themselves through that.

What was left was self-help. And by late 1968, at least among people my age, that meant drugs, lots of them. I would let them take over and, as in *Love's Body*, burn my error up. I even imagined they'd so frighten my mother she'd change her tune, although I knew that was pure fantasy. Being gay was too sinful, too ruinous for a reputation like hers. No, my mother would never come around.

I'd gambled she loved me more than her status as a respectable middle-class lady and lost. Now, I just needed to live with the consequences, although every time I got close to acceptance, my inner crybaby started wailing *no! no! no!* while the rebel inside me demanded I dig in and fight harder. "Give it right back to her!" he'd chant until all sympathy was squashed and, consumed by bloodlust, I got even higher still.

"I thought I might find you here," Ben smiled as I stood in a line outside a theater on East Genesee Street where Timothy Leary, the psychedelic guru, was scheduled to speak. He said he'd come up from Binghamton in hopes of seeing me. "Can we talk?"

I asked what he wanted to talk about.

"I made a mistake. I miss you."

I told him I had a ticket for Leary's lecture and wanted to hear what he had to say. Rumor had it he was starting to talk revolution, a topic I was beginning to think a lot about too. I laughed when Ben asked if I was still doing drugs. "Is the Pope Catholic?"

He asked if we could get together after the lecture. "You know, maybe go to my parents' place. They're out of town." He leered at me. "Or maybe the drive-in. I have their car."

I shook my head. I had no desire to ball Ben. He was the past: weak, neurotic, ambivalent—an "aesthete." What I wanted was a warrior: strong, self-confident, and fighting mad. "Sorry," I replied.

He pointed to the marquee. "'Death of the Mind,' is that really what Leary's lecturing on?"

I nodded and smiled cattily. "What's the matter, a bit too prosaic for you?"

He grimaced and accused me of sounding bitter.

"No," I replied. "Just straightforward. We're on different wavelengths, Ben." I shuffled forward as the line started to move and noted he wanted to be an avant-garde poet living in a Parisian garret, while I wanted to be a hippie faggot freak holed up in an East Village tenement. "You want to make a name for yourself. I want to fight back."

"Look, I'm sorry if I hurt you."

I told him not to worry about it. The break-up cleared up a lot of illusions. I understood my trajectory much better now. I told him I was seriously thinking about dropping out. "No, out of everything," I said when Ben asked if I meant just school.

He asked what I intended to do about the draft.

I shrugged and confessed I had no idea. "I just know I can't keep this up."

He said he couldn't see me in the jungles of Vietnam.

"Neither can I. But I can't take my family much longer either." I shook my head. "It just keeps getting worse and worse."

"Still your mother?" he asked.

I nodded sullenly. "Yup, still her."

He looked at me sadly and shivered against a blast of cold air. "So, I guess this is goodbye then..."

I nodded. "Yeah, I guess it is," I replied and turned to enter the theater. I stopped at the doors and looked back at him. Our farewell felt oddly momentous, as if I was saying goodbye to more than just Ben. He smiled, blew me a kiss, and then disappeared up East Genesee.

Blue, green, and red nebulae swirled on the scrim behind him. Dressed in white linen, Timothy Leary sported a daisy over his left ear. Smiling impishly from the podium, he peered at the crowd through granny glasses shaped like half-moons. Shaggy gray hair fell to just above his shoulders. "Better living through chemistry," he shouted into the microphone and thrust a V into the air like a tripped-out Nixon. The crowd roared.

"It is no coincidence," he intoned, holding up a sugar cube meant to symbolize LSD, "that this was invented in the same decade as the atomic bomb." The crowd murmured. He announced we were on the cusp of a vast evolutionary leap forward. He smiled and said a universal dream-state of peace, love, and happiness was within our reach. "Millions have taken LSD. The psychedelic battle is won!" Waves of applause washed over him.

He frowned. "I look around me and all I see is metal. All my cells hate metal. I see the pollution of the air and the poisoning of the rivers and the concrete over the earth and I say, baby, it's time to mutate."

A man at the end of my row tossed rose petals into the air. A woman across the aisle shot up from her seat and danced like a whirling Dervish. The man in front of her chanted Om.

Leary popped the sugar cube into his mouth. The scrim behind him pulsed with color. Squatting on the floor next to him, a man in a white turban strummed a sitar. Leary leaned into the microphone. "You must run away! Be freaks! Flip out!" He smiled and flashed a peace sign. "Turn on! Tune in! Drop out!" His fingers collapsed into a clenched fist with which he pummeled the air.

We rose to our feet and chanted: *Turn On! Tune In! Freak Out!* Leary beamed.

That night, back in my dorm room, I popped a black beauty and re-read Brown's *Life Against Death*. At the start of his last chapter, entitled "The Way Out," he quoted Henry Miller: *The cultural era is past. ... Man will be forced to realize that power must be kept open, fluid and free. His aim will be not to possess power but to radiate it.*

I popped another beauty and, glowed, baby, glowed.

On my third black beauty, I smoked a pack of Camels and re-read Genet's *Our Lady of the Flowers*. Demented, I told myself I was the dead Divine, "from head to foot, forever a ship breaking up ice-flows, motionless and rigid, drifting toward infinity." Finally, I was there, fierceness personified.

On my fourth, I fractured into a thousand parts, a collage of tumult and trauma. I was the carving knife Arnold used to shred his red silk kimono, the revolver in my father's dresser drawer, the syringe Gino used to bring himself down from a bum trip. I was the black eye that Mary, the Continental Room's barmaid, sported—a gift of love from her cretin husband, Karl, the bartender. I was the pool of piss she had to stand in to fill his ice bucket.

I was the blow job I gave the guy in the Cadillac. I was Randy crawling on all fours to please him. I was Larry blowing kisses to a dorm full of haters. I was the typewriter he left me, the cab that whisked him away.

I was a Betsy Wetsy doll, a pink tutu, an aquamarine bracelet. I was my mother demanding to know who'd been rummaging through her jewelry box. I was the girdle and bra she had no idea I'd also worn.

I was a rampaging hippie-terrorist in Godard's *Weekend*; a tripped-out jet-setter in Antonioni's *Blow Up*; the couple in Resnais's *Last Year at Marienbad* who could never connect. I was the painter beset by demons in Bergman's *Hour of the Wolf;* Severine fantasizing her own rape in Buñuel's *Belle de Jour;* Clay, the hapless victim of Lula's predations in Leroi Jones' *Dutchman*. I was Odetta singing "Sometimes I Feel Like a Motherless Child" in Pasolini's *Gospel According to St. Matthew*.

I was a painting by Francis Bacon, a photo by Diane Arbus, a poem by Sylvia Plath. I was the man in the Beatles' song who blew his mind out in a car. I was a mourner saluting Bobby Kennedy's funeral train, a rioter avenging the assassination of Martin Luther King.

I was a Buddhist monk dousing himself with gasoline on a Saigon street. I was Elisabet in Bergman's *Persona*, watching him incinerate on TV. I was her nurse, Alma, leaving a shard of glass for her to step on. I was the film ripping apart inside the projector when she did.

I was Eldridge Cleaver, the Yippie pig, Allen Ginsberg chanting Om at a Central Park Be-In. I was a Red Guard declaring war on the old order, the star child in *2001* announcing the birth of a new one. I was the White Knight talking backwards, the Red Queen who'd lost her head. I was Alice when she's ten feet tall.

I was Bonnie and Clyde's Ford V8. I was my father's Corvair. I was the odometer I'd disconnect to cruise Market Street, the clutch I'd burned out to fetch Valerie and her tripmates in New York. I was the Purple Haze we'd dropped in Longwood Gardens, the seven silver dollars I'd spent to suck my first cock, the porno flick I'd refused to watch so a high school teacher couldn't suck mine.

I was a boy begging for mercy behind a Catholic church. I was the pointy boots his assailant wore, the zipper I opened to take him, the fist sandwich I got instead. I was the bloody lip I went home with, the lie I told my parents about how I got it. I was the shame that kept me from telling anyone what had happened, even my shrink.

I popped another pill.

I was vomit. I was my mother begging God to make it all go away; my brother promising everything would work out. I was the bottle of aspirin I'd intended to swallow to get them all off my back. I was Dr. Radin warning me I'd never be happy. I was Arnold locked up in the loony bin.

I was a sissy on LSD, claiming an epiphany. I was Sal running away. I was Valerie insisting we deserved better. Much, much better.

I was the Four Tops' "Reach Out, I'll be There"; Mitch Ryder's "Sock it To Me, Baby"; James Brown's "Say It Loud: I'm Black and I'm Proud." I was Aretha singing "Ain't No Way."

I was the product of an overbearing mother and a distant father. I was an abomination. I was a castration complex. I was the reincarnation of my twin sisters, Nan and Jane; a girl trapped in a boy's body. I was a fumbled baseball, a Dying Swan. I was mentally ill.

I was the son whose father said he hated him. I was the sick queen Arnold said would be better off dead. I was the black bitch Paul saw in the Evil Queen's mirror. I was T snarling, *Once a queer, always a queer.* I was Junior chiming in: *Yeah, you piece of cocksucking shit.*

I was revenge, a hippie faggot freak, my parent's worst nightmare. I was self-destruction, a shed on the banks of the Brandywine, ready to blow. I was defeat, Dr. Radin's beady-eyed next patient, nervously stroking a plucked plastic chicken. I was defiance, the chant thousands of war protesters used against Chicago's charging, club-swinging bullies-in-blue: *The whole world is watching!* Or Donnie in my father's Corvair channeling Edward Albee's Martha: *I'm not a monster! I'm not!! I'm not!!*

The next night, Sal called and I told him I needed to get away. My parents, I said, were out to destroy me. I told him I wanted to move to New York.

He asked about college.

Still on fire, I snarled I'd burned all that out of me. I had no more dreams. I no longer wanted to be anything at all.

"You high?" he asked hesitantly.

My jaws were clenched. My sweat smelled of error. I'd been dancing, I mumbled. Soon, I'd be ash.

He said he didn't understand.

I told him about spontaneous combustion.

He agreed it sounded like I needed a change. I thanked him. For once, someone had heard me.

He asked about the draft. I reminded him the Army didn't take people like us. He asked if I really wanted that on my record. "It's permanent, you know."

"Yes," I replied. When he warned it could ruin my chances for a career, I simply said good. I just wanted to be gay. "A flamer," I added.

Sal laughed.

I asked if we could get a place in New York together.

Sal paused but only briefly. "Sure, man, that'd be cool," he said before noting he'd left the East Village. He said the gig with Otto had run its course and he was crashing on West 10th Street with another refugee from the Summer of Love, Bruce, the only cat he knew who'd read everything by Alain Robbe-Grillet.

I asked if he recalled Robbe-Grillet had written the screenplay for *Last Year at Marienbad*, the first film we saw together at SU's Film Club.

"Oh yeah, I'd forgotten that," he replied. "I remember you really liked that one. Said it was about homosexual panic." He chuckled. "Never did understand that one."

I replied there was a lot neither of us understood but contended the black beauties were a big help. Through them, I was finally figuring things out.

Sal advised me Bruce had only one room. I'd have to sleep on the floor. He also noted Bruce didn't do drugs. "Seen too many minds blown," he explained. Noting Bruce's boyfriend, a grad student at NYU, was a frequent visitor, he also said I'd need to go for some very long walks.

Before hanging up, he also warned me to watch out for the pills. He said word on the street in New York was that speed kills, although he confessed more and more freaks seemed to be doing it, especially the gay ones. In Bruce's building, where he said everyone but the crone across the hall was gay, speed was definitely the preferred high. It was, he said, a very "happening" kind of place.

I told him I was thrilled to finally be putting my parents behind me and then launched into a long, breathless rap about Genet. When I got to the part about Divine's death, the operator came on and told Sal if he wanted to continue the call, he'd have to deposit two more quarters. He said he'd gone through all his change but before hanging up he had me write down his address: 250 West 10th Street. "Halfway between the Trucks and the Stonewall," he whinnied. "You'll love it."

I was all set. Four days earlier, I'd charged a mountain of textbooks on the credit my father had set up at the campus bookstore. Returning them the next day, I'd reaped over two hundred dollars, more than enough to tide me over until I found a job in New York. I chuckled over my timing. Three days earlier, Nixon had moved into the White House with a secret plan to end the Vietnam War. Now I was heading off to Greenwich Village with a secret plan to escalate mine. I popped my last black beauty and smiled. My parents were gonna freak.

At 6 p.m., right on schedule, Trudy honked the horn of her brand-new 1969 Mustang. My signal to begin firing, I ran to the pay phone in the hall outside my dorm room to break the news to my parents: I was dropping out of college, turning my back on them and, yes, most likely my future too. I didn't care anymore. I was moving to New York City, their code for confirmed homosexual.

No, I said over my mother's whimpers, there'd be no way to reach me. No, I replied, I couldn't say when I'd see them again. Yes, I assured her, I still loved them but, no, my mind was made up. That time, it was my turn to vomit. That time, I was telling them what I thought of closed minds—*their* closed minds.

Breaking into sobs, she cried out for my father, "Honey, come quick. It's Dale." Over his muffled shouting at the dog—"Come on now, Jeff, git, git outta my way"—my mother pled with me to hang on. "Dale, please, please, I'm begging you, honey, please don't do this to us."

Click! I hung up on her. I didn't want to hear one more time about how I was upsetting my mother, ruining my parents' lives, or bringing shame onto the family name. It was my time now, life against death.

With the help of my dorm mate, Doug, a nervous, wiry first-year library sciences major who'd confessed the night before he thought he was gay too, I trundled up my belongings—a suitcase, my portable stereo, an old Boy Scout sleeping bag and a cardboard box full of LPs—and loaded them into Trudy's car. I wished Doug well—Syracuse, I warned him, would be a tough place to come out—and, hopping into her car, told Trudy to gun it. "Let's split this flat tire."

"Whee!" she squealed as she floored it and, tires squealing, we careened up the street. Smiling, I turned and admired the two streaks of burnt rubber we'd left behind, the last trace of my time in Syracuse. Waving from the curb outside the dorm, Doug looked particularly forlorn. Although I'd promised to stay in touch, I knew I wouldn't. Doug didn't do drugs and I did. In fact, by the time I left Syracuse, they were just about all I was doing.

When we got onto I-81, Trudy told me to hold on. She wanted to see how her car performed on the open road. *Boom!* The Mustang roared as my head snapped back and I grabbed the edge of my seat. I tried not to look but, alarmed, noticed the speedometer hit 120 before she finally took her foot off the gas. As she explained, I was on my way to freedom. She wanted to know what that felt like.

She was, she confessed, jealous. Boys got to do things girls couldn't. I didn't bother noting Valerie had left Syracuse almost a year earlier to live by herself in the East Village. Trudy loathed Valerie; a degenerate, she even called her. Instead, I took a swig from the flask Trudy had brought along for the ride and smiled darkly. Where I was going, everyone would be a degenerate—hippie faggot freaks, every last one of them.

Thirteen years later, after my father died, I found a handwritten note from my mother in his top dresser drawer. It was part of a pile of papers tucked between his revolver and a candy tin full of silver dollars.

Thursday, Jan. 23, 1969, 6 p.m. Dale called (collect) to tell us he would not be going to school the second semester. He is going to New York City where he expects to rent an apartment with someone named Sal. His last name is unknown to us, although I think Dale did mention it. Sounds very foreign.

Sal was Italo-American. His last name ended in a vowel.

13
Driving Nails Home

"You fucking douche bag, where're all my reds?" a low, gravelly voice bellowed from deep inside the rooming house. Outside, Trudy's Mustang turned north onto Hudson Street and disappeared into a raging storm. When I'd asked if she wanted to come in, she'd shaken her head and told me to just go on. New York scared her. Besides, Sal's book talk made her feel stupid.

I let the door to the street slam behind me and examined the vestibule's two rows of ravaged mailboxes—one, Sal said, for each of the building's nine tiny rooms. On the first, he'd handwritten his last name under Bruce's, the ex-monk and scholar of modern French literature who'd agreed to put me up, sight unseen, on the condition that Sal and I find our own place in no more than three weeks. At the other end was a nameplate that simply read "Eden."

The bellowing resumed. "Girl, you better get your leaky ass up here. If I find out you ate all my pills, I'm gonna take a blow torch to your wigs."

Sal held the vestibule's inner door while I peered apprehensively down the building's hallway. Lit by a buzzing fluorescent coil that clashed with the townhouse's stern Federalist symmetry, it traversed the building's depth and ended in a stairwell from which the shouting came. Thick globs of white paint bubbled from its walls and the floor's four wide planks, painted chocolate brown, were pitted and gouged, as if by a giant claw.

When describing it over the phone, Sal had said the building was among Greenwich Village's oldest, one of the first built by a bourgeoisie eager to escape the sweaty, smelly ribaldry of New York's docks. Feeling slightly off-balance, I noticed a precipitous tilt to the right, as if, bored with the straight and narrow, the building wanted to return to that which its builders had fled—to the river and the docks where gay men cruising for sex had replaced stevedores unloading the produce of slave labor: tobacco from Virginia, sugar from Cuba, rum from Jamaica, and mahogany from Belize.

"You hear me, Miss Pig Bitch?" the voice at the top of the stairs demanded.

Sal picked up my box of LPs and rolled his eyes. The building's resident drag queens, Stephanie Lisa and Miss Barbara Eden, were at it again. "Although I don't think Barbara's in a position to do much talking right now," he snickered before explaining she was holed up in the building's only bathroom with a cop from the precinct house up the street. He giggled. "He's got a wife and kids way out in Queens but she still calls him her husband."

"A cop?" I cried, clutching my suitcase.

Sal assured me I had nothing to worry about; most New York cops were into drugs. "Besides, they don't hassle freaks, just the drag queens." He said, a few months earlier, the one upstairs had picked Miss Eden up for loitering down by the docks, thrown her in the back seat of his cruiser, rammed his billy club between her legs and proposed a deal: in exchange for letting her go, he'd swing by every other Friday night for a cut of her welfare check, a handful of pills and a long, sloppy blow job. He whinnied Miss Eden insisted it was a small price to pay for her freedom. "Honey, the Tombs is no place for a drag queen," Sal crowed, mimicking her.

He said Stephanie and Miss Eden called themselves "pre-ops," meaning that, while they still had dicks, they'd recently acquired breasts. He explained that, about a month ago, they'd purchased the silicone off the street and injected it themselves. Stephanie, however, had been so loaded on reds when she'd done up Barbara, one tit had ended up lower than the other. "Miss Eden was wrecked. Locked herself in her room and ate all the Seconal in sight. Next thing she knew she was in St. Vincent's with a tube down her throat."

Stephanie clomped down a flight of stairs and pounded on the bathroom door. "Miss Thing, I'm serious. I need you! You know I can't face the street without Mother's little helpers."

"Poor things," Sal sighed, "one week, it's Stephie, the next, Miss Eden. The medics come here so often they know what room to go to. Third floor, first door on the right."

A door directly above us flew open and a pair of flip-flops pattered across creaking floorboards. "There, there, princess," a man's soft, sultry voice purred. "Why don't we go back upstairs and let mama make things pretty again." Stephanie instantly quieted down and then, over the flapping of slingbacks and flipflops on bare stair treads, the man inquired about the status of Stephanie's supplies. "Oh, darling, please say you still have that point I gave you. Mine's so dull I have to practically hammer it in."

"That was Peter," Sal groaned, again rolling his eyes. "I know him from San Francisco." He shook his head and complained there had to be something wrong with his karma; of all the flophouses in New York, he and Peter had to end up in the same one. He said he'd met Peter at the Capri, San Francisco's infamous gay freak bar. "Wild, wild place," he murmured. "Lesbian hookers, gay bikers, drag queens shooting up in the john, hippies dancing naked on the bar, runaways sleeping in the booths. Never seen anything like it. Not even at the Stonewall." He said Peter and Forrest, the man who gave him hepatitis, were leaders of a pack of junkies called the Speed Queens. "Stars of the show," Sal called them.

I laughed. "Speed Queens? My mother had one of those in the basement."

Sal chuckled. He said Peter and Forrest had been tight, real tight. "Crazy Catholic queens," he called them before noting they'd met in the seminary. "Even left together. Decided they'd rather be hippies than priests." He shook his head and grimaced. "And now look at him. Peter's a total junkie."

Sal said I would've really dug Forrest. "He wasn't sleazy like Peter. Just wanted to be outrageous. He said his favorite pastime was blowing people's minds." A giggle welled up as he recalled the time he'd visited Forrest's Haight Street pad. He'd marched Sal up to the roof and told him to piss on his jewelry. He broke into a loud guffaw. "Said it enhanced their street value."

Sal said Peter claimed he'd fled San Francisco to get away from the speed. "Then, not two weeks later, he was hooked up with this speed freak named George." Sal shook his head; George was nothing like Forrest. "He lives in this shooting gallery over on East 4th Street. Never says much, just kinda hangs out in the background." Sal cleared his throat and tugged on the end of his moustache. "He's here a lot too—you know, on the second floor with Peter. Sometimes, I think all they do is shoot up and ball. Stay away from the cat, man." He looked at me and flushed slightly. "I don't know, maybe what they say is wrong. I mean, Peter's older than me. But people say George is a terrible chicken hawk."

He squatted on the floor and thumbed through my box of LPs. He pulled out *White Light/White Heat*, the Velvet Underground's second, so-called "black album," one even more hardcore than their first, and said he'd pretty much lost his taste for decadence. "New York freaks have really gotten carried away with all this evil shit—you know, the occult, S&M, shooting up, songs like "Sister Ray." Even the gays are starting to get scary." He flicked a cockroach off his pants leg and squashed it with the heel of a work boot. "I mean, take that cat, George. He leads some gang called the Horrible Fags."

I laughed. "The Horrible Fags? Who'd ever want to call themselves *that*?"

"I'm serious, man," Sal said, slipping the album back into the box. "They all got their start in Warhol's Factory. Every last one of them is a junkie."

"*The Factory*?" I cried. "So does that mean he knows Lou Reed?" I felt my face flush. "Or Joe Dallesandro?" My heart started to pound. "And what about Viva and Ultra Violet?"

Sal groaned. "I don't know who the cat knows, man. I'm just warning you. Stay away from him. George is bad news—a real death trip."

Sal rose from his haunches and, turning, pointed at the battered metal door on my left. "Well, here it is," he said, "Bruce's room, the place where you'll be crashing." He warned me we'd have to be quiet; every night from ten to one was what Bruce called "study hall," the time he devoted himself to scholarly pursuits. "The Bible," he said when I asked what Bruce was currently studying.

"Wait a minute," I cried, grabbing his arm, "you mean this guy's a Jesus freak?"

Sal sighed and shook his head. "I don't know, man. He never used to be like this." He said, the previous weekend, he'd found him reading passages from Revelations to strangers at Keller's, a new leather bar down by the docks. He'd so upset the patrons the bouncer had to kick him out. "I'm afraid he's flipping out, man. I mean, how many people do you know who've been kicked out of a gay bar?"

"But I thought you said Bruce didn't do drugs."

"He doesn't," Sal replied. "That's why I don't get it. I mean, the man's a fucking genius. Before he dropped out of Berkeley, he was finishing up a dissertation on France's Nouvelle Vague." He reminded me he'd read everything by Robbe-Grillet. "How many other cats do you know who can claim that?"

I didn't bother asking why Sal thought an expertise in the writer who'd done the screenplay for a film as bizarre as *Last Year at Marienbad* proved anyone sane and instead inquired about the status of Bruce's love life. "Does he still have that boyfriend you mentioned?"

Afraid I was up to something, Sal told me he didn't want any trouble with the landlord. Bruce, he noted, could be quite prickly. "And, yes, to answer your question. He and Greg are still together. You might even meet him tonight." He noted that Greg, a grad student at NYU, was around a lot.

I assured Sal I had no intention of bedding the landlord. "Besides, I don't do vague. I do drugs, remember? I drive nails home into fact." At that, I shoved Bruce's door open with my portable stereo and waltzed in to check out my new digs.

The room was dark and so thick with cigarette smoke I had to stop and wait for my eyes to adjust to the gloom. "Jeez, is it always like this?" I asked, gulping in the air leaking into the room from a window whose bottom three panes were covered in moldy cardboard. "Yeah, pretty much," Sal muttered before noting Bruce was more a beatnik than a freak. A "mystic," he called him.

I peered out the window at a tidy, well-manicured courtyard in the rear of the building and asked what that was all about. "I mean, you don't exactly expect something like that outside a dump like this." Sal chuckled and explained it was the interior of a block bounded on one side by the gay bars of Christopher Street and another by the folk and jazz venues of Bleecker Street. "The intersection of the hip and the gay," he crowed. "No other place like it on earth!"

"Quiet!" a voice suddenly bellowed from the opposite end of the room. Turning, I spied through the gloom a tall, gaunt man with sunken eyes, hollow cheeks, and thick black hair shorn to a stubble sitting on a filthy mattress in a raised alcove strewn with dirty clothes. Above his head, a small window rattling against the storm bathed him in the pale sickly glow of a streetlight. Peering over his wire-rim glasses, he gave me a quick once-over and returned to his book without even so much as hello.

"And fuck you too," I grumbled, clearing a space for my things amidst a clutter of dusty books and cardboard boxes. If I was expected, there was not a shred of evidence to indicate so.

Sal laughed nervously and returned to a description of the courtyard. He said that, while, around Easter, it was supposedly awash in daffodils, no one had ever been seen tending it. He woozily pulled out his pack of cigarettes and offered me a Camel. His breath reeked of cheap wine. "Miss Eden calls it the end of the rainbow."

I smiled and handed Sal the chunk of hash I'd brought along as a hostess gift and then stumbled over a pair of legs while trying to reach the open jug of Cribari next to Sal's sleeping bag. "Oh, I'm sorry," I mumbled, squinting into the darkness at a man with long, greasy blond hair and skin the color of milk paste. Sprawled across the room's bare floorboards and furiously fussing with the dials of his transistor radio, he too ignored me.

"Oh, don't mind him," Sal said between puffs of a hash pipe. "That's Freddy. He just kinda, well..." He turned to the hollow-cheeked ghoul at the other end of the room. "I don't know, what would you say Freddy does, Bruce?" He paused to release a thick cloud of hash smoke. "Hangs out?"

Bruce looked up from his Bible and, scowling, finally acknowledged my presence. "Have you ever noticed how difficult it is for your friend to follow rules? It's the third time this week he's broken one." He peered disapprovingly at the two of us. "How many times must I remind you, Salvatore? Every night between ten and one is quiet time." Glancing at his watch, he noted there was still an hour-and-a-half to go. He pulled a hand-rolled cigarette from the breast pocket of a rumpled t-shirt and lit it with a withering flourish. "Or perhaps you children would prefer to go outside and play?"

I bristled but Sal assured Bruce we'd quiet down. Sliding onto the floor next to Freddy, he handed me the hash pipe in exchange for the jug of Cribari and toyed coquettishly with a button on Freddy's shirt. "Whaddya think?" he asked as Freddy, oblivious to Sal's advances, continued to twist the dials of his transistor.

Not wanting to be rude, I merely noted Freddy was a bit too vacant for my tastes. "I like my men more in the moment," I said, smiling perhaps a bit too cattily. "You know, sexually speaking."

Sal giggled.

Suddenly, Bruce bellowed from the other end of the room: *And he gathered them together in a place called Armageddon. And the seventh angel poured out his vial into the air; and there came a great voice out of the temple of heaven, from the throne, saying, It is done.*

Frightened, Freddy slid under a side table and, waving the radio over his head like it was an F-11 strafing the Plain of Jars, made loud buzzing noises.

"Oh, don't worry about him," Sal said, noting my alarm. "Freddy's just showering."

"Showering?"

Sal nodded woozily. "Yeah, you know, with radio waves." He snatched the pipe away from me and snickered. "He channels them through his transistor."

I asked what drug Freddy was on so I knew what to stay away from but Sal insisted Freddy no longer got high. He brushed a strand of hair from Freddy's brow and explained that somewhere along the line he'd taken too much LSD and never came down.

I scoffed that Sal sounded like one of those newspaper articles designed to scare people away from psychedelics but he insisted the story was true. "There aren't even any batteries in the damn thing," he said, pointing at Freddy's transistor. He said Miss Eden had found him one night wandering the docks in his underwear and brought him back to her room where she fed him a Sara Lee cheesecake and gave him her half-empty pack of Newports. Ever since he'd slept outside her door. "She calls him her poodle," he giggled.

He said once she and Stephanie had even done Freddy up in drag. "It was fucking weird, man. He just sat there, buzzing his head with his transistor radio while they painted his face and ratted his hair out into this big blond bouffant." Sal sat up and finished off the jug of wine. "He'll let you do anything you want but get into his pants. He's not gay, straight, bi or anything."

I waved my hand in front of Freddy's face but he just looked right through it. Shuddering, I recalled the aphorism from *Love's Body* "Transparency. To let the light not on but in or through...as in the sky at night, or in the space on which our dreams are traced."

"Everybody calls him *Electric* Freddy," Sal exclaimed. "So fucking turned on and tuned in he's completely dropped out."

Oblivious, Freddy mutely stared at a crack in the wall.

Drunk, Sal jumped up and said he felt like celebrating. "We'll do the town and stay up all night!" he slurred, imitating the queens who imitated Miss Garland. Dragging me into the hallway, he slipped me a five and told me to go up to the third floor where a guy named John sold black beauties for a buck a pill.

Snickering, Sal suggested I might want to linger. John was, he said, a "real looker." Then, giggling, he darted back into Bruce's room and I crept up the stairs wondering who or what I'd run into along the way: a cop, a drag queen, the missing batteries to Freddy's transistor radio, a Horrible Fag, or the old hag across the hall from Bruce who Sal said banged on her pipes every morning right before dawn.

"Come in," a voice as soft and plush as velvet said in response to my knock on a door with a peace sign and a Day-Glo decal of a goat. I pushed the door open and stepped into a thick cloud of pot and incense smoke. A few feet in front of me, an Indian print of yellow cockatoos resting on red branches covered a mattress and box springs placed in the middle of what appeared to be a perfectly square room, larger, airier, and better attended to than Bruce's dark, dingy garret. Behind it, a line of votive candles flickered on the sills of two small windows overlooking the corner of West 10th and Hudson. To my left, on a surprisingly elegant marble mantle, two brass incense burners filled the room with the treacly scent of patchouli, while in the corner, a tinny stereo played "White Bird" by a group called It's a Beautiful Day.

I smiled. It was one of my favorite songs.

I heard a match strike and turned to find a man sitting at a makeshift desk encircled in the light of a brass goose-necked lamp. He was long, thin, and sultry, with hair that cascaded to below his shoulders in thick, auburn waves. A shy smile softened high chiseled cheekbones, a square jaw, and thin lips, while a hint of blue darted nervously behind tinted aviator glasses. As I watched him light a joint as sleek as an eyebrow pencil, I wondered if perhaps I was already too high. All I could think of was Tchaikovsky's swan.

He didn't introduce himself or ask my name. Instead, he jiggled three brass coins in the palm of his left hand and informed me he'd just cast the *I Ching*. I didn't dare say I had no idea what that was and instead just smiled vaguely and replied as nonchalantly as I could, "Far out." He said his hexagram had been "Inner Truth," with a nine in the second place that read: *I have a good goblet. I will share it with you.*

Blushing, I stammered that Sal, the guy crashing downstairs with Bruce, had said I could cop some pills from him. Nervously waving Sal's five-dollar bill in front of me, I asked what he had to offer. Clearly amused by my awkwardness, John chuckled and opened a drawer packed with bottles of pills. "Take your pick. I've got Obetrol, Desoxyn, Doriden, black beauties, Dexedrine, and the three "nal" sisters: "Nembu," "Seco" and "Tui." He said he even had some niacin. "Ever tried it? Makes you tingle like your insides are on fire." He held up a little brown bottle and asked if I wanted some. "They're free."

I shook my head and, handing him my cash, said I only wanted black beauties. He dropped six in the palm of my hand for what he called "good measure" and snickered as I stumbled over a pink bathmat and banged my head on my way out the door.

Back downstairs, Sal and I each popped a beauty and launched into a drunken speed rap. And though we managed to honor Bruce's rule by keeping our discussion of Norman O. Brown's work within bounds—Sal insisted *Life Against Death* was his best, while I favored *Love's Body*—the resumption of our long-running feud over Andy Warhol's *Flesh* quickly got heated. Sal loudly dismissed the flick as the work of a mindless swish, while I even more volubly asserted it was a trailblazer, the first to portray gay life without a hint of hysteria or judgmentalism. When we started in on whether or not Warhol was even involved with the flick—Sal noted the director was a man named Paul Morrissey, while I claimed anything that came out of the Factory was by definition Warhol's—Bruce informed us our squabbling was driving him insane. Escorting us into the hall, he told us not to come back until we'd settled the dispute. "And don't be any too quick about it, either," he instructed. His boyfriend, Greg, was expected any minute.

Fortunately, the storm that had greeted my arrival had passed and, since it was Friday night, Sal suggested a tour of the Village's gay hot spots. First stop was two blocks east where, at the Stonewall, we danced with a roomful of drag queens and hustlers until 3 a.m. Then, he took me five blocks west where, in the shadow of the elevated West Side Highway, we joined an orgy of men in the darkened hulls of a half-dozen delivery vans that Sal said were known simply as the "Trucks." After that, he took me three blocks back east to a storefront on the corner of Christopher and Hudson that he said was the world's first gay bookstore. "Yeah, right," I sneered, cupping my hands on the window to see if the sex booths were visible from the street. "Even Syracuse has one of these."

Sal shook his head and said I had it all wrong; the guy who owned the shop didn't even carry porn. "Says it makes sex dirty," he snickered. He pointed to the section inside the store devoted to Walt Whitman and beamed. The other day, he'd been in and discovered a rare first folio of *Leaves of Grass*. Calling it his "ballsiest," Sal quoted from memory a poem, "To You," which Whitman had expunged from all subsequent editions: *Come! vouchsafe to me what has yet been vouchsafed to none/Tell me the whole story/Tell me what you would not tell your brother, wife, husband or physician.*

I looked at the sign over the door—The Oscar Wilde Memorial Bookstore—and felt a heavy weight lift. Finally, I was where I belonged—Greenwich Village, the one place on earth where our love dared to speak its name. Then, as I took in a notice taped to the door—*Gay is Good* it proclaimed in a large lavender script—I caught out of the corner of my eye the retort vandals had spray painted along the building's foundation: *Kill All Fags*! it screamed in a lurid orange.

Neither of us mentioned the scrawl on our way back to W.10th Street, although when we approached our building, I suggested I go back upstairs and cop some reds from John. I had a feeling our crash was going to be bad and I was in no mood for any more of Bruce's Bible rants. Then, sure enough, right as we opened the door, the crone on the first floor greeted us with a whack of her pipes that made the building's walls come suddenly alive.

"Fucking vermin!" Sal cried as we warily ventured inside. As he noted, on top of everything else—drag queens turning tricks in the john, Horrible Fags shooting speed, Jesus freaks ranting about the apocalypse, crazy-ass crones whacking her heat pipes, and New Age-types selling pills—the building had rats. "Lots of 'em," Sal grumbled.

Shuddering, I confessed I'd never lived around rats before, although I complimented the crone on her timing. "She's right on schedule," I murmured, tapping my watch face. "It's the hour of the wolf."

Sal looked at me blankly. "The hour of the *what*?"

"You know, from the Bergman film—the one he made right after *Persona.*"

Sal confessed he'd lost his taste for Bergman. "Too intense," he called him.

I nodded and noted I'd had to take a sleep cure after seeing *Hour of the Wolf.* "The time right before dawn when dreams turn into nightmares," I said when Sal asked what the flick was about. "When madness takes over."

"They shoulda called it F," Mike grumbled as he scanned the wall of high-rise projects lining the other side of Avenue D. In his second year at NYU's Drama School, Mike, who'd grown up on the mean streets of South Philadelphia, had his heart set on leaving the ghetto behind.

"F?" I asked.

Mike nodded and grimaced. "Yeah, you know, as in failure. F for failure."

Facing the opposite direction, I gaped at the crumbling hulk on the corner of D and East Fifth Street. Nailed over a hole that had once been the building's entry, a chipped and peeling sign from the City proclaimed new hope for the people of the Lower East Side. With help from Sargent Shriver, the recently sacked head of the federal Office of Economic Opportunity, Mayor Lindsay and the local community action agency, Mobilization for Youth, had pledged to rebuild the now roofless wreck into a methadone clinic, the area's first.

"Fat chance of that," I sneered quietly so Mike, who thought me a communist, wouldn't hear. Like student strikes, Freedom Rides, protest songs and Be-Ins, the War on Poverty had become just another quaint but futile gesture against our country's rising tide of violence and inequality. With Nixon in the White House and drugs suddenly everywhere, heroin, not hope ruled the area's streets.

From his perch in the blasted hulk's second-floor window, a man with an eye patch and a red bandana on his head watched our every move. One gaping hole over, a darker-skinned man in a wide brimmed hat hissed at two women in leopard-skin pedal pushers and curlers passing by. He caught my stare and, smiling lewdly, grabbed the crotch of his yellow polyester pants. "Hey, puta, wanna suck?"

I turned away as he yelled at me again—"Hey, come on inside, baby, I won't hurt you"—and examined the next-door tenement. Five flights up, in the rear of the building, Sal and I had moved into a furnished, two-bedroom sublet for only ninety bucks a month. The apartment came with two police locks and iron grates on all the windows, precautions against the junkies who used the roof to shoot up. On the first floor, a package store specializing in nips enjoyed a brisk business.

"I told you not to wear your hair like that," Mike sneered, glaring at my ponytail. "These people think you're a drag queen." I glanced at the purple scarf with gold threads he'd draped over his shoulders "á la Isadora" and laughed. A plump, pimply "mama's boy" who'd had to be rushed to the ER after his first— and only—puff of marijuana, Mike had no stomach for the changes I was going through. He still couldn't bring himself to call me a freak, although, unlike his best friend Dominic, he at least hadn't written me off. Indeed, the day before, he'd even asked to move in with Sal and me.

Sal was less than thrilled about having a nelly show tune queen like Mike for a roommate but he'd agreed we could use help with the rent. Besides, as he'd grumbled when he first saw the place, no one was ever gonna visit us. "The other side of the moon," he called Avenue D.

Mike took one last look up and down the street, crossed himself, and, before heading for his new address's battered front door, grumbled, "Oh well, anything's better than the dorm." Indeed, three days earlier, members of NYU's football team had dangled him over the sixth-floor railing of his dorm and informed him he either agreed to move out or they were letting go. As they'd noted, they didn't countenance living with "pervs." The very next day, he'd asked if he could have one of Avenue D's two bedrooms. He hadn't cared that we were the only white people on the street or the only gays in at least four blocks, or that Spanish, not English, was the street's lingua franca. All that mattered was keeping his NYU scholarship, his ticket to a career on Broadway where, he'd been told, it didn't matter how gay he was. And as even Mike acknowledged, he was a screamer. The minute he walked into a room everyone knew.

"And, of course, I was cruised!" Mike crowed as he followed me down the building's tiled entry hall—his own campy way of taming spaces he found threatening. I didn't dare tell him that, the night before, two Puerto Ricans had pulled a knife on me, dragged me into the cul-de-sac at the base of the stairs and demanded all my cash. Nor did I mention that when I'd handed over the buck fifty Sal and I had scrounged together for a six-pack of beer, they'd just shaken their heads and handed the money back. "You call yourself white, man?" the cuter of the two had sneered before they'd swaggered off. "You're worse off than us."

Mike claimed he needed the sunny north-facing bedroom to bolster his mood, although three days after moving in, he complained its view of the housing projects was "too depressing for a white woman" and covered the window with a swath of rose-colored satin he'd stolen from NYU. Claiming it took a "fairy to make things pretty," he painted the walls puce and arranged on the childhood dresser he'd hauled up from South Philly his collection of antique perfume bottles. On the wall with the window, he tacked up a poster of Carole Channing in *Hello, Dolly!* and above his bed he put another one of Zero Mostel in *Fiddler on the Roof.*

I didn't have the heart to tell him the only fiddlers on our roof were junkies. All night long, they clomped up and down the fire escape outside the rear bedroom into which I'd flung my sleeping bag. I'd painted the walls black and the floor a screaming yellow and, for decoration, tacked up a photo of a naked Joe Dallesandro, the star of Warhol's *Flesh*, that I tore from the pages of *After Dark*, a new "entertainment" magazine popular with West Village's "bourgie" gay set.

Mike claimed the room scared him and refused to enter it, even to dust. But Sal, attracted by what he called its "nihilist vibe," threw his sleeping bag in the corner opposite mine. On the floor between us, I placed a vial of black pills for getting up, another of red ones for going down, and an alarm clock whose hands glowed like they'd been dipped in Strontium 90.

At first, the nightly parade of junkies on our fire escape unnerved me, although when a February blizzard forced the city to abandon the neighborhood, I realized they weren't the problem, the authorities were. Suddenly, without a cop car or fire engine in sight, crime plummeted. Abandoning our fire escape, the junkies took to the streets, where they built bonfires all across the Lower East Side. Street parties proliferated.

After that, I claimed I was safer on Avenue D than I'd ever been in suburban Wilmington, although Sal accused me of romanticizing the poor. Maybe, I retorted, although, as I reminded him, he hadn't lived two doors away from a bully in a place called Carrcroft or been beaten up multiple times in a high school called Mount Pleasant. I'd take dope fiends and welfare queens over smug, self-righteous, God-fearing haters any day.

And it was true. We really were quite safe. After my aborted mugging, word must've spread about the impoverished white guys who'd moved onto D because no one bothered us again. Even when we walked home at 4 or 5 a.m. after a night at the Stonewall or the Trucks, the junkies let us be.

And it wasn't like we didn't stand out. We did. Like sore thumbs. With his scarves, his campy outbursts and his swishy mincing and prancing about, Mike especially turned heads, although no one threatened us or, other than an occasional "puta," called us names. Once around 3 a.m. on my way home from a night of dancing at the Stonewall, a cute Puerto Rican guy sitting on a stoop on East 5th Street between Avenues B and C—allegedly the most dangerous stretch on the trek back to D—asked for a blow job. When I refused, I was sure I was in for a beating but he just shrugged and went back inside his building. After that, I knew I was right where I was supposed be to—a judgment-free zone where people had more important things to fret over than who or what I did in bed.

Sal liked to say Avenue D was too freaky even for the freaks, while Mike likened it to the Palermo slum his immigrant parents had fled. For me, it was something altogether more favorable—a place so far-out, so lawless and written-off, so utterly devoid of smugness and pretense, that I was finally free to break all the rules—the hip, as well as the gay—and flesh out the new me: neither one or the other, but something entirely, scarily brand-new.

Every few nights, on my way back to Avenue D from my job loading trucks for a West Village book depository, I stopped by John's for more pills. After a while, he ceased selling them and, pointing to the drawer where they were kept, told me to take what I wanted. "You're family now, dear. What's mine is yours."

By then, I'd sampled just about all of his offerings. The night I'd tried the niacin, I'd even sampled John. High on psilocybin, we'd banged it out under a black light that made our skin translucent and the ceiling glow like the evening sky. The next day, afraid I might be falling for him, he'd noted the glyph on his horoscope that showed he wasn't what he called the "marrying kind." Pointing to a circle with a blue dot in its center, he'd explained he was a Capricorn, the sign for people who thought mostly of themselves. "Nixon's one too," he'd chuckled before declaring himself a whore.

I'd thought it an odd trait to brag about but, not wanting to come across as uptight, I let it slide. John had already made it clear he thought I was too judgmental. Claiming we'd suffered enough from the rules straight people made, John resisted passing judgment on just about everything gay. "Nothing is wrong; it simply is," he'd declare every time I railed against some aspect of gay life that I found retrograde, tacky, or crude. He even kept his cool when James, the Black hippie who'd turned him on to the *I Ching*, had started shooting meth behind a blanket in the back of his Hudson Street antiques shop. "New York's just a speedy town," he shrugged. Pulling out the astrological chart he'd done on the city, he pointed out the significance of Neptune's placement in what he called the city's "first house." That, he explained, indicated a propensity for excess, drugs especially. He'd slid the chart back into his stack and smiled slyly. "Homosexuality too."

Sal dismissed John as just another Aquarian crank, but I saw him in a much more favorable light. Approaching thirty—the age, John joked, when the so-called "youth culture" claimed he could no longer be trusted—he quickly became the self-appointed older "gay mother" whose example proved I too could make it as an out gay man. "Fuck 'em if they can't take a joke," he snickered when I told him how my parents had reacted to my coming out. No one had ever dismissed them quite so peremptorily. Even Sal, who liked to think of himself as a hip New Left radical, drew the line at family. "You gotta understand where your folks are coming from," he'd once chided. "You're gay. You expect too much."

John thought Sal blew a lot of hot air, especially when accusing me of expecting too much. "Nobody's gonna tell me I can't be gay," he growled. "It's the way I was born." I loved it when John talked like that. No one else ever had, at least so unequivocally. As with Ben, the Syracuse boyfriend who'd broken up with me because he thought me prosaic, John was determined to be fully out but, unlike Ben, he refused to distance himself from gay life. Sure, he agreed elements were hidebound and tacky—hopelessly mired in guilt and shame— but, for John, gay life was also a touchstone. Like Blacks who'd migrated north but for whom the South continued to beckon, John wanted to have a heritage, be a part of something with deeper roots than just the latest fad. "A people," he called us and eager to join his crusade, I gobbled up his stories almost as hungrily as I did his pills.

Like many gays, John acknowledged he'd grown up a loner, tormented by bullies. Raised around the railroad yards of gritty Hammond, Indiana, by parents whose marriage his birth was supposed to have saved, he'd quickly learned to be wary of what others called love. He'd been seven when his parents had finally divorced but only fifteen when, six weeks apart, they'd both died— his father of drink and his mother, grief. "They couldn't live with or without each other," John sighed in the same soft way with which he'd called himself a whore.

"Fine," he shrugged when I asked how he'd handled the trauma of such a sudden orphaning. He hadn't cried once, even when his mother had taken to her bed and died a few weeks later. As he noted, Capricorns wore thick armor; rarely were others able to break through. Besides, he acknowledged the lessons he'd learned fending off bullies in hardscrabble Hammond. "You gotta be tough to be a sissy," he advised.

That was something else I liked about John. Most everyone else, including many gay men, looked down on sissies. Not John. He was the first gay man I knew who claimed effeminacy was a gift, rather than a shameful burden. Sissies, John said, were fun; butches, he countered, were bores. That was one of the reasons he liked living where he did. Except for Bruce, an intellectual he said blew even more hot air than Sal, and, of course, the old crone who banged on her pipes every night right before dawn, everyone who lived in the building was a sissy.

After his mother's death, John said he'd been shipped off to live with a married, older sister in Buffalo. She'd been as cold and stiff as the winter wind that blew off Lake Erie and, as soon as he'd finished high school, he'd enlisted in the Army. Stationed in DC, he'd overheard stories about men congregating around the Iwo Jima Monument and one night crossed the Potomac to check things out. Next thing he knew, he was having sex with a man inside a bramble. A week later, his commanding officer, an older man named Wally, had come out to him and, declaring himself John's "gay mother," helped him navigate his new gay life.

"Pow!" John exclaimed about the color his life took on once he came out. When he got out of the Army, he'd moved to West Hollywood where for six years he and four other guys threw a non-stop party in a big house with a pool down the hill from Marlo Thomas. Then, one night in the spring of '68, he'd picked up a hippie on Sunset Strip who'd given him a tab of something called Orange Sunshine. Always eager to try something new, John had popped it. "Pow!" he exclaimed again about what he could only describe as a second coming out. Two days later—the very one, he snickered, that LBJ had announced he wouldn't be running for re-election—he'd donned the faux-leather jacket he called his "Persian Plastic," stuffed his portable stereo and the Naugahyde sectional he'd gotten as a Christmas bonus from the furniture store where he worked into the back of his Volkswagen Beetle and headed east on Route 66.

"Ended up right here," he crowed as if he, the building, and everyone in it had been fated for each other. He'd painted the walls of his room sky-blue, glued Day-Glo stars to the ceiling and trimmed the windowsills and baseboards in contact paper that Woolworth's called "Flower Power." At night, he put so many candles in his windows that hippies would often stand on the corner across the street and trip out on the light show. "Wow, man," I heard one of them crow one night when I ventured out for cigarettes, "some really cool cat must live up there." Stopping, I smiled and assured him one did. "Very cool," I murmured.

John was convinced something big was about to blow in Greenwich Village. "There's no other place like it on earth," he said of its witches' brew of freaks, Beats, Blacks, Reds, gays, Puerto Ricans, dykes, and drag queens. Like Timothy Leary, John believed passionately in the power of drugs but, like me, he'd recently switched his allegiances from LSD to speed. "Acid may be love," he once observed, "but speed is power. It's time we started standing up for ourselves."

That was another first. I'd never heard a gay man talk about speed like that. Through John, I started to see gay speed freaks as warriors. With John, I quickly graduated from popping black beauties to snorting crystal meth. While beauties made me feel strong, crystal made me feel fierce—like one of those Speed Queens Sal had talked about, the ones who ruled the roost in that San Francisco freak bar, the Capri. A "living Hieronymus Bosch," he'd even once called it.

One night, on my way up to John's to learn the *I Ching*, I encountered the Horrible Fags Sal had warned me about on my first night in town. Peter had a stunning halo of strawberry blond curls but was shorter than I'd expected and, shirtless, he had a pale, Pillsbury doughboy physique that I'd hoped would be taut and lean. He fidgeted with a purple polka-dot scarf and babbled incoherently about principessas and marchesas and Carthaginian elephants that I simply had to see, darling, simply had to.

Behind him a man in a woolen black cape, crumpled jeans, and a loose-fitting, navy-blue t-shirt crept into the landing's light. He was tall and lean, with baby-fine, pitch-black hair, a brutish brow, and thick, bristly forearms. He stopped a few feet outside Peter's door and, smiling shyly, introduced himself as George. I knew instantly from his gaze that he was interested in me.

I was not impressed. His hair was short, banker's style; his Dracula outfit ridiculous; and, although I thought his scuffed, spray-painted silver wingtips cool, the silk scarf tied around his neck was pure West Village fag. Worse, he was coming on to me in full view of his lover.

"I hear you're new in town," he murmured in a Southern drawl that told me he too had once been a newcomer. Although he seemed much too mild-mannered for someone supposedly so horrible, his pupils confirmed at least part of Sal's story. Only speed freak eyes got that dilated.

I nodded and mumbled a curt reply: "I've been here a little over a month."

"So how do you like it?" he asked.

I noticed his dimples and sensed a certain sadness about him that I found touching. Then, despite myself, I glanced at his crotch. Noticing the shift in my gaze, George smiled and nodded slightly, as if to confirm that, yes, that too would be available, should I be interested. Blushing, I mumbled I liked it fine, just fine.

Meanwhile, Peter continued his babbling—this time about the Carthaginians making it across the Alps. Draping his scarf across his face, he strutted to the bathroom door and, claiming he was the barbarian princess Salambo, exhorted Hannibal and his elephants to continue their trek. We simply had to storm Rome, he cried. We simply had to.

I mumbled yes, we certainly did, then, nodding at George, politely excused myself. Although I'd been around lots of people on drugs, I'd never seen anyone as high as Peter. His eyes were literally rolling around in their sockets. George, on the other hand, seemed much too cool. Except for his pupils, I would never have suspected he was even high.

Blocking my way, George asked if I often visited the building.

"Enough," I replied. I pointed up the stairs and explained I was there to see my friend, John. Glancing at my watch, I told him I had to be going. "He was expecting me a half-hour ago."

"Ah yes, the astrologer," George persisted. "I understand you're a Pisces."

I considered asking how he could possibly know that about someone he'd just met but wanting to bring our encounter to a close, I again excused myself. "I really do need to be going," I explained, circling around behind him. I smiled warily. "John's going to teach me the *I Ching*."

"I hope we see each other again," George smiled, moving slightly aside. Glancing inside Peter's room as I passed by, I spied on the floor, next to a tube of KY and a crusty cum rag, a syringe sitting in a glass half-full of water. Other than a tousled bed and a grocery bag overflowing with dirty clothes, there was nothing else to the room—no photos of a naked Joe Dallesandro or posters of Carole Channing, no Flower Power contact paper or Day-Glo stars on the ceiling, no books, no TV, no stereo, no curtains, not even a transistor radio. Even the light bulb was naked.

Shuddering, I raced up the stairs to the safety of John's room and the soft, treacly sounds of It's A Beautiful Day—*White bird in a golden cage/on a winter's day/ in the rain....*

When I told John I thought George was interested in me, he warned me, as Sal also had, to be wary of him, although he couched his reservations in purely astrological terms. He said he'd done George's chart at Peter's request and had found aspects of it deeply troubling. As a result, he'd nicknamed him 'George Wrong' to distinguish him from the other Village speed dealer whose chart he'd found so favorable he'd dubbed him 'George Right.' "Imagine that, George Right and George Wrong," John chuckled. "Right here in River City."

John strongly suggested that, if it was a reliable source of speed I was after, I focus on George Right. He even volunteered to introduce us. As he noted, George Right was tight with his friend James, the Black hippie who'd started shooting meth in the back of his Hudson Street antiques shop. They were, he said, both Texans, although I wasn't sure why that mattered.

While John noted that George Right was also very good looking, he admitted his lover Danny, a runaway two years younger than me, was more to his liking. John even speculated that if George and I hit it off, maybe he'd have a chance with Danny, whose chart indicated they'd be well-suited for each other. Noting I was no homewrecker, I pointed at the three Chinese coins John kept next to his bed and reminded him he'd promised to teach me the *I Ching*.

My first casting led to a hexagram called *Difficulty at the Beginning*. In the Chinese, it was Chun, connoting "a blade of grass pushing against an obstacle as it sprouts from the earth." The image of its lower trigram, The Arousing, was thunder while its upper, The Abysmal, stood for danger. Together, they signified a profusion of chaos teeming with rain and wind. Its Judgement advised perseverance and "the appointment of helpers."

Its top line was solid yang and read: "Horse and wagon part. Bloody tears flow." It warned of great danger. "The difficulties at the beginning are too great for some persons. They get stuck and never find their way out; they fold their hands and give up the struggle. Such resignation is the saddest of all things. Therefore, Confucius says of this line: *Bloody tears flow. One should not persist in this.*"

Two weeks later, I was pushing pills in the Ninth Circle, a new gay dance bar the Mafia had opened across Sheridan Square from the Stonewall. I kept the joint jumping, supplying the bouncer, bartenders, busboys and a crowd of hungry college kids with beauties I sold for two bucks a pop. On a really good night, I made almost two hundred dollars, nearly every penny of which I spent in the hip boutiques on St. Mark's Place.

Sal accused me of cavorting with the enemy, by which he meant gay bar Mafiosi as well as New Age capitalists, but I no longer paid any attention. Sal couldn't keep up. Something was always holding him back. His liver hurt; his conscience bothered him; he spent too much time cruising The Ramble; he'd lost touch with poetry; he was becoming too gay; he wasn't gay enough. Worse, he'd even started talking about moving to the country. The city, he said, was too louche, too dirty, too dangerous, too commercial. "Depressing," he'd even started calling it.

I was moving beyond Sal. While he remained stubbornly right-on, I was working on becoming "fabulous," a new gay word I'd picked up from Peter, the Horrible Fag who'd urged me to join in on the sack of Rome. "Well, of course, I'm fabulous, darling. I'm a speed freak," he'd boasted on the night he, Sal, John, and I had first snorted crystal meth together. Sure, I'd heard drag queens bandy that word about, but never a gay man. Most were too crippled by guilt and shame to show that kind of chutzpah. Not Peter. He was the most flamboyant, in-your-face, hip gay man I'd ever met and I wanted to be just like him.

By then, I'd taken over John's job at Lodox Drug Wholesalers after he'd started to worry he was getting hooked on its fare. Knowing I had no such qualms, he'd informed me of the vacancy and suggested I run right over and apply for the job. "Use my name," he'd advised. "I'm sure they'll hire you right on the spot." As he'd noted, he'd been a model employee, always on time and never a shirker. If they knew he'd been robbing them blind, no one ever let on, although he suspected everyone who worked there was in on the steal. After all, no one could survive on what Lodox paid.

John predicted I'd be perfect for the job, which consisted of stocking an aisle with prescription drugs and filling orders as they passed by on a conveyor belt. His aisle, he'd said, was mostly uppers and downers, although the union steward worked the one with the harder stuff—morphine, methadone, cocaine. Tending that aisle was the plum position. As he noted, the union guy, a handsome, well-dressed Black guy from the Bronx, drove a Cadillac convertible to work. Everyone else walked or took the subway.

The boss, a trim, white-haired WASP who seemed too nice to be in on the grift, hired me on the spot. As predicted, he complimented John on his work habits and said any friend of his had to be a safe bet. I smiled sweetly and inquired about a start date. "How about tomorrow?" he replied. "9 a.m.?" I asked. "See you then," he said before shaking my hand.

My biggest theft at Lodox was a bottle of pure liquid meth that I traded to Peter for his copy of Flaubert's *Salambo* and a promise to accept my invitation as soon as I got it together for my first-ever gay dinner party. John, who'd dealt Lodox fare for almost a year, complained I had no head for business; the vial I gave Peter was worth at least two months' rent on Avenue D. But I didn't care. I didn't know how to cook either. I was just obsessed with Peter. I wanted to be his new Forrest—a Speed Queen.

John said this was because Peter was "on fire," meaning that with a sun in Sagittarius and a moon, Mars and Venus in Leo, he was pure will. In contrast, John said I was "all wet," meaning that my chart was a swamp of water signs with no fire, hardly any air and barely enough earth signs to ground me. My moon and rising sign were in Cancer, while my sun and Mars, a planet that was supposed to give me backbone, were in equally watery Pisces, placements which John's astrology book said made me dreamy and idealistic but overly accommodating, highly impressionable and "subject to misuse by others."

I protested he must've gotten something wrong. Sure, I was shy, insecure and a bit starstruck, but I rankled at the suggestion I was overly accommodating. After all, hadn't I come out to my parents when I was only eighteen? "Who else do you know who's done that? Or stood them down when they demanded I submit to a cure?" I challenged John to name one other person who'd fought as hard just to be gay.

He double-checked his calculations and even had me confirm the hour of my birth with my mother. But once he determined his findings were correct, I had no choice but to accept the chart as my own. If I wanted to live my life as I wanted, I needed to do as the *I Ching* advised and appoint helpers.

When John noted that Peter's rising sign was Scorpio, I knew he was the one. *Scorpio Rising* was an underground film whose review in *Time* had so blown my mind I'd cut it out and used it as a bookmark for Selby's *Last Exit to Brooklyn*. Every time I returned to it to read up on Georgette the hip queer, I'd stop and savor *Time*'s summation of the film's strange, scary pull: *Kenneth Anger's notorious Scorpio Rising is a jaggedly cubistic piece of black cinema that examines the big strong she-men who gun along with a motorcycle cult. The movie concludes with a satanic black-jacketed bacchanal that looks like the last stages of an amphetamine nightmare.*

Although Peter wasn't yet aware, I'd appointed him my helper. He was the big strong she-man who'd show me the ropes of the satanic bacchanal on whose periphery I lurked—a sister in the struggle to break free, to be something never-before-seen: a hip, in-your-face, out gay man.

I got fired from Lodox even before the end of my three-week probationary period. On my last day, the boss met me at the door and told me not to bother clocking-in. For the third time that week, I'd taken too many Tuinals and slept through my alarm. That day, I was almost three hours late.

I begged him to give me another chance, but I knew from the smirk on the union guy's face the gig was up. Stealing merchandise was fine but interfering with production wasn't. I lacked the self-restraint necessary for the job. As I headed for the stairs back down to the street, the owner took two cigars from a box on his desk and, handing one to the steward, wished me well. "Good luck, son."

"Yeah, brother, peace," the steward added, with a weariness that indicated I was by no means the first who liked their work perhaps a little too much.

I didn't bother telling them both to go fuck themselves. I didn't need to. I had the drugs I'd stolen from them to do that for me. That night, I popped two reds and panhandled outside the Stonewall with my new pal Joey, a tall, lanky, wiry-haired runaway from Staten Island who'd made the mistake of falling in love with John. That's how we'd met. I'd sold him the pills to help him forget.

We made good money that night, mostly because of the novelty—people said they'd never seen gay panhandlers before—although when we tried to get into the Ninth Circle, my old friend the bouncer told us we were too loaded. I thought that was hilarious given all the beauties I'd sold him and, from there, we stumbled off to the Trucks where we giggled at all the goings-on until two men in dog collars came up to us and complained we were ruining their mood. "Wouldn't you girls be happier outside?" one asked, while the other shoved us onto the street.

Joey wanted to go back in swinging, but I calmed him down with another red. From there, we returned to Avenue D, where I snorted a line of crystal meth John had copped for me from George Right and scrawled my parents a long, furious, drug-crazed letter. I'd tried to bare my soul but, bullied by my mother's refusal to countenance the word gay, I reverted to the code which shielded her from knowing anything about who I really was or what I might be going through as a result of that.

In the letter, I wrote, *I am doing 'it,' will continue to do 'it,' and remain convinced not just of 'its' necessity but 'its' total reality.* To a stranger, which my parents were fast becoming, 'it' could just as easily have been moving to an ashram, starring in an underground film, blocking munitions shipments to Vietnam, or standing on a soap box and screaming the word "fuck." Instead, 'it' was merely code for being gay, the biggest outrage of all.

For news, I told them I was struggling against a deep depression brought on by the "heavy changes" going on around me. For details, I mentioned only that Sal had fallen into "a very bad head." I didn't bother noting that I'd been fired from my job—mostly because they didn't know I'd been hired for it—or that George Right, the Village's biggest supplier of speed after George Wrong, had asked John if I might be interested in hooking up. And while I wrote that Valerie, the hippie chick from SU, and her new boyfriend were curled up in a corner of my living room, I didn't say they were coming down from an acid trip. Nor did I mention that Joey, the runaway from Staten Island, was crashed out in the opposite corner on reds. As my mother had said, she wanted to hear no more about "that"—a term so all-encompassing only the weather was left as a suitable topic.

Of Mike, about whom she'd professed some interest, mostly because he was still in college, I said only that he'd left town unexpectedly to be with his mother, with whom he was, in stark contrast with me, unusually close. What I didn't explain was how I'd finally gotten him to split. The night before, he'd paraded around the apartment with a feather duster and a scarf tied around his head "á la Carmen Miranda" squealing he felt just like a stage mother for the cast of *Hair*. I'd gritted my teeth and endured as much of that as I could but when he started belting out "Good Morning Starshine," I'd retaliated by putting the Velvet Underground's "Sister Ray" on the stereo full-blast. While he'd quieted down for the part about sucking on a ding-dong, the business about searching for a mainline and not being able to hit it sideways had gotten him up and out the door real fast. With Mike gone, we could finally do our drugs out in the open, rather than sneak off to the bathroom.

I concluded my letter by advising my mother to take care with its insane jumble of paper scraps: *I don't want you to drop them on your way to the <u>den</u>.* As I underlined "den" in black and blue ink, I wondered if she'd get the allusion or if, as Mike had said of straights, she too suffered from an "irony deficiency." The den was the room where she and I had always had it out—the place where I'd told her I was gay and where, in retaliation, she'd told me she never wanted to hear any more about "that"—code for me, homosexuality, long hair, drugs, downward spirals, all-consuming rages and the terrible drive to get back, to hurt her as badly as she'd hurt me.

I sealed the envelope and shook my head at the dizzying pace of my fury. Only a little more than a year ago, I'd pulled back the swaddling and revealed the face of my mother's last little bundle of joy, only the second of four to have survived the journey from her womb. *It's Black!* Mike had shrieked in mock horror when I'd told him how she'd reacted to the news that I was gay, a moral breach at least as sinful as race-mixing. *My baby's Black!*

Decades later, when my mother and I finally tried to talk about my time in New York, she told me the story of my letter's delivery. Alarmed by the return address, as well as the insane scribbling along the envelope's edges, the postman had decided to ring the bell rather than just drop the letter through the mail slot. "I'm sorry, Mrs. Mitchell, I don't want to intrude," he'd said, handing my mother the letter. "But do you have any idea where Avenue D is?"

She'd numbly shaken her head. "No, why?"

"Oh dear, I don't want to alarm you. But I think you should be concerned." The postman had smiled faintly and explained he'd once delivered mail in New York City just a few blocks from Avenue D. "Very, very concerned."

My mother had been so upset by his description of what went down on the street and its environs that she immediately took to her bed. That afternoon, she'd become so distraught my father had to leave work and come home early. "I felt so helpless and ashamed," my mother stammered before confessing she'd even gone to Dr. Connolly, the family minister, for counseling.

Still crippled by her gag order, I didn't bother noting those were emotions I'd shared with her even back then. Nor did I mention that, instead of Dr. Connolly, I'd turned to a speed freak junkie named Peter for guidance. And although he'd said I was not yet Speed Queen material, he'd agreed I had potential. I just needed to dispense with some inhibitions. Like John, Peter thought I was too judgmental.

"Kay Hoopes Harrington," Peter had started calling me, after a friend of his mother who'd shown up for bridge games in white gloves and a string of pearls. "Oh, Kay," Peter would cry every time I'd claim I'd reached my limit; I couldn't possibly break another taboo. "You're such a proper lady!" I'd assumed that meant I needed to snort more speed, although I never seemed to snort enough to stop being Kay.

After a while, I'd assumed the problem lay elsewhere, although whenever I contemplated shooting up, Peter's preferred means of getting high, I'd nearly always wanted to jump out of my skin. Then, one night when Peter again started babbling about the storming of Rome—although that time he was in my living room on Avenue D rather than on the second-floor landing of West 10th Street—I'd realized that was the point. Jumping out of her skin was exactly what Kay Hoopes Harrington needed to do.

14
Getting Real

Disgusted, I tossed my cigarette into my plate of spaghetti and listened as it hissed back at me. Across the kitchen table, Sal, John, and Peter, who'd recently left West 10th Street to live with George in his East 4th Street shooting gallery, mutely stared into their laps as a cockroach crawled from the garlic bread's tin foil wrapper. "What the fuck?" I cried, swatting it onto the floor and smashing it with my foot.

My first gay dinner party, a send-up of my mother's post-church, pre-game Sunday suppers, had been a fiasco. I'd dumped cayenne instead of black pepper into the spaghetti sauce and baked the garlic bread into a charcoal briquette. Even the joints I'd rolled had been a mistake. They'd sent Sal and John deeper into their shells, while Peter, normally irrepressible, had become tongue-tied. "It's why I never do marijuana," he'd sheepishly confessed after a particularly long, awkward silence. "I become a bore."

Determined to break through, I asked if he'd brought along his works. Peter flinched as if I'd dropped a plate on the floor and then, turning to Sal and John, asked if I was always so forward. John continued to mutely stare into his lap, although Sal actually disavowed me. "Hey, don't look at me," he stammered, nervously tugging on the end of his moustache. "The cat's doing his own thing now."

It was a bald-faced lie. The night before, the three of us had agreed we were ready for what John called the "next phase" and vowed one of us would ask Peter to shoot us up. While I'd waited and waited, neither of them had spoken up. Indeed, they'd hardly uttered a word. *Useless chickenshits*, I muttered under my breath.

Peter turned back to me. "Why, no, darling, as a matter of fact, I left my works with George." He smiled sweetly. "He promised me a new point."

"Don't lie to me Peter. You said just the other day junkies are always carrying."

His face reddened. As I knew well, nothing bothered Peter more than being caught in a lie. "Okay, so what if I am?"

I looked him squarely in the eyes. "Because I want you to shoot me up."

"Oh, darling, I mean, *really*..."

"I'm serious, Peter. I want to feel it. You know, the rush. The one you say only comes from injecting it."

"But it's not ladylike," Peter retorted. "Kay Hoopes Harrington may take a poke of vitamin B-12 every now and then but it's only in the ass. She never, ever mainlines."

I groaned and rolled my eyes. If I heard one more time how I reminded Peter of his mother's bridge partner, I was going to start throwing things.

"And what about those evening gowns?" he continued, running his fingers through what was left of his strawberry blond curls. Two days earlier, complaining he was sick of hippies flashing him the peace sign, he'd sheared his halo down to a stubble. "You can't have tracks in a strapless! What would people think?"

John snickered into a paper napkin he'd nervously folded into a party hat, while Sal desperately tried to clear a frog from his throat.

"Then, I guess I'll just have to wear opera gloves, won't I?" I snapped, glaring defiantly back at him.

Peter cackled loudly. "You know, I like you best when you're riled. I mean, you should see your eyes. They're positively blazing!"

I continued to glare at him.

He sighed and reached across the table to take my hand. "Listen, darling, you're a really sweet kid. Don't ruin it. Shooting up is not for you."

"Oh, Peter, please," I groaned, yanking my hand away. "Cheap sentiment does not become you." I grabbed a napkin and wiped my brow. The room was stifling. From the living room, Nico's "Femme Fatale" egged me on: *Here she comes/ You better watch your step...*

I leaned across the table and stared into Peter's eyes. Their color reminded me of the vast, silvery lake on whose shoreline my family had once waved into the eye of some forgotten neighbor's camera. Long before I could remember, my father had rowed me out into the middle of that lake to give me a bath. Soapy, I'd slipped out of his grip and nearly drowned. When we'd finally made it back to shore, my father had collapsed onto a cot in our lakeside cabin and cried his eyes out. "Just like a baby," my mother had said, relaying the story. "I'd never known him to be so upset."

Having never seen my father cry, I'd tried to envision the scene but never managed to conjure up anything more than a murderous intent. Most of the time, I'd imagined him waiting to rescue me until I was just a faint blur in the water, although, a few times, I'd actually visualized him tossing me overboard. No matter which, I was always left with the same harrowing question: how bad did a child have to be to be so hated by a parent?

No matter what, I always ended up with the same answer—I brought out the worst in my parents. "That's why I want it, *darling*," I hissed back at Peter. "I want to burn it out of me. I want the guilt and shame *dead*."

Peter shrieked as if I'd just said the magic word and then, pushing off from the table, asked John and Sal if they wanted a shot too. "You'll like the rush. It's not the least bit jangly." While I wondered why their sweetness didn't also warrant a comment, they looked at each other and shrugged sure, why not. They had nothing better to do.

Nothing better? I almost cried. *What could be better than becoming someone like Peter*? Instead, I mutely followed them into the living room and watched as Peter sat on the end of the sofa and pulled an Altoid tin from a beaded rawhide shoulder bag, a relic from his time as San Francisco's reigning Speed Queen. When I'd first seen it, I'd used a David Hemmings line from Antonioni's *Blow-Up* and told him to get rid of it; the bag was diabolical. Peter, who credited the film for his decision to leave the seminary, had squealed with delight. Later, when I'd confessed that Veruschka, the supermodel who'd played one of the film's drug-addled jet setters, was my fantasy alter ego, Peter had even called me "fabulous." It was then I'd known I was close. Soon, I'd be the new Forrest, Peter's sidekick.

Pointing back into the kitchen, Peter told me to fetch a glass of water and a spoon and, when I returned, patted the space on the sofa next to him. "Sit here. I'll do you up first," he murmured. He then proceeded to line the contents of his Altoid tin in a neat row to his right—a glassine dropper; a sharp, shiny needle; a red rubber bulb; a bright blue elastic; a ball of cotton; a book of matches; and a one-inch square of tin foil. "There," he murmured after affixing the point and the bulb to his dropper, the latter with the bright blue elastic. "All set?"

I looked across the room at John and Sal—John in a chair against the rear wall by the fire escape, busy even then with junkies, and Sal by the window looking north toward 14th Street. Both were ashen, with Sal continuing to try to clear his throat. Neither looked willing or even able to speak. "Yes!" I cried as the screech of an electric violin announced the start of the Velvet Underground's "Venus in Furs." *Shiny, shiny, shiny boots of leather/ whiplash girlchild in the dark....*

Peter nodded, filled the dropper with water and squirted its contents at a nest of flowers in the center of a badly-stained rug that Sal and I had hauled up from the street. "You must always make sure your dropper is clean," he instructed. "Do up someone else's blood and you'll know why they're called bonecrushers." He refilled the syringe and again squirted the carpet. "They're a junkie's nightmare. Feels like your insides are in a meat grinder. I got one in San Francisco and promised myself never again." He looked at me sternly. "Clean your dropper before you use it, understand? Every time!"

"You sound like I'll be doing this again," I replied, smiling coyly.

"Of course, you will, darling. No one does this just once," he said, opening his square of tin foil. Sal nodded, his throat suddenly clear of its frog. As he noted, he too had done this before. "With Forrest," he mumbled, although Peter, thinking Sal a bore, didn't bother to respond.

"Not too much, okay?" I stammered as Peter dusted the bottom of the spoon with his drug.

"What's the matter, don't want to end up like Electric Freddy?" Peter smirked as he doused the speed with water. "Don't worry, darling. I'm not like George Wrong." He chuckled; he loved the nickname John and I had given his lover. "I don't do overdoses."

Mesmerized, I watched as he waved a match under the spoon until the powder dissolved into a pale murky brine. He dropped a cotton ball into the mix, drew the elixir up into the dropper, emptied it, drew it up again and then clenching the syringe between his teeth, motioned for me to roll up my sleeve. "Uh-uh," he grunted as I unbuttoned a cuff, "the other one. Your left arm."

He untied the blue paisley scarf from around his neck and, after twisting it tightly around my upper arm, told me to hold it firmly in place. "No, tighter," he instructed, "as tight as you can make it." Then, he ordered me to make a fist. "Oh, come on, can't you do better than that?" he grumbled as I limply curled my fingers into a ball. "A *fist*!" Finally satisfied, he kneaded the soft inner flesh of my arm until the dark blue shadow of a vein appeared. "Mmmm," he murmured, poking it with his forefinger, "you've got good veins."

I blushed.

Slipping off the couch, Peter crouched between my legs and looked up into my eyes. Beads of sweat dripped from his brow onto the knees of my jeans. "I need to know you want me to continue. You must be absolutely certain." On the stereo, Nico's "All Tomorrow's Parties" issued a warning: *A blackened shroud/a hand-me-down gown...*

I looked out the window at the slant of shadows on the roofs lining Avenue D. At that very moment, my mother would be at the dining room table, her tiny hands folded over her plate, solemnly nodding as my father invoked Sunday grace: *Give us this day our daily bread and forgive us our debts as we forgive our debtors*...Twisting the scarf still tighter, I flashed on Jeff's snout, snarling through the porch screen at the garbage men. I heard his low-pitched growl—a long, deep moan that was as much anguish as wrath, nurture as nature, and murmured, "Oh, yes, Peter, please."

I winced as his needle pierced my flesh and then marveled at the bright red plume of blood that gushed into the dropper. "Just like a mushroom cloud!"

"Hush," Peter chided and then, cradling the syringe in the palm of his hand, flicked the barrel with a forefinger until the liquid was the color of pink lemonade. As Sal had warned the night before, even the tiniest bubble would mean instant death.

"Okay, now hold very, very still," Peter demanded. Then, gently rocking on his knees, he slipped his left hand under my elbow and instructed me to loosen the scarf. "Quickly," he barked as I fumbled with its folds. "All the way." He nodded as I finally unfurled it. "That's it. Now drop it. Yes, that's right. Onto the floor!"

I held my breath as Peter emptied his syringe into me and then, even more quickly, removed it. "Shit," he muttered as a thin stream of blood trickled down my arm, although I swore the windows also rattled and the black light over the now booming stereo flickered on and off. *Whoosh!* My eyeballs puckered and my head snapped back as a blistering wall of heat slammed into me. Flames leapt up my throat and a roiling burst of chemical exhaust rolled off my tongue. I collapsed into a heap.

Bang! My cells exploded. A line of cannons let loose deep inside me and I vanished into a thunderous roar. Leaning over me, Peter wiped my brow with his scarf and asked if I was alright. I peered through a hoop of flames and moaned, *Oh my God, yes*. I looked down at my feet. They were on fire.

As the Velvet Underground's "Heroin" thundered across the room, I rolled off the sofa into a pool of molten lava. I jumped up and materialized as a knife. Flames shot from my fingertips as I pointed at John, into whose outstretched arm Peter again emptied his syringe. He slumped over and quivered slightly as, that time, Peter congratulated himself; he hadn't shed a drop of John's blood. Straightening himself up, John's eyes also blazed. Then, he too burst into flames.

"Spontaneous combustion!" I cried.

Tracers of me raced for the walls and engulfed Sal, ashen and trembling as Peter ordered him to tighten his fist. "What is it with you sissies, anyway?" Peter sneered. "Can't you at least *try* to be butch?"

"Jesus," Sal moaned after he finally worked up a vein for Peter to jab and then curled into a tight fetal ball. Then, Peter, squatting in a corner with a needle in his arm, also burst into flames.

The ceiling cracked. Walls warped. Brains exploded. Wild-eyed, the four of us embraced in the middle of the room and even John, who had no sense of rhythm, danced until we were panting and drenched in sweat. *And I guess but I just don't know*, Lou Reed bellowed from the stereo.

I darted down the hall and stared at my reflection in the bathroom mirror. My face was flushed and my pupils were swirling tar pits. The vein in the crux of my arm was swollen and had darkened slightly. Below it was a patch of dried blood. "Stigmata," I murmured.

I reached for a towel to wipe my still-smoldering brow and recalled the aphorism from *Love's Body*: *Truth is error burned up*. Vulcan had finally come knocking. The she-man I'd anointed my helper had fired her gun. Nothing was left of the old me but ash.

Three weeks later, Mike ran into the living room on Avenue D with a bloody syringe he'd found in the bathtub soap dish. Throwing everything but his perfume bottles and his posters of *Hello, Dolly*! and *Fiddler on the Roof* into a duffel bag, he shrieked he hadn't come this far in life to let a bunch of junkie losers ruin him. He didn't care that George Right, George Wrong's rival for control of the Village's burgeoning speed market, had used it to loosen me up for a fuck in a bubble bath or that, three hours later, we'd turned the bathwater the color of pink lemonade. He didn't find the story the least bit sexy, decadent, or amusing. Instead, he looked me straight in the eyes and spat that I was a sick fucking queen and a perversion of everything good in the world. I handed him his Ethel Merman and Barbra Streisand LPs and told him thank you; finally, he got it. He left saying he never wanted to see me again.

Mike was my last connection to straight gay life and with him gone, the needles came out into full view. George Right, who'd taken to calling me his boyfriend even though Danny was, technically speaking, still his lover, likened Avenue D to a shooting gallery, although John, who'd stopped paying rent on his West 10th Street room in anticipation of a return to the West Coast, was content to simply call it home. Only Sal was conflicted, although he quit his job at a midtown bookstore to regularly avail himself of the speed George so generously offered, free of charge.

I knew from the start Sal wasn't going to be able to keep up. And so, one morning, only a week or so after Mike had fled, he emerged with his sleeping bag tied to the top of his backpack and announced he was splitting for Cambridge, where an old friend promised to put him up until he figured out where he'd go from there. The speed, he explained, had become too much. His liver was killing him. Worse, he feared New York was becoming a death trip.

He admitted he had no idea where he'd go after Cambridge. Maybe he'd return to Syracuse and help his aging parents out. His mother's heart was bad; his father's hearing worse; and the old neighborhood wasn't what it used to be. Vandals had even torched a building a few doors away.

Or maybe he'd join his hippie friends Karen and Murdoch in their teepee out on the Olympic Peninsula, or maybe he'd head off to Lake Placid. Someone, he couldn't remember who, had said it was a good place to get one's shit together, whatever the fuck that meant, although I suspected it primarily involved getting away from other gay people. Every time Sal hung around them for too long, he started blathering about death trips.

I shook my head in disgust. That was Sal in a nutshell. He simply could not take a stand. I looked around at the growing chaos of our lives on Avenue D and vowed I was staying put. Some things were worth dying for. And being gay was definitely one.

When Sal left, I didn't bother wishing him well. He was a coward, as well as a deserter. Besides, I no longer needed him for my war. I had speed and, better, fellow warriors who injected it. As Peter had noted, I even had good veins—very good. And then there was George Right, not just a speed freak, but a speed *dealer*, who said I was a really good fuck. I wasn't just gay. I was *fabulous*.

I'd forgotten the warning from my first casting of the *I Ching*: "Horse and Wagon part. Bloody tears flow...One should not persist in this."

John's face floated in a pool of candlelight above a ripped armchair and rickety side table, part of the rag-tag ensemble—a kitchen table and two chairs, some pots and pans, a wastebasket—that the landlord claimed made the Avenue D apartment furnished. His cheeks were sunken and his eyes had the same wild gleam as my mother's on the day she'd demanded I submit to a cure. "But it's Miss Eden's big moment," he cried. "She's going to be *real!*"

He was referring to Barbara's impending return to Washington, DC, in whose drag bars she'd gotten her start as a skinny, sixteen-year-old Puerto Rican runaway. A rich john had promised her a luxury pad off Embassy Row and an all-expenses-paid stay at John Hopkin's sex change clinic in exchange for a regular go at her freshly-made parts and her companionship at the whirlwind of diplomatic events he was expected to attend. Hoping to wrangle more inducements out of him, Miss Eden had held off agreeing to the arrangement until, miffed by her delays, the john had issued her an ultimatum. She either claimed her new apartment by the end of the month or the deal was off. With only a week to go, Miss Eden had immediately turned to John. Would he drive her down to DC in his VW Bug?

John had agreed and asked me to tag along, although I wasn't at all sure I was up for the next phase he intended the journey to usher us into. Actually, his plans frightened me. I was even trembling. Visibly. "My God, look at you!" John exclaimed. "This really has you spooked, doesn't it?"

Everything he'd gathered for the trip was arrayed around him. The license plate he'd stolen to make his VW Bug roadworthy was by his feet, while the syringe he'd jury-rigged from odds and ends he'd lifted from Lodox and the nickel bag of crystal meth he'd copped off George Right were on the side table. And propped against the side of the chair was the two-toned blue vinyl VW door panel behind which everything was to be stashed, safe from all but the most thorough searches.

But it was on the left arm of his chair where he'd laid out his proudest take—the stash of hot credit cards, each of which Barbara called a "love child." At first, she'd refused to give them up, saying her reward for all those hours spent on her knees down by the docks was too steep a price for a lift to DC. But five days later, with time running out on her john's offer, she'd finally relented. "What's a girl to do? He said he wouldn't take me unless I handed them over," she'd whimpered when Peter demanded to know why she'd given her babies to a milquetoast like John rather than a sleaze like him. "Besides, he's the only queen I know with a car."

What Peter didn't know was the sweet, shy John he thought a crashing bore was about to be history, replaced by someone as cold and calculating as he claimed to be. "Oh, come on," John urged. "Don't be so uptight. The trip's our chance to prove ourselves sleazes, too."

I took a long drag of my Marlboro and shuddered; the speed had ratcheted things up to a breaking point. Even the words and phrases we used to telegraph our hipness—like 'far out,' 'fucked-up' and 'right-on'—had become suddenly square. In the brave new world of New York speed freaks, one no longer pushed the envelope; one crashed the plane. One was either 'demented,' 'loaded' and 'sleazy' or simply no one at all—what Peter dismissed as a bore. Even being strong or in-your-face was no longer enough. One had to be bad too, although horrible was even better.

This is it, I thought, the spiraling that was the start of what Sal had called a death trip. Even someone as hardcore as Miss Eden was freaked out by what John was up to. "Have you lost your mind?" she'd shrieked when, earlier that day, he'd shown her the stash he intended to take along for the trip. "Don't you know it's now ten years for crossing state lines with a hypodermic? And I'm not talking the Tombs either. Honey, this shit means *Sing Sing*."

When John replied that was a risk he was willing to take, she'd sputtered about crazy, head-in-the-clouds hippies who didn't know their asses from their elbows. Then, ushering us out the door of her tiny room, she'd declared the trip too risky for drag and announced she'd be passing as a man—or at least as much as one with tits, long fingernails, and shaved eyebrows could. "I hope you faggots are happy," she'd snarled before slamming the door in our faces. She hadn't been out of drag once since she'd come to New York. Indeed, so disgusted was she by the sight of her own penis, she no longer even stood up to pee.

Barbara's reaction had only emboldened John. "When a drag queen says you've gone too far," he'd murmured while testing out the stolen license plate on a spin up Broadway, "you know you're finally onto something." When I'd mentioned even Peter thought he'd been too hard on Barbara, he'd gotten surly. Barbara, he'd snapped, was a big girl and more than capable of fending for herself. Besides, her dream was different from ours. She wanted to come in from the cold and "be real." Ours was to burn our bridges and go so far out we'd be beyond the reach of straight people. "Taking control," John called it. "Just like the Blacks."

"I can't. It's too dangerous," I said of John's request. "Besides, I think I've gone far enough out." For weeks, I'd told myself the speed's assaults on my sense of propriety were good for me—that, as Peter had said when he'd named me after his mother's bridge partner, I was just too damn uptight. But John's plans went too far. I told him I had no interest in breaking rules just for the sake of breaking them. Besides, I didn't want to be a sleaze. Or, for that matter, a junkie either. "Just strong," I muttered.

"That's just your fear talking," John replied. "Just think what would happen if one day all the fags and dykes, hippies and freaks, spades and spicks, hustlers and drag queens—even those poor slobs, the ekers, struggling to make a go of it—all of us just stopped and said we're not playing by the straight world's rules anymore. We're going to do what we think is right. My God, there'd be a fucking revolution!"

John insisted only our guilt was holding us back. To conquer it, we had to be as bad as possible. He waved his jury-rigged syringe at me. "Only then will we be free." He chuckled. "*Real*, just like Miss Eden."

"Oh, I see," I sighed. "Our own version of a trip to Johns Hopkins."

"Ahh, finally, you get it!" John cried, whacking the arm of the chair so hard he raised a cloud of dust.

"But what if we get busted? I don't want to end up in a place like Sing Sing."

Freedom, John countered, was something we needed to risk everything for. He smiled and tapped the ash from his joint onto the floor. "Besides," he murmured, "we can't go on like this. Something's got to give."

I watched the candlelight flicker across his face and shuddered. When Sal had once asked what I saw in someone who only read astrology books, decorated his room with contact paper from Woolworth's, ironed even his underwear, and claimed to be too much of a whore to ever fall in love, I hadn't quite known what to say. Suddenly I knew. John was the first gay man I'd ever met who hated his predicament enough to stake everything on the notion he could discover a way out—a gay Captain Cook searching for his own Northwest Passage. As he'd said over and over, he was no thinker like Sal or dreamer like me. He was just a doer—a good, practical Capricorn, indifferent to means. All he wanted was to be free.

"Okay," I muttered, "I'll go along. But only if Miss Eden agrees to get us off." As I noted, while John was bringing along a set of works, neither of us had yet mustered the courage to do ourselves up. For that, we needed someone more experienced and, next to Peter, no one we knew fit that bill better than a drag queen named Miss Barbara Ann Eden, the 'Ann,' a recent addition so she could imagine herself the object of The Beach Boys' ardor: *Tried Peggy Sue/Tried Peggy Lou/Tried Mary Lou/But I knew she wouldn't do/...You got me rockin' and rollin'/Rockin' and reelin'/Barbara Ann/Ba-Ba-Ba-Ba Barbara Ann...*

Bored, I stuck my head between the front seats of John's VW Bug and asked my travel companions to guess who I was. Assuming a look of mock outrage, I placed both hands on my hips and hollered in my best Southern drawl, "Hey boy, what you doin' in my mama's *caaar?*"

John and Miss Eden looked blankly at each other. Knowing my interest in film, John guessed I was a character from a movie, although he didn't know which one. "Is it foreign or Hollywood?" he asked. I replied neither really, although I acknowledged it had at least been made in this country,

Miss Eden asked if the movie was new or old. When I told her it was more or less new, she gave up. As she noted, the last film she'd seen was a re-run of *Cobra Woman* with Maria Montez.

Noting the last movie he'd seen was *It's a Mad, Mad, Mad, Mad World*, John also gave up. "I know you're not Ethel Merman or Edie Adams," he said of its two female leads. "I've seen it five times and know they never had a line like that."

"So, who are you?" they asked in unison.

"Faye Dunaway in *Bonnie and Clyde*!" I cried before noting it was the line she used when the dashing Clyde, played by Warren Beatty, had turned Bonnie's dreary Dust Bowl life on its head. I turned to watch the monotony of central New Jersey whizz by and giggled. "That's what we're doing. Turning life on its head."

Staring out the VW's passenger window, Miss Eden tried to imagine what life would be like after the "change." She envisioned wide brim hats, garden parties, and season tickets to the symphony. Maybe even a maid. "No more blow jobs down by the docks, that's for sure." She turned to John and chuckled. "Maybe I'll even stop doing drugs."

"Don't go too far, dear," John warned. "Even ladies need their little helpers."

I played with the pink and turquoise boa Miss Eden had stuffed into the mountain of shopping bags with which I shared the VW's back seat and envied the stark clarity of her trajectory. All she needed to do to gain respectability was to change the offending parts of her anatomy. For John and I, there was no offending appendage which, once altered or removed, would render us whole. To become respectable, we needed to bring the whole fucking mess down and start over.

Be as bad as possible, John had urged—break every rule in the book. "Straights say we're evil. Well, let's show 'em just how bad we can be," he'd cried. I chuckled over the simplicity of his logic. "Getting real," he called it.

An hour or so later, the shot Barbara had given us at the start of our journey started to wear off and, noting the Turnpike's sign for an upcoming service area, I suggested a booster. It turned out to be the Walt Whitman stop, which I thought a good omen, although a state trooper pulled up behind us as soon as John started searching for a parking space.

"Uh-oh, looks like he's serious," John grumbled, peering into his rearview mirror. "His lights are flashing."

"I told you not to bring that thing along," Miss Eden snarled, glaring at the VW door panel next to her. She shook her head. "A fucking *hypodermic*!"

"Shhh," John hissed, still staring into his rearview mirror. "He's heading right for us."

"Hail Mary, full of grace," Miss Eden muttered, pulling her rosary beads from the jeans she'd donned in lieu of a dress.

"Okay, fellas, outta the car," the cop bellowed from about twenty paces away.

"Oh my God, he thinks I'm one of you—a *guy*!" Miss Eden cried. She turned to me and then to John, her eyes wide with fear. "What do I do now?!"

"*Act butch*!" John spat while reaching across her to make sure the door panel hiding his stash was securely in place. Satisfied, he glared at her. "And, for God's sake, don't let him see your tits."

"Hey, you guys deaf?" the officer shouted before whacking the VW's rear bumper with his billy club. "I said outta the car."

John turned to me. "And not a word from you, understand? You give him any lip and we're done for." Then, exiting the car, he peered over the roof of his VW Beetle and smiled sweetly. "Good afternoon, officer. What seems to be the problem? Have we done something wrong?"

Ordering us to line up in front of him, the trooper admitted he didn't much like what he saw. "You don't seem to like barbers much. People around here take pride in how they look. Pay taxes too." His eyes narrowed. "You guys pay taxes?"

On my left, John smiled and assured him we did, while, on my right, Barbara wheezed into a breathalyzer.

He asked what our business was in New Jersey. When John told him we were passing through on our way to DC, he seemed mollified, although when he asked where we'd come from, he again grew suspicious. "Greenwich Village? Don't like the sound of that. They got drugs and who knows what else up there." He even called it a "den of iniquity."

He pointed at John's VW and announced he was going to have to conduct a search. "From stem to stern," he added ominously. "And I better not find any contraband, I can tell you that right now." Then, announcing he'd be starting with the pile of shopping bags in the back seat, he climbed into John's car.

"Yeah, that's it," John muttered as he tore into one of Barbara's bags.

"But my gown's in that one!" Barbara wheezed. "The one Stephie and I stole from Bendel's. It's for my DC debut!"

"So, what do you think is worse," he shot back, "a man with a dress or one with a syringe?"

"One with both," I snapped and then told the two of them to shut up. A bust was no time for a bitch fight.

Quickly coming to a halt, the trooper held up a red lacy G-string in one hand and a pink marabou slipper in the other. "Who the fuck do these belong to?"

Stuffing her breathalyzer into her jeans pocket, Miss Eden bravely stepped forward and cleared her throat. "They're mine," she quaked, hunched over to hide her tits. "I'm a performer."

The cop locked eyes with her. "Oh, yeah, what kind of performer?"

"I'm a female impersonator," she replied.

"A *what*? You mean, a fucking faggot cocksucker, don't you?" he bellowed, his face red and the veins in his thick pig neck bulging. Without waiting for a reply, he gathered up Barbara's bags, backed his fat ass out of the car and dumped their contents onto the parking lot. "Here's what I think of performers like you," he bellowed as he ground her belongings into the asphalt with the heel of his knee-high boot. When he was finished, he implanted both fists on his hips and growled, "Now, I want you to get the hell out of my sight before I impound the car and throw the three of you's in jail."

Stunned, we mutely stared back at him. Then, Barbara turned to John. "You mean, he's letting us go?"

"Yeah," he muttered, "looks like your drag saved the day."

"Yeah, but too bad about your boas," I added, pointing at the multi-colored remnants the breeze had sent drifting across the parking lot. One was even ensnared on the cop car's antenna.

Barbara's eyes welled up. "My babies." She looked at the heap of torn and ripped clothing the cop had ruined and whimpered, "I've lost everything."

"What's the matter, you perverts have a problem following orders?" The trooper stepped forward and slapped his left palm with his billy club. "I said get the fuck out of my sight before I puke all over myself and have to call in for reinforcements."

John saw me bristle at the word 'puke' and grabbed me by the arm. "Yes, sir, of course, right away, sir," he stammered, dragging me back to his VW. Shoving me into the backseat, he turned back to the cop and gave him a big toothy grin. He even thanked him. "We appreciate your patience, sir."

On our way out of the parking lot, the trooper stood astride the flattened pile of Barbara's drag and bid us farewell with a raised middle finger. "Fucking pig," I muttered, returning his glare.

For the next ten miles, Barbara sucked on her breathalyzer and recounted all the ways the cop had gotten on her very last nerve. "I mean, do you have any idea what a New Jersey jail cell is like?" she whimpered. When we admitted we didn't, she noted she did—she'd spent two nights in one with Stephanie Lisa—and she wouldn't wish anything like that on her very worst enemy, not even that cunt Francine, the Roman Catholic prelate she'd sworn on a stack of Bibles she'd once had a run-in with at an Upper East Side drag party.

Then, when she finally quieted down, John started in on the cop. "The finger!" he growled. "Did you see how he gave us the fucking finger? I mean, who does he think he is, anyway? After all, aren't we citizens, too?"

I wanted to remind him that, no, we were sleazes; we took the law into our own hands, remember? But my head felt like it was about to split open and so I instead focused all my energies on trying to levitate the panel on the VW's passenger door, inside of which was John's nickel bag of speed. If we could just have another shot, I told myself, everything would be fine: John could go back to imagining himself a sleaze; Barbara, a lady with a maid and season tickets to the symphony; and me, Bonnie on her wild ride across the Dust Bowl with the dashing Clyde.

On the crest of the Delaware Memorial Bridge, I pointed out the industrial sprawl of Carney's Point, the DuPont explosives plant my father helped manage in the marshlands of southern New Jersey, and, further on, across the river, the smog-blurred skyline of Wilmington, in whose suburbs I'd become someone I wanted to incinerate. After that, I'd clammed up until, crossing into Maryland, I spotted the exit for my old Boy Scout camp, Camp Rodney, named after the Delaware slave-owner who'd been the first to sign the Declaration of Independence, and told John about the filling station down the road whose bathrooms locked from the inside, where Barbara finally got the three of us off.

As we drove through Baltimore, Barbara pointed out the exit for Johns Hopkins, where she'd soon be rid of the person she wanted to incinerate. When we entered the tunnel under Fort McHenry, whose bombardment had inspired Francis Scott Key to pen our national anthem, I led us in singing what we knew of "The Star-Spangled Banner." John dropped out after the first line and, while Barbara made it through the third, I actually sang the entire first verse, a feat Miss Eden found highly suspect. "Now, I see why you do so many drugs. You got a lotta crap inside that head of yours." She looked at me strangely. "No queen's supposed to know shit like that."

When we got to DC, John drove us past the Iwo Jima Monument, where he'd first had sex with a man, and the Quonset huts near the Lincoln Memorial, where he'd been stationed while in the Army, part of a typing pool supervised by a sergeant who'd ended up his gay mother. From there, Barbara directed us to her old haunts, a string of drag bars located directly across from the FBI headquarters. When I asked if the rumors about J. Edgar Hoover were true, she said she couldn't say for sure, although she'd always found it strange that, unlike the city's gay venues, DC's drag bars never got raided. She also noted that, while every faggot she knew considered Hoover an enemy, DC drag queens considered him a protector. "Or should I say 'protectress?'" she asked with a roll of her eyes.

After that, we drove to Embassy Row where John parked his VW Bug down the street from the modern four-story glass apartment building where Miss Eden was to live out her dreams, a lady at last. As we approached, an older white man, dressed in saggy black pants, a rumpled white shirt, and an ill-fitting cap, stood at attention by its entry. "Oh my God, that's Eva. She used to be my Queen Mother!" Barbara cried as we got closer.

"Oh, you-hoo, Miss Thing!" she bellowed right as a rat darted from a nearby sewer grate. John, who was closest, danced a little jig to get out of its way but, with big feet and a bad sense of rhythm, he glanced the rat's head with his Beatle boot. *Eeeee*, it squealed as blood splattered up his right pant leg. Baring its teeth, it circled us three times and then disappeared into the building's freshly-clipped hedge of bright green cherry laurel

For a few stunned seconds, we stared at the rat's bloody trail and then, running into each other's arms, screamed bloody murder. Mortified, the doorman, who was in fact Eva, Barbara's Queen Mother, came running and chastised us for breaching local decorum. "You're not in Greenwich Village anymore," he snipped. "This is the South. People down here don't go in for screamers."

"Well, excuse us," Miss Eden huffed before sashaying into her new domicile's gleaming marble lobby. "I guess we forgot our smelling salts."

When we got to Barbara's glass and balconied pad, John sat down with his astrology books to decipher the meaning of our encounter with the rat. While Barbara dutifully washed the blood from his jeans, she insisted it had nothing to do with the stars but was instead a curse, a version of what they called back in Puerto Rico the "evil eye." Stubbornly materialistic, I refused to go that far, although I did admit that, of everything one had to deal with in New York—the filth, the heroin addicts, the cops, the crime, the rip-off landlords, the cockroaches—rats were the worst. "Disease carriers," I called them.

Barbara instantly corrected me. "No, honey, you just haven't been around long enough. You'll see. They're messengers of the devil." As she noted, the rat had circled us exactly three times. "Once for each of us."

Shortly after John and I returned from DC, Peter stopped by Avenue D to say he'd left George and moved back to the rooming house on West 10ᵗʰ Street. "The mother of us all," he quipped before noting he'd even taken over Miss Eden's old room.

I told him I remembered it well. "On the third floor, across the hall from John. The one Electric Freddy used to sleep outside of." I laughed and noted it was also the room where I'd made Barbara swear on a stack of Bibles that she really had met Cardinal Spellman—"Francine"—at an Upper East Side drag party.

Peter laughed. "Yeah, the city's not gonna be the same without her."

I asked if the second-floor bathroom was still as filthy as ever.

Peter rolled his eyes and assured me in that regard nothing had changed. He laughed, however, that someone was now using it to beat off to the sex ads in the back of the *East Village Other*. Crusty newsprint was now scattered across the floor along with the plastic syringes and the pots of dried and caked depilatory Miss Eden and Stephanie Lisa, now ensconced in Bayonne with a new "husband," had left behind.

We both howled.

I asked about Bruce, the ex-monk on the first floor who'd put me up when I'd first come to town.

"Oh, God, no, he flipped out and ended up in Bellevue," Peter replied, although he'd heard he'd since gone back to Berkeley to finish up his dissertation. He again rolled his eyes. "On the Nouvelle Vague, no less. Can you imagine?"

Peter shrugged when I asked about Electric Freddy and informed me he'd simply vanished when Barbara left for DC. "And what about you?" he asked. "You still seeing George Right?"

I shook my head and said Danny, his eighteen-year-old lover, had overdosed on reds when George told him he wanted to break up and, guilty, George had gone back to him. I sighed and told him I hadn't had a drop of speed since. I glanced at Peter. "How about you? You got any?"

"Ha! I haven't had a drop since George and I broke up." Peter grimaced. "He expects me to pay for it now. Cash on the line. But that's alright." He smiled slyly and announced he'd gone back to hustling.

"Now, Kay, don't look at me that way," he replied when I cast him a disapproving glance. "How else am I supposed to pay for my drugs? God knows, my welfare check won't." He looked at me coyly. "Besides, a girl has to stay on her toes. Being a sleaze requires practice."

I rolled my eyes and asked what went wrong between him and George Wrong.

Peter shrugged and said the arrangement had simply run its course. "I mean, let's face it, neither one of us is exactly the marrying kind." He looked at me and flushed slightly. "Besides, I'm a bit old for George." When I noted twenty-seven was hardly old, Peter sighed. "It is for a chicken hawk." He ran his fingers through his strawberry-blond stubble and shifted nervously in his chair. "And you're what, nineteen?"

"No, twenty. You shot me up a few days after my birthday, remember?"

Peter shook his head and sighed. "I still regret that. Should never have done it. I mean, you're practically jailbait."

"Peter," I groaned.

He smirked and said he was glad to have found me at home; he wouldn't have wanted to leave a note. He flicked his cigarette ash into an ashtray on the floor and leaned forward. "Besides, I have a message for you." He smiled sheepishly. "It's from George—George Wrong."

"But I hardly know him. What could someone like him possibly want from me?"

"I'm not sure I should tell you," Peter replied, smiling coyly.

Confused, I asked why.

"Because a woman of your social standing does not accept messages from lowlifes like him. George is a junkie and a drug dealer. You have a reputation to uphold."

I shot him a withering glance. "Peter, please."

"Okay, darling," he sighed and spat out the message: "He thinks you're cute and wants to get into your pants."

I turned beet-red. "That's it?"

"I told him I wouldn't tell you. I mean, let's face it. John's right. George is all wrong for someone like you." Peter blew a thick cloud of cigarette smoke into the center of the room. "And, after all, I do have *some* pride. I mean, we'd only just broken up."

We watched in silence as his cloud of cigarette smoke slowly descended and then, a few inches above the carpet, dissipated into thin air.

"But he turned nasty. He threatened to cut me off." Peter's hand trembled as he picked a speck of tobacco from his tongue. "I'm a speed freak, darling, have been for years." He gazed out the window at a cloudless blue sky and grimaced. "I mean, what else is there? Open an antiques shop and turn into one of those horrid little fags?" His jaw stiffened as he shook his head. "Please, I'd rather die."

I asked why George hadn't delivered the message himself. "I mean, East 4th Street is only a few blocks away. West 10th is all the way across town."

"Because he's like every other faggot I've ever known," Peter sneered. "A crybaby. Afraid somebody is gonna reject him. Make him feel bad." He scrunched up his face and cried mockingly, *W-a-a-a*, just like a kid, and then, pulling on a tuft of hair his buzzcut had missed, confessed he wished he had the balls to be a drag queen. "They don't give a shit what anyone thinks. They're gonna be who they are no matter what."

As proof, Peter recalled Miss Eden's last night in town, when he'd paraded up and down Christopher Street with her on one arm and Stephanie Lisa on the other. Peter had loved it, especially when two leather queens in dog collars and chaps blocked their way and told them to get off what they'd called their street. They'd even complained drag queens were giving decent, law-abiding, respectable gays like them a bad name. Stephie had gotten so bullshit over that one she'd pulled out her nail file and threatened to cut their balls off right then and there—provided, of course, she could find them. Terrified, the men had run off like scared little rabbits. "God, I hate chickenshit fags," Peter groaned.

"But everyone says George is so horrible," I countered. "You know, a Horrible Fag."

"Do you know who gave them that name?" Peter asked, smiling mischievously. "Me, that's who, on my first night on East 4th Street, shortly after I'd arrived in town. You know, from San Francisco. They were all there, all the die-hard speed freaks George grew up with at the Factory—Ronnie Vile, Rotten Rita, Norman, and that horror Peter Point—and after I'd danced for them..." He blushed slightly before confessing he'd performed Salome's 'Dance of the Seven Veils.' "Anyway, I suggested they rebrand themselves the Horrible Fags." He shrugged. "I guess they liked it. At any rate, it took."

He said that before, at the Factory, they'd been known as the Moles. "I guess because they only came out at night, I don't know." He paused to roll his eyes. "I mean, a *mole*? How bland and colorless! And closeted! I mean, this is 1969, darling. We're supposed to be out around-the-clock, not just at night!"

I fidgeted with my pack of Marlboros and confessed I feared George's scene was a bit too hardcore for me. "I mean, I can't even shoot myself up." I smiled shyly. "Besides, I don't think I'm Andy Warhol material."

Peter groaned and snarled if he heard that queen's name one more time, he was going to scream. "I mean, he's just another nelly uptown fag. Who cares what he thinks? All the action is downtown now. We're where it's at, dearie."

"But still, George..."

Peter stubbed his cigarette out in the bayberry candle John had brought over from West 10th Street. "You'll go, of course." When I asked him what made him so sure, he looked at me for a moment and then fluffed the scarf around his neck á la Bette Davis in *All About Eve*. "Cause you're like me, that's why. You want to

be turned inside out. And there's nobody who does that better than George."
He chuckled softly. "George Wrong."

When I asked what time the invitation was for, he replied curtly,
"Tomorrow at 4." When I asked if he'd mind me going, meaning was he still in
love with George, Peter simply looked at his watch and said he had to be
running along. His john, a gentleman in his fifties who paid fifty bucks just to
watch Peter dance, was expecting him. After that, he'd be heading over to East
4th Street to cop some speed, his first since the break-up. He confessed it'd be
nice to be high again; since he'd gone cold turkey, he hadn't been feeling
himself. "I'll also confirm I delivered the message." He licked his lips
lasciviously. "Maybe George'll even give me a tip."

"Oh, Peter, *please...*"

He smiled and admitted he still found George sexy. He again turned toward
the window and flushed slightly. "I suspect it's just his dick, though. When push
comes to shove, I am, after all, just another size queen."

"Stop putting yourself down like that," I clucked. Size queens, I contended,
were among the lowest of the low. "You're fabulous," I gushed.

At that, he smiled slightly, rose from his chair and walked across the room
to stand in front of me. "You're gonna be swimming with sharks soon, babe,"
he declared before dropping his pack of Gauloises into the fringed rawhide
shoulder bag I'd once called diabolical. "If you're gonna survive, you're gonna
have to toughen up." His jaw quivered slightly. "And I do mean fast."

I stood and returned his gaze. "I've been swimming with sharks my whole
life, Peter."

He shook his head. "But these are Horrible Fags, darling. Speed junkies.
They like their meat raw."

I looked him in the eye. "I know how to take care of myself, Peter."

At that, he threw out his arms and we hugged, awkwardly. "There," he
murmured, "it's done." Then, turning, he ran down the hall and out the door.

I listened to his footsteps clatter down the building's five flights of stairs and
then, realizing I was once again all alone, ran and bolted the front door's two
police locks. The novelty of my Avenue D freak show had started to wear thin.
I hadn't had an out-of-town visitor in weeks and I'd gone through almost all
the money I'd made pushing pills. Soon, I'd be behind on the rent and the
landlord, a hip capitalist who lived on 14th Street, would be threatening
eviction. Worse, with George Right back with Danny, I'd lost my access to
speed and there was no way I'd turn to hustling to pay for my drugs. In that
regard, Peter was right. I was too much a Kay for that.

Also broke, John was again threatening to return to the West Coast. Two friends from LA had moved to Chicago and he'd figured he could make it at least that far on a really good hit of speed. He'd asked me to accompany him but I couldn't be bothered. Chicago was too uptight. All that ever happened there were police riots. Besides, San Francisco, his intended destination, held no fascination for me. The Summer of Love had died an ignominious death and, although John predicted the city would soon overtake the Village as America's gay capital, the last thing I wanted to be was a gay barfly again.

No, Peter was right. I wanted to be turned inside out. The next day at 4, the turning would start.

That night, I dreamt my mother and I had it out. Claiming she was sick with worry over my move to New York, she grabbed a fistful of hair and showed me her roots. "See," she sobbed, "pure white. I never had a gray hair before all this!"

"Good," I replied coolly. "My plan is working. You're starting to hurt too."

Suddenly, she reappeared in a teased-out helmet of bright orange, the color of her hair the day I'd returned from the Bobby Kennedy funeral train and she'd told me I needed to straighten up and face things like a man.

"What a hideous color!" I cried. "And so much spray!" I touched it. Her hair felt like the fiberglass drapes I'd grabbed the day she'd told me I'd become too much; she'd wanted to hear no more of me. A shard even pricked my finger and drew blood.

My mother just looked at the blood and smiled. "You think you're so smart, buster, but let me assure you, you'll never get to me. Understand? I'll never accept who you are. It's wrong—an abomination!"

"Oh, yeah, then take this!" I hissed and pulled back a curtain behind which George Wrong stood, in his black woolen Dracula cape and holding, in one hand, a plastic baggie of crystal meth and, in the other, a sharp, shiny syringe. I grabbed my mother by the arm. "Please, just say the word and I will stop. I'll even go back to college. Anything, just not Vietnam."

She looked at George and then at me. She knew the word I wanted. It was the one that had torn us apart, the one she refused to utter—the word 'gay.' "You've made your bed," she spat. "Now go lie down in it."

I awoke in a cold sweat.

15

A Place I've Never Been

I stood on the curb next to a busted floor lamp and a smoldering mattress and glanced nervously around me. I'd made it to the place Sal had warned me to never go near—the stretch of East 4th Street between Avenues B and C that he'd called "junkie heaven." Next door, a small brick church with a boarded-up Palladian window and a rotting portico stubbornly insisted God was Love. From a roof across the street, a familiar-looking man with a black eye patch and a red bandana over his head gestured to a colleague standing guard on the corner that I was okay.

Turning, I threaded my way through a phalanx of overturned garbage cans—the early warning system junkies used to alert them to an impending police raid—and smiled darkly. Anywhere else, the man's signal would've been the prelude to a beating. Here, I was just another strung-out white kid in search of a fix.

I threw myself against the bullet-riddled door of George's building and stumbled into a crimped vestibule of cracked tiles and jimmied mailboxes. A crumpled newspaper whose shit-smeared headline warned of a growing impatience—*Nixon to Ho: No More Warnings*—skittered out of a corner, revealing a fresh human turd. Shuddering, I let the door slam behind me only to be instantly enveloped in darkness. Just as Peter had predicted, junkies had stolen all the light bulbs.

I lit a match and groped my way up a stairwell that reeked of piss and rancid cooking oil. On the second floor, a growling Doberman Pincher chained to the banister let me be but, one flight up, a woman with pink lipstick stuck her tongue through a crack in the door and hissed at me. Two doors later, a man shouted over clanging pots and a blaring TV that if somebody didn't do something about the screaming baby, he was tossing it out the window. On the next floor up, a knot of burly, dark-skinned men with pistols tucked under their belts argued loudly in Spanish. Terrified, I inched past them but only the youngest seemed to notice me. "Five dollars," he murmured while groping himself and flicking his head toward a doorway bathed in red neon.

One flight up, I banged on George's door, dripping with sweat and close to tears. When he finally threw the last of his three police locks, I pointed to the neighboring unit and asked what the fuck was going on. Sealed by orders of the New York City Police Department, its door was covered in a crisscross of bright yellow crime tape. When he explained that, two nights earlier, the cops had raided the apartment and busted a group of gun-runners called Up Against the Wall Motherfuckers, I folded my arms across my chest and vowed not to take another step until he assured me I was safe. "Sorry, call me uptight, whatever," I whimpered, closer than ever to tears, "but I draw the line at guns."

"Oh, baby, it's all right. Don't worry, no one's gonna hurt you," George cooed, taking me by the hand and escorting me down a narrow, pitch-black hallway. "You're with me now." Emerging into a grimy, dimly-lit kitchen with a string of red Christmas lights illuminating a sink teaming with cockroaches, I encountered a short, beady-eyed man with dark, closely-cropped hair and thick, black-framed glasses. He thrust a limp hand across a plywood-covered bathtub stationed in the middle of the room and puffed himself up to his full five-and-a-half feet. "Hi, I'm Norman," he crowed, "George's best friend." He glanced nervously at George and smiled, revealing a mouthful of teeth so rotten they looked like shards of coal. "Aren't I, George?"

Without waiting for a reply, Norman rifled through one of the shoe boxes lined up across the tub's plywood cover. "I want to show you these," he said, holding a string of pale-yellow cat's eyes into the light. "They're from Egypt. Very ancient, very occult. The witch Orion..." He again glanced at George. "Gave them to me." He arched his right eyebrow. "They're for a necklace I'm making for a client on the Upper East Side. Lovely, don't you think?"

"Mmmm," I murmured, still reeling from the state of his teeth. Turning away, I glanced into an adjoining room draped in tie-dyed sheets and guessed it was where Peter had predicted George and I would start off. The shooting gallery, he'd called it, the place where, dancing Salome in a G-string and a flurry of scarves, he'd rechristened the assembled Moles—the die-hard A-heads from Warhol's infamous Silver Factory—the Horrible Fags.

Peter had said the tie-dye was his idea. "Not that it mattered but the neighbors could see right in," he'd explained. Once, he'd caught a girl in pigtails from a room across the air shaft watching him get off. He'd admitted that was a bit too sleazy even for him, although George had insisted the girl was better off for it. Living around junkies, he'd claimed, built character.

I stared at the bathtub sitting in the middle of the kitchen like it was a prop for the staging of *Marat/Sade* and wondered what had possessed me to come. I was no match for the likes of Peter. I couldn't even take a bath in public let alone prance around in a G-string and a swirl of scarves.

"You know, I've heard so much about you I feel like I know you," Norman prattled on. "Pisces with Cancer rising, right?"

I wanted to ask who'd told him that, but not wanting to seem paranoid I merely noted my moon was also in Cancer. "I'm told that makes me impressionable." I flushed slightly as I recalled John's precise wording; I was, he'd claimed, "all wet." "Accommodating, too," I added, although I left out the "subject to misuse by others" part John had also read from his astrology book.

"Oh, but that's good!" Norman cried in a shrill nasally whine. "You're open to new experiences." He smirked noticeably. "I mean, people are so uptight these days, don't you think?" Again, without waiting for a response, he glanced at George. "George is a Pisces too, aren't you George?"

George took my hand and blushed slightly, although I couldn't tell which he found more embarrassing: his fawning friend or his own astrological make-up. I hoped for his sake it was Norman. Personally, I found him repulsive.

Norman dropped the cat's eyes back into their shoebox and tapped its side with a long, filthy fingernail. "You know the timing of things can sometimes be so strange. I mean, take your arrival. Not two minutes before you knocked, I'd just finished reading George's Tarot." He swept up a set of brightly colored cards arranged in the shape of a cross on his plywood work surface and fanned them in front of him. On the far left, a card labeled Strength showed a massive red lion licking the arm of a young garlanded woman. On the right, another called Judgement showed a robed angel trumpeting the resurrection of a half-dozen corpses. In the middle, an upside-down devil with ram's horns and bat wings glowered at me. "We were very excited by this reading, weren't we George?"

Again, without waiting for a reply, Norman explained George's Tarot had predicted he'd soon find the one he'd been searching for. "His mirror," he said, flashing another mouthful of rot.

I looked warily at George and wondered what kind of a fool did he and his roommate take me for? I mean, a witch named Orion? Cat's eyes from Pharaonic Egypt? A Tarot reading predicting I was the one George had been searching for? Shaking my head, I turned to walk out. "I think maybe I better be..."

"No wait," George protested, grabbing my hand. "I've got something I want to show you." Leading me to a doorway into what looked like a pantry, he parted a curtain of blue and green glass beads and bowed slightly from the waist. "Welcome to the doctor's office," he murmured, grinning broadly.

"But I thought..." I stammered, pointing across the kitchen into the shooting gallery. "I mean, aren't we going to...?"

George pulled me closer to him and grinned. "I thought we'd get to know each other first." He looked askance at Norman. "You know, alone. In private."

"Oh," I mumbled and warily peered at a space just big enough for the single mattress lying on the floor. On the right wall, a sconce draped in a fringed silk scarf bathed the room in a soft golden glow, while a stick of burning frankincense lent it an air of pagan solemnity. On the floor, squeezed into the narrow space between the mattress and the wall, a glass half-full of water held a dropper with a sharp, shiny needle and a pale pink bulb. Behind it, a fine white powder sparkled inside a clear plastic baggie. At the far end of the mattress, barely visible under a pillow, was a tube of KY.

I idly fondled the curtain's beads and recalled the last doctor's office I'd visited, the one in Syracuse where Dr. Radin, the shrink my parents had hired to cure me, had insisted homosexuality was a serious mental illness. I kicked off my Bass Weejuns, stepped onto the mattress and muttered to myself, *This one's for you, motherfucker.* To George, I merely nodded and murmured, "Far out."

George dove onto the mattress and removed a navy-blue t-shirt with a swift gesture up and over his head. Still standing, I discretely studied the contours of his chest. It was lean and taut with a light dusting of fine black hair and nipples that rose from aureoles as pale and pink as his dropper's bulb. A thick tuft of pubic hair spilled from the waist of low-slung, loose-fitting blue and white striped rayon pants and flowed, like the Nile, upstream toward the flat plain of his belly. He smiled and put a hand behind his head, revealing a thick patch of dark armpit hair flecked with traces of baby powder. He smelled heavenly. "Ready for your appointment?" he cooed, patting the space next to him.

I laughed nervously and, fumbling with the buttons of the green velour shirt I'd picked up at Limbo on St. Mark's Place, worried I'd overdressed. Like George, I kept on my pants, a pair of hiphugger bellbottoms, and slid down next to him. I idly ran my fingers through his chest hair, stopping first to play with his nipples and then with the waistband of his pants. "Mmmmm," he moaned, as the bulge below my hand quivered in the room's perfumed glow.

At first, our love-making proceeded smoothly. We groped and kissed each other, blew into each other's ears, and sucked on one another's nipples. At one point, I even told him he had nice lips, a compliment he returned by saying he liked my buns—his signal that, like the tube of KY, he'd at some point want to fuck me. But when he rolled on top of me and thrust his tongue so far down my throat our teeth clashed, I started to have my doubts. I tried to slow the pace down but, squatting on my knees, George unzipped my bellbottoms and swallowed me whole. I started to relax when he moved on to my balls but when, on the climb back up to kiss me, he clumsily elbowed me in the ribs, I finally had to throw him off me. "My father used to jab me there," I explained, sliding my back up against the wall and protectively placing a pillow over my lap. "Always when my guard was down."

I asked if he wanted to know what it felt like. Before he had time to reply, I started yelling *Raskob*! *Raskob*! and jabbed him in the ribs with both hands until he begged me to stop. "Okay, okay, I get it!" George cried, retreating into a corner. "It hurts!"

"Raskob is one of my father's heroes," I explained—the son of dirt-poor eastern European immigrants who'd worked his way up DuPont's corporate ladder to become one of the family's most trusted lieutenants. In contrast to me, a sissy my father claimed would never amount to much of anything, Raskob possessed what my father called "gumption," the secret ingredient behind every self-made man's success. I felt my face flush. "Needless to say, my father and I don't have much in common." My fist curled into a tight ball. "Once he even told me he hated me."

"Oh, baby, I'm sorry," George groaned, "your father's the last person I want to remind you of." He slid back down onto the mattress and, tracing a crack in the wall with his right index finger, admitted he was nervous. As he noted, he'd wanted everything to be so perfect, he hadn't even gotten high. When I asked if that was unusual, he nodded and confessed he couldn't remember the last time he'd had sex without doing speed first.

"So how long have you, uh, you know, been doing this?" I asked.

"Which?" George smirked. "Shooting meth or balling boys?"

I grimaced and objected to the word 'boy.' "An insult," I called it.

"Only if you choose to make it one," George countered, playing with the fuzz sprouting across my belly. He smiled slyly. "I try not to let pride get in my way of having fun."

Ignoring the crack, I returned to my question. "So, how long have you been, uh, shooting up?"

He paused for a moment and then replied, "Seven years. Like you, I started shortly after I came to New York." He chuckled softly and noted that seven was also the number of phases in the karmic life cycle. "Guess I'm due for something new, huh?" He smiled sweetly. "A rebirth."

"*Seven years*?!" I gasped. "But that's not possible. I mean..." I pointed in disbelief at the crux of his left arm. "You don't even have needle tracks."

"Preparation H," he chuckled. "Clears 'em right up." He noted Vitabath also worked wonders, although only the green version. The pink, he claimed, was mostly for just smelling good, although he said he preferred baby powder. "Johnson's and Johnson's," he smiled.

"But no one's supposed to be able to do speed that long," I countered. "I mean, you must be very strong. Your brain's obviously not fried and your body, well…" I turned beet red. He was far sexier than I'd expected. "I mean, it's not the least bit wasted."

George claimed everything I'd heard about speed was a lie. "It doesn't kill. In fact, it's a miracle drug. Whatever you get—a cold, a fever—the speed burns right out of you." He even claimed he hadn't been sick once since he'd started shooting it.

"Besides," he continued, "why do you think so many Beautiful People do it?" When I replied I didn't know they did, George said that back in the early Sixties he'd met more celebrities in the waiting room of a Park Avenue physician known as Dr. Feelgood than he had at Factory parties. "Tennessee Williams and Truman Capote were both regulars. Judy Garland too."

He said Feelgood told his patients he was giving them Vitamin B-12 shots but George knew it was really pure pharmaceutical meth. He chuckled. It hadn't taken long before many of them were hooked. "They'd be so desperate for another shot some would even show up in their bathrobes." Once, Judy had arrived in curlers.

I noted his mention of Factory parties. "So, is it true what they say—that you're friends with Andy Warhol?"

George cringed. "Andy doesn't have friends. He doesn't need them. He's a machine—a Pop machine. Besides, only tourists use his last name. You should just call him Andy."

"But that would sound pretentious," I protested. "Like I know him or something."

"But I do," George purred, snuggling up against me. "And you're with me now, right?"

I laughed. "But we just met."

George corrected me. "No, we met in the hallway of West 10th Street. Remember? I was with Peter." He threaded a leg through mine and confessed he'd been thinking of me ever since.

I noted that had been over two months ago. "No one pines away that long. At least, not here in New York." I smiled coyly. "Besides, you're a drug dealer. You must have to fight the guys off."

George insisted I had him all wrong; he wasn't like other New York fags. "I don't care how cute a guy is, I won't ball him unless I feel a connection." He blushed slightly. "I feel a connection with you." He shifted onto an elbow and reminded me I still hadn't answered his question. "So, are you with me or not?"

He buried his face in the pillow and begged me to please say yes. "Oh, please, *pretty please!*"

Stunned by the intensity of his come-on, I rolled onto my back and, staring up through the wall sconce, tried to figure out my next move. Spying a tiny burn hole in the silk scarf draped over it, I recalled the scene in *Persona* when Alma leaves the shard of glass for her mutely haughty charge to step on—an act so gratuitously violent even the film recoils, blistering and melting inside the projector. Yes, I thought, here it was -- the shard of glass by which I'd prove to my tormenters I could be just as scary. I turned to George and smiled bravely. "Yes," I replied, my voice quavering only slightly, "I'm with you now."

"Cool," was all he murmured in return, although his dimples deepened and his eyes seemed suddenly ablaze. After that, we lay quietly next to each other, barely even touching, and listened as WBAI played on the kitchen radio Nico's cover of Dylan's, "I'll Keep It with Mine," a song we both agreed was one of our favorites. *I can't help it if you think I'm odd/for saying I'm not loving you for what you are/but for what you're not.../Come on, give it to me/I'll keep it with mine....*

"So, I suppose you know the Velvet Underground too," I finally ventured.

George nodded and said he'd danced back-up for them in Andy's Exploding Plastic Inevitable. "Lou," he added, almost as an afterthought, was even an ex-lover.

I raised myself onto an elbow and, as coolly as I was able, said I hadn't known Lou Reed was gay.

"I didn't say he was," George replied. When I asked if that meant Lou was bisexual, he noted he hadn't said that either. Lou was, he said, just Lou—like Andy, a machine. I wanted to ask if that meant Lou had simply used him as his cocksucker but, not wanting to embarrass him, I simply murmured, "I see..."

George said he too hoped to someday be a machine but feared he was too romantically inclined. "I don't know, I just feel so out of shape when I'm not in love," he sighed. When I asked what bars he had the best luck meeting guys in, he assured me he wasn't that kind of a gay. He didn't trick, had never visited the Trucks, and couldn't remember the last gay bar he'd been to. In fact, he didn't even like the word 'gay.' When I asked what he called himself instead, he replied, "Pop—you know, after Andy." Andy, he explained, was what he called his "avatar," the most brilliant man he'd ever met. "A genius."

"Almost a year," he said when I asked how long he'd been without a lover. Lou, he said, had been his last; they'd broken up shortly after the Velvet's disastrous trip to LA. He retraced the crack in the wall with his finger and sighed. "Sometimes, I worry I'm losing my touch. I've never gone this long without one."

When I asked about Peter, he got suddenly testy. "What, he said we were lovers?" When I confirmed he had, George insisted they'd been nothing more than friends. When I countered I didn't think Peter would lie about something like that, he scoffed. "Peter's a pig. He's taken so much speed you can't believe a word he says."

He calmed back down when I inquired about Norman. "He's the only person I know who's shot drugs his whole life," he said, explaining their bond. "At the Factory," he replied when I asked how they'd met. He said Norman had shown up one day looking for heroin—Norman, he explained, had been born a junkie—and George had given him a shot of speed so big he never went back to smack. George chuckled. "He says I saved his life."

When I admitted I found Norman repulsive, George shrugged. "Yeah, that's why we're friends. Norman's a total sleazebag. All he wants to do is fuck boys and shoot speed." George added that someday he hoped to inherit Norman's mantle as the most horrible fag in all of New York. In the interim, he was teaching George everything he knew.

When I inquired about his own upbringing, George said that, unlike Norman, he came from money, namely North Carolina tobacco, although he noted his parents had cut him off years ago. When I asked if the breach had been over drugs, he shook his head and noted that, back then, in the summer of 1962, at least in Winston-Salem, where he'd grown up, only Blacks did drugs. He pointed to the syringe in the glass next to him and chuckled. "Guess times have changed, huh?"

When I asked about college, George said he'd been all set to enroll at Duke, which he claimed one of his forebears had helped found, when his father came home early from a golf game and found him in bed with the maid's son. George chuckled. He still didn't know which was worse, balling another guy or breaching the color line. "Or, who knows, maybe it was the kid's age. I mean, he was only thirteen." At any rate, his father had kicked him out of the house so fast he hadn't had time to grab so much as a toothbrush. They hadn't spoken since.

"I'm sorry, I can't imagine..." I murmured. I told him that, while my parents also knew I was gay, we were at least still talking. "Sorta anyway." I traced the contour of his Adam's apple and felt my cheeks flush. "That must've really hurt, huh?"

George shrugged. He and his father had never gotten along, although he did regret losing his trust fund, which he said would have been more than enough to support his drug habit. "Besides, it'd be nice to not have to deal." He confessed he worried a lot about getting busted. Prison, he added, was not a place he thought he'd survive.

When I asked about his mother, George stared into the beaded curtain separating us from the kitchen and replied in a voice so soft I had to raise my head to hear him. He said she used to call on birthdays and holidays but she'd stopped after his father caught them talking and had ripped the phone cord out of the wall. "Almost exactly five years ago," he murmured when I asked when that had been. "On my twenty-first birthday."

I confessed I lived in dread of my mother's rejection but George again insisted everything had turned out for the best. His mother was a "juicehead," by which he meant alcoholic, and had mostly just cried through their calls. George confessed he hated tears almost as much as the word 'no.' "The only sins," he called them. Both, he said, made him see red.

He said his parents explained his disappearance on a fatal car crash and boasted he even had a tombstone to prove it. His sister, with whom he was still in touch, had even sent him a photo. He slid his hands between my legs and, playing with the hair on the back of my thighs, murmured, "Bet you've never had sex with a dead man, huh?"

He saw me blanch and laughed. "Am I scaring you yet?"

"You mean, do I want to jump up and flee?" I peered deeply into eyes the color of dark chocolate and assured him I did not. Nor did I fall for his Horrible Fag routine. "You're no more evil than I am," I asserted. I even called him a "pussycat."

"Wow, you can tell that much about me already? You must be pretty insightful, huh?" George smirked slightly. "So, tell me, what was it that gave me away?"

"Your smile," I replied, running a finger down his left cheek. "And then there're those dimples." They were, I confessed, adorable.

He buried his head in the pillow and groaned, "Please, stop, you're making me blush."

I persisted anyway. "You've been hurt. So, you put on a scary mask. I get that. We all want to keep the bullies at bay. But as an end unto itself, being bad is just another cop out—like your mother's drinking..." I thought about stopping there and then decided what the hell; if we were going to be an item, I needed to at least be able to speak my mind. "Or you being a junkie."

I told him I had no intention of following his lead. For me, shooting up was merely a means to an end, my way of breaking with my past. "I need to be about doing good. You know, liberation—life, not death; Eros, not Thanatos." I paused and squirmed, certain I was blowing it. "Like the Panthers say, if you're not part of the solution, you're part of the problem." My cheeks started to burn. "I want to be part of the solution."

George admitted he'd long ago given up wanting to be a part of anything. Getting high, he said, was the best one could hope for. Failure, he added, was the only success.

I kicked our cover sheet to the foot of the bed and insisted there had to be more to life than sticking a needle into our veins. I invited him to join me in trying to find out what. "Who knows, together we might actually get somewhere."

George ran the same finger that had traced a crack in the wall down the side of my cheek and murmured, "You're cute, you know that? And unspoiled. Not at all like the others." He turned onto his back and complained New York was overrun with what he called "pigs"—gay men who, like Peter, were interested only in his drugs. "You seem different. Like you really care."

"I do," I whispered, blushing slightly. "Sometimes too much."

He looked at me plaintively. "I need someone I can trust." He smiled warily. "Someone who can cure me."

I smiled wistfully. "Me too."

There was no more need for talk. We'd both admitted we needed each other to help break with our pasts: George with the drugs; me, my upbringing. Moving in close, I ran my tongue around his left nipple until his breath quickened and then slowly licked my way down to his belly button. "Oh, yes," he moaned before lifting his hips and begging me to rid him of his pants.

I did as he asked, although intimidated by the size of his cock – it was bigger by far than any I'd ever encountered—I did little more than lick it. However, when he pleaded with me to put it in my mouth, I somehow managed to get my lips around it and sucked. My jaw, however, quickly knotted and soon even my gag reflex kicked in, provoking a round of hacking and coughing that forced Norman to pack up his shoe boxes and move from the kitchen into the shooting gallery.

Embarrassed, I buried my face in a pillow and suggested we call it quits. "You're too big." I glanced warily down at his still-engorged cock. "I don't think I can take you."

George would hear none of it. "Oh, baby, don't talk like that. Lots of people can't take me. I understand. I'm big." Sliding his hand between my thighs, he murmured, "Besides, I think I have just what the doctor ordered." He chuckled softly and nodded at the syringe in the water glass to his right. "Bet you've never been fucked on speed before, have you?"

I thought briefly about lying but decided instead to stick with the truth. I told him his rival, the other George, George Right, had already beaten him to the punch. "He's big too," I noted. "But he took his time. We went at it for hours." I blushed slightly. "In a bubble bath—Vitabath, actually," I added, perhaps a bit too cattily. "The green version."

George flinched but, wiggling his finger way up inside me, vowed to do me one better. "I'll take you to a place you've never been," he promised while his other hand gently stroked my cock. Melting into his grip, I chewed on his lower lip and accepted the offer. "Take me," I panted.

At that, George threw my legs over his shoulders, mixed up a shot, tied me off with a rubber tube he kept under the mattress, and injected me with what he said was some of the best methamphetamine New York had ever seen. Then, after mixing a shot for himself—much stronger, he explained, because of his greater tolerance—he thrust himself into me so hard and fast I was sure I'd been struck by lightning. Fusing, we writhed on the mattress for what seemed like hours, although I was so high it could've been mere minutes.

Then, just when I thought I was all fucked out, he tied me off again, shot me up a second time, and rode me until right before dawn. By the time George finally came, my hole burned like the mouth of a volcano but my old SU pal, Larry—the one who'd happily finished off the guy in the red Corvette I'd walked out on—would've been proud. I'd slopped up buckets of him. George asked if he could stay tucked, safe and sound, way up inside me and, as his cock quivered against my lining like a fish stuck in a net, he confessed he'd been hooked since the moment he'd laid eyes on me. Then, starting to stiffen, he thrust himself still deeper into me and, moaning he was back ready for more, confessed he loved only me.

I wanted to protest things like that weren't supposed to happen so quickly but, after two monster shots of pure methamphetamine, my tongue had turned to dust; I was literally unable to speak. My boundaries had also collapsed and I was beset with dread—the burn hole in the scarf over the wall sconce was about to burst into flame; the crack in the wall George had traced with his finger was splitting open; the band of gun-running terrorists had returned to their next door hideout; the cops were out on the street preparing for a raid; the second-floor Doberman had broken free and was roaming the hallways, looking for fresh meat.

Under siege, I limply offered up my arm and mutely let George administer yet another shot, my third of the night, more speed by far than I'd ever dared to take. Then, as the room's glow turned a sickly pea-green and its perfumed air became so charged with danger it crackled, I pulled him on top of me and begged him to fuck me again, certain that sex would at least keep the demons at bay.

I was wrong. I spent the entire fuck convinced that Norman and his boyfriend, a Broadway dancer who'd arrived sometime in the middle of our first fuck, were on the other side of the beaded curtain laughing at me. Terrified, I listened to what I was sure were rats in the wall and asked George if he'd seen Bergman's latest film, the insane one, the one with vampires and birds that peck your eyes out—I was too bewitched to dare utter its name—but, an old hand with speed-induced paranoia, he merely pulled me close, placed my head on his chest and, after saying he hadn't seen a film since Andy had sold out and gone commercial, told me to listen to his heart. "The best machine ever invented," he murmured.

Certain I was going mad, I latched onto his words as if they were gospel. While razor blades strafed the air around my head and a voice inside the wall alleged I was the victim of a monstrously sick joke, I focused on the beat of his heart until I finally came down enough to realize I was wrong. I hadn't lost my mind. I'd merely taken too much speed. As George said, I just needed to work on my tolerance. Eventually, I'd be able to handle the rough patches like the best of them. "A Horrible Fag," he murmured.

Two speed-crazed days later, after the second-floor Doberman tried to take a chunk out of me, George left Norman behind and moved in with me on Avenue D. Since John was staying there too, biding his time until the stars were aligned for his much-anticipated return to California, George kept him in speed too, although he quickly tired of the arrangement. Not only did John's astrology raps suck all the air out of the room, John proved to be almost as piggy with the speed as Peter. After only a week, George insisted we get a place of our own.

The very next day, I found a room at "the mother of us all," the flophouse on West 10th Street, across the hall from Peter and next door to John's old room. It was barely big enough for a chair and a single mattress, although it had a hand sink for cleaning George's works, a windowsill for storing food in the winter and a balcony for cooling off in the summer. "Everything we need," George chuckled as he slathered the walls with sheets of silver Mylar, an homage to his days at the Factory, when speed was plentiful and the energy high. "Our little love nest," he called the room—the place where he vowed to crawl inside me and never, ever leave.

Sitting on the bed, I pondered how to start the letter informing my parents of yet another address change, my third in as many months. In my lap was the black faux-leather funeral home guest ledger George had given me as a trip book. "Just a little token of my affection," he'd smiled as he showed me the inscription he'd penned in a pulsating duet of green and yellow magic marker. Entitled *Stephanie Lisa and the Rings,* it was a quote he'd overheard while Miss Eden and her roommate had been loaded on reds: *"I'm gonna be in a movie," purred Stephanie. "Yesss—umhumm. Gonna star in my own movie—that means it's all about me and everything."*

I re-read George's inscription and smiled. I was now the star of my own movie—one all about me and my life with my new live-in gay lover—proof positive, if there ever was one, that I was not only a confirmed homosexual but a drug-shooting freaky one, at that—my parents' absolute worst nightmare. I wondered which of his personae they'd find most horrifying: speed freak, junkie, drug dealer, Horrible Fag, or Silver George, a former mainstay of Warhol's Factory and ex-lover of Lou Reed, rock 'n roll's darkest angel. I picked up an orange felt-tip pen and scrawled my parents my greeting: *Mom & Dad, go fuck yourselves.*

16
Gas, or the Rat Inside

As the elevator doors rattled to a close, George sidled up next to me, grabbed my hand and guided it into his crotch. "Feel it?" he asked, smiling sheepishly. When I noted we'd already balled twice that day, he explained it was our destination, not my ass that was turning him on. Twelve floors up, his "Grand Poobah," the man who kept him and downtown's growing network of street dealers stocked in crystal meth, awaited our arrival. "He likes it when I bring a boy along," he explained.

"But I thought you said he was straight."

"He is," George chuckled. "But he likes to see me with a boy." He explained that whenever he had one in tow, his Grand Poobah would dip into his secret stash of pure liquid meth—the best, George claimed, that money could buy—and together they'd get what he called "demented." George said they were highs like no other. He slipped his hand down the back of my jeans. "Whenever I visit, I try to bring along someone I think he'll like." His breath quickened as he reached my sphincter. "I'm sure he'll like you."

Sensing my discomfort, George assured me there'd be no sex. As he said, his Grand Poobah just liked to observe what he called George's "prowess." "He says what I get from a boy he's never been able to get from a woman." When I asked what that might be, George smiled and murmured, "Docility." When I asked what my role in this charade was supposed to be, George said all I needed to do was sit there and look pretty. "You know, be seen and not heard."

I bristled at the notion of being so slavish but he insisted the visit was just another stop in the round of introductions that he called showing me off. Two days before, he'd introduced me to the young childless couple who kept his bail money in a cookie jar in the kitchen of their Hudson Street apartment. "Any time you need help, reach out to them. They're like family," he'd said before confessing I was the first lover he'd ever introduced them to. Even Lou, he'd said, had met them only as a friend.

"Oh, I don't know, I just didn't want to rub their noses in it," he'd explained of his previous reticence. When I'd asked what he'd been protecting them from, he'd admitted many of his previous lovers had been pigs. "You're different. Gay life hasn't ruined you yet."

The next day, George had me meet Harry, a smarmy underground playwright he knew from his days hanging around the San Remo. While I'd clearly not been the first lover he'd seen George with, Harry had gone out of his way to make me feel special. "Don't hesitate, any time, my dear, to drop by," he'd purred as we'd gotten up to leave his dark, cramped Christopher Street flat. He'd glanced at George and smiled slyly. "With or without you-know-who."

Afterward, George had warned me that Harry was a lech, although he'd agreed he was not nearly as predatory as the Horrible Fag he'd next introduced me to. A pederast known as Peter Point, supposedly because of his fondness for needles, he'd barely acknowledged me, an indifference George attributed to my age. 'The Point,' he'd explained, preferred his boys prepubescent. When George had suggested we follow that visit up by dropping in on the man he called Rotten Rita, one of the Factory speed freaks who'd turned him into a junkie, I told him I'd met enough old friends for one day and we'd instead gotten egg creams at the Orange Julius on West Eighth Street and gone back to our room and balled.

I must've made a good impression on George's Grand Poobah because the shot he mixed up for me was so strong it didn't matter how humiliated I was to be introduced as George's boy. Rendered mute and consumed with paranoia, I watched them pass the needle back and forth convinced I was the center of a vast conspiracy. Every word I took as code for the plot they were hatching against me.

When offered a second shot, George accepted for me and, although it nearly lifted the top of my head off, it did at least keep me in my place. As the Grand Poobah noted, unlike all the women he knew, I wasn't the least bit mouthy. He even called me "sweet," a word that, had I not been so demented by the speed, I would've made him eat, letter by letter.

When we got up to leave, I had to pry my tongue off the roof of my mouth to even mutter a goodbye. Other than the few pleasantries we'd exchanged upon meeting, it was the first word I'd spoken the entire afternoon. On the walk back to West 10th Street, George had to reassure me we weren't being followed, and my hand shook so badly he had to light my cigarettes. When we got to our room, I finally felt safe enough to confess my paranoia. I even admitted I was afraid George was out to get me. "By making me the butt of some horrible sick joke," I said when he asked how. "To laugh at."

I blamed the speed. "I think I'm taking too much. I may need to cut back."

"Sure babe, anything you say," George murmured. When I asked if he thought less of me for handling the speed so poorly, he assured me that, on the contrary, he was quite proud of me. My time with his Grand Poobah had gone so well he'd even asked George to bring me back. "Says you're a real find," George cooed.

"Really, you're not angry or disappointed I can't keep up?"

George smiled indulgently. "No, of course not, why would I be?" He pulled me to him and assured me I had nothing to worry about. As he noted, I was still learning the ropes. I just needed to sit back and watch. I was, he added, lucky. "Not everyone gets to learn from a Horrible Fag."

I admitted I wasn't used to being so understood. "My family never talked anything out. Things just got swept under the carpet."

George nodded. His upbringing had been equally stifling. "You can trust me with whatever's bothering you," he murmured. "I understand." He leaned over and kissed me. "I'm here to help you." He nibbled on my earlobe and whispered, "Just what the doctor ordered."

We hadn't had sex the day George suggested we pace ourselves and get some sleep. We'd never gone so long without balling, although when I started to worry George had found someone else, I realized once again how paranoid the speed made me. Except for brief runs to the corner bodega for cigarettes and cherry Cokes, George hadn't been out of my sight for almost two weeks.

Still, I was filled with dread. I didn't know why, except that, once again at George's urging, I'd taken too much speed and had been up for too long. I asked for a Seconal to quiet my nerves, but George said he didn't have any. That worried me too. I feared he was saving them for someone else—someone younger and less "prideful," as George had started calling me. He didn't like me objecting to being called his boy.

We had only a single mattress, so George and I had to wrap ourselves tightly around each other. George laughed that it was an arrangement only speed freaks, who rarely slept and used a bed mostly for sex, could tolerate. I started nibbling on an ear, but George claimed he just wanted to sleep. "Later," he promised before calling me his little sex pig.

He'd never called me that before and, though it stung, I didn't protest. At George's instigation, our sex had recently taken a nastier turn, involving more role-playing and verbal jousting. While I hadn't objected to being called some names, I'd drawn the line at 'boy.' That, I'd reminded him, I'd never be. George had, in turn, reminded me he didn't like to be told no. A "prude," he'd even called me.

Outside of sex, George had never called me a name before. I'd let 'prude' pass too, but it had worried me. We'd started squabbling. I worried I was taking too much speed; George thought I was doing too little. I wanted to make something of my life; George vowed to leave me if I ever got a job. I kept in touch with my parents; George said I should've dropped them months ago. Same with John. Both he called bad influences. They made me weak. "Insipid," he called it.

Drifting off, I felt something scamper across my shoulder and tickle my chin. At first, I thought I was dreaming but George, who was threading his legs through mine, suddenly froze. "A rat!" he gasped and bounded out of bed.

I leapt up, rushed around the room and, gathering up my clothes, demanded we move out. "Right away," I said, pulling my suitcase from the closet. "The building is cursed." I even quoted Miss Eden. Rats, I claimed, were "messengers of the devil."

George grumbled I was acting paranoid again. "You're not in the suburbs anymore, you know. Rats are all over New York." Picking up the scales I'd pulled from the trash so I could keep track of my weight loss, he dropped them over a hole in the floor under the hand sink and wedged them into place with his big toe. "There, feel better?" he asked as he sized me up through the hand sink mirror. "No more devils."

"But, George, I can't use the scales there," I said, climbing back into bed. "The sink's in the way." I didn't get it. The speed never seemed to affect George. He hadn't lost so much as a pound; I'd shed almost ten. "If I move them, the rat'll jump out." I held out my hand and watched it tremble. The speed had turned the world into one big jack-in-the-box.

George glared at me. "You know what your problem is? You're too uptight. Everyone has a rat inside them. You need to accept yours." He smiled at his reflection as he tousled the hair around a small bald spot on the back of his head. "I have."

I stared at the tuft of bristles on the toe he'd used to shove the scales over the rat hole and worried George had paid too high a price to be him. When we'd moved in together, he'd brought nothing with him but a torn Lufthansa flight bag in which he kept an Altoid tin containing his works; a tattered deck of Tarot cards; a dog-eared copy of Aleister Crowley's *Magick in Theory and Practice;* and his old Factory party clothes—a pair of black velvet bellbottoms, a ruffled white silk shirt, and his silver spray-painted wingtips. Other than the couple two blocks up Hudson who kept his bail money in a cookie jar, he had no one, just an ever-changing band of speed freaks banging their heads against the wall of IV drug abuse and competing for the title of the most Horrible Fag in all of New York.

George claimed the moment his father had kicked him out of the house for bedding the maid's son was the start of his campaign to be, as John had vowed on the eve of our disastrous trip to DC, as bad as possible. Penniless, he'd stuck out his thumb and let an old man blow him in exchange for a lift to Manhattan. At first, he'd drifted around the Village's Beat scene and then, on a dare, went to the Factory for a party. He'd heard from a friend at the San Remo, a hustler bar off Washington Square, that Andy was looking for people to take their clothes off on camera and George, having nothing better to do and nowhere else to go, thought what the hell, people had always liked him for his dick.

Word had quickly spread about the tall, lanky, eighteen-year-old with the southern drawl, a Cro-Magnon brow, and a thick eight inches between his legs. Everyone had wanted a taste and George, who loved getting his cock sucked, had been only too willing. Whenever he arrived, the Factory's back room suddenly filled.

One day, three of the Factory's scariest speed demons—Ondine, Binghamton Birdie and Rotten Rita—hatched a plot to make George one of their own. Using a fifteen-year-old runaway as bait, they'd lured him to the Upper East Side coop of a fat, demented bull dyke known as the Duchess. The heiress to a publishing fortune, she and her window queen husband were hosting a round-the-clock party to see how quickly they could go through her inheritance. There, they'd handcuffed George to her bed while she'd mixed up a syringe of pure pharmaceutical meth—the best, he said, money could buy.

For a week, she'd used him as her pin cushion and they their sex toy until he'd become so full of holes he claimed he could see light streaming through him. Then they'd spray painted his shoes silver and released him back to the streets as one of them—an "A-Man," the 'A' standing for amphetamine, alchemy, androgyny, anal sex, apocalypse and, of course, their avatar, Andy. After that, everyone called him Silver George.

Eventually, even Andy took notice and starred George in one of his *Screen Tests*. While many of Andy's sitters were intimidated by the relentlessness of his camera's stare, George reveled in it, his face in half-shadow, chewing bubble gum. After blowing a bubble, a slight smirk emerged as he applied Chapstick to lips the lighting made almost impossibly voluptuous, studied the tube's label and, right before his *Test's* end, started flossing his teeth. A master of insouciance, George looked for all the world to be having the time of his life.

From there, the stories grew murky. George had impersonated Andy for media interviews or had he merely turned Andy on to the news photo he'd used in his silk-screen, *Tuna Fish Disaster*? He'd helped Billy Name plaster the Factory walls with tin foil or had he only dyed his hair to match? He'd hung out with Edie Sedgwick, Nico, and Brigid Polk at Max's Kansas City, or had it just been Ondine, Rene Ricard, and the Sugar Plum Fairy at the Tenth of Always? Some claimed he'd even starred in *The Chelsea Girls'* last reel, "George's Room," but no one could say for sure. That reel had disappeared shortly after its initial screening.

George refused to be of any help. An aspiring Pop machine, he claimed the past was dead and only the moment was real. Initially, I took him seriously but after a while I realized all I had to do was sit back and wait until he got so loaded that he returned to his salad days with Andy, Gerard, Ondine, Brigid, and, if I kept real quiet, his ex, Lou Reed.

At first, I was proud I'd snared the former lover of a rock star. But as the stories piled up, I worried nothing had quite measured up for George since Andy, recovering from his shooting, had had the Factory swept clean of its crazies. In that regard, George's reverence for Aleister Crowley, the black magic guru whose notoriety the Beatles had revived by putting him on the cover of *Sgt. Pepper's*—a glum jowly man surrounded by Mae West, a Hindu swami, George Orwell, and Aubrey Beardsley—was perhaps more prescient than even George cared to admit. Like George, Crowley had been a drug and sex fiend who cultivated a reputation as the "Great Beast," the wickedest man alive. And yet he'd died lonely and bitter, forgotten by everyone but the doctor who mailed him his monthly heroin prescription.

I stared at the stack of Tarot cards on the drop-down desk George and I had hauled in from the trash that morning and recalled what he'd told me on that first night on E. 4th Street. Seven years of shooting speed was long enough. He needed a change. A "rebirth," he'd called it. Me.

I picked a card from the top of the Tarot deck and examined it. Called The Fool, it featured a wandering minstrel in green tunic and tights who, holding aloft a white rose, eagerly marches off into a bright, sunny future. When it had appeared in my first Tarot reading, John had pointed to the cliff edge a few steps away and said the dog barking at the Fool's feet was trying to warn him of the danger ahead. But the Fool was so blinded by vanity he was oblivious. Disaster, he'd said, was imminent.

I turned back to George, determined to strike a deal. He could be the Fool but, in exchange, I got to be his barking dog. "No, you're wrong, George," I blurted out as he stood at the sink, scrubbing the head of his dick.

"Oh?" he replied, peering at me through the hand sink mirror.

I watched his balls dangle over the lip of the sink and fought an urge to pin him against the wall and do him right then and there. He was the biggest, baddest, motherfucking faggot I'd ever known, and I was crazy about him, absolutely mad.

"Yes, George, love kills all rats," I asserted, riveted by the dark brown eyes staring back at me. "Together, we're gonna make it through." I smiled and straightened my back. For a moment, even my hands stopped trembling. I'd spoken a truth not even a Pop machine could refute.

"Think so, huh?" he replied as he wiped his hands on the pink and white checked terry cloth towel I'd stolen from the laundromat around the corner.

"Yes," I replied.

"Be careful," he warned, draping the towel over its bar, "I know exactly what I'm doing."

"But we can't...It's too dangerous," I stammered. "Even you said seven years..."

George put a finger to his lips. "I said *exactly*," he repeated. Then, crawling back into bed, he peered under the sheet at his freshly-scrubbed crotch and chuckled he'd found another rat that needed stuffing back into its hole.

At first our lovemaking went well. However, at the first whiff of shit, George pulled himself out of me and, red-faced, snarled I was a filthy mess. Pointing at our Mylar-slathered door, he ordered me out of his sight until I'd cleaned myself out. He even called me disgusting.

For a moment, I thought he was joking. After all, shit was as much a part of butt-fucking as rats were of life in New York. But there was something about his tone and the look on his face that made me do as I was told. And so, wrapping myself in a sheet, I slunk like a kicked dog down to the second-floor bathroom where I sat on the john and pushed everything out until I was as clean as a whistle. The toilet bowl, on the other hand, was a bloody mess and my asshole burned like it had been seared with a red-hot poker—the start of a debilitating case of hemorrhoids that eventually got so bad I smelled like I was rotting from the inside out—which, of course, in a way, I was. George's rat had crawled up inside me and built a nest.

I rose and numbly stared at my reflection in the bathroom mirror. I listened as a faint scratching worked its way toward the naked bulb dangling from a glut of wires in the center of the ceiling and wondered how bad one had to be to be called "disgusting" by a lover—a gay one, no less—my very first. For a moment, I considered walking out on him just like I had the guy in the red Corvette, but I had only a sheet to cover me and, even if I went back upstairs and got dressed,

I had no money. Or drugs. Not even a cigarette. I'd given up everything to be with George. Besides, I was in love with him. Besotted. Hooked.

And so, I rewrapped myself in the sheet and trudged back upstairs for the conclusion to George's fuck. Figuring that, since he knew exactly what he was doing, I must also be getting exactly what I deserved, I even made my peace with the hand-job he finished me off with. When and if I warranted more, he'd give it to me, although the enormity of the changes George had started saying I needed to go through predicted a very long wait indeed. After all, as I'd learned from my mother the day I came out to her, 'disgusting' was a handicap one didn't overcome overnight.

Still, a question gnawed away at me. How could someone who claimed to have made peace with the rat inside him get so bent out of shape over a dirty bum—a lover's dirty bum? Something, I told myself, didn't add up.

Living across the hall from Peter—a mere ten feet apart—was at first a challenge. George was wary of my relationship with Peter; I was wary of his with Peter; and Peter was wary of mine with George. None of us expected the arrangement to last. Exhausted by its awkwardness, either Peter would move out or George and I would. It was merely a question of when.

John, who'd stayed behind on Avenue D, was even starting to make noises about taking over Peter's room if he should leave, a prospect that so disturbed George he went out of his way to ingratiate Peter into our lives. At first, he did this by offering him an occasional hit of speed, a move he insisted was merely intended to keep Peter a customer, although I suspected more was involved. While Peter was no longer what he called George's "inamorata," he still managed to amuse George. The two had even invented their own language— an arch conflation of gay talk, pigeon-Italian, and the Latin Mass. On the other hand, I became so tongue-tied on speed, I feared that, outside of bed, George thought me a bore.

The speed never tongue-tied Peter. Indeed, it turned him loose in ways that I was utterly unable to mimic. Of course, George attributed this to the inherent differences in our characters. I was an uptight, middle-class kid from the suburbs, while Peter was a madcap, in-your-face speed freak with an unquenchable thirst for sleaze. In this instance—that is, socially, rather than sexually—my youth worked entirely against me. At twenty, I was still green, while, at twenty-seven, Peter was thoroughly—and, for George anyway, delightfully—hardcore.

Eventually, the three of us worked things out and became a family of sorts, although no one dared use a word so uncool, so hideously bourgeois, as that to describe us. George, who stood firmly at our apex, was the one who graciously rewarded our fealty with regular injections of speed. Peter functioned as the court jester who, in exchange for a free shot or a deeply discounted nickel bag, kept George amused, while I was the courtesan who, when he was ready to retire, satisfied him sexually, also for drugs, which, in contrast to Peter's, were always freely given, if not always lovingly administered. While I repeatedly asked for smaller doses, George insisted he knew better and invariably gave me what he deemed I needed—the amount necessary to rid me of the hang-ups that kept me from being a boy eager to learn the ropes of gay survival from a master and a sex pig happy to settle for the hand jobs he doled out in exchange for another go at my ass.

After a while, the three of us settled into a routine. Days we spent together, Peter jesting and me struggling to keep up, while at night, I did in bed what George liked, and Peter went off "sleazing" in search of the purloined fare George agreed to accept as payment for his drugs.

The arrangement was not without its tensions. George demanded much more fealty than Peter, otherwise his peer, was able to tolerate. Blow-ups inevitably ensued—hissy fits and bruised egos that generally required me to function as a go-between. Sometimes, my diplomacy worked; sometimes not, although I always managed to stay out of the crossfire. A few times, I even sneaked Peter some reds to tide him over until George finally relented and, hungry for the levity Peter provided, welcomed him back into the fold.

One morning, after a three-day spat that George, offended by one of Peter's more pointed barbs, had initiated, Peter burst in from a night of pickpocketing the Trucks and announced a restructuring of our arrangement. "Turning over a new leaf," he called it.

Sitting at the opposite end of the bed from me, George, who bristled at even the slightest challenge to his authority, noticeably stiffened. "Oh?" I, his dutiful intercessor, asked.

"Uh-hum, I'm going to get a job," Peter declared. "Something I can do loaded, of course. You know, like go-go dancing or working the box office of one of those dirty movie theaters up on 42nd Street." He paused to light a Gauloises and explained the Trucks had simply become too creepy. "My God, some of those ghouls have been in there so long they're starting to glow in the dark."

He tossed his night's take onto the space on the bed between George and me and waited for George to announce the tally. "God, I hope it's at least a dime bag's worth this time. Three days is too long to be left high and dry." He glowered at George. "Really, sometimes it's like Fort Knox over here."

"Not bad," George murmured after declaring the results of his count—eighty-four dollars in cash, three photo IDs, four credit cards, two checkbooks, a brass cock ring, and a silver ID bracelet. He placed the cock ring on the windowsill next to a rolled-up tube of KY and examined the ID bracelet. "Hmmmm, Bruno," he said of the name engraved on it.

Peter blushed and said he'd slipped it off the wrist of the man he'd let fuck him. "From Hackensack," Peter said, rolling his eyes.

A slight smile crept across George's face. "Jersey, you say. Was he any good?"

"Not really," Peter grumbled, running his hand through the strawberry-blond curls he was finally letting grow back. "You know me, I need a sledgehammer."

George clasped the bracelet onto his wrist and, clearly amused, chuckled softly. "A new leaf, eh?"

He then turned and glowered at me. Earlier, he'd complained we were spending too much time together, although when he'd suggested we try a three-way, I'd put my foot down. "And what about you? What new leaf are you planning to turn over?"

I looked at him blankly. We'd been up for three days. Things were starting to get weird. "Huh?"

"Well, I certainly hope you're not gonna sit around while everybody else goes out and..." George looked at Peter. "What do you call it?"

Peter smiled sweetly. "Singing for your supper?"

"Yeah, that's it," George snarled and turned back to me. "What are you going to do to earn your keep around here?"

I noted the fifty dollars I'd weaseled out of my parents to pay our tab at the corner bodega but George said that was all in the past; he was talking about now. When I reminded him that he'd threatened to leave me should I ever got a job, he replied he wasn't talking about going straight. "I'm talking about being a sleaze." He pointed across the room at Peter. "Like him."

George's face reddened. "I'm sick and tired of you playing the princess, lying around smoking cigarettes and drinking cherry Cokes while everyone else goes out and brings home the bacon. You need to get your hands dirty too." He picked up the checkbook and wallet Peter had stolen from a guy on Jane Street whose photo ID looked remarkably like me. "It's time you turned over a new leaf too," he sneered, tossing the ID and checkbook at me.

I noted I'd never passed bad checks before and asked if he intended to show me how it was done. "Or perhaps you'd rather have me thrown in jail?" I snipped, glaring back at him.

George replied he'd be busy all day dealing drugs but, turning to Peter, assured me he would help out.

Peter smiled slyly and said he'd be happy to show me the ropes, although he was concerned that I might be a bit of a challenge. I still had a lot of what he called "Kay Hoopes Harrington" in me. "We'll need to be good and loaded," he added, winking at me.

"And make sure he only goes after the gays," George told Peter after he got both of us off. "It'll be so much sleazier that way." He chuckled as Peter and I headed for the door. "You know, his own kind."

When Peter suggested we first hit up Balducci's on Sixth Avenue, I was too freaked out by what we were doing to accompany him, although when he emerged with five tins of Beluga caviar, two bottles of champagne, and a shopping bag full of Godiva chocolates, I started to suspect our assignment was easier than I'd feared. At the hip boutiques on St. Mark's Place, I was at least able to go in with him and match the sales clerks darling for darling while he wrote bad checks for enough ruffled silk and brushed velvet to rival Oscar Wilde. However, it wasn't until we hit up the antique stores along Bleecker that I finally found my voice. Taking over from Peter, I posed as the younger but butcher half of a proudly out gay couple shopping for their new Upper East Side love nest.

My breezy chatterbox blatancy so dazzled the two older queens who owned the shop they waived all their rules. "Oh, no, I won't insult you by even looking," a balding red-nosed nelly with a pinkie ring and two yapping poodles cooed when I offered him my stolen Jane Street ID. "I can tell you're upstanding." His partner, a taller, thinner old man with a bejeweled cigarette holder and a walking stick inlaid with silver, shook his head and clucked. "Most of the sissies who come in can't even look us in the eye."

As we lugged our haul back to West 10th Street, Peter admitted our last caper had blown his mind. "I mean, we just breezed in and told those two queens we were gay. Even I've never been that brazen." He stopped and laughed. "I must admit, darling, I had no idea you had it in you. You seem so, well, you know..." He paused and smiled warily. "Timid."

"Just wait," I replied. "There's a whole new me coming out." I smiled as Peter roared his approval. "A brazen hussy," he even called me.

When we returned, we dropped our booty on the bed for George to inspect. In addition to the food and drink, there was a paisley silk scarf, a red velvet smoking jacket, a pair of white linen pants, a cut-glass vase, two dozen peacock feathers, a fringed Victorian shawl, a hand mirror framed in whalebone, and a sterling silver gazing ball that Peter had picked out as a personal gesture. "A peace offering," he said, holding it up for George to admire. "You know, so we can be friends again."

Peter nodded as George responded by noting that, of all the loot, the gazing ball was his favorite. He examined it more closely. "Is it really sterling?"

"Of course," Peter murmured. "What else for Silver George?"

As thanks, George mixed up monster shots for the two of us. "You did good, hon. I'm proud of you," he purred as he slipped the needle into my vein. Then, right before doing up Peter, he said he'd left his trip book out on the balcony and asked if I'd retrieve it. "Thanks, babe," he cooed, slipping the needle into Peter's vein. "You're a sweetheart."

When I returned, the silver gazing ball was on the table in the corner and Peter was nearly in George's lap. It occurred to me something was up but I figured I was just once again being paranoid. After all, George's shot had been much bigger than what I'd asked for.

Later that night, after Peter had returned to his room and George and I had finished balling, George slipped out of bed and announced he was going across the hall to pay Peter a visit. "Sorry, hon, but I gotta," he said, when I protested his departure. "I promised."

I rolled onto my side and, burying my face in the musk he'd left behind, asked if I could tag along. As I noted, Peter and I had had a particularly good day together. I smiled at the recollection. "A brazen hussy," he'd even called me.

Turning on the tap, George peered into the hand sink mirror and shook his head. "I don't think that'd work," he said, before reminding me of my aversion to three-ways. "Peter and I are going to have sex."

I froze. "You're going to *what*?"

"But he said he was horny," George cried, trying to calm me. "You don't want him to have to go back to the Trucks, do you?" When I just glared at him, he pointed at the silver gazing ball and shrugged. "Look, he insisted, okay? He said I couldn't have it unless I agreed."

"I see," I muttered as I recalled George asking me to retrieve his trip book from the balcony. "Let me fuck him first. He'll take it better then," I imagined him telling Peter while I'd been out of the room. When I'd returned empty-handed, I'd noted George's trip book was on the drop-down desk and Peter's hand was almost in George's crotch.

"Don't look at me that way," George groused, dousing his balls with baby powder. "He's just gonna give me a blow job." He stood up straight and returned my glare. "At least somebody will."

"Fuck you," I spat and hurled the cum rag he'd again jerked me off into at him. The night before, George had warned me our sex life was getting stale. When I'd asked him in what way, he'd suggested I blow him. "Sometimes I like to just lie back and get worked on, you know what I mean?"

I'd almost asked, "Like Lou?" but instead turned over and clammed up. I'd given George my ass. That was enough. I'd be damned if I was going to be his cocksucker too. It was his turn to vary his routine. Indeed, I was sick of his hand jobs. I'd go down on George when he went down on me.

George pulled the plug on the sink and a dam suddenly broke deep inside me. "What have I done?" I whimpered. "Why are you doing this to me?"

"Doing what?" George snarled, turning back to the mirror. "Driving you mad? Making you a laughing stock?" I huddled in the middle of the bed as he tied the drawstring of the same blue and white-striped rayon pants he'd worn on our first night together. "No one's doing anything to you but you. It's all in your head. You're too clingy and uptight, too Puritanical. You need to understand sex is different from love."

"But it isn't with me," I countered. "At least with you anyway." I took a deep breath. I didn't care how square or uptight I sounded. I just needed to speak directly from the heart. "You're all I want, George. All I think about. I even masturbate to you."

George flinched but only for a second. "Look, you've got to stop this. You're suffocating me. You need to accept that I like sex and I'm going to have it with whoever I want. The more you try to change that, the more you're going to drive me away."

When I pointed out he was using the speed to try to change me, George claimed I had even that wrong. "No, I'm trying to help you. Someday you're going to thank me for all this."

I watched him walk out and then, after some whispering in the hall outside Peter's room, the building fell into a fretful stupor. I tried writing in my trip book but, too humiliated to focus, retreated to the balcony. Too high to sleep, I smoked the pack of Marlboros George had left behind—his sole consideration—and watched the clock tick off the minutes to dawn. No, I told myself over and over, I'd never thank George for putting me through this. I'd prove him wrong instead. I knew he loved me. He was just too afraid to admit it.

I tiptoed to the hand sink and listened as the rat scratched at the scales covering the hole in the floor. "No, go away! I'm not letting you in," I cried. I felt moisture on my cheeks and shuddered; as George had repeatedly warned me, tears were the only sin. "Do you hear me?" I whimpered, wiping away every trace of my weakness.

I turned and faced the door. Across the hall, a mere ten feet away, the friend I'd hoped would someday call me his sister was giving the only man I'd ever called a lover a blow job. And I was to think so little of myself I was supposed to be okay with it. "I won't!" I cried as the rat resumed its scratching. *"I won't! I won't!"*

George returned from Peter's the next morning and, patting the space on the bed next to him, told me to sit down. I hesitated—no blowjob took all night— but he sounded serious and so I did as I was told. He motioned for me to hold out my arm and, after tying me off, jabbed me with his syringe. "There," he said after emptying its contents into me. "Now we need to talk."

Struggling to stay upright, I waited for George to mix up a shot for himself but his time with Peter must've been a really doozy. His pupils were swollen and he was sullen like he got when he'd taken too much. "Yes?" I asked, bracing for another bombshell.

"I'm tired of doing all the work around here," he said, capping the syringe's point and placing the dropper back in its Altoid tin. "You need to contribute more."

"I see," I said, determined not to provoke him.

"I want you to go to Bellevue and apply for welfare. Peter says it'll be just enough to cover the rent." He looked at me and managed a faint smile. "He says it's easy."

"Bellevue, eh?" I asked, staring at the dimes in my Bass Weejuns. A high-rise fortress on First Avenue, Bellevue was the lunatic asylum where they routinely locked up people like me. There were rumored to be hundreds, maybe thousands inside, so many it was widely known as the city's gay prison, a Bastille of sexual deviancy whose inmates were rumored to have only two options: either rot away alone in a six by nine, rat-infested cell or escape via one of its many unsecured, upper-story windows. Warhol had even commemorated their suicides in a silkscreen called *Purple Man Jumping*, a lesser known but more overtly gay contribution to the electric chairs, lunging police dogs, and fatal car crashes of his *Death and Disaster* series.

"Just tell 'em you're crazy," George instructed before shepherding me out into the hall. "You're high enough now so they'll believe you," he added before slamming the door.

On the walk over, I realized just how right George was. His shot had sent me over the edge. Everyone I encountered was a threat: an old lady sweeping her sidewalk; a cop pounding his beat; a sidewalk vendor hawking his wares; a turbaned cabbie discharging his fare. As I approached the hospital, a little girl walking her poodle called me a sex pig, while across the street a construction worker in a hardhat and overalls grabbed his crotch and asked for a blow job. Faggots, he noted, were so much better at it than chicks.

At Bellevue, I nearly lost it when two dark-skinned men in white coats walked toward me, laughing. Then turning down a hall they disappeared. I waited for reinforcements but the receptionist, a pale, gum-chewing broad in a ratty bouffant, called my name and motioned me towards a door the color of gunmetal. On it, a sign read "Social Work." I feared the worst.

A buxom matron in a paisley mumu and hair pulled back into a tight bun greeted me by rising from her chair and offering me her hand. "Yes, I was just looking over your application," she said. Her bracelets clanged as she fumbled with a stack of papers. "Now where is it? It was just here." She sighed and peered at me over the half-moons of her bifocals. "Oh well, let's just talk, shall we?"

I scanned the ceiling for gas jets and then her arms for needle tracks. As George had repeatedly claimed, everyone in New York was a junkie for something. "Well, I'm, I mean, I..." My hand trembled as I lit my last cigarette. I glanced at her warily, certain she was going to have me locked up. George had called in advance to work out the arrangements. Like Peter, she was blowing him for drugs.

"Stop!" she cried, waving her hands in the air. "You don't have to say another word. I can feel the anxiety in the air!"

She checked off a series of boxes, signed her name at the bottom of my application and flung it into her out-box. Then, assuring me I'd get a check as soon as a home visit could be arranged, she pried me out of my chair and ushered me into a blindingly bright, fluorescent-lit hallway.

"A home visit?" I asked as the two orderlies I feared she'd called to escort me up to my cell breezed past us.

"Yes, yes, but don't worry. We just have to make sure you're not living beyond your abilities." Before I could tell her that might be a problem, she said someone would be out in about two weeks and then disappeared back into her office.

George pretended he was a trick when the man from the city showed up for my home visit. "See ya 'round," George drawled as he slipped on the Converse high tops he kept under the bed. "Yeah," I replied, wondering who he was rushing off to this time. After the night with Peter, George had disappeared three or four times, once for an entire day, although he refused to say who he'd been with. "Free love," he called it—his right.

The inspector turned on the faucet, checked out the heat and, then claiming everything looked good, asked me to sign another form. When I pointed out the rat hole, he nodded and said I was lucky. Most of the places he visited had at least two.

"Where you from?" he asked, flipping through my file. "Hmm, Wilmington, Delaware." He smiled and stroked a neatly-trimmed, sandy-colored beard. "DuPont Country." He looked at the syringe I'd left on the drop-down desk as a cry for help and smiled. "Not too many rats down there, huh?"

George called me in from the balcony and, grimacing, complained of gas. He'd pinned a fraying towel over the window to block out the light and the room, dark and airless, reeked of nervous sweat.

"What you need is some fresh air," I said, walking to the window. As I noted, the daffodils in the interior courtyard Miss Eden had dubbed the "end of the rainbow" had just opened. "A riot of yellow," I called it.

"No, no, leave it," he moaned before grabbing his groin. "It hurts. Bad, real bad." He rolled onto his side and speculated it was the strychnine the Mafia had started cutting the speed with. Drugs, he grumbled, weren't what they used to be.

"Mmmm," I murmured distractedly.

George took my hand and mustered a wan smile. "I need you to do me a favor, hon."

"Why, of course," I said, thinking he wanted me to run out and grab some Alka Seltzer.

"There's really only one remedy," he murmured. He nodded and motioned for me to come in closer; as he said, he didn't want the others to hear. He lifted his head off the pillow to make sure no one else was in the room and then smiled sweetly. "You listening?" he asked.

I assured him he had my full attention.

He waited for another spasm of pain to pass and brushed a strand of hair from my face. "You really are cute, you know."

"George, please," I groaned, nodding in the direction of the balcony. "We have company. Quit beating around the bush and tell me what it is you want."

"Okay, okay," he mumbled and, squeezing my hand, blushed slightly. "I need you to give me a blow job."

I yanked my hand away. "You want me to *what*?"

"It's the only thing that works," he murmured, again grabbing his groin. "You know, for the gas."

"Just like that? I mean, you lie back and I, uh, pull your dick out and suck you off?" I pointed to the balcony. "And what about them?" Six feet away, Peter was scribbling in his trip book; Norman was stringing beads; his Broadway dancer boyfriend was staring mutely into space; John was trying to decipher some obscure astrological aspect; and Adrian, George's latest recruit into the Horrible Fags, was composing another scene for a play he was writing for John Vacarro's Theater of the Ridiculous. The ashtrays were overflowing. No one had slept in two days.

"Ah, go on and forget it, if that's the way you want to be," George grumbled.

"It is," I huffed and turned away.

"Oh, and when you get back on the balcony," George added as I rounded the base of the bed, "ask Peter to come in, will you? I'm sure he'll be more than happy to help out." His eyes burrowed two holes into me. "Thank God everyone's not a spoiled little brat like you," he sneered.

I stared at the silver gazing ball on the table opposite the bed and shuddered. There was no bottoming out with George. Only falling.

I stumbled up the two steps to the balcony and explained to the others that George and I had some business to take care of. Reaching for the door, I assured them I wouldn't be long. Norman snickered but the ruined Broadway dancer he paraded around as proof of his perverse powers stared numbly at the floor. John looked nervously at Peter who, turning to me, quietly shook his head. I couldn't tell if he was disappointed in me for giving in or jealous that George had chosen me to do his bidding. Oblivious, Adrian babbled away about the bloodlines of European royalty and Catherine the Great's alleged fondness for stallions.

I walked back to the bed and, after waiting in vain for some sign of life from George, removed his jeans. I waited again for some movement, but he remained as still as a corpse. I recalled the night in Syracuse when I'd walked out on just such a man and vowed this time things would be different. This time, I was going to get what I needed too.

George was soft when I took him in my mouth, but it wasn't long before I had him where I wanted. I waited until his breath quickened and his moans turned sharp and husky and then went in for the kill. "I want you to tell me you love me," I demanded.

"Yeah, baby," he replied huskily. "Anything you want. Just please keep going..."

I stopped again and repeated my demand. "I want to hear you say the words." I pointed at the wall between us and the balcony. "Loudly, so the others can hear."

He grabbed my hand and gnawed on my palm. "No, please, keep going," he begged. "I'm so close, so, so close..."

"Come on, you bastard, say it!" I hissed. When I resumed my sucking, his breath quickened, his back arched and he pounded the mattress so hard the room shook, but he finally did as he was told. "Yes, I love you," he bellowed so loudly I was sure even the neighbors could hear.

"Who else?" I demanded.

"Only you," he cried, again slamming his fist against the mattress. Then, trembling all the way down to his bones, he gave up a thimbleful of power that, for one glorious instant, reversed our roles and made me George's master and him, my slave.

Cured of his gas, George wasted no time getting even. The next morning, after he'd left for another visit with his Grand Poobah, his first without me, Peter knocked on the door and announced he had another message to deliver. He stammered he didn't quite know how to say it but George had insisted and, as was his wont, had backed it up with threats. "He said he'd cut me off if I didn't."

I stared at the scales covering the rat hole and told Peter not to worry. I understood. He was a speed freak; yes, of course, drugs came first. Besides, I was a grown-up. I could take whatever George meted out. I looked at him grimly. "So, what does he want this time?"

"It's your teeth."

I looked at him blankly. "My teeth?"

Peter nodded. "George says you use them too much." He fidgeted with the hem of his t-shirt and said George had complained my blow jobs hurt. He'd even shown Peter the tooth marks. "Red ones," he added, blushing. He stepped forward as I started to tremble but then, dropping his hands to his sides, stopped. "He says next time you need to be more careful."

Peter watched me turn ashen and then, reaching for the door, asked if I was going to be all right.

Fighting back tears, I turned away and mutely stared at the bed. A single mattress with box-springs that George and I had dragged in off the street, it framed a collage of the turn my life had taken since he and I had hooked up: a half-empty tube of KY; a crusty cum rag; a shot glass and the ball of cotton he'd used to draw up our last shot; a deck of Tarot cards; an empty Sara Lee pie tin; our matching black faux-leather trip books; and, at the base of the bed, a paperback of Pauline Réage's *The Story of 0* Peter had lent me. He'd said the sex was kinky but hot and suspected I'd like it too. Turning pain into pleasure, he'd added, was almost as decadent as shooting speed.

"Okay," Peter murmured, stepping into the hall. "I'll be in my room if you need me."

"Yeah," I replied as the rat scurried about beneath the floorboards, searching for another way in.

At the tail end of a marathon speed high, Norman launched into his favorite topic, the corruption of youth. Personally offended, I tried to cut him off but George, for whom no topic was too deranged or perverse, especially when high, only egged him on. "Yeah," he cried, "tell us how a real Horrible Fag does it!"

Norman noted the selection of prey was critical. "Any boy won't do. You've got to find one with a broken wing." While runaways were easy, he claimed most were too morally compromised to be much fun. Some threw their legs up in the air before you were even ready to fuck them. "And, after all, let's face it. Sex is just a pretext." For what, he didn't say.

Hippies, he argued, were the best. Motivated by idealism and operating from a strong sense of scruples, they were the ones who tended to fall the hardest. "And the look of horror on their faces when they realize just how low they've sunk is priceless," he added. He smiled wryly. "Better even than a shot of pure pharmaceutical meth."

I'd never heard George laugh so hard. When he finally recovered, he congratulated Norman on staying so on top of his game. Well into his forties, he was still the sleaziest, most horrible fag in all of New York. He even called Norman an inspiration.

I wanted to tell George he was wrong on both counts; I was worse than either of them. Anyone with an ounce of self-respect would've walked out on him weeks ago. But without a dime to my name and nowhere to go but back to my parents, I instead suggested we do up some reds. As I noted, we'd been up for four days and the crash ahead was bound to be unpleasant. Something to knock us out would do us all a world of good.

To my great relief, George agreed. And so, after he hit each of us up with Seconal, we passed out, George and I on our single mattress and, Norman, curled up on a towel on the floor.

A few hours later, George awakened me, complaining again of gas. "Be a good boy, okay?" he whispered, gently nudging me down towards his crotch. "It hurts really, really bad."

I knew better than to protest Norman's proximity. For George, modesty was as much the mark of a prude as an aversion to three-ways. And so, I crawled down the bed to perform my duties, although on my way I was sure I spied Norman grinning lustily at me in the moonlight.

I had to work overtime to get George hard but once I did, he grabbed the back of my head and shoved himself all the way down my throat. Struggling to control my bite, I quickly sank into a heaving, gasping heap that apparently turned George on even more. Soon, my gagging and George's pounding aroused Norman enough for him to try to join in. And though I was able to swat his hand away, I could do nothing about the snicker which greeted the sound of my innocence choking on the vomit of its own self-disgust.

On my way back up from George's crotch, I gazed out our window at the moonlit interior of the block Miss Eden had christened the "end of the rainbow." I tried telling myself this wasn't happening, it wasn't real, gay people didn't treat each other like this—anything to keep the horror at bay—just like I had the night of my beating behind the Catholic church, when the phone started ringing off the hook with bullies asking where their silver dollars were. And then suddenly the Seconal kicked in again and I passed out, of all places, in George's arms. When I awoke the next day, Norman was gone and George was pressed up against me, hard as a rock, ready for more.

17

The Ultimate Fuck You

Holly was a barefoot Puerto Rican Jew drag queen who knocked on our door one rainy May night looking for George. Dripping wet, she said she'd heard he had connections to Andy Warhol, whom she hoped would make her a star. "Honey, I'm too fabulous to be out on the streets," she purred, drying her feet with a hand towel. "I'm a..." She paused and looked around her, as if suddenly confused. "What does he call 'em?" After a prompt from George, she pulled her mane of frizzy auburn hair back from her chiseled face and laughed like a buck-toothed Ninotchka. "Yeah, that's it, a *superstar*!" she crowed, the Kirk Douglas cleft in her chin twitching madly.

She sat on the edge of the bed and wrung out the hem of the grimy, white lace tablecloth she'd fashioned into a tunic. "Oh, no, pussycat, they're real," she replied when Peter asked about her tits. She let the tunic drop to her waist and showed us two small mounds with nipples as sleek as nose cones. "I don't need silicone like those fakes Andy has around him. My tits are real," she boasted.

"A hermaphro-*what*?" Holly cried when I asked what she called herself. When I explained hermaphrodites were people with both male and female sexual parts, she stood up, pulled down a Chinese red thong and snarled somewhere between the growl of Lauren Bacall and the whine of Phil Silvers, "Honey, this wiener's no schnitzel. I'm an illusionist, not a freak."

As Peter and I roared with delight, George mixed up what he called her "welcome home" shot. The Horrible Fags, he announced, had just landed their first drag queen.

Frazzled by the speed, Holly soon forgot all about Andy Warhol and instead imagined herself the star of her own movie. Most of the time, this entailed sitting on the floor of our tiny room, rummaging through the A&P grocery bag in which she kept all her possessions and mumbling to herself like a guttersnipe Norma Desmond preparing for her close-up. One minute, she was searching for her eyebrow tweezers; the next, a bottle of Jungle Red nail polish; a tube of neon-pink lipstick; a string of beads she was making for a girlfriend whose name kept changing; the bolt of chiffon or the mangy boa she'd fished out of a trash can; the scraps of paper she called her to-do lists; the needle and thread she used to repair the straps on her size 14 wedgies; or, whenever George issued the call, the Carmen Miranda headband she twisted around her arm to raise up a vein.

"Just look at her, she's completely demented," Peter complained when, ten days into her tenure at West 10th Street, she finally left for a day of trash picking. "If she doesn't change that tablecloth, you're going to have to fumigate. And, oh my God, have you seen those feet? They're starting to sprout mushrooms!"

Peter accused George of intentionally dementing Holly. It was one thing, he said, to amuse himself by fucking with the minds of other gay men; we had resources to fall back on. Drag queens had only the streets. If they didn't keep their wits about them, they'd end up like those two queens Miss Eden knew—floating face down in the Hudson. "You need to let up on her, George. She can't handle it."

Furious, George accused Peter of going soft and, claiming he needed a dose of his own medicine, instantly cut him off. When, a few days later, I tried to intercede, George warned me to stay out of it. "Peter's dead to me," he snarled. And indeed, the next time we encountered him in the hallway, George looked straight ahead and kept on walking.

I felt badly for Peter but at least I had George all to myself—or, at least, so I thought. Peter, on the other hand, had to go back to hustling to keep himself in drugs. He never did patch things up with George and eventually turned to reds to get high. A "deadhead," George called him.

One afternoon, George sent Holly and me on a shoplifting spree at a supermarket that had just opened a few blocks up Hudson. Walking in the door, she told me she was going to show me what she called her "superstar" approach to theft. "Now don't be alarmed, darling," she advised while leading me up the store's center aisle. "When they come running, head for the baked goods and grab everything you can. I'll meet you at the door." Sashaying back toward the front, she suddenly grabbed her throat, gasped for air, and collapsed into a stack of 20 Mule Team Borax. As boxes skittered across the floor, Holly twitched, gurgled and kicked her legs in the air until her mini-skirt slid up to her waist and everyone in the store came running.

Noting the tell-tale bulge in Holly's thong, the manager broke through the crowd, escorted her to the front of the store and demanded to see the contents of her shoulder bag. "But this is an outrage," Holly protested. "I'm a sick woman. I have epilepsy and diabetes and am at high risk of paraplegia." When he just glared at her, she shrugged, upended her bag, and mumbled quietly to herself as her massive collection of porn tumbled onto the check-out counter. "Hey, look, whaddya want?" she grumbled as the line of gray-haired matrons behind her gaped at a photo of two men, one Black, the other white, fucking. "I'm a single girl and it's all they sell down here." She shrugged. "I mean, this is Greenwich Village, ain't it?"

Holly ran her fingers through her auburn locks and adjusted her top as the manager, beet-red, gingerly picked his way through her mountain of filth. However, when he came to her dildo, she got huffy. "Leave that alone," she snipped, grabbing it from him. "That's my feminine hygiene device, you filthy little man."

At that, the manager pointed to the door and shouted for her, him, or whatever the hell Holly was to get out of his store. A few minutes later, I followed with my own shoulder bag stuffed full of stolen goods. I'd even nabbed a quart of Häagen-Dazs rum raisin ice cream, George's favorite.

George loved the story and, later that night, after Holly had gone out for more trash picking, he rewarded my efforts by pulling from his Altoid tin a brand-new set of works. It had a sharp shiny point, a long glass neck and a bright blue elastic around the throat of a pale pink rubber bulb. Handing it to me, he smiled and said I'd finally passed what he called the "sleaze test." It was time I learned to get myself off.

I gazed at my reflection in the sex mirror George had propped opposite the bed and smiled. I looked fabulous. My hair had grown to below my shoulders and I'd dropped just enough weight for the new skin-tight hip-huggers and rayon shirts in burnt oranges and soft greens that were all the rage. "Oh George, thank you," I murmured, certain the syringe was his way of saying he loved me.

While I made a bloody mess of my arm the first few times that I got myself off, by the end of the next day I was slipping the syringe in and out of a vein like a pro—nary a drop of blood. Soon, I told myself, I'd be just as good at it as George—no longer a boy but his equal, a Horrible Fag too.

Holly moved on after a couple of weeks, although she'd regularly reappear for a hit of speed which George, who loved the demented spectacle she put on, happily gave her free of charge. Holly complained the speed was bad for her career—she'd forget her lines or miss her cues for the Off-Off-Off Broadway plays she was perpetually auditioning for—but she never dried out for long. Hardly a week went by without her showing up at least once for one of George's hits—"the bigger, the better," as she liked to say.

I never understood why people wanted to get as high as Holly. It wasn't fun—other than Peter, speed freaks rarely laughed—or liberating—only the truly perverse could equate speed's paranoia with enlightenment. Nevertheless, addicts like George, Peter, and Holly just kept at it, getting higher and higher until—well, they were exactly what they said they were: demented—drooling-in-their-shoes, out-of-their-minds schizoid-psychotic.

A few days after Holly's departure, George brought home two hits of Orange Sunshine he wanted us to shoot. He tried to entice me with claims of how good the sex would be but, as I countered, I'd seen what insanity looked like up-close by mainlining methamphetamine. I didn't need to see the technicolor version by doing the same with LSD. "No, I don't want to end up like Electric Freddy," I added. "So tuned in and turned on I'd be completely dropped out."

Clearly put off, George dismissed my suggestion that we instead pop the two tabs of LSD. As he noted, he didn't do drugs he couldn't inject into a vein. Even skin-popping, the intramuscular "poke" of Seconal Gino had offered after we'd tripped out in Longwood Gardens, was beneath him. And though his face flushed slightly, and he sullenly retreated to his trip book for the rest of the afternoon, I thought that was the end of it; I'd never have to deal with the topic of injecting psychedelics again.

Silly me, I clearly failed to take George seriously when he'd told me the only word in the English language that he truly hated was 'no.' I'd even thought he was joking around when, one night with Peter and me, he'd picked 'perverse' as the word he thought best suited him. (Peter had chosen 'decadent' and I, 'radical.') After all, 'perverse' was just a few stops short of 'evil' and, as I'd said on our first night together, George was no more that than I. A "pussycat," I'd even called him.

Oh, sure, George could be mean and nasty, especially during his so-called "mind games," the cruel, sadistic methedrine-fueled power-plays by which he established his dominance. But all that was just bluster, I told myself—the posturing of another victim of the hurt, humiliation, and abandonment I'd come to think of as the engines of gay life.

No, I still stubbornly insisted that— even though he no longer said it and refused to show it through anything more than a hand job—George did indeed love me. Like Peter had said of so many other faggots, he was just too scared to admit it. "A crybaby. Afraid somebody is gonna reject him. Make him feel bad," Peter had snarled before scrunching up his face and crying mockingly, *W-a-a-a-a-a*, just like a little kid.

"Here, I think you'll like this," George murmured, handing me a nickel bag of crystal he'd gotten for my return to Wilmington, my first visit with my parents since he and I had gotten together. "I took a taste. It's pretty good stuff."

"Wow, you came through," I said, stunned by the sudden change in his mood. All week, he'd been so sullen over my plans that I'd begun to suspect he resented the fact that I still had family to go back to. "That's really nice, George. Thank you." I threw my arms around his neck and, inhaling his mix of musk and baby powder, told him I'd miss him.

"Yeah," George said, slipping his hand between my legs, "I'll miss you too." As he flashed me a smile so big his dimples showed, I marveled at how attentive he'd been. Since Peter's banishment, he hadn't cheated on me once. "Have a good time, hon," he said before giving me a goodbye kiss so passionate I almost changed my mind and stayed.

The next night, I got together with my old high school pal, Angie, who took me to a pot party friends at the University of Delaware threw every weekend in their Newark apartment. On the drive down, I showed her my syringe and the packet of speed George had given me and asked if it'd be okay if I shot up once we got there. "Yeah, sure, why not?" Angie replied in the same squelched monotone she'd adopted since high school. "People down here think they're cool just because they've dropped LSD. But nobody's seen a real-live junkie before." She said she even thought it'd be good for them. "The ultimate fuck-you," she called my syringe.

She stared out the passenger window of my father's Corvair and complained about how uptight everyone in Wilmington was. Even the crowd of gays she'd started hanging out with were square. "You're so lucky to have gotten out," she grumbled. "Wish I could."

"Yeah," I murmured, admiring my reflection in the car's rearview mirror. The last time I'd seen Angie, I was a simpering, budding gay man pleading for acceptance. Now, I was an in-your-face Greenwich Village fag with hair down to his shoulders and a look that screamed St Mark's Place. All I wanted to do was blow minds.

An hour later, Angie and her friends crowded around the bathroom door while I sat on the john of their Newark apartment and set myself up. I walked them through each step of the process: cleaning out the works; mixing up the drug in a spoon; drawing the liquid up through a cotton ball; twisting a scarf around my arm and making a fist; and piercing my vein with the sharp, shiny point of my syringe. Wide-eyed, they gasped as blood gushed up my dropper's neck and then fell silent as I mixed the shot with the flick of a forefinger, unfurled the scarf and, gently squeezing the syringe's pale pink rubber bulb, sent the elixir hurtling into me. Huddling into a tight bunch, they laughed nervously as I pulled the needle out, wiped away the droplet of blood from the puncture wound and, collapsing against the hopper, awaited my rush.

"You alright, man?" our host, a short stocky kid Angie said we'd gone to high school with but whom I couldn't recall, asked as I stared mutely at a towel bar.

Embarrassed, I shook my head and admitted I felt nothing. "I don't get it. My, uh, friend, George said it's really good stuff," I stammered, again reaching for the nickel bag. "I must not have mixed up enough."

"This is too freaky," our host's girlfriend, a pretty, pert blonde with a pink ribbon around her ponytail, complained as I sprinkled more crystal into the spoon. "I think I'm going to be sick." I offered to get up if she needed to use the toilet bowl, but she just twirled on her heels and, dragging her boyfriend behind her, told me to go fuck myself. I was sure she also called me a faggot, although Angie insisted I was just being paranoid.

Groaning they'd seen enough, the rest of the party quickly followed suit. While Angie shuttled between me and the others, I emptied another dropper into me and again waited in vain for a rush. "Shit!" I cried as that time even Angie deserted me. Frantic, I tied myself off again and, filling the spoon with a heaping dose of crystal, yelled for someone to bring me more matches.

Angie and her friends responded by slamming the front door of the apartment behind them. Grumbling about chickenshit pot heads, I wandered into the bedroom, found a box of stick matches next to a still-smoldering bong, and sat on the edge of a bed to complete my third shot of the evening. Pissed that it also failed, I pinched a nickel bag of grass lying on the floor and fifty dollars in cash I found in the bottom of a sock drawer. On my way out, I taped a note to the bedroom mirror thanking them for their hospitality and signed it "A Horrible Fag."

On the drive home, the drug suddenly kicked in with a flash of light and a boom so deafening it rattled the Corvair. Twisting back onto itself, the road splintered into ribbons and wrapped the car in bright Day-Glo knots. From the edge of a nearby forest, ghosts beckoned, while the radio station dissolved into static, and a sulfurous slime oozed from the heat vent.

It was then that I realized the pale pink crystal George had given me as a going-away gift hadn't been speed but was instead some weird, timed-release psychedelic—the one drug I'd told him I'd never shoot. In the back seat, his disembodied voice rebuked me for my pridefulness. "Serves you right, you spoiled little brat. Didn't I tell you to never say no to me?"

How I managed to make it back to Carrcroft in one piece was itself a miracle. I was so out of it I could barely distinguish the clutch from the gas pedal, while red lights suddenly meant go and green, stop. Pulling into our driveway, I was at least able to discern that the garage was empty—meaning that, if nothing else was going my way, my parents were still out drinking and dancing the night away at the DuPont Country Club. If they ever saw me like this, they'd surely have me locked up.

Desperate, I ran upstairs and somehow managed to phone Angie. In my mind, my message was clear—I was in a jam; I needed a place to crash; could she put me up for the night?—but my words came out gibberish. Cackling she was fucking the devil, she replied sure, come on over. Slamming the phone down, I watched in horror as it melted into a thick glob of black plastic that oozed down the stairwell. Racing to bed, I cowered under sheets crawling with spiders and spent the rest of the night listening to ghouls curse me from the cauldron of my closet.

The next morning, I waited for my parents to leave for church and, reeking of nervous sweat, ran to the bathroom to wash up. Stepping into the shower, I prayed I'd come down enough to at least be around other people, but when the water turned to blood as soon as it hit me, I realized I was still hopelessly out of it. Throwing on some clothes, I retreated to the creek at the edge of our backyard where I hoped to sit out the rest of my high. And although I managed to keep from screaming when a nest of snakes disappeared up my pants leg, I knew the gig was up when, several hours later, my mother called me in for Sunday supper. My pupils were still as big as saucers. "What the hell are those for?" my father growled as I sat down at the dining room table in dark shades. "You're *inside* now!"

Convinced my mother had pissed in the potatoes and laced the pot roast with lye, I mutely picked at my meal until my father announced he'd had enough and told me to leave the table. After that, I sat on the living room floor with the family Bible and spent the rest of the afternoon tracing Dore prints of raging skies cleft with light and angels wrestling with dragons onto sheets of my mother's typewriter paper. I'd never felt quite so insane.

An hour before I was to catch my train back to New York, my mother knelt on the carpet beside me and, picking up my tracing of Dore's *Samson Slaying the Philistines with the Jaw Bone of an Ass*, told me how nice it was to see me back with the Bible. "It's been such a long time," she cooed. She brushed a strand of hair from my sweaty brow and gave me the same sickly-sweet smile she used when doing her rounds as a candy-striper at one of the local hospitals. "Why don't you forget about going back to New York and stay here with us?" she asked. "Where you're loved," she even had the temerity to add.

I glared at the red slippers with gold arabesques she'd worn the day I came out to her—the day she'd run to her bathroom and vomited—and chomped so hard on my pencil a sliver of wood broke off in my mouth. Snatching my tracing back from her, I spit the sliver out and told her to get away from me; I couldn't bear the sight of her. I even called her a warthog from hell. Of her offer to stay, I simply said I'd rather die first.

Horrified, my mother looked at me as if I was one of those ghouls that had taunted me all night from inside my closet. For a moment, I even thought she might run to my father's dresser for his pistol. But instead, she just fled the room in tears.

After that, I prepared myself for some rough stuff but, by then, my mother at least knew what not to tell my father, although he must've suspected something was up. When I left, he refused to even look at me, let alone say goodbye. At the train station, my mother grabbed my arm as I was about to board my train back to George and again begged me to stay. Sobbing, she even said I was destroying the family.

I pried myself loose and replied she should've thought about that a long time ago. "Before you sent me to that shrink. Remember?" I recalled the time she'd denied seeing me dress up in her clothes and felt my face flush. "Or are you gonna say that never happened either?"

After that, I boarded my car and watched her pale, stooped figure vanish as the train lurched into the slow, jerky roll that signaled the start of its journey north. When it reached the bend at the little stone church the Swedes had built to honor their victory over the heathens, I craned my neck to see the factory parking lot where, surrounded by razor wire, I'd first had sex with a man. All this, I thought, because I was now in love with one.

Then, switching sides, I stared out over the acres of rubble that still marked the rage over Martin Luther King's assassination and gloated over my victory. I was, my mother had said, destroying the family. *Destroying.* Soon, there'd be nothing left of it but ash.

Although I came down from my high before I arrived back in New York, I had to wait two days to confront George over the mess he'd made of my trip home. He refused to say where he'd been or who he'd been with, although he did say my weekend away had rekindled his interest in other guys. Doing his own thing, he called it. "Free Love."

He was equally unapologetic over what he called the drug "mix-up," although I knew from his smirk that he'd intentionally given me a psychedelic. When I told him the drug, whatever the fuck it was, had so crazed me I'd called my own mother a warthog from hell, he laughed. "Well, isn't she?" he cried. As he noted, he'd heard me call her much worse. "You should've dropped her months ago," he sneered.

I warned him not to try to come between me and my parents ever again. "I don't want to end up like you. Disowned and motherless." I even vowed that someday I was going to change my parents' minds and get them to accept me. I smiled defiantly. "You'll see."

At that point, he claimed I was a bigger fool than he thought. As he noted, people as prudish as my parents—"Calvinists," he called them—would never come around. Exasperated, he asked why I couldn't just sit back and learn from his example. "Not everyone, you know, gets to sit at the feet of a master." He smiled at his reflection in the sex mirror. "A Horrible Fag, a born survivor."

I reminded him this wasn't ancient Greece. The days of older, wiser men teaching younger guys the rules of the game in exchange for a regular piece of ass were long gone. "Get with the times, George. We're equals."

Furious over my challenge, he announced that, like Peter, I deserved a dose of my own medicine and stormed out, presumably back to the less prideful, more compliant arms of his latest find. When he finally returned a few days later, I was so lonely and desperate for his touch, not to mention his drugs, I pretended to be the docile, be-seen-and-not-heard boy that he wanted.

But still I seethed.

18
The Redistribution of Karma

"You're lucky no one's around to hear you," George sneered after I made the mistake of calling Sixth Avenue the Avenue of the Americas. "You sound just like a tourist."

Refusing to be baited, I merely muttered a distracted *hmmm* and kept on walking. As I knew well, tourists – along with Hare Krishna, Calvinists, Jesus freaks, hippies, preppies, peaceniks, protesters, panhandlers, Bowery bums, juiceheads, potheads, heroin addicts, pill poppers, leather queens, surfers, interior decorators, hairdressers, poodle walkers, the Beatles, Sonny and Cher, Maharishi Mahesh Yogi, Eugene McCarthy, Shirley Temple Black, and everyone from New Jersey, LA, and San Francisco – were part of the vast conspiracy of creeps, phonies, and prudes George regularly railed against. Persisting, George stopped a few storefronts later and, clearly determined to freak me out, pointed out the dimness of his reflection in a haberdashery's window. "Be careful," he warned. "Vampires cast back no light. Soon, I'll be wanting to drink your blood."

Fed up, I glared at him and told him I was in no mood for any more of his mind games. The day had been difficult enough, stifling hot—"riot weather," the owner of the bodega across W. 10th Street had called it—and the night offered little in the way of relief. Worse, a luridly orange full moon hung over the city like a giant heat lamp.

"You've taken too much speed, George," I hissed. "You're a mess." After that, he shut up and we walked on in silence, me counting the cracks in the sidewalk and George dementedly chain-smoking Marlboros.

We'd spent the evening on the top floor of a Riverside Drive coop with one of George's regular clients, a Madison Avenue ad man he knew from the Factory. George claimed the guy was straight, but I'd suspected from his look of disappointment when he'd seen me in tow that he'd hoped to cop more than just his usual three ounces of speed from George. Crystal meth was like that. It made everyone a cocksucker. Everyone but George, that is. He was a machine, a man with no heart. All I ever got out of him were hand jobs.

Refusing all but the first shot, I'd sat quietly off to the side while George and his client got higher than I'd thought humanly possible. After the fourth shot, the ad man, his skin crackling like parchment and his pupils the size of lotus blossoms, had pulled out a revolver and suggested a game of Russian roulette. I'd waited for George to come to his senses and say no but, of course, that was the word he hated more than any other, so when he agreed, I'd stood up, pointed at the revolver and said, in a voice so calm even George took notice, that if anyone so much as touched that thing I was calling Bellevue.

For the rest of the evening, I'd watched the houselights across the Hudson flicker against a curtain as black as roof rubber and marveled at how superficial the changes I'd put myself through were. Growing up, my family had done its screaming around the dinner table, at each other, generally my father at me, although sometimes me back at him, or my mother at the two of us for ruining another meal she'd spent all day preparing. Now, George and I did our screaming, alone, in the crux of our arms. When George had finally agreed it was time to go, he was so high I'd had to help him to the door, although at least the gun remained on the coffee table, loaded but still unused.

Disgusted by the subway's smells, and paranoid the cop staring at us was wise to the half-kilo of crystal meth he had in his shoulder bag, George had insisted we get off the train at Union Square. While waiting to cross 14th Street, I'd pointed back through the trees and suggested we stop in at his old haunt, Max's Kansas City. I'd wanted to be around other people, ones who weren't in his thrall, who weren't Horrible Fags. I'd rattled off as many names as I could remember—Brigid, Gerard, Ondine, Billy, Rotten Rita, Binghamton Birdie, the Sugar Plum Fairy—but he'd just stared numbly ahead. Desperate, I'd even mentioned Lou Reed, his ex-lover. "For old time's sake," I'd pled.

Shaking his head, George had grumbled there was no point. After Andy had the Factory cleared of its crazies, the A-heads had mostly scattered. Some had died of overdoses; a few had simply vanished; but most had dried out, found jobs and, like Ondine, turned into crashing bores. "Come on," he'd grumbled, motioning me across the street to the narrow stretch of Manhattan he called "Bohemia" where, despite the growing incursion of pot-smoking hippies and poodle-walking gays, the depravity of the Factory's early days still sputtered on. "I hate uptown. The air's too thin." He'd grimaced as he gazed back toward Max's. "Too many phonies."

From Sixth Avenue, George and I turned into the Village at the Women's House of Detention, a grim Victorian fortress rumored to be as full of dykes as Bellevue was of fags. As if in proof, we quickly encountered a cluster of young Black lesbians shouting messages of love up at the jail's impassive granite facade. "Frankie, I love you, baby." "Johnette, the lawyer'll be in tomorrow. Hang in there, honey." "I be true, Bettye. Don't you worry." One even lifted her top so her lover, waving a t-shirt from high above us, could see her breasts.

Fascinated, I wanted to stop and admire the spectacle but George, appalled by their blatancy, insisted we move on. While being demented on speed was cool, being out in public—"obvious," he called it—wasn't. "Besides, I need your help," he added, smiling sheepishly. "I have gas."

"*Again*?!" I cried. "You know, George, you're always saying I need to take more speed. But maybe it's you who needs to take less." I shook my head; the night had been hard enough. There was no way I was going to spend the rest of it being his cocksucker.

Ignoring me, George forged ahead, although once he crossed onto Christopher, a street he didn't like to be seen alone on, he turned back to me. "Coming?" he inquired. Knowing he'd only find someone else if I refused, I reluctantly caught up, although a cluster of flashing blue police lights at the end of the next block quickly brought us to a halt. "What do you think that's all about?" George asked, nervously clutching his shoulder bag. "Think it's another drug sweep?"

"Not at this hour," I replied, recalling the sweep I'd evaded a few days ago. "They only do those in daylight." Squinting down the street, I guessed the cops were instead raiding the Stonewall. "Come on," I said, venturing a few steps forward. "This shit happens all the time. I bet it's over before we even get down there."

"But what about the speed?" George whimpered. "I haven't even cut it with milk-paste yet."

"George," I grumbled, "you're acting like you've never seen a gay bar raid before. The cops don't care what's in your shoulder bag. It's their bribe they want. Once the Mafia pays them off, it'll be back to normal. Like I said, these things happen all the time."

Unconvinced, George told me to check the situation out. "I'll wait here," he mumbled, retreating into the basement stairwell of a nearby apartment building. "But don't take long." He again looked at me sheepishly, although that time his complaint wasn't gas; it was fear. He even claimed to be paranoid, a word he'd previously used only on me.

I wanted to say I was tired of being the one who always stuck his neck out—the one who passed the bad checks and stole pills from his clients' medicine cabinets—but I knew he was too high to argue with. Besides, for once, I was in charge and he was the whimpering, helpless, needy one. "Sure, babe," I replied, recalling the last time I'd been on top. Then, I'd even weaseled a confession of love out of him. Who knew what this time might bring.

I ventured down Christopher as far as Waverly Place, where I found three older, nattily attired gay men huddling together on a granite stoop. When I asked what was going on, they confirmed my suspicions; the cops were raiding the Stonewall. "Again! It's the second time this week," one of them groused, a portly white guy who, despite the brutal heat and humidity, sported a paisley silk ascot. "When are they finally going to shut the place down?" Another with tweezered eyebrows and thinning peroxided hair nodded and grumbled, "Seems like every other night there's something."

"This time, I hope they lock 'em up and throw away the key," their host, a grayer older man who was perspiring heavily, snipped. "I mean, we'd just sat down to opera." He smiled haughtily. "*La Boheme,*" he purred.

He furrowed his brow and pointed a ruby-ringed finger at the paddy wagon idling on the corner of Christopher Street. "It's getting so you can't even have friends over!" He pulled a cigarette from his pack and waited for one of his guests, the man with the ascot, to light it. He sighed and blew a thick cloud of blue smoke into the steamy night air. "The Village used to have such a nice cozy feel. Now you can barely walk the streets without being accosted by some panhandler."

The one with the tweezered eyebrows scowled as he gave me the once-over. "It's you fucking hippies and those goddamn drag queens. You're giving us self-respecting gays a bad name." The others nodded. "Why do you all have to act like such..." He paused to blot the sweat from his brow. "*Trash*?!"

I wanted to tell them to go fuck themselves but instead I politely thanked them for their time and returned to find George crouching behind a dumpster in a darkened service alley. "I was right," I said, trying to coax him back into the light. "No drug sweep, just the usual cop thing—raiding gay bars and busting drag queens."

When George suggested a detour around Sixth Avenue, I insisted we stay the course. Christopher Street, I said, was ours. "The gay street," I called it. I glanced back at the lesbians defiantly shouting their love up at the impassive face of the Women's House of Detention. "Besides," I added, "it's time we start taking a stand too."

To my surprise, George acquiesced, although the closer we got to the Stonewall the more agitated he became. He kept whimpering that he didn't want to end up in jail, just the thought of it made his gas worse, until I finally had to take him by the hand and, telling him not to worry, I was in charge, lead him the rest of the way. As I had to repeatedly remind him, I'd kept my dosage low. He hadn't. He was out of his mind. I was barely even high.

Among the first to arrive, we found a spot on the curb directly across from the bar. "Front row seats," I quipped, although George was much too unnerved by the police presence to do anything but grimace. At first, there was so little action only the number of people streaming into the Square seemed noteworthy. Whereas before, a gay bar raid would have warranted only a few furtive glances, on that hot, steamy night, hundreds were streaming into Sheridan Square.

Indeed, except for the weekend I'd gone with Donnie to Atlantic City's gay beach, I'd never seen so many gay people in one place. Even the Ninth Circle, the Mafia dance bar on the other side of the Square where I'd tried my hand as a pill pusher, was engulfed, as was Waverly Place, where the three nellies I'd encountered earlier were holed up, no doubt by then thoroughly beside themselves. I chuckled. *La Boheme*, indeed.

The crowd's mood was surprisingly festive, with everyone seemingly high on something or other. Scores of joints were being passed around, as were beers from the area's numerous gay bars, all of which had purportedly emptied out as soon as word spread that something was brewing over at the Stonewall. A group of hippies had even started a snake dance around the paddy wagon, a dead giveaway that some were tripping.

Attitudes hardened, however, when two cops emerged from the bar, escorting their first batch of drag queens to the waiting paddy wagon. The tripping hippies dispersed, replaced by a band of beer-guzzling bull dykes. "Let 'em go!" a group from deep inside the crowd demanded. "Now!" the dykes replied, their fists pumping the air.

As a hailstorm of coins started whizzing over our heads, I reached into my pocket and pulled out the dregs of that month's welfare check, a handful of quarters I'd been saving for a pack of Marlboros and a Sara Lee cherry cheesecake. "Don't you dare," George hissed. Cackling, I hurled them anyway.

George sneered I'd lost my mind but the guy behind us, a short, wiry Black man in a brightly colored dashiki, congratulated me on my aim; surprisingly, several of my quarters had hit their target, one of the cops with a drag queen in tow. "Right on, brother," he murmured. I raised a fist and smiled proudly. "Right on!" I bellowed.

"Okay, that's it, I've had enough," George snipped before storming off. As he struggled to make his way through the throng, I recalled the night he'd challenged Peter and me to choose the word that best fit our stance toward life. While he'd praised Peter's selection of 'decadent,' he'd ridiculed mine. 'Radical,' he'd complained, betrayed a lack of imagination. "Insipid," he'd even called it.

Suddenly alone, I surveyed the crowd around me and let out a loud whoop. My wish from earlier that night had finally come true; there wasn't a Horrible Fag in sight. Thrilled, I turned to the man in the dashiki and confessed I'd thought I was the only one. "But look, the Square's full of us! Radicals! *Gay* radicals!" He smiled and nodded. "Yeah, fucking mindblowing, huh?" he muttered before spotting a friend and running off.

Unable to break free, George returned a few minutes later, appalled by the crowd's fury. Why, he wondered, was everyone so uptight? Didn't they have any drugs to go home to? He listened to the coins whizzing overhead and sneered outbursts like this weren't the least bit Pop. Andy, he grumbled, would be appalled.

Grimacing, I glanced up at the moon, as fat and full as I'd ever seen it, and shook my head. No one gave a shit what Andy Warhol thought. Even Andy had moved on, dropping Pop in favor of celebrity portraiture and transforming the Factory from a faggie freak show into a high-class corporate salon. Only George had stayed the course, certain the silver spray painted wingtips he kept in our closet would still come in handy, ready for the moment his avatar repented and turned back the clock to a time when, before Black Power, the Viet Cong, LSD, Watts, the Paris uprising, and Prague's Spring, 'perverse' was a stand-in for 'radical' and speed was as close to powerful as gay men got.

Somewhere behind us a high-pitched voice shouted over the chaos, "Gay is good!" Others around him took up the chant until the entire Square rang with it. Turning, I smiled at George, hoping he too recognized it as a clarion call: we no longer had to be bad; good was where thing were now at. Sensing the threat, George made it clear he was staying the course. The day gay became good, he growled, was the day he'd be going straight.

Suddenly, a drag queen, a dark-skinned Puerto Rican in a halter top and leopard skin tights, broke free of the cops and ran to the curb. Standing a few feet in front of us, she wobbled woozily on her stilettoes, shrieked "Come on, you faggots, let's riot!" and then dove head-first into the mob. Roaring, it surged forward.

"Off the pigs!" a group in the back chanted as the fusillade over our heads shifted from coins to bottles and bricks.

"Uh-oh, looks like things are starting to get ugly," the man to my right, a tall, thin hippie with long stringy hair, grumbled as a beer bottle shattered in front of us. His companion, a stockier, bearded guy in an NYU t-shirt, nodded and said he'd heard a rumor that SDS had shown up. "Back there," he said, pointing at the far northeastern corner of the Square where the bricks and bottles were coming from. When the hippie next to me countered that couldn't possibly be true—he'd heard SDS hated gays—the NYU guy shrugged; all he knew was they had to be straight. "Gays would never call cops pigs. We're too polite. And besides," he added between puffs of a joint passing through the crowd, "everyone knows sissies can't throw straight."

Meanwhile, terrified of the mob, a contingent of cops had barricaded themselves inside the Stonewall. Enraged, the crowd responded by attacking the building. A tall, muscular Black guy battered its entryway with a parking meter he and a friend had ripped from the sidewalk, while, to his left, a short, shirtless blond in cut-offs hurled a trash can at the bar's tinted plate-glass window. "I'm tired of being fucked with!" he shouted as shards of glass showered the sidewalk around him. Drunk, he woozily turned back to the crowd and, pumping the air with his fist, proclaimed Christopher Street a liberated zone. Not to be outdone, the Black guy ramming the Stonewall's doors tossed aside his battering ram and shouted out the clarion call for every American riot since Watts: *Burn, baby, burn!*

At that, all hell broke loose. A mob surged toward the paddy wagon on the corner of Waverly and demanded freedom for its imprisoned haul. Quickly surrounded, the cops guarding its rear door retreated into the van's cabin. Pumped, a group of young toughs rocked the holding tank on its axles, while the queens trapped inside made the most of their escape. One curtsied and bowed; another pumped a fist in the air; a third cried like she'd just been crowned Miss America; and a fourth egged the melee on. "Flatten the motherfucker's tires," she shouted huskily.

The paddy wagon at first tried to inch its way free of the mob. But when the toughs managed to nearly topple it, the driver panicked, flicked on its siren and flashing lights, and gunned the vehicle up Christopher Street. "Hey, you're going the wrong way!" the crowd shouted as a cascade of rocks and beer bottles pummeled the fleeing vehicle's backside. "Arrest them!" others laughed.

The crowd paused as it watched the paddy wagon disappear onto Sixth Avenue and then a deafening roar engulfed the Square. People jumped for joy. Strangers hugged. We'd won! We'd beaten the cops! They'd fled! From us— *gay people!*

"Power to the people!" the bull dykes on the corner of Waverly shouted. "All power to all the people!" the group rumored to be SDS replied under a hail of debris.

Meanwhile, a contingent of cops from the Sixth Precinct, a half-block up from our building on West 10th, arrived to rescue their beleaguered colleagues. "What's the matter, faggots?" a short, beefy hustler shouted as the first two were escorted out of the then-ravaged Stonewall. "Scared?!" A few feet away, a white drag queen in a leather miniskirt and a towering bouffant grabbed her crotch.

"Here, pussies," she snarled as two more cops, one a woman, emerged from the bar. "Wanna suck on this?"

"Okay, that's it," I said to George. "We can go now. Things are starting to degenerate." As we slowly worked our way toward Seventh Avenue, I shook my head as a shirtless hustler with a bandana tied around his neck called the cops cocksuckers. A few feet away, a tattooed dyke in a tank top accused them of being fairies. "I hate it when we act like them."

"Them?" George asked.

"Yeah, you know, like straight people. Haters."

Suddenly, Peter ran up to us shrieking, "It's the queens. The drag queens. They're absolutely beside themselves!"

Noticing a splotch of dried blood in the crux of his left arm, I wet my thumb as discretely as I could in the midst of a riot and blotted the stain away. "Really, darling," I muttered, "you need to be more careful. There're cops everywhere."

Embarrassed, Peter blushed and admitted that perhaps he'd done a few too many reds. "It's just the night's been so crazy."

"Yeah, tell me about it," I replied, recalling the game of Russian roulette I'd had to squelch. I glanced nervously at George, who, ignoring Peter, stared stonily off into the distance. "Now, what were you saying?" I asked, turning back to Peter. "What about the drag queens?"

"What, you don't know?" he gasped. "Judy's funeral was today. You know, up at Campbell's on East 81st Street." He wobbled slightly and grabbed my shoulder for support. "Stephanie Lisa went and said every queen worth her salt was there." He paused to light a Gauloises and smirked. "So many, in fact, the cops had to call for reinforcements."

I told Peter I had no idea what he was talking about. "Who did you say died?"

"Why, Judy Garland, of course! Didn't you know?!" When I admitted I didn't, Peter shrieked, "Why, the girls have been in sackcloth and ashes all week. Where have you been—living under a rock?" He picked a tobacco shard from his tongue and glanced maliciously at George. "You speed freaks need to tear yourselves away from those trip books and get out more. Things happen!"

Peter took a long drag from his cigarette and chuckled. "Rumors kept swirling that Judy's coffin was lined with Seconal and so, when it emerged from the hearse, the queens rushed it." Everyone, he cackled, had wanted a souvenir. "Stephie swears the crush was so bad she was almost trampled to death." He smirked. "Says her heel got caught in a sewer grate."

At that, even George laughed. "That's our Stephie," he muttered. "A sewer grate, huh?"

Peter said as soon as they got back downtown, the queens were at his door, clamoring for reds. Everyone wanted at least one. "For Miss Garland!" he squealed, imitating them. Then, spotting the one to whom he'd promised his last three, he ran off noting he'd made a small fortune. "Best night I've ever had," he cried before disappearing into the crowd.

Next, we ran into John, who a week earlier had moved onto our balcony after the landlord had locked him out of the apartment on Avenue D. "It's Pluto. I just know it," he said of the planet he was convinced ruled all things gay. He prattled on about how it was trine with Venus and conjunct with Jupiter but when he got to its opposition with Leo, George stormed off.

So caught up in his own rap, John didn't even notice. "I had to look it up. I'd never seen that aspect before. It said karma is being redistributed!"

He pointed to a kid squirting lighter fluid on the wooden frame of the Stonewall's shattered plate glass window. "Look! We're doing it! We're getting even!" Then, as the frame burst into a ring of fire, John did something he'd never done, even on the night we'd made love. He hugged me. "And do you know what else?"

"Sorry, John, but I can't," I cried as I spotted George a few yards away, cruising another guy. "George is getting impatient. He's going to..."

John grabbed my arm. "Wait, just wait 'til you hear this," he cried. "Aquarius is rising!"

"Oh, John, please," I groaned before asking if he too had been sampling Peter's reds.

"No, he gave me a black beauty," he replied, blushing slightly. "Two, actually." Then, pointing at the flaming face of the Stonewall, he cried, "Oh my God, there he is. I've got to tell Peter, too!" Dashing off, he shouted over his shoulder that it was the dawning of the Age of Aquarius and then, giggling, he too disappeared into the throng.

George was scowling when I found him standing alone on the corner of Seventh Avenue, although the guy he'd been cruising was only a few yards away. Pointing out the phalanx of cops in riot gear massing several blocks north, he said there was no time to waste; we needed to be splitting. He then stepped off the curb but, sensing my hesitancy, stopped after a few paces. "Unless, of course, you'd rather spend your night with these cretins." He chuckled softly. "I'm sure I can find someone else to help with my, uhm..." He paused just long enough to smile at the other guy. "Gas."

Next to me, a tattooed hustler in a tank top picked up a stray brick and aimed it at the Stonewall.

"No, there!" I shouted, pointing at the two plate glass windows on the corner. "*The Village Voice!*"

"You mean the fucking rag?" the guy asked, numbly peering into the office.

"Yeah, that's right. Smash its windows!"

Appalled, George snarled that if I said one more word, he was leaving without me but, thrilled to finally be saying my piece, I persisted. "It refuses to print the word 'gay!' Here, right here on Christopher Street!" I pointed at the trashed and burning hulk of its neighbor. "At least the Stonewall let us dance."

The hustler replied he didn't give a shit what the *Voice* printed or who-the-fuck the Stonewall let dance, he just wanted to raise some hell. Then, dropping the brick and muttering about goddamn motherfucking pigs, he woozily stumbled off.

By the time I caught up with George, his rage had shifted from the rioters to John. Turning onto Bleecker Street, he announced he was cutting him off. "No more speed. The guy's an idiot. If I hear one more word about the planets and their effect on a bunch of doped-up drag queens, I'm gonna explode."

The next night, on our way back from another drug deal, George and I encountered more action outside the Stonewall. The crowd was larger—so large, in fact, it blocked traffic on Seventh Avenue. And not only had the Ninth Circle again barricaded its door, but so had Rikers, where the Village's growing cohort of street queens hung out. United Cigars, the bustling corner newsstand with the Village's largest selection of gay porn, was also shuttered, although across the street, at *The Village Voice*, business went on as usual. Not a single window was broken.

At first, the crowd behaved itself, entertained by the legion of drag queens parading up and down the street under the glare of TV klieg lights and leading the crowd in campy, off-color chants. But when the drugs finally kicked in and the queens started taunting the cops' manhood, New York's armed and notoriously brutal Tactical Patrol Force rushed Christopher Street with batons swinging.

A group in the back of Sheridan Square, that time rumored to be the Weathermen, an ultra-left spinoff from SDS, responded with a volley of beer bottles. When one almost clipped George in the head, we fled across Seventh Avenue and watched the crowd take baseball bats to an errant taxi full of terrified tourists. I felt a momentary urge to rescue them but when their attackers cried this was our part of town, the gay section, and they didn't belong there, weren't even welcome, I left them to their own devices. As John had said the night before, karma was being redistributed. Finally, straights were learning what it felt like to be hated too.

Looking away, I noticed the face of the Women's House of Detention was awash in a sea of white flags. At first, I feared the rioters had set the jail ablaze but the lesbian next to me, a librarian in a nearby elementary school, said the prisoners had been at it all night. "They're saying they're with us," she said excitedly. "That we should keep it up." She looked at me. She was flushed and sweat was dripping from her brow; the heat wave had still not broken and the moon remained a lurid orange. "Can you believe what's happening?"

I confessed I didn't know what to think. Was it just a bunch of doped-up drag queens grieving the loss of their diva, Judy Garland, as the run on Peter's reds had indicated, or was it the start of something big, what John had called, only half in jest, the dawning of the Age of Aquarius?

She admitted she wasn't sure either. As she noted, everyone seemed very high. She smiled warily. "A little crazed even."

I nodded and chuckled softly. "Yeah, being gay'll sometimes do that to you."

She laughed and then bid me farewell with a raised fist and a hearty right-on, a salute I'd never before seen anyone but straight men give each other.

On our way home, George went on another rant about people who should be home doing drugs rather than out on the streets behaving like lunatics. "I mean, don't they know the world is perfect just the way it is?" he cried, paraphrasing his avatar, Andy Warhol. Ignoring him, I recalled the message we'd seen spray painted across the Stonewall's now boarded-up facade. "Gay Power," it had read in a big drippy scrawl. While I'd seen "Black Power" and "Power to the People" scrawled across numerous walls, I'd never seen or even heard of "Gay Power." Maybe John was right. Maybe a new day was dawning.

Crossing Seventh Avenue, we'd even encountered two men holding hands on their way to the subway. George had been even more appalled by their blatancy than he had been by the lesbians we'd encountered the night before. But I'd actually stopped and stared. Two men holding hands? In public? No, I'd never seen that before either.

That night, we found John huddled on the landing outside our room poring over his astrology books. "Did you see the TV cameras?" he asked of the action outside the Stonewall. "People are starting to say we mean business."

He followed us into our room and instantly started up on the stars. "I can't believe last night's aspects. Jupiter was in a really strange position: conjunct with Uranus, sextile with Mars, in opposition with Leo. And, look here, Neptune's in Pisces," he cried, pointing to a circle covered with glyphs. "There's something very spiritual going on...."

Recalling George's fury from the night before, I ran onto the balcony and slammed the door behind me. An hour later, I ventured back out and found George alone on the bed, quietly writing in his trip book.

"I shut him up good and tight," he said when I finally worked up the courage to ask about John. "I'm not sure I could've handled it. It was one of the biggest shots I've ever given anyone."

Chuckling, he described the aftereffects. As John collapsed into a heap, George had leaned over and whispered in his ear that he'd worn out his welcome. John's eyes had rolled around in his head a few times and then, pale as a ghost, he'd grabbed his astrology books and the jacket he called his Persian Plastic and run out the door.

No, George snarled, he hadn't said where he was heading or how long he'd be gone. He'd simply vanished into thin air. "Poof! Just like a fairy godmother," he said, flicking his fist into a starburst. His eyes narrowed. "*Your* fairy godmother."

He dropped an orange felt tip pen on the bed, picked up a blue one and resumed his scribbling. "Just like I wish all those little people out on the street would do. Where'd they come from anyway? They're ruining New York."

The next night, Holly stopped by for a hit of speed, which George, always eager to dement a drag queen, gleefully administered. Afterward, she left for the Stonewall, where she hoped to get on TV. As she noted, the media was out in force, covering the drag queens and the trickle of VIPs who'd stopped by to show their support for what had suddenly become known as a "cause." Homosexuals, people were starting to say, had rights too—grievances even, especially when it came to the cops.

Holly had heard Allen Ginsberg had shown up that afternoon and she was hoping Andy, whom she still hadn't met, might also. "I mean, I've tried just about everything else. Who do you have to fuck in this town to meet the queen, anyway?"

Holly hung around the Stonewall that Sunday night until the rioters dispersed, although Andy never did show. When Holly later expressed her frustration at Andy's aloofness, George counseled patience. After all, the

Stonewall crowd was much too obvious for a master of deflection like Andy Warhol. And much too political. As he noted, protesters bored Andy to tears.

Besides, he claimed the rioters outside the Stonewall lacked the glamour Andy liked to surround himself with. No one who was anyone, George said, would want to fuck people like that. Indeed, if I hadn't insisted, he wouldn't have given any of them so much as a passing glance. But then, he sneered, I was radical. I longed to be good. He was perverse. He loved being bad.

"Junkies don't take to water," Peter explained, modeling the denim hot pants he'd fashioned from an old pair of jeans. "They aren't supposed to have bathing suits." He dabbed the sweat from his forehead with the bath towel draped over his shoulders and gave me a smile so tender I almost burst into tears.

Abandoned by George, I hadn't spoken to another human being in four days. Worried about me, Peter had suggested we cool off at the municipal pool a few blocks down Hudson. "Come on, it'll be fun. We'll have a pool party," he murmured. He picked up my trip book and ripped out a page. "Look, we'll leave a note in case George comes back. It's only a few blocks away. He can walk over and join us."

"He won't come," I grumbled. "He says only little people use municipal pools."

"Yeah, and what about the heat?" Peter cried. "Do only little people get hot?"

The heat wave that had begun the day of the Stonewall riots had still not abated. Worse, I hadn't had a drop of speed since George had left for who-knew-where. For Peter, it had been even longer. Weeks, he said. He'd even run out of reds. "The Great Dope Famine," the *East Village Other* called it.

"I don't know," I whimpered. "I think I'm losing it, Peter." Afraid I'd miss him, I'd left our room only to grab a cherry Coke or buy a pack of cigarettes at the corner bodega. Still, once, George had gotten past me. When I'd returned, I'd found a smoldering Marlboro in the ashtray and a smattering of baby powder on the floor next to the hand sink. "Why is he doing this?" I started to tear up. "What have I done?"

"Come on," Peter murmured, grabbing my hand and leading me to the door. "You need a change of scenery."

At the pool, Peter dangled his feet in the water and leaned in close to me. "You know, darling, I don't care what you say. You really are a Kay Hoopes Harrington.

You think you can burn it all out of you. But, deep down, you know you'll never be one of us. You're too sweet. You should treasure that and get out while you can."

"Oh, but the speed has done such wonders for my cheek bones," I countered. I leaned back and struck a vampish pose. "Soon I'll be as svelte as Veruschka."

Peter groaned. "Personally, I can't figure why you're still hanging around. It's certainly not the speed. My God, you should see yourself when you're high." He leaned over and dipped his fingertips in the water. "You're pathetic."

"Peter, please don't," I pled. "It's my armor. Being a speed freak makes me something. A somebody." I reminded him of what he'd said of his prospects off drugs. "I don't want to be just another ordinary fag, afraid of his own shadow. I want to be strong and in-your-face." I looked at him wistfully. "Like you— fabulous."

Unconvinced, Peter rose and walked back to our towels. When I rejoined him, he started back in on me. "Look, you have options. Your family still loves you. Not everyone's does, you know." He watched two kids in the pool splash each other and, donning shades, suggested I rethink college. "You really should go back, you know. You have a future." He chuckled. "I've seen your drive. You may not recognize it yet, darling, but when you set your mind to something, you get it."

I told him I'd rather die than end up back in my parents' clutches. "They're hateful, Peter. They can't even bring themselves to say the word 'gay.'"

He shook his head. "It's George, isn't it? You really are in love with him, aren't you?"

I stared at a tuft of crab grass poking through a crack in the concrete and fought back a wall of tears. "I can't help it," I whimpered. I started to tremble. "I'm lost, Peter, I know it. But it's true. He's all I think about."

"Oh, honey, come on. You've been around long enough to know the difference between love and a big dick." Peter swatted a fly buzzing about his head and laughed. "Let's face it, even George doesn't know what to do with it. He just lies there, expecting you to do all the work. Well, a girl gets tired after a while. Sometimes she wants some attention too!"

Stunned, I watched Peter reach into his shoulder bag and pull out his pack of Gauloises. Rivals didn't talk like this. Girlfriends did.

"Sometimes, you just have to stand back and watch that bloated flounder flop around, hoping it'll finally exhaust itself." Peter blew out his match and took a long drag from his cigarette. "It's hilarious when you think about it." He poked me in my ribs and laughed. "Am I right? Now, come on. Be honest!"

I nervously glanced around the pool to make sure George hadn't snuck in to witness my betrayal and then nodded. "Okay, looked at in the right light..." I played with the frayed edge of my towel. "I mean, yeah, I guess it is sorta ridiculous, huh?"

At that, Peter started shouting *Bloated flounder*! *Bloated flounder*! so loudly a girl two blankets down joined in. Then collapsing onto a sheet stained from enough hand jobs to convince me I was as ugly in body as I was in spirit, Peter and I laughed until we cried.

I struggled back to my knees as the Beach Boys' "Wouldn't It Be Nice" blared from a speaker atop the pool's concession stand. "Oh my God, in high school this was one of my favorite songs! I'd put my 45 on the living room stereo, stand in front of our dining room mirror and lip-synch the lines. Tears would just stream down my face."

Peter started to clap. "Oh, how fabulous, that's so you! *So Kay!*"

"Wait," I said, holding up my hand. "Here comes the best part..." Then, as Peter bounced on his knees to the beat, I sang along in the half-soprano, half-tenor warble puberty had left me with about the happiness that came from being deliriously in love.

I enviously watched the straight Puerto Rican couple next to us snuggle and coo and then, turning to Peter, asked why we had it so hard. Nothing, after all, seemed more basic than the right to be in love.

"Oh, Kay," he groaned, "you know why. Straights are *supposed* to love each other. We aren't." I asked him to say more but he just put his finger to his lips. "You're getting too heavy, darling." He laughed nervously. "We don't want to be bores, now do we?"

"I'm sorry," I replied, glumly staring at the pool's concrete surround. "Heavy, I guess, is just the way I am." I fumbled with my pack of Marlboros and told him what Trudy, the resident "fag hag" from Syracuse's Continental Room, had once said of me. "She was right, you know. Something always does seem to be bothering me."

"Come on," Peter cried, jumping up and dragging me to the pool's edge, "let's play Esther Williams." He grabbed my hand and we dove off the deep end, embracing and slithering around the bottom of the pool like two demented eels. Muffled by the water, our howls and screams, giggles and sobs formed bubbles that raced to the surface like blood in a dropper. When we finally got out of the pool, Peter regretted waiting so long to have what he called "girl time" with me. "Sorry, but that fag hag was wrong. You really are a lot of fun."

On the walk back to West 10th Street, Peter put his arm through mine and, ignoring the stares of passersby, apologized for what he called "the mess" with George. "All I'd ever wanted was speed. I mean, I don't think I even like the guy." When an old crone in a babushka stopped and scowled at us, Peter glared back at her and asked what she was looking at. "I mean, we are, after all, sisters," he said before breaking into a loud cackle. Stunned, the crone raised her cane and shook it at us. "Yeah, that's right, honey," he bellowed back at her. "We're *gay*! *G-a-y, gay*!"

In the middle of the next block, Peter credited me for his outburst. "Remember the time you had us play lovebirds when we ripped off those two queens who owned the antique shop on Bleecker?" When I confessed I still felt guilty about that day, Peter grabbed my arm and swung me around to face him. "Oh no, darling, you were an inspiration. I know it sounds crazy but I'd never seen anyone be so matter-of-fact about being gay before." He smiled. "You weren't outrageous in the least bit. Just, well, kinda *normal*, you know what I mean? It blew my mind." He again threaded his arm through mine. "It really did."

As we continued up Hudson, I quietly went through the list of names I'd been called over the years. While I was familiar with a host of slurs—homo, sissy, pervert, queer, pansy, cocksucker, faggot, fairy, fruit—no one had ever called me an inspiration. Indeed, hearing someone like Peter say that about me was almost as mind-blowing as watching "doped-up drag queens," as George had called them, battle the cops outside the Stonewall. "I need to start standing up for myself more, don't I?" I asked as we turned the corner onto West 10th.

Peter stopped, glanced up at our building's crumbling façade, and put a finger to his lips. "Shhh, you never know. George might be listening." I thought that was strange coming from Peter, especially since neither of us were high, but he persisted. "He has powers, you know," he muttered before entering the vestibule. "You don't want to cross him."

On our third-floor landing, I thanked Peter for the day, although, heeding his warning, I didn't mention his critique of George's sexual prowess or my performance as a speed freak. I focused on our Esther Williams routine, which I said I'd enjoyed even more than dancing 'The Dying Swan' as a kid. I smiled shyly. "At least with you I had a partner."

"Yeah, but it woulda been so much better high," Peter replied, fumbling with the key to his room. "I mean, who does a girl have to fuck to get some drugs around here?" At that, he winked and disappeared into his room.

The next morning, I found a note tacked to Peter's door. Addressed to me, it said he'd fled New York for his mother's house on Long Island. When, that evening, I showed it to George, who'd finally returned from whoever he'd been fucking, he gave me a dime and told me to go to the pay phone up the street and call him collect. "Tell him we want to come visit. See what he says," he mumbled darkly.

When I called, Peter sounded tired but he made it clear he wanted nothing more to do with George. Warning me he was dangerous, Peter advised me to get out of New York as soon as I could. "Don't hesitate, just go." Then apologizing for his abruptness, he told me not to call again and hung up.

I listened to the dial tone buzz in my ear while a rat skittered down the curb and disappeared into a sewer grate. Peter was my last New York friend. After him, all I had left was George.

"Oh really, he said that, did he?" George sneered when I returned and reported on the call. "So, what else have you and Peter said behind my back, eh?"

"What do you mean?"

"Oh, I don't know," he said. "I just want to make sure you're not conspiring." He peered into the silver gazing ball on the table next to the bed—a gift Peter had called a "peace offering." "You know, just being cautious. I am, after all, a drug dealer." Then, reaching for his works, he asked if I wanted a shot.

"Just a light one," I said, wiping the sweat from my brow. The room was hot and airless. "You know, I'm tired of being paranoid," I added, mustering a smile. I opened the window and savored the evening breeze. The heat wave was finally starting to break. "Maybe speed isn't for me, after all."

Dropping a ball of cotton into the spoon, George looked askance at me. "Mmmm, Peter tell you that, too?"

His shot hit me like an avalanche. Flattened against the bed, I listened as a cacophony of bells rang inside my head. Gasping for air, I inched my head up from the pillow and saw a message written in hieroglyphics on the wall next to the hand sink mirror. I couldn't tell what it said but the lightbulb over the hand sink could. Flickering, it suddenly went dead.

"Oh my God, please, George, get help. Your shot was too big. You gave me too much." Struggling to lift my head up, I pointed at the wall. "Do you see? It's a message. A warning." Dropping back to the pillow, I moaned, "Oh my God, the bells. Do you hear the bells?"

George waved the empty syringe in my face. "Don't you ever talk to anyone about me again, do you hear?"

Too terrified to speak, I simply nodded.

"Good," he snarled and motioned for me pull down my pants. He wanted to fuck me. "And you better be clean this time, you filthy little shit."

19
All That Glitters Isn't Gold

"Honey, you're too young to be cooped up like this," Holly chided while ratting her hair out in the sex mirror opposite the bed George and I shared with a growing infrequency. "You're not a monk, you know." She pulled a tube of neon-pink lipstick from her shoulder bag and suggested a night out at Max's Kansas City, Andy Warhol's Union Square hangout.

I recalled the time I'd tried to convince George to take me to Max's and sighed. "Too many phonies," he'd grumbled. Later that night, we'd stumbled upon a mob of drag queens and street hustlers fighting the cops outside the Stonewall. "Little people," George had called them.

"Oh, come on, they'll usher us right in," she said when I told her I was too broke to afford Max's cover charge. "Everyone knows me now." She adjusted the strap to her size 14 wedgies and frowned slightly. "Everyone but Andy, that is." Since landing the role of Princess Ninga Flinga Dung in Jackie Curtis' new play, *Heaven Grand in Amber Orbit,* Holly had thrown her campaign for Factory superstardom into overdrive. Hearing Andy no longer worked with junkies, she'd even stopped shooting speed.

"But tonight's gonna be different. I can tell. He's gonna show," she said, fluffing the confection of scarves she'd whipped into a dress. "He has to. After all, everyone else has."

"Oh yeah?" I asked, my interest suddenly piqued. "Who?"

"Oh, you know, the whole crowd," she muttered before listing Viva, Brigid Polk, Taylor Mead, Gerard Malanga, Ultra Violet, Eric Emerson, and a guy she called "Little Joe."

"You mean, Joe Dallesandro?"

"I guess so," she shrugged, dabbing her tracks with Preparation H. "You know, the guy whose dick everyone wants to suck."

"Okay, okay, I'll go," I said, heading for the closet to find something to wear. "And what about Lou? Have you met him?"

"Lou?" she asked as I came across the t-shirt with a fish staring at a hook that I'd worn as a kid. Thanks to the speed, I could get into it again. "Who's that?"

"Lou Reed. You know, from the Velvet Underground," I said, smiling at my exposed midriff—the latest in New York "flash" trends.

"The Velvet Underground?" Holly asked. "What's that, one of those boutiques on St. Mark's Place?"

"Oh, God no. The Velvets were Andy's house band when George hung out at the Factory. George and Lou were lovers."

"No way," Holly cried. "I'm plucked!"

"I'll point him out if you promise to introduce us," I said, ushering her out the door. I stopped on the second-floor landing and anticipated the encounter. "Hi," I'd say, "we have a friend in common." I'd wait for Lou to ask who someone like me could possibly have in common with someone like him and then go in for the kill. "I'm Silver George's lover," I'd say and wait to see what he said.

Just as Holly had promised, Max's doorman, a Botticelli look-alike in a tank top with a halo of blond curls, broad shoulders and dreamy blue eyes, let us breeze right in. The front room was packed, although Holly waved off a table of drunken tourists who mistook her for Candy Darling, one of the Factory drag queens she called fakes, and headed instead for the bar. When no one offered her a drink and the bartender informed her she had to settle her tab before he could serve her, she grumbled the place was dead and dragged me to the back where, next to a wheezing ice machine, a scowling linebacker in a muscle t-shirt and hot pants guarded a door with a porthole and a sign below it that read "Private."

The bouncer leaned forward to accept Holly's peck on the cheek and looked blankly away as she sought his permission to enter. He continued to ignore her until she lewdly promised a tip the next time she showed up. "You know, alone," she added, glancing at me. At that, he reached behind him, gruffly threw open the door and pointed to a steep, unlit stairwell. "And no shenanigans in the bathroom this time," he grumbled.

"Well, here we are, the inner sanctum," she gushed as we entered a smelly, dimly lit, low-ceilinged room at the top of the stairs. "Hmmm, looks kinda dead up here, too, huh?" she grumbled as she stalked its perimeter of empty booths.

"Must be the time of year," I ventured. "I mean, it is, after all, the Fourth of July weekend." I listened to the air conditioner rattle behind me and mustered a wan smile. "Anyone who's anybody's gonna be at their beach house."

"The Fourth of July?" Holly gasped, forlornly fluffing the scarves of her improvised dress. "I'm plucked. I had no idea."

"George says Andy has a place out on Long Island. In Montauk. You know, with the rest of the art crowd," I said, mimicking his sneer. By then, realizing his banishment from the Factory was permanent, George had even turned against Andy. A "sell-out," he'd started calling him, although he saved his harshest words for Paul Morrissey, the director of *Flesh*, who'd carried out Andy's orders to clear the Factory of its A-heads. "The anti-Christ," George called him.

"Oh, how fabulous, a garden party at Andy's summer cottage," Holly cooed, batting her glitter-caked eyelids. She stepped onto the dance floor and gazed up at a tiny disco ball. "Next summer," she added dreamily.

"So, this is it, Max's Kansas City, Andy's home away from home," she crowed, twirling in her size 14 wedgies. "I'm plucked! I mean, isn't it fabulous?"

I scowled at the fake knotty pine paneling, the ripped red vinyl booths and the buckled linoleum floor tiles and said Andy's inner sanctum looked just like a tacky gay bar. I spied the pool of piss outside the bathroom door and, recalling Holly had also spent time in Syracuse, asked if she'd ever been to the Continental Room. "Yeah, well, that's what this reminds me of," I grumbled when she noted the only Syracuse dives she'd ever hung out in were the joints where she'd worked as a stripper. "A dump."

I met her glare and wondered why I'd bothered tagging along. Other than a taste for speed and a cache of unfulfilled dreams George dismissed as romantic delusions, Holly and I had little in common. She was always up, a gender-bent Holly Golightly distracted by glittery surfaces, while I was most always down, a judgmental wet blanket obsessed with the undercurrent of meaning running through things. The one time I'd seen her favorite film, *Breakfast at Tiffany's*, I'd turned the TV off. When I'd told her about mine, *Persona*, she'd looked at me blankly. The only Bergman she'd ever heard of was Ingrid.

Holly pointed to the bathroom and boasted that on a really good night it was so full of junkies shooting up, people had to piss off the fire escape. I tried to pretend that was one of the coolest things I'd ever heard but it only sent me deeper into my funk. George was right. I was too uptight for all this. Depravity wasn't what I was into. Revolution was.

I dropped my last quarter in the jukebox and played for Holly her favorite tune, Donovan's "Lalena." As she twirled around the dance floor, her scarves opening up like some weird psychedelic flower, I recalled the night in my father's Corvair when, driving to Philadelphia for my first gay party, my old high school pal, Donnie, and I had repeated Martha's line from *Who's Afraid of Virginia Woolf?*—*I'm not a monster! I'm not! I'm not!* Ever since, I'd been trying to prove how wrong Martha was. Somehow, I needed to find my way back to good.

I wandered into a dark, deserted room overlooking Park Avenue and looked out a grimy bank of windows at a row of Beaux Arts mid-rises on the other side of Union Square. In one of them was the Factory and, a few floors away, the headquarters of the Communist Party USA. I gazed up at a crescent moon hanging over the Square, amazed that two of the country's biggest bogeymen— one, Andy Warhol, the Pop pervert, and the other, Gus Hall, the Red menace— shared the same lobby and elevators—maybe even the same men's room. When I'd asked George if the two groups ever got together, he'd looked at me like I'd gone mad. Communists were superego, he'd growled, while the Factory was id. The two were incompatible. Indeed, they canceled each other out.

Too bad, I thought, as I turned to rejoin Holly. From their coupling, a future outside of the gutter just might have been possible.

I watched Holly flit about the dance floor and wondered if George was right; maybe I was crazy. No one had dreams like mine. After all, mixing sexual liberation with Marxist-Leninist orthodoxy was as loony in its own way as a drag queen like Holly trying to break into the big time. As George had said, some things were incompatible. They cancelled each other out.

I waited for Donovan's lament to end and suggested we head back to West 10th Street, guessing by then that George had returned. I glanced down at my needle tracks. After all, it'd been two days. Rarely did he stay away longer.

"Yeah, I can't believe how dead it is. Besides, I hate this song," she grumbled of the other jukebox offering I'd selected, Dylan's "Visions of Johanna."

"Funny, it's one of my favorites," I countered.

"Figures," she scoffed before heading down the stairs, hoping against hope that on the way out she'd run into Andy.

When Holly and I returned to West 10th Street, George was sitting on the bed, quietly writing in his trip book. We barely spoke but Holly instantly launched into the story of her life since she'd last wandered off, loaded to the gills on another one of George's shots.

"Upstairs, huh?" George muttered when she got to her nightly vigils at Max's Kansas City. "No wonder you've never met Andy. The second floor's what they call "Siberia." It's where they send the nobodies."

Slouching forward like she'd just been sucker-punched, Holly slowly shook her head. "You mean what they said was a lie?" She looked around the room as if bewildered; she'd only just met most of them. "A sick joke?"

George chuckled and asked if she wanted a shot. "Nothing like a good hit of speed to get over a shock," he added, with a smile so big his dimples showed.

"Yeah, sure, why not? Do me up good," she muttered. "Who the fuck cares if Andy doesn't like tracks? I'm never gonna meet him."

"Yeah, who cares," George purred, removing his dropper from its Altoid tin. He dropped a ball of cotton into a shot glass. "Nothing matters, nothing at all."

While George helped Holly get off, I examined my worry lines in the sex mirror across from the bed. No matter how hard I tried, I couldn't shake the feeling that I too was the butt of a horrible sick joke—the bird with a broken wing whose ruin proved, like the mute Broadway dancer Norman paraded around, how monstrous George really was.

For the next three days, Holly sat on our floor, babbling to herself and playing with the contents of her shoulder bag until George finally ran out of speed and she returned to her boyfriend, a seventeen-year-old runaway from upstate New York George seemed much too eager to meet.

After that, thinking it would spice up our flagging sex life, he had me watch him fuck me in the sex mirror. At one point, I wondered who that wretch was George was calling his little sex pig. It couldn't possibly be me. At twenty, I was supposed to be at the peak of my sexual powers, while the guy staring back at me was so repelled by how low he'd sunk he couldn't even get hard.

Not that George noticed. After he came, he even seemed relieved he didn't have to bother with another hand job. We'd barely even kissed.

I noted the look of dismay on George's face when I returned from a shoplifting spree and wondered if something was up. After all, he'd been so faithful the past few weeks that I'd started to take him at his word. As he'd said upon his return from his last tryst, it was time for him to settle down. He'd even resumed telling me how different I was from the others, not the least bit piggy or self-serving.

No one was more surprised by the change than I. Sparked by a three-day blowout that had landed the other guy in Bellevue and George nearly in jail for assault, we'd settled into a routine so domestic that Adrian, the tall, lanky redhead who was George's latest recruit into the Horrible Fags, had started likening us to a boring old married couple. High, we mostly just smoked cigarettes, drank cherry Cokes, wrote in our trip books, balled and rapped with other speed freaks who stopped by for drugs. "Straight," or not high, we mostly caught up on our sleep, gorged ourselves on fare from the Pink Teacup, a diner on Bleecker Street, or the Silver Dollar, another down by the Trucks, and looked for ways to get high again, although sometimes I got George to work up the energy to ball then too. In fact, I so enjoyed having George all to myself I'd even started to feel sexual again.

Besides, George and I worked best together when straight. Then, we made love rather than just fucked. That afternoon—the one I'd gone off shoplifting—both of us were high, although we'd just come off a dry spell during which George had been unusually affectionate. The previous night, we'd fallen asleep in each other's arms and in the morning—before he'd run off to his Grand Poobah for more speed—he'd even asked if I knew I was the first lover he'd ever trusted enough to move in with. I, of course, instantly thought of his time with Peter but not wanting to ruin the moment let it slide. And, in truth, it'd been a while since George had called me a lover, although, as I also noted, he still would not say he loved me. That, he insisted, should be apparent from his deeds, not his words.

I'd expected to find Adrian when I returned—after all, he'd been there when I'd left—although his greeting also seemed odd. "Why darling, you're back so soon!" he cried, blocking my entrance. "We hadn't expected you for hours."

"What are you talking about?" I replied, pulling from my jeans the two Sara Lee cheesecakes I'd stolen from the supermarket up on Hudson—the same one in which Holly had introduced me to her "superstar" approach to shoplifting. "See," I said, shoving the door open. "I've been out doing my part." I smiled proudly. "You know, being a sleaze."

It was then I realized I was right; something was up. In the far corner opposite George, sitting in the high-backed wicker chair I'd hauled in from the trash two days before and spray painted neon orange, was none other than Lou Reed, George's ex and the rock star I'd hoped to meet the night I'd gone with Holly to Max's Kansas City.

I quickly checked out the distance between the two of them and breathed a sigh of relief. If their intentions were sexual, my timing had been perfect. George's trip book was still in his lap, while Lou's hands were securely tucked under arms tightly folded across his chest. Indeed, Lou seemed so uptight—his legs were also crossed and his right foot manically sliced the air in front of him—I wondered if sex was even on the agenda. Perhaps, I thought, they were just reconnecting as old friends.

Relaxing, I leaned against the hand sink and briefly scoped our visitor out. Dressed in sparkling white tennis shoes and pressed khakis, with the collar of a pink polo shirt turned feyly upward, Lou looked more like a patron of Julius's, the bourgie gay bar a few blocks up West 10th, than the writer of songs like "Heroin," "Venus in Furs," and "Sister Ray." Only his halo of curly black hair and his presence in the shooting gallery of one of New York's biggest speed freaks indicated Lou was even remotely hip.

"Hello," I ventured as nonchalantly as possible. I knew gushing would be uncool and, besides, I felt the hint of an affinity. Maybe it was that foot slicing the air or the queeny flamboyance with which he puffed on his cigarette—or maybe it was just that he'd also been George's lover—but he seemed so profoundly ill at ease that I sensed he too knew he was over his head. Way over. "Swimming with sharks," Peter had called it.

Perhaps discerning my intent, Lou quickly disabused me of any hope of a connection. Arching his left eyebrow, he shot me one of those bitchy, don't-fuck-with-me looks the drag queens at the Stonewall used to throw around before rioters torched the joint and then, turning to George, sneered, "*Who's she*?"

Even Adrian, who'd been manically flitting about the room since I'd arrived, froze.

I let out a low-pitched moan that I hoped sounded like laughter and turned to George. I waited for him to repeat what he'd told me that morning—that I was the first lover he'd ever trusted enough to move in with—but he just sat there, grinning stupidly at the red Converse high-tops I'd bought for him with silver dollars I'd stolen from my father's dresser drawer. My mind went blank and my knees buckled, although I did at least hold back my tears.

Sensing I was about to lose it, Adrian grabbed my arm and, mumbling he had something to show me, dragged me onto the balcony.

"*She*?! Did you hear him? He called me a *she*!" I stammered as Adrian slammed the balcony door shut. "Like some tacky piano bar queen." I slumped onto the floor and tried to collect my wits. "I mean, who the fuck does he think he is, anyway? It's my goddamn welfare check that pays the rent around here."

Blocking my way back into the room, Adrian stuffed a Gauloises into an alabaster cigarette holder and slowly shook his head. As he reminded me, who paid the rent was hardly the issue. "Presence" was what this was about. And in that regard, the room and everything in it was George's—*Silver George's*.

"So, what are you saying, I don't count?" I cried, banging my fists against the floor. "That I'm just the boy?!"

Adrian sighed and, reddening slightly, nodded.

"No, I refuse, do you hear me? I won't sit back and be seen and not heard. I won't! I won't!"

A few minutes later, George crept onto the balcony, put his arm around me and informed he was leaving. "Yes," he replied when I asked if Lou was accompanying him, although he kissed me and told me I had nothing to worry about. As he noted, he always came back.

"Gee, thanks," I grumbled. "But when?"

"It won't be long, I promise. I've even left some speed for you. It's on the drop-down desk," he said before stepping off the balcony.

I waited until I heard the front door close behind them and then started to tremble uncontrollably. When, worried, Adrian asked if I was going to be okay, I admitted I was starting to lose it. "I've begged George to meet me halfway but he just says I'm uptight." I stopped and shook my head; it had been the same with my parents, the bullies too—an uninterrupted line of blame and recrimination that stretched all the way back to the note my kindergarten teacher had written, begging my parents to do something about my piercing screams. "No matter what, it's always me. My fault."

I struggled to regain my cool but the tumult that had been building up inside me kept pouring out. "I've tried telling myself he's just doing his own thing. That all this isn't about me—that there's no reason to be ashamed, to feel like a failure but...." I wiped the sweat from my brow. Suddenly, I was dripping wet. "But I can't help it, Adrian. I've given up everything for George. Is it really asking too much that he at least tries to be true?"

"*True*?" Adrian sneered before jumping up and tapping the floor with an ebony cane whose sterling silver wolf's head he said fended off vampires. He peered at me through the pince-nez perched on the end of a beak nose and then, tugging on the lavender brocade vest his mother, a Boston Brahmin, had sent him as a birthday present, straightened his back. "What rattling noise is this at which my snakes all hiss?"

"Huh?" I asked, looking around me. "What snakes? What hissing?"

Adrian glared at me, snatched my trip book from the floor, jotted down a note, and threw it back at me.

I watched him storm off the balcony and then opened the book to the page where, in a crisp composed script, he'd written: *You'd be much more successful if you could but only learn to hide the fact that you're a virago, at least when you're in public.*

"What's a virago?" I yelled after him.

Adrian clomped back up the balcony steps and waved his cigarette holder in my face. "Dissembling, you know that word?" he asked. "Good. Remember it. Repeat it to yourself every time you get upset. Never let him know your weak spots. Once you do, you're lost."

I told him I thought lovers were supposed to share weaknesses, but Adrian corrected me. "Not when your lover's a bully."

Stunned, I asked how he could possibly know that about someone he'd only recently met. "Because I've seen his aura," Adrian replied without the slightest trace of irony. Like his own, he said George's was very powerful, although with darker, more sinister undertones. "Brutish," he even called it.

When I asked if he'd also seen mine, he flushed slightly and nodded. "Very weak," he said of it. "More glimmer, really, than an emanation." When I asked what that meant for being able to better stand up to George, he sighed and said he was afraid that, until I had a few more lifetimes under my belt—I was, he claimed, a new karmic being—the best I could hope for was to endure. When I assured him there was no way I could wait that long, he just shrugged. "Nothing you can do about it," he offered.

Certain someone as obvious as Adrian had also had to face down bullies, I asked how he'd dealt with people like George. Instantly offended, he puffed up like a Prussian general and gasped, "What do you take me for, some *ordinary fag*?" With the blood of European royalty coursing through his veins and a soul as ancient as the Ptolemies, he assured me he was far too evolved to be anyone's punching bag. "Besides," he added, "that's why I keep my tongue razor-sharp." As he noted, there was nothing quite like a cutting barb to make a bully turn and run. "Works every time," he crowed, smiling wryly.

After we shot the speed George had left behind, Adrian returned to the lab he'd set up in his cold-water flat at the bottom of 9th Avenue. A week earlier, he'd announced he'd merged with his astral projection and was devoting his remaining time on this plane of existence to converting lead into gold. He asked if I wanted to assist him but by then I'd had enough of his mumbo jumbo. Besides, I'd decided my time would be better spent staying put, working on my poker face. A mask for the pain was all the alchemy a karmic newbie like me could hope for—that, and the patience to make it through until the no-good cheating louse I called my lover returned to plug all my holes. Like Adrian had warned, once I showed him my weak spots, I'd be lost.

I kept my cool when George returned the next day—apparently, his reunion with Lou had not gone well and, although he refused to elaborate, he didn't disagree when I called Lou a fake—and again a few days later when he disappeared with someone new. But when, three days later, he still had not returned, I told Adrian, who'd been reading me the latest scene from a play he was writing about Transylvanian speed freaks, a Carthaginian princess, and her Nazi transvestite lover, I'd had it. "I've waited around long enough. This time, I'm going out and getting my own drugs."

"But darling," Adrian cried as I ran for the door. "There are bad people out there. You have no idea what you're getting into."

I told him I didn't care how weak my aura was or how new I was to the karmic life cycle, I was taking charge. "I refuse to be at anyone's beck and call. Least of all, George's."

I even knew exactly where to go—around the corner to the Christopher Street flat where Harry, the underground "camp" playwright who was one of George's most regular clients, lived alone in drug-crazed splendor. Ringing his buzzer, I glared at the card above his nameplate that, in a florid script overlaid with sequins, read *All that glitters isn't gold*. When George had first brought me there, I'd thought it delightfully wicked. Now it just seemed like another cruel sick joke.

I adjusted my crotch and took a deep breath as my hoped-for benefactor threw the last of his three police locks. "Vampires, my dear," he'd murmured when, on my first visit, I'd asked why all the security. "You never know when one might try to get in."

As soon as Harry opened the door, I knew I'd made a mistake. With heavily pomaded hair, mascara, and a red silk robe with yellow dragons straining to cover a belly matted with black fur, he was even more repulsive than I'd recalled. "Hi," I said, fighting an urge to flee. "May I come in?"

"Why, of course, my dear," Harry cooed, ushering me down a narrow, windowless hallway to a room draped in purple velvet. "I hope you don't mind the heat," he said, clearing a space on a red satin sofa, "but it's the only way I can write."

I admired the Japanese paper umbrellas hanging from the ceiling and wondered if his plays made any more sense than Adrian's. The scene Adrian had read before I'd run out had seemed particularly crazed.

Harry smiled from an ornately carved, straight-back chair and urged me to remove whatever I needed to make myself comfortable. "After all," he said, raising an eyebrow, "we're all men here."

"Mmmm," I said, crossing my legs.

"So, to what do I owe the honor of your lovely presence?" Harry asked, stroking his sagging jowls with a raven's quill.

I fondled a crouching ceramic black panther at the base of a table lamp next to the sofa and thought what the fuck, Peter had done worse for a Tuinal. I smiled as sweetly as my churning stomach allowed and asked if he had any speed. "You know, crystal," I said, opening my legs. "It's been a while."

"Why, of course, you little angel, I'd be delighted," he said, sliding his chair up to a drop-down desk strewn with papers. He pulled a tin-foil square and a steel syringe from a cubby hole stuffed with vintage postcards and reached for a glass of water and spoon on top of a stack of dusty books. When I pointed out I'd brought my own works, he replied, "Oh no, darling, you're in my trip now. We'll do this my way."

"Hey, whatever you say," I said, hoping his trip didn't also include sex.

He dropped to his knees, slid across the floor, and nestled himself between my legs. He removed the belt to his robe and exposed a pair of black lace panties that I pretended not to see. He wrapped the belt around my arm until a vein popped up. "Oh, yes, very nice," he purred, stroking it. He glanced at my crotch and then up at me. "Delicious even."

I returned his smile. "Yes, I've been told I have good veins."

"Why, of course, you have—someone as angelic as you," he replied, licking his lips. "And where is that lovely man of yours anyway?" he asked as he jabbed my arm with the point of his ancient syringe. "He is, as of course you know, such a dear," he purred as blood streamed down my arm.

Wincing in pain, I wiped the blood away and nodded. "Oh yes, quite," I added, avoiding the question of George's whereabouts.

"Oh my, silly me," Harry murmured as my vein continued to seep blood. "I seem to be having difficulty hitting it." He smiled again, although even more lasciviously than before. "And it is such a lovely vein too. Guess I'll just have to try again, won't I?"

Nodding, I mumbled yes, please. As I noted, I really needed to get high, although the truth was I simply wanted to be someone in my own right, someone other than George's boy—someone to be seen and not heard.

The second time, Harry leaned as far into my crotch as he could, although he missed my vein that time too. The third time, he told me he'd lick the blood off my arm if he missed, which of course he did, although I refused to let him lick past my elbow. The fourth time he actually hit his target, a success that prompted him to finally get up off his knees, return to his chair, and cover his belly with the folds of his robe.

"So how was it?" he asked, smiling at the bloody mess he'd made of my arm. "As good as you were hoping?"

At first, I thought he'd been stingy with the speed but when I felt the energy drain out of me, I knew something was wrong. "I don't know. I feel kinda weak," I muttered, collapsing back onto the sofa. I looked around me bewildered. I could barely lift my head. "Way down in my bones."

I noticed the glass of water on his desk and shuddered as I realized Harry had neglected to clean his syringe before injecting me. "You shoot someone else's blood and, believe me, you'll wish you'd never been born. They're called bonecrushers," Peter had warned the first time he'd shot me up. "They're a junkie's nightmare. Feels like your insides are in a meat grinder."

"What, so soon?" Harry cried as I hauled myself off the sofa and lunged down the hall. "And I was so hoping we'd spend the afternoon together."

He stood in his doorway, the folds of his belly draped over his panties, and waved goodbye as I staggered down the stairs. "Oh, and darling, do remember me to that boyfriend of yours," he cooed. His eyes narrowed and he flushed slightly. "He is, after all, such a dear."

"Fucking vampires," I panted, crawling on all fours up the stairs to the room on West 10th Street. Collapsing into bed, I cried out for help but, of course, no one came. Adrian had gone back to his cold-water flat and George was out hammering fresher, presumably younger, more compliant, less prideful meat. And so, as the drop of Harry's blood tore through me, crushing everything in its path, I wondered how long it would be before someone found me. Whenever it was, I was sure I'd be dead.

Toward dawn, I awoke from my delirium and saw my friend John smiling at me from the end of the bed. Beaming next to him was Mack. the tall, beefy blond with a halo of curls who I'd had an affair with in Syracuse.

"Small world, huh?" John chuckled as I fell back onto my pillow, certain they were hallucinations. When I drifted off, they wrapped me in a blanket, laid me in the back of Mack's VW bus, the same one in which he and I had fought over Buñuel's *Belle de Jour*—he'd thought it a cruel, sick joke and I, a hilarious sex romp—and drove me, sick and crying, to Provincetown, where in a garret overlooking the sea, they nursed me back to health.

I emerged from my sick bed the day after men first landed on the Moon. Sitting at the kitchen table in the attic apartment he shared with Mack, John pointed at the photo on the front page of the Provincetown paper and chuckled. "Guess it's not made of cheese after all, huh?"

I stared at the imprint of Buzz Aldrin's space boot, seared into the moon's surface as if by the coils of a toaster, and smiled wearily. A "magnificent desolation" was how the photo's caption described the lunar landscape. I glanced at my still inflamed needle tracks and thought, that's what I was too— a magnificent desolation. "Got any drugs?" I asked.

John replied that, other than two reds he'd copped off a visiting drag queen and a tab of acid he'd dropped with a trick, he'd been clean since he'd left New York. When I asked what he did to fill the void, he acknowledged life had slowed down. He spent most of his days at the beach working on his tan, while at night he earned beer money by swabbing down the floor of a clam shack out on Town Pier.

When I asked about the gay scene, he said it was, for a fishing village out on the end of Cape Cod, surprisingly active. He said there were several gay bars, a nude beach, and even an after-hours cruising area known as the "Meat Rack." "It's amazing. Right in front of Town Hall, in the middle of everything." He lit a cigarette—he'd switched from Larks to Old Golds—and chuckled. "Come 1 a.m., when the bars close, everyone congregates there. Even the cops are cool about it." It was, he said, very cruisy.

I rubbed my bloodshot eyes. "And right out in the open, in full view of everyone?"

John nodded before noting that Provincetown had a long history of attracting what he called "freethinkers." First, it was the transcendentalists, then the bohemians and a smattering of Reds, followed by beatniks and, a few years back, hippies. "Now," he said, "it's the gays."

He attributed the town's appeal to its isolation. "It's literally at the end of the road. You go any further and you're in the ocean." He said that while Provincetown was very open-minded, he did, however, note a pronounced hostility to New York-style sleaze, especially speed. He guessed it was the sea air; he said it brought out the best in people. In contrast, he said New York's air was filthy; every morning he'd have a thick layer of soot on his West 10th Street windowsills. He shook his head. "Bad air, bad vibes. I can't believe I put up with it for as long as I did."

When I asked if he intended to settle down in Provincetown, he admitted he missed big-city life and predicted he'd go stir-crazy if he spent a winter out on the tip of Cape Cod. As he noted, Boston, the nearest big city, was over three hours away and New York almost five. When I asked where he thought he'd end up next, he said he wasn't sure, although one thing he'd learned from his time in the Village was how much he needed to be around freaks as well as gays. Bars, he said, were no longer enough. He needed an air of rebelliousness, too. "You know, someplace where another Stonewall might break out." He smiled. He still couldn't get over how mind-blowing those two nights in June were.

I wished him luck. As I noted, there weren't too many places where gays and freaks co-existed.

John nodded and ticked off what he considered his options. There was, of course, New York, although he'd already ruled that out. "Too speedy," he said of its scene. As for Chicago, he acknowledged he at least had friends there, although he'd heard the cops hassled gays almost as much as freaks. Being both, he thought, would only invite trouble. He said LA, which he'd also already done, was too plastic, while DC, where he'd come out, was too buttoned-down. Detroit was too bombed-out, Atlanta, too Jim Crow and, while he didn't know Boston, he'd found Cambridge, where he'd visited Sal, too serious. All the freaks there wanted to talk about was revolution. Other than a handful of college towns—Madison, Ann Arbor, Austin, Berkeley, all of which he dismissed as too bookish—and a few gay enclaves he thought too bourgie—Fire Island, Key West, Palm Springs—San Francisco was the only place left, although he'd heard teenyboppers and panhandlers had thoroughly curdled its scene. "After that, what else is there?" he asked and pointed at the photo on the paper's front page. "The Moon?"

He said he sometimes feared there was nowhere for gay freaks like us—the "freakiest of the freaks," he called us—to go. Even in Provincetown, it was mostly just him. Mack, he grumbled, was still mostly a hippie, while the town's other longhairs were little more than potheads. No one had ever gone near a syringe—what John called the dividing line between us and the everything straight.

He fumbled with his pack of Old Golds as he told me about his hike from the day before, when I was still in bed recovering from my bonecrusher. He'd trekked out to the lighthouse on a spit of land at the entrance to Provincetown's harbor called Long Point. He said it had taken him a good two hours to get there but as soon as he'd arrived an angry seagull started dive bombing him. He showed me the gash on his left arm and the tear in his t-shirt and admitted the encounter had spooked him. "It was like saying get out, you're not wanted here, even out there, in the middle of nowhere." His eyes widened. "In nature!"

He said the gull had even followed him back into town, dive bombing and squawking at him the whole way. He said he'd been so shaken by the experience he hadn't slept a wink. "I mean, what if it's true? That we really don't belong anywhere at all?" He blanched. "That the only thing left is to give up and go back."

"You mean, back into the closet?"

John nodded.

I bummed an Old Gold from him and sighed. There, in a nutshell, was the difference between John and me. While he'd fled New York after only one of George's monster shots, I'd stayed and endured scores. "You should've stood your ground and fought back," I grumbled. "I would've."

Claiming I needed some of the Cape's vaunted sea air, I left John to his musings and strolled Commercial Street, Provincetown's main drag. Festooned with bunting and photos from the Apollo 11, the street only increased my sense of dislocation. How could I not have known there'd been a manned moonshot?

I recalled Peter's shock when I'd admitted I knew nothing of Judy Garland's death. "Where have you been?" he'd cried. "Living under a rock? The girls have been in sack cloth and ashes for days!"

Still woozy from my bonecrusher, I took refuge from the blazing sun under the canvas awning of a hardware store and was soon joined by a hippie chick in bangles and a long flowing granny dress unbuttoned halfway to her navel. "Pretty cool about the moon thing, huh?" she gushed, pointing at the photo in the store's window. "My old man says they might even see angels." She smiled in that goofy, spaced-out way that hippies did when they got too stoned and asked what I thought. "You look pretty groovy. I mean, do you believe in angels too?"

I was tempted to tell her one didn't have to go into space to find things like that. I'd just been rescued by two right here on Earth. Their names were Mack and John, did she want to meet them? But still reeling from the shock of having been injected—presumably intentionally—with someone else's blood, I replied that no, I didn't believe in angels. I was, I explained, from New York.

"Oh, yeah, New York, I've never been. So, what're freaks down there into?"

I inhaled the treacly-sweet scent of the patchouli oil she'd doused herself with and squinted into the narrow space between the store and its listing, boarded-up neighbor. Caught in its frame was the lighthouse where John's avenging angel, the angry seagull, had convinced him there was no place for freaks like us. "Destruction," I replied, "that's what we're into. We believe in tearing things down. Everything. All the way to the ground."

"You're kidding, right?" she said, her eyes wide with alarm.

"No, actually I'm dead serious," I said, smiling darkly. Then, I rolled up my sleeve and showed her my needle tracks. "See?"

She stepped back and gasped, "Oh my God..." She grasped her hippie beads and looked at me like I'd suddenly sprouted horns. "But that's, that's..."

"Evil?" I interjected as the rosiness drained from her cheeks. Then, smiling politely, I excused myself by saying I had some business to attend to out on Long Point. "With a seagull."

"Peace," she cried after me, a plaintive benediction I found so vapid I almost responded by giving her the finger. But, fearing she'd start shrieking she'd seen the devil, I decided to simply move on. Provincetown was, after all, a quaint little fishing village—the Puritan's first stop on their way to the New World. Who knew how the locals might react.

When I finally made it across the jetty to the lighthouse, I called the gull out. But when it failed to show, I drove a stake in a small rise of sand to mark my victory and then stripped and swam as far out to sea as I could without losing sight of land. Before I'd left on my walk, John had encouraged me to check out the water, which he contended someone with as many water signs as I would find almost as comforting as home. He was wrong. I felt as alien at sea as I did on land.

When I got back to town, I lied and told John I'd beaten the seagull to death with a piece of driftwood. When I realized he actually believed me, I prided myself on how convincing my mask was. Finally, I was scaring others almost as much as I was myself.

I woke from a nap to the sound of shouting. In the next room, Sal, who'd hitchhiked from Cambridge as soon as he'd heard I was in Provincetown, was arguing with Mack. Groggy and still weak from my bonecrusher, I slipped out of bed and tiptoed to the door. Startled, I heard Mack use my name.

"Tell me this," Mack cried. "Would you ever be so desperate for drugs you'd shoot somebody else's blood? Where is this shit going, anyway? This isn't what we started." He jabbed his finger at Sal's chest. "Come on, you were there. The Be-Ins, the levitation of the Pentagon, the Summer of Love. Tell me this is what we had in mind."

"Hey listen, man, I've shot up. I know where that's at," Sal replied. "It's like walking the gang plank. There's nothing but you and the end." He threw his Camel into the sink and listened to it hiss. "The world's fucked up, man. Maybe tearing down is the only thing left to do. *The Upanishads* say the only real prayer is to want the world to go up in flames."

"Oh, come on, Sal," Mack scoffed. "Don't wrap junkies in the mantle of mystics. He's not praying. He's shooting up, for Christ's sake. He's lost, man." He shook his head. "Everyone has to believe in something. Otherwise, there's no point. It's all just suicide after that."

"Sorry to interrupt," I said, strolling into the room. "But do either of you know who I have to fuck around here to get some drugs?"

Sal snickered but Mack bellowed he wanted me gone. He wasn't having a junkie in the house. If John, who was off swabbing down the floors of the clam shack out on Town Pier, had a problem with that, he'd have to go too.

Sal volunteered to put me up in Cambridge but first had to find a phone booth to clear it with his roommates. When he returned to announce they were cool, Mack agreed to let me stay the night. "But no drugs." He looked at Sal sternly. "Not even any pot, okay?"

"I think we can handle that," Sal murmured and turned to me. "Right?"

"Oh, I suppose," I grumbled and retreated back to bed, where I at first managed to keep the tears at bay, although eventually my weaker nature took over and I let my horror over what Mack had seen in me show. I cried my eyes out.

By mid-morning the next day, Sal and I were out on Route 6, thumbing our way to the Cambridge pad he shared with four freaks—three cats and a chick—all of whom he said were straight. I made light of Mack's expulsion by claiming I'd been kicked out of better places, a lie that Sal gleefully accepted as proof that I was as impervious to rejection as I pretended. He watched a car whiz by, ignoring his thumb, and grumbled, "I don't know, maybe you look too freaky for this. Think we should take the bus?"

"Here," I said, stepping in front of him, "let me try." To my surprise, the very next car stopped, a VW bus driven by a straight freak who said my look—what he called "flash"—had been too good to pass up. "Not too many like you out here," he said. "You from New York?" When I acknowledged I was—the Village, in fact—Sal, sitting quietly in the backseat in his baggy Army pants and his threadbare denim shirt, smiled proudly. As John had said, I was one of the exalted few: the "freakiest of the freaks," willing to stop at nothing in order to be free.

I sat on a broken chair in the cluttered back room of the Cambridge pad Sal called a commune and watched him roll a joint. Next to me, a stack of cardboard boxes left behind by the horde of crashers who'd preceded me sagged into itself. As Sal had said, lately it seemed like someone was always fleeing something. Before me, it'd been a draftee AWOL from boot camp and, before him, two teenyboppers on the lam from their pimp. A month earlier, they'd even put up a cell of anarcho-syndicalists wanted for torching an ROTC office. In between, they'd dealt with so many bad acid trips they'd started stocking Thorazine. He pointed to a kitchen cabinet with an orange Day-Glo "Amerikkka" scrawled across it and shook his head. They'd just gotten a refill and it was already half-empty.

"Anybody ever show up with a bonecrusher?" I warily asked. Any more receptions like Mack's and I'd need more than just Thorazine. I'd need a straitjacket too. I lit one of Sal's Camels and flashed on the night George had kicked me out of bed for having a dirty bum. "Disgusting" was the word he'd used on me—the sane one my mother had used after I'd come out to her. Ever since, it had bounced around my head like a tripped grenade.

Sal put down his rolling machine and laughed that there were only two kinds of freaks his roommates had never seen. One was a speed junkie and the other a hip, in-your-face fag. "I can't wait 'til they meet you," he gushed. "You're gonna blow their minds."

I tugged on the drooping knee of the bellbottoms I'd worn for five days straight and sighed. Stick thin and dead broke, I relied on Sal for even my cigarettes. I'd offered to repay him when I got my next welfare check but he'd been adamant. Money was meant to be shared. He'd even said that's what friends were for.

I stared at the purple and green Op-Art cover of Allan Watts' *The Wisdom of Insecurity* that Sal had given me and tried to get my bearings. Claiming hippie pads and marijuana bred weaklings and fools, George had insisted we avoid both. I flicked my cigarette in the ashtray on the floor between us and confessed I was nervous about the impending arrival of his roommates. "I have a hard time trusting straights, especially guys." I looked at him apprehensively. "It's been months since I've been around one."

Sal licked the seam of a joint and frowned. "They aren't all monsters, you know." He said one of the guys he lived with, an old friend from Syracuse named Fenton, had even gone through San Francisco's Summer of Love with him. When I reminded him that I was over the hippie thing, Sal moved on to Eugenie, a raven-haired groupie who'd just returned from a gig with the Kinks. "She thinks all that Factory shit you're into is cool."

I told him star-fucking was hardly my bag but Sal insisted I'd find Eugenie a soulmate. "She tells everyone she's a gay man trapped inside a woman's body," he chuckled, his cheeks turning bright pink.

When I noted I was as wary of fag hags as I was of star-fuckers, he assured me I had her all wrong. "Eugenie likes to ball too much to be a fag hag." He leaned in close and snickered. "But the only way she'll take it is up the ass. Says she hates it when a guy goes for her pussy."

"Huh, I don't get it. So how does she get off?"

"She doesn't," Sal replied. "Eugenie says sex is a head trip." He handed me the joint and crowed she was the first real sexual freak he'd ever known. "Keeps this book called *Story of O* under a tub of Vaseline next to her bed. Ever heard of it?"

I took a long hit of pot and noted that it was Peter's favorite book, although, determined to hide every vulnerability, I lied and said I'd never read it.

"Oh man, you should check it out. You'd love it. It's totally sick."

"Hmmmm," I murmured, recalling how close to the bone O's descent into masochism had cut.

Sal laughed about the morning Eugenie had showed off her bruises from the nineteen-year-old with Mick Jagger lips she'd picked up in a Boston dive bar called the Rat. She'd been radiant and, for someone so manic, surprisingly calm. "Oooh, Sallie, he was so *good,*" he cooed, imitating her. "She's wild. I'm telling you, you're gonna love her."

I tried to argue, as much to myself as Sal, that S&M was a cop-out, a turning inward of anger that should be directed outward, but Sal would have none of it. "She's just doing her own thing," he said and smiled slyly. "Besides, people say shooting up is a cop-out too. But that doesn't seem to have stopped you." He lit another joint and handed it to me. "Eugenie's fine. Unlike your friends the Panthers, she's at least not hurting anyone."

I puffed on the joint and grimaced. On our way in, Sal and I had argued over the Black Panthers, whose takeover of a nearby housing project had sparked a rash of shoot-outs with the cops. He hadn't cared how worthy the cause. Violence of any sort, he insisted, was wrong. I, on the other hand, had countered everyone had a right to self-defense, especially when it came to the cops. I'd even cited Malcolm X: "By any means necessary."

Refusing to revisit the argument, I merely shrugged and noted that sometimes people ran out of cheeks to turn. I glanced at my needle tracks. "I know I sure have."

Sal asked if I knew anything about what had allegedly gone down outside the Stonewall. He'd heard rumors that gays had fought back against a police raid and the bar had been torched. "It sounded too crazy to be true. I mean, *gay people?*"

I confirmed the rumors were true; George and I had ringside seats for the riots' first two nights. When Sal asked what had precipitated them, I noted everyone had their own theory. Peter blamed them on drag queens grieving the death of Judy Garland; John, on the influence of stars like Pluto and Neptune; George on uptight newcomers he called "little people;" and the guys next to us on the riots' first night on outside agitators, possibly SDS or even the Weathermen.

I told him I had a different take. I attributed the riots to the street queens and hustlers who the cops had pissed off and, inspired by groups like the Panthers and their Puerto Rican counterparts, the Young Lords, decided to fight back. As I noted, most of the rioters had been people of color, Puerto Ricans mostly. "By any means necessary," I added, smiling slyly.

"Hmmm," Sal murmured, flushing slightly. "So did they do any good? I mean, has anything changed?"

I acknowledged that, except for the "Gay Power!" slogan spray painted across the front of the Stonewall's burned-out hulk, Village life went on pretty much as before. The bars were still packed, the Hare Krishna still did their thing in Washington Square, the *Village Voice* still refused to print the word 'gay' and, every Saturday, day trippers still descended on Bleecker Street looking for nickel bags of pot. "And what they get is still pretty much oregano," I added, chuckling.

Sal laughed. "Sure sounds like the Village I know."

I noted most of the changes seemed to have occurred down by the docks. "Come 2 a.m. the cruising is everywhere. It's no longer confined to the Trucks. Whole streets are taken over." I also noted a lot more bars had opened. "Mostly leather, though, and filled with bourgie types from New Jersey." I smiled warily. "Crystal meth's gotten big too. Even the straights are doing it." George's business, I added, was booming.

Sal sighed and said he'd pretty much lost touch with gay life since moving to Cambridge. He hardly ever went into Boston for the bars—Cambridge, he said, had none—and, for sex, mostly just relied on an area along the Charles River up by the Harvard bridge that he said was cruisy. When I asked what he did to fill the void, he admitted he still preferred to hang out with straights. Gay men, he complained, were too superficial; all they talked about was dick. Almost as an afterthought, he noted he'd also started getting into Zen. "The detachment," he said when I asked why. "I want to get to a state of non-belonging."

I didn't bother saying a sense of belonging was what I missed most in life and instead returned to the subject of his roommate, Eugenie, who I agreed sounded cool. "I mean, anyone who claims to be a gay man trapped inside a woman's body has got to be fun." I looked at Sal and smiled wistfully. He'd even said I'd find her a soulmate.

Sal's face darkened as he lit another joint and admitted he was getting worried about Eugenie. "No matter how hard she tries, nothing ever seems to come together for her." When I noted the same could be said for the two of us, he got suddenly testy. "Sorry, man, but I've never felt more together than here in Cambridge. Besides," he huffed, "I don't know what you're complaining about. You at least have a lover."

I almost laughed out loud over that one but, still determined to hide every vulnerability, merely nodded and confirmed that, yes, he was correct. A lover was something I did indeed have. A live-in one, no less. As Sal had already noted, no one he knew had that.

Sal blamed Eugenie's problems on a mother who'd abandoned her when she was six. "I mean, what kind of a mother does something like that?" he cried. I almost replied one like mine and George's—and probably his too if he ever worked up the courage to tell her he was gay—but Sal and I had been over all that. Coming out to parents was my trip. Protecting them from the shame of knowing was his.

"You know, love can really do a number on you," Sal blithely pattered on. "Every few months, Eugenie'll try to reconnect with her mom. But each time, she comes back rebuffed. Then, a few months later, she's back at it, banging her head against a brick wall for the acceptance she'll never get." He puffed on the joint and gave me one of those pothead grins that George found so insipid. "It's really too bad. She's got a heart of gold. And there isn't anything she won't do for you. I mean, she paid for everything when I first came to town. And I'd just met her." He handed me the joint and sighed. "I try to help—you know, boost her spirits, tell her she's fine. But no matter what, she still thinks she's a shit."

"Yeah, most of the nice ones do," I grumbled, stubbing the joint out in a blue plastic ashtray. If I took one more hit of pot, I was sure my head was going to explode. As Sal again crowed about all the changes I'd gone through—about how hard and cynical I'd become, not at all like the sweet young thing he'd seen dancing with Paul and the other Black queens in the back of the Continental Room—I reached for another one of his Camels and hoped my shattered nerves didn't betray me. His was the only bridge I hadn't burned. After Sal, all I'd have left was George.

"So, Sallie, why didn't you tell me he was so cute?" Eugenie chided, eyeing me from a chair next to the pile of cardboard boxes in their commune's back room. She ran her fingers through her thick black mane and smiled coquettishly.

Sal snickered and warned me to watch out; Eugenie liked her men young. "Come on, Eugenie," he said, glancing at his other three roommates, all straight men, sitting on a battered sofa directly across from me, "tell him how old your youngest guy was."

She tugged on the hem of her black leather mini-skirt and blushed slightly. "Fifteen?"

At that, Sal and the others erupted into a loud, almost obscene guffaw. Clearly, Eugenie's sex life was the subject of much household banter.

Refusing to play along, I flicked my hair from my shoulders, crossed my legs, and queenily folded my hands over my knees. "Thanks for the warning, but I think I can handle myself," I said, glaring at Sal.

Eugenie pointed out the seams she'd drawn with eyeliner on the back of her hose and asked if I approved. "I like to look vampish," she noted with a giggle the guys met with a groan and a roll of their eyes. When I agreed they were glamourous, she admitted she liked fishnet too. "But all the guys think you're a whore." She crossed her legs, tugged on her neon-pink tube top until it covered a roll of belly fat and sighed. "Same thing if they think you're a hippie." She said her boss, a fat, greasy wop from Somerville, had trapped her in the bathroom of the auto body shop where she worked as the bookkeeper as soon as he found out she lived in a commune. "Said he wanted some of my free love too," she grumbled.

She rolled her eyes as her roommates laughed at that like it was one of the funniest things they'd ever heard and then turned her attention back to me. "So, Sallie says you're in the Village." She flinched slightly when I corrected her by noting I lived in the West, not the East Village. "Of course," she said and smiled knowingly. "With the gays, not the freaks."

I again corrected her. "No, with the speed freaks." I paused for effect. "The *gay* speed freaks."

"Cool, very cool. Speed, I hear, is the latest thing, although you'd never know it in boring old Cambridge town." She again adjusted her tube top—that time, to cover her ample breasts—and shook her head. Cambridge, she complained, was still mostly hippie. "You know, granny dresses and jeans."

She confessed she'd love to be in New York too but needed to be near her grandmother, a Lebanese immigrant who lived alone in Lawrence, a dying mill town north of Boston. "So, you ever go to Max's Kansas City?" she asked. "I hear it's really cool."

"Oh sure, love it," I lied. I even claimed to know Lou Reed. "He used to be my lover's boyfriend."

"I didn't know Lou was gay!" Eugenie cried and looked accusingly at Sal. "You never told me that!"

Sal shrugged and mumbled he hadn't known either. "Besides, who gives a shit who the cat balls."

"Me, I'm a groupie, remember?" Eugenie cried, rolling her eyes. "I ball rock stars."

I took a drag from another Camel I'd bummed from Sal and noted my lover's name was George. "Silver George was what he went by at the Factory."

"The Factory, oh wow!" Eugenie exclaimed.

I smiled. "He danced in the Exploding Plastic Inevitable."

"That means he knows Andy!"

I nodded, hoping Eugenie wouldn't ask if I did too.

"So," Fenton, the straight roommate Sal had gone through the Summer of Love with, said by way of introduction. He leaned forward, placed both elbows on his knees, and slowly rubbed his hands together. He was short and stocky with a full beard, suspicious eyes and mud-caked work boots. Earlier, Sal had said he worked in construction.

"Yes?" I replied, meeting his gaze. I didn't care how butch he was. I refused to be intimidated.

He cleared his throat and glanced at the two straight guys with whom he shared the couch. Both had long stringy beards. Neither had said so much as a word to me, although both pierced me with a gaze so steely, I wondered if I was under interrogation.

Fenton smiled slightly. "So, you like the Velvet Underground?"

"Yeah, I do, I like them a lot," I replied, flicking my cigarette into the ashtray on the floor. "Why?"

He smirked and again glanced at the two guys next to him. Next to me, Sal squirmed nervously in his chair. Clearly, this was a test, although of what I wasn't sure. "Cuz, I think they're sick," Fenton replied.

"Yeah, that's why I like them," I shot back, returning his smirk. "I like sick."

It was as if I'd just said the magic word; suddenly everyone in the room was cheering and clapping. Eugenie even reached into the quilted leather bag she kept at her side and tossed a handful of glitter into the air. "Didn't I tell you?" Sal cried, the pink returning to his cheeks. "A real-life fleur du mal!"

"And look what I have!" Eugenie added, holding aloft a tin foil square she'd pulled from her bag. "Crystal meth. I went to Harvard Square and got it on my lunch break." She giggled. "I had no idea what I was doing. I mean, I've never copped drugs off the street before. And so, I went up to the cutest guy who looked like he might be a dealer and voila!"

She looked at me and smiled. "We decided last night, right after Sal called to say you'd be coming." She noticed a run in her stockings and frowned slightly. "We want you to shoot us up."

"You want me to *what*?"

"Oh, come one, don't act so shocked," Eugenie scolded. "Sal told us all the stories. About you and Peter on Avenue D." The other heads in the room bobbed in agreement.

"Yeah, just like old times, huh?" Sal cried, jumping up to fetch the works John had slipped him on our way out of Provincetown. He stopped at his bedroom door and turned back to the others. "I told him you'd be cool. He thinks all straight people hate gays."

At that, Eugenie and the others broke into another round of raucous laughter, although I just glared at the dimes in the flaps of my Bass Weejuns. Suddenly, I wished I was anywhere but there.

"But I've never shot anyone up," I protested, before recalling Peter's reaction the night I'd asked him to do me the very same favor. Even he'd had qualms. "I can't. You don't know what you're asking. It's not right."

"So, when did that ever stop you?" Sal scoffed, dropping the syringe in my lap. He turned to the others. "My God, you should hear the way he treats his own mother."

"Yeah, you're the crazy one, the freak who'll try anything once!" Eugenie cried.

I flinched but, desperate for their approval, reluctantly agreed to get them off. And while I was careful to mix up the stingiest of shots, only Eugenie, who instantly took to tossing more glitter, got into her high. Within minutes, Sal started to complain about his liver, while the three straight guys grumbled about paranoia. As they noted, speed wasn't at all like LSD.

Within an hour, Fenton said he wanted to come down and suggested a walk across the Charles River to cop some reds at an open-air drug bazaar outside the People's Drugs at the bottom of Beacon Hill. Setting off, we trudged across acres of rubble cleared for a NASA mega-lab that Nixon had just pulled the plug on, while Sal went on and on about how much Zen was helping him detach, Eugenie tossed more glitter into our hair and squealed about how cool it was to be around someone as flashy as me, and Fenton and the other two straight guys fell into a long tedious rap about which group they thought would end up leading the revolution—the Weathermen or the Panthers. I flitted so seamlessly among them that, by the time we reached the bridge to Boston—Sal said it was named after the poet Henry Wadsworth Longfellow, but Eugenie said the locals referred to it as simply the "salt and pepper" bridge, after its ornamentation—I felt so at home I actually broached the subject of staying. Might they be into having a sixth roommate?

Sal pretended he didn't hear me, while Eugenie said I'd be a fool to leave a set-up as cool as the one I had with George. And though the straight guys refused to say what they thought, each had an East Village war story to share, all involving a junkie, and agreed Cambridge was a much better place for getting one's head together. When I replied the head was a trap the speed freaks I hung out with were trying to free themselves of, Fenton suddenly got testy. "So, what are you people into anyway?"

"You people?" I asked, turning to Sal.

"Hey, don't look at me, man. This is your trip," he snipped. "I don't even like most gay men."

Fenton's eyes narrowed. "Okay man, so we've read about Warhol's Factory and heard about the riots. So, tell us what you gay freaks are up to anyway."

Over his shoulder, I spotted a wedge of moonlight floating on the river and felt a rush I knew as Peter pulse through me. "We're into being outrageous and decadent. And fabulous, fabulous for days," I replied. That the words were as hollow as the paper tiger who'd once uttered them didn't matter. A straight man had confronted me and the power to shock was all I had. I played with my scarf the way Peter had the night he'd urged me to join the sack of Rome. "We're into blowing minds 'til we no longer know who or what we are." I stepped so close, I could hear Fenton grinding his teeth. "Then we want to start all over."

Eugenie laughed but, appalled, Sal slunk off toward Boston.

"Sounds like a fucking power trip, man," Fenton groused.

"It is," I retorted. "But what isn't? Your hippie trip, all that peace and love crap? Or all that talk about the Panthers versus the Weathermen? *Revolution*?" I hunched my shoulders and pursed my lips like Miss Eden had the night she'd gotten dolled up for a Harlem drag ball, and continued. "Without power, everything's just one big drag show, with us prancing around in our do's and our get-ups, thinking we're the most gorgeous, we know the judges, we're on the inside track to win the prize, while the ones who know the deal, the real one, the master plan, sit back and laugh at us." I grabbed the bridge's railing for support as another surge I knew as George whipped through me. "Well, I'm sick of being laughed at. So, yeah, that's what I'm into—getting to a place where what they think no longer matters." I straightened myself up. "*They* no longer matter."

"Wow," Fenton exclaimed, stepping into the light of a street lamp. "A master plan? People laughing at you? Man, you better watch out. You're sounding paranoid."

"Only someone like you could say something that," I coolly replied. "As if paranoia is just something you get when you're high and you take something—a Seconal or a Thorazine—to come back down." I shook my head. "People like you think there's always a way out. People like me know better. We know there's no coming down from where we're at. All we got is the power—yeah, that's right, *man*, the power—to say fuck off. We're gonna do things *our* way."

"Wow, man, that sounds really uptight." Fenton clenched both fists and took a step toward me, as if preparing for an attack. "Kinda fucked-up, actually."

Standing firm, I nodded and smiled sweetly. "Thank you. Like I said, I like sick."

"Come on, let's get outta here," Fenton said to the others before, trembling with rage, he ran off to catch up with Sal.

Staying behind, I leaned over the bridge's railing and stared into the black, rain-swollen face of the Charles. Earlier, Sal had dismissed it as a piddling thing, more creek than a river, but to my parched ego it might as well have been the mighty Ohio, on whose banks I'd played as a child. Behind me, a subway train shot from a tunnel and raced across the bridge toward Boston. Sparks from its wheels arced over a granite parapet and then a deafening roar rose out of the river that engulfed me and everything around me—the train, the bridge, the giant Cambridge Electric clock looming over me, the neon Citgo sign blinking off in the distance, the lapping water, the cloud bank rolling in from the east, extinguishing a blanket of stars. Even the speed, an old adversary I'd made it my mission to best, was my friend again. I'd stood up to a straight man. He'd even backed down. I chuckled. My very own Stonewall...

Sal stopped at the crest of the bridge and pointed at the spire of a Boston office tower whose flashing blue light he'd said predicted rain. "You don't need a weatherman to know which way the wind blows!" he cried, quoting the Dylan line the Weathermen had adopted as their slogan. I smiled, knowing it was a message meant just for me, the end of the argument we'd had over the Panthers. He'd changed his mind. Ends did sometimes justify means. We were free to risk everything.

"Hey, wait up," I shouted as Fenton and Sal raced each other to the traffic circle on the Boston side of the bridge, across from which, in a crowd that gathered every night to buy and sell drugs, Fenton hoped to score the reds that would bring him back down—to himself, the person he'd never been horrified by or ridiculed and beaten up for being. "I don't know where I am!"

No sooner had I spoken than Sal darted down a granite stairwell and across a metal catwalk leading to a park along the Charles. I waited, but when no one followed I panicked and ran to Eugenie. "But we're supposed to be a group." I pointed into the trees where Sal had disappeared. "Why aren't we following along?"

"I don't think Sallie'd much like that," Eugenie chuckled. "He's doing his own thing now."

"What do you mean?" I asked, squinting into darkness. After all, I was supposed to be the night's thing. It was part of the deal, the reason I'd shot them all up—I get them high and they treat me special. Like I was cool. As Sal had said, a real-live fleur du mal.

"Oh, come on, you know," Eugenie replied, "he's looking for guys. Doing the fag thing." She picked at the glitter on her fingernails and scowled. "What, they don't do that in New York anymore?"

"No, I was just hoping I wouldn't have to deal with that for a change." I watched her readjust her tube top and wondered if, as Sal had claimed, she really might be a soulmate. "I mean, don't you ever want to just hang out with friends?"

"You're kidding, right? I mean, don't get me wrong. I like my girlfriends. But I'd much rather ball a guy than hang out with them any day. I mean, who wouldn't?" Eugenie looked at me suspiciously. "Hey, you're not into Sal, are you?"

I assured her I hadn't looked at another man since I'd met George. I'd even rebuffed Paul America, the hunky star of Warhol's *My Hustler,* who'd come over with one of George's old Factory friends to cop some speed and who'd made it clear he wanted to ball me. "No, I've had my fill of free love. What I want now is something solid. Like this bridge—a way to get from here to there without having to swim it." I admitted I was tired; before long, I feared I'd be going under.

"Really? I mean, you get everything you need from just one guy?" she asked. "Wow, I need to get down to New York. Things are changing more than I thought."

"I'm not talking about just sex," I replied. "I mean, take Sal. All I've ever wanted was to be his friend. But every time we start to click, he splits." I spotted his silhouette on a bridge over one of the park's canals and then, poof, as if in a dream, he again disappeared. "I don't know, maybe it's us—you know, gay men. Maybe what they say is true..." I paused and shuddered. "You know, that we're not supposed to get it together."

"But you guys are where it's at," Eugenie countered. "It used to be the spades but Black Power ruined all that. I mean, I can't even ball a Black guy anymore without getting shit for it. Now, Andy and the Factory—glamour and decadence and, like you said, being outrageous and blowing people's minds— are where things are at." She chuckled as she unraveled a strand of hair from a hoop earring. "What did Sallie say you call yourselves?"

I looked at her and blanched. "You mean the Horrible Fags?"

"Yeah, that's it," she chuckled. "You guys got it right. Go on welfare, ball whoever and whenever you want and fry your brain cells on drugs." She pointed out the Prudential Tower, lording over the faded glory of Boston's Back Bay like a young, polyester-clad upstart. "I mean, what are brain cells good for anyway? So you can spend your life pushing paper in some office tower?" She brushed the glitter off my shoulder and smiled. "Besides, you're just doing your own thing."

I glared up at Beacon Hill, looming against Boston's soot-tinged horizon like an angry, festering boil. Earlier, Sal had said so many gays were moving onto its north slope that people had started to talk; where, they wondered, were they all coming from? They had no idea there were so many. Sal, of course, was unimpressed. As he'd said, he'd given up on gay life. Zen was his new thing, his antidote for the need to belong, his ticket out of identity.

"You know, if I hear 'do your own thing' one more time, I think I'm gonna scream. I mean, look at us. We can't even come together for a single night."

"Huh? But that's what makes us cool." Eugenie paused to throw out her arms. "*Free!*"

I told her I'd also come to hate that word too. "Free to do what?" I sneered. "Run off whenever you want and fuck whoever you want? Shoot people up with your own blood? Hurt and humiliate them? *Degrade* them?"

"Hey, wait a minute," she said before noting how badly my hands were shaking. "You seem kinda uptight. You, okay?"

Turning, I glanced back at the park into which Sal had disappeared and shuddered. I'd let her see my weaknesses: my need to belong, to find a home, and be loved—all the qualities George had promised the speed would burn out of me but which were still holding me back. "I need to be getting back to New York," I mumbled. "I've been gone too long." Over my left shoulder, the office spire that Sal had said predicted rain flashed its rebuke: while others might know which way the wind blew, I still needed a weatherman. "I miss George."

"Oh, I get it," Eugenie cried, racing after me. "You mean, instead of 'do your own thing' they say something different in New York. Like getting demented instead of high, right?"

At dawn, I shot the rest of Eugenie's speed and asked Sal for directions out of town. On the stoop where we'd argued over the Black Panthers and ends versus means, he smiled and told me how well the visit had gone. Eugenie, of course, thought I was the very next thing, but the straight guys were freaked. Fenton had even used the word 'monster' to describe me. I smiled but left without saying what a fool they were for believing my lies or how terrified I was to be trapped inside them, alone now except for George.

I crept up the stairs to our room on West 10th Street, worried over what awaited me. After all, I'd left sick as a dog, without so much as a word as to where I was going. I doubted George would be there; he hated being left alone—"deserted" he called it – and wondered how long I'd have to wait for him to turn up.

I feared he wouldn't. After all, a week was more than enough time for him to find someone new. Someone less prideful. Someone who got off on being seen and not heard. His sex pig. A "boy."

I thought I heard rustling as the door creaked open and then I saw them. George with his dick up the other guy's ass. In my bed. Our little love nest—the one where he'd promised to crawl up inside me and never ever leave.

No! I cried and grabbed a straight razor from the shelf next to the hand sink. At last, the truth, I thought, as my rival, younger and smoother by far than me, grabbed his clothes and ran naked out the door. Just as I'd suspected, he was Danny, the other George's, George Right's former boyfriend. The week I'd spent recuperating from my bonecrusher, my George, George Wrong, had spent fucking him. What a nice little piece of karmic justice, I thought—shy, sweet, retiring Danny stealing my lover in retaliation for me almost taking his. Yeah, a real goddamn mindfuck. A truly horrible sick joke.

George grabbed a hammer from the windowsill and leapt onto the bed. "Come on, you motherfucker, just try to cut me," he shouted, his still-flushed cock glistening with KY. "I dare you."

Suddenly, Miss Eden, who'd moved into John's old room after she'd decided against the surgery her DC john had promised her, rushed in and dragged me out the door. Throwing me onto her bed, she told me I looked terrible. "Oh, I know, honey, love's tough. But you keep this up, you're gonna end up in Bellevue just like Electric Freddy."

I wiped my face with the cool washcloth she handed me and scoured the ceiling for a trace of the Day-Glo stars John had covered it in. I couldn't find one.

20
The Nine of Swords

Lynn was a pretty, petite blonde with an ingenue's smile and a peaches and cream complexion even the speed couldn't curdle. Straight, she was shy and nervous, the tongue-tied remnants of the tomboy her father, a Toronto surgeon, had beaten out of her. Loaded, she was a smoldering ruin of rage and paranoia I tolerated mostly for the light she cast on things. With Lynn around, there was finally someone else who got more twisted on speed than I. Through her, I started to see the problem wasn't, as George insisted, me. It was the drug.

When Lynn revealed she too was a Pisces with Cancer rising, George joked that the only way to tell us apart was by our appetite for meth. While I always complained I'd taken too much, Lynn never seemed to get enough. That was why, only three days after her return from a two-year hiatus back home in Canada, he named her the Horrible Fag's first female, while, six months into my tenure as his live-in pin cushion, I remained a mere wannabe. I still had limits. Lynn had none.

George and Lynn had met during the Factory's heyday, when every night was a party and everyone, fabulous. Like him, she'd been young and green and quickly caught the eye of the Factory speed freaks known as the Moles. At first, the speed had made her feel powerful. But, as was her wont, she took too much and, one night in the summer of '67, the so-called Summer of Love, she'd stood in the middle of the West Side Highway, screaming about alien vampires sucking her dry. A kid from Hackensack picked her up and, thinking he'd landed a real-live Factory superstar, agreed to drive her back home to Toronto on one condition, that she balled him every two hundred miles. Thinking him her savior, she offered him one better, a fuck every hundred and a blow job every other fifty.

By Albany, she'd given him crabs and, by Niagara Falls, the clap. When a doctor told her she'd had syphilis for so long her uterus was ruined, she'd been secretly relieved. As she said, kids needed things—love, affection, food, clothes—and, after two years of doing nothing but crystal meth, Lynn only knew how to take. The giving part, like her womb, she'd burned up.

Back in Toronto, she'd hooked up with a tribe of hippies who dropped acid like the Moles shot speed: as if their lives depended on it. But she grew tired of giggly group gropes and long walks in the woods, looking for the godhead. As she said, she needed to see her own blood to know she was alive; and while she'd tried razor blades, there was nothing quite like a syringe to prove she was real. And so, after she and her tribe drove to Woodstock in a caravan of VW buses for three days of rock 'n roll, rain, and bad acid, she'd decided she'd had enough peace and love and snuck off to New York in search of her old pals.

Only I was surprised at how quickly she'd found George. Holed up in a Village flophouse with no phone or even his name on the mailbox, he was someone a private eye would've had a hard time tracking down. But, like Adrian had once said, the dark side of the moon was always just around the corner for anyone who bothered to look.

Of course, I lacked the eyes to see such things. That was why I'd decided to stick with George. He was going to correct my vision. With him, I'd learn to see people and things as they really were and not care. Like my mother, who'd vomited when I told her I was gay, or my father, who said he hated me after I'd fumbled multiple throws of a baseball, or the shrink who claimed I was severely mentally ill, or the speed, which kept insisting I was the victim of a horrible sick jok, or even George, who refused to say if he even still loved me.

One night in October, George invited the Horrible Fags over for a shooting party to honor the Weathermen's failed Days of Rage. I thought it an odd choice, given his disdain for so-called revolutionaries, but, as usual, George contended he knew exactly what he was doing. Anyone who marched in shin guards and football helmets through the hometown of a thug like Mayor Daley, tossed nails under the hooves of police horses, and fought the cops with baseball bats, had to be demented on speed. "Besides," he chuckled, "I like failures."

That night, Lynn mixed a hit of windowpane acid she'd bought off a hustler on 42nd Street with one of George's monster shots of pure liquid meth. Instantly crazed, she stripped, draped herself in one of the black sheets I'd stolen from a laundromat on Bleecker Street and wandered around the room speaking in tongues. After turning all our mirrors to the wall—George had hauled so many in from the trash, the room had started to look like a funhouse—she squatted next to our bed and, smiling lewdly, pissed on the floor. She then ran down the stairs and into the rear courtyard where she darted buck-naked from one corner to the next, whooping and flapping her arms like a baby bird that had just fallen from its nest.

"Don't worry. No one's gonna call," George said as I hurriedly gathered up all the drugs in anticipation of a police raid. As he noted, freak-outs were as common in the West Village as overdoses were in the East. He glanced at Norman and chuckled. "After all, isn't that what gay people do best?"

"Yeah," his black-toothed mentor drolly replied, "without us, Bellevue'd be just another apartment block."

At that, Adrian stepped forward, his pupils as big as salad plates and his red hair a burst of wiry static. "I can still remember the day they hauled Brendan Behan out of here in a straitjacket. I was on my way to Caffé Cino—you know, for one of Harry's plays—and encountered a paddy wagon at the front door. The EMTs said he'd drunk himself crazy."

He spotted a cockroach on the floor and smashed it with the careful aim of his ebony cane. "He lived in this very room, you know," he smiled before recalling his obituary; he couldn't remember if it had been in the *Post* or *Daily News*: *Too young to die and too drunk to live*. At that, he pulled out the syringe he kept in the brocaded velvet smoking jacket his Brahmin mother had sent him on his birthday and suggested another round of speed. He said we had a tradition to uphold. We weren't quite "Brendan Behan" enough.

Sensing I was about to lose it, George patted the space on the bed next to him and told me he had something he wanted to show me. He reached into his jeans pocket and pulled out an uncut turquoise the size of a raisin attached to a thin brass chain. "It's for you," he said with a smile so big his dimples showed. "A token of my affection." He even said he and Danny were through.

A voice inside me warned it was another trick, but I put a pillow over its mouth and bravely accepted his gift. Paranoia was the old uptight me. The new one was learning to be content with whatever crumbs got tossed my way. As I clasped the chain around my neck and mumbled a shy, tongue-tied thanks, Lynn pointed up at our silhouettes in the window next to our bed and shrieked that they, the Horrible Fags, were poisoning her mind.

"Ah, yes, the mind. It's a terrible thing to waste," George smirked, slipping his hand down the back of my jeans. Norman flashed him a black-toothed grin and broke out into a loud guffaw. By his side, the ruined Broadway dancer he paraded around as the symbol of his dark powers mutely stared at the rathole. In the alcove next to the closet, Adrian stood in front of the dressing mirror George had dragged in from the trash—"to get a larger view," he'd said—and prattled on about the Rosicrucians and the teachings of Madame Blavatsky. A few feet away, two other Factory exiles, Rotten Rita and Ronnie Vile, tried to outdo each other by re-enacting scenes from *Cobra Woman*. Lounging against a pile of dirty sheets on the steps up to the balcony, another Horrible Fag, the cretin everyone called Peter Point, presumably because of his fondness for needles, bragged about the underage boys he'd lured into his lair, a fetid shooting gallery off Washington Square. "Some don't even have pubic hair," he repeated so many times that by dawn it was—like Lynn's drug-crazed ravings and the old hag on the first floor's insane pipe-banging—nothing more than background noise, the aural equivalent of wallpaper.

John peered at me through his tinted aviator glasses and drew my last card from the top of the Tarot deck. He paused and told me to recall the query I'd asked at the start of the reading. I nodded, closed my eyes, and mutely repeated the question that had been tormenting me since Lynn's freak-out—where was life with George heading? More and more, I was sensing disaster.

We were sitting on the bed in the room on West 10th Street that George and I shared, John at one end and me, the other, with the Celtic cross John had been building with George's Tarot deck splayed out in the space between us. John's tan was a rich butternut and his hair, pulled back into a ponytail that fell between the straps of a tie-dyed tank top, was flecked with gold. He'd said the tan was natural but admitted he'd helped his hair along with lemon juice. "When you look good, you feel good," he'd said, repeating one of the platitudes that, despite the tie-dye, the length of his hair, and his obsession with the occult, still pegged him as a square. Cool people looked good no matter how they felt, while the coolest had no feelings at all.

John had dropped in on his way from Cape Cod to Chicago to see if I might also be ready for a change. "You know, what with summer over and winter coming," he'd said, as if Mother Nature herself demanded something new. He'd smiled when I'd asked what spending a summer working on a tan was like. "Provincetown's a spa. Boring, but I caught up on my sleep and had lots of good sex." He'd run his hands down the jeans he kept pressed, even when on the road, and chuckled. "You know us Capricorns. We like our creature comforts."

"Yeah," I'd replied, looking around at the monk-like squalor of my surroundings: a bed, a tube of KY, a shot glass, a cum rag, my syringe, and my tattered and dog-eared copy of *Love's Body*. Everything but the man who brought it all to life. I hadn't seen George in four days. When John had asked, I'd lied and said he was out on a drug run.

John had said the best part of life in Provincetown was the absence of a drug scene. Oh, sure, everyone smoked pot—everyone but the fishermen, that is, who stayed pretty much in a world of their own. When I asked how he'd handled his withdrawal from speed, he said by the end of July, a month after he'd landed in town, he'd stopped craving the drug. And by Labor Day, when a trick from New York offered him a snort, he'd actually kicked him out of bed. Speed, he'd said, was the past. It was time we found something new. He'd even expressed surprise that I was still doing it. "After your bonecrusher, I thought maybe you'd have given speed up."

"Yeah, I thought about it," I'd replied, idly toying with my syringe. "But George says he'll leave me the minute I stop."

John placed my final Tarot card atop the column of my three previous draws. "So, there it is," he said with a flourish. "The answer to your question."

"Oh," I mumbled, staring numbly at an androgynous-looking blonde in a long white robe weeping on a bed. Covering her legs was a patchwork quilt of red roses alternating with glyphs I vaguely recognized from John's astrology charts. Above her, nine long swords were suspended in a pitch-black void. I looked across the bed at John. "So, what is it?" I asked plaintively. "More bad news?"

John cleared his throat and reached for another Old Gold. The reading, a relentless litany of bad news, had been a strain for both of us. "It's the Nine of Swords, the Tarot's torment card," he said. "It isn't total defeat—the Ten of Swords is that—but almost. The swords represent conflicts you can't get past. The quilt's roses are your desires. And its astrological signs are forces working against them."

John reminded me that each draw of the Tarot represented a person or event in my life affecting my question. So far, nearly everyone I'd known in New York had appeared: Norman, Holly, Sal, Peter, Adrian, Miss Eden. Even George had shown up as the Four of Swords—reversed of course—a position John had said indicated turmoil. "Have any idea who this card might be?"

"It's Lynn, I just know it," I sighed, burying my face in my hands like the distraught figure on the card. I told John of the night Lynn had freaked out on a double dose of LSD and pure pharmaceutical meth. "It was terrifying. I've never seen anyone so crazed. Then, the next day, she was back at it, begging George for more speed."

I said, of all the Horrible Fags, only Norman, the whiney, black-toothed troll who was George's coach in the fine art of being horrible, would've been a worse final draw. Fortunately, he'd already turned up as the Magician—like George's card, reversed—in the sixth place, a position John had said governed only the here and now. This card, my final one, was the one that predicted my future.

"Whoever it is, it sure doesn't look good, that's for sure," John said. He bent over the card and pointed at the bed's plinth with the arm of his aviator glasses. "See the frieze? It's hard to make out on these old beat-up cards of George's. One soldier is killing another. That signifies persecution." He glanced at the door and lowered his voice, as if he too had heard someone on the stairs. "Often from a loved one."

I looked out the window and nervously fondled the turquoise George had given me, claiming it signified a fresh start. After much prodding, Adrian had finally revealed that too had been a lie. George and Danny were as strong as ever.

John offered me another Old Gold. "Look, I don't want to interfere but why don't you come to Chicago with me? I could use the company." He lit his cigarette and then mine. "If you don't like it, you can always hitch back."

I stared numbly at my feet and shook my head. I still had things I wanted to do in New York, like go to the top of the Empire State Building, attend a Fillmore East concert and see the Unicorn Tapestries at the Cloisters. More than any of that, though, I still hadn't heard George link me with the only word that mattered in life, the one the shrink had insisted no gay person could ever possibly know—the word 'love.'

I picked up and examined the card I'd drawn for the Tarot's seventh place, the one that John had said signified how I wanted things to be—not how they were or might become, but how I wished they were. "The Tower's my favorite Tarot card," John had smiled when I'd drawn it. "See the bolt of lightning? It's knocked off the tower's crown. And those yellow spots that look like raindrops? They're called Yods, the Tarot's symbol for the life force. Here they're washing away everything that's old and tired. Like those two old farts," he'd said, pointing to the lord and lady stiffly plummeting from the tower into the abyss. He chuckled. "I like to think they're straight. And the Yods, us gays."

I felt my face flush. George was supposed to have been my Yod—the act of righteous retribution that in *Persona* had suddenly wiped the screen clean and, after a brief interlude of howling demons and dancing ghouls, established the humiliated Alma as a force to be reckoned with—the mutely haughty Elisabet's equal. But nothing had happened like it was supposed to. My demons had just kept on coming—Norman; his boyfriend, the ruined Broadway dancer; Holly; Adrian; Lynn; even that horror, Peter Point. I glanced back at my final draw, the Nine of Swords. As John had said, it wasn't quite total defeat—the Ten of Swords was that—but close.

John waited around after my Tarot reading for George to return and offer him a hit of speed big enough to last him all the way to the Midwest. But, of course, he never showed and, eager to hit the road before nightfall, John left with a promise to keep in touch. As he noted, we were family now. "Sisters," he even called us.

Once again alone, I dropped the slip of paper with John's Chicago address into the cigar box I kept in the top drawer of our drop-down desk. A gay couple he knew from LA had moved there and started up a three-way with a younger leather queen. Not one for group sex, let alone leather, John had no interest in joining in, although he had taken them up on their offer of the living room couch. On his way to San Francisco, he figured Chicago was as far as his battered VW Bug would go before burning out. How he'd manage the rest of the trip, he'd deal with there.

I pulled from the cigar box a stack of letters from my mother, a long rant of worry I saved primarily to prove someone cared, and looked out the window at a sky so blue John had laughed when I'd called it heartbreaking. Only dreamy Pisceans like me, he'd said, talked like that. Practical Capricorns like him would merely note the lack of clouds and deduce umbrellas weren't necessary. When I'd finally confessed I was depressed, he'd come right out and said he was glad he wasn't me. I let my emotions get the better of me. He always kept his in check, although, unlike Adrian, he at least didn't call me a virago. Nor did he, as George did nearly every chance he got, once accuse me of being paranoid.

I picked up the Tarot card that had capped off my reading and examined the frieze on the base of the androgyne's bed. Persecution" was what John had said the two soldiers' struggle signified. He pointed to the soldier on the right who was about to impale his opponent with his sword, and flushed slightly. "Often from a loved one," he added so softly I had to ask him to repeat himself. It felt like the story of my life. "Often from a loved one...."

I lay motionless in bed and listened as they crept into the room. The night was moonless and there wasn't a shred of light, but I knew from the waft of baby powder that one of them had to be George. But who was he with? I knew it couldn't be Danny. Since I'd caught him in bed with George, he'd given me a wide berth. The last time he'd seen me he'd actually turned and run. Adrian would've been chattering away while Norman would've had his boyfriend in tow. And there were definitely only two sets of feet. When they stopped at the sink to fill a water glass, I peeked and realized George's companion wasn't a he at all. It was my Nine of Swords, Lynn, the Horrible Fag's first female.

"Don't you want to wake him?" she whispered.

"Shhh. Let's go out to the balcony," George replied, his back to me.

I heard a syringe tinkle against the side of the glass and the whoosh of a tie being wound and then unwound around an arm. When Lynn whimpered, I was glad they'd let me be. Once again, George's shot had been too strong for even a pig like her. But when I heard George's belt buckle hit the floor, I sat bolt upright and looked into the dressing mirror opposite the balcony door—the one George had hauled in from the trash to give us what he'd called a "larger view." There, in the glow of a candle, I saw George's face in Lynn's breasts. In her left hand, she held George's still flaccid cock.

I grabbed a stack of books—my copy of *Love's Body*, Peter's *Story of O*, and George's *Magick: In Theory and Practice*—and hurled them at the mirror, shrieking, "Get out! I won't let you! This is my place, do you hear?" Shards of glass careened across the floor. "*MINE*!"

The two of them pulled themselves together and rushed out so quickly that, for a moment, I feared I'd dreamt the whole scene up. But when, at dawn, I stepped out of bed and sliced my foot open on a shard of glass—just as Elisabet had in *Persona*—I knew everything was as it seemed. As Lynn had said, there was one good thing about seeing your own blood. You knew you were for real.

For the next two days, I stayed in bed, smoking the cigarette butts I'd found lying around the room. From time to time, I caught glimpses of myself in the remnants of the mirror I'd smashed and thought about doing myself in. But the prospect of rotting in that horrid little room while George fucked his way across town sickened me back to life. I'd rot alive instead.

I scrawled a message to myself on the door to our room in the only magic marker that hadn't gone dry. *Dale—Sorry I missed you. Been thinking about you. Stop by sometime. Love, G.* The 'G' was for the other George, George Right, the tall, thin Texan John had said I'd been a fool to give up. The one I'd chosen instead was the one he'd dubbed George Wrong, Silver George, the source of all my Tarot's swords.

I stepped back and admired my scribble. I added a flourish under the closing "Love" and smiled at my cleverness. When George returned, he'd think I was back to being courted by his rival. That it was a lie, that I was so abjectly in love with George Wrong I couldn't even look at anyone else, didn't matter. If George was going to fuck around, I'd at least pretend I was too.

"Trying to make me jealous?" George chuckled, waltzing through the door two days later. He went straight to the closet and, changing his clothes, said he was surprised I hadn't heard. The other George had left town more than a month ago. "Took too much of his own speed," he said before again walking out on me. I didn't see him again for another three days.

No one visited and the only mail I got was a letter from my mother saying how much they were looking forward to my father's upcoming transfer to the new ordnance works DuPont had opened up in Indiana. She boasted they'd even started calling themselves Hoosiers again, even though the house they'd purchased, a two-story Colonial with a family room and two fireplaces, was across the state line in Illinois. She closed by assuring me they'd have a room for me any time I was ready to return to the place where she again claimed I was loved, although not once did she indicate either she or my father was prepared to utter the word 'gay.' Two years into our war and me near total defeat, they hadn't budged an inch.

By the time George finally returned, I was so desperate for company I stuck out my arm every time he offered me a shot. I didn't even bother asking for small ones. Dosage no longer mattered or even sex, really—by then, my abjectness so horrified me I'd become totally impotent. I just didn't want to be left alone anymore with my thoughts about how worthless I was, how disgusting and degraded, how sad and utterly, unalterably shameful I'd become.

My draft notice arrived in the letter from my mother informing me the family dog, Jeff, had died the same day they'd moved into their new Midwestern home. Of the notice, she'd said only that she and my father hoped I did the "right thing." She'd meant, of course, enlist. What the shrink hadn't accomplished, my parents hoped Vietnam would. Like my father had repeatedly professed, there was nothing quite like the Army for a good swift kick in the butt. Obviously, he'd never met George.

As was her habit, my mother blamed herself for Jeff's death. She'd been so distracted by the movers' damage—three dining room chairs were broken and one of the doors to the hutch where she displayed her cut glass and sterling silver had been ripped off its hinges—she hadn't noticed he'd wandered off. Deaf and crippled with arthritis, he hadn't even heard the car coming. "I wish I'd been there," I said to George, my voice cracking. "Jeff and I grew up together." I fumbled with his *I Ching* coins and smiled wistfully. "Guess I'm no longer a kid, huh?"

George dipped his straight razor— the same one I'd grabbed when I'd found him in bed with Danny—into a sink full of hot water and glowered at me through the mirror. After two drugless days, he was in no mood for the mooning of a twenty-year-old over the loss of his childhood pet. "So, what are you going to do?" he asked, nodding at the draft notice. "December 6 is only a few days away."

I suggested a hit of speed, certain that what had gotten me onto welfare would surely keep me out of the Army.

"Sorry, babe," he said, resuming his shaving, "but the town's completely dry."

I watched the razor glide down the side of his face and decided that time I'd believe him. Straight, George generally told the truth. My eyes followed the line of his back, the slightly flattened curve of his ass, the cyclone of hairs on the backs of his thighs and across to the cinder block I'd put over the rat hole. Since he'd run out of speed, George hadn't left my side once. The night before, after I'd worked on him for so long he'd finally gotten hard, he'd almost slipped and said he loved me. In the morning, we'd awakened as if fused, his cock still inside me.

"But something's bound to turn up," I said. "It has to. You said yourself you've never seen New York so dry."

George wiped the last of the shaving creme from his face. "I don't know what to say, hon. I'm as much a victim of this as you." He dried his face with a hand towel and shrugged. "More so, actually. I mean, I've been at this for almost eight years. You've been at it, what, eight months?"

"Oh, come on, George, this is the Army we're talking about. Vietnam. You're really going to tell me you can't find one measly shot of something to get me out of this?" A rush of panic overtook me as he slipped on the pair of white silk panties Lynn had given him. "What about some of that shit you gave me that time I visited my parents? You know, the time I called my mother a warthog from hell?" I paused for the pang of guilt to subside. "What was that called? Angel Dust?"

George unplugged the hand sink drain. "I don't know what you're so worried about," he said. "Just think about all those horny grunts who'll be dying for a piece of ass like yours."

"Stop it, George. You know I hate it when you talk like that." I glared at my feet. "Like I'm a piece of meat."

He ran a comb through his hair and shrugged. "Sorry, babe, but there's nothing I can do. The town's dry." Pivoting on bare feet, he turned and faced me. The silk panties Lynn had given him outlined in perfect detail the head of his cock. "Que sera, sera."

"Then I'll just tell them I'm gay," I replied, battling a desire to bury my face in his crotch. "There's no way I'm going to Vietnam."

George's face reddened and his eyes narrowed. "But what about your future? Employers check things like that. You'll never get a job."

It was then I realized that the night before—the tenderness and the near-miss of his profession of love—had been just another lie. George didn't do people with futures. When we'd moved in together, he'd made it clear the day I got a job was the day he left me.

I tossed my draft notice onto the drop-down desk across from the bed and glowered at him. I was staying anyway. My war was there with him, not in some jungle nine thousand miles away. Vietnam wasn't getting me. George was.

I stood in a line that snaked out of a crenellated, yellow brick armory and down a sunny Philadelphia side street. I was the only one with hair down to his shoulders and the only one dressed in hip-huggers and a gray Red Army coat. I didn't know if anyone else had needle tracks on the inside of his arm or had devised a plan quite like mine. I spoke to no one, and no one spoke to me.

Like everyone else, I stripped down to my briefs and folded my clothes into a neat pile on a table the color of gun metal. I didn't know if I was the only one they said looked a little gaunt or whose balls had already been cupped in a man's hand. Like everyone else, I coughed when the sergeant squeezed them.

"Fine," the officer in charge muttered before patting me on the butt. He instructed me to get dressed and, pointing to a cubicle off in the distance, told me I could see a psychiatrist if I liked. Otherwise, I'd be all set or, as he put it, "ready to go."

I didn't know if I was the only one who opted to take him up on his offer, although the open newspaper on the shrink's standard-issue, gunmetal gray desk indicated he hadn't been particularly busy that day. Tall, trim, and clean-shaven with a square jaw, straight back and short cropped gray hair, he looked nothing like Dr. Radin, nor did his cubicle display any of his credentials. Indeed, there was only a business calendar turned to the month of December hanging from a nail in the wall, and from a hook on the door behind me, his civilian clothes—a starched white shirt, a sports coat, and a pair of dress slacks—covered in a clear plastic dry-cleaner's bag.

He didn't bother introducing himself and instead got right down to business. "Do you have anything you'd like to tell me, son?" he asked. I didn't know if I was the only one who replied yes, although I gathered from his smirk that he was steeled to confessions like mine. I was, I told him, gay.

"So, have you ever liked girls?"

I didn't know if I was the only one who stumbled and almost said why, yes, of course, for half my life, I'd thought I was one. Instead, I shook my head and said no sir, never.

I waited for him to ask about the bars I frequented but he instead mumbled, "I see," and reached across his desk for a black felt-tip pen. I didn't know if mine was the only form on which he placed a check inside the box marked 4-F, the Army's category for mental and moral defects. But I guessed from the force with which he wrote "*OBVIOUS AND OVERT*" across the bottom of mine that I had sparked a particular disgust. He slid the form to the edge of his desk's gray felt blotter and turned it so I could read it. "I think that just about says it all, don't you?"

I leaned forward, read the insult that George claimed would trail me for the rest of my life and then peered into his steely gray eyes. I didn't know if I was the only one who wanted to leap onto his desk and gouge them out with my own two thumbs. Instead, I returned his smile and, like everyone else he'd encountered that day, mumbled a polite, "Yes, sir."

He dismissed me with a nod toward the door and a crisp, "Good luck, son."

Back out on the street, my long hair and my attire quickly aroused suspicion. "You lost or somebody come for you?" a crone in a black shawl and a hairy chin asked in broken English.

"Neither," I said and moved to the corner. When a police car showed up, I decided it was time to move on and hitchhiked back to my brother's house, a suburban Wilmington split-level with a two-car garage, an all-electric kitchen, and a dining room with a picture window framing a sand box and a brand-new swing set. A rising star within DuPont's Explosives Division, with a baby on the way and a stay-at-home wife whose job was to give his first-born the best of everything, Dean had graduated from the ne'er-do-well my father had railed against to a success my parents bragged about with friends over drinks at the country club. Thank God, at least one had turned out well.

"A letter from my shrink," I said when my mother, clearly disappointed, asked how I'd managed to avoid my duty to God and country, although she was at least relieved to hear I was back in therapy—her code for a cure. The shrink I told her I saw once a week in Bellevue's welfare clinic—I got a special thrill every time I told her I was on the dole—was, of course, a fiction. Injecting methamphetamine was instead my course of treatment—the cure on which I'd had her pin her still-fervent hopes for the return of her wayward son—once the apple of her eye and now a drug-shooting, hippie faggot freak on welfare, a true-blue 4-F if there ever was one. It was the cruelest joke I could think of. So blinded by my need for revenge, I couldn't see—or when I could, care—the joke was entirely on me.

21
The End of the Sixties

Ben sat on the edge of the bed in the room George had once called our love nest and stared at the dropper in the water glass. A bead of sweat on the end of his nose glistened in the room's rising heat. A shudder swept up from his gut and then he mumbled, yeah, he was sure; he wanted me to shoot him up. Outside on the windowsill, a carton of orange juice was speckled with frost, the season's first.

An old boyfriend from Syracuse, Ben had tracked me down after hearing from Trudy, the Continental Room's resident fag hag, that I'd fallen into a really sick, decadent scene. He'd started off apologizing for our break-up but I'd told him not to bother. None of it mattered anymore. Besides, I'd found someone else. "George," I'd said when Ben asked his name, although I didn't mention I hadn't seen him in three days. "To a fault," I'd replied when he asked if I was faithful, a question I took as an oblique—and unwelcome—come-on.

Ben smiled as I squirted a jet of water through the syringe. "You know, I've always fantasized about shooting up. I think it's erotic." He looked up at me and blushed. "You know that, right?"

I washed a spoon in the hand sink and shook my head. I recalled the times we'd balled, at his insistence, on his parents' bed and, at the drive-in, in the back seat of their brand-new, 1968 Chrysler Imperial. And I remembered the night of the Democratic National Convention when, as the Chicago cops assaulted thousands of war protesters, I'd puked all over his mother's prized Persian rug. But, no, I recalled nothing about a syringe. "I think that would've stuck," I said. "At the time, I was terrified of needles."

"So, what happened?" Ben asked, fumbling with the pack of Marlboros I'd gotten from the corner bodega on credit.

"You mean to my fear of needles?"

Ben took a Marlboro from the pack without asking, lit it and nodded.

"I fell in love with someone who doesn't have any," I replied and reached for the dime bag of speed George had given me, half of which I was to sell to Valerie, the hippie chick I'd befriended in Syracuse. She too had looked me up as soon as she'd moved back to New York, hungry for a taste of the harder stuff.

Suddenly, it seemed like everyone was. Even Tom, the old boyfriend from Philadelphia who was the first man to ever say he loved me, had come looking for meth. He'd quit his job selling ladies shoes at Wanamaker's and moved to Greenwich Village, as he'd said, to "freak out." He'd also let me know he was shopping around for a drug connection and asked if I'd be his dealer. George, always eager to expand his customer base, gave me a nickel bag and told me to give it to him for free. "An investment," he'd called it, although the speed was mostly just milk paste.

"I've never heard anyone say they think a syringe is sexual," I said, sprinkling a pinch of crystal into the spoon. "Except for maybe Peter. But he'd say anything to shock."

"So why do you do it?"

I looked at Ben and laughed. "You mean, because it isn't sexual?"

Ben nodded.

"Because I'm afraid of guns and I don't know how to make a bomb," I snarled as a blue jay in the ailanthus tree outside our window peered in at me. "Deep down, I tell myself I'm a Weatherman."

"Well, I don't care what you say, I think it's erotic," Ben said. "And decadent." He asked if I remembered how much he was attracted to decadence. "It was why I broke up with you. You liked *2001: A Space Odyssey* and I didn't. I didn't think it was decadent enough."

"Hmmmm," I replied as the blue jay flew off. "I believe 'prosaic' was the word you used."

He watched me wave a match under the spoon and then looked longingly at me. "I was stupid to send you away like that. I think about you all the time." He ran his hand through the curly brown frizz he called his "Art Garfunkel" and blushed. "I think I'm still in love with you."

"No, you're not," I sneered, recalling Tom had said the same thing. "You just want to get high." I picked up the red, white, and blue-striped tie I'd worn to Sunday school as a kid and tossed it to him. "Here, make yourself useful and tie yourself off."

Ben flinched. "What's happened to you, anyway? You seem so hard and cynical." He looked around the room as if suddenly noticing its squalor. "I thought you said you were in love."

"I am. That's what happened to me. I wouldn't wish it on a dog." I stared into the yellow-pink alchemy my match had wrought in the bottom of the spoon and cursed my folly. In the great Greco-Roman tradition of homosexuality, I'd sat at the feet of an older, more experienced man and, in exchange for sex whenever he wanted it, learned what he knew of life—that everyone was a junkie for something.

"Hey, that's just a small one, right?" Ben quaked, distracted by the liquid I drew up into the syringe. "I mean, I don't want too much. You know that, right?"

I squirted a drop onto a finger and savored its cum-like bitterness. I felt a pang of longing for George and wondered who he was balling this time. I supposed it was Danny but knew it could be anyone. As long as he had a mind to fuck with and a vein to pierce, George was happy.

"You know how I hate acid," Ben continued. "It's not like that, is it?"

I held the dropper up and flicked the air bubbles out of it. If any got into his bloodstream, he'd die instantly. "No, it's the exact opposite actually—much more physical and not nearly as spiritual." I smiled wearily. "But, trust me, it'll still blow your mind."

"It won't send me to the hospital, will it? You know how neurotic I am about my heart."

I rolled my eyes. "Ben, really...."

"I know, I know, but I can't help it. I'm a hypochondriac. Don't you remember?"

"Even that can be burned out of you," I said, tightening the tie until he winced. "Anything—pain, fear, decency, pride..." I paused and grimaced. "Everything, that is, but cock. That, the speed'll make you a fool for."

I ran my hand over the measly swell of Ben's vein and wondered if he too would go on to do this with someone else. I recalled my first time and George's story of his own, tied to a bed and shot so full of holes he'd claimed he could see the light streaming through him. I wondered if, like George, Ben would look back on this as the dawning of a new day or, like me, the start of a long free fall. I wondered how long we'd keep doing this to each other, confusing degradation for love and decadence for rebellion. I flashed on my mother retching into the toilet. The boys in Larry's dorm shouting *Two, four, six, eight, who do we obliterate?* My shrink foretelling a life of anguish and regret: *You are going to be unhappy as long as you persist in this choice.*

I went stone-cold dead inside and then pierced Ben's vein with my syringe. Speed was the cure, the hazing that hardened us off for the long hard winter of a faggot's life. "Good," I said after pulling the needle out. I hadn't shed a drop of his blood.

"Oh my God, oh my God," Ben cried, twitching and flopping about the bed like he'd stuck a finger into the wall socket. He even mumbled something about bells. When I explained they were brain cells bursting, he looked startled, then rose from the bed and groped for the door, as if his eyeballs had also exploded.

Out in the hall, he turned to face me. He was pale and trembling and his pupils were swollen black moons. "But I asked you for a small one."

"It was," I replied coldly. "For me, anyway."

His legs wobbled as he headed down the stairs. At the landing, he cast a terrified glance back at me. "How long will this last?"

I shrugged and said it'd be over in about six hours, not counting the crash. For that, I recommended a downer. He could get one from just about any drag queen.

"But my heart!" he gasped. "I can't wait that long."

"There's nothing you can do," I said. "Speed's like everything else in life. It just must be endured." I warned him not to take any downers until he crashed—earlier, the shock might be too much for his system—then shut the door and locked myself in. I listened to his footsteps as he raced down the stairs and recalled Peter's warning after he'd come to Avenue D to deliver George's invitation to a tryst. "You're gonna be swimming with sharks soon, babe. If you want to survive, you're gonna have to toughen up."

I staggered to the hand sink mirror and confronted the face staring back at me. Its eyes were blank, its cheeks, hollow, and its color, pallid. Its mouth, contorted somewhere between a grimace and a scream, reminded me of the Francis Bacon portraits I'd seen as a teenager in the pages of *Time*. Behind me, a naked light bulb illuminated the tableau Ben had found so alluring or, as he'd preferred, "decadent"—a spoon, a shot glass with a used cotton ball, a syringe in a drinking glass and a red, white and blue-striped necktie—now that Jeff, the family dog, was gone, my only memento of a youth a privileged, white, middle-class kid like me was supposed to recall as happy but which I knew as mostly a living hell.

I recalled what Bacon had told *Time* of his vision: *Everything in life is violent, even a rose.* One of the sharks Peter had warned me about was now me.

George breezed in after five days with Danny, warning me on his way to the closet that he had no time for a scene. His Grand Poobah, the straight man on Broadway and 12th who kept him in speed, had summoned him to another taste test. He tossed the pair of striped rayon pants he'd worn on our first night together and a pair of crocheted lace panties I'd never seen before onto a heap in the closet and foraged for something clean to wear. "He's finally forgiven that mess with me and Norman. Says he was sure it was all Norman's fault," he said of their attempt to cheat him out of three kilos of pure crystal meth. He grabbed a pair of bell bottoms and chuckled; anyone who trusted a Horrible Fag deserved to be sleazed. He walked naked to the hand sink and smirked. "Now don't get your hopes up," he said, filling the sink with hot water. "I'm just here to freshen up."

I sat on the bed and fixed my gaze on my trip book, the same black faux-leather funeral home guest ledger George had given me after we'd moved in together. On the left, *Marquis de Sade* shrieked at me in a thick swirl of dark blue curlicues and crosshatches. On the right, my newest entry—the Jefferson Airplane refrain, *And all I see is draining me of my plastic fantastic lover*—bespoke a quieter, more resigned rage. Alone in the middle of the page was *draining*, the spine of its 'd' a thick spike of angry red but the tail of its concluding 'g' a gaping, empty hole. Above it, the "I" was split down the middle, as if by an axe.

"You been here the whole time?" George asked, cleaning the head of his dick with a soapy washcloth.

I nodded, digging my felt-tip pen deeper into the spine of draining's 'd.' Except for the owner of the bodega across the street who let me buy my Marlboros and cherry Cokes on credit, I'd spoken to no one in five interminable days.

He dried his crotch, doused his balls with baby powder, and peered at me through the hand sink mirror. "You don't look well. Why don't you come along? The fresh air'll do you good."

I watched a sparrow peck at the crumbs of a cheesecake I'd left on the windowsill, amazed at how easy it was when I wasn't high to see through George's lies. He hadn't stopped by to, as he'd said, "freshen up." George had stopped by because, after five days of serving as his pin cushion, Danny was in no shape to be seen, let alone shown off, and that was exactly what his Grand Poobah expected—someone in tow to prove George was still at the top of his game, the Horrible Fag who shot more speed and fucked more boys than anyone else in New York. In need of an emergency back-up, George had come for me, the other boy.

He slipped on a pair of white cotton briefs, stepped into his bellbottoms, and turned to face me. "What's the matter, cat got your tongue?"

I closed my trip book and looked across the room at him. It no longer mattered that he was a no-good lying cheat or that I was nothing more than sloppy seconds. I just didn't want to be left alone anymore. Trapped in my own thoughts, I'd convinced myself I was to blame for everything—even Danny. If only I'd been cleaner or handled the speed better—or renounced my parents, turned on my friends, agreed the rioters outside the Stonewall were cretins, thought the world was perfect the way it was, embraced sleaze more enthusiastically, enjoyed curing him of his gas, being his boy, his little sex pig—George and I might still be together. In love, like we were supposed to be. Happy, like gay people weren't supposed to be.

"Or maybe it's this?" George said, toying with his zipper. He threaded his belt through the first two loops of his jeans and leered at me. "Who knows, I might even fuck you when we get back. I haven't done that in a while, now have I?" He stepped so close I could smell the baby powder on him.

I whimpered like a beaten dog and shamelessly pulled him to me.

"Hungry, eh?" he chuckled as I took him in my mouth. He lit a cigarette, waited a few moments and then, still flaccid, grabbed my chin and turned my face upward toward his. A cloud of blue smoke enveloped me. "Still my little sex pig?"

I moaned as he ran a finger around the inside of my ear, certain it was as close to a profession of love as I was ever going to get.

His smirk deepened and then, turning to face the wall, bared his ass. "Now rim me," he ordered.

I wanted to protest I was too good for that but, knowing better, I merely pulled the frayed bath towel that functioned as a curtain across the window, dropped to my knees and did as I was told.

After what seemed like an eternity, he finally said he'd had enough, although of what I wasn't sure; he still wasn't hard. "Besides," he chuckled, zipping himself back up, "I have an important business meeting to attend." He again ran his finger around the inside of my ear and smiled. "You don't want to make me late, now do you?" He donned his pea coat and admired his reflection in the sex mirror. "So, you coming or not?" he asked, idly adjusting his hair around a small bald spot.

I glanced at the Maxfield Parrish print above the drop-down desk—other than the silver gazing ball he'd accepted as tribute from another man he'd used as his cocksucker—our room's only decoration. Two young androgynes lounged next to a blue alpine pool. One was naked and supine; the other stood, robed and garlanded. "Have you ever noticed how Parrish never shows any body hair?" George had asked after retrieving it from the trash. "I'm sure he was an ephebophile." Delighted, Norman had let out a high-pitched squeal that careened around the room like a rat on the loose. "An e-pheb-o-phile," George had repeated, relishing the roll of its syllables off his tongue.

"Good," George mumbled as I rose from the bed and mutely trudged to the closet for my pea coat. There was no point in trying to extract a concession: only one of the Grand Poobah's shots; a promise to stop seeing Danny; or even a full night together. Nothing worked. I just needed to accept that I was nothing more than an ornament to be seen, not heard—until, of course, I wasn't. I glared back at the Maxfield Parrish and flushed. In three months, I'd be twenty-one. Obsolete. An adult, not a boy.

I followed George down the stairs but, once out on the street, knew I was too far gone for the remaining humiliations George and his Grand Poobah had in store for me. For five interminable days, I'd stayed holed up in my room, venting my anguish and growing paranoia onto my trip book. Page after page was filled with a pathetic, insane howl: *Time's Up! BONG!! Human Life is Obsolete. Hidden Ideals #1: To Control the Electrical Waves of the Universe. For President: Master Brainwasher, George M_____.*

One page I'd filled with the mindless drivel of a pop song: *Doobie-doobie-doobie/laadie-laadie-laadie/Doo-doo-doo.* At the bottom, I'd written *HEAR ME-E-E* in jagged red caps. Four pages later, I'd written in razor-edged blocks George's only ground-rule: *No Remorse, No Blame.* The 'o' of Blame's *No* was a hideous, hectoring mouth with bared teeth and lurid red lips. Further on and clearly worn out, I'd scrawled in purple the last line of Dylan's song: *And these visions of Johanna are all that remain.* The a's and o's were all filled with bars, like the windows in a jail cell, while the j's tail was a thin, wasted sliver ending in a needle's point.

On day three of his five-day sprint with Danny, George had returned for a change of clothes and taken pity on me. As he'd also noted then, I didn't look well. Opening my trip book, he'd attempted a dialogue by writing in purple: *Oh well, sighed the Principessa, at least one thing is certain. We can't live forever.* Next, he'd written in red: *You must...* and handed the book back to me to complete his sentence. *Make the most of even the most disgusting situations*, I'd mutely fumed in blue. Furious, he'd snarled that I was hopeless and stormed back out.

We walked in silence past the precinct station and a row of brick tenements that cast long, mournful shadows across West 10th Street. At the corner of Bleecker, I tasted George's shit on my lower lip and panicked that it was smeared across my face. I wiped my mouth with the back of my glove and glanced at a passing couple. "Can you believe it?" I heard the woman gasp. Her companion glared at the sidewalk and shook his head. "Terrible," he murmured, "just terrible."

Down Bleecker, one of the fag antique dealers Peter and I had ripped off stepped out of his shop. He squinted in our direction as one of his poodles raised a leg and peed on a tree trunk. Afraid he'd recognize me, I hid my face with the collar of my pea coat just as a police car whizzed by, its blue lights flashing. My knees buckled and I grabbed a stop sign before telling George I felt strange. "Like I'm high," I stammered, although I hadn't had a drop of speed or even so much as a puff of marijuana in almost a week. They were the first words I'd spoken since he'd returned.

"Come on, you're going to make me late," George grumbled, stepping off the curb. I almost told him to go ahead without me; I was in no shape for the half-day of drug-shooting that lay ahead. Indeed, the idea of getting that high terrified me. But George was halfway across the street. I'd have to shout.

Two doors into the next block, I stepped onto a metal grate in front of an abandoned storefront. Below me, a rat skittered through a clutter of newspapers and broken bottles. Shuddering, I stumbled, just slightly, and pressed my hand against the shop's window. The glass, blackened up to my chest, wobbled, mixing my reflection with George's. Inside, upended chairs were scattered across the floor. Behind them, a counter was draped in a white sheet, like a corpse. On it, an old cash register was stuck on "No Sale."

I braced against a blast of cold air that suddenly swept down West 10th Street. Odd, I thought, and then someone shouted. I couldn't tell who; it could've been George, one of the people walking toward us, the couple who'd just passed, or maybe it was the fag antique dealer coming after me. As I raised my head, I felt the flesh on my face suddenly slip away. Panic-stricken, I turned to George.

He smirked, as if he could see inside me. "Now everyone can tell what a selfish little shit you are," he sneered, although his lips didn't move once.

"What?" I whimpered.

"Come on," he replied, tugging on the arm of my pea coat. "You know how he hates to be kept waiting."

Paralyzed with fear, I watched in horror as a straight couple approached. Suddenly, the man burst out laughing. Then the woman pointed at me. "Oh my God, look at that, will you?"

"No, please, I can explain," I stammered, backing into the glass. Beneath me, the rat squealed like it had been stepped on. "I'm not like that, not at all."

"You should be ashamed," the woman said, wagging a long gnarly finger at me.

"What's going on with you?" George growled. "Have you lost your mind?"

Certain I had, I turned and, muffling a scream, ran back to our room and shoved the drop-down desk in front of the door. When I was sure no one had followed me, I warily approached the hand sink mirror. Relieved I still had a reflection, I sat down on the bed, smoked a half-pack of Marlboros, one right after the other, and took heed of the warning. Before, I'd freaked out only after taking too much speed. That day, I'd lost it without having taken any. As Miss Eden had once cautioned, if I didn't take care, I was gonna end up in Bellevue just like Electric Freddy.

When George returned later that night, he accused me of intentionally making him look bad for his meeting with the Grand Poobah. "Like I've lost my touch. You know how much he likes me to show up with a boy." When I asked if that meant we wouldn't be having sex, he snarled he didn't fuck crazies. "Contagious," he even called me.

I didn't bother noting that was the most paranoid thing I'd ever heard anyone say nor, fearing his dosage, did I ask for a compensatory shot of speed. Instead, I just sat at the head of the bed with my back against the wall and, owl-like, stared at him while he scribbled in his trip book. Finally, my silence and the relentlessness of my gaze so unnerved him that he packed up his blue Lufthansa flight bag and left, stopping only at the door to call me a menace. "You should be locked up, you know that, locked up!" I looked serenely back at him and, for the first time ever, laughed in his face.

I awakened from a two-day sleep cure to realize it was New Year's Eve, the end of the decade known as the Sixties. With no plans and no sign of George, I decided to drop in on my old Syracuse pal, the hippie chick Valerie who, along with her new boyfriend, were staying in the Second Avenue brownstone of a middle-aged gay man she'd met through an ad in the *East Village Other*. In exchange for home-cooked gourmet meals, fine wines, and a house furnished in modernist classics, she'd agreed to be his lifestyle coach, a live-in guru on the counterculture's ever-changing tastes in language, fashion, and drugs. As she'd said when describing the arrangement, the guy wanted to be both gay and hip. "You know, like you," she'd smiled. I hadn't bothered asking why anyone would want something like that; not even my own lover could stand being around me. I hadn't seen George in over a week.

I was more depressed than surprised to discover that the guy Valerie was coaching was none other than Sal's old roommate, Otto, in whose East 10th Street pad I'd stayed the first two times I'd visited New York. Almost two years and at least one address change later, he was still groping around, searching for a way out of his box—an alternative to the tedium of gay bars, the tawdriness of subway tearooms and the claustrophobia of the closet. As Sal had once noted, Otto was too bourgie to drop-out and too gay to fit-in. "Stuck," he'd called him, although I was clearly in no position to judge. A year earlier, I'd dropped out of college in order to be gay and had ended up a strung-out, drug-shooting speed freak on welfare. If that wasn't stuck, I didn't know what was.

"Oh my God, I can't believe it! Look at you!" Otto cried, ushering me up a flight of stairs to a high-ceilinged room with ornate moldings, a gilt-framed mirror over the mantle, and a Mies van der Rohe chaise lounge in the front bay. Grabbing his wine goblet, he perched himself in front of a marble fireplace in which a small fire flickered and noted the length of my hair and the stylishness of my threads—a pair of wool hip huggers and a glossy red form-fitting shirt I'd lifted from Limbo on St. Mark's Place. "And to think he used to be such a shy, sweet thing!"

Valerie, reclining on a plush cream-colored sofa where she and her boyfriend were rolling joints, beamed. "I know, I sold him his first tab of acid." She sat up and giggled. "You should've seen the shirts he wore back then. Great colors with lots of stripes and checks. But every collar was buttoned down. I'd never seen anyone so straight."

"Yeah, thank God, that's over with, huh?" I said, smiling valiantly. When my family had gotten together over Christmas at my brother's suburban Wilmington split-level, my father had taken one look at me and sneered that I looked like a carnival barker. My mother had burst into tears.

"I see you still have your Aubrey Beardsley," I said, pointing to a print on the wall that opened onto a large, elegant dining room. "I remember it from when I stayed at your place over on East 10th Street. It's *The Dream*, from his *Rape of the Lock* series."

"Oh God, that place was such a dump," Otto sighed. "All those hideous bars on the windows. And, oh my God, the cockroaches. I swear they carried away one of my Eames chairs."

"Oh no, I loved that place," I said. "I remember you even had a mixer in the kitchen. That really blew my mind." I chuckled. "A man with a mixer." I played with the fringe of my floor cushion. "You know, that was my first exposure to gay New York." I took a sip of wine from the goblet Otto had filled— "Baccarat," he'd murmured as he poured—and smiled. "My mind was blown."

"Hey, wait a minute," Valerie cried, lighting a joint. "What about that time you tripped out with Gino and me in Central Park?" She turned to Otto and giggled. "He thought the rocks were stage props."

"Yeah, but that time I was just a freak. The times I visited Sal at Otto's place, I was gay too."

"What do you mean, you and Sal balled?"

"Oh, God no, Sal and I have never had sex." I watched Valerie take several puffs on a joint and then turned to Otto. "Although I did see Edward Albee in Julius's."

"Oh, her," he sneered. "You see her *everywhere*."

"And Andy Warhol's *Flesh*. I saw that too." I paused to think. "Except that was on my second visit—in the Fall, not the Spring of '68." I took a long drag from the joint Valerie finally relinquished and recalled the sights I'd seen on those two visits. Of all of them—the student take-over of Columbia, hippies snake-dancing to *Sgt. Pepper's* in

Washington Square, Allen Ginsberg blowing into a conch shell at a Central Park Be-In, Coretta Scott King reading her husband's *Ten Commandments Against the War in Vietnam*, Edward Albee sipping a beer at Julius's—none had blown my mind as much sitting in the Garrick Theater—renamed the *Andy Warhol* Garrick Theater—and watching *Flesh*. "Sal and I had a huge fight over it. He thought the flick was crap. I loved it. The first film to show gay people as we really are, not as the wrecks and monsters straight people make us out to be." I smiled at the recollection. "Sal accused me of having 'gay on the brain.' By the time we got to Karen and Murdoch's, we were barely speaking."

"Oh, I remember those two. The hippies over on St. Mark's Place." Otto smiled mischievously. "I called them 'the blonds.'" He took another sip of wine and pursed his lips. "I don't think they approved of me much." He ran his hand through a thick mane of wavy black hair that curled over the collar of a paisley Nehru jacket. His pants, an expensive-looking pair of dark blue bellbottoms, were pressed, while the arabesques on his wine-colored opera slippers reminded me of the shoes my mother wore the day I came out to her.

"*Mildred Pierce*," he replied when I asked what he thought the problem had been. "I'd told them it was my favorite film and, of course, they were appalled. They'd just finished yammering about this hideous Godard flick they'd just seen—you know the one where a gang of hippies terrorizes these rich people stuck in a traffic jam on their way to their country homes."

"*Weekend*," I said. "I saw that with Sal too. I liked it. A lot, actually." I smiled. "It blew my mind almost as much as *Flesh*."

Otto looked at me like he expected as much from someone who shot hard drugs. "Anyway, Sal and the blonds were boring me to tears with all their talk about Brechtian alienation—you know, as if it's some kind of badge of honor or something." He took two rapid tokes from the joint and then immediately exhaled.

"Oh no, Otto," Valerie interjected. "You've got to hold the smoke in. You know, in your lungs. That's how you get high."

"Oh, sorry," Otto sighed and shook his head before passing me the joint. "I don't know why, but I just can't seem to get the hang of this drug thing." He took another sip of wine and settled back onto the floor cushion he was reclining on. "I mean, who in their right mind wants to be alienated? It's painful." He sat up again and fidgeted with an ashtray on his Noguchi coffee table. "Just like the despair Sal used to blather on and on about. Nobody can really live like that. They'd blow their brains out after just a week of it." He lifted his wine goblet as if to make a toast. "The point is to be in the world. And succeed!" He looked at me and laughed heartily. "Just like Mildred Pierce!"

"Hear, hear!" Valerie and her boyfriend, who hadn't uttered a word since I'd walked in, cried. Giggling, they collapsed into each other and cuddled on the sofa.

"Straights." Otto said, rolling his eyes.

"Okay, okay," Valerie cried, untangling herself. "Can we please change the subject?" She lit another joint and frowned. "I don't know why you guys always have to make such a big deal about being gay. Besides, I think Andy Warhol's a bore. I saw *Flesh* and fell asleep."

I took the joint from her and smiled wearily. She hadn't even been impressed that her old trip-mate, Gino, had starred in one of Andy's earliest underground films, *Beauty #2*, along with Edie Sedgwick, the Sixties "It Girl."

"You know the cops raided Warhol's last movie," Otto said. "*Fuck*, he called it, although I think he changed the name after the raid. It played over on Bleecker Street, probably in the same theater you saw *Flesh*. I suppose that was the joke. You know, rub hard-core sex in the noses of those sanctimonious, love-is-all-you-need hippies who're taking over the West Village." He handed the joint back to me and chuckled. "It opened right as they all came back from Woodstock. And I do have to say it was filthy. Even I walked out."

I looked out the bay at a phalanx of taxis hurtling down Second Avenue, amazed at how quickly things had fallen apart. In less than two years, we'd gone from the shock of *Flesh* to the tedium of *Fuck*. I wondered who George was with and how high he was. "Yeah," I murmured. "After too much repetition, I guess everything becomes just smut, huh?"

"Oh, don't get me wrong. You can never get too much of a good thing," Otto replied. "I walked out because the sex was straight."

"Talk about a good thing," Valerie interjected. "We're breaking in the New Year by taking Otto on his first acid trip." She held up a gelatin square and giggled. "It's windowpane. Wanna join us?"

"I don't know," I stammered, recalling my recent freak-out.

"Oh, come on, a head like you?" Valerie cried as I stared numbly at the hit of LSD she'd handed me. "Besides, it's the end of the Sixties! What better way to usher in a new decade?"

I listened as Valerie recounted for Otto the acid trip we'd taken in Longwood Gardens with Gino and his girlfriend, Sandrine. "He's a fantastic trip guide," she said, nodding at me. "One of the best." I met Otto's worshipful gaze and sighed. That and being a good fuck were just about all I seemed to have going for me. "Thanks," I murmured and popped the gelatin square in my mouth.

"That's all you do? Just take it like it's an aspirin?" Otto gasped. "I thought we were supposed to sit around in a circle and listen to Ravi Shankar or something." He turned to Valerie with a look of bemused irony. "Sal said acid trips were supposed to be spiritual."

"Oh, God no, they're supposed to be fun!" Valerie pointed at the tab still sitting in the palm of his hand. "Go ahead, pop it! You'll see."

Otto looked wide-eyed at me. "Will I see God?"

"No, but you might see the insides of your eyeballs," I replied dryly.

"Oh, but that's so gross!" Otto cried. "I don't want to see anything like that."

"Funny, I always thought that was the best part," I said as the edges of the room started to wobble.

I tried to make the most of our trip but Valerie's manic hilarity, her boyfriend's silence, and Otto's squealing about the acid's colors only sent me deeper into my funk. And so, I snuck out a few minutes before midnight and wandered the streets of the Village alone. A block down Second Avenue, a marquee for Ingmar Bergman's latest film, *Shame*, rebuked me for the waste I'd made of my time in New York. I hadn't seen a flick, gone to a concert, or even so much as taken a walk in Central Park since I'd been with George. The only two books I'd read were Flaubert's *Salambo* and Pauline Reage's *Story of O*. On George's instructions, I'd even shipped my portable stereo back to my parents. Music, he'd contended, made people insipid.

Same with peace marches. The Vietnam War, he claimed, had done wonders for the American drug trade. Only a prude would want to stop something like that.

On St. Mark's Place, a prostitute mistook me for a junkie and offered me a blow job in exchange for a hit of smack. I told her she was barking up the wrong tree and kept on moving. Under the arch in Washington Square, a strung-out runaway offered me a nickel bag of Angel Dust for five bucks. I wanted to ask her what it was about horse tranquilizers that got her off, but I knew too well the hell people put themselves through for an escape. Instead, I grumbled she'd have to pay me to take shit like that and walked on.

At the Women's House of Detention, I stopped and surveyed the various calls-to-arms plastered across the prison's fortress-like base. One demanded revenge for the deaths of Fred Hampton and Mark Clark, two Black Panthers murdered in their sleep by the Chicago cops; another wished a long life for the Thought of Chairman Mao and his Great Proletarian Cultural Revolution. Next to it, someone had milk-pasted a cover from the *New York Review of Books*, a drawing of a Molotov cocktail, complete with instructions on how to make it. Below it, a red scrawl shrieked *Fork Power*!—a Weatherman slogan inspired by the inscription the Manson murderers had etched into the belly of Roman Polanski's very pregnant wife, Sharon Tate. I recalled the interview one of the Weathermen leaders, Bernadine Dohrn, had given the *East Village Other—That's what we're about, being crazy motherfuckers and scaring the shit out of pig America*—and felt suddenly nauseous. She sounded just like a Horrible Fag.

Two blocks down Christopher, the Stonewall's plywood-covered window sported graffiti that proclaimed *Gay Is Love*, an assertion so at odds with my reality that I almost burst into tears. Across Seventh Avenue, a drag queen stood outside Riker's and threatened three others with a nail file. Someone had stolen her reds and she wasn't letting anyone go until she found out who. I recalled the scene from my first night in town almost exactly one year earlier—Stephanie Lisa banging on the bathroom door of West 10th Street demanding Miss Eden hand over her reds—and sighed. What had previously been kept behind closed doors was now out in the open, for the whole world to see. Next to me, a bundle of a new underground gay newspaper, the nation's first, lay in a doorway. *Come Out!* its masthead bellowed.

Down by the river, I watched a swarm of men dart in and out of the Trucks, looking for sex. When one in leather chaps and a muscle shirt motioned for me to join him, I shook my head and moved on. I didn't care how cool S&M had become; I'd had my fill of degradation. As John had said of speed, it was time we found something new. I recalled the "gay is good" chant I'd heard the first night of the Stonewall riots and, for the first time that trip, smiled. That was the way out, I thought. Like James Brown had sung that day I'd tried to get my mother to talk through our rift: *Say it loud, I'm Black and I'm proud.*

I ended my wandering in the fetid, rat-infested square at the bottom of 9th Avenue where Adrian had his cold-water flat. I was certain George had been hiding out there, possibly with Danny or maybe even someone new. With George, anything was possible, except, of course, for being what I wanted most. As he'd sneered that first night of the Stonewall riots, when gay became good, he'd be turning straight.

For the rest of the night, I stood in a doorway across the square and focused all my energy on the light in Adrian's front window, convinced by the acid I could make George feel what he refused to hear. I told him it was time to crawl back from the edge. We'd gone too far out. The first step needed to be the drugs. The speed was killing both of us. I told him I'd help and stay with him all the way through. All he needed to do was come out and join me. The moonlight was as beautiful as any I'd seen. From there, we'd figure the rest out.

At dawn, when George failed to emerge and the effects of the acid started to wear off, I dragged myself back to our room on West 10th Street. As soon as I entered the building, the old hag on the first floor greeted me with a whack of her pipes that rattled even the rats. I tried to shrug the assault off, but the sound kept bouncing off the insides of my skull until I knocked on Miss Eden's door and begged her for a down. "Sure, baby," she said, handing me a Nembutal. "But only one. We don't want any more Judy's, now do we?"

Two days later, EMT's rushed her to St. Vincent's for another stomach pumping. From there, they sent her to Bellevue for what the queen who came for her feather boas described as a long overdue rest. "She just never got over it," she clucked. I looked at her blankly; there was so much. "Oh, you know, Miss Garland." I didn't bother asking if she'd meant her life or her death. To me, both had been wastes.

The next day, I learned from WBAI, New York's underground rock station, about an alleged massacre at a South Vietnamese village called My Lai. American soldiers were rumored to have gone in, slaughtered hundreds of unarmed peasants, including scores of women, children and old people, and then torched the village. True to form, the Pentagon dismissed the rumor as communist propaganda. Ever the liar, Nixon had weighed in by claiming we couldn't possibly be the culprits; our side only went after the guilty.

I'd stumbled across the report while turning the dial of the same Sony pocket transistor Electric Freddy had used to channel electrons from the universe on my first night in town. The queen who'd cleared out Miss Eden's room had told me to go ahead and take it; Bellevue didn't allow music. I didn't tell her neither did George.

22
The Brutality of Fact

We crossed 14th Street in Valerie's brand-new 1970 T-bird convertible, a gift from her father for graduating from Syracuse only a year late. On the drive through the Village, we'd figured that, if I ever re-enrolled, I'd be at least two years older than the rest of my classmates, a gulf Valerie thought too vast to bridge. "Better to stay dropped out," she'd advised. "Besides, you've gone too far out. You'll never fit back in."

We turned onto Park Avenue, passing Warhol's Factory on the left and Max's Kansas City on the right, and then, at the corner of 19th Street, faced the rising canyons of midtown Manhattan. I squinted through the smog and street steam and wondered what lay ahead. The last time I'd been uptown, I'd had to threaten to call Bellevue when one of George's clients had pulled out a revolver and suggested a game of Russian roulette. Back downtown, we'd found the drag queens in high dudgeon and the Stonewall under siege. It'd been more than six months.

"Isn't it outasight?" Valerie cried as two Black men stopped in the crosswalk to ogle her car. She gunned the engine for them and squealed with delight as they responded with power salutes and a loud *Oh baby*! When the light turned green, she floored it, leaving behind a trail of burnt rubber and a chorus of admiring "Right on's." At the next light, she pulled a joint of Acapulco Gold, as fat and stubby as her pinkie, from her glove compartment, dabbed the tip with the coils of her dashboard lighter and squealed, "Don't you just love blowing minds?"

I clenched my jaw and nervously played with a shirt button. After nine months of doing nothing but blowing my mind on speed, I was close to a collapse. To the northwest, the tall, gleaming needle of the Empire State Building rose gloriously into view. I thought of King Kong, swatting at attack planes, and cringed at what George would say if he saw me cruising up Park Avenue in a red Thunderbird convertible and smoking pot with someone as plastic as Valerie. Of all my friends, he detested her the most. "I don't want her around me ever again," he'd growled after just one encounter. "She's hideous, a complete fake."

I watched her puff greedily on her joint and sighed. What had bothered George most wasn't her shallowness or her need for attention or even her looks, although he had said he thought women that ugly should be gassed, an assertion he'd only doubled down on when I'd noted Valerie was Jewish. What had bothered him most were Valerie's limits. When George had offered her one of his shots of speed, she'd declined by noting the last time she'd used a needle she'd contracted hepatitis. "Besides, I only skin-popped. I'd never mainline."

That had been it. According to George, only uptight uptown types refused to shoot up. That Valerie lived in the Village only a few blocks away from us was irrelevant. For George, 'uptown' was a state of mind—as in "I'm too good for needles" or "my body is my temple" or even, as I'd once ventured, "love will get us through." 'Uptown' meant insipid sentimentality; 'downtown,' the brutality of fact.

I peered wistfully down 34th Street at the tour buses ringing the Empire State Building and confessed it was the closest I'd gotten since I'd been in New York. "George refuses to cross 14th Street." I paused to extinguish my Marlboro in the dashboard ashtray. "Except to sell drugs, of course. He says everyone who lives uptown is a creep and a phony."

"But that's crazy!" Valerie cried. "I mean, you can't cut yourself off like that. It's totally paranoid."

"But look around," I protested before pointing out all the men in suits and the women in skirts and ratted-out bouffants. "We're here, in the middle of it, the belly of the beast. It's everything we're supposed to be against."

"Here, smoke this and lighten up," she replied, handing me the joint. "Nobody talks like that anymore. The world is our oyster. Remember, this is the Woodstock Nation now."

I stared straight ahead and puffed anxiously on the joint. I'd spent the weekend of Woodstock holed up with George in our room on West 10th Street, shooting speed and relieving him of his gas pains. No, Altamont, the West Coast debacle where peace and love had finally curdled into freak-outs, overdoses, and gang violence, was the nation I belonged to.

"Besides, Gino lives uptown and nobody's cooler than him," Valerie said of the man we were on our way to visit. She cracked her window to let out some pot smoke and asked if I'd looked him up since I'd been in New York.

I shook my head and noted the last time I'd seen him was the acid trip we'd taken in Longwood Gardens. "Oh, wasn't that the best?" Valerie gushed. "Gino talked about it for months!"

"Yeah," I replied. "It was the first time I saw anyone shoot up."

"Really? You mean, I turned you on to that too? Far out!" Valerie cried and smiled proudly. "You've come so far."

As we crossed 42nd Street, I watched a hustler work a john in wingtips and a belted trench coat and felt a long tether of fear and shame snap deep inside me. Finally, I was far enough out of George's range to open up. "So has he ever been faithful?" Valerie asked after I told her about Danny. "Only at the beginning," I replied, glowering at the face of the Pan Am building staring down on us. "He claims he's just doing his own thing," I said when she asked why I put up with it. "You know, free love and all that."

"No, uh-huh, sorry," she sneered over the clanging of her Bakelite bracelets. "If Bill ever cheated on me, I'd kick him out so fast he wouldn't know what hit him."

I watched her steer her T-bird around Grand Central Station, the Pan Am building's majestic Beaux-Arts base, amazed at her ability to pick and choose which countercultural strictures to follow. With George, you were either all in or out the door—totally cool or one of the hordes of creeps, phonies, and prudes he'd have nothing to do with.

"I suppose it's the drugs, huh?" Valerie mused, turning back onto Park Avenue. "I mean you are, after all, an addict."

I stared up the tree-lined straightaway and shrugged. Everyone had a theory for why I'd stuck it out with George but me. Peter had blamed the attraction on an obsession with dick; John, a preponderance of water signs; Adrian, a weak aura; Norman, a broken wing; and Eugenie, Sal's Cambridge roommate, the allure of the Factory. Ever the romantic, Sal had simply chalked it up to love. I watched my hand tremble as I raised a cigarette to my dry, cracked lips. Whatever it was, I'd reached my limit. The struggle to bend George to my will was doing me in. I was a physical and emotional wreck.

Up ahead, the slender, blue-green tower of the Lever House, a soap maker's homage to openness and light, shimmered in the sun. Across from it, the Seagram building stood proud, an icon of virtuous living—all clean sight lines and crisp, sharp angles. Unlike my dark dingy hovel, no one ever gets lost in a building like that, I thought. No matter where you were, you could always see light.

Valerie cleared her throat and then grimacing fell silent.

"Yes?" I said, my stomach knotting. Valerie rarely hesitated for words.

"Bill and I are talking about getting married," she finally revealed.

"Married?" I gasped. "But that's so *straight*."

Valerie shrugged and confessed she needed a change. New York's scene was becoming a drag—not at all like the last time around, the glorious, freaked-out summer of '68 that she and Gino spent together in the East Village. In the year and a half since, the drugs had only gotten harder and the vibe more uptight. Worse, everywhere she went she got hit up for money. Panhandlers, she said, depressed her. The homeless, too. The other day, she'd seen a guy sleeping in a cardboard box. "He'd even pissed himself!" she shrieked.

I watched her light one of my Marlboros and quietly fumed. No matter how broke I was, Valerie regularly bummed cigarettes off me.

"Besides, my father says he'll buy me a house if we get hitched. You know, back in St. Louis." She assured me the pad would be groovy—with a trip room, a dance floor, and a pool in the back, way out in the suburbs.

"The suburbs?!" I cried. "But only squares live in places like that." Freaks like us, I contended, belonged in cities with the other rejects. "Like in the Village," I added, before noting we hadn't seen another long hair or drag queen since Union Square. "Not even a poofter walking his poodle," I grumbled.

"Now, see, there's your problem," Valerie chided. "People are people no matter where they are." She straightened her back and noted she'd never had a problem in the suburbs. "And I'm just as freaky as you."

"Yeah, but you're not gay," I grumbled.

"That's just a word you use to keep yourself apart—alienated," Valerie countered, spitting the last word out like Otto, the older gay man she'd coached on how to be cool until, freaked out by all the drugs, he'd kicked her and Bill out. Then, she repeated the refrain that she'd used since I'd come out to her: "No one cares what you do in bed."

I tried explaining that being gay was about more than just sex, but she insisted I was missing the point. "Look, you've done acid. You know all those boxes are there to just keep us apart, thinking one group's better than the next." Everyone, she professed, was the same.

"Still, I'd rather die than go back to the suburbs."

Valerie stopped at a light on 53rd Street and flicked on her turn signal. "I don't understand why you and Gino never got it on. I mean, you're both freaks." She chewed on a fingernail and then spit out a tiny sliver. "And, after all, he is bisexual."

I looked at her blankly.

"What, you didn't know?"

"No, how would I? Every time I saw Gino, he had a woman hanging all over him." I glared at her. Everything might've turned out differently had Gino and I balled. "Besides, you never said a word."

"Well, I didn't think it was important. Anyway, Gino didn't like it when people called themselves gay. He thought it was uncool."

"Yeah, that seems to be a New York thing," I sighed, looking out the car's passenger window. With Sal, Peter, and John gone, I was the only one left who called himself that. Miss Eden identified as a straight woman, while Holly simply called herself an illusionist. Adrian hated the word so much he claimed to be a werewolf, while George preferred either Pop or fag, although only if the latter was preceded by the word 'horrible.' 'Gay,' he said, referred only to "little people," like the cretins who'd laid siege to the Stonewall—the uncool, uptight ones he complained were ruining New York.

"And what about you?" I asked, hoping to change the subject. "Did you ever get it on with Gino?"

"Oh, God, no," Valerie replied, picking at a pimple on her chin. "I mean, a fat, pushy broad like me?" No, she said, Gino got off on her energy, not her body. After their first acid trip together, he'd admitted he'd never had so much fun with a woman. After their second, he'd wanted Valerie as his permanent trip-mate. "I drove all those Waspy model-types Gino used to ball crazy," she crowed. "None of them could take the drugs," she added before mimicking them, high on LSD: *Oh, Gino, I'm scared. Please don't leave me. Everything is melting.* She said the hardest part had been the laughter, the soul-rattling, everything-is-absurd convulsions the acid nearly always brought on. None of them could handle it. "It ruined their make-up," she sneered and shook her head. "I mean, can you imagine not being able to belly laugh?"

"Hmmm," I muttered, trying to recall the last time I had. Of all that I'd given up to be with George—music, a regular paycheck, my self-esteem, even, at times, my sanity—a good belly laugh was the one I perhaps missed the most.

Valerie pulled into a parking space across from the converted brick warehouse where Gino had his loft and confessed she was nervous. As she explained, she hadn't seen Gino since the four tripped-out months two summers ago when they'd ruled St. Mark's Place as its freakiest odd couple— she, a short, squat troll in jeans and a t-shirt and he, a tall, sleek fashion model in a spangly vest and velvet pants. When, burned-out on LSD, she'd announced she was returning to Syracuse, Gino had turned on her. College, he'd charged, was a cop-out; people like them, the cool ones, were supposed to live life, not study it.

"But I thought you said you left because you got hepatitis."

"That was just an excuse. It's not cool to say you can't keep up with the drugs." Valerie turned and looked at me plaintively. "I thought I was losing my mind."

I laughed when she asked if I knew what that felt like. "Obviously, you've never had one of George's shots," I mumbled. I watched my hand tremble and shook my head. After nine months of them, I shook so badly I could barely even light my own cigarette.

Valerie grimaced; by the time she'd left New York, she and Gino weren't even speaking. "I was surprised he even took my call to set this meeting up," she said, barely above a whisper. When I tried to assure her everything would be fine, she turned to me, her face streaked with panic. "You do know why I asked you along, don't you?"

I shook my head. I only knew I was glad to be out of my room, free from the grind of waiting for George to return.

"I need you for moral support," she said.

"*Me*?" I exclaimed, stunned she'd choose someone she'd twice caught stealing Obetrol from her medicine cabinet.

"Yes, you. Gino intimidates me. He always has. You're the only one I know who's on his level, who he'll respect."

"But he's hardly ever spoken to me. If he had something to say, he'd always say it through you." My face flushed. I was sure it had been because I was gay.

"Yes, but you were just a silly college kid then. Now, you're a freak, a real one. A speed freak." She opened her door, stepped into the street and explained that, by the time she'd left New York, speed was just about the only drug Gino did.

I asked if he'd been shooting it.

"Of course," she purred and smiled at me. "Isn't that what the coolest people do?"

I bounded out of Valerie's car and stared up at Gino's building, amazed at the sudden turn in my luck. If Gino and I hit it off, maybe he could keep me stocked in speed. Then, it wouldn't matter who George fucked or how long he stayed away. Finally, I'd be in control.

I stood outside the doorway to Gino's fifth-floor loft and waited while Valerie and her old friend embraced. Gino dropped his arms first, then Valerie turned and pointed at me. "Remember him?" she asked and then broke into loud, nervous giggles.

Gino glanced at me coolly. "Sure," he said, his long mop of dirty blond hair still wet from a shower, "he's the one from the trip in that garden. The one with all the fountains."

"Longwood. Longwood Gardens. It's an old DuPont estate," I replied, my face flushed.

Dressed in purple velvet pants, cream-colored Italian loafers, and a white Cossack shirt unbuttoned halfway to his waist, Gino was, if anything, even more glamorous than before. I looked at Valerie and waited for her to remind him of my name. "Dale," I finally said, following them into his loft.

"Yes, I remember," Gino murmured. "You lived in this fabulous house with a stream in the back."

"It was a tacky suburban Colonial," I protested, brushing the branch of an avocado tree out of my way.

"No, it was fabulous," he said and walked to a card table on which stood a tall two-reel tape player. He pointed at two Stickley-style chairs facing him and asked if we'd like to hear a piece he'd composed on the Moog synthesizer. "It's short, barely more than a minute." He pulled the tape from its box and, without waiting for a reply, threaded the end through the machine. "I just sold it," he said, smiling proudly. "It's gonna be the music for a TV ad Dow's doing." His smile broadened. "Dow Chemical."

"Oooh, the big guys," Valerie gushed, at which Gino flicked a switch and filled the room with a tune so treacly it made my teeth ache. Valerie, on the other hand, loved it and congratulated him on the sale. "I think it's great the suits are finally using heads like us to sell their stuff," she said. "Pretty soon, we'll be turning the whole world on."

I groaned and looked at Gino. "But Dow makes napalm. I mean, I've protested against it. Thousands have. People like us. Freaks."

Gino turned to Valerie and laughed. "I see he hasn't changed a bit, huh?"

"But don't you care how your work is used?" I persisted.

"No," he replied. "What matters is that people are finally taking notice. Someone the other day even called me a composer." He chuckled at the irony of it all. After two years of searching for inspiration through drugs, he'd finally found it after just six months of hard work. "I've never felt so turned on. I'm even making money."

"But aren't you worried about selling out?" Puzzled, I looked at Valerie. We were supposed to be throwing our lives away. "Refusing to cooperate," I called it.

Gino bristled. "That's just a guilt trip losers and deadheads use to keep people like us, people with talent"—he looked at Valerie, not at me—"stuck in the same nowhere place as them." After a summer of fashion shoots in Italy, he'd decided that what he called "luxe" was the new Cool. "All the fun people are rich," he said to Valerie, whose trust fund had fueled their summer of LSD.

Valerie reached for another one of my Marlboro's and giggled. "Yeah, I'm over the hippie thing, too. The poverty just got to be too much. A real drag." She leaned forward to accept Gino's offer of a light. "I mean, if you've got it, why not flaunt it, right?"

"Oh, God, I'd almost forgotten how fabulous you are," Gino murmured as he snapped shut the sterling silver cigarette lighter an admiring duchessa had given him. He sat back in his chair and shook his head. He couldn't believe the number of people who still hadn't forgiven him for leaving the East Village. "As if living around junkies is a privilege," he said in a voice too close to a whine for someone so cool. "After you left the city, they just took over. Nothing was sacred." He pointed to his Moog. "I even had to put that in storage."

Gino looked around him and smiled proudly; he finally felt safe. With the money he'd made composing Madison Avenue ditties, he'd found a loft in the lower Fifties only a few blocks from his old stomping grounds—the fabled Warhol Silver Factory where he'd starred in *Beauty #2*, Andy's sadistic assault on his drug-addled alter-ego, Edie Sedgwick. In a corner opposite me, he'd set up his Moog and started work on his magnum opus, the score for *Ciao Manhattan*, the countercultural epic his old co-star Edie hoped would catapult her into the big time.

I told him I'd heard a lot about the film. "The world's first above-ground underground flick," I said, repeating the buzz. I lit my own Marlboro and blew a thick cloud of smoke at the ceiling. "I hear things aren't going well. You know, a bit...." I smiled knowingly. "Out of control."

Gino rubbed his palm on the thigh of his purple velvet pants and acknowledged he wasn't sure either Edie or the film were going to make it. Everyone involved was doing drugs, especially Edie, whose post-Factory switch from speed to barbiturates made her too out of it for most of her scenes.

"Yeah," I interjected. "That's the problem with downs." I suggested someone intervene. "Like you. I mean, you're her friend, right?" I said brightly. "She probably just wants to know someone cares. You know, a cry for help, that sort of thing."

Gino sneered that I sounded like a social worker. "Besides, one never interferes in other people's trips," he intoned, citing Cool's cardinal rule.

"Even if they're standing on the ledge, threatening to jump?" I asked. I pointed to the bank of grimy windows behind me, five floors up from the street. "What if I bolted for them right now?"

Gino smiled wearily and nodded. "Even then."

After that, I just sat back in my chair and watched the shadows from his avocado tree dapple his tin-lined ceiling. More than a steady supply of speed or even a hit to tide me over until George returned, I wanted someone to tell me no, I'd gone too far; it was time to step back from the edge and stop.

Bored, Valerie quickly shifted the conversation back to herself. "I have a lover now," she announced, glancing shyly at Gino. "You'd probably find him a bore. He isn't flashy and he smokes way too much dope. But the sex is great. We do it practically every night." She laughed bawdily. "We've been living together for almost four months."

"Yeah, I just moved my first lover in," Gino replied, pulling a rumpled pack of Gauloises from his shirt pocket. "He's a student at Julliard," he said, staring at his lighter's flame.

"Oh, really," Valerie said, her voice trailing off. She furtively glanced at me. "A he..."

I sat up and smiled; finally, Gino and I had something in common. "I've been living with a lover for the past nine months." I looked him in the eye and smiled. "I think you may even know him."

"Oh?" he replied, arching a brow.

"Yes, from the Factory." I watched Gino's back stiffen; clearly, he hadn't taken me for quite that caliber of a fag. "He's the one they called Silver George, remember?"

Gino paused and scowled, first at the floor, then at me. "So, you're mainlining now, is that it?" he replied, his voice suddenly clipped and flat.

I flinched but nodded, certain he'd find that as fabulous as a summer of fashion shoots in Italy. After all, hadn't George said all the Beautiful People shot up?

"Yeah, he's gone hardcore now," Valerie interjected and pulled a joint from the pocket of her jeans jacket. "Pretty amazing when you think back, huh?" She lit the joint, took a toke and then handed it to Gino.

"Sorry," he said and pointed at his Moog. "But I still have work to do." He looked at her sadly and then at me, angrily. "After you leave, of course."

"Oh, I see," Valerie muttered, stubbing the joint out. Red-faced, she turned to me and said it was time to go.

"But I don't understand. I mean, we just got here."

Valerie shut me up with a brusque wave of her hand. "We've interrupted his work," she said stiffly.

While Valerie retreated to the bathroom, I followed Gino into a galley kitchen he also used as a dark room and asked if he had any speed. "I've been going through a bit of a dry spell," I explained.

Gino took a water glass from a shelf and opened the refrigerator door. "I stopped doing speed months ago," he said, snapping open a carton of orange juice. "I found that I couldn't work on it."

Stunned, I asked if it'd been hard to quit.

"No, not really. But then, I never mainlined." He gulped down the juice. "I have too much respect for my body for that," he added, setting the glass next to the sink. He asked me to roll up my sleeve and then examined my tracks in the harsh light of the refrigerator. "I'd be blacklisted if I ever showed up for a modeling gig with those," he said, shaking his head in disgust.

"Really? But I thought all the Beautiful People shot up," I stammered as the trembling in my hand shot up my arm and consumed first my shoulder and then my entire torso. I pointed to the orange juice and asked if I could have some too; my throat was parched. "Help yourself," Gino said and walked out, leaving the refrigerator door ajar. When I lifted the glass to my lips, I shook so badly I spilled the juice down the front of my shirt.

At the door, Gino gave Valerie a peck on the cheek but refused to even look at me. On the drive back downtown, she complained Gino was turning straight and doubted she'd ever see him again. "I mean, he wouldn't even take a hit off my joint. And what was all that shit about work, anyway?" Supported by her father, Valerie had never worked a day in her life.

"Hmmm," I murmured, "some moral support, huh?" Lighting a cigarette with her T-bird's lighter, I tried desperately to control my trembling. "I'm sorry I ruined your time together," I added, both hands grasping the lighter. "As soon as I mentioned George's name, Gino acted like I was poison."

"Just please, stop apologizing," she snarled before cursing the taxi driver who cut in front of her. "You're starting to sound like those chicks who used to hang all over Gino. Needy and uptight. Wimpy. A *crybaby*."

At the Empire State Building, I tried to redeem myself by pointing to a crowd of middle-class fatties pouring out of a Gray Line tour bus and announcing that someday I too was going to the tower's top. "I don't care how straight it is. Or tacky. Or how many people from New Jersey there are," I said, repeating George's litany of objections. "I'm going." I turned to Valerie. "I really am."

"Okay, okay, so go. Who's stopping you, anyway?" she cried, her voice dripping with contempt.

For the next three days, again alone in my room, Valerie's contempt ate away at me. While I tried to blame my misery on others—the hostility of my parents, the repressiveness of society, the relentlessness of George's infidelities—she was right; only I could make myself so pathetic. And so, one pre-dawn morning in January—just two weeks shy of my first anniversary in New York—I finally told myself I'd had enough, crawled out of bed, and hauled myself over to Adrian's, in whose cold-water flat I was sure George was holed up.

I found Adrian sitting in the bathtub in the middle of his kitchen, fully clothed and madly typing away on an old Underwood. As before, his hair was a crazed fright wig of red sparklers, his pallor, pale and ghostly, his pupils, swirling black holes. He immediately jumped up and tried to block my way but I'd have none of it.

I raised my arm and pointed a trembling finger at the door I was certain George was hiding behind. I glanced at the dimes I kept in the flaps of my Bass Weejuns and fought back a wave of nausea. It was either this or call my parents, a defeat to which not even George could drive me. "Get out of my way, Adrian. I know he's in there."

"But, darling, I haven't read you the latest installment of my play," he cried, waving a fistful of paper scraps at me. "The lesbian princess shoots up the vampire speed freaks with dildos filled with lye. They turn into a pack of werewolves who roam the countryside looking for the blood of virgin transsexuals." He shot me a yellow, nicotine-stained grin. "I gave a copy to Vaccaro yesterday. He promised it'll be the very next thing the Ridiculous does."

I glanced at the jumble of beakers and tubing he'd set up in the back of his kitchen to turn lead into gold and shuddered over how demented we'd become. Adrian had no more chance of getting John Vaccaro's Theater of the Ridiculous to stage his play than I did of getting George to say he loved me. "Some other time," I said, brushing him aside. "George and I have some business to discuss."

Just as I suspected, I found him in the next room sitting on a day bed, quietly stringing beads. He appeared to be alone, although, except for a pair of cotton briefs, he was naked, generally a sign he'd just finished fucking someone. On his left was a shoe box filled with feathers and beads, and on his right a half-full ashtray and the Altoid tin in which he kept his works. On the wall above him, a cuckoo clock ticked away, while beneath his feet, a dingy hooked rug gathered dust. In the far corner, under a window overlooking a garbage-strewn square, a radiator hissed.

He pulled a striped purple bead from the shoe box and pierced it with a needle. It slipped onto a leather strap dangling between his thighs and fell into place, the third in line. He looked across the room and smiled at me. His eyes sparkled and his dimples deepened. "Hey, babe," he cooed in his thickest North Carolina drawl, "how are you?"

"How do you think I am?" I snapped. "I have no drugs and I've done nothing but sleep for three days. I've smoked every cigarette butt and gone through all the loose change I could find. My nerves are shot. I shake constantly." I held out my right hand as proof but he wasn't interested. "Hmmm," he replied, searching his box for a bead. "I know it's in here somewhere."

"It's been over two weeks, George. You've never stayed away this long." I wiped the sweat from my brow with the back of my hand and shuddered. The room was stifling. "I can't keep this up. It's driving me mad."

George held a pale-yellow cat's eye up to the light. "Poor baby," he clucked.

My face flushed. "I need to know what's going on. You can fuck whoever you want. I just need to know if I still mean anything to you. Are we even living together? Should I toss your stuff onto the street?" I waited for a response but heard only the clock tick off the seconds. I persisted, "I think I'm entitled to a response, George."

He looked up from his bead work and glowered at me. "You're entitled to nothing. Got that? Nothing."

My knees buckled and I grabbed the back of the chair next to me for support. "It's Danny, isn't it?" I whimpered.

Still, George ignored me.

My fury rising, I pressed on. "You know, I've been wondering about something, George. Do you take Danny in your mouth when you make love? Or am I the only one you ignore?" I released my grip on the chair and rocked on the balls of my feet. "Just why is that, George?"

The cuckoo in the clock above him announced the hour with a series of sharp, bright chirps—6 a.m., the start of a brand-new day.

I counted backwards from one hundred. At eighty, I decided to try again. "Come on, George. I'm not leaving until I get some answers. Why is it all I ever get is a hand job?"

An eerie smile crossed his face as he looked up from his handiwork. "Because I'm not interested in cock, that's why."

"What?!" I cried. "So, you're straight, is that it?" I laughed derisively. "Trade, I suppose, eh?" I dug my nails into my palms and quietly seethed. I'd put up with too many lies to let him end it with one as demeaning as this. "Look at me," I demanded.

George glanced up from his string of beads and, for a moment, a flicker of fear crossed his face.

"Good," I said. "Now, I want you to say that one more time. Only this time I want you to look me straight in the eyes when you do."

"You heard me," he said, peering into the closet behind me.

I pivoted, convinced that Danny, Lynn, or whoever he'd been fucking was hiding there. For a moment, I even suspected Adrian. Seeing no one, I wheeled back around and stepped to within striking distance. "You know what, George? Everyone's warned me about you. Yes, everyone has talked about you behind your back. Sal said you were a death trip. John called you George Wrong. Peter told me to get away from you—a danger, that's what he said you were."

I stopped to catch my breath. My heart was pounding; my mouth had gone dry; and the room was starting to spin. "Even Gino, remember him from the Factory? Well, Valerie and I visited him the other day." I smiled as his face registered the news; I'd traced him all the way back to the beginning, to the origins of his myth. "Turns out he doesn't think too much of you either. He kicked us out as soon as I said we were lovers." I shook my head. "Yes, I was so foolish as to claim even that."

George grabbed the edge of the day bed and lowered his head as if readying to charge me.

"But you know what? They've given you too much credit." Months of George's abuse—the repeated sexual humiliations, the lies and overdoses, the relentless drive to isolate and control me, the abandonments, each longer than the one before—flashed in front of me. All of it, he'd argued, had been my fault, the price I paid for being either too willful and proud; too green and insecure; too uptight and guilt-ridden; too spoiled and bratty—the list went on and on, as endless as it was ever-changing. "You're no Horrible Fag, George. You're the most ordinary one around, a frightened homosexual," I spat. "A coward." I smiled as he hunkered down over a shoe box full of feathers and beads. A straight man, indeed.

"I may be uptight and judgmental. And my dreams may be middle-class." I turned and reached for the door. In the kitchen, Adrian banged away at his old

Underwood. "I may even be a virago. But I'm no coward. It's the one failure in life I'm too good for."

I opened the door. For the first time in months, I felt my full 5'11." "I'm too good for you, too, George," I growled and then did what only he'd ever done to me—I walked out on him.

"But, darling," Adrian called out as I bolted for the stairs, "you haven't let me read to you." I stopped halfway down, shouted back that I'd heard quite enough for one day and then stormed out into the garbage-strewn, rat-infested square outside his building. I even woke a junkie nodding out next to a pile of half-frozen lettuce.

As I raced down Hudson Street, dawn burst out of the side streets like flowers from a giant bouquet. I was two months behind on the rent; the corner bodega had cut off my credit; and my welfare check wasn't due for another six days. Yet, I was still proud of myself. Dignity had finally trumped drugs, dick, maybe even love. From a half-open window three stories up, Aretha greeted the new day, *Hello, sunshine, so glad to see you sunshine/It's been dark for a very long time...*

Two nights later, George crept onto the balcony of our room on West 10th Street and curled up next to me on the mattress we'd once called our summer retreat. Behind me, the wind whistled through a tear in the clear plastic sheet that, at the onset of winter, we'd nailed across the opening to keep warm. It was the last domestic chore we'd done together.

In the corner, against a whitewashed brick wall that, the day before, I'd banged my head against in a futile effort to stop thinking about him, the coils of a space heater glowed a lurid red. In the valley between my pillow and the balcony's other brick wall, the tiny jeweled light on the controls for the electric blanket my parents had given me as a college send-off flickered and clicked, its signal that the juice was flowing.

George nibbled on an earlobe. "I've missed you," he whispered.

I buried my face in the pillow and pushed back against him. That time, it wasn't a dream; he really had come back—hard, as hard as a rock. "I've missed you too," I quaked.

He reached under the blanket and played with the hair on the inside of my thighs. I returned the favor by reaching behind me and fondling him. He moaned slightly and then, as his fingers slipped between the cheeks of my ass, asked if he could fuck me. "It's been too long," he murmured, his voice thick, his breath heavy.

I rubbed the sleep from my eyes and stared at the brick wall in front of me. I'd promised myself there'd be no sex until we talked a few things through. The first needed to be the speed. I needed to cut back. Way back. The second was Danny. George and I needed to spend more time together. A lot more. The third was Andy, as in his avatar, Andy Warhol. I'd heard from Adrian he'd introduced Holly to him. I wanted to know I was at least as worthy.

I pulled myself away and sat up on the end of the mattress. "No," I said and trembled. It was the first time I'd ever refused him sex. I glanced down at my cock. It was also the first time in months I'd gotten hard.

George sat up next to me and nibbled on my neck. "Are you sure?"

"Yes," I said, wrapping myself in the top sheet. "Positive."

George stepped off the balcony and stood in front of the hand sink. He filled a water glass and opened the Altoid tin in which he kept his works. He looked at me through the mirror and smiled wistfully. "Will you at least join me in a shot?"

I listened to the wind whistling through the tear in the plastic and sighed. There was nothing George hated so much as the word 'no.' If I refused him twice, I knew he'd pack up and leave, probably for good.

The arc of water he shot to clean out his syringe splattered at my feet. I also knew my need for him was slowly driving me mad.

"Okay, but only a small one," I replied. I turned and looked through the plastic at the blurred outline of the trees in the courtyard. "I need to keep it together. In the morning, I'm looking for work."

"A job, eh?" George replied, sprinkling crystal into a spoon. "That's pretty drastic, don't you think?"

I shrugged. "It's better than sitting around here waiting for you."

"Ahh," he said, dissolving the crystal with a match. "I see."

"That's a small one, right?" I asked as he drew the shot up into his dropper. The sheet fell to my waist as I leaned into the doorway and caught his eye in the mirror. "Remember, I said I only want a small one."

George tasted a drop of my shot and nodded. His lips were full and his lashes, long and silky. "Sure, babe. It's whatever you say now, right?"

"No, that's not it," I replied, crossing my legs to hide my erection. "I just want some control too." I watched him slip the tin foil packet of speed into his hip pocket. "Is that so bad?"

George stepped onto the balcony and sat on the end of the mattress between me and the railing. He tied me off with the red, white, and blue necktie from my childhood and caressed the vein that rose to greet him. "You have good veins," he said, poking it like a cat with a mouse.

My arm tingled at his touch. I nestled my head in the crook of his neck and inhaled the heady mix of musk and baby powder that, for weeks, he'd denied me. I glanced down at his crotch and wondered if he was wearing the silk panties Lynn had given him that so perfectly outlined the head of his cock. My cheeks flushed and my mouth went dry. *Remember your promise*, a voice inside me cautioned, *no sex*.

He slipped the needle into my vein and loosened the scarf. I opened my fist. The heat in the room rose; the walls between us collapsed. *But he's come back*, I replied. *To me, not Danny, to me...*

From the corner of my eye, I noticed the thickness of the shot draining into me and knew that, once again, I'd been duped. "Stop!" I yelled, trying to jerk my arm away. "It's too big!" George tightened his grip and continued squeezing the dropper's rubber bulb. "That's enough, George!" I yelled, blood streaming down my arm. "I said I wanted something small..."

By the time he pulled the needle out of me, I was already hearing voices in the courtyard's trees. A scratching worked its way up inside a wall and the pot over the rat hole rattled and shook. A whooshing, like razor blades slashing the air, whistled in my ears and, in the doorway, monks in tunics with gray hoods chanted in a language I'd never heard.

"Coptic," George said without moving his lips.

"What?" I cried as he stood and unzipped his jeans. Terrified, I crawled into a ball and covered my face with my hands.

I heard the thud of shoes in the corner by the space heater. A belt buckle clanged against the balcony floor and then the sheet I'd wrapped myself in flew off me. Hands grabbed my feet and splayed me across the mattress. A mouth spit into the palm of a hand.

"No!" I shouted as George's prick pried open the clenched cheeks of my ass. I reached behind me and grabbed a fistful of hair. "I said no!" I screamed and pulled as hard as I could.

"Arghhh," George wailed and bit my hand.

I tried to bolt from the bed but George's shot had been too strong. My head was too heavy to even lift off the pillow.

"You little brat," George snarled, repositioning his cock in the crack of my ass. When he reached the bleeding hemorrhoids that surrounded my pucker, I stopped flailing and begged for mercy. "Please, George," I whimpered. "I promise I won't move. Just go into the other room and get the KY."

"Shut up," he replied. Then, in a single violent thrust, he rammed everything he had—a full eight inches, all the way up to his balls—into me.

I bit the pillow and howled out in pain. "*No-o-o-o-o-o!*"

"I said shut up," he barked and shoved my face into the brick wall. He twisted my arm and pressed it into the small of my back. His breath, rancid and oily, seared the down on my neck.

For once, George came quickly, without asking me to suck on his balls or calling me his little sex pig. "Uhhh," was all he grunted and then he collapsed next to me, one hand holding my body close, the other shoving my head away. A shudder welled up inside him and then he pulled his dick out of me like a stopper in a sink. "Oh, God, please, no!" I wailed as the stench of shit quickly filled the room. "Please, not that too…"

I dug my fingers into my eyes and prepared for the final insult—the verbal abuse George heaped on me every time my bum was dirty. *Just look at the mess you've made, you filthy little shit. Can't you do anything right?* But spent of his venom, he simply rose from the bed, slipped on his shoes, wiped his dick clean with the sheet and left without so much as a word. Terrified that too was a trick, I stayed curled up in a ball and listened as the effects of my overdose—the voices in the trees and the chanting in the doorway—slowly faded away.

At dawn, I crawled out of my ball and surveyed the damage from the night's carnage. A line of dried blood streaked down my left arm and a larger, darker stain marked the spot on the sheet where George had impaled me. A drop of dried cum matted the hair on the back of my left thigh and the room reeked of terror and shit. I'd even pissed the bed. Next to my pillow, a fistful of jet-black hair was the only sign I'd been more than just a victim. Before fear and pain had stripped me of my dignity, I'd fought back. If only for a moment, George had hurt too.

I wrapped myself in the filthy bedsheet and stumbled into the hall looking for someone to comfort me. But with Miss Eden in Bellevue and a straight man in Peter's old room, I had no one left to turn to. A full-time speed junkie and live-in lover of New York's most Horrible Fag, I'd become the building's persona non grata—a hippie faggot freak no one with an ounce of decency or a shred of self-respect dared get near. Even the building's only other gay, a second-floor NYU grad student who wore a peace sign on the lapel of his pea coat, refused to make eye contact with me.

I ended up in the second-floor bathroom where I sat on the john and shit out the remains of George's assault while listening to the rat scratch around the nest of wires surrounding a naked light bulb. For once, I wasn't afraid. I'd already done battle with a rat, the inner one the man I called my lover had let loose on me. There was nothing left to scare.

I stood and stared at the bloody glob of George's cum floating in the toilet bowl and wondered what words to use to describe what had transpired between us. Overdose, certainly—the chanting monks and the voices in the trees, not to mention my still-dilated pupils, were more than enough proof of that. And, yes, of course, assault, too—the scrape on my forehead from when George had shoved my face into the brick wall and the dried blood on my arm from when we'd struggled over his shot clearly showed that as well.

But what of rape? I wasn't even sure a word like that existed in gay life. After all, as my former friend, Donnie, had once said, no self-respecting gay man ever refused cock. Least of all, one as big and fat as George's. A "bloated flounder," Peter had once called it, although that night it felt more like a wrecking ball.

I reached for the flush cord and then hesitated. For a moment, I thought about bottling the bloody mess, a memento of my time with George, knowing there'd be no more. And then, catching a glimpse of my reflection in the hand sink mirror—I was ghostly pale and my eyes were sunken pits of despair—I pulled, certain the deadness inside me was more than memento enough. I wanted to cry but couldn't. I repeated the word no, just to make sure I still could, only to realize it too had been stripped of its meaning. I listened to the whoosh and gurgle of the toilet's flush and nodded. My long free fall was over. I'd finally hit rock bottom. Nothing was left but the hard, cold brutality of fact.

I tossed my sheet into the corner with the pots of dried and caked depilatory Miss Eden and Stephanie Lisa had left behind and walked naked into the hall. As I climbed the stairs, I stopped at the landing and recalled the headless goose that had chased me and the two kids next door into our Jeffersonville back alley. "Bodies can live off their own energy," their father had said of the fowl's terrifying stamina. "But only for a while. To survive, the head and the heart must be connected."

I'd been six, a sissy addicted to dancing 'The Dying Swan' in a frilly pink tutu. In two months, I'd be twenty-one, an out gay man addicted to shooting meth amphetamine with a lover who called himself a Horrible Fag. Trembling from head to toe, I looked up at the door to the room I shared with that man. In the span of only nine months, George had done what a host of haters—a score of high school bullies, my parents, a shrink, the cops, the Mafia, the draft board—had tried but failed to do. He'd severed my head from my heart. I hated what I'd become. I wished I was anything but gay.

I frantically rooted through my things for my parents' phone number. I knew it was somewhere. My mother had sent it as soon as they'd settled into their new home somewhere out in the Midwest. What was the name of the town? It began with Dan. Dan-something.

Ahhh, there the letter is, tucked inside George's book on black magic. Strange, I thought, before examining its postmark. Yes, that's it, Danville—Danville, Illinois. Another Midwestern hellhole, I'd thought at the time. A lot had happened since then.

My mother accepted the charges for my call and instantly started to whimper. I told her to stop. For once, she needed to just listen. I wanted to come home. Yes, for good. She broke into sobs and asked if I needed cash. I told her no; just send me a one-way ticket to the airport nearest to them. I no longer trusted myself. I just wanted to get out of New York.

An hour before I left for the airport, George responded to the message I'd left with Adrian and showed up to say goodbye. As a send-off, he gave me a shot so big the room darkened. For once, though, it didn't matter. I was no longer his prisoner. He handed me a plastic baggie of uppers and a handful of reds and said they were the best he could do; New York was completely dry. He asked for my parents' phone number and promised he'd call. He leaned over and whispered, "I want you back. I need you."

I didn't dare ask what for. Instead, I rose from the bed and, careful not to brush up against him, dragged my suitcase to the door.

"You know, I really do love you," he murmured, smiling shyly. He acknowledged he didn't often act like it, but he wanted me to know it was true and repeated his desire that we get back together. "After you rest up and regain your strength. Spend some time with your folks."

"But I thought you hated them."

He shrugged and said he was sorry he gave that impression. "I don't know, maybe I'm jealous of what you have." He looked down at his feet. "That, you know, you have someone to turn to."

I knew better than to wrap him in my arms and beg him to let me help; as our previous encounter had revealed, love had little, if anything, to do with getting through things. Instead, I merely confessed I dreaded what lay ahead. "Trapped with my parents in a place like Danville, Illinois." I tried to control my rising panic. "In the middle of the Corn Belt." I confessed I was thinking about calling the trip off. As I noted, at least in the Village, I could be gay.

George encouraged me to stick to my plans. I was, he said, stronger than I gave myself credit for. Besides, he promised he'd be calling soon. "Within a week or two," he said. Then he again said he loved me.

I opened the door and, staring numbly into the hall, waited for my knees to gel. After trying every trick in the book, it turned out all I needed to do to get him to say those words was threaten to leave him. I turned and smiled warily. "See ya," I muttered.

He nodded and patted the pocket into which he'd slipped my parents' number. "I'll call. I promise."

As I closed the door behind me, the note I'd scrawled across it in a futile effort to make George jealous rebuked me. *D: Sorry I missed you. Been thinking about you. Stop by sometime. Soon. Love, G.* The G was for the man John had called George Right, the dealer who'd taken too much of his own speed and had to flee back to Texas. The one I'd fallen for instead was George Wrong, the dealer for whom there never was too much and who had nowhere to flee, except, of course, to the North Carolina cemetery where a headstone, courtesy of the parents who'd disowned him, noted his dates, 1944 to 1962, the latter being the year his father had found him in bed with the maid's son. I looked at the landing a half-flight down and reminded myself all I needed to do was put one foot in front of the other. Before I knew it, I'd be gone.

I lingered outside the taxi waiting to take me to the airport and took one last look at the building's crumbling façade. Except for three months on Avenue D, it had been my only New York address, the eye of a small storm that, one hot night in late June, collided with a thousand others outside a drug-infested, Mafia-run dive called the Stonewall. Batting his eyes and whirling his Gauloises, Adrian had once said of the building: "Pee-tah, whut-t-t ah dump-p-p," a Horrible Fag imitating an ordinary one imitating a drag queen imitating a movie star imitating real people starved for dreams. George had been the only one who hadn't laughed. He didn't traffic in dreams, just the brutality of fact.

I gazed down West 10th Street toward the docks. There, every night around 2 a.m., hordes of men, far too many to be contained in the backs of the trucks they'd once trolled, spilled into the streets to cruise for furtive, anonymous sex. Only George had thought it a step backward. "How can they fall in love if they don't know who they're fucking?" he'd once asked. At the time, I'd thought it a quaint, almost charming objection—proof that the romantic he claimed his inner rat had killed off struggled on somewhere deep inside him.

Once again, I'd given George too much credit. Love between men was a fact too brutal for even someone like him. I worried it was for all of us. To each other, we were all horrible fags.

"Cam on, de meter's runnin'," the cabbie barked. "Ya wanna miss your plane?"

Mumbling a lie, I told him no, it was just that, for a moment, I thought I'd left something behind. As I settled into the taxi's backseat, I glanced once more at the building and then told him to step on it. "Let's split this flat tire," I grumbled, the same farewell I gave Syracuse right before Trudy hit the gas pedal for my flight to New York, almost exactly one year ago.

On our way to La Guardia, the cab's radio played Donovan's "Lalena," Holly's favorite song. I smiled as I recalled Adrian's story of how, a few weeks earlier, she'd taken his advice and, in preparation for the big break Warhol had promised her, adopted the name of a Bronx cemetery. As he'd noted, Woodlawn would look so much better on a movie marquee than whatever her real surname was. Like everything else about her—her address, the age of her boyfriend, the play she was always on the verge of landing a part in, her lip color, her feather boa, her fondness for speed—it always seemed to be changing.

I watched the cars whizz by and marveled at the resolve of the drag queens I'd met during my time in New York: Miss Barbara Eden; her roommate, Stephanie Lisa; and, of course, Holly Woodlawn, the most ambitious of them all. No fact was too brutal for a drag queen—least of all their gender, supposedly the most immutable of all, or society's hatred, certainly the most debilitating. Unlike nearly every gay man I'd met, they stuck together and, when confronted—as Stonewall had so gloriously shown—fought back. "Sisters," they even called each other, although sometimes, mostly after standing down a particularly contemptible adversary, they added "fierce" for emphasis. Sisters *fierce*!

Approaching the airport, I slid onto my lap the suitcase in which I'd packed my syringe and George's baggie of pills—just enough, he'd said, to tide me over until he called. I watched my hand tremble from the shot of speed George had given me and wondered if he really would call—and, more importantly, if he did, what I would say in response to his request that I rejoin him. I knew that would be a disaster, but I'd long ago given up believing that would keep me away. As Peter had said after delivering George's first invitation to a tryst, "You'll go, of course." Why? Because, like Peter, I wanted to be turned inside out. And, as he'd so astutely noted, nobody did that better than George. George Wrong, a contender for the title of the most Horrible Fag in all of New York.

Peter had been correct, of course; I'd hooked up with George because I had indeed wanted to be remade. But what he'd failed to note was that I also wanted to turn the world inside out. As that drag queen had bellowed at the start of the first night's melee outside the Stonewall—"Come on, you faggots, let's riot!"— I wanted to bring the whole motherfucking mess down and start over.

If I ever did go back to George, I knew only one thing for certain: it would not be as his boy or, God forbid, his sex pig. It would be as something fiercer by far than a Horrible Fag, something never before seen—an in-your-face, upfront gay militant. Like those two men George and I had seen on their way to the subway on the second night of the Stonewall riots, we too would walk down the street holding hands. Gay was no longer gonna be bad. It was gonna be good, goddamnit, *good*.

23
Dick Van Dyke Likes It

My parents met me at the Indianapolis airport and knew instantly from the dark shades that I was high. As my father had sneered upon greeting me, the sun had set hours ago; what, exactly, was I hiding from? The college football team that heckled me on our way out to the car only added to our tension, although it was the cockroach that crawled out of my suitcase as my father loaded it into the Oldsmobile's trunk that sent my mother over the edge. "I swear, if you bring anything like that into our home," she seethed. "I don't know what I'll do." Her face was red, and her tiny hands were curled into two tight fists. "I just don't..."

I didn't dare mention the syringe or the pills, a going-away gift from my male lover that I'd also packed away, although I suspected my presence was more than enough to foul their nest. The prodigal son or, as the football guys had preferred, their "he, she, it, or whatever the fuck" I was, had returned from his Greenwich Village sabbatical a strung-out, in-your-face, hippie faggot freak. "God's country," as my parents called the Midwest, was no more ready for me than I was for it.

During the two-hour drive to Danville, they both started in on me. My mother complained about the length of my hair and my weight loss, while my father grumbled about my clothes and how people "out here" didn't go for "that type." Huddled in the backseat, I caressed my needle tracks and wondered which type he meant. Fag and freak were so intertwined I no longer knew where one started and the other stopped.

The next day, my mother lent me her Olds, and told me to drive around town to get my bearings. She suggested I start with the K-Mart out on Route 136 where she said there were lots of job openings but I headed instead for downtown where I wandered a deserted pedestrian mall bedecked with Christmas wreaths and looked in vain for something familiar: a gay bar, a drug den, a cruisy corner, a hip boutique, a drag queen, a bookstore, a record shop, a movie theater, even a drunk passed out on a bench. Desperate, I ducked into a corner drugstore where, determined to prove I was, as George had claimed, stronger than I gave myself credit for, I slipped a bottle of Vitabath under my pea coat and wandered the aisles, mouthing to the gaping customers I passed a silent "fuck you."

I must've made an impression because, on my way out, a security guard nabbed me, had me hand over the Vitabath, and escorted me to a windowless back room where he held me until the cops arrived. When my father came to bail me out of jail, he glared at his wingtips as the cops snickered about the long-haired hippie faggot freak they'd caught, their first in them-there-parts. I tried my best to keep it together but even the two Dexedrine I'd popped to keep the crash from George's shot at bay didn't steel me to the look of humiliation on my father's face. I burst into tears and, right there in front of everyone, cried like a baby.

On the drive back to Denvale, the suburban tract next to the Danville Country Club where my parents had purchased a two-story Colonial, my father didn't say a word—although my mother more than made up for his silence. Cornering me in the family room of their new suburban box, she hissed I'd really done it this time; a reporter from the local newspaper had already called asking for a comment. The next morning, everyone in town would know their son was a criminal.

"And we just moved here!" she shrieked before claiming she'd never again be able to look the neighbors in the eye. She first tore at her hair and then raised her hand to slap me. "And for what? *Bubble bath*?!" Her eyes narrowed as she stepped in closer, but she at least dropped her hand, knowing, I suspected, that if she hit me, I'd be out the door and on my way back to George in a heartbeat. "I bet that warped mind of yours thinks this is all funny, huh? Showing us Midwestern hicks what a big city slicker you are?" Her face reddened. "A real cool cat, huh?"

I offered an apology but, in high dudgeon, she refused to accept it. Instead, she informed me that, from that point on, she was taking charge of my life. I steeled myself for the appointment she'd made with the latest shrink who'd promised her a cure but, at least that time, she knew what not to do. That would've sent me back to George too. College, she informed me, was where I'd be heading next and she knew just the right one—Indiana University, the bucolic Hoosier godsend that had transformed my father from a bathtub-gin-swilling, Charleston-dancing dandy into a God-fearing pillar of his community: a church deacon, Rotarian and loyal company man. At that point, my father chimed in and brought up his old fraternity, Kappa Sigma, whose rush I'd rebuffed when I first arrived at Syracuse. "Why, if you play your cards right, they might even call you Mitch too," he murmured, smiling proudly.

I looked at him and wanted to burst out laughing—I was as far from a Mitch as he was a Miss Eden—but instead, I turned and walked to a sliding glass door that opened onto a windswept, snow-packed patio. Beyond was my new prison yard, a flat suburban expanse of winter-killed crabgrass, edged in tightly clipped yews and enclosed with a fence whose wide horizontal planks were painted a blinding white. In the far corner, where my parents' property line met that of three neighbors—like them, all white Anglo-Saxon Protestants and members in good-standing of the Danville Country Club—they'd buried the family dog, Jeff. Behind the small mound that marked his grave was the yard's only tree, a thin, cankerous dogwood that looked too weak to have even formed buds.

I tugged on the slider's handle, but it refused to budge. "What about Syracuse?" I asked, my panic rising. "I at least know people there." That they were all denizens of a Mafia-run dive called the Continental Room was beside the point. They were at least gay. At Indiana University, located in another Midwestern hellhole smaller and even more isolated than Danville, I was sure I'd be the only one.

"*What*?! And start this horror show all over again?" my mother shrieked. "Absolutely not." She turned to my father who, drawing her in close, nodded solemnly. "Those people have done quite enough to this family," he intoned. "You're safe now, here with us. We'll have no more talk of the East Coast in this house."

After that, I begged off the dinner my mother had said I'd already ruined and retreated to the room at the top of the stairs that, the night before, she'd insisted on calling mine. As proof, she'd pointed out the print of *Christina's World* above the bed and, to the right of a window that looked out over the expanse I likened to a prison yard, the charcoal portrait of me done on a car trip to Cape Cod. Under it was the bookcase in which I'd kept my most prized childhood mementoes, although, other than my three high school yearbooks and a tattered Boy Scout manual, all my books had disappeared. "The movers," my mother had clucked when I'd asked about them. "It was a disaster. You should've seen what they did to the dining room chairs." Gone were the ones that had stoked the start of my teenage rebellion: Tolstoy's *Anna Karenina*, Golding's *Lord of the Flies*, Sontag's *Against Interpretation*, Sinclair Lewis' *Babbitt*, Dreiser's *Sister Carrie*, D.H. Lawrence's *Sons and Lovers*, Isherwood's *A Single Man*, John Barth's *Giles Goat-Boy*, Fanon's *Black Skin, White Masks*, and my two teenage sex manuals: Hubert Selby's lurid tale of life on the edge, *Last Exit to Brooklyn*, and John Rechy's overtly gay, *City of Night*. Even Dr. Spock's *Baby and Child Care*, a tome I repeatedly turned to for its no-nonsense approach to childhood sexual development, had gone missing.

Oddly, my mother's dog-eared copy of Norman Vincent Peale's *The Power of Positive Thinking* was on the bedside table, under the clock radio she'd made a point of noting I'd need once I found a job. Even more strangely, next to it, staring straight at the bed, was the white ceramic troll I'd picked up on the Jersey shore the same summer I'd tried to steal my first kiss from a boy. I'd gotten caught then too. "Faggot," the boy had spat before shoving me into the sand and running off.

I reached under the bed, pulled out the bag of pills I'd taped to the bottom of the box springs and popped a red. What the hell, I thought, my parents could send me wherever they wanted; I still had my syringe. Besides, I could find drugs anywhere—even at a nowhere place like Indiana University. Probably even Danville, too. I smiled knowingly. As George had said, everybody was a junkie for something. Even upright, God-fearing, flag-waving Corn Belters.

I walked to the sales counter and handed the cashier my purchase, a 1940s sleeveless golf sweater with a large green snowflake on the chest. "I found it in the sale pile," I said, pointing at a handwritten sign on a library table that nearly ran the length of the store. I handed her two quarters and smiled. After four days of scouring Danville's half-dozen thrift stores, I'd finally found something worthy of the meager remains of my last welfare check. "Sorry for the mess," I said. "But it was way down at the bottom."

"Yeah, not too much demand for this old stuff," the cashier replied, folding my sweater. She was dark-skinned and razor-thin, with a processed do and a gold cross dangling from her neck. "Most guys come in lookin' for somethin' a little more practical." She pointed at the rack of drab brown and beige clothing at the back of the store, above which a sign in stocky black letters read "MEN'S." "You know, dress pants and sports coats, stuff they need for job interviews." She glanced at my ponytail. "You got a job?"

I shook my head. "No, I haven't worked in a while."

She looked at me warily. "You're not from around here, are you?"

"No," I replied. My smile widened. "I'm from New York."

She nodded. "Not too many people around here look like you."

"So I noticed," I said and sighed. I glanced at the dress on the mannequin in the window, a strapless purple sequin number with red marabou trim, and heaved a sigh of relief. Except for the house museum where Lincoln had spent his last night in Illinois, I'd been stared and pointed at everywhere I'd turned in Danville. "Mommy, is that a man or a woman?" a freckled girl in pigtails had asked in the last thrift store I'd visited, a church-run bungalow with a gravel parking lot on the white side of town. "Both," I'd snarled before storming out.

"Last summer, we had a few like you stop in," the cashier informed me. "They said they were heading for that music festival they threw out your way."

"You mean, Woodstock?"

"Yeah, that's it," she said. "We saw some of it on TV. Looked pretty wild." She shook her head. "Gotta say, I don't approve of nudity and all that other stuff." She again looked warily at me. "You go?"

I grimaced, as I recalled George's elation over the exodus that had emptied the Village of its hippies. "Finally, no more people flashing us peace signs," he'd crowed at the start of the festival. The rest of that weekend, I'd spent holed up on West 10th Street, shooting speed and relieving George of his gas pains. I hadn't laughed or listened to music once. "Nope, missed that one," I said.

"So, where you heading?"

"Nowhere," I replied. "I'm staying here, with my parents."

"Oh, yeah? Whereabouts?"

"Out on Denvale Avenue. You know, on the other side of Lake Vermillion, up by the country club." I grimaced slightly, hoping she wouldn't think less of me. As I was sure she knew, there wasn't a Black household within miles of my parents.

"Oh sure, my sister cleans one of the houses up there. For nice people. The Buchanans. You know 'em?"

"Yeah, we've met," I groaned. The Buchanans were part of the country club set my parents partied with nearly every weekend. The minute they'd met me, they'd made it clear they disapproved. Mr. Buchanan had even refused to shake my hand, an affront my father, who carpooled with him to the ordnance works DuPont ran across the Indiana state line, blamed on me. "What do you expect, looking the way you do?" he'd sneered.

I turned and looked across the street at the two bulldozed blocks my mother said had once been Danville's tiny but raucous, mostly Black Skid Row. She'd said before the city had sent in the wrecking ball it'd even been the site of some trouble during what she called "all that mess" around Martin Luther King's assassination. "I don't know why you don't check out the new K-Mart," she'd said of the suburban box store with four acres of free parking out on Route 136. "It's done wonders for Danville. Besides, nobody goes downtown anymore except for the coloreds."

"Blacks," I'd replied between clenched teeth. "They call themselves Blacks now, Mother."

"Okay, Blacks," she'd continued, lighting a Virginia Slims with the Florentine cigarette lighter I'd gotten for her on my 10th grade Latin class tour of Italy. "I still don't know why you go downtown."

"Because it's the only place I can find anyone who's different," I'd replied. Although I'd found a few winos and even a crowd of scrawny, pimply-faced glue-sniffers, I hadn't found a single freak or gay person. I'd even started to worry I was the only one.

The cashier dropped my two quarters into the register and rang up the sale. "Excuse me for askin'," she said, "but I bet you come from a good family. Just like the Buchanans, right?"

My smile curdled into a grimace. "What do you mean by good?"

"I mean your father's got a good job and your mother gets to stay home and cook." She pointed at the Oldsmobile 88 coupe I'd parked outside the store. "I bet that's even her car you drove up in."

I blushed. I'd wanted my father's Corvair but it'd been his week for the carpool.

The cashier shook her head. "A lot of the folk who come in here'd give their eye-teeth to be drivin' a car like that." Her eyes narrowed. "And you say you don't even have a job?"

I glanced at the clock on the wall behind her; there was no time to argue or explain. In half an hour, my mother needed the car to dash off to her bridge club. After that, she had a meeting of her PEO chapter, a Christian charity that offered scholarships to girls who needed financial help getting into college. When I'd asked if they'd ever helped a Black girl, my mother had evaded the question by saying she didn't think any had ever applied. "Can't help those who don't want it," she'd breezily added.

"Yeah, I guess they're okay," I replied to the cashier's question. "You know, comfortable," I said, hoping to end the discussion there.

Refusing to cooperate, the cashier pointed at my hair. "They like the way you look?"

"No, not particularly."

She leaned across the counter. "So, tell me, why on God's good earth do you go breaking their hearts by parading around in stuff that makes you look, well…" She pulled my sweater out of the used Kroger's bag she'd dropped it into and held it up for the two women at the dress rack next to her to inspect.

"Peter Pan," a large buxom woman in a Kente cloth turban replied.

"Uh hum," a darker woman still in the white robe she'd worn to church choir practice dismissively murmured. "A fruit."

I grabbed the sweater from the cashier, dropped it back into the Kroger's bag and walked to the door. "No, I don't think so," I said in response to her query about a receipt. "There's no way I'll be returning it." I felt my heart race. "It's for my lover. His name is George."

As I climbed into my mother's Olds, the cashier stood at the shop's plate glass window, shaking her head at me. I watched the tightly processed wave she'd molded her hair into glisten in the sun—a long, stringy "S" that repeated itself multiple times as it rounded her head. "At least I'm not trying to be someone I'm not," I grumbled before whipping the car out of its parking space. In Danville, Afros were as hard to find as homos. I'd been in town over a week and hadn't seen one of them either.

The next morning, I followed my mother's advice and visited the new K-Mart out on route 136 to see what, if anything, I had in common with the people she insisted on calling my "own kind." As soon as I arrived, the store manager started tailing me, even though, as I informed him on my way out, his store had nothing I wanted to buy, let alone steal. The so-called "book department" consisted of a cardboard display box of Jacqueline Susann's latest potboiler, *The Love Machine*, while the record department's "rock and roll" section was stocked with dreck from the likes of Tom Jones and B.J. Thomas, whose "Raindrops Keep Fallin' on My Head" had made Danville radio unlistenable. Although the "soul" section had the latest from Smokey Robinson, Marvin Gaye, Aretha Franklin, and James Brown, I knew better than to purchase any of it. The only Black singers my parents tolerated were Nat King Cole and Ray Charles. The others, they complained, were too "course," by which they meant too sexual, although my mother took a particular dislike to James Brown, whose "Say It Loud: I'm Black and I'm Proud" was the only 45 she'd ever said made her want to vomit.

"Never heard of 'em," the gum-chewing, peroxided blonde behind the record counter replied when I asked about the Velvet Underground.

I persisted. "What about the Beatles, ever heard of them?"

She nodded and said, of course, but informed me that K-Mart had removed their records from its shelves the day after the Manson murders. "One of their songs supposedly drove 'em to it," she said, jabbing the sharpened end of a No. 2 pencil through her beehive. "I can't remember the name, but it was the Beatles all right."

"You mean "Helter Skelter?""

"Yeah, that's it." She gazed dreamily into the center of K-Mart's fluorescent-lit cinder block box. "It's too bad. I used to really like the Beatles. You know, 'I Wanna Hold Your Hand' and stuff like that." Her face darkened as she examined me more carefully. "You look kinda like those Manson kids. You don't by any chance know 'em, do ya?" When I assured her that I had no connections to any of them, she glanced nervously at the store manager, who stood off to the side observing my every move. "That's good cuz Danville's a nice, quiet town. We raise our children right here."

"Hmmm," I murmured, fighting an urge to start hurling things.

I arose from my third nap of the day, dragged myself down the stairs and collapsed onto the family room's Naugahyde sectional. Above me, a brass lamp shaped like a flying saucer was suspended from the ceiling by a frayed nylon cord. Across from me, a framed photo of the family my mother alleged I'd ruined rebuked me for my folly. To my right, a pale-blue princess phone mutely taunted my vanity. I'd thought I'd be in Danville at most a week. After three weeks, I still had not heard from George.

I held out my right hand and watched it tremble. Although I'd managed to stay away from the pills, it still shook like I'd seen a ghost. I rested my feet on a spindly ottoman upholstered in the same cream-colored Naugahyde as the sectional and fished through the stack of magazines my mother had neatly fanned across a Parson's table stained to look like walnut. Pulling out the *TV Guide*, I perused the evening's offering—*The Brady Bunch* at 7 and *Bonanza* at 9—and groaned. *Saturday Night at the Movies*, my only salvation, was still three nights away.

"For heaven's sake," my mother grumbled from the recliner at the far end of the room, "what's the matter? You act like you've lost your very last friend."

"I'm bored," I replied, using the only word left me. Earlier that day, when I'd tried to talk out New York's lingering pull, she'd instantly shut me up. "I don't want to hear a word about it. You're with us now. It's time to put all that sordidness behind you." I tossed the *TV Guide* back onto the Parson's table and sighed. "There's no one to talk to in this town."

"I don't know why you'd say something like that," my mother chided. "There's a very good-looking crowd of kids who go to the country club. And the church youth group is always up to something." She took off her reading glasses, the ones with rhinestones in the corners, and smiled. "Your father and I are having the time of our lives here in Danville."

I picked up the latest issue of *Life* and grimaced. On the cover was Robert Redford, the star of the "New Hollywood" hit, *Butch Cassidy and the Sundance Kid*, whose blue-eyed wholesomeness only made me miss George's dark-eyed sleaziness that much more. "Guess that means I'm not like you, huh?" I countered.

My mother dropped the *Saturday Evening Post* she'd been reading into her lap. "Well, if you cut your hair, people might warm up to you more."

"Mother," I groaned, noisily leafing through *Life*.

"Why don't you just let me trim it?" she persisted. "I promise I'll only take off an inch. Your ends are split. It's unbecoming."

"I know," I murmured, stopping at an article on the Black Panthers. On the facing page was a large photo of a young man in tattered pants crouching by an open window. On the look-out for the cops, he held in his hands a gun, which the caption noted was "trigger ready." I looked at my mother and smiled sweetly. "I want to be unbecoming."

"Oh, you can't possibly mean that," she clucked.

I quickly scanned an accompanying interview with Eldridge Cleaver, the Panther leader-in-exile who *Life* had dubbed "Papa Rage." Next to it was a full-page photo of him with his wife, Kathleen, a tall, steely-eyed beauty with the biggest, baddest Afro I'd ever seen. The perfect blend of rage and glamour, she was everything I wanted to be but had failed to pull off. "I most certainly do, Mother," I muttered.

"Well, you certainly weren't brought up to think like that," she snipped. "Your father and I take great pride in the way we look."

Across the top of the next two pages were mug shots of the nineteen Panthers whose murder the police—like the rioters outside the Stonewall, the Panthers called cops "pigs"—had deemed "justifiable homicides." Of them, the youngest, Bobby Sutton, had been only seventeen. The most recent, Fred Hampton and Mark Clark, had been killed in their sleep on Chicago's South Side, only a few hours north of Danville. Like the unfolding news of the slaughter of scores of Vietnamese peasants at My Lai or the persistence of my own homosexuality, their murders had not warranted even a mention by my parents. "Appearances aren't everything, you know, Mother."

"And neither is ugliness, young man," she retorted, snapping the recliner into its upright position. She stood, glanced at the clock atop the TV console and headed for the kitchen. As she noted, my father would be home soon—it was time to get what she called a "head start" on dinner.

A few minutes later, she returned and stood in front of the glass sliders onto the backyard patio. She'd donned a blue apron and, in her right hand, she held a vodka and water. "Dick Van Dyke likes it," she said.

Confused, I dropped the magazine into my lap and looked at her. "Likes what?"

My mother's chin quivered. "And Jerry too."

"Jerry?"

She nodded and took a sip of her drink.

"You mean from *My Mother the Car*?"

"Why, yes, of course," she replied. "Who do you think I meant, Jerry Lewis?"

I removed my feet from the ottoman and placed them firmly on the carpet. "Okay, Mother, I give up. What are we talking about?"

"They both grew up in Danville, that's what. And they come back every chance they get. They love it here." Her eyes welled up. "Their family is here."

I listened to the wind whistle through the family room chimney and thought about the pills George had given me, still in their plastic baggie and taped to the bottom of my bedroom's box springs. All I needed was one to get me through this. Or, okay, maybe two.

"Mother, this is not a TV show."

She pulled a crumpled Kleenex from her apron pocket and blew her nose. "I thought you liked Dick Van Dyke." The ice cubes in her glass tinkled softly. "You used to laugh so when you watched his show."

"But that was years ago!" I grabbed a strand of my hair and pulled it in front of my face. It was finally long enough to chew on. "Look at me, for God's sake." For a moment, I even considered dragging her upstairs and popping my pills by the handful, right in front of her. "Do I look like someone who has anything in common with Dick Van Dyke?"

"But you used to be so happy," she whimpered. She took another sip of her vodka and water. "I just want you to be happy again."

I watched her dab her eyes and sighed. 'Happy' was, along with 'clean-cut' and 'well-mannered,' code for being straight. "I'm sorry, Mother," I said, knowing just how impossible that was.

While she resumed her dinner preparations, I returned to *Life* and its article on the Black Panthers. In its last photo, five men in leather jackets sat around a table in a spare storefront and stared warily into the camera. The caption quoted their leader, David Hilliard, as saying, "After four hundred years of struggle and death, revolution is the only thing left."

Two beams of light washed across the room as my father's Corvair turned into the driveway, home from another day at the DuPont explosives plant where he helped make bombs for the war in Vietnam. While I'd seen gay men stick needles into their arms and blow their brains out on drugs—I'd even known a few who'd grown tits and threatened to have their dicks cut off—I'd never known one to call himself a revolutionary. I recalled the two nights of rioting outside the Stonewall and slumped deeper into the sectional. What at first had seemed like a breakthrough had turned out to be little more than a fluke. Within a week, Village gays had gone back to business as usual: getting high, cruising for sex, and keeping up with the latest fashion trends. If there'd been talk of revolution, I certainly hadn't heard it. As with 'rape' and possibly 'wrong,' I wasn't even sure the word existed in gay life. "Boring," Peter had called it. Gino too.

I tossed the magazine aside and, yawning, felt another nap coming on. While the Panthers at least had revolution to fall back on, all I had left was sleep.

Two days later, after the trembling in my hand worsened, I asked to borrow my mother's Olds to check out Champaign-Urbana, the twin cities an hour west of Danville, where the University of Illinois's main campus was located. I desperately needed to be around people like me and other than Indianapolis, a city so uptight it even had a Republican mayor, they were as close to a metropolis as the Corn Belt got.

I gazed out the family room window at the house across the street—except for the green shutters, an exact copy of ours—and imagined myself in a large rundown hippie house, listening to music I hadn't heard since New York and calming my frayed nerves with tokes of a joint my newfound friends had rolled for me. Maybe, they'd even have the new Velvet Underground album, the one with the song about the drag queen, "Candy Says," or that other one George had complained made Lou sound like he'd gone soft, "Pale Blue Eyes."

My mother coolly watched me retrieve the cigarette a new tremor had knocked from my hand. "And if I refuse?" she asked.

"Then I'll hitchhike," I replied, tightening the scarf around my neck.

"You wouldn't," my mother gasped.

I assured her I was serious. "Maybe one of your friends will even give me a ride," I said, mostly just to torment her. "Wouldn't that be a hoot!" I smiled at my daring. 'Hoot' was a word only gay people used.

My mother ran a finger along the edge of the mantle and grimaced. "If I lend you the car, will you be home for dinner?" she asked, inspecting her fingertip for evidence of dust. She walked to the sliders and stared at the back of another neighbor's house—like the one in front, identical in every way but its color to our own. "I wouldn't want you out after dark."

I groaned over the relentlessness of her oversight. Like 'living in a city' and 'returning to the East Coast,' 'out after dark' was code for being around other homosexuals. "Of course," I said bitterly. In Danville, I hadn't been out of the house once after dark. I might as well have been fifteen again.

"I don't know," she replied, eyeing me skeptically. "I think Champaign-Urbana may be a bit too big for you." When I reminded her that I'd just spent a year in a city of eight million, her worry lines deepened. "Precisely, and look what happened to you." She walked to the Parson's table and reached for her pack of Virginia Slims. "No, I think you're better off here," she said, lighting a cigarette. She exhaled a thick cloud of blue smoke and smiled smugly. "In Danville, where things are safe."

I glanced at the antique clock on the mantle, a hand-me-down from her mother whose working parts my mother had long ago had removed. If I didn't get out of town, I'd end up as hollow on the inside as that clock. "I'll let you cut my hair if you do," I said, desperate.

"Really?"

"But only half-an-inch," I said. I took a handful of hair and nervously held it up for her inspection. "You know, the split ends."

"When?" my mother asked.

"Tonight," I replied, my heart starting to race. "After dinner."

I looked at her anxiously as the grandfather clock in the foyer struck eleven. If I didn't leave soon, I wouldn't have enough time to get high.

"All right," she said, reaching for the black patent leather purse at the end of the sectional. "But I want you to be careful. Any more messes like before and, well..." Her chin quivered as she handed me the car keys. "I just don't know what I'd do."

"I know, Mother, I've ruined your life," I said, racing for the garage.

"Just promise me you won't get into any more trouble," she yelled after me.

"I promise," I lied before jumping into her Olds. After three weeks of nothing but good, trouble was just what I wanted.

I sat at a small round table by a plate-glass window hung with spider plants and tiny prisms and warily checked out my surroundings. Although I'd driven around Champaign-Urbana for over an hour, a coffee house was as close to what I was looking for as I could find. I read a flyer for a hootenanny the cafe sponsored every Friday night and groaned. I hated folk music. Almost every gay person I knew did. Besides, short hair, chinos, and button-down collars abounded. No one looked even remotely like me.

After a few minutes, a blonde in a gray University of Illinois sweatshirt and a pleated navy-blue skirt asked me to join her table. She said she and her friends were all members in good standing of the campus Young Democrats club and, while debating Nixon's latest peace initiative, had come to an impasse. "We've tried and tried but no one can figure out what's wrong with it," she said, clearly flustered. She pointed at the orange and red sunbursts on my t-shirt, part of a batch George and I had tie-dyed while loaded on speed, and smiled. "We're hoping you'd give us a more..." She blushed slightly and turned to her boyfriend, a guy with short-cropped hair sporting a faded Eugene McCarthy for President button. "You know, a more radical perspective."

I walked over to their table and apologized in advance for not being much help—I really hadn't been keeping up with current events. As I explained, I'd spent the last year in Greenwich Village. I watched them shift nervously in their seats and then asked if they might be able to help me out; where in town did people who looked more like me hang out? "You know, freaks, heads, hippies— whatever you call them out here," I said. I looked around to make sure no one else could hear and then confessed I was looking to get high.

A stunned hush fell over the table. "Oh no, we're not into that," a guy in a blue blazer said.

"Oh, don't worry," I continued. "I'm not a narc or anything." I smiled at the horrified expressions around the table. "Honest. I just really wanna get high." I felt my face flush. I hadn't uttered those words in almost a month.

The guy at the head of the table, a buzz-cut blond in a football jersey, shook his head. "Sorry, man, but you'd have to go to Chicago for stuff like that."

"You're kidding," I groaned. Chicago was much too far away. I could never be home before dark if I went all the way up there. "Look, all I want is to smoke some grass," I pled, my voice rising. I looked down to make sure my needle tracks weren't visible. "Nothing harder."

A rush of cold air announced a new customer, a tall, thin, bespectacled man who flashed us the peace sign as he passed.

"But this is a college town. I thought everyone in college smokes grass," I persisted as he settled into the chair I'd just vacated.

A straight couple across the room looked up from their books and frowned.

"Hey," the manager, a big burly man with a thick gray beard called from behind the counter, "everything alright over there?"

The people around the table again shifted nervously in their seats. "Look," the guy with the McCarthy button said, "we don't want any trouble. But you're in the wrong place, okay?"

"Okay, okay," I muttered, my desperation rising. "So, what about a gay bar? Is there anything like that around?" I smiled bravely, certain that good liberals like them could tolerate a query like that.

"Hey, man, now you've really gone too far," the short-cropped blond in the football jersey snarled, his back stiffening. "We don't go in for that kind of stuff, got it?"

"Yeah, just leave us alone, okay?" the girl's boyfriend, the one with the McCarthy button, chimed in. "Or do you want us to have to call the manager over?"

Afraid the trouble my mother had warned me about was starting to brew, I nodded and slunk out of the coffee house like a kicked dog. After that, I drove around the countryside looking for something, anything out of the ordinary: a hippie commune, a farmer-turned-folk-artist, a cruisy rest stop, even a biker bar or a Holy Roller church would do. However, after an hour of nothing but desiccated cornfields, I pulled over, banged my fists on the steering wheel and screamed so loudly I scared off a nearby buzzard feasting on roadkill. When I was finally so hoarse I couldn't get anything more out, I headed back, hyperventilating the whole way, to the white vinyl-clad suburban box my mother insisted on calling home, the one place on earth where I was loved.

That night, after trimming my hair, my mother announced a package had arrived for me in that day's mail. "From Ginny Pritchards," she said, smiling.

"Oh?" I asked apprehensively. A family friend from Wilmington, Mrs. Pritchards claimed to have served tea to the Virgin Mary. "But I thought you said she was in a mental hospital."

"Oh, no, she's better now," my mother replied, handing me the package. She smiled as I opened it to find a thin volume of prayers entitled, *Are You Running with Me, Jesus?* "I hear all the kids your age are reading it," she said.

"No one I know," I snipped, tossing the book aside. Word on the street was that its author, an Episcopal street-priest named Malcolm Boyd who'd dared to include a prayer for the patrons of a gay bar, was a closet queen. "Not a one."

"Well, maybe you're not as 'with it' as you think," my mother countered. "It's supposed to be on the *New York Times* bestseller list."

"And what makes you think I care about that?" I cried before running out of the room. "About any of it? About anything at all?" I continued on my way up the stairs to my bedroom where, again hyperventilating, I threw myself across the bed and tried in vain to force myself to sleep.

The next morning, I locked myself in the bathroom, crushed three of the uppers George had given me and shot them with the syringe I'd taped "just in case" to the bottom of my bedroom dresser. The rush was so weak I barely felt it but at least I was breaking rules again—a Horrible Fag in deed, if not exactly in fact. That afternoon, I gathered up Boyd's book, my three high school yearbooks and my old Boy Scout manual, drove my mother's Olds to a ravine on the edge of a cornfield—I'd told her I was going to the K-Mart—and doused them with gasoline from a can my father kept in the garage next to the snowblower. As I watched all trace of the old me—the good, wholesome straight kid my mother still insisted I be—go up in flames, I felt a rush that I once knew as peace overtake me. For a moment, my hands even stopped trembling.

"Go ask your mother," my father muttered after I requested the Corvair for my first evening out. He pushed the recliner back another notch and returned to reading the latest issue of *Forbes* magazine. "She's handling all that now."

"What do you mean, 'all that?'" I persisted.

"Just go talk to your mother, okay?" he grumbled, his face hidden behind the magazine.

I turned and walked out of the family room, bristling over the abruptness of his dismissal. When, two nights earlier, he'd suggested my mother back off and give me what he'd called "some slack," I'd hoped he'd be, if not exactly an ally, at least a buffer.

I stood in the entry to the kitchen and watched my mother load a stack of dinner dishes into the dishwasher. I considered lending a hand but knew she'd only take my offer as a rebuke. After over a month of monitoring my every move, she'd grown prickly and defensive, freighting every incident between us with the shame and sense of failure she'd picked up from the books on homosexuality she turned to for help—the ones that argued only mothers made their sons gay. "Why, so you can again tell me what a terrible mother I am?" she'd cried when, that morning, I'd offered to wash my own cereal bowl.

"There's a movie I want to see at the drive-in," I said, my voice quavering. "Dad says I have to ask you if I can have the Corvair." I smiled wanly, hoping she'd say he had it all wrong; I needed to go back to him. The Corvair was my father's car; the Oldsmobile was hers.

"That's right," my mother replied.

"So?" I asked, my face reddening.

My mother wiped her hands on a dish towel and sighed. "I don't know. What kind of movie is it?"

"What, you're monitoring the movies I see?"

She looked at me coldly. "That's right."

"You can't do that. I'm twenty years old."

"I most certainly can," she replied. "Until you start acting like a responsible adult, that's exactly what I intend to do." Her chin stiffened as she pointed at the local paper lying on the peninsula between the kitchen and breakfast room. "Show me the ad."

Furious, I grabbed the paper and opened it to the ad for Russ Meyer's latest film, *Beyond the Valley of the Dolls*. A bevy of buxom beauties, naked except for their minks, lay across a heart-shaped bed, beckoning the viewer to join them. "Here," I said, thrusting the paper at her.

"Oh, well, now aren't they attractive," my mother said of the women. Ignoring the X-rating in big boxy letters at the bottom of the ad, she asked what the film was about.

I recited the few decent tidbits I'd picked up from *Time*'s review. "Three girls from the Midwest form a band called the Carrie Nations and head off to LA to become rock stars," I explained before glancing nervously at the stack of magazines in the family room. If she demanded to see the review, the gig would be up. In it, *Time* had also revealed the villain was a crazed homosexual named Z-Man who overdoses on LSD and takes revenge on all his bullies by killing them. Apparently, there'd been quite a few. *Time* said the film ended in a bloodbath.

I felt my face flush as I awaited my mother's verdict. I didn't care how crude or insulting the Z-Man caricature was. He was gay and, after five weeks in the white-bread straitjacket known as the Corn Belt, that was all I cared about.

"The Carrie Nations, huh?" my mother murmured. "Well, that certainly sounds wholesome." Her smile broadened. "And those girls are attractive." She looked at me and narrowed her eyes. "Don't you agree?"

"Uh, sure," I stammered as my mother's eyes bore deep holes into me. Despising her for the lie she was forcing me into, I even managed a smile. "Very," I murmured.

"What do you think, honey?" she shouted into the family room. "Think it's safe?"

"I don't see any harm in it," my father muttered, still buried behind his issue of *Forbes*.

"Okay, but I want you to come right home after the movie," she said, escorting me to my father. "No more of that joyriding you used to do."

I winced. A marker of my days in the closet, 'joyriding' was the lie I'd used to explain the half-tank of gas I'd consumed while cruising Wilmington's Market Street. "Not to worry," I said as I took from my father the keys to the car in which I'd first had sex with a man. A grade-B Hollywood version of a homosexual was as close to a real one as life in Danville, Illinois, was going to get.

The next morning, my mother was at the kitchen sink peeling potatoes when I came down for breakfast. She waited until I got settled, put down her paring knife, and asked how my time at the drive-in had gone.

I glared into my cereal bowl and recalled the spectacle. Every time Z-Man had appeared on the screen, people had leaned out of their car windows and screamed obscenities. The young straight couple in the car next to me had been the worst. "Kill the faggot," the guy, a football type with short-cropped hair and a deep penetrating baritone, had bellowed. "Yeah, blow the motherfucker away," his drunken companion, a squeaky babe with big tits and ratted-out hair, had added. When, at the end, Z-Man had obliged them and finally died—like a good homosexual, by his own hands, of course—the drive-in had come alive with so many blaring car horns and flashing headlights you'd have thought Danville had just won the state basketball championship. It hadn't even mattered that Z-Man was later revealed to be a woman in male drag. As the guy in the car next to me had so loudly noted, just playing a faggot was grounds for an offing. The bitch got just what she deserved.

I put down my spoon and reached for the cigarette lighter DuPont had given my father for twenty years of service to its Explosives Division. I hadn't seen such hatred since a mob of dorm mates had forced Larry to flee Syracuse for his life. I lit my Marlboro and turned to my mother. "I need to get out of this town," I said from behind a veil of cigarette smoke. "It's not for me."

Once again, my mother took my complaint as a personal rebuke and ran from the room in tears. In disbelief, I stared out the breakfast room window as she threw on a coat and flung open the front door, shrieking she couldn't take it anymore; everything was always her fault. I went to her and, lying, tried to convince her my need to get away had nothing to do with her, but she raced for the garage, hopped in her Olds and drove off anyway.

Determined to stay away from George's pills—there was only one thing worse than being gay in Danville and that was being high—I tried to stay calm by playing over and over my 45 of Martha and the Vandellas' "Nowhere to Run," all the while wondering who was more likely to end up like Z-Man, me or my mother. When, two hours later, she returned, her eyes puffy and her helmet of sprayed hair a wild, disheveled mess, I realized just how close to a dead heat we were. I was killing my mother as surely as she was me.

My parents and their new Denvale friends, the Freemans, stood around the family room fireplace, admiring my mother's mantle arrangement. "Yes, I'm quite pleased with the way it turned out," my mother murmured between sips of her vodka and water. She noted how the blue and green plastic balls in the two apothecary jars on the left brought out the color of the room's drapery and then turned to the bouquet of gold plastic flowers on the right. "I spray painted them myself," she said, flushing with pride.

"Oh, you didn't," cried Mrs. Freeman, a thin, wiry woman with a needle nose and brown, beady eyes. "But they look so real!"

My mother nodded. "Right there in the garage." She took another sip of vodka and frowned at the gaudy brass eagle the house's previous owners had installed over the fireplace. "I wanted to tone that down," she said. She paused while my father lit her Virginia Slims. "I don't like things to stand out. Everything in a house should blend together."

"Of course," cooed Mrs. Freeman. "Well, it's absolutely lovely. Very tasteful."

My mother turned woozily to me. "Dale says he hates it. 'Tacky,' he calls it." She took another sip of her drink and swept her free hand from one end of the mantle to the other. "All of it. The whole thing."

"Well, I see you're a man of strong opinions," Mrs. Freeman said, eyeing me. Ordered by mother to look presentable, I'd put on bellbottoms, my tight-fitting red rayon shirt and matching Converse high tops, although I'd refused to let her again trim my hair. "So," she asked, her beady eyes fixed on a ponytail that fell between my shoulder blades, "you have a girlfriend?"

I played with the tiny turquoise hanging from a chain around my neck—other than a rapidly depleting baggie of pills, an increasingly dull syringe, and a bad case of bleeding hemorrhoids, my only memento of George—and stiffened. "No," I replied. "Can't say that I do."

"What, a handsome guy like you?" She turned and a bit too drunkenly elbowed my mother. "Well, we'll certainly have to fix that, won't we, Jane? It just isn't right."

My mother downed the last of her vodka and numbly shook her head. "It most certainly isn't. Not right at all."

"So," chimed in Mr. Freeman, a thin-lipped, barrel-chested man decked out in a pale blue sports jacket, checked polyester pants, and white shoes, "I hear you spent the last year in New York City."

"That's right," I replied.

"Lots of niggers in New York," he said.

My parents shook their heads. "Terrible, terrible place," Mrs. Freeman clucked.

Mr. Freeman took a sip of his Scotch and soda and stepped closer to me. "You know any?"

I listened as the strains of the Ray Conniff Singers, a group I found particularly loathsome, drifted in from the living room stereo and let the wave of disgust and rage I'd been holding inside since my flight from New York wash over me. "Why, yes," I coolly replied. "As a matter of fact, my roommate was Black."

The room fell into a stunned silence.

"Dale," my mother gasped, "you know that's not true." She looked apologetically at her friends. "He's joking, of course." She turned back to me and, pale as a ghost, pled with me to tell them the truth.

I looked at their smug, self-righteous faces and smiled darkly. I'd rather be back with George, loaded out of my mind on speed, listening to him call me his little sex pig, than within a hundred miles of these, these... I recalled the insult I'd once hurled at my mother, high as a kite on a psychedelic George had tricked me into shooting. Yes, I thought, they really were warthogs from hell.

"You know, I really don't like that word," I said, my voice suddenly clear and sharp. "It's insulting and degrading. The respectful term is Black."

"Respectful?" Mr. Freeman scoffed, puffing out his barrel chest. "To what, a bunch of jungle bunnies?"

Ignoring him, I turned to his wife, whose mouth was ajar. "As for a girlfriend..." I said.

"Alright, alright, that's quite enough," my father interjected, his face red and his jaw set like he wanted to throttle me. He nodded at the doorway into the kitchen. "You may be excused now."

"Thank you," I replied and, without another word, retreated to the upstairs bedroom my father called his office. I sat at his desk, picked up the phone, and listened for a few seconds to the dial tone. I'd promised myself George would have to be the one to call but I couldn't bear another minute of this agony.

I took a deep breath and dialed the number for the young, childless couple who kept George's bail money in a cookie jar. If anyone could get a message to him, they could. The phone rang twice and then a woman's voice suddenly came on. "Hello?" she asked.

I looked at the photo on the opposite wall of my father accepting a citation from DuPont for a perfect safety record. There'd been no accidents that year at the munitions plant he'd helped manage. He'd forgotten when the photo was taken but I knew from the cut of his trousers and the width of his tie that it had to have been before I was born. "Hello?" the woman repeated. "Is anybody there?"

I slumped over the desk, shamed by my capitulation. "Is that you, George?" the woman asked. "Are you alright?"

"Oh, I'm sorry, wrong number," I mumbled and slammed the phone down. I numbly stared at the stacks of bills and cancelled checks my father had arranged along the top of a gray felt desk blotter and, suddenly disoriented, tried to get my bearings. Almost out of pills and with no hope of returning to George, I was completely and utterly adrift.

I heard the rumble of the garage door and walked to the window as my parents drove off with the Freemans to the country club for another night of dancing and drinking. I turned and spied the bundle of yarn my mother had left on the arm of the chair facing my father's desk and recalled the wedding ring that Randy, one of the Continental Room regulars, had worn to work so no one would suspect he was gay. If I didn't get out of Danville soon, I was going to end up just like him: a guilty closet case afraid of his own shadow—my parents' dream come true and my very own worst nightmare.

24
Like Bernadette

I took a bite of my tuna fish sandwich and watched the neighbor's German Shepherd descend into a paroxysm of rage. As with Jeff, the Dalmatian my father had buried in the corner of the backyard, trash day transformed him from a docile, tail-wagging pet into a ferocious, jaw-snapping beast. "Jesus Christ," I muttered.

My mother stood a few feet away at the kitchen peninsula, folding napkins. The tiny gold bell on her charm bracelet tinkled softly, while next to it, a small diamond inset into my father's Kappa Sigma fraternity pin—a memento of his two years at Indiana University, the school my parents hoped would finally straighten me out—caught the low, winter light and sparkled. "Now, you know we don't take the Lord's name in vain in our house," she chided.

"You know, you once told me Jeff thought the garbage men were thieves," I said, pointing at the two men facing down the dog across a white picket fence. "But you were wrong. It's because they're Black. The dog knows they're not welcome here." I turned and looked at her. Her chin was set and her face was flushed, like it got when she felt under attack. "In the city, dogs don't act like that. Not a one. Ever." I returned the sandwich to my plate. "People are more tolerant and open-minded in the city."

My mother patted her stack of napkins and sneered, "So, why don't you go back if you like living in filth so much?"

I took a sip of my Pepsi and felt my face redden. Neither one of us had recovered from the incident with the Freemans. "I plan to," I said and pointed at the X on the wall calendar marking my court date. "Right after my trial."

"Oh, no, you won't," my mother snipped. When I asked what made her so sure, she smiled. "Because you're too smart for that."

"Well, I'm certainly not staying here," I said. "I'm depressed, all I do is sleep, my nerves are shot..." I tossed my napkin onto the table and held out my right hand. "See?"

My mother's brow furrowed as she watched my hand tremble.

"Every day it gets a little bit worse," I said.

I watched one of the garbage men hurl an empty trash barrel at the now thoroughly berserk canine. *Stay the fuck away from me, you honky-ass bitch*, he hollered.

My jaws clenched and the muscles in my neck knotted. If I didn't get away soon, I was going to explode just like him.

When the garbage truck rumbled off and the neighbor's dog finally quieted down, my mother placed her hands on her hips and looked gravely at me. "Your father and I have made a decision," she announced.

I stiffened. The last time she'd made a pronouncement like that, she'd ordered me to submit to a cure. "Yes?" I replied warily.

"We want you to start attending church," she said. "With us. As a family."

I folded my napkin and, returning it to the side of my plate, slowly shook my head. After learning our Presbyterian minister, Dr. Connolly, had been the one to recommend a cure to her, I'd vowed never to enter another church again. "Absolutely not," I said.

"You will if we say you will. This Sunday, I want you downstairs..." My mother pointed to the entryway into the family room. "In a coat and tie and ready to go by 9 am."

"No," I repeated. "You have no right to demand this."

"I most certainly do. As long as you're living in this house, we have every right to demand that you live by our values." She reached behind her and loosened the belt of her apron. "It's time you started making other choices."

"Choices?!" I cried, pushing my plate away. "What choices?"

My mother's chin stiffened. "You know perfectly well what I mean."

"I see," I said. We'd slipped all the way back there, to the heart of the matter—my mother's shame at having a gay son. I put my hands in my lap and took a deep breath. "That is not a choice, Mother. It is who I am."

"You don't know what you're saying," she scoffed. "That's those people in New York City talking." She glared at the half-eaten sandwich on my plate—more evidence of her failure as a mother. "They've brainwashed you."

"Let me tell you something, Mother. Everything I have done..." I paused to catch my breath; no one I knew had been as headstrong as me. At fifteen, I'd propositioned my first man for sex and, three years later—against the advice of everyone I knew—come out to my parents. Over the next year, I'd fought off the shrink they'd hired to cure me, dropped out of college, turned my back on what might have been a bright future, and fled to New York to be a full-time, in-your-face hippie faggot freak. I'd even stuck it out with an abusive lover, mostly because I refused to go back to them. "Everything," I repeated, "has been my own doing. No one else's. I am the author of me."

"No," my mother spat, "we raised you too well for that." Her face hardened into the stern, unforgiving mask by which she repelled every unpleasantness. "It's those people, I know it. They've ruined you."

"But you know nothing of them. You've never even asked their names."

"Nor will I, ever. There's nothing worth knowing about people like that."

"What if I said I was in love with one of them, Mother?" I asked, my voice quavering. "Madly, desperately..."

"I don't want to hear about it," she interrupted. "Not one word."

"His name is George," I persisted.

Her face reddened and the rhinestones in the corners of her glasses flared. "I'm warning you..."

I leaned forward and reached across our divide for her. "He's called for me, hasn't he? You've taken the message and kept it from me."

"I said I don't want to discuss it! If you continue like this one more second, I'm going to..." She stepped away from the counter and pointed down the hall to the powder room whose tissue dispenser she'd decorated with seashells and on whose walls she'd hung two very piss-elegant Louis XIV sconces. "To vomit," she shouted. "Do you hear me? *Vomit!*"

That was it. I lost it. "I'm sick to death of all this guilt and shame!" I bellowed, bursting out of my chair. I grabbed the jar of mayonnaise I'd watched my mother make from scratch the day before and hurled it across the room. "It's killing both of us!" I shouted as shards of glass careened across the kitchen's dark-blue linoleum floor and gobs of pale-yellow goo oozed down the avocado green of her refrigerator door.

My mother froze. Then, without uttering a sound, she slowly walked to the closet, grabbed a broom and started to clean the mess up. "That's okay, I'll take care of it," she said when, horrified by what I'd done, I came over to help. She tightened her grip on the broom and glared at me. "Like I always do," she added, her eyes swimming in tears.

I turned away from the TV—*Saturday Night at the Movies* was showing *Song of Bernadette*, a film I recalled Dominic and his gay mother, now a transgender lesbian, had both liked—and reached for the phone. I leaned my head back and, like I did every time it rang, prayed it was George. I exhaled a thick cloud of cigarette smoke, cleared my throat—I hadn't spoken to a soul since I'd refused my parents' invitation to join them for a family reunion in Evansville—and lifted the receiver. "Hello?" I murmured.

"Dale?" the voice on the other end asked.

My heart stopped. "Yes," I replied hesitantly.

"I was just doing your chart and noticed your moon had returned to Cancer..."

"John!" I cried, sitting bolt upright. "Oh my God, John!" I smiled and, for the first time in months, even managed a laugh. The gay mother who'd once nursed me back to health from a bonecrusher had re-appeared out of thin air. "How did you ever find me?"

John said he was surprised at how easy the search had been. He'd gotten my parents' phone number from Sal, the very first person he'd turned to, who'd gotten it from Eugenie, who'd looked me up on a visit to the Village and gotten it from George, still holed up on West 10th Street. "Sal says she now understands why you split," John added. "I guess George gave her one of his shots."

"Sounds right, huh?" I said, wondering if they'd also had sex. "The fucker was supposed to call for me. But, of course, he hasn't." I glanced at the TV just as Jennifer Jones' luminous face—she'd won an Oscar for her portrayal of Bernadette—filled the screen. It'd been seven long, heartsick weeks.

"He gave me a baggie of uppers to tide me over," I continued. "Dexies mostly." I lit another cigarette and said that while I'd been pretty frugal—I noted getting high in Danville wasn't much fun—my supply was almost gone. After that, I had no idea how I was going to make it. "My parents still refuse to say the word 'gay. They monitor my every move."

"Well, fuck 'em if they can't take a joke," John chuckled, repeating the mantra by which he rebuffed every challenge.

I smiled and said I wished I could. "But I can't, at least not for a while anyway." I told him about my shoplifting bust—laughing, he admitted he'd also used Vitabath to clear up his tracks—and explained that, since my parents had posted bail, I felt an obligation to stay at least until my trial. "I've ripped them off too much as it is."

"Too much?" John sneered. "That doesn't sound like a sleaze."

"No, I guess it doesn't," I said, cringing at how puerile the word, stripped of its Horrible Fag context, sounded. I took a long drag from my cigarette and recalled the time on Avenue D when John and I had first decided to embark on the process of becoming totally bad. Two months later, he'd fled New York after one of George's monster shots while I'd hung on, George's mute, impotent, drug-addicted boy. "I don't want to be a sleaze anymore," I announced before recalling the 'gay is good' chant George and I had heard the first night of the Stonewall riots. "I'd like to try that out for a while. You know, kinda like you in Provincetown." I smiled. "Boring but good."

John chuckled and suggested that, if boring was what I was after, I come to Chicago and live with him. As he noted, he had just enough floorspace in his studio for another mattress. He said he was in a gay area called "New Town," mostly to distinguish it from "Old Town," where Chicago's head shops were located—although, other than its two gay bars and a proximity to Lincoln Park, which he called cruisy, there was little to recommend it. There were, he said, no sex shops or bookstores and no flash to speak of. "Straight," he even called the vicinity.

He said only a few locals were freaks and, of those who were, most were just potheads. Some had tried LSD but only once or twice, while no one had ever gone near a syringe. Most seemed baffled by his stories of the Stonewall riots and few seemed bothered by the Vietnam War. Motown was the preferred bar sound, although Judy Garland and Barbra Streisand ran close seconds; the gay bar closest to him, he said, was strictly show tunes. Neither New Town jukebox offered fare from groups like Jefferson Airplane, Big Brother and the Holding Company, or The Doors, while no one he'd encountered had ever even heard of the Velvet Underground. "I could use your company," he murmured.

He also noted that, while Chicago had a multitude of ethnic groups—Irish, Italians, Poles, Lithuanians, Albanians, Puerto Ricans, Blacks—each had its own territory. Rarely did they interact and, when they did, it was often violently, through street fights and riots. New Town, he said, was lily-white, as were its gay bars. He'd never seen a Black face in either and suspected it was intentional; Chicago Blacks, he said, had a tough time of it, much worse than gays. And while there were several drag bars, he'd also never encountered a street queen. Miss Eden and Stephanie Lisa, he speculated, would hate it there.

"I don't know, Chicago sounds kinda uptight," I said of John's invitation and then listed my own, more political objections: the police riot outside the Democratic National Convention; the Weathermen's failed Days of Rage; and the previous December, the cop killings of two Black Panther leaders, Mark Clark and Fred Hampton. "And then, let's not forget the Chicago Eight trial," I said, shaking my head. For that one, the judge had ordered a gagged and bound Bobby Seale, another Black Panther, shackled to his chair. "Besides," I grumbled, "I think I'd rather go back to George than be a gay barfly again."

"Well, it isn't Greenwich Village, that's for sure," John conceded. Chicago's cops, he acknowledged, kept the locals on a pretty tight leash, while the gay bar scene was what he called "old world." Outside of the two newer ones around the corner from him, most were either drag or piano bars, with a few particularly sleazy ones devoted to rough trade. He also noted he had no intention of staying long; as soon as he saved up enough from his job making beer signs for local bars—he noted that while Chicago had a paucity of decent gay bars, it had lots of raucous straight ones—he'd be splitting for the West Coast. "Maybe we could even go out together. You'd like San Francisco," he said before calling it the new gay capital.

"No, I'm an East Coast type, remember?" I replied, recalling our debate over which side of the continent we were more suited for. I said I hoped to go back to the Village but admitted I was afraid of running into George. I flushed as I recalled beating off to a fantasy of him earlier that day. "I don't think I've fully weaned myself of him yet."

"Yeah," John replied. "We all wanted to say something but..." When I said I wished he had, he reminded me of judgmentalism's slippery slope. Once started, it always seemed to end up blaming the gay part.

I told him my parents, who never hesitated to castigate, were adamant that I go back to college. While I admitted I found the prospect of engaging my mind after a year of doing nothing but blowing it enticing, I felt hemmed in by the limitations my parents had placed on my options. So far, only Indiana University, situated in the heart of what my father called 'God's Country,' had been deemed suitable. "My parents think I'll turn straight there."

John laughed at the prospect. As he noted, short of a few drag queens, he'd never met anyone quite so determined to break free of the closet as me. He encouraged me, though, to seriously consider a return to college. Not having taken advantage of the GI Bill when he got out of the Army was one of his biggest regrets. He was, however, concerned about the timing. September, the start of the new academic year, was almost seven months away. "Remember, I've been updating your chart. You can't last that long where you are," he warned.

"But my mother will freak if I just pack up and split." I wiped a bead of sweat from my brow and trembled. Outside, the wind howled, while the patio snow cover glowed in the moonlight like it was lit from within. "Totally, totally freak."

"So?" John scoffed. "She survived it before, didn't she?"

"Yeah," I sighed, "but I guess I'm tired of hurting her." The muscles in my jaw and the back of my neck twisted taut. "It would be one thing if I could just end it, you know, leave and never see her again." I slumped back against the sectional and welled up. "But I can't. I want things right between us again."

"Gawd, you Pisces," he cried, "always worried about what's going on with other people. It's too bad you're not a Capricorn. We're selfish. We do whatever we want."

On that note, the operator broke in and told John he'd have to deposit two more quarters if he wanted to continue the call. Noting it was freezing inside his phone booth, John declined but, before signing off, told me to think more about joining him in Chicago. He said he was on a street called Surf, directly behind Shari's, one of New Town's two gay bars. The other one, he added, the Annex, was only a half-block away. He even said on weekends I could dance there. "Remember, you need to think about your needs too," he said before the connection was cut.

I returned to the TV and watched as Bernadette rebuffed a group of officials determined to get her to renounce the vision of the 'beautiful lady' she'd seen in a grotto. Of all their warnings—her future would be ruined; she'd never be able to marry; she'd have no children—the most devastating was the one my mother had used on me: she was ruining the family. Sticking to her guns, Bernadette let the chips fall where they may. Her fealty was to her vision, not her comfort.

"I don't know, honey. Do you think it's drugs?" my mother asked over the clanging of dinner dishes. Her last word was dry and clipped, as if she was ashamed having to even utter it.

I crept two more steps down the stairwell and stopped. My heart was pounding so loudly that, fearing my parents could hear it, I muffled it with my hand. The depression that had sent me to bed for three days had finally forced them to confront a situation they'd otherwise refused to see. I was in trouble. "Falling apart," my mother had called it. Right in front of them. She even said they hadn't seen anything like it since Bo, my paternal grandfather, had drunk himself to death way back in 1951.

"No, of course not," my father said, clearing the dishes for a dinner from which my sleep marathon had blessedly excused me. "This is God's Country. There's nothing like that within fifty miles of Danville."

More like one hundred and fifty, I thought recalling my trip to Champaign-Urbana. I traced with a forefinger the wallpaper's blue curlicue and recalled John's offer of a refuge. At least in Chicago, I could smoke pot. The tightness in my neck slackened. I could even be gay. Laugh and dance. Be out. No more closets.

"But have you seen how he shakes? He never did anything like that before."

"But everything about him is different," my father countered. "His hair, his clothes, the language he uses. I mean, whoever heard of calling money 'bread?'"

I imagined my father's grimace and the way his cheeks fired whenever the topic of conversation turned to me. "Sometimes, I think he's in the wrong family."

"Do you think he might be having a nervous breakdown?" my mother ventured. "You know, like Ginny Pritchards."

"If he is, it'd be one of the best things that ever happened to him," my father replied.

My mother closed the dishwasher door and secured the latch. "Now, why on earth would you say something like that?"

"Because it just might be the kick in the pants he needs to see the error of his ways. All this whining and moping around as if the world owes him something has got to stop. It's time he realized he's his own worst enemy. If he wants to get something out of life, he's got to go out and get it." Gumption, he added, was what I lacked.

"Maybe we should find him a doctor," my mother said.

"You mean a psychiatrist?" The dishwasher roared as it filled up with water.

"Yes," my mother replied.

"Over my dead body," my father snapped. "The last one nearly bankrupted us and what did we get out of it? A kid who's throwing his life away and a lecture about how we're the ones who need to change." He banged his fist on the kitchen counter. "No, after that, I promised myself I'd never let another Jew bastard tell me how to run my family. Now, you can send him to a doctor if that's what you want but I'm not spending one red cent on it. Do you understand?"

"But he's threatening to go back to New York," my mother whimpered. "I don't think I could live through that again. I just really don't."

"Well, I suppose we could commit him to the state hospital up at Manteno," my father said. "It wouldn't cost us anything. But we'll have to act fast. Once he turns twenty-one, it'll be out of our hands."

I sank to my haunches and covered my face with my hands. It had come to this. They'd rather have me locked up than have me be gay. Turn me into a zombie, I thought, as I recalled the electroshock treatments places like that routinely meted out to people like me. Or a eunuch, I shuddered, recalling the stories I'd heard about enforced castrations.

"But what would we tell people?" my mother asked.

"We tell 'em whatever we want. I mean, it wouldn't be the first time he just ups and disappears."

I waited for my mother to put her foot down and say, like my father had about the prospect of another Jew-bastard shrink, over her dead body, no way were they going to send her baby to a torture chamber like that. But all I heard was more clanging of dishes, followed by an announcement on the family room TV that it was time for Lawrence Welk, the champagne music maker, to return them to a world where gay still meant happy and people like me remained stubbornly locked up in closets, suffocating on fear and shame.

"Come on, honey," my father yelled. "The Lennon Sisters are about to come on."

"Ooh," she squealed. A cabinet door slammed shut and slippers pattered across the breakfast room floor. "I'm on my way!"

The magistrate read the shoplifting charge against me and, noting I was underage, asked if I had an adult with me. I bristled at the question—I'd been through more at twenty than most people twice my age—and turned as my mother rose from her seat in the gallery. "Yes, your honor," she replied. Her chin quivered slightly. "I'm with him."

Intrigued—other than the stenographer, my mother was the only white woman in his courtroom that day—the magistrate motioned her forward. She glared at me as she opened the gate—as she'd said on the drive in, she'd never been inside a courtroom before—and waited for the bailiff, a towering, thickly built Black man with a pomaded pompadour, to nod his assent. She strode to my side, straightened her tiny 5' 2" frame and, grim-faced, gave for the record the information asked of her: "Mrs. Hardin D. Mitchell, 216 Denvale Drive, Danville, Illinois." She tightened her grip on her black patent leather purse and grimaced at the bailiff's final query. "His mother," she replied bitterly.

The magistrate, a round-faced white man with silver hair and ruddy cheeks, peered at her over the half-moons of his glasses. "I see we're neighbors," he said, picking up a pencil. "My wife and I live in Denvale too. Right off the golf course." He tapped the pencil on the stack of folders in front of him and cocked his head to one side. "Do you play?"

My mother nodded. "My husband and I both do." She noted, though, that, having only moved to Danville in November, they hadn't yet had a chance to test out the course. "The first warm day, though," she added, her face brightening, "I'm sure we'll be out on that fairway, teeing off."

"Yes, won't we all," the magistrate sighed and glanced out the window at a large maple an overnight ice storm had topped off. "This winter's been tough. I think everyone's just about had it."

"I know I certainly have," my mother said, glancing at me.

The magistrate asked where she'd lived prior to Danville.

"Wilmington, Delaware," she replied before noting my father worked for DuPont's Explosives Division. She fondled her strand of pearls and added with an air of importance, "We were transferred here. My husband runs the Human Resources office of the new ordnance works over near Terre Haute."

"Ah, DuPont," the magistrate murmured. "We're very lucky to have it in the area."

My mother smiled. "DuPont's been good to us." She glanced down at the blue and white wingtip pumps she wore with her navy-blue suit. "Very good."

The magistrate folded his hands over his paunch and leaned back in his black leather chair. "So, Mrs. Mitchell," he said, "it's not often that a young man with your son's background comes before this court on a shoplifting charge."

My mother blanched. "We're a good family, your honor." Her chin again quivered. "We've never denied him anything."

I bit my lower lip and, turning to a window, stifled a groan.

The magistrate glanced at me and then back at her. "So, do you have any idea why he would steal..." He leaned forward, opened my folder, and re-read my arrest report. "A bottle of bubble bath?"

My mother winced as people in the gallery behind us tittered and then nodded gravely. "Yes, your honor, you see my son is very impressionable. Some would say gullible even."

Furious, I looked up and watched the courtroom's ceiling fan whir.

She took a deep breath and sighed. "I'm afraid he got caught up in the wrong crowd."

Skeptical, the magistrate asked where my supposed corruption took place.

"New York City," my mother replied, her voice squelched with suppressed rage. When he asked which part—as he noted, his wife had grown up on the Upper East Side—she pointed at the ponytail I'd refused to let her cut off, even for my court date. "Oh no, we're talking Greenwich Village."

"Oh, I see," the magistrate muttered, removing his glasses. He rubbed his eyes and glanced nervously at me. "And what about college? Has there been any of that?"

"Why, yes, of course," she said, explaining they'd paid what she called "full freight" for three semesters at Syracuse, where, for two, I'd studied architecture. When I'd switched majors—"to English literature," she said with a distinct sneer—they'd kept on paying top dollar to avoid what she'd called "any further disruption." As she noted, I'd been going through a difficult phase.

She shook her head and said she could still remember the date—January 23rd, 1969—when everything came to a head. That evening, shortly after they'd finished dinner, I'd called—"collect, of course"—with the news I was dropping out of college and moving to New York. "We were devastated," she said, pulling a starched hanky from her purse. "I must've cried for two weeks straight."

The magistrate waited for her to regain her composure and then, noting that that had been over a year ago, asked about my Selective Service status. "Surely, the draft's caught up with him by now."

My mother turned pale and told the magistrate I'd have to be the one to tell him about that. She dabbed her eyes and grimaced. "I can't."

The magistrate looked at me accusingly. "I certainly hope you're not one of those draft dodgers."

I clasped my hands behind my back and cleared my throat. So far, I hadn't been allowed to utter a word. "I am 4-F, your honor," I said with the same sense of pride with which my mother had identified DuPont as my father's employer.

The magistrate gaveled the gallery quiet. "4-F?" he murmured. "But you certainly look fit."

"I am, your honor."

Stunned, he dropped his voice and, leaning over his bench, asked if I'd been diagnosed with a mental illness.

I glanced warily at my mother, whom I'd told my rejection was due to a letter I'd obtained from a Bellevue shrink. "No, your honor," I answered, relieved to finally be free of that lie, "I am not mentally ill." I watched the stenographer record my words. There was no more room for doubt. The only other option was gay.

The magistrate's face froze. He shook his head and, again leaning back in his chair, looked at me long and hard. I stiffened against the expected invective, but he simply sighed and, in a voice so soft I barely heard him, confessed that, in all his years on the bench, he'd never encountered anyone who'd thrown quite so much opportunity away. "I mean, it's really quite remarkable."

I returned his gaze and nodded. What he'd meant to say was that he'd never encountered a homosexual like me. Like Bernadette, I was letting the chips fall where they may. "Thank you, your honor."

"Do you have any goals at all?"

I shrugged and confessed I'd like to return to college. "Provided it's Syracuse." Through the sleeve of the dress shirt my mother had ironed for me, I massaged the needle tracks the growing dullness of my syringe had turned into a throbbing bruise. "I want to be around people I know," I added, glancing defiantly at my mother.

"My husband and I think he should stay here in the Midwest," she interjected, "where we can keep an eye on him."

"Ah, yes, the Midwest, a much better idea," the magistrate intoned. "After all, if it wasn't for the Eastern Establishment, your son probably wouldn't be standing here in front of me." Permissiveness, he grumbled, that was what was ruining the younger generation. "That, and mollycoddling. We've been much too lenient with our young people." He straightened a pleat in his robe and asked if they'd considered his alma mater, the University of Illinois. He noted that, unlike on so many other campuses, where deviance had replaced the straight and narrow and rioting had become a required course, U of I still offered the same wholesome education that he'd enjoyed as a youth.

My mother thanked him for the suggestion but said she thought Champaign-Urbana, where I'd failed to find so much as a joint, was too wild. She asserted I needed a smaller, "more manageable" environment with as few outside distractions as possible. For a moment, I thought she was describing the state mental hospital up at Manteno but then she added, "We're hoping on Bloomington, Indiana, where my husband went to college." She noted both she and my father, after more than a decade in Delaware, still called themselves Hoosiers. "We were both born and raised in Indiana," she explained, tearing up slightly. "The southern part, on the Ohio River. What my husband calls 'God's country.'"

"Well, then," the magistrate said, glancing at the clock at the far end of the courtroom, "there's certainly no arguing with that." He congratulated her on the care with which she'd approached such a difficult situation, adding only that he wished every parent he saw in his court was as devoted. He looked at the rows of Black faces filling the gallery and sighed. "Perhaps then we wouldn't have the problems we have in this great country of ours."

He turned to me and said he hoped I was grateful for the support my parents were giving me. "Many wouldn't have bothered," he added, narrowing his eyes. "You know, given your, uhm, lifestyle." At that, he gaveled my case closed, dropping the shoplifting charge against me on the condition that I reported back to him on my search for a suitable college, which he defined as one located somewhere between Nebraska and the Pennsylvania/Ohio line, no later than Tax Day, April 15th. In the interim, he ordered me to find a job, a task my mother assured him would be done with dispatch. She said there were openings at the local Arby's Roast Beef where, she announced with noticeable relief, they'd also make me cut my hair. I watched her chin stiffen and knew that Sunday church services wouldn't be far behind.

On the drive home, she confirmed my suspicions by announcing that, after lunch, she was taking me shopping for a sports coat. "And I don't mean at one of those thrift stores you like so much," she snarled. "It's a new day. I want you to look respectable. Like you're one of us."

I had other ideas. While she prepared lunch, I shot the last of George's uppers, threw the few belongings I had into my suitcase and announced from the foyer that I was leaving for Chicago. "For good," I added with the same relish with which she'd looked forward to my haircut.

"Oh, no, you're not," my mother shouted, rushing in. "I won't let you." She pressed her back against the front door and challenged me to remove her. "Go ahead. Throw me across the room," she hissed, pointing at the spot on the floor where she imagined she'd land, a bloodied and crumpled heap. "After all, isn't that what this is all about, what you've always wanted..." Her eyes narrowed and her face flushed a bright coital pink. "To hurt me?"

"No, no, you've got it all wrong," I stammered, horrified by her invitation to violence. "I want the hurting to stop. All of it. On both sides."

"Sides?" she shrieked. "What sides? There aren't any sides in a family."

I wiped the sweat from my forehead. I'd never seen her quite so deranged. "Look, Mother, we're making each other miserable. Surely, you can admit to that."

"How dare you even say such a thing!" She wagged a finger in my face as the vein in her neck turned thick and purplish. "A mother made miserable by her own son."

"Look, just let me go, okay?" I pled. I grabbed my suitcase and suggested that, with some distance between us, we might even relearn how to talk to each other. "Like before," I added, recalling the way we used to giggle together. The clench in my jaw tightened as I gripped the suitcase's dried and cracked handle. Of all my setbacks, the loss of my mother would be the hardest to bear.

"I'll show you the kind of talk people like you get," she spat and ran for the breakfast room phone. "I'm calling the police." She lifted the receiver and pointed it at me. "They'll be here in fifteen minutes."

"Fine," I replied, opening the front door, "tell them I'll be waiting outside." I pointed at the end of the driveway and smirked, knowing that, in full view of the neighbors, she'd at least have to quiet down. "Maybe they'll even give me a lift to the highway."

"What do you mean?"

I pulled the driver's license from my wallet and pointed at my birth date. As I noted, at twenty, I was entitled to do as I pleased. An "emancipated minor," I called myself.

"*A what*?!" my mother shrieked, slamming the phone down mid-dial. She ran back into the foyer and grabbed the edge of a small cherry console on which my father had placed a stack of outgoing bills. "Where you'd ever learn a term like that?"

I looked at her coolly. The term was, along with learning how to mix up a shot of speed and hit a vein with a hypodermic needle, one of the lessons I'd picked up from George—once we turned eighteen, our parents had no more power over us than what we gave them. It was, he'd said, one of the few times the law was on our side, the gay one. "From my time in New York," I told her.

"So, does that include crawling back into the gutter and ruining your life all over again?"

At that, my patience snapped. "Maybe," I replied before I stuck my face in hers and acknowledged that, while Chicago was still safely within the confines of the Midwest—"God's country," I sneered—I would be moving in with John, a friend from Greenwich Village. "You know, from the wrong crowd," I said, recalling her courtroom performance.

"No," she whimpered.

I again picked up my suitcase and nodded. For insurance, I'd even packed up my syringe.

"But you've made such progress," she mumbled.

"No, that's just what you and Dad tell yourselves so you can pretend everything is fine. But it's not, Mother. I'm miserable—more miserable, I think, than I've ever been." I stepped onto the front stoop into a vortex of wind-whipped sand and snow melt. Two years after I'd come out to her, she and I were still stuck in the scene that had followed it: my mother on her knees, puking her disgust out into the toilet bowl and me, running for the door, shouting the word 'gay' at her as if it were a rebuke. It was time for another take.

"I'll never be what you want, Mother," I said calmly. "I didn't choose this but neither am I unhappy about it. It is something that simply is." I smiled at her, knowing the burden of shame that she also struggled with. As the books she'd read had told her, mothers were the ones who made their sons gay. I glanced at the row of brown, spindly yews which, planted under a deep overhang that even my mother had acknowledged was a design flaw, were slowly dying of thirst. "Until you accept who I am, we will never again be a family."

For a moment, we stood facing each other, trembling at the prospect of another breach—perhaps the final one, the one from which neither of us would recover.

I reached into the pocket of my greatcoat and pulled out my application to IU, complete except for a stamp. I held it up, proof that my escape was, that time anyway, about recovery, not revenge. "I'll send this off soon," I offered. "I promise."

Her face hardened as she contemplated the imminence of my departure. "No, you won't. You're just saying that." She gripped the edge of the door, looked at me bitterly, and repeated the charge she'd used against me since the day I'd come out: "You're so lost you no longer know truth from lies." Her face reddened. "Fact from fiction."

I bristled but, at that point, I just wanted our encounter over. "Goodbye, Mother," I said and, walking off, gave her my back. She responded by slamming the front door so hard the Christmas wreath my father wanted to keep up until the first sign of spring went flying.

I thought for a moment about retrieving it and then said fuck it, let it rot; Christmas wreaths had bookended my time in Danville. They were what had decorated the pedestrian mall on my first day in town, the one when I'd been busted for stealing a bottle of bubble bath. And they were on the door of the suburban Colonial I'd finally freed myself from on the day the judge, seduced by my mother's invocations of middle-class respectability, had given me a pass and let me go on the promise that I'd become what I was supposed to be: a white guy with a future. The others in his courtroom, all young Black men, well, let's face it, they were *supposed* to end up in prison—their lot in life, as Donovan sang in "Lalena," the last song I'd heard before fleeing New York.

I followed the road out of Denvale, heading for Route 136, the two-lane highway where I hoped to hitch a ride to Chicago. In the middle of the causeway across the still-frozen Lake Vermillion I stopped and watched two men fish through a hole cut into the ice. One waved to me and, for a moment, I felt like I was dreaming and then, suddenly, my mother's Olds pulled up alongside me. "Come on, get in," she said, lowering the passenger side window. "I'll give you a ride to the bus station. You know how I hate the idea of you hitchhiking."

She stubbed her Virginia Slims out in the dashboard ashtray and grimaced when I told her I was fine catching rides from strangers. "Oh, don't be silly. It's freezing out." She pulled a fifty from her purse and waved it at me. "Besides, you'll need this to get yourself settled."

On the drive to the bus station, she asked what I planned to do in Chicago. When I told her I'd have to find a job, her mood suddenly lifted. "Really, you mean you won't go back on welfare?"

Stunned, I felt my face redden. Coming from her, the word 'welfare' sounded suddenly infantile, like, in a tantrum, I'd willfully squandered talents only she still believed in. "No," I mumbled, not sure even then I was telling the truth, "I want to do something…" I paused to search for the word that, along with 'family,' 'decency,' and 'pride,' George and the speed were supposed to have burned out of me. My voice cracked. "Constructive."

In the parking lot outside the bus station, my mother leaned across the console and hugged me. She apologized for any hurt she'd inflicted and said it was only because she loved me. "You know all I want is for you to be happy."

I recalled George's farewell—he too had professed to love me—and groped for the door handle. As for happiness, well, I'd pretty much given up on that too. Strength, that's what I needed now. The kind that George had, only without the speed. I wondered if there even was such a thing.

"You're a very brave young man," my mother said. "Not many people could do what you're doing." She brushed a strand of hair from my face and caressed a cheek with a hand redolent of glycerin and rose water. "I may not like what you're doing but I am proud of you for sticking to your guns." She leaned back in her seat and smiled sheepishly. "Very proud."

I acknowledged her change in tone but only warily, with a nod. "Thank you," I said, fighting an urge to hug her. The only thing better would have been to hear her say the word 'gay.'

In the bus station, I bought a stamp and, as I'd promised my mother, dropped my application to IU in the mailbox. I then pulled out my application for readmission to Syracuse, complete except for an essay describing what I'd done with myself since last there. I'd tried several times to write something but there simply was no way I could explain what I'd been through, let alone how or why. Fighting for my rights might have been an angle, something on the order of going South for Freedom Summer, although, a mere six months after Stonewall, no dean of admissions would have accepted my struggle as legitimate. Besides, the suggestion that sticking a needle in a vein might be an act of resistance was, well, frankly beyond the pale. Protesters were supposed to sit-in, march, leaflet, get busted, organize, not self-destruct. Hitting rock bottom was a victory only for those from whom nothing else was expected—or wanted.

Oh well, I thought, as I grabbed my suitcase and, on my way to boarding the bus, tossed the Syracuse application in the trash. In her own hysterical, hyperjudgmental way, my mother was right. Syracuse would have been just a waystation back to George or, as she preferred to call it, the "gutter." If I wanted to disconnect gay from bad, I needed to start by somehow learning to feel good about myself.

I handed the driver my bag, stepped onto the bus, and stared down its darkened aisle. I had no idea if I was up to the task. As Peter had once said, gays were supposed to hate themselves.

As the bus headed north, I turned to the window and, staring at field after field of desiccated corn, thought about John, whose offer to put me up had finally pried me free of my family. Of all my friends, he'd been the one who'd rankled George the most, no doubt because he'd been the most steadfast. When I'd been at one of my lowest points—the night I'd come down with a bonecrusher from having shot someone else's blood—John had been the one who'd shown up and nursed me back to health. Where love had proven to be a feckless humiliation, friendship had turned out to be astonishingly true-blue. My "fairy godmother," George had even called him.

The land flattened to a relentless monotony. A flock of crows descended on a cornfield, cawing loudly. I knew nothing about where I was going except this: Chicago was run by a hateful thug named Richard Daley and I had a friend who lived there. A gay one, one of the few who was as determined to break free as me. I pulled out the slip of paper on which I'd written down John's address and smiled. Surf Street—I'd even be around water again. For the first time in a very long time, I felt like I was heading home.

25
Two, Four, Six, Eight

I arrived in Chicago in late February 1970, two weeks before my twenty-first birthday, the age at which my parents could no longer commit me, and stayed until the end of August when, barring another student strike against the war in Vietnam, Indiana University's orientation for new enrollees was set to begin. After the waste I'd made of my life in New York, I was surprised IU had accepted me, although my mother was so relieved, she wrote me a note announcing she was relinquishing what she called her "apron strings." Finally, she said, I'd earned the right to set my own course.

I was so moved by her message I folded it up and slipped it into my wallet for safe keeping. John, on the other hand, whose offer to share his Surf Street studio had triggered my Danville flight, was more impressed with the note the magistrate overseeing the discharge of my shoplifting conviction had sent. "Congratulations," he'd written of my decision to return to college. "And thank you for keeping your word."

"Boy, I bet it's been a long time since anyone's said something like that to a sleaze like you, huh?" John chuckled. Nodding, I smiled and replied that was why I'd done it. I needed to know I still could. "Drying out," I called it.

I weaned myself off the speed and, except for the night I shot a red John had purchased off an itinerant drag queen, my syringe too. Although I was fired from the job John got for me at Embossograph, the beer sign manufacturer a few blocks up Diversey where he'd worked since coming to town, I managed to keep the one I found on my own, working as a file clerk for a big downtown law firm. The pay was just as lousy and I had to shell out for the bus, but at least there I didn't I have to raise my hand every time I wanted to use the toilet. I just stopped what I was doing and took a leak.

My second week on the job, I came out to my fellow file clerks—two Blacks and three whites, all guys, none of whom had ever ventured more than an hour outside of Chicago. John, who claimed to know the local mindset better than me, had warned me against it, claiming I'd be fired but, inspired by a special supplement that Chicago's underground rag, *The Seed*, had published on a new group called the Gay Liberation Front, I decided I needed to start doing my part for the cause too. And, although one of the guys, an older, white middle-aged father of two from way out in Cicero, called me a pervert and refused to speak to me again, the others were mostly just perplexed why I'd admit to such a thing. As one of the Black guys put it, none of the other homos he knew—the dirty old man who gave free blow jobs two floors up in his building, the bachelor English teacher a few blocks over with a penchant for the poetry of Langston Hughes, and a great aunt who maintained the woman she'd lived with for over twenty years was only a roommate—had ever felt compelled to talk about it.

Soon, word spread about the open homosexual the firm had on staff until even the partners knew, or so I was told, although they didn't seem to be bothered much either. Just that co-worker, the white guy from Cicero, although later another one, also white, an amateur bantam-weight boxer with acne scars and a bad stutter, wrote me off too. That, however, wasn't because he hated gays. In fact, I suspected he was one or so he indicated when, cornering me in the law firm's attic archive, he asked if I'd give him a blow job. While I admitted I was flattered by the interest, I informed him I was different from the neighborhood cocksuckers he was perhaps used to. My kind of gay, a newer, more "liberated" version, believed sex should be between equals. Whatever I did to him, I said, I'd expect him to do to me too.

Pissed, he stormed off saying he didn't care what I called myself, he'd never put a dick in his mouth, what did I take him for, *pussy*? After that, he refused to speak to me, even to say good morning, and while I missed his company—of my co-workers, he was the only one interested in books—I was proud that, after nine months of settling for nothing but George's hand jobs, I'd finally stood up for my own sexual rights. Pride, I'd decided, was something one practiced everywhere, even in bed.

In early May, I made another break with my past by joining my first anti-war protest since Syracuse—a massive, mile-long march against the killings at Kent State. It was a somber affair, with thousands gathering in Civic Center around the sculpture Picasso had donated to the city and then marching in silence to Grant Park, where two years earlier Mayor Daley had unleashed his cops on peaceful protesters outside the Democratic National Convention. The memory of that violence was still fresh on everyone's mind and so, when, at the rally, a bearded Yippie in battle fatigues mounted a massive Civil War monument and unfurled a giant Viet Cong flag, a red and pale blue-striped banner with a gold star in the center so big it seemed to rival the sun, I girded for trouble. However, the crowd was so large—with over a hundred thousand participants, the protest was, a speaker had claimed, the largest in Chicago's history—and its roar of approval so deafening—finally, people cried, we were bringing the war home—the cops actually retreated. As I watched them pull back, a rush of adrenalin surged through me just like the one I'd felt that first night of Stonewall, when the cops' paddy wagon had been forced to flee under a hail of beer bottles and rocks. *Yes,* I joined in, *home!* I flashed on Junior slugging me behind the Catholic church, my mother vomiting into a toilet bowl, then Dr. Radin's warning—"You're going to be unhappy as long as you persist in this choice"—and cried again, *Yes, the war! Bring it home! Now!*

As the rally started to break up, I stumbled, hoarse and drenched with sweat, into a small clearing where a barefoot hippie chick in a granny dress ran up to me and asked if I was alright; I looked like I was freaking out on the bad acid going around that day. "Not to worry, though, my old man's got just what you need," she said, pointing to a strung-out, seedy-looking character with long brown hair sitting in the shade of a tree. When I asked what he was peddling, she giggled. "Thorazine. Two bucks a pop."

I scanned the faces of the crowd streaming past me. I'd never seen so many different types in one place, even at New York Be-Ins. Black and brown; young and old; hippie and straight; student and worker; blue-collar and white were all there, as angry and fed up as me. Earlier, during the march, I'd even spotted two lesbians bravely holding hands. "Oh no," I replied, my face still flushed, "I'm fine, really, just the way I am." Dazed—I couldn't remember the last time I'd said anything like that without already being high—I turned back to the Yippie still waving the Viet Cong flag, an outrage more brazen than anything I'd ever seen a Horrible Fag do, and pumped the air with my fist. In the midst of protest, I'd finally found peace, a place where I no longer needed—or even wanted—drugs.

The next month, John and I marched in Chicago's first gay pride event, a small affair of a few hundred mostly freaks that was held on the anniversary of what its organizer, Chicago's nascent Gay Liberation Front, called the "Stonewall Rebellion." John and I thought that a bit of a stretch for the drug-fueled street brawl we'd witnessed the previous June but, after a few blocks of marching through the streets chanting "Two, four, six, eight/gay is just as good as straight" to stunned passers-by, we agreed the hype was worth it. Like John had said after the second night of Stonewall, the one where the TV cameras had shown up, people were starting to think we meant business.

In July, John and I got swept up in our first real riot, one that made the "Stonewall Rebellion" look like mere child's play—a rock-throwing, car-burning, Molotov cocktail-tossing melee sparked when Sly and the Family Stone failed to show up for a free Grant Park concert. When a roving gang of young toughs in keffiyehs shouting "Eat the Rich" headed off to loot downtown, I tried to drag John along. "Come on, it'll be fun. We might even get to smash some windows."

"Uh-huh, it's not safe," John demurred, scowling at the plume of acrid black smoke billowing from a cop car the mob had set ablaze. "So?" I replied as a fusillade of Molotov cocktails set a stand of nearby trees afire. "Neither is sticking a needle in your arm. But that never seemed to stop you." I watched a band of young dykes—a dozen or so tough-looking Black lesbians in cut-offs and do-rags—run amok and recalled the chant I'd heard at the Kent State protest. "This is it, John," I cried, trembling slightly. "Our chance to bring the war home."

John grimaced over the growing din—of strafing police choppers, wailing sirens and popping tear gas canisters—and shrugged. "Do what you want," he said. "But I'm going home." He removed the red bandana he'd tied over his head to protect it from the blazing sun and covered his mouth against the drifting tear gas. "I'm hot. I'm hungry. And I'm sick of all these fucking crazies." He paused to glower at a mob undone by cheap wine, acid laced with too much speed, and Sly's broken promise of free fun and then stormed off.

Afraid to join the melee all on my own, I caught up with him and we returned to our room on Surf Street, where we spent another desultory evening smoking pot and swapping stories of New York depravity, a game of one-upmanship that I invariably won. After that, claiming we needed to wash the day's riotous vibe from our system, he had me tag along for a couple of beers at Shari's, the corner gay bar whose jukebox featured the Broadway show tunes I loathed, but which its clean-cut, mostly white, middle-class and, by then, thoroughly drunken clientele loved to sing along to. I tried my best to abide the revelry but the contrast with everything else that had gone down that day—the promise of a Grant Park Woodstock, Sly-and-the-Family-Stone-style, curdling into another Altamont, Chicago-multiracial-style—proved too much. I lost it.

I told John I wanted to tear Shari's up just like I would've, if I'd only had the balls, some posh downtown store, say Marshall Field or Bloomingdale's. But, as he so wisely pointed out, I'd only end up in jail and then the Mafia would retaliate, most likely by tossing a firebomb through one of our Surf Street windows, and he wasn't into being caught up in any more craziness. Besides, he didn't have the bread to put down on another place, nor did he think a landlord would ever dare rent to anyone the Mafia had on its hit list, at least in Chicago anyway.

And so, I instead slunk back to our room, retrieved my syringe from the suitcase I'd hidden it in, and shot the red John had purchased from a drag queen a few weeks earlier for what he'd called "just in case." The needle was so dull I had to practically hammer it in, but the high at least kept me from running off to the nearest pay phone and calling the straight couple who kept George's bail money in a cookie jar. "Hello, I need you to get a message to George. It's urgent," I imagined myself saying before the Seconal kicked in and I finally passed out.

The next week, I found in one of the law partner's offices an *Esquire* with an article on the Weathermen, whose Greenwich Village bomb factory had blown up a few months earlier, killing three militants. One of those killed, Ted Gold, was quoted in the article as having said of the difference between the Weathermen and the rest of the counterculture, of which it claimed to be the revolutionary vanguard—"We don't think in terms of being happy. We think in terms of being strong." I was floored. Except for the context, it was exactly what I'd told Dr. Radin two years earlier when he'd asked if I'd be open to a cure. "I don't want to be straight, Doctor. I want to be strong."

That night, I informed John I'd found the new direction we'd both been searching for since we'd fled the drugs and sleaze of New York. I wanted to become a revolutionary. John, who had no use for organized politics, let alone street fighting, tried to dismiss my new-found resolve as a passing astrological phenomenon. "That's only because your Mars is squared with Jupiter," he said of an aspect supposedly common to rabble rousers. "Besides, you didn't do so well making beer signs. What makes you think you'll be any better at bombs?"

I agreed bomb-making was a bit butch for a sissy like me, although I noted the types we'd seen at the "Stonewall Rebellion" commemoration had opened my eyes to a different kind of radical—neither one nor the other, but both, butch and fem, all mixed up together. "Crazy quilt," I called it. I recalled the big, heavyset bulldyke in overalls with whiskers on her chin who'd led us in shouting, *Two, four, six, eight/ gay is just as good as straight.* That chant, I confessed, had blown my mind even more than the one I'd learned at the Kent State protest, the one about bringing the war home. "I want to be just like her," I declared, pausing to recall what the march's organizers had called themselves. "A gay liberationist."

John grimaced. As he noted, he liked his creature comforts too much to ever be a revolutionary. Besides, the change he most wanted in his life was geographic, not political—a return to the West Coast, in whose New Age vibes he insisted we'd once again find ourselves. At that, he arose from the mattress on his side of a room we only half-jokingly likened to a jail cell and suggested a beer at Shari's. Saying I was in no mood for another night of show tunes, I declined, although, after he left, I sensed trouble brewing. I was starting to think for myself and John didn't like that. A starry-eyed Pisces, I was supposed to be the confused kid so distracted by dreams I needed a practical Capricorn like him to keep me grounded. My "gay mother," John still liked to call himself, even though, as I'd repeatedly told him, after almost a year of George, I was eager to retake control of my life. "Seizing the time," I called it, in a nod to the Panthers.

That weekend, John picked a fight over how I'd scrambled the eggs. He said they had to be cooked in butter and I'd used Mazola. The argument quickly escalated until we came so close to blows that I packed up and moved out. Fortunately, an older gay man, Horace, who lived in grand style across from New Town's other gay bar, the Annex, offered me a spare bedroom, where I crashed until I left for IU. Horace had a kept boy, Isaac, a bleach-blond runaway from Wisconsin who had pierced nipples and a thing for leather and who'd asked him to put me up, hoping my long hair and New York flair would enhance his freak bona-fides. As he said, he wanted to be cool too, although, while I tried my best, Isaac was too much a screamer to ever be hip. He didn't like Jefferson Airplane, loved to lip synch to Judy Garland songs, and got paranoid every time he smoked pot.

The only real friend I made in Chicago was Tom-Tom, a freak hairdresser with long Veronica Lake locks and a Mae West swagger who greeted everyone with the line, "Hi ya, tomata." Except for the local premiere of *Myra Breckenridge*, which we agreed was the gayest film we'd ever seen, we never got together outside of the Annex, where we'd teach each other the latest dance steps, or the Riviera, the gay Lake Michigan beach at which Tom-Tom practiced his swan dives and I worked on my tan. Next to the Riviera, the freaks maintained their own beach, which they called Acapulco, although the two groups rarely interacted. The freaks thought the gays, few of whom did drugs, uptight, while the gays thought the freaks, nearly all of whom did, degenerate. Tom-Tom and I were the only ones who mixed with both, although some on the gay side called us criminals for smoking pot, while a few on the Acapulco side thought us narcs for never having our own.

The cops, whom John called the Blue Meanies, after the villains in *Yellow Submarine*, the Beatles movie, kept both groups on a short leash. They routinely harassed the freaks—on my first day in town, I'd witnessed them strip-search a hippie in plain view of everyone on N. Clark Street—while they regularly raided the Annex, which, unlike Shari's, maintained an illegal dance floor which the owners opened up every Saturday night when the cops were too busy keeping the Blacks on the South Side down to bother with us North Side gays.

Everyone I knew complained bitterly about Chicago's ban on gay dancing, although no one seemed inclined to do much about it, mostly, I suspected, out of fear. In fact, there was much to be fearful of in the Chicago of 1970. Mayor Richard J. Daley, the thin-skinned petty tyrant whose cops had the previous December brazenly murdered in their sleep two local Black Panther Party leaders, Fred Hampton and Mark Clark, was rumored to loath gays almost as much as Blacks. Word got out that if you spoke up too loudly you might end up like those two Panthers—corpses, riddled with bullets.

Then, one hot sultry weeknight, emboldened by the gay pride march in which we'd openly defied the police by marching down the middle of Chicago's streets, Tom-Tom and I cleared the tables and chairs from the Annex's dance floor and "liberated" it to Freda Payne's hit, "Band of Gold." Certain the cops were on their way, the crowd at first tried to dissuade us but, by the end of the night, when the Blue Meanies failed to show, everyone was on the dance floor, whooping and hollering along to Freda's refrain, *Since you've been gone...*After that, people were free to dance at the Annex whenever they wanted, except, of course, on Sundays, which Mayor Daley proclaimed a day of rest for everyone, straight as well as gay—no dancing allowed.

Except for brief affairs with a motorcyclist who never got it up and an ad man who did but only when high on psylocibin, I kept my sex life confined to a small patch of bushes in Lincoln Park. I thought I was safer there, no worries about falling in love, getting hurt, finding another George Wrong, just the hard, cold reality of anonymous sex. Then, one Sunday afternoon, two thugs with murder in their eyes tried to drag me off to a car idling in a nearby parking lot. I fought them off with a ferocity that clearly surprised them—fairies, after all, were supposed to be easy marks—but by then I'd had my fill of groveling; they could've slit my throat before I would've begged them for mercy. Indeed, once I got far enough away, I even turned and taunted them: *What's the matter, pussies, can't beat up a fag?* If they'd had a gun, I was sure they would've shot me. As it was, they just kept hanging around, waiting for the next guy to come along, looking for company.

They must've found him because, a few days later, stories began circulating about Lincoln Park "fag bashings," a term those gay liberationists I wanted to become had coined. Someone had supposedly been badly beaten; one story even had him killed, but, of course, there was nothing in the papers about it. Back then, violence against gays was so commonplace it wasn't deemed newsworthy. For a while, there was talk of a gay neighborhood watch—Horace even donated money to get it started—but, as with so much else in town, nothing came of it. Everyone in Chicago was paranoid, afraid to take a stand. Indeed, it was the closest I'd ever come to living in a police state. The cops were truly horrible. Every last one was a pig.

Two weeks before leaving Chicago, I picked up a tall, lanky blond named Richard, in town on business from, of all places, Bloomington, Indiana. "Trust me, you'll love it," he said when I informed him of my impending IU enrollment. "The town's wild. And very gay."

When I asked about the bar scene, he laughed; Bloomington, he said, didn't have one. Gay people got together in other ways. "Parties, mostly," he explained when I asked how, although he noted a campus tearoom called "Sugar and Spice" was also quite active.

I assured him I was no tearoom queen nor, for that matter, did I much care for gay parties. The last one I'd been to, an orgy after a Chicago GLF dance, had been an unmitigated disaster, with the host putting a halt to any action he wasn't a part of. Other than my Philadelphia debut, at which my arrival had been announced with a cry of "fresh meat!" and the Syracuse after-hours bash where our host had tried to off himself with a carving knife, the rest of the parties I'd attended had been small Greenwich Village get-togethers of Horrible Fags, blowing their minds on speed. "Pretty scary," I said of those.

"You've been in big cities too long," Richard replied. "You'll see." He added there was even talk of starting a Gay Liberation Front there, a prospect I admitted washed away a number of concerns. "I thought it'd be all yahoos and hicks down there. You know, Bible thumpers and Nixon freaks."

He chuckled and noted that, in addition to being gay, Bloomington was also quite radical. He mentioned the previous spring's strike against the war that had shut the campus down for over a month. "And trippy," he added. "LSD is very big." He said the town even had a 'People's Park,' where a band called the Screaming Gypsy Bandits played for free and freaks got high right out in the open.

The next morning, "Penny," as Richard said he was known in Bloomington—every gay man, he explained, was expected to have what he called a "drag name"—gave me his number and told me to call as soon as I got to town. He even said he had a lover he wanted me to meet. "Ever been Lucky Pierre?" he asked of the guy who got to be in the middle. "Great," he murmured when I confessed my expertise mostly involved drugs, "you can get us high and we'll get you off." Blushing, I didn't bother noting that, in my world, 'getting off' was also about drugs.

On my last day in town, I stopped by John's Surf Street pad to say goodbye. We hadn't spoken since Horace had taken me in and I was startled by the changes he'd made in the décor. The space where my mattress had been was filled with marijuana plants he'd grown from seed and he'd cut what he called portholes into the blue contact paper he'd used to cover the room's two rickety windows. "So, I can feel like I'm out to sea," he explained. "Anywhere but Chicago."

He chuckled when I told him about Bloomington's rising prospects. "Your poor parents. Some cure, huh?" he murmured before we laughed about all the money they'd spend putting me through college while I earned my BA in gay liberation. After that, the conversation started to lag, as it often did with John, although as I got up and headed for the door, he confessed he might want to visit. "Anything to get away from these bars," he grumbled, staring through a porthole at the back of Shari's, whose jukebox even John, whose favorite film was still *Auntie Mame*, had come to loathe.

I gave him the address of the Bloomington room I'd rented in the back of a building owned by an entity called, of all things, "Greenwich Village Trust" and assured him he'd be welcome anytime. "What's mine is yours," I said, repeating the mantra we'd used to get ourselves through the trauma of New York, the trial by fire that would forever bind us.

Out on the street, I headed east for the lake, mostly to avoid seeing John sitting and staring out the windows he'd transformed into portholes so he could imagine being anywhere but where he was. Other than his job at Embossograph, the Diversey Street display manufacturer where he was a model worker, and the two N. Clark Street gay bars where he was drinking more and more, sitting alone by his window and smoking pot were just about the only things John did. He'd even let his astrology slide, while he'd shifted the site of his geographical cure from San Francisco to a remote, hardscrabble corner of the Ozarks, where an ailing great aunt, Dora, promised him her chicken farm. John knew nothing about farming, let alone chickens, and hadn't lived more than a few city blocks from a gay bar since he'd come out. But Dora didn't have long to live and, as he'd said, anywhere but Chicago.

At the lakefront, I sought out the granite slab with the refrain from the Rolling Stone's "Paint It Black"—*No colors anymore, I want them to turn black*—scrawled in tar across it. John and I had stumbled upon it on the only acid trip we'd taken in Chicago and he'd had to literally drag me away. It was, I'd claimed, the one spot in the Midwest where I felt like I was back in Greenwich Village, in whose witch's brew of decadence and drugs I'd tried in vain to concoct my own way out. After we'd come down, John had tried to explain away the slab's draw as another passing astrological quirk, but I knew better. Every chance I got, I snuck back to that slab, each time letting a little more of George go, until one day his pull simply vanished, and I was free to start over.

I listened to the waves lap against the granite slabs and the gulls squawk overhead and shuddered at how close a call it had been. I'd telephoned the couple on Hudson Street who kept George's bail money inside a cookie jar twice since I'd come to Chicago. The first time, I'd hung up on the second ring but the next I'd waited until the woman, a shy, tongue-tied 'plain Jane' who'd been even more enthralled by George's Factory past than I, had actually picked up. "Hello? Hello?" she'd cried into the receiver as I'd stood trembling in a phone booth outside the drug store a few doors up Diversey from the corner of N. Clark. Rising from the slab, I pulled my address book from my back pocket, tore out the page with their number on it and, after ripping it into pieces so tiny no one could possibly reconstruct it, scattered it to the winds. "There," I murmured, "be gone."

At sunset, I headed back to N. Clark Street and sat on the stoop of Horace's building across from the Annex, whose open dance floor had transformed it into a venue so popular a line regularly formed to get in. Watching the moon rise over the trio of billboards that marked the start of New Town, Chicago's sorry excuse for a gay ghetto, I recalled an aphorism from *Love's Body,* Norman O. Brown's meditation on apocalypse that I still kept bedside: *To let the light not on but in or through...as in the night sky, or the space on which our dreams are made.* Like the boy at the start of Bergman's *Persona*, a film I'd also been unable to shake, I'd been groping for an image that, flickering on the screen of my dreams, stubbornly resisted coming into focus—that of a man who paid no price for the simple fact of being gay.

I spied a star off to the far left of the horizon and smiled. It was, I knew, Venus, the goddess of love, the planet John called a Piscean's "protectress." I thought for a moment about returning to ask him what sign it had moved into but quickly decided against it. My sights were set on the future and astrology was, like the Tarot, *I Ching*, black magic, and all the rest of a speed freak's mumbo-jumbo, the language of my past. It was time I found new answers—modern ones, ones that put me, not fate, in the driver's seat.

"Hi ya, tomata!" Tom-Tom shouted from across the street. "You gonna shake your tail feather tonight?" He clicked his fingers and bobbed his hips to Stevie Wonder's "Signed, Sealed and Delivered," blasting out of the Annex. I shook my head and wistfully waved him on, knowing I'd probably never see him again. I'd had my fill of gay bars and Tom-Tom, upon learning that Bloomington had none, had instantly declined my invitation to visit. "What would we do?" he'd cried, incredulous. "Play *canasta*?!"

As he slipped past the doorman into the already hopping bar, I wondered what gay life would be like in a rural college town like Bloomington, Indiana. While I dreaded the prospect of returning to my Hoosier roots, I was eager to put my failures behind me. I held out my hand, the barometer of my battle-readiness, and nodded. The chronic trembling and self-doubt that had marked my addiction to speed—and, by extension, to George—had subsided in favor of a nascent pride and a growing hunger for a new kind of solidarity with people like me—one that had nothing to do with syringes, shooting galleries or, for that matter, even sex. As the ragtag crowd of long-haired liberationists at

Chicago's commemoration of the "Stonewall Rebellion" had done, I clenched my right fist and raised it, a salute to a future of which only one thing was certain—that whatever came next had to be better than what had come before. "Gay power," I murmured quietly to myself.

I glanced back toward Venus and spied a scrawny kid—he couldn't have been more than fifteen, awkward, with that hunted look sissies got when they were being bullied—hiding behind a mailbox and gawking at the line of men that had formed waiting to get into the Annex. It was an unusually raucous crowd, at least for Chicago, with lots of camping and squealing—a great sight, I thought, for a kid starved for images of who he knew he'd someday be. I recalled my first sightings of a homosexual—the dirty old man who'd groped himself as I was leaving a downtown Wilmington movie theater and then the other, the lecherous high school teacher who'd tried to seduce me with dirty movies—and felt myself flush. A torrent of bad memories overwhelmed me— me hurling a glass of milk into my father's face after he'd called me a sissy; Junior and T beating me up behind the Catholic church; my mother vomiting after I told her I was gay; the shrink lecturing me about how degraded gay sex was; George overdosing and raping me. Then, just as suddenly, their opposite, a swell of purpose and protest, washed those memories away. While I couldn't undo the damage that had been done to me, I could at least try to make sure others weren't so maimed.

I thought of the prospect of finding something like the Gay Liberation Front in rural Indiana. It seemed so far-fetched but who knew? After all, the Bloomington trick I'd picked up, "Penny," he'd said he was known as, seemed like a together kind of guy—a bit too bourgie, perhaps, but certainly not one prone to tall tales. I reached for my address book and searched for his name. Yep, there it was, his phone number too, the one I was supposed to call as soon as I got settled. I chuckled. "Lucky Pierre," he'd said he'd make me.

Looking around, the boy saw me spying on him and, frightened, ran off. I wanted to yell after him, don't be scared, I'm one too, but I knew the really important business lay ahead. No one should have to go through what I did just because they were gay. Not that kid, not anybody.

The next morning, I caught an 8 a.m. train to Danville and from there my parents drove me to the dark dingy back-alley hovel overlooking the Monroe County jail that I'd taken as soon as the real estate agent had shown it to me. As I'd defiantly muttered to my horrified parents, still holding fast to the notion that Bloomington would be my path back to normal, "Anywhere but the dorm." True to form, my mother had burst into tears, while my father's face had hardened, like he'd wanted to slug me.

It was then that my parents finally realized they'd lost their long, drawn-out war against the person I insisted on being. Anyone who'd choose to live alone in a back-alley hovel looking out onto the county jail in a town in which he knew virtually no one rather than be among a dorm-full of Hoosier-wholesome buddies, some of whom he might even end up rushing a fraternity with, was clearly not someone who was returning to the straight and narrow. And although, for the next three years, they dutifully paid my rent and tuition and my father, as he had at Syracuse, resumed sending me my monthly allowance, a crisp fifty-dollar bill in a security envelope with no note, from that day forward I did as I pleased, even spending my summers where I wanted, no questions asked—provided, of course, I did not rub their noses in what I was up to or tarnish the family name. As my mother would much later say, after my father had died and I insisted on having David, my partner—later my husband—accompany me on visits, discretion was key.

Of course, even that was a tall order, although, if my parents had any idea how militant a gay man I became, they closed their eyes to it, while, fed up with beseeching and begging, I stopped trying to make them see who I really was. The love and respect I'd once demanded of them, I instead got from others, a new "chosen family" of gay brothers and sisters who were collectively defining something brand-new, revolutionary even—the first out-of-the-closet, self-affirming generation of homosexuals in the entirety of human history.

My parents never knew that, by the end of my second week in town, I joined thirty-five others in IMU-44 of IU's Student Union building to found Bloomington's Gay Liberation Front or that, six months later, I was attending class in a dress and a beard as part of GLF's "genderfuck" protest against sex stereotyping. Nor did they know that, at the start of my second year at IU, the house at 447 S. Henderson Street that I moved into with five other guys—Eric, a tall, rail thin, Ichabod Crane-type who'd arrived in town fresh off a regimen of electroshock treatments; Mark, a breezy, apple-cheeked chatterbox who cruised me at GLF's first meeting and with whom I had a brief affair; Wilson, an older chainsmoker and lapsed student of serial music whom I found in People's Park reading *Quotations from Chairman Mao* while sporting a "How Dare You Presume I'm Straight" button; Don, a troubled, acid-tongued, opera queen dropout from nearby Bedford whom Eric, a collector of lost souls, had brought into the mix; and my friend John, who'd come down from Chicago for a weekend visit and stayed eight months—was Bloomington's first gay male collective and de facto community center that we androgynously named Pat

Henderson House, although my parents dutifully paid my share of the rent there too.

Nor did they know what went on in that house: the raucous parties that often spilled into the street and which the cops, whom we derisively called Alice Blue Badge, were invariably called to break up; the consciousness-raising "rap sessions," during which we shared our pain and trauma and discovered our solidarity as a new oppressed group—a people, *gay people*; and the monthly "visiting hours" we kept at which people from all over southern Indiana—Evansville, Versailles, French Lick, Madison—who were having trouble coming out could sit down and just talk, no sex allowed. Nor did they know of the protests we organized, like the boycott of Nick's English Tavern, an off-campus watering hole that hung a "This is a bar, not a fruit stand" sign over its cash register or the "zap" we did of the Young Democrats' screening of *Boys in the Band*, whose line "show me a happy homosexual and I'll show you a gay corpse" so enraged us we pulled the plug on the projector, turned on the lights, and demanded equal time.

But it was our "come out, come out, wherever you are" GLF dances that were our crowning achievements, the first of which was a 1970 Halloween celebration held in the cafeteria of Wright Quad, a men's dormitory complex across from the campus library. Like many that night, I'd dropped acid and was so high I thought the gang of young toughs who'd come to break the gathering up were revelers too. When the cops arrived, no one was sure who they were going to side with, but then word spread that IU's long-term president, Herman Welles, a lifelong bachelor who allegedly still lived with his mother, had ordered that our event proceed without incident. No one knew if the rumor was true, but one thing was certain: the fag bashers disappeared within minutes, as if by magic.

After that, GLF dances, held every Halloween and Valentine's Day, became events attended by hundreds, straights as well as gays, from all over the Midwest. After the Wright Quad incident, IU even moved us to the safer, more defensible and much more elegant ballroom of the Student Union building. There we even had a stage on which the more outrageous among us could perform—Chris, drag name Bianca—or 'B' for short—dressed as a grief-stricken Jackie Kennedy in a blood-splattered pink Chanel suit who later stripped down to a girdle and bra was perhaps the most infamous. Thank you, President Welles, gay liberation owes you a lot.

My parents knew nothing of those dances or the outfits we concocted, nor did they have any idea that I was part of a GLF contingent on the cover of the special edition of the local underground rag, *Common Sense,* called *Common Sense Comes Out*! However, they might have seen me on the front page of the

IU Daily Student—the first open homosexual elected to IU's Student Senate—that ran on the Saturday my parents came to town for a football game. If they did, they didn't mention it, just like the time they showed up unexpectedly at the dark, dingy hovel I rented behind the county jail only to be greeted by GLF's genderfuck superstar, Eric, drag name Rhoda Dendron in a dotted Swiss dress and Cleopatra eyes.

Nor did they know that, one dark, moonless night, I went out with Mark and Bridget, a raven-haired, boot-stomping radical lesbian, and spray-painted anti-war slogans—*Off the Butch in Southeast Asia!*—all across campus. Nor did I mention that a year earlier, Eric, Mark and I tested Huey Newton's embrace of gay liberation by attending a Black Panther-sponsored "All People's Revolutionary Conference" in Ann Arbor, Michigan. Amazingly, the Panthers welcomed us, even when Eric and a contingent of genderfuckers showed up for the conference's closing dance in dresses. Back in Bloomington, however, GLF's "moderates," all white men, were outraged by our embrace of revolutionary politics. Gay men, they said—by then, the women had split off to form their own lesbian separatist organization—had no business getting mixed up with women's liberation, the anti-war movement, or even, for that matter, Blacks. We had our issues; they had theirs; and, according to them anyway, never the twain should meet. "Bourgies," we called them.

They in turn complained we were too obvious—to them, the ultimate putdown. We instead called ourselves "radical fems" and adopted a chant based on the Mickey Mouse Club theme song to announce our presence: *R-A-D/I-C-A/L-F-E-M-S/Radical fems/Off the butch!/Radical fems/Off the butch!!/Forever, let us raise our voices high, high, high, high...* We'd get in line and sing it, kicking our legs in the air, Rockettes style, and upping our registers until, by the end, we were exactly what we weren't supposed to be: out, proud, in-your-face, no-holds-barred, stereotypical sissies. It drove the bourgies crazy, which we, of course, took as very high praise indeed.

What I did make sure my parents knew about was my arrest during the 1971 May Day "If the Government Won't Stop the War, We'll Stop the Government" week of demonstrations in Washington, DC. And while I didn't let on that I was there as part of a large GLF contingent—the first gay group to march under its own banner in a national anti-war action—or that, as we were carted off to waiting paddy wagons, we chanted—to thunderous applause from our fellow protesters—*An Army of Lovers Cannot Lose!*, I was sure my message got through, loud and clear. Tread carefully next time you think about straightening me out, Mom and Dad. I was willing to risk everything—even jail time—to be me.

On that late August drive from Danville to Bloomington, I was anxious over what lay ahead—syllabi, textbooks, exams, term papers, grades. After all, it'd been almost two years since I'd been in a classroom and, in the interim, I'd burned more brain cells on drugs than I cared to think about. But I was also eager to start over. For once, I'd have only myself to answer to—no hectoring mother intent on returning me to the straight and narrow; no abusive, drug-addicted lover determined to get me to embrace my inner rat; no sleazy Horrible Fag friends; no bullies to hide from; no employers for whom I had to tone myself down; no overbearing gay mother telling me how I was supposed to scramble my eggs.

I could let my hair grow as long and dress as freaky as I wanted. Do drugs or not, act fruity or not, fall in love or not. And, of course, most importantly, make new friends—none of whom would be gay barflies or Horrible Fags. Just people like me, people eager to take a stand and say the word that George had hated most in the world, the word no—as in no more; no way, get used to it; no, I'm never again pretending I'm straight, never, ever, ever.

I examined my reflection in the rear window of my parents' Olds and sighed. With hair to below my shoulders, dressed in threads I'd either shoplifted from hip boutiques or purchased from secondhand stores, with a scar still visible in the crux of my left arm and only six months off a live-in love affair with a Horrible Fag, I doubted anyone in Bloomington would know gay life as I did. Arriving from various Hoosier backwaters, many fresh out of high school, some straight off a farm, I suspected few would have ever seen the insides of a gay bar, let alone a shooting gallery. "Welcome to the doctor's office," George had said that first night on East Fourth Street. "Ready for your appointment?" I hadn't been, not at all, but there you have it. I stayed anyway, all the way to the bitter, rock-bottom end.

As practice for my debut in the blank slate of a small Indiana college town in the middle of "God's country" at the tail-end of the decade-long upheaval known as "the Sixties," I muttered the word over and over—*no, no, no, no*. No, if the locals were hateful or I really was the only one, I wasn't going to stay. And no, I didn't care how bad things got, I wasn't going back to George, nor would I be following John to San Francisco. And, no, even though I'd packed it, I wasn't returning to the syringe either. Junkies were my past. Liberation was my future. *Gay* liberation. No to career, privilege, hypocrisy, lies—but, most of all, no to the closet. Like Bernadette, I was letting the chips fall where they may. *No, no, no, no.*

"What's that you're mumbling?" my mother grumbled, turning and scowling at me from her perch in the Olds' front passenger seat. "You sound like you have marbles in your mouth." Through the rear-view mirror, my father glared at me.

"Oh, nothing," I murmured, smiling sweetly, "just something I picked up along the way." I waited until she returned to hectoring my father over his driving—he'd just passed a truck without putting his turn signal on—clenched my fist, and raised it as high as I could without either of them noticing. Then, I mouthed the heresy—*Two, four, six, eight/gay is just as good as straight*—that would be my guide for the rest of my life. As the numbing flatness of cornfields gave way to the gentle roll of wooded hills and the monotony of Jesus Saves! signs morphed into billboards for the Holiday Inn, Ethan Allen furniture and the Hoosiers, IU's football team, my mother once again turned and announced, in the same high-pitched squeal with which she'd greeted Lawrence Welk's the Lennon Sisters, we were almost there. Bloomington was only a half-hour away.

www.ingramcontent.com/pod-product-compliance
Lightning Source LLC
Chambersburg PA
CBHW021657120626
46545CB00004B/1275